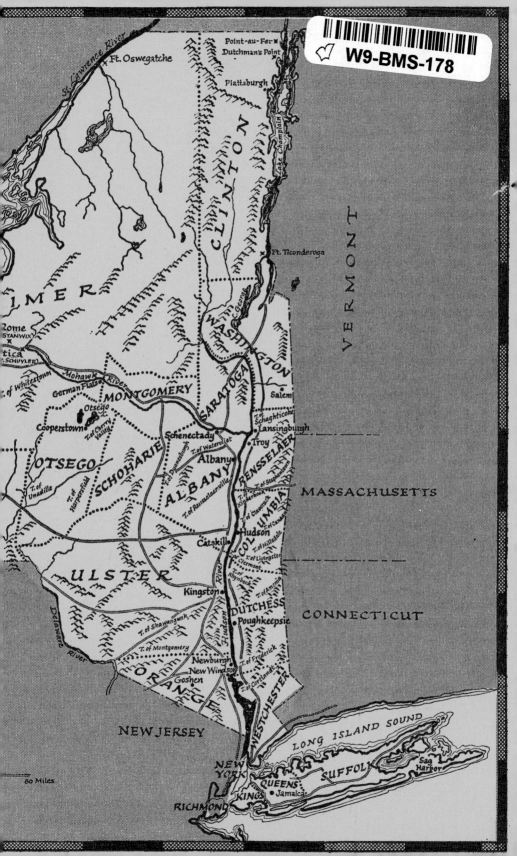

St. Lawrence River

× Ft. Oswegatche

Point-au-Fer
Dutchman's Point

Plattsburgh

CLINTON

Lake Champlain

VERMONT

× Ft. Ticonderoga

L MER

Rome
STANWIX

tica
SCHUYLER

WASHINGTON

L. George

SARATOGA

T. of Whitestown

Mohawk River

German Flats

MONTGOMERY

Salem

T. of Schaghticoke

Lansingburgh

Otsego

Cooperstown

T. of Cherry Valley

Schenectady

T. of Watervliet

Troy

RENSSELAER

OTSEGO

T. of Unadilla

SCHOHARIE

T. of Duanesburgh

Albany

ALBANY

T. of Stephentown

MASSACHUSETTS

T. of Harpersfield

T. of Rensselaerville

T. of Kinderhook

COLUMBIA

T. of Canaan

T. of Claverack

Hudson

ULSTER

Catskill

T. of Hillsdale

T. of Livingston

Clermont

Hudson River

T. of Rhynbeck

T. of Amenia

Kingston

CONNECTICUT

Delaware River

T. of Shawangunk

DUTCHESS

Poughkeepsie

T. of Montgomery

T. of Frederick

Newburgh
New Windsor

ORANGE

Goshen

T. of Cortlandt

WESTCHESTER

NEW JERSEY

LONG ISLAND SOUND

80 Miles

NEW
YORK

SUFFOLK

Sag
Harbor

QUEENS

KINGS

Jamaica

RICHMOND

THE DEMOCRATIC REPUBLICANS
OF NEW YORK

The Origins, 1763-1797

The Institute of Early American History and Culture is sponsored jointly by the College of William and Mary and Colonial Williamsburg, Incorporated.

THE
DEMOCRATIC
REPUBLICANS
OF NEW YORK

The Origins

1763-1797

ALFRED F. YOUNG

Published for
the Institute of Early American History and Culture
at Williamsburg, Virginia
by The University of North Carolina Press · *Chapel Hill*

To Mally

Preface

This book is an attempt to re-examine the Democratic-Republican movement as a whole by an intensive study of one state, New York. I make no claims to project my findings to other states, although I would hope that my approach has some validity beyond the confines of New York. I began this study many years ago to fill a gap in the monographic literature about the state between E. Wilder Spaulding's *New York in the Critical Period, 1781-1789*[1] and Dixon Ryan Fox's more famous *The Decline of the Aristocracy in the Politics of New York, 1801-1840*.[2] In the present volume I deal primarily with the origins and growth of the movement during the two Washington administrations. A second volume will carry the Republicans through the testing in the administration of John Adams, from 1797 through 1801 and beyond.

My research has been directed towards answering four large questions about the Democratic Republicans and, within the framework of these, a host of lesser ones.

First, I have asked, who were the Jeffersonians? Carl Becker in his famous monograph, *The History of Political Parties in the Province of New York, 1760-1776*,[3] portraying the Revolution in New York as a question of "who should rule at home" as much as "a question of home rule," projected the conflict of "popular" Whig vs. conservative Whig into the conflict of Federalist vs. Republican in the 1790's.

1. (New York, 1932).
2. (New York, 1919).
3. (Madison, 1909).

Charles A. Beard, in *The Economic Origins of Jeffersonian Democracy*, to sustain the thesis in his earlier work on the Constitution argued that the battle of Federalist and Republican in 1800-1801 continued the alignment of Federalist and anti-Federalist of 1787-88, making major use of evidence from New York.[4] Where does the emphasis belong in New York politics in the last quarter of the eighteenth century—on the continuities suggested by Becker and Beard or on the discontinuities? One cannot avoid the question because most of the leaders of the 1790's were also the leaders of the preceding two decades.

Nor can one escape the question of how classes were aligned. New York had a unique landlord aristocracy which no amount of revisionism is likely to erase from the Hudson Valley. Where were the manor lords in the party battles? And where were Republicans when the strife between landlord and tenant, quiescent since the Revolution, erupted again in the 1790's? How, in particular, can one account for the presence among Republicans of the lower manor Livingstons, led by Chancellor Robert R. Livingston? In the battle over the Constitution in 1787-88, mechanics and merchants were almost unanimously Federalist. How did Republicans win back from the Federalists the mechanic following once enjoyed by the "popular" Whigs? Why did merchants begin to break away from the Federalists, albeit in small numbers? How can one explain why the frontier, proverbially Jeffersonian, in New York was Federalist? It is to these sometimes enigmatic groups that I have directed particular attention: Republican landlords, merchant and mechanic Republicans, and frontier Federalists.

Second, I have asked what issues produced the Democratic-Republican movement? It has been argued that the Republican party of the 1790's was "a new growth that sprang from the divisions in Congress and the national government," essentially a "product of national rather than state politics."[5] The subtitle of a book on Pennsylvania politics of the 1790's is *A Study in National Stimulus and Local Response*.[6] To what extent does New York conform to this pattern? Granted a role for national issues, which ones stimulated New York? To what extent did Hamiltonian finance, traditionally assigned a

4. (New York, 1915).
5. Noble Cunningham, *The Jeffersonian Republicans: The Formation of Party Organization, 1789-1801* (Chapel Hill, 1957).
6. Harry M. Tinkcom, *The Republicans and Federalists in Pennsylvania, 1790-1801: A Study in National Stimulus and Local Response* (Phila., 1950).

large role by historians, produce opposition? Why did Federalists increase their popular support at the end of Washington's first term and Republicans fail to acquire a mass following until 1794? Why, even after the emergence of the Republican movement, were Federalists able to elect John Jay governor in 1795, and in 1796 sweep New York's congressional and presidential elections at the end of Washington's second term? To answer such questions I have tried to measure the scope and intensity of the reaction to Federalist measures, a procedure too often neglected by historians prone to confuse the popgun of a newspaper article with the cannon of a mass movement.

Towards the same end I have focused on the relationship of state issues to party politics. To what extent, I have asked, was Republicanism a positive movement in response to the policies of George Clinton and his party who were in power in New York from 1777 to 1795. In recent years the role of the state in the economy has attracted the attention of scholars.[7] I have attempted to put the politics into the study of this question for New York.

Inevitably state history becomes local history. While I have tried not to neglect any area of the state I have singled out for special attention: New York City, then as now the largest commercial center, unique by virtue of its size; Ulster and Orange counties, the home of the yeomanry, the most consistent stronghold of the "popular" Whigs, anti-Federalists and then Republicans; Columbia County, a center of landlordism and home of the Livingston families; and Otsego County, bailiwick of Judge William Cooper, Federalist chieftain of the western frontier. Ultimately, a number of the questions I raise will only be fully resolved by more intensive investigation of politics at the county, town, and ward level.

Third, I have directed research to the Democratic Republicans as an organized movement. Standard textbooks usually treat the New Yorkers only in terms of their famous leaders, the Clintons, the Livingstons, and Aaron Burr, projecting back into the 1790's the factional strife characteristic of the early nineteenth century.[8] More recently historians dealing with the national scene have directed attention to the political party, to the Democratic-Republican Societies, and to the Republican newspapers. What role did each of these components play in New York? To what extent did political practices show a

7. Summarized in Carter Goodrich, "Recent Contributions to Economic History: The United States, 1789-1860," *Journal of Economic History*, 19 (1959), 25-43.

8. For example, Samuel E. Morison and Henry S. Commager, *The Growth of the American Republic*, 3d ed., 2 vols. (N.Y., 1942), I, 342-44.

process of change over this period? What were the secrets of success and failure for Republicans and Federalists? And how did Republicans function as a party in national politics?

Fourth, what was the philosophy of the Democratic Republicans, if indeed they had one? To what extent did they differ from their opponents the Federalists, from their predecessors the anti-Federalists, and from their partners the Virginians, whose views are widely accepted as those of the movement at large? This question will be taken up at length in the volume that follows. Certain questions still seem particularly appropriate for the formative era of Republicanism. What was the attitude to the Constitution of a party that was an amalgam of "feds" and "anti-feds"? What did Republicans mean when they attacked the Federalists as "aristocrats" and affixed the name "Democratic" to themselves? Jefferson, by convention, is characterized as an agrarian. What was the credo of New York Republicans whose constituents included not only farmers but merchants, mechanics, and manufacturers as well? Jefferson is also thought of as a proponent of limited government. What were Clintonians who for years had power in the state government to apply their philosophy? May one call the New York Republicans "Jeffersonian"?

A word perhaps is necessary as to the structure and style of the book. I have adopted the form of narrative history for two reasons: it best conveys a sense of the growth of the movement, my major concern, and it alone enables me to blend in the concurrent strands of national, state, and local history. To tell my story I have also relied a good deal on the language of contemporaries, on incidents, and description. If the detail is tedious to some who are impatient for analysis, I am hopeful that it will find favor with others who believe as I do that presenting the texture of history is as important as drawing conclusions. I am grateful to a publisher who did not insist that it all be boiled down.

It is a pleasure to express my appreciation to the many scholars, librarians, and institutions who have helped me prepare this book.

Ray Allen Billington guided the doctoral dissertation version of this study at Northwestern University with his customary sound judgment and high standards. Julian P. Boyd first expressed confidence in the merits of publishing it with its formidable detail and documentation intact and gave me the benefit of a criticism based on his deep understanding of the period. Both scholars have been an unfailing source of encouragement.

I am especially indebted to all connected with the Institute of Early American History and Culture: to Lester J. Cappon, Director; to James M. Smith who brought to bear the experience of many productive years as Editor of Publications trying to help me achieve clarity of thought and presentation; to E. James Ferguson who as Visiting Editor and in subsequent years read the manuscript with acumen; and to Susan Lee Foard and Marise Rogge, who prepared the manuscript for the printer with patience and precision.

Clarence Ver Steeg, the late Dorothy C. Barck, Librarian of the New York State Historical Association, and Robin Brooks gave me expert, detailed criticism of the doctoral dissertation and of several chapters in later drafts. Richard B. Morris, Staughton Lynd, Jackson T. Main, and Emory G. Evans read drafts of Part I and sharpened my perspective of the Revolutionary and Confederation era. Over the years Staughton Lynd shared with me his perceptions and passions for early New York history. Jackson T. Main made available to me drafts of his work as well as much of the raw material of his painstaking scholarship. Richard T. McCormick helped me to puzzle out some of the mysteries of the suffrage question.

Scholars who read drafts of chapters, correcting my errors and challenging my analysis, are: Kurt Beermann (ch. 16), Donald O. Dewey (ch. 9), James A. Frost (chs. 12, 23), Ralph L. Ketcham (chs. 9, 16), Leonard W. Levy (ch. 22), Bernard Mason (chs. 1, 2), and Peter Paulson (ch. 22). The late Arthur Bernstein, Roger Champagne, Milton Cantor, Noble E. Cunningham, Jr., Merrill Jensen, Milton Klein, Stephen G. Kurtz, and Dumas Malone offered instructive comments on convention papers I delivered whose findings have been incorporated in this book.

Many scholars responded to my queries, offered suggestions, or helped me to track down elusive material. They are Harry Ammon, Roland Baumann, Robert E. Cushman, David H. Fischer, Paul Goodman, Winthrop Jordan, Clifford L. Lord, Forrest McDonald, John Platt, Beatrice Reubens, Ann Barus Seely, David Syrett, Glenn Thompson, Dorothy L. Webster, and Edmund P. Willis. David Armour, Linda Grant DePauw, and Nicholas Varga allowed me to read their manuscripts.

I am also grateful to the directors of several publication projects and their associates who generously took time from their own editorial labors either to answer my queries, or to provide me with information about documents, or to permit me to examine transcripts of specific items. I thank Dr. and Mrs. Harold Syrett, Cara Miller, and Dorothy Twohig of the Papers of Alexander Hamilton; Richard B. Morris and Mary-Jo Kline of the Papers of John Jay; Julian P. Boyd of the Papers of Thomas Jefferson; Donald O. Dewey, formerly of the Papers of James Madison; and Robert G. Wheeler, Director of Research, Sleepy Hollow Restorations, Tarrytown, N.Y. Finally, Mrs. Alfred Nicoll of Washingtonville, N.Y., kindly let me read her collection of the *Goshen Repository*.

I also wish to thank the librarians on whose resources I have drawn most heavily: Lewis M. Stark and his staff at the rare book room and Robert W. Hill and his staff at the manuscripts room, New York Public Library; Geraldine Beard, E. Marie Becker, and Wilmer R. Leach of the New York Historical Society; Juliet Wolohan and Donald C. Anthony of the New York State Library; Clifford K. Shipton, Director of the American Antiquarian Society; and David C. Mearns's staff in the manuscript room of the Library of Congress.

Grants from the American Philosophical Society and the Dixon Ryan Fox Fund of the New York State Historical Association made possible two summers of research and writing. Northern Illinois University lightened my teaching load and contributed toward typing the manuscript.

A. F. Y.

September, 1966
DeKalb, Ill.

Table of Contents

PART III

The "Republican Interest" Emerges

1790-1792

PART IV

The Battle Joined

1793-1797

PART V

The Republican Movement Deepens

1795-1797

List of Tables and Maps

TABLES

MAPS

PART I

Who Shall Rule at Home?

1763-1788

———•———

CHAPTER 1

The American Revolution

in New York

1763-1783

On June 10, 1789, George Clinton walked from the governor's mansion in New York City to the home of Rufus King, recently settled in the city from his native Massachusetts and even more recently elected a member of the New York Assembly. King was not at home. The governor left his card and returned the next day but King was out again. On June 12 King returned the visit, and Clinton moved quickly to his purpose: sounding out the well-known Federalist on accepting anti-Federalist support for a seat in the United States Senate.[1]

Clinton's puzzling offer is explicable only in the context of New York's tangled political history. After dominating New York politics as governor since 1777, George Clinton had suffered a series of setbacks that left him with his back to the wall: the unanticipated Federalist victory at Poughkeepsie the previous summer which had secured the state's ratification of the federal Constitution; the subsequent stalemate in the state legislature over the choice of federal senators as a result of a split between the "adopting" and "non-

1. Substance of a Conversation with Governor Clinton, June 12, 1789 [a memorandum], Rufus King Papers, New-York Historical Society, N.Y.C., reprinted in Charles R. King, ed., *The Life and Correspondence of Rufus King . . .* , 6 vols. (N.Y., 1894-1900), I, 354-60. The circumstances are discussed below, ch. 6, sec. V.

adopting" anti-Federalists; and Clinton's near-defeat in the recent gubernatorial campaign after going all but unchallenged in the three elections since 1777.

In his extraordinary interview with King, Clinton began by explaining the controversy in the legislature over the selection of senators, pointing out why Melancton Smith and John Lansing would not or could not be the anti-Federalist choice. When Clinton asked King whom he had heard spoken of as candidates, King named besides Lansing, Robert Yates, another anti-Federalist, and Philip Schuyler, Robert R. Livingston, James Duane, and Richard Morris, leaders of the conservative Whig nationalists during the Revolution and now leaders of the state's Federalists. Each of the Federalists was a member of New York's unique landed aristocracy, the estate holders of the Hudson Valley: Schuyler was the most powerful figure of the Albany area; Duane was son-in-law of the upper manor Livingstons, owner of Duanesburgh in his own right, and the mayor of New York; Livingston was chancellor and the head of the Clermont or lower manor branch of his family; Richard Morris, associate justice of the supreme court, was son of the late Lewis Morris, lord of the manor of Morrisania of Westchester.

Deftly, Clinton explained his objection to each of the men mentioned by King. He "questioned whether any gentlemen in the state judiciary ought to take a share in the national Legislature, that this might be confounding the judiciary and Legislative Department," a comment that clearly eliminated Judges Morris, Livingston, and Yates. Lansing could not serve for personal reasons. Then, with a mounting impatience, Clinton warmed to a history lesson for the newcomer to New York politics:

> besides that it had uniformly been his opinion that the Offices of Great Power should not all be concentrated in a certain party, or family association—that their abilities and wealth already gave them great influence, and that the addition of great Offices to the entire exclusion of other characters might endanger the public liberty—That he was desirous that they should be allowed their reasonable share according to their abilities, and that he would pay a proper consideration to their property, but that such allowance should be a distinct thing from a monopoly of the public office.

This took care of Schuyler, Livingston, and Duane. Duane, Clinton knew, considered it his right to be chosen senator, but no man had such a right. Who then should be senator? "Some Persons," Clinton said, "had thought that there should be a mercantile character" in the Senate but "it was a little difficult to find one in all points suitable."

Clinton was ready to be direct: what about King? His visitor was properly coy; he was "but lately an inhabitant of the state"; many of "the old and very reputable citizens would claim it as their right"; he had no desire to stir up controversy. Clinton dismissed King's objections one by one. When King brought up Duane's name again, Clinton replied heatedly, revealing his conception of his own role in New York politics. Before the Revolution, he said, "there were two great families or parties named Delancey and Livingston" in the state; "now the case was different," for "all the great opulent families were united in one confederacy." His "politicks" were "to keep a constant eye to the measures of this combination."

As if to clinch his argument, Clinton ended by pointing out who had put forward King's name: "some gentlemen from the country" in the legislature, the men he might have added who for more than a decade had been the backbone of Clinton's support in his battles with "the great opulent families." They were "men of sound judgment," the Governor explained, defensively, "but not used to public speaking," and they resented the ridicule heaped upon them by polished orators. They would be gratified, the Governor suggested to the new assemblyman, by having the legislature meet occasionally, not in New York—the sophisticated metropolis, the center of Federalism—but at Poughkeepsie, or the even more bucolic hamlet of Esopus, near Kingston. The Governor perhaps was drifting. King, sensing that Clinton had exhausted his purpose, excused himself. The interview was over.

Clinton's history lesson had laid bare the antagonisms of a quarter-century of New York politics: the domination of colonial political life by "the great opulent families"; the rivalry between the two greatest, the Delanceys and the Livingstons, which dominated colonial politics from the 1750's until the strife of the era of Revolution ushered in new political movements; the conflict during the Revolution between the "popular" and conservative wings of the Whig party; Clinton's unexpected elevation to the governorship and his forging of the instruments of power. What Clinton had not discussed with King was implicit in his story: the harsh conflict between tenant and landlord which thrust across the better-known political struggles;

the elimination in the wake of the Revolution of not only the Delanceys but also a wing of the landed and mercantile aristocracy
which made it possible for "new men" to gain political and economic
power; and finally, the quest of a frustrated aristocracy to regain as
nationalists and Federalists the prize that had eluded them as conservative Whigs. All this, and more, was in the marrow of the men
who were making New York politics as Clinton's interview with King
signaled the end of an era.

I

What George Clinton and his contemporaries took for granted
about the politics of colonial New York was made a commonplace
among historians by Carl Becker in his classic monograph in 1909.
"A small coterie of closely related families," wrote Becker, "was able
in large measure to control provincial politics."[2] In recent years
Becker, like the other giants of the "progressive" school of scholarship, has been subject to review. Yet the question in dispute is not
whether the aristocracy held power—Becker's most persistent critic
agrees that "the local aristocracy did occupy a commanding position
in the colony's politics"[3]—but how they maintained it.

The evidence for their power remains impressive. Examining the
major officials for the period from 1750 to 1776, Irving Mark identified as "the landed gentry": ten of the thirteen justices of the supreme
court; six of the seven registrars and principal surrogates; all four
admiralty judges; twenty-five out of twenty-eight members of the
council, the appointed upper house; and fifty-two of seventy-seven
members of the elected assembly.[4] The most recent scholar to subject New York's provincial legislature to scrutiny modifies the traditional picture only in degree. The appointed council, like its counterparts elsewhere, was, according to Jackson T. Main, "dominated by a
local social and economic elite," men who could be regarded as part
of "the native upper class" or who had been recently admitted to it.
Of the New York councilors, 94 per cent were wealthy and 75 per
cent were of "prominent old families," although merchants and mer-
chant-landholders, rather than landholders alone, were dominant. The

2. Carl L. Becker, *The History of Political Parties in the Province of New
York, 1760-1776* (Madison, Wis., 1909), ch. 1.
3. Milton M. Klein, "Democracy and Politics, in Colonial New York," *New
York History*, 40 (1959), 240, and in general, 221-46.
4. Irving Mark, *Agrarian Conflicts in Colonial New York, 1711-1775* (N.Y., 1940),
89-94.

assembly was a shade more representative. In the assembly elected in 1769 "the great landowners and the merchants held almost all of the twenty-eight seats" while "the voters elected only seven farmers." Merchants together with lawyers "furnished one half of the membership," making townspeople a majority of the legislators. Of these men, "at least 43 per cent were wealthy," holding property valued at more than £5000; "an equal number were well-to-do," holding property valued at from £2000 to £5000; while "at most five men, and probably fewer, belonged to the middle class of moderate men" who owned property valued from £500 to £2000. The aristocratic background was also pronounced. Ten of the twenty-eight assemblymen came from "the colony's foremost families who had, for the times, a distinguished ancestry, and two thirds or more were born of well-to-do parents." As a group, they "had either always belonged to or had successfully entered the colony's economic and social upper class."[5]

These findings thus confirm Lieutenant-Governor Cadwallader Colden's observation of 1764 that the assembly "consists of the Owners of these Extravagent grants, the Merchants of New York, the principal of them strongly connected with the Owners of these great Tracts by family Interest, and of Common Farmers, which last are Men easily deluded and led away with popular Arguments of Liberty and Privilege."[6]

How these men of wealth secured power is another matter. Although aristocracy in New York, as in the colonies as a whole, "had no formal institutional role in government," the institutions clearly were weighted in its favor. The aristocracy may have been "competitively maintained and dependent on continuous, popular support,"[7] yet it had most of the advantages in the competition.

The electorate, recent research has made clear, was considerably broader than scholars have believed. According to the student who has made the most serious effort to assemble the scattered statistical data, approximately 65 per cent of the adult white males were entitled to vote for the assembly under the prevailing £40 freehold

5. Jackson T. Main, "Social Origins of a Political Elite: The Upper House in the Revolutionary Era," Huntington Library Quarterly, 27 (1964), 155; Main, "Government by the People: The American Revolution and the Democratization of the Legislatures," William and Mary Quarterly, 3d Ser., 23 (1966), 394.

6. Cadwallader Colden to the Lords Commissioners of Trade, Sept. 20, 1764, The Colden Letter Books (N.-Y. Hist. Soc., Collections, vols. 9, 10 [New York, 1876-77]) I, 363-64.

7. Bernard Bailyn, "Political Experience and Enlightenment Ideas in Eighteenth Century America," American Historical Review, 67 (1962), 348-49.

qualification.[8] Tenants who held leases for twenty-one years or more, as most of them did, were counted as freeholders, which meant that a good proportion of them could vote.[9] In New York City and the port towns of the Hudson Valley, all the merchants and most of the "respectable mechanics and tradesmen" could qualify, although not the mass of cartmen, journeymen, petty tradesmen, and laborers.[10]

On the other hand, the sole elective body, the assembly, was small, even when enlarged to thirty-one members in 1773. Three manors, Cortlandt in Westchester County and Livingston and Rensselaer in Albany County, were entitled to their own assemblymen; the merchant centers, New York City and Albany, were overrepresented, and the few counties where the yeomanry were numerous were outnumbered. Moreover, the electoral machinery was at best pre-democratic, with elections on short and poorly publicized notice, polling places relatively few, voting by voice, and broad discretionary power given to the sheriff in taking the poll, opening the way to favoritism and fraud.[11]

Landlord dominance of their own bailiwicks was a fact of life, not immutable, but sufficient to discourage most men from challenging it. The proprietors of the three tracts entitled to send representatives to the assembly, Colden explained, "are become Hereditary Members." "The owners of the other great Pattents being Men of the greatest Opulence in the several Countys where the Tracts are, have sufficient influence to be perpetually Elected for these Countys."[12] The lord of Livingston Manor claimed that normally he could "carry" four hundred or so tenant voters. Between the Livingstons and Van Rensselaers, it was said that "it is in their power to determine every election in the county of Albany."[13] In every county south of Albany along the east bank of the Hudson there were other large estate holders to be reckoned with: in Dutchess, the lower manor Livingstons, allied with the Beekmans, and the owners of the Beverly

8. Chilton Williamson, *American Suffrage: From Property to Democracy, 1760-1860* (Princeton, 1960), 27, 107-8, 111; Klein, "Democracy and Politics," *N.Y. History*, 40 (1959), 237.

9. Williamson, *American Suffrage*, 7, 13, 27-29; E. Wilder Spaulding, *New York in the Critical Period, 1783-1789* (N.Y., 1932), 91-92.

10. Staughton Lynd and Alfred Young, "After Carl Becker: The Mechanics and New York Politics, 1774-1801," *Labor History*, 5 (1964), 221-23.

11. Nicholas Varga, "Election Procedures and Practices in Colonial New York," *N.Y. History*, 41 (1960), 249-77.

12. Colden to the Lords of Trade, Sept. 20, 1764, *Colden Letter Books*, I, 363-64.

13. William H. W. Sabine, ed., *Historical Memoirs of William Smith . . .* , 2 vols. (N.Y. 1956-58), I, 136.

Robinson and Philipse estates; in Westchester, the Philipses and Van Cortlandts, who together with the "manors" of Fordham, Pelham, Morrisania, and Scarsdale occupied two thirds of the county; in Manhattan, the Delanceys. To the west along the Mohawk was the powerful Sir William Johnson family; to the northeast several lesser estate holders. Only in Orange and Ulster counties on the west bank of the Hudson and Suffolk on eastern Long Island were yeomen farmers numerous enough to set the tone for their counties. It was these counties and sometimes Dutchess and Tryon which sent Colden's "common farmers" to the assembly.[14]

The landed gentry could not expect to have their candidates automatically elected; they often had to court and treat the voters, just as did their better-known Virginia brethren. Bribery was common, and even so, more than a few elections went awry.[15] But to Abraham Yates, stormy petrel of Albany County politics, New York's assembly districts resembled England's rotten boroughs: "for what material difference is there," he asked, "whether one elector by his own voice sends a member to Parliament or a manor settled with a hundred or a thousand tenants, under the influence of one person," sends a member to the assembly. Men like Yates, one-time sheriff and later a bitter enemy of "the manor lords," were advocates of electoral reforms, especially of a written ballot, by means of which Yates said, quoting Harrington, "no man in this way need fear the disobliging of his landlord, customer or benefactor."[16]

Politics in colonial New York prior to the crisis with Great Britain very likely was more than the rivalry of "family interest" and of "personal connections" that Carl Becker portrayed. The student of provincial politics "must work his way through a tangled morass" involving "the interplay of family alliances and rivalries; conflicting economic interests—land and trade, monopolists and freetraders, wholesalers and retailers; ethnic and national differences; religious tensions; and sectional divisions."[17] Even so, the competition between

14. For surveys, see Edward P. Alexander, "The Provincial Aristocracy and the Land," in Alexander C. Flick, ed., *History of the State of New York*, 10 vols. (N.Y., 1933-37), III, ch. 5; Lawrence Gipson, *The British Empire Before the American Revolution*, 12 vols. (N.Y., 1939-65), III, ch. 5; David M. Ellis, *et al.*, *A Short History of New York State* (Ithaca, N.Y., 1957), ch. 7.

15. Varga, "Election Procedures," *N.Y. History*, 41 (1960), 254-55.

16. Abraham Yates, "Speech to the Delegates" [Continental Congress, 1786-87], Abraham Yates Papers, New York Public Library, N.Y.C.

17. Milton M. Klein, "Politics and Personalities in Colonial New York," *N.Y. History*, 47 (1966), 8.

the Livingstons and Delanceys seems to be the warp and woof of politics to which the other tangled threads were tied, at least until the Stamp Act crisis.[18] The Livingstons were known as the "popular party" who represented "the landed interest," the lawyers, and in matters of church and state the Presbyterian meeting house. The Delanceys, known somewhat unjustly as "the court party," spoke for "the mercantile interest," the prerogatives of the crown, and the established Anglican church. The celebrated "Whig Triumvirate" who led the Livingston party through the 1750's and 1760's—William Livingston, William Smith, and John Morin Scott—had an aura of aristocratic liberalism about them.[19]

From 1752 to 1761 the history of New York politics "is essentially the story of the formation of the Livingston party." From 1761 to 1768 the Livingston party was dominant; thereafter, until the collapse of British government in 1775, the Delanceys were on top.[20] As late as 1774, John Adams could conclude after a visit to New York that "the two great families in this province upon whose Motions all their Politicks turn are the Delanceys and Livingstons."[21] In the Revolutionary era, however, new elements had entered into the competition for power.

II

Carl Becker's famous formulation for the period from 1763 to 1776 was that there was a question of "who should rule at home" as well as a "question of home rule" in New York. Although he doubtless overstated his claim that the two questions were "about equally prominent" and that the movement "for the democratization of American politics and society" was "fundamental,"[22] recent scholarship

18. See Nicholas Varga, New York Government and Politics During the Mid-Eighteenth Century (unpubl. Ph.D. diss., Fordham Univ., 1960), conclusions, 491-502.

19. Dorothy R. Dillon, The New York Triumvirate: A Study of the Legal and Political Careers of William Livingston, John Morin Scott, William Smith, Jr. (N.Y., 1949), chs. 1-6; Milton M. Klein, ed., The Independent Reflector . . . By William Livingston and Others (Cambridge, Mass., 1963), introduction, 20-48.

20. Beverly McAnear, Politics in Provincial New York, 1689-1761 (unpubl. Ph.D. diss., Stanford Univ., 1935), pp. 914-18, Parts 4 and 5.

21. Lyman H. Butterfield, ed., Diary and Autobiography of John Adams, 4 vols. (Cambridge, Mass., 1961), II, 103. In the same vein: "There are in this province two ancient and respectable families, viz the DeL-n-y and the L----n who are the only competitors in it for power," N.Y. Journal, Apr. 5, 1770, cited in Varga, New York Government, 156.

22. Becker, Political Parties in New York, 5, 21-22.

has not eliminated his basic contention about New York; it has only refined it. If anything, New York had not a two-way, but a three-way conflict: between Whigs and the British abetted by Loyalists, who were more numerous and powerful than in any other northern colony; between "popular" Whigs and conservative Whigs who vied for control of the Revolution on behalf of different interests; and between tenants and "manor lords," both Whig and Tory, for land.

The city of New York in the 1760's and 1770's was a center of one brand of "popular" Whiggery: militantly anti-British and in time democratic.[23] The leaders of the Sons of Liberty—John Lamb, Isaac Sears, and Alexander McDougall—were, according to conservatives, "a number of demogogues . . . not distinguished by birth or breeding," "upstart merchants" of humble origin or mechanics of the middling sort. Their followers, who to the elite were "the mob," "the inferior people," and "the lower sort," were mechanics, journeymen, laborers, sailors, and dockworkers. They were by no means "creatures" of the Livingstons, as their enemies claimed; one faction, in fact, supported the Delanceys. By 1776 the Sons of Liberty were replaced by the Committee of Mechanics, an aggressive, independent, and self-conscious political force.[24]

As events developed in the Revolutionary period, the democratic threat implicit in a mass-based Whig movement—public meetings at which everyone voted, petitions signed not only by freemen and freeholders, but by the "other inhabitants of all ranks"—became explicit. There were demands for a written ballot in assembly elections and for taxpayer suffrage in the election of delegates to extralegal bodies.[25] Gouverneur Morris, the scion of a landed family,

23. I agree with Merrill Jensen that the term "popular" is preferable to "radical" Whigs; see Jensen, *The Articles of Confederation: An Interpretation of the Social-Constitutional History of the American Revolution, 1774-1781* (Madison, Wis., 1940, 1959), preface to third printing, xxi. For contemporary use of the term "popular," see Cadwallader Colden's report of 1765, cited in Don R. Gerlach, *Philip Schuyler and the American Revolution in New York, 1733-1777* (Lincoln, Nebr., 1964), 99, in which he refers to "the popular leaders" who led the opposition to the Stamp Act, and William Smith, who in Sabine, ed., *Memoirs of William Smith*, II, 280, 306, refers to the division between "the popular and the landed interest."

24. Roger B. Champagne, The Sons of Liberty and the Aristocracy in New York Politics, 1765-1790 (unpubl. Ph.D. diss., Univ. of Wisconsin, 1960), especially 439-40, ch. 7, 504-8; Milton M. Klein, The American Whig, William Livingston of New York (unpubl. Ph.D. diss., Columbia Univ., 1954), ch. 13; an older account is Herbert Morais, "The Sons of Liberty in New York," in Richard B. Morris, ed., *The Era of the Revolution* . . . (N.Y., 1943, 2nd ed.), 269-90.

25. See Williamson, *American Suffrage*, 74, 77-78, 80-81, 83-85; Becker, *Political*

described one famous mass meeting in the spring of 1774 at which "I stood in the balcony and on my right hand were ranged all the people of property with some few poor dependents, and on the other all the tradesmen." Then his "fellow citizens fairly contended about the future forms of our government, whether it should be founded upon Aristocratic or Democratic principles."[26] From January to June 1776, almost every issue of the city's three newspapers "carried some lengthy discussion of the different kinds of government," including proposals for universal adult suffrage, annual elections, rotation of office, equal apportionment, the secret ballot, popular election of all local officials, complete religious tolerance, and the abolition of slavery.[27] On the eve of Independence, according to another close student of the city's politics, it was "clear that a battle over fundamentals was shaping in such a way as to pose a threat to aristocratic control."[28]

The yeomanry and small-town bourgeoisie of the state were the source of a less extreme popular Whiggery: militantly anti-British but less reformist on internal questions. At Albany, the Sons of Liberty were "formed and led by representatives of the older property holding dominant social class"—the Lansings, Yates, Douws, Vischers, and Rosebooms, especially the young sons of the leading Dutch burgomasters. Among them was the youthful heir to Rensselaerswyck, Stephen Van Rensselaer.[29] The Whigs of Ulster and Orange counties were led by the solid prosperous farmers and "lesser gentry," among whom were the Clintons, Tappens, DeWitts, and Wynkoops.[30] At the vote taken in 1775 on supporting the association authorized by the Continental Congress to enforce non-importation, the centers of freehold farmers were almost unanimously patriotic.[31]

Parties in New York, 106, 124-25, 134, 182; Dillon, New York Triumvirate, 104, 109-10.

26. G. Morris to Mr. [John] Penn, May 20, 1774, Peter Force, comp., American Archives: A Collection of Authentic Records, State Papers, and Letters . . . up to the Ratification of the Constitution, 9 vols. (Washington, 1837-53), I, 342-43.

27. Staughton Lynd, "The Mechanics in New York Politics, 1774-1788," Labor History, 5 (1964), 230.

28. Roger Champagne, "New York Politics and Independence, 1776," N.-Y. Hist. Soc., Quarterly Journal, 46 (1962), 302, 281-304.

29. Alice P. Kenney, "The Albany Dutch: Loyalists and Patriots," N.Y. History, 42 (1961), 339-41; Beverly McAnear, "The Albany Stamp Act Riots," Wm. and Mary Qtly., 3rd Ser., 4 (1947), 486-98.

30. E. Wilder Spaulding, His Excellency George Clinton, Critic of the Constitution (N.Y., 1938), ch. 3, 4.

31. Becker, Political Parties in New York, 215 and ch. 9. See ch. 4, n.27. For the Whig movement in the state as a whole, see Hugh M. Flick, "The Rise of the Revolutionary Committee System," in Flick, ed., History of State of N.Y., III, ch.

The tenants, by contrast, were a source of political toryism and social radicalism. The Whig-led Stamp Act riots began in October 1765 and recurred in the spring of 1766. In February 1766 a tenant rebellion began on the Philipse estate in Dutchess County which by spring engulfed most of the great Whig estates of the valley: the Van Cortlandts, the upper manor Livingstons, and the Van Rensselaers. Several thousand tenants were in motion, forcing the British to deploy against them regulars who were standing by in Albany and New York to prevent further agitation against the Stamp Act.[32] The popular Whigs were indifferent to the tenants; as a British captain wryly observed, "they are of the opinion that no one is entitled to riot but themselves." John Morin Scott and William Smith of "the Whig Triumvirate" sat on a special panel of judges which convicted the Westchester ringleaders.[33] In the ensuing election the Delanceys exploited tenant sentiment to topple the Livingstons from office.[34]

By 1775 tenants were disaffected to the point of believing the promises spread by royal agents that "if they take up arms against the Whigs the King for their services will give them the Whigs possessions." In 1777 the British were told that a promise to make freeholders of the tenants of Albany, Dutchess, and Westchester "would instantly bring you at least six thousand able farmers into the field."[35] When war came, tenants of Whig landlords in Albany County were actively Tory or at best indifferent to the patriot cause. Tenants along the Mohawk Valley followed the leadership of their Tory landlords, the Johnsons, and tenants in the occupied southern district, Westchester in particular, cooperated with the British. Only in southern Dutchess County, it would seem, did tenants of Tory landlords

7; [A. C. Flick], New York State, Division of Archives and History, *The American Revolution in New York: Its Political and Economic Significance* (Albany, 1926), ch. 2, 3.

32. Mark, *Agrarian Conflicts*, ch. 5; see also Oscar Handlin, "The Eastern Frontier of New York," *N.Y. History*, 18 (1937), 68-75.

33. James and John Montresor, *The Montresor Journals* (N.-Y. Hist. Soc., *Collections*, vol. 14 [New York, 1882]), 363; Dillon, *New York Triumvirate*, 164-69.

34. Champagne, "Family Politics Versus Constitutional Principles: The New York Assembly Elections of 1768 and 1769," *Wm. and Mary Qtly.*, 3d Ser., 20 (1963), 57-79.

35. John Watts in Philadelphia *Pennsylvania Ledger or the Weekly Advertiser*, Oct. 29, 1777, cited in Mark, *Agrarian Conflicts*, 13; Samuel Dodge to President of Provincial Congress, Dec. 5, 1775, *Journal of the Provincial Congress, Provincial Convention, Committee of Safety and Council of Safety of the State of New York, 1775, 1776, 1777*, 2 vols. (Albany, 1842), II, 106.

become "middling Whigs," anticipating and forcing the state's confiscation of their masters' estates.[36]

In 1776 the landed and mercantile elite of New York split asunder, confronted in effect by a triple threat of the British from without and tenant and urban political radicalism from within. "Two thirds of our gentlemen," the Whig landlord Robert R. Livingston, Jr., wrote, "fell off early in this controversy."[37] In New York City about a third of the 104 merchants in the Chamber of Commerce were Loyalist, and another third neutralist. But if among the landlords the Delanceys, Philipses, and Johnsons were Tory, the Livingstons, Schuylers, Van Rensselaers, and Van Cortlandts, who matched them in landed wealth, were Whig. And if William Bayard, James Jauncey, Isaac Low, and John Watts, Sr., of New York City were loyal to Britain, such prominent merchants as the Lows, Roosevelts, Rutgers, and Livingstons joined the patriot cause, becoming refugees from the occupied city.[38]

In this crucible the "Whig Triumvirate" dissolved: William Livingston continued his career in New Jersey, becoming its patriot governor in 1776; William Smith became a Tory under house arrest during the war and then an exile; and John Morin Scott became a popular Whig in search of a constituency.[39] The leadership of "the Livingston Party" was assumed by a new group of remarkable conservatives, chief among whom were James Duane and Philip Schuyler of the older generation; and John Jay, Robert R. Livingston, Jr., and Gouverneur Morris among the younger men. All were born into or married into the "great families" of the colony. Ever on the lookout for "men of talent," they soon took into their circle William Duer, a former aide to Lord Clive of India and heir to a West Indian plantation, who became the "prince of speculators" in the new nation; Egbert Benson, an extremely able Dutchess County lawyer; and in time Alexander Hamilton, another young migrant from the West

36. Richard B. Morris, "Class Struggle and the American Revolution," *Wm. and Mary Qtly.*, 3d Ser., 19 (1962), 12-13; Staughton Lynd, *Anti-Federalism in Dutchess County, New York: A Study of Democracy and Class Conflict in the Revolutionary Era* (Chicago, 1962), chs. 3, 4.

37. Robert R. Livingston to Edward Rutledge, Oct. 10, 1776, cited in George Dangerfield, *Chancellor Robert R. Livingston of New York, 1746-1813* (N.Y., 1960), 87.

38. Sidney Pomerantz, *New York An American City, 1783-1803: A Study of Urban Life* (N.Y., 1938), 76-77; A. C. Flick, *Loyalism in New York During the American Revolution* (N.Y., 1901), 32-36.

39. Dillon, *New York Triumvirate*, ch. 8.

Indies, a Columbia student who would make good first as Washington's aide-de-camp and after 1780 as Philip Schuyler's son-in-law.[40] These men consciously embarked on a course of steering the Revolution in New York in a safe direction. The metaphors of their private correspondence reveal their frame of mind. In 1774 Gouverneur Morris was fatalistic, comparing the mob to "reptiles struggling to cast off their winter's slough . . . ere noon they will bite" and to a horse that had to be whipped.[41] By 1777, however, Robert R. Livingston was convinced of "the propriety of Swimming with a Stream which it is impossible to stem." Observing the defeat of the Pennsylvania conservatives at the hands of their popular Whig party, Livingston remarked that "I long ago advised that they should yield to the torrent if they hoped to direct its course—you know nothing but well timed delays, indefatigable industry, and a minute attention to every favourable circumstance, could have prevented our being exactly in their situation."[42] Hamilton wrote to Jay that "in such tempestuous times it requires the great skill in the political pilots to keep men steady and within bounds."[43] It was this temporizing, accommodating approach that the aristocratic Whig leadership adopted.

Over the years the "pilots" varied in their political success. Jay was to Becker "the most perfect embodiment of that boldly cautious spirit that carried the revolution through in New York." "He had . . . the associating mind . . . which easily shapes its thinking to the exigencies of action."[44] James Duane was similarly successful; "very sensible I think and very artfull," said John Adams.[45] On the other

40. Many of these men belonged to the same clubs in New York City. Members of "The Moot" from 1770 to 1775 were Robert R. Livingston, John Jay, Gouverneur Morris, James Duane, William Livingston, and Stephen Delancey; members of a social club which met at Fraunces Tavern included Jay, Morris, Egbert Benson, Morgan Lewis, and Robert R., John, and Henry Livingston; see Rufus Griswold, *The Republican Court; or, American Society in the Days of Washington*, 2d rev. ed. (N.Y., 1867), 148.

41. See n.26 above.

42. Robert R. Livingston to William Duer, June 12, 1777, R. R. Livingston Papers, N.-Y. Hist. Soc.

43. Alexander Hamilton to John Jay, Nov. 26, 1775, Harold C. Syrett, Jacob Cooke *et al.*, eds., *The Papers of Alexander Hamilton*, 9 vols. (N.Y. 1961-66), I, 176-78.

44. Carl Becker, "John Jay and Peter Van Schaack," in *Everyman His Own Historian: Essays on History and Politics* (N.Y., 1935), 289; Joseph Dorfman and Rexford Guy Tugwell, *Early American Policy: Six Columbia Contributors* (N.Y., 1960), 43-98; Frank Monaghan, *John Jay, Defender of Liberty* (N.Y., 1935).

45. Butterfield, ed., *John Adams Diary*, II, 106-7; Edward P. Alexander, *A Revolutionary Conservative, James Duane of New York* (N.Y., 1938).

hand Gouverneur Morris, the youngest son of the landed family, marred his effectiveness by panic, a reaction that foreshadowed his response to the French Revolution twenty years later.[46] Robert R. Livingston was not "by temperament or training or background capable to play mentor to rural lawmakers" and at crucial moments retreated from the political battle in a pique.[47] By contrast Egbert Benson, the Dutchess lawyer who was close to Livingston, became a grey eminence in the state government.[48] Philip Schuyler was handicapped by manners an early biographer called "austere and aristocratic," but in time he became a major behind-the-scenes potentate in state affairs, practical, enterprising, and aggressive.[49]

In the years before, during, and after the Revolution these men worked together closely, corresponding, conferring, consulting. Their tactics varied. When the "torrent" of social radicalism threatened to engulf them, they had no choice but to fight it head on. But to a remarkable extent they taught themselves the tactics of "swimming with the stream"—of giving a little to save a lot more, of wooing away talented members of the opposition, of "minute attention to every favorable circumstance," in short, of beating the popular leaders at their own game. The combination of the two tactics was the secret of conservative survival in New York.

When Independence came in 1776, the New York patriots were locked into a coalition in which both political extremes were seriously weakened. They ruled a truncated state the southern part of which was occupied by the British, the rest of which, north and west, was a battlefield. There were more Tories and a greater proportion of them in New York than in any other northern state, enabling the British to recruit perhaps half of their 25,000 native troops there. The southern district, with the exception of Suffolk, was overwhelmingly Tory as were the western frontier along the Mohawk Valley, the northern frontier near Lake Champlain, and the tenanted areas on the east bank of the Hudson.[50] The popular Whigs of New York City lost their mechanic constituents either to the British occupation

46. Jared Sparks, The Life of Gouverneur Morris . . . , 3 vols. (Boston, 1832), I.
47. Dangerfield, Chancellor Robert R. Livingston, 114.
48. See Charles W. Spencer in DAB s.v. "Benson, Egbert"; Lynd, Anti-Federalism in Dutchess County, passim.
49. Bayard Tuckerman, Life of General Philip Schuyler, 1733-1804 (N.Y., 1903), ch. 8; Gerlach, Philip Schuyler, introd. and ch. 1.
50. Flick, Loyalism in New York, 112-13 and ch. 5; for a more recent estimate, see Bernard Mason, The Road to Independence: The Revolutionary Movement in New York, 1773-1777 (Lexington, Ky., 1966), chs. 2-4.

or the patriot army. Radical voices continued to be heard in the army and among the refugees from the southern district who swarmed over the Hudson Valley, but their best-known leaders, Lamb, Sears, and McDougall, were out of public life.[51] At the same time conservatives lost the support not only of the merchants of New York City but also of their upstate tenantry who were on the verge of rebellion and utterly beyond control at the polls. The military and political burden of the war fell on the popular Whig leaders of the middle Hudson Valley, on the west bank from Orange and Ulster, on the east bank from Dutchess and Albany. Their yeoman constituents provided the sinews of war. As a result the George Clintons of Ulster, the Melancton Smiths of Dutchess, and the Abraham Yateses of Albany rose to the fore.

III

In the early years of the war New York's patriots achieved a rough consensus within which they continued their political conflict. The constitution adopted in May 1777 registered the political center of gravity in the coalition. Contrary to a view widely held among historians, the document which provided the framework of New York politics for the next quarter of a century and the basis of George Clinton's political power was not the exclusive handiwork of conservatives.[52] The drafting committee selected by the Provincial Convention was headed by Abraham Yates who soon was anathema to conservatives. The popular Whigs were represented by Robert Yates of Albany, Henry Wisner of Ulster, and Charles DeWitt of Ulster, the conservatives by Jay, Robert R. Livingston, Gouverneur Morris, and Duer. John Morin Scott squeaked in by a vote of 21-20.[53]

Conservatives were frankly alarmed at the debate over political

51. Roger Champagne, "New York's Radicals and the Coming of Independence," *Journal of American History*, 2 (1964), 39-40; for hints of radicalism in the army, a much neglected subject, see R. R. Livingston to John Jay, Dec. 6, 1775, Jay Papers, Columbia Univ., and Isaac Q. Leake, *Memoirs of the Life and Times of General John Lamb* (Albany, 1850).

52. For traditional views, see Curtis Nettels, *The Roots of American Civilization: A History of American Colonial Life* (N.Y., 1937), 668; Spaulding, *New York in the Critical Period*, 87-95; Dangerfield, *Chancellor Robert R. Livingston*, 88-92; Elisha P. Douglass, *Rebels and Democrats: The Struggle for Equal Political Rights and Majority Rule During The American Revolution* (Chapel Hill, 1955), 62-66; Monaghan, *John Jay*, 95-97.

53. The best recent analysis is Mason, *Road to Independence*, ch. 7, richer in detail than the author's Ph.D. diss. (Columbia Univ., 1958), ch. 6, which I used. See also Champagne, *Sons of Liberty*, 452-57.

fundamentals the prospect of constitution-making had precipitated. "We have a government to form, you know," John Jay wrote, "and God knows what it will resemble. Our politicians are like some guests at a feast, are perplexed and undetermined which dish to prefer."[54] Robert R. Livingston was sick of the heavy diet of political philosophy; he would not "give one scene in Shakespeare for 1000 Harringtons, Lockes, Sidneys and [John] Adams."[55] The "diversity of opinions," however, as Abraham Yates pointed out, was "not whether the government should be the republican form partaking of monarchy, aristocracy and democracy; but what proportion of the ingredients out of each should make up the compound."[56]

As political theorists the popular Whigs were no match for the aggressive young conservatives on the committee. The latter were able to stretch out the drafting over eight months—a good example of Livingston's "well timed delay"—but they were unable to resist the pressures of the revolutionary situation "out of doors." As Abraham Yates later recalled, the framers "had to consider that the strength of a country lays in the yeomanry thereof, who already in the preceding campaign had been upon hard militia duty, in which a man worth no more than 10 pounds had to do equal duty with a gentleman of 10,000 pounds, and it was like to be the worse in time to come; that if the rich intended to avail themselves of the yeomanry of the country to fight for their riches, it would require to shew them by the confederation and the constitution that they intended no partiality and that there was no difference but in militia duty."[57]

The clash over voting qualifications epitomized the conflict within the Whig consensus. "All agreed," Robert Yates later explained, "that the rights and liberties of a country were ever in danger from the rich and the poor, and their safety was in the middle sort of yeomanry of the country, still the difficulty occurred in establishing the mean."[58] According to Yates, one draft was "handed about, to try

54. Cited without exact reference in N.Y. Division of Archives, *The American Revolution in New York*, 84-85.
55. R. R. Livingston to Philip Schuyler, Oct. 2, 1776, Philip Schuyler Papers, N.Y. Pub. Lib., cited in Dangerfield, *Chancellor Robert R. Livingston*, 87.
56. Abraham Yates, "Rough Hewer" notebook, Feb. 23, 1789, Yates Papers, N.Y. Pub. Lib.
57. *Ibid.* Yates compared both the constitution of New York and the Articles of Confederation to "the confession of a person on his sick bed dangerously ill whose assertions carry with them a greater presumption of truth because his future safety depends on it."
58. "Sidney" [Robert Yates], *N.Y. Journal*, June 13, 1788, reprinted in W. C.

it was supposed the temper of the members"; it proposed that the governor and senators be chosen from men holding estates of £10,000 by freeholders worth £1000 and more. A variant proposal suggested voting "in proportion to the value of a man's estate," i.e., one vote for a man with £100 estate, ten for a man of £1000, "and so on in the same ratio." "Others on the contrary supposed there ought to be no other criterion than the age of twenty one, a citizen born and resident in this country." But universal male suffrage was not to the taste of most popular Whigs; lowering the £40 freehold qualification to £20 was probably their limit. A written ballot was of greater concern, along with stiff regulation of election procedures "to guard against undue Influence, Partiality, Fraud and Corruption."⁵⁹

The provisions for voting typify the compromise written into the entire document. The provincial requirement for voting in assembly elections was lowered from a £40 freehold to a £20 freehold or "renting a tenement to the yearly value of forty shillings." But in elections for governor and senators the £40 freehold was raised to £100. The result was that the total electorate was somewhat larger than the provincial electorate but only half the voters could vote for the higher offices. The compromise on the type of balloting was more tortured. The constitution recognized that "an opinion hath long prevailed among divers of the good people of this State, that voting at elections by ballot, would tend more to preserve the liberty and equal freedom of the people than voting 'viva voce.' " The framers were willing for "a fair experiment" to be made and provided that the governor be elected by written ballot. They also specified that during the war senators and assemblymen would be elected by voice voting, but they authorized the legislature after the war to abolish voice voting altogether by a two-thirds vote. To accompany the new constitution the legislature enacted an election code to prevent fraud or coercion at the polls.⁶⁰

Ford, ed., *Essays on the Constitution of the United States* (Brooklyn, 1892), 307-08.

59. See the votes in *Journals of the Provincial Congress*, I, 866-67, 891-92; for the secret ballot, Sabine, ed., *Memoirs of William Smith*, II, 121, 129, 157; for what may be a popular Whig draft, see "Minutes of the Convention which formed the Constitution of the State of New York," Abraham Yates Papers, N.Y. Pub. Lib.

60. For the first census, 1790, see Table 1, Appendix; for analysis, see below, ch. 4; for the constitution, Benjamin Poore, comp., *The Federal and State Constitutions, Colonial Charters and other Organic Laws of the United States*, 2 vols. (Washington, 1877), II, 1328-39; and N.Y. State Division of Archives, *The Revolution in New York*, 326-29; for the election code, *Laws of the State of N.Y.*, 1st Sess., ch. 15.

The constitution of 1777 retained many "aristocratic" features. Estate owners were guaranteed their land grants whether fraudulent or legal. A Council of Revision composed of the governor, chancellor, and judges of the supreme court was empowered to veto legislation. The senate would be composed of twenty-four freeholders elected on staggered four-year terms from four large districts. Like his royal predecessor, the governor, elected to a three-year term and re-eligible, could convene and prorogue the assembly. By establishing a Council of Appointment made up of the governor and four senators and giving it the power to select county officials, conservatives expected to keep the courts in respectable hands, preventing the appointment of "ignorant and inattentive clerks."[61]

At the same time the constitution made several democratic departures from provincial precedent. Assembly elections were annual and the governor and senate, unlike the royal council, were elective. The number of representatives in the assembly was increased from thirty-one to seventy, and the three manor seats were abolished. Populous rural counties like Ulster and Dutchess, which formerly had but two representatives each, would now have six and seven, respectively. An electoral census and reapportionment were made mandatory at intervals. The assembly would "enjoy the same privileges" as its provincial predecessor but in electing senators to the Council of Appointment the assembly would share the appointive power with the governor; the two houses could override the governor's veto by a two-thirds vote. There was no Bill of Rights—"our situation resembled a people in a state of nature," Robert Yates explained, for "the constitution to be formed would operate as a bill of rights"—but trial by jury, due process of law, and religious liberty were guaranteed.[62]

Had extreme conservatives had their way, they would have gotten elections at four-year intervals by voice voting, an upper house indirectly chosen, a governor elected by an upper house, and a governor with more of the powers of his royal predecessors. Had the most democratic elements had their way, there would have been taxpayer

---

61. For continuing conservative concern with the appointment of county court and law officers, see Robert R. Livingston and Gouverneur Morris to John Jay, Apr. 26, 1777; Jay to same, Apr. 29, 1777; Schuyler to Jay, May 30, 1785, Henry P. Johnston, ed., *Correspondence and Public Papers of John Jay*, 4 vols. (N.Y., 1890-93), I, 126-36, III, 151-52; Robert R. Livingston to John Armstrong, Jan. 2, 1790, R. R. Livingston Papers, N.Y. Hist. Soc.

62. "Sidney" [Robert Yates] in Ford, ed., *Essays on the Constitution*, 315.

suffrage, a secret ballot for all elections at once—Abraham Yates fought for this on the floor of the convention—annual election of all state officials, and popular election of county and local officials; furthermore the appointive power would have been vested exclusively in the assembly and the governor's veto power would have been eliminated.[63]

In the context of these alternatives the final document has an unmistakable middle-of-the-road ring to it. According to Robert Troup, it proved popular in Albany, a center of moderate Whiggery, precisely because it "preserved a proper line between Aristocracy on the one hand and Democracy on the other." It was so delicately balanced, John Jay said, that "another turn of the winch would have cracked the cord."[64] Historians can hardly improve on these judgments.

The reactions among patriots confirm the "all things to all men" quality of the constitution. Only ultra-conservatives were unhappy; the upper manor Livingstons, whose manor seat had been "plucked from a family without any more ceremony than a crab from a tree," complained peevishly that it "savors too much" of the "levelling principle."[65] But Peter R. Livingston of the upper manor was the only member of the Provincial Convention to vote against the final document. Even Gouverneur Morris saw the new government as an "unwieldly" machine which "will require much oiling, winding and the like before it works well for the state." Hamilton was positive,[66] while the two chief architects, John Jay and Robert R. Livingston, Jr., were long proud of their handiwork.[67]

Equally important, the popular Whigs found the constitution to their liking. In his inaugural message in 1777 George Clinton pro-

63. Mason, *Road to Independence*, 224-29, discusses the various drafts.

64. Troup to Jay, May 15, 1777, cited in Monaghan, *John Jay*, 97; George Pellew, *John Jay* (Boston, 1890), 76.

65. William Duer to John Jay, May 28, 1777, Johnston, ed., *Correspondence of John Jay*, I, 137-40; Gouverneur Morris to Alexander Hamilton, May 16, 1777, Syrett, ed., *Hamilton Papers*, I, 253-54; Walter Livingston to John Carter, Aug. 11, 1777, Walter Livingston Letterbooks, R. R. Livington Papers, N.-Y. Hist. Soc., cited in Dangerfield, *Chancellor Robert R. Livingston*, 97; Sabine, ed., *Memoirs of William Smith*, II, 136-38 (May 13, 14, 1777).

66. Gouverneur Morris to R. R. Livingston, Feb. 1, 1777, R. R. Livingston Papers, N.-Y. Hist. Soc.; Hamilton to Gouverneur Morris, May 19, 1777, Syrett, ed., *Hamilton Papers*, I, 254-56.

67. Jay to Grand Jury of Ulster County, [July] 1777, in Johnston, ed., *Correspondence of John Jay*, I, 158-65; R. R. Livingston to John Armstrong, Jan. 2, 1790, R. R. Livingston Papers, N.-Y. Hist. Soc.; "Aristedes" [Robert R. Livingston], "To Timothy Tickler," *N.Y. Journal*, Apr. 4, 1792.

nounced it "our free and happy constitution"; ten years later he still found it "our excellent constitution."[68] During the debate over the federal Constitution Robert Yates contrasted the New York document he had helped shape in 1777 with the work of the federal convention he had abandoned in 1787. And Abraham Yates endorsed the comment of his opposite, Robert R. Livingston, agreeing that the New York constitution "has all along been considered unexceptionable."[69]

IV

Whigs next clashed in the contests to fill the high offices in the new state government. The skirmishing began in the Provincial Convention over the choice of judicial and legal officers. In the voting for chief justice of the supreme court John Jay defeated John Morin Scott, 19 to 15; Robert R. Livingston then defeated Scott, 21 to 15, for chancellor.[70] Scott himself rejected one of two other places on the supreme court, which then went to John Sloss Hobart, the proprietor of Easton Manor, associated with the Suffolk County Sons of Liberty, and Robert Yates, a moderate Whig from Albany. As attorney general the convention selected Egbert Benson, correctly characterized by a contemporary as "a Person of Probity and plain Understanding who will be guided by John Jay and R. R. Livingston."[71] Scott understandably "railed at an *Aristocratic Faction* which he pretends has formed and organized the new government," accurately identifying his enemies as Robert R. Livingston, Philip Livingston, James Duane, William Duer, and Gouverneur Morris. To placate Scott, the convention made him chairman of the Council of Safety, the Revolutionary body authorized to assist the governor when the legislature was not sitting.

In the popular campaign for governor there were three candidates,

68. "Speech to the Senate and Assembly, Kingston, Sept. 10, 1777," George Clinton Miscellaneous Manuscripts, N.-Y. Hist. Soc., also in draft form in Robert R. Livingston's hand as "Speech to the Legislature made and for Govr. Clinton," R. R. Livingston Papers, N.-Y. Hist. Soc.; Charles Z. Lincoln, ed., *Messages from the Governors* . . . , 11 vols. (Albany, 1909), II, 256 (Jan. 16, 1786).

69. "Rough Hewer" notebook, Feb. 23, 1789, Yates Papers, N.Y. Pub. Lib.; for Livingston's original statement, Robert R. Livingston, *An Oration Delivered Before the Society of the Cincinnati of the State of New York; in Commemoration of the Fourth of July* (N.Y., 1788).

70. *Journals of the Provincial Congress*, I, 910; Dillon, *New York Triumvirate*, ch. 8.

71. B. F. Stevens, *Facsimiles of Manuscripts in European Archives Relating to America, 1773-1783* (London, 1889-95), No. 438, Box 4, cited in Spaulding, *George Clinton*, 88.

each representing a different element in the patriot coalition: Philip Livingston, delegate to the Continental Congress, for the conservative Whigs;[72] General John Morin Scott, for the urban-based popular Whigs; and General George Clinton, for the yeoman-based popular Whigs of the Hudson Valley.[73] However, with William Livingston, Philip's brother, recently elected governor of New Jersey, his cousin, Robert R. Livingston, chancellor of New York, and John Jay, his nephew by marriage, chief justice, Philip's candidacy gave the impression that the Livingstons were "grasping at all the offices," as General Alexander McDougall growled.[74] The "impropriety of having two brothers Governors," Robert R. Livingston informed Duer, "made it absolutely necessary to change our battery." If they were not flexible, they might suffer the fate of the Pennsylvania conservatives.[75] The conservatives promptly switched to a ticket of General Philip Schuyler for governor and Clinton for lieutenant-governor.

The chaotic conditions of war and tenant rebellion in the upper Hudson made for confusion in the campaign. Conservative leaders backed the Schuyler-Clinton ticket. So did a committee of the Council of Safety which included John Jay and two of Clinton's in-laws from Ulster.[76] But in Albany there was talk of a ticket of Schuyler and James Duane and support for still another ticket of Schuyler and Abraham Ten Broeck, an Albany merchant and uncle of Stephen Van Rensselaer. Elsewhere there was support for John Jay for governor which he tried to squelch. Conservatives made John Morin Scott their chief target, unaware that Clinton's supporters were secretly backing their man for first place.[77]

At the polls voting qualifications were not strictly observed. Melancton Smith, the new sheriff of Dutchess County, probably already a supporter of Clinton, "took no list," i.e., he allowed all and

72. Gerlach, *Philip Schuyler*, 300-310, has the fullest account; see also Spaulding, *George Clinton*, 89-93.

73. William Duer to Philip Schuyler, June 19, 1777 (two letters), Schuyler Papers, N.Y. Pub. Lib.

74. Henry Beekman Livingston to R. R. Livingston, June 30, 1777, R. R. Livingston Papers, N.-Y. Hist. Soc.

75. R. R. Livingston to William Duer, June 12, 1777, *ibid.*

76. "A Statement of the Committee of Safety," John Jay, Charles DeWitt, Zephaniah Platt, Matthew Cantine, and Peter Tappen to George Clinton, June 7, 1777, Hugh Hastings and J. A. Holden, eds., *Public Papers of George Clinton, First Governor of New York, 1777-1795, 1801-1804*, 10 vols. (N.Y., 1899-1914), I, 855-56.

77. Gerlach, *Philip Schuyler*, 300-307.

sundry to vote.[78] As a result of John Morin Scott's efforts in the Council of Safety, soldiers were also permitted to vote in the forts where they were stationed; thus, no one could question whether they were £100 freeholders.[79]

As Schuyler lamented, Clinton "played his Cards better than was Expected,"[80] winning with 1828 votes; Schuyler had 1199, Scott 368, and Jay 367. Clinton also won the contest for lieutenant-governor, receiving 1647 votes to 1098 for Pierre Van Cortlandt, the Westchester landlord, and 748 for Abraham Ten Broeck. When Clinton resigned the office Van Cortlandt became lieutenant-governor.

The vote foreshadowed a pattern that would prevail for many years in state elections. In the civilian vote, the contest was between Clinton and Schuyler. Clinton swept Ulster, his home county, 464-12, neighboring Orange, 223-10, Dutchess across the river, 206-132, and the small northern part of Westchester not occupied by the British, 68-7. Schuyler carried Albany, his home county, 589-125, frontier Tryon to the west, 237-10, and frontier Charlotte to the northeast, 35-2. The soldier vote, counted separately, seems to have been divided between Clinton and Schuyler, 963-187.[81] Thus Clinton's major support rested in the yeomanry and the soldiers, mostly yeomen, while Schuyler's came from his own center of tenantry. Schuyler blamed his defeat on the low turnout in Albany County where the upper manor Livingstons were unable to deliver their rebellious tenants to the polls.[82] Clinton's strength, conservatives knew, rested partly on his military reputation,[83] but also on anti-Livingston sentiment. "The

78. Sabine, ed., *Memoirs of William Smith*, June 11, 14, 1777, 157, 159-60.
79. Dillon, *New York Triumvirate*, 150-51.
80. Schuyler to Jay, June 30, 1777, cited in Gerlach, *Philip Schuyler*, 308.
81. N.Y. Secretary of State, *Calendar of Historical Manuscripts Relating to the Wars of the Revolution in the Office of the Secretary of State*, 2 vols. (Albany, 1868), II, 242, reprinting "Canvass of Votes for Governor and Lieutenant-Governor of New York, 1777," from Miscellaneous Papers, 37, 225-33. This lists the votes for six counties, Westchester, Dutchess, Ulster, Albany, Tryon and Charlotte. A Memorandum (photostat), Pierre Van Cortlandt Papers, Sleepy Hollow Restorations, Tarrytown, N.Y., which also presents the vote for each county, adds Orange. The Secretary of State's *Calendar* reports the following figures "on a separate slip . . . without the names of any place": for governor, Clinton 963 and Schuyler 187; for lieutenant-governor, Clinton 569 and Van Cortlandt 642. These doubtless were the votes of soldiers cast at their encampments. Thus Clinton with 1130 civilian votes to 1013 for Schuyler, won even without the soldier votes, a point not hitherto recognized by historians. John Morin Scott's 368 votes were scattered in six counties, and John Jay's 367 votes came from Westchester, his home county, and Tryon.
82. Schuyler to William Duer, July 3, 1777, Schuyler Papers, N.Y. Pub. Lib.

people of Dutchess and Ulster," William Smith recorded, were "persuaded in chusing a Governor to name no Livingston nor any in Connection with that family."[84]

Conservatives were ruffled by Clinton's election, but not alarmed. "His family and Connections," wrote Schuyler, "do not Intitle him to so distinguished a predominance," but he added that "General Clinton's having the chair of Government will not cause any divisions amongst the friends of America . . . he is virtuous and loves his Country, has abilities and is brave, and I hope he will Experience from Every patriot what I am resolved he shall have from me, Support, Countenance and Comfort."[85]

The new legislature moved to bind up the wounds in the patriot coalition. As speaker, the assembly elected Walter Livingston of the deprived upper manor. To represent the occupied southern district the Council of Safety chose John Morin Scott a senator, whereupon the senate elevated him to the Council of Appointment; in time he also became New York's secretary of state.[86] The legislature with Clinton's blessings sent John Jay and Robert R. Livingston to the Continental Congress.[87]

Thus the elections, taken as a whole, found a place for leaders from all wings of the Whig party. The Livingstons unquestionably had returned to a place of influence long denied them by the Delanceys. Conservatives were entrenched in the supreme court and in the Court of Chancery, especially important for protecting their dubious land titles. They also had a strong foothold in the Council of Revision where they could check the legislature. What the legislature might do, however, what an untried governor dependent for support on the "popular interest" might do, was beyond prediction.

V

Social issues soon split the fabric of Whig unity. William Smith proved correct in his prediction that there would be a "Severence between the Popular and the landed interest," but he let his Tory

83. Hamilton to R. R. Livingston, Aug. 7, 1777, Syrett, ed., Hamilton Papers, I, 308.

84. Sabine, ed., Memoirs of William Smith, II, 151, 326.

85. Schuyler to Jay, July 14, 1777 in Johnston, ed., Correspondence of John Jay, I, 147; Clinton to Schuyler, Aug. 7, 1777, George Clinton Papers, Library of Congress, cited in Spaulding, George Clinton, 93.

86. Dillon, New York Triumvirate, ch. 8.

87. Clinton to Hamilton, Mar. 5, 1778, Syrett, ed., Hamilton Papers, I, 437.

sympathies mislead him in contending that "they will mutually pull each other down."[88] What Smith should have remembered from his own experience was that the popular Whigs were not levelers when it came to the property of the landlords.

The first test came in the tenant rebellion of 1777. In October 1776 there was a foreshadowing of trouble when the Van Rensselaer tenants in the militia deserted en masse at the prospect of being ordered out against the British; the patriot militia rounded them up in the woods. Then in May 1777, as Burgoyne's army approached Ticonderoga, almost the entire Livingston tenantry, some five hundred from both the upper and lower manors, plotted to seize their Whig landlords. The popular Whigs were true to their role in the Great Rebellion of 1766. To suppress the insurrection the Provincial Convention dispatched a commission on which the Clintonian Zephaniah Platt of Dutchess served with the landlord Robert R. Livingston. Generals Scott, McDougall, and Clinton stood by with the patriot militia of Dutchess to move against the tenants if necessary. When it was clear that the British would not arrive and that patriots would overpower them, tenant spokesmen approached the Livingstons "offering to give up their arms . . . if they might be left undisturbed on their farms." Rejecting the offer, the Livingstons and the militia carted three hundred rebels off to jail. Two ringleaders were hanged, thirty were kept there as hostages, and the rest were made to swear an oath of loyalty to the patriot government.[89] George Clinton, it was said, was sorry more did not hang. The old lord of the upper manor, Robert Livingston, was "greatly agitated," raging hysterically at his disloyal tenants, "the new government," and the outrageous state constitution.[90] Considering the circumstances of war and invasion he was an ingrate; the popular Whigs had helped the landlords suppress their tenants just as the British had done a decade before.

Although conservatives were relieved that the popular Whigs rejected tenant radicalism, they were appalled at the new class of men risen to influence in the legislature. "The new raw hands," one

---

88. Sabine, ed., *Memoirs of William Smith*, II, 306, 280.

89. Staughton Lynd, "The Tenant Rising at Livingston Manor, May 1777," N.-Y. Hist. Soc., *Qtly. Journal*, 48 (1964), 163-77; Kennedy, "The Albany Dutch," *N.Y. History*, 42 (1961), 339-41; Robert R. Livingston, Zephaniah Platt, and Matthew Cantine to the Provincial Convention, May 4, 8, 1777, *Journals of the Provincial Congress*, I, 910, 912, 918-19.

90. Sabine, ed., *Memoirs of William Smith*, II, 127-28, 132-34, 136, 280.

Livingston called them. William Smith labeled them "the meaner hands," and Robert R. Livingston agreed that they were men "unimproved by education and unrefined by honor." Philip Livingston claimed there were not four men in the assembly or three in the senate who could draw up a bill, and Walter Livingston doubted that there were that many.[91] It was an assembly of working farmers; raising a quorum "at the eve of Harvest" was unthinkable.[92] On the county level it was even worse. Gone as judges, county clerks, and sheriffs were the Tory gentry: Cadwallader Colden, Jr., in Ulster, Guy Johnson in Tryon, James Delancey in Westchester, Stephen Delancey in Albany. In Dutchess County Beverly Robinson, the Tory landlord, gave way as chief judge to Ephraim Paine, son of a farmer and blacksmith, a Separatist preacher who wore the plain garb of a workingman. Mr. Melancton Smith replaced Philip Livingston, Esq., as sheriff; he was a self-made merchant, a farmer's son who had risen from the station of a clerk in a retail store.[93]

As the "raw hands" legislated, conservatives in the Council of Revision resorted to the veto: on an election regulation that would have made pressuring the voters more difficult, on a tax levy of £50 on each £1000 gain by war profiteers, and on validating as laws the acts of the quasi-legal Council of Safety. Time and again, however, assembly and senate overrode them. A bill was even brought in to impeach the council.[94]

Taxes were a running sore. Over the council's veto the legislature levied a tax of three cents a pound on improved land and a half cent a pound on personal property. At best it would hit hardest at large estate holders.[95] What made it unbearable, however, was that the

91. Robert L. Livingston to Peter Van Burgh, Apr. 4, 1780, R. R. Livingston Papers, N.-Y. Hist. Soc.; Sabine, ed., *Memoirs of William Smith*, II, 159-60; Robert R. Livingston to Edward Rutledge, Oct. 10, 1776, Bancroft Transcripts, N.Y. Pub. Lib., I, 229.

92. George Clinton to R. R. Livingston, June 6, 1782, R. R. Livingston Papers, N.-Y. Hist. Soc.

93. A. Werner, comp., *Civil List and Constitutional History of the Colony and State of New York* (Albany, 1884) lists sheriffs, clerks, first judges and surrogates by county with dates of appointment.

94. Lincoln, ed., *Messages from the Governors*, II, 21-24, 26-31, 34-39, 40-41, 59-65; R. R. Livingston to John Jay, Mar. 4, 1779, R. R. Livingston Papers, N.-Y. Hist. Soc.

95. N.Y. State Division of Archives, *The American Revolution in New York*, 124-25. "From July 4, 1776 to Oct. 1, 1781 from taxes collected the counties paid the following sums into the State Treasury: Albany, £875,720; Dutchess, 1,116,141; Ulster, 620,008; Orange, 280,741; Westchester, 79,598; Tryon, 32,450; Charlotte, 3,821." Thus Dutchess and Albany, the two centers of landlordism, paid almost

"executors of the new laws," as Gouverneur Morris put it, were "men who like the Laws themselves were new."[96] Assessors and collectors were elected by a vote of the local "inhabitants"—not even freeholders —and as Hamilton later excoriated them, they had "little disposition to risk the displeasure of those they elect." Their assessment was determined by "the exterior figure a man makes, the decency or meanness of his manner of living, the personal friendships or dislikes of the assessors."[97] Margaret Beekman Livingston complained to Egbert Benson, the attorney-general, about her assessment, and her son the Chancellor pleaded with the Governor, but when these temporal sources refused to intercede she prayed, "May the Almighty give us Peace, Independence and deliverance from the persecutions of the Lower Class."[98]

The tests of inflation and profiteering also drove a wedge in the ranks of the patriots. Spontaneous Committee meetings petitioned for price regulation, Ulster and Orange county Whigs demanding action against the "unrestrained practises of monopolizers and engrossers." John Holt's Whig New York Journal, re-established at Poughkeepsie, fumed against "the selfish avaricious spirit" of profiteering merchants.[99] Legislation initially sponsored by John Morin Scott was passed regulating prices and designating local Committees of Safety to police the law. Robert Livingston was furious at being challenged on the price of iron from the upper manor's forges, and his son Walter saw nothing objectionable in a 700 per cent profit on pork rations which he as deputy commissary-general offered to supply the army. Justice Hobart provided the conservative rationale for opposition to price regulation with a jeremiad about the loss of the "spur" of the "liberty of acquiring property."[100]

two-thirds of the £3,048,481 collected; see also Thomas Cochran, New York in the Confederation: An Economic Study (Phila., 1932), ch. 3.

96. Gouverneur Morris, fragment, n.d., Gouverneur Morris Papers, Columbia Univ., cited in Staughton Lynd, The Revolution and the Common Man: Farm Tenants and Artisans in New York Politics, 1777-1788 (unpubl. Ph.D. diss., Columbia Univ., 1962), 20.

97. Hamilton to Robert Morris, Aug. 13, 1782, Syrett, ed., Hamilton Papers, III, 135-36.

98. Margaret Beekman Livingston to R. R. Livingston, Dec. 30, 1779, Benson to R. R. Livingston, Mar. 20, 1780, Livingston to Clinton, May 21, Clinton to Livingston, July 7, 1780, R. R. Livingston Papers, N.-Y. Hist. Soc.; for Duane's furor over taxes, see Alexander, James Duane, 217.

99. Cited in Bernard Mason, "Adjustment to a War Economy: Entrepreneurial Activity in New York State During the Revolution," Business History Review, 40 (1966), 201.

100. Ibid.; Richard Morris, "Labor and Mercantilism in the Revolutionary Era,"

The disposition of Loyalist land was the most divisive issue of all, the battle over it unfolding in stages, first in 1777 over the sequestering of land, then in the fall of 1779 over confiscation, and finally in the spring of 1780 over the sale of confiscated land. The pressures for confiscation and sale were diverse: the urgent financial needs of the state, in light of the failure of price regulation; the clamor of tenants on Tory lands, particularly from southern Dutchess; the need to counteract British propaganda among tenants. The popular Whigs were divided. There was talk in Dutchess and Ulster that "when the Independency is established the Manors would be parcelled out to such tenants as were in favor with the New Established Government."[101] Abraham Yates, however, opposed sale on the grounds that the land would fall into the hands of speculators, and Governor Clinton opposed it on the grounds that it was neither "sound policy" nor constitutional.[102] In the winter of 1779-80 when patriot fortunes were at a perilously low ebb and the Dutchess tenants threatened direct action, the pressure mounted. Much to the disappointment of the Whig estate holders, Egbert Benson chose this moment to "yield to the torrent" in the legislature. The result was a law for the sale of the estates of fifty-five attainted individuals, passed over a veto of the Council of Revision. The session, said Benson, was "a continual wrangle from first to last," with the atmosphere "poisoned by distrust."[103]

Although "the popular" and "the landed interest" thus drew apart, they maintained their consensus as patriots behind George Clinton. When Clinton ran again in the spring of 1780, this time with Pierre Van Cortlandt as his running mate, he had no opposition and was returned with 3624 votes, only a few less than the total cast for all candidates in 1777.[104]

---

in Morris, ed., *The Era of the Revolution*, 115-39, *passim.*; see also Cochran, *New York in the Confederation*, 30-32.

101. Staughton Lynd, "Who Should Rule at Home? Dutchess County, New York, in the American Revolution," *Wm. and Mary Qtly.*, 3d Ser., 18 (1961), 343-53.

102. Clinton to John Jay, Mar. 17, 1779, Charles DeWitt to John Jay, Apr. 20, 1779, Jay Papers, Columbia Univ.; Carol M. Spiegelberg, Abraham Yates: An Eighteenth Century Public Servant (unpubl. M.A. thesis, Columbia Univ., 1960), 46ff.

103. Egbert Benson to Robert R. Livingston, Mar. 20, 1780, R. R. Livingston Papers, N.-Y. Hist. Soc.

104. F. B. Hough, *New York Civil List* (Albany, 1860), 29, speaks of Clinton's "majority" as 3284 without indicating any other vote. Robert R. Livingston to George Clinton, June 29, 1780, R. R. Livingston Papers, N.-Y. Hist. Soc., speaks of "the great superiority of ballots in your favor at the last election," claiming

That conservatives supported Clinton is not surprising. As war governor his record was excellent. In his talk with Rufus King in 1789, Clinton might well have pointed to these war years for proof that he "would pay a proper consideration" to the property of the "great families." In the Council of Revision if Clinton ever challenged the vetoes of Livingston and Hobart, there is no evidence for it. Moreover, he gave ample proof that he would allot the landed families "their reasonable share" of the offices, "according to their abilities." Jay, Robert R. Livingston, Philip Livingston, Duane, Duer, Gouverneur Morris, Hamilton—in short, the entire galaxy of conservative leaders—served as New York's delegates to Congress during the war. Thus it is not strange that Chancellor Livingston or Lewis Morris, the Westchester landlord, should congratulate Clinton on his victory in 1780.[105]

Robert R. Livingston had more special reasons for his warm wishes: the Governor and the Chancellor had in effect a personal and political partnership. The Chancellor wrote the first message to the legislature for the General fresh from the battlefield.[106] The two sat together on the Council of Revision. Egbert Benson, who was considered Clinton's confidential friend and advisor, was even closer to Livingston.[107] When it came to favors on taxes, appointments, or exemptions which Livingston unabashedly requested, the Governor kept the Chancellor at arm's length.[108] But when Abraham Yates and John Morin Scott attempted to oust Livingston as Chancellor—apparently to replace him with James Duane—while he was in Philadelphia serving as Secretary for Foreign Affairs, Clinton protected his office, true to "the firmest reliance upon your friendship" which Livingston placed in him. When the legislature retaliated, failing to pay the Chancellor the money the state owed him, Clinton even arranged for a personal loan of $2000.[109] Many years after the Chancellor and Governor had parted ways politically, they could look back

that "the people notwithstanding the endeavors of some designing men are disposed to do justice to your merits." See Clinton to Livingston, July 7, 1780, *ibid.*, for the reply.

105. Spaulding, *George Clinton*, 131-32.
106. See n.68 above.
107. Alexander Hamilton, "Letters of H.G.," No. 3, Mar. 1789, Syrett, ed., *Hamilton Papers*, V, 267-68.
108. Clinton to Livingston, Apr. 16, Nov. 6, 1778, Mar. 9, 1780, Livingston to Clinton, Nov. 4, 1778, May 21, July 7, 1780, R. R. Livingston Papers, N.Y. Hist. Soc.
109. Livingston to Clinton, Dec. 19, 1781, Feb. 23, July 31, Aug. 28, Dec. 5, 1782, Apr. 2, 1783, Clinton to Livingston, Mar. 19, 1783, *ibid.*

to this wartime collaboration. In Livingston's eyes he was fulfilling what he later called the historic connection of his family with "the democratic interest."[110] From Clinton's point of view he was preventing the formation of a "confederacy of the great and opulent families" against him.

In Clinton's second term, however, the coalition of patriots was on the way to dissolution as the conservative Whigs embarked on their quest for a stronger, less republican national government. Hamilton was convinced of the need for "a solid coercive union," Schuyler of the need for a national "dictator" with "vice-dictators" for the states.[111] In 1780 Schuyler, Benson, and Hobart went off to the convention at Hartford, on the road that would lead to subsequent nationalist conventions at Annapolis in 1786, Philadelphia in 1787, and back to Poughkeepsie in the summer of 1788.

In the closing years of the war, 1781 and 1782, the conservative Whigs were all in the thick of service to the cause of nationalism: Gouverneur Morris as assistant to Robert Morris, Superintendent of Finance at Philadelphia; Hamilton on his return to public life as Robert Morris's appointee as federal receiver of taxes; John Jay as minister to Spain, and New York's most distinguished diplomat; Robert R. Livingston as the first Secretary for Foreign Affairs; and James Duane as a near boss of the Continental Congress.

In 1782 as war turned to peace Hamilton railed at Abraham Yates as a man of "ignorance and perverseness" while Yates, whom Hamilton replaced as receiver, fumed over the machinations of the Superintendent of Finance and his minions. In the spring of 1783 Philip Schuyler ran against George Clinton for governor but made a pitiful showing. Late in 1783 as the patriot refugees returned to New York City, Robert R. Livingston expressed his shock to John Jay when New York City elected to the assembly a ticket of "warm and hot headed whigs" made up of the old Liberty Boys. Gouverneur Morris wrote Jay he thought "the superior advantages of our constitution will now appear, to the repressing of those turbulent spirits, who wish for confusion, because in the regular order of things they can only fill a subordinate sphere." But Jay could hardly have been as confident as he fumed to Hamilton at the anti-Tory policies of the New

110. Robert R. Livingston, "Political Essay on Elections" [n.d. but 1792], *ibid.*
111. Hamilton to Duane, Sept. 3, 1780, Schuyler to Hamilton, Sept. 10, 18, 1780, Syrett, ed., *Hamilton Papers*, II, 400-418, 425, 432-33.

York legislature which ran counter to the peace treaty he had just helped negotiate.[112]

By the end of the war it was clear that two interests were in the process of formation in New York based on the antagonism between conservative and popular Whigs that had predated the Revolution. Without exception, the conservative Whig leaders of the 1770's became the nationalist leaders of the 1780's and the Federalist leaders of 1788. Governor Clinton, on the other hand, became the center of an interest composed of the popular Whig leaders of the 1770's who with only a few significant exceptions became the anti-Federalist leaders of 1788. The struggle over "who should rule at home" would continue in peace as new issues spurred contesting factions to reach for the fruits of republican victory.

112. Hamilton to Robert Morris, Aug. 13, 1782, Jay to Hamilton, Sept. 28, 1783, *ibid.*, III, 137-38, 459-60; Robert R. Livingston to Jay, Jan. 25, 1784, R. R. Livingston Papers, N.-Y. Hist. Soc.; Gouverneur Morris to Jay, Jan. 10, 1784, Sparks, ed., *Life of Gouverneur Morris*, I, 266.

CHAPTER 2

The Clintonians:

From Popular Whigs To

Anti-Federalists

————•————

As the war drew to a close, one of "the great and opulent families," the Delanceys, had been removed from New York politics, and the other prewar "party," the Livingstons, were confronted with the fact that the "new raw men" they despised, the "country members" of the legislature who, Clinton mentioned to Rufus King in 1789, had come to stay. In the Confederation period party politics in New York no longer revolved exclusively around the rivalry of the two great families. One party, the Federalists, was led by "a confederacy" of the landed families. The other revolved around Governor Clinton who left the unmistakable imprint of his personality and principles upon it. It was led by men of the "middling classes," who were cemented to Clinton by the perquisites available to the powerful governor of New York and who differed markedly from their Federalist counterparts.

I

By the mid-1780's George Clinton was virtually unassailable at the polls. In 1783, he was re-elected over halfhearted, divided opposition. Schuyler ran against Clinton, but despite his friends' taking "infinite pains for him" he got only 643 votes, all from his home county. Robert R. Livingston's family backed Clinton, the upper manor

Livingstons were indifferent, and New York City was still in enemy hands. Ephraim Paine, in Hamilton's eyes a "fiery" and "primitive" radical, received 520 votes, all very likely from his home county of Dutchess and conceivably a protest against Clinton's moderation on land confiscation. With about 1100 more votes cast than in 1780, Clinton got 3584, almost his previous total and still "a very disproportionate vote," as a Livingston noted.[1]

Three years later conservatives were unable to muster any candidate at all against Clinton. In pleading with Jay to run in 1786, Schuyler conceded that "none have a chance of succeeding against Clinton" but "you, the Chancellor or myself." Robert R. Livingston would fail "on account of the prejudices against the family name"; he himself would run well only in the north where he was known, but Jay, alone, had a statewide following. Jay refused to make the race, recognizing that "disgust and discontent" with Clinton was not widespread.[2]

George Clinton, the dominant figure in New York politics of the 1780's, like democratic leaders of other times and places, epitomized in many ways the background and aspirations of his followers; in him their characteristics were writ large. Clinton had a better start in life than most of those in his party. He "had noble blood in his veins," his biographer asserts, as a "direct descendant of Henry, the second Earl of Lincoln." "He was also a distant cousin of that other George Clinton, the son of the Sixth Earl of Lincoln who was the governor of the province of New York from 1743 to 1753." His grandfather, a Scottish Presbyterian, had acquired an estate in central Ireland which had been "planted" by the Stuarts. Clinton's father, happy neither in his estate nor the state of religion, migrated to New York in 1729. He settled at Little Britain, a hamlet in what became Orange County, a few miles inland from the Hudson and not many years removed from the frontier. George Clinton's mother may have been of "common" Irish stock; in later years the Governor regularly attended the dinners of the Friendly Sons of St. Patrick and does not seem to have minded the affectionate sobriquet of "the Old Irishman." His father

1. Margaret Beekman Livingston to Robert R. Livingston, Apr. 30, 1783, Thomas Tillotson to R. R. Livingston, Apr. 27, June 1, 1783, R. R. Livingston Papers, N.-Y. Hist. Soc.

2. Philip Schuyler to John Jay, May 30, Sept. 18, 1785, Jay Papers, Columbia Univ.; Jay to Schuyler, June 10, 1785, Johnston, ed., *Correspondence of John Jay*, III, 154-56.

acquired land, became a surveyor and a farmer, and through his connections with the royal governor, first judge of Ulster County.[3]

George Clinton, the youngest son among six children, was born in
the family's unpretentious cottage in 1739; he was educated by the
local Presbyterian minister. In 1757, still in his teens, he went off to
sea as a sailor on a privateer preying on French vessels; on his return
he joined an expedition to Montreal as a lieutenant in his brother's
militia regiment. Settling to a career, Clinton studied law in the
office of William Smith of the Presbyterian Whig Triumvirate and
then returned to Ulster to assume the rounds of a small-town lawyer.
Skilled in his father's craft, he also did an occasional turn at surveying, a job in which he kept an eye cocked for likely land speculations of his own.

In 1768 Ulster County elected the twenty-nine-year-old lawyer to
the provincial assembly in which he would serve until 1775. In 1770
Clinton married Cornelia Tappen, characterized by Thomas Jones, the
Tory historian, as "the daughter of an eminent substantial burgher"
of the corporation of Kingston, and the brother of Christopher Tappen, clerk of the corporation. "This match," claims Jones, "was the
foundation of all his after greatness. . . . In the Dutch towns in the
Province of New York, (Kingston is entirely so) the inhabitants are
all related. Cousins in the fifteenth degree are looked upon as nearly
related, as cousins-german in an English town. The Tappen family,
in consequence of this kind of consanguinity, was related to almost
the whole town."[4] He bought a farm at New Windsor with a beautiful
vista on the Hudson and soon owned diverse tracts of land, and bonds
and notes worth almost £1500.

As the crisis with Britain deepened, Clinton earned the reputation of a staunch Whig in the Livingston party. Elected a delegate
to the Continental Congress in 1775, he was "silent in general and
wants (when he does speak) the influence to which he is entitled."[5]
At the outbreak of hostilities he chose to fight rather than make laws.
Appointed a brigadier general in the militia, he contributed more in

3. Spaulding, *George Clinton*, the major source for other biographical data
below; Richard C. Murphy and Lawrence J. Mannion, *The History of the Society
of the Friendly Sons of St. Patrick in the City of New York, 1784 to 1955* (N.Y.,
1962), 535-37.

4. Thomas Jones, *History of New York During the Revolutionary War* . . . , ed.
E. F. DeLancey, 2 vols. (N.Y., 1879), II, 326.

5. Edward Rutledge to John Jay, June 29, 1776, Edmund C. Burnett, ed., *Letters
of Members of the Continental Congress*, 8 vols. (Washington, 1921-36), I, 517.

the opening months "to the waging of the war than any other general officer from New York with the exception of Schuyler."[6]

Clinton's estate grew during and after the Revolution. He was wealthy enough to lend the state money and to finance George Washington's share in a 6000-acre speculation in Mohawk Valley land. By 1789 Hamilton said with accuracy that "he has applied the greatest part of his public allowance to the accumulation of a large fortune." He had made "several profitable speculations in land," some publicly known, others Hamilton alleged in the name of a third person, and had received "a handsome fortune" from the state in a "few accumulated payments" for his loans.[7] Most of Clinton's speculations were in undeveloped frontier land, the largest a 40,000-acre tract in Oneida County which he shared with five others; others were in confiscated estates in Dutchess which tenants continued to farm. As a landholder Clinton could be stern with tenants or squatters. He also owned several gristmills and sawmills, and had a modest investment in state and federal securities. He had what his sympathetic biographer calls a "bourgeois love for investments and speculations."[8]

Neither his land holdings nor social status, however, raised him to the ranks of the "great families." He was, as it was said by the historian-politician Jabez Hammond who knew him personally, "in grain and in principle a republican."[9] "His behavior in society," one New Yorker recalled, "was plain but dignified." His home at Little Britain was a farmhouse; his personal residence in Manhattan at Greenwich was "a long low venerable irregular white cottage-like brick and wood building, pleasant notwithstanding, with a number of small low rooms and one very spacious parlour."[10] Seen through the eyes of a member of the city's fashionable society in 1789, "he and his family neither visit nor are visited by any families, either in public or private life. He sees no company, and is not much loved or respected." As to the Governor's wife, she "is not showy, but is a kind, friendly woman."[11]

Plainly Clinton was "anything but a man of learning," an observa-

6. Spaulding, *George Clinton*, 91.

7. Hamilton, "To the Electors," Apr. 7, 1789, Syrett, ed., *Hamilton Papers*, V, 326-27.

8. Spaulding, *George Clinton*, 228 and ch. 18.

9. Jabez D. Hammond, *The History of Political Parties in the State of New York . . . to 1840*, 4th edn. corrected and enlarged, 2 vols. (Cooperstown, 1846), I, 5.

10. "Scenes and Characters in New York as remembered by Mr. Francis Herbert" in Griswold, *Republican Court*, 454.

11. Mrs. William Smith, John Adams' daughter, cited in *ibid.*, 94-95.

tion made by Brissot de Warville in 1788 and one repeated by Jefferson years later when he observed he was not "a man of mind." His conversation, contemporaries recalled, was "shrewd, sensible and commonly about matters of fact—the events of the Revolution, the politics of the day, the useful arts and agriculture."[12] As a lawyer he had "served with reputation though not with distinction"—Hamilton's acid phrase.[13] His messages to the legislature and his correspondence were concise and to the point. He left it to others to write pamphlets and newspaper articles. As a speaker he "had unassuming and modest pretensions," although he commanded respect.[14] He was best, obviously—this man who had been a farmer, sailor, soldier, surveyor, country lawyer, assemblyman, land speculator, general, and governor—with practical matters, people, and politics.

He had many of the attributes of a democratic politician, not least of which was his ability to wield patronage. George Clinton did not initiate the "spoils system" in New York but he did not need either his nephew, DeWitt Clinton, or Thurlow Weed to teach him the uses of appointments, land grants, and political favors to further his "interest." Anyone familiar with the techniques of the royal governors knew that, and the constitution by making the governor the head of a Council of Appointment and vesting in it the royal governor's power to select judges to the supreme court, the mayors of New York and Albany, county sheriffs, clerks, judges, and other minor officials made the governor the inevitable cynosure of pressure for the "loaves and fishes."

The fact that Clinton did not turn several political opponents out of office in the 1780's has misled some historians into thinking he was nonpartisan.[15] Actually he could hardly remove Richard Morris or John Sloss Hobart from the supreme court or Robert R. Livingston from the chancery court without grounds for impeachment. He continued Egbert Benson as his attorney general, long after he parted with him politically, probably because first-rate legal talent was scarce among his followers. And he appointed James Duane mayor of New

12. J. P. Brissot de Warville, *New Travels in the United States of America, 1788,* trans., Mara Soceanu Vamos and Durand Echeverria (Cambridge, Mass., 1964), 146; Thomas Jefferson to Benjamin Rush, Aug. 17, 1811, Ford, ed., *Writings of Jefferson,* IX, 327-29; Griswold, *Republican Court,* 455.

13. Hamilton, "Letters of H.G.," No. 1, Feb. 20, 1789, Syrett, ed., *Hamilton Papers,* V, 263-64.

14. William Kent, ed., *Memoirs and Letters of James Kent* (Boston, 1898), 306.

15. Linda Grant DePauw, *The Eleventh Pillar: New York State and the Federal Constitution* (Ithaca, N.Y., 1966), 25-27, 134-35, 162-63.

York in 1784 very likely to reward him for past services and to divide "the great families."[16] Federalists, moreover, took it for granted that Clinton's appointments were partisan. In the election of 1789, in fact, they made his partisanship a major campaign issue, Hamilton deriding Clinton as *"artful,"* leaving the impression that he was "CUNNING." A friend who watched Clinton maneuver a measure through the legislature spoke of "old George with his private Irish ways." He was good in taking the measure of a man. Francis Adrian Vanderkemp considered "his knowledge of men . . . a distinguishing trait of his character . . . and one of the chief means of his political success," an opinion Jabez Hammond shared.[17] He was stubborn, impressing opponents as conservative as James Kent with his "great decision of character and stern inflexibility." The "old Irishman" also had a temper. " Though of an irritable temper," wrote Hamilton, "when not under the immediate influence of irritation he is circumspect and guarded, and seldom acts or speaks without premeditation or design." The total picture calls to mind the better known self-made Scotch-Irish democratic hero of the southern frontier who entered the White House in 1829.[18]

Clinton's popular reputation always rested fundamentally on his role in the Revolution. The judgment Hamilton made in 1777—that "General Clinton is an excellent officer, the people have Confidence in him, will once act with zeal and Serve with Spirit and perserverence under him"—was never erased by all of Hamilton's later propaganda. As one soldier, an active Republican at Plattsburgh, later recalled, "he led me into military rank when I was but a boy—I have shared the perils of the field by his side . . . I have admired him for his simplicity of manners, ease of access, decision and firmness."[19] Thou-

16. Alexander, *James Duane,* 146; Spaulding, *George Clinton,* 142-48; see below, ch. 3.

17. Hamilton, "Letters of H.G.," No. 1, Syrett, ed., *Hamilton Papers,* V, 263; Peter W. Yates to Joseph C. Yates, n.d. [probably mid-1790's], Yates Papers, N.Y. Pub. Lib.; Francis Adrian Vanderkemp, Diary, in "Extracts from the Vanderkemp Papers, From the Hudson to Lake Ontario in 1792," Buffalo Historical Society, *Publications,* 2 (1880), 54-55. Hammond, *Political Parties,* I, 33. For recognition by other contemporaries of the importance of Clinton's appointive power, see Robert R. Livingston to Marquis de Lafayette, Sept. 17, 1788, Bancroft Transcripts, N.Y. Pub. Lib.; Samuel B. Webb to Killian K. Van Rensselaer, Mar. 22, 1789, cited in I. N. Phelps Stokes, comp., *The Iconography of Manhattan Island, 1498-1909,* 6 vols. (N.Y., 1915-28), V, 1236; James Parton, *The Life and Times of Aaron Burr,* 2 vols., 2nd ed. (Boston, 1892), I, 168-70.

18. Kent, ed., *Memoirs of James Kent,* 306; Hamilton, "Letters of H.G.," No. 11, Syrett, ed., *Hamilton Papers,* V, 290.

19. Hamilton to Robert R. Livingston, Aug. 7, 1777, Syrett, ed., *Hamilton Papers,*

sands of others in New York had the same emotional experience. In the opinion of the historian who has studied the governors throughout the colonies his administration as wartime governor was one of the best.[20] All of this added up to the record that his followers would emblazen on his banners in many campaigns: George Clinton, the "tried and tested Whig," "old seventy-six," George Clinton, "the publican general."

II

Conservatives were obsessed not so much with George Clinton as with the "new men" he helped raise to power. In the spring of 1782, as Alexander Hamilton surveyed the New York political scene in a report to his new chieftain and mentor, Robert Morris, he clearly recognized two sides to George Clinton.[21] He had, on the one hand, wrote Hamilton, "declined in popularity, partly from a defect of qualifications for his station and partly from causes that do him honor—the vigorous execution of some necessary laws that bore hard upon the people, and severity of discipline among the militia." On the other hand, said Hamilton, "the preservation of his place is an object to his private fortune as well as to his ambition; and we are not to be surprised, if instead of taking a lead in measures that contradict a prevailing prejudice, however he may be convinced of their utility, he either flatters it or temporizes; especially when a new election approaches."

By contrast, to paint the portraits of the leading politicians in the legislature, Hamilton dipped his pen in acid. The senate, planned as a bastion of conservative interests, presented the greatest problem. The foremost thorn was John Morin Scott, whose "only aim seems to be by violent professions of popular principles to acquire a popularity which has hitherto coyly eluded his persuit." Zephaniah Platt of Dutchess was "a man of plain sense, thoroughly acquainted with agriculture. He intends to do well whenever he can hit upon what is right." Ephraim Paine, of the same county, was "a man of strong natural parts and as strong prejudices; his zeal is fiery, his obstinacy unconquerable. He is as primitive in his notions, as in his appearance.

I, 308; M. T. Woolsey to John Williams, Apr. 13, 1797, John Williams Papers, III, 33, N.Y. State Lib.
20. Margaret McMillan, *The War Governors in the American Revolution* (N.Y., 1943), 54, 238, 274.
21. Hamilton to Robert Morris, Aug. 13, 1782, Syrett, ed., *Hamilton Papers*, III, 137-38.

Without education, he wants more knowledge, or more tractableness."
For Abraham Yates of Albany, Hamilton saved his greatest spleen;
he was "a man whose ignorance and perverseness are only surpassed
by his pertinacity and conceit. He hates all high-fliers, which is the
appelation he gives to men of genius. He has the merit of being always the first man [in attendance] at the Legislature. The people have
been a long time in the *habit* of choosing him in different offices; and
to the title of prescription, he adds that of being a preacher to their
taste. He *assures* them they are too poor to pay taxes. He is a staunch
whig that deserves to be pensioned by the British Ministry."

The leading assemblymen, although on the whole not as bad,
were also infected with democratic prejudices. John Lansing of Albany was "a good young fellow and a good practicioner of the law;
but his friends mistook his talents when they made him a statesman.
He thinks two pence an ounce upon plate a *monstrous tax*." Cornelius
Humphrey of Dutchess was "pretty remarkable for *blunder* and
vociferation"; at the end of the last session of the legislature he had
complained that it was very inconvenient for "the country members"
to be detained. Somewhat better was William Malcolm of New York
City who was able and "pretty right" but too close to Scott and "too
fond of popularity and too apt to think every scheme bad that is not
his own."

The picture was not completely grim according to Hamilton.
Philip Schuyler had "more weight in the legislature than the Governor" yet not enough to get his bills through. James Duane was a
positive influence in the senate as was John Laurance of New York
City in the assembly. The judges of the supreme court gave Hamilton
cause neither for enthusiasm nor complaint.

Hamilton was lamenting what was in effect a shift in the political
center of gravity in New York from one class to another. That such
a shift did indeed take place has recently been verified by Jackson T.
Main's careful comparison of the postwar assembly and senate with
the prewar assembly and council as to occupations, wealth, and social
origins. The assembly, Main concludes:

> differed from the old in many respects. The voters selected
> fewer townspeople. In the 1769 Assembly some 57 per cent of
> the members had been engaged primarily in a nonagricultural
> occupation; by 1785 the proportion had been halved. Farmers,
> exclusive of large landowners, had made up 25 per cent of the
> total in 1769; now they furnished about 42 per cent. In con-
> trast, one half of the 1769 legislators had been merchants and

lawyers, but now such men held less than one third of the seats. Similarly the proportion of wealthy members dropped from 43 per cent to 15 per cent, whereas the ratio of men of moderate means increased from probably one seventh to nearly one half. New York's elite families, which had contributed ten out of twenty-eight Assemblymen in 1769, contributed the same number in 1785, but in a House twice as large. Meanwhile the number of men who had started without any local family background, newcomers to New York, increased from two to twenty-three. In general, the yeoman-artisan "middle class" which in colonial days had furnished a half-dozen members, now actually had a majority of the legislature.[22]

The senate had also changed drastically. Among the senators who served from 1777 to 1787, descendants of prominent old families held from one-fourth to one-third of the seats compared to three-fourths of the provincial council. The number of men newly risen was about the same, but the greatest change was in the appearance of a large bloc of men comprising about 40 per cent of the total from old respectable families but not of the elite. Wealth was still noticeable, but where the old council was composed almost completely of wealthy men, in the new senate about 40 per cent were wealthy, about 36 per cent were well-to-do, and 25 per cent were of moderate property. An occupational shift also took place. The council was dominated by merchants, large landholders, and lawyers; about a third of the postwar senate was made of large landholders and a third of farmers.[23]

"Did the sons of the old established prominent families oppose the newcomers who were just rising to power?" Main asks. His answer is yes, based on an examination of the roll call of votes in the senate from 1777 to 1787. On two-thirds of the votes, seventy-nine to be exact, the senators "resolved into two major groups of about equal numbers," groups which were "remarkably cohesive." "The senators who came from prominent old families voted almost unanimously on one side; they were opposed by the great majority of the new men just arrived to power." Insofar as wealth and occupation is concerned, "wealthy New Yorkers, including most of the merchants, lawyers and large landowners voted almost to a man on one side, while on the other were farmers and other small property holders." "The

22. Main, "Government by the People," *Wm. and Mary Qtly.*, 3d Ser., 23 (1966), 400.
23. This and the following paragraph are based on Main, The Upper House in Revolutionary America, ch. 6, the manuscript version of which Professor Main has kindly permitted me to read.

members of the pre-revolutionary upper class," he concludes, "were overwhelmingly opposed to the Clintonians, while the new men who came from outside the state, or were born of humble families within it, almost invariably supported the Governor."

III

A survey of the men recognized as the major anti-Federalist leaders in 1788-89 in the key centers of "the interest"—Albany, Ulster, and Dutchess counties, and in New York City—supports the same conclusion Main drew for the legislators of 1777-87. Indeed many are the same men.

Politically, the anti-Federalist leaders were men more or less new to power who had risen during the war. Tories among them were rare. Few could be reckoned members of the old colonial "ruling class," few even held elective office in the province. They were assemblymen and senators who had been elected during and after the Revolution and had gravitated to Clinton's leadership. They were county officials, sheriffs, clerks, and judges, appointed by Clinton. An exceptionally large proportion were obligated to Clinton's administration, if not for an office, for a grant of land or a favor.[24]

In social origin they were either from respectable old families of the middle rank or were *nouveaux riches* who had risen often from humble ranks in the era of the Revolution. They included at most a few members of what contemporaries recognized as the lesser branches of "the ancient families." Anti-Federalists who were large landholders usually owned uncultivated frontier land which they had acquired fairly recently. If they owned tenanted land, they either had acquired it since the war or owned small scattered parcels which did not permit them to rival the Van Rensselaers or Livingstons in wealth, much less in social status. They were men who hoped to make their fortunes in the newer forms of wealth: confiscated estates, securities, the public domain, manufacturing, or in trade with countries other than England. Local leaders who did not conform to these economic or political patterns often had "connections" as relatives, business associates, or clients with those who did. The "connections" of these middle-class men served them no less than the formidable network of intermarriages and partnerships served the "great."

At Albany, the major anti-Federalist leaders were Robert Yates,

24. See the discussion, ch. 3, sec. II, of the political pattern of the distribution of confiscated Loyalist estates.

John Lansing, Abraham Yates, Jr., and Jeremiah Van Rensselaer. Of neither Robert Yates nor Lansing, two of the state's three delegates to the Philadelphia convention, could it be said that "they were members of high rank in their local aristocracies." While it is true that Yates had "a comfortable estate" and a "lucrative practise in law," his family was hardly "of high station"; indeed, he was chosen by the Federalists as their gubernatorial candidate in 1789 precisely because they wanted a candidate who did not hail from the "great families." From a family of prosperous lesser gentry, he had married into the same level, choosing a daughter of the prosperous but undistinguished Van Ness family. After reading law in William Livingston's office, he made his living as a lawyer. An Albany alderman and a member of the Committee of Safety, he had been elected to the supreme court in 1777, raising him beyond his expectations although not beyond his abilities. "Judge Yates is upright and respectable in his profession," Hamilton reported in 1782. Almost unique among Whig leaders, he turned his back on buying confiscated estates: "No I will sooner die a beggar than own a foot of land acquired by such means," a near contemporary reported him as saying; perhaps as a result, he died poor.[25]

So far was John Lansing from being "one of the patricians of the Hudson" that he served in the Revolution as Philip Schuyler's military secretary and in effect man of all work. He remained on friendly terms with Schuyler, who tried to woo him from Clinton, but he was not at all in the same social class. Lansingburgh did not belong to him as has been contended, but to Abraham G. Lansing; moreover, it was not an estate but a very new town whose lots were laid out in 1771.[26] Lansing was not poor; he bought 40,000 acres of confiscated

25. For a distorted claim, see Forrest McDonald, *We the People: The Economic Origins of the Constitution* (Chicago, 1958), 50; for Yates on speculation, [Robert Yates], *Secret Proceedings and Debates of the Convention Assembled At Philadelphia, in the Year 1787* . . . (Richmond, Va., 1839), introduction (a biographical sketch), *passim*; for his modest house, see, George R. Howell, ed., *History of the County of Albany, N.Y. from 1609-1886* (N.Y., 1886), 674; for Hamilton's judgment, see Hamilton to Robert Morris, Aug. 13, 1782, Syrett, ed., *Hamilton Papers*, III, 140.

26. McDonald, *We the People*, 49; for the relationship with Schuyler see Lansing Family Papers, *passim*, N.-Y. Hist. Soc. and N.Y. State Lib.; for land see A. J. Weise, *History of Lansingburgh, New York* . . . *1670-1877* (Troy, 1877), 7, 11. "Abraham Jacob Lansing early in the year 1771, had a portion of his farm surveyed by Joseph Blanchard, and named the newly laid out streets, alleys and lots, the City of Lansingburgh." There were 288 lots which ran about 120 x 50 feet, hardly a tenanted estate.

land (presumably with depreciated securities) and eventually funded $7000 in public securities. Yet while he may have been "one of the wealthiest members of his party," he depended for his income on his law practice, not on his land. He "would not serve," if elected to the United States Senate, Clinton told King in 1789, because "his prospects were good in his profession," and "he owed it to a numerous young family not to go into public life."[27] Clinton appointed him mayor of Albany, a job whose numerous fees were probably necessary for his livelihood. At the Philadelphia convention, he impressed others not as a "patrician" but as "a man of good sense, plain in his manners, and sincere in his friendships."[28]

Abraham Yates, Jr., was an object of special venom, and not to Hamilton alone. Schuyler sneered at him as the "late cobbler of laws and old shoes"; Dr. Thomas Tillotson, a Livingston in-law, called him "an old booby."[29] It was not only that he was a man of humble origins, who as the ninth son of a prosperous farmer had indeed been apprenticed to a shoemaker; it was more particularly that he bit the hand that fed him. He became a lawyer and was appointed sheriff of Albany County (1754-58). In that post he learned the facts of life in the landlord's domain. While attempting to evict some Livingston tenants who claimed land titles from Massachusetts, he was held incommunicado for a day by a band of men who threatened his life and then carted him off to a Springfield jail. When he ran unsuccessfully for the assembly in 1761 he had the financial backing of Robert Livingston, lord of the upper manor. He was a foe of the tenant rebellions,[30] but at some point in the Revolutionary era—precisely

27. Rufus King, "Substance of a Conversation with Governor Clinton," June 12, 1789, King, ed., *Correspondence of Rufus King*, I, 354-56.

28. William Pierce, cited in Joseph R. Strayer, ed., *The Delegate from New York: or, Proceedings of the Federal Convention of 1787, from the Notes of John Lansing, Jr.* (Princeton, 1939), introd., 19; Spaulding, *New York in the Critical Period*, 237.

29. Thomas Tillotson to Robert R. Livingston, May 1784, R. R. Livingston Papers, N.-Y. Hist. Soc.; Schuyler to Gouverneur Morris, Feb. 3, 1778, Gouverneur Morris Papers, Columbia Univ., cited in Lynd, ed., "Abraham Yates's History of the Movement for the United States Constitution," *Wm. and Mary Qtly.*, 3d Ser., 20 (1963), 223-45, and esp. 225.

30. See a lengthy correspondence of Robert Livingston [upper manor] to Abraham Yates, 1755-61, *passim*, Yates Papers, N.Y. Pub. Lib.; Handlin, "Eastern Frontier of New York," *N.Y. History*, 18 (1937), 60-64, 69-74; Spiegelberg, *Abraham Yates*, chs. 2, 3; Mark, *Agrarian Conflicts*, 123-25 for a likely claim that Yates also opposed the tenant rebellion of 1766.

when is not clear—he also became a confirmed foe of "the manor lords," a New York Hinton Rowan Helper, as it were.[31] Yates rose during the Revolution: as chairman of the county Committees of Correspondence, of the county Committee of Safety, then chairman of the committee that drafted the state's constitution in 1777. From 1777 to 1790 he was an influential state senator; he was also continental loan officer until 1781 when he was replaced by Hamilton, leaving him "very hurt," as he put it, and embittered at Robert Morris. Throughout the Confederation era he was a trenchant polemicist, writing as "Rough Hewer" and "Sidney." In the Continental Congress in 1786 he won a reputation as a churlish delegate who often cast the only "nay." He was, in his own words, "a Suspicious Man," given to seeing plots by all "high fliers," a populist prototype.[32] He seems to have depended on officeholding for his income; in 1790 Clinton rewarded his long services to anti-Federalism by appointing him mayor of Albany, in which post he served until his death in 1796 at the age of seventy-two.

Jeremiah Van Rensselaer was the only anti-Federalist member of the landed family, and perhaps for this reason his colleagues made him chairman of the Albany anti-Federalist committee and then their first candidate for Congress. Years before he had been clerk and secretary of the Albany Sons of Liberty. Educated in the manor house and at Princeton, he was one of the heirs to Rensselaerswyck and a brother-in-law of Philip Schuyler. His holdings lay within Clavarack, the lower manor, an estate considerably smaller than the ducal upper manor; according to family history, moreover, at some time there was a falling out between Jeremiah and the principal figures in the family. His activities suggest a need for income aside from his estate. He was, for example, Inspector of Pot and Pearl Ashes at Albany in 1772. He was also a skilled surveyor—Schuyler recommended him for surveyor-general in 1777. Clinton appointed him Commissioner of Forfeitures for the western district instead, a post that proved even more rewarding personally. Early in the 1790's he promoted an abortive

31. See in Yates Papers, N.Y. Pub. Lib., An Historical Account of the Manor of Rensselaerswyck in an Action at Law, 1762, Revolutions of New York: Notes on Ancient Revolutions of New York, [a history of Albany], and Notes on Early History of Albany, all incompleted MSS, together with voluminous note books on the same subjects.

32. Yates to Jeremiah Van Rensselaer and Henry Oothoudt, Aug. 29, 1787, Burnett, ed., Letters of the Continental Congress, VIII, 641, 642; for his reputation in Congress see Nathan Dane to Rufus King, July 16, 1787, ibid., 622.

scheme to manufacture maple sugar and a more successful glass factory. He also became director of the Bank of Albany and the Western
Inland Navigation Company—all signs of the aspiring entrepreneur.[33]

At Albany a numerous tribe of Yateses and Lansings, together
with a good sprinkling of Dutch burghers, swelled the anti-Federalist
committees. The names of most can be found on the rosters of the
Albany Sons of Liberty and the Committees of Correspondence. Often
they were appointees of the Governor.[34] In 1788 when Albany Federalists announced that their slate of delegates had been nominated
at a meeting of "very respectable citizens, and some of the first characters in the county," the Albany anti-Federalists were not inaccurate
in rejoining that their candidates were chosen by "very respectable
citizens . . . though perhaps not the *first characters* in point of property."[35]

In Ulster and to a lesser extent Dutchess it is remarkable how much
Clinton rewarded his family connections, the center of his interest.
In Ulster Dirck Wynkoop, of his wife's family, was first judge of the
county; Clinton's brother-in-law, Christopher Tappen, was deputy
clerk—the Governor himself kept the sinecure position as clerk from
1760 to his death in 1812; Simeon DeWitt, Clinton's nephew, was the
state's surveyor-general. The sons of Clinton's brother, James, first
Alexander, and after 1788, DeWitt, served the Governor as private
secretary. In Dutchess, John DeWitt, a relative of James Clinton, was
sheriff, and Gilbert Livingston, the surrogate, was Peter Tappen's
brother-in-law. All were active in the Governor's "interest."[36]

The Dutchess anti-Federalist leaders, as their most recent analyst
has demonstrated by examining their property holdings, "were a long

33. For a sketch, *Biographical Directory of the American Congresses, 1774-1927*
(Washington, 1928); Spaulding, *New York in the Critical Period*, 74, 82, 223; for
his holdings in land and slaves in 1797-1798 see Jeremiah Van Rensselaer Miscellaneous Manuscripts, N.-Y. Hist. Soc. and Van Rensselaer Papers, N.Y. State Lib.;
for genealogy, see Howell, ed., *History of Albany*, 291; for the family dispute,
Alexander, *James Duane*, 43.

34. Abraham G. Lansing was surrogate for Albany, 1787-1808; Matthew Vischer
was clerk of Albany, 1778-1790; Richard Lush was clerk, 1790-1808; Dirck Swart
became clerk of Saratoga, 1791-1804; Christopher P. Yates was clerk of Tryon
County, 1777-1800 and surrogate, 1778-1787 and Commissioner of Forfeitures; Henry
Oothoudt, fellow Commissioner of Forfeitures with Jeremiah Van Rensselaer, was
the owner of forfeited lands and a silver mine which received an exemption from
the state; Anthony Ten Eyck was first judge of Rensselaer County, 1791-1803. For
grants of state land to these men see below, ch. 3, n. 22.

35. Broadside, Albany, Mar. 15, 1788, N.-Y. Hist. Soc.

36. For some background on county leaders see Nathanial Sylvester, *History of
Ulster County, New York . . .* (Phila., 1880), 101-3.

step up the social ladder from their constituents, yet still well below the Federalist landlords."³⁷ They too were appointees of Governor Clinton, beginning in 1777 with Melancton Smith as sheriff. They were also entrepreneurs, often tied to each other by business partnerships: Livingston and Peter Tappen were shipbuilders during the Revolution; Tappen later started a stocking factory. Smith and Jonathan Lawrence had been partners in army contracting; so had Lawrence and Zephaniah Platt. Smith, Lawrence, and Jacobus Swartwout shared in Platt's large speculation in state land at Plattsburgh, near Canada.

Of these Dutchess leaders, Gilbert Livingston alone bore the name of a prominent family, yet he was descended from a line of the Livingstons in which it has been shown that no member "became a landlord or planter or gentleman." Their land holdings were small, their marriages undistinguished, and their pursuits strongly middle class; as a result "local public offices tended to be a means of livelihood for them."³⁸ Gilbert Livingston owned tenanted land of his own but made his living as a lawyer, collecting rents and filing ejection suits for his uncle and other large landlords. In the debate at the Poughkeepsie convention Robert R. Livingston had no compunction in lashing out at him with a "mingling of sarcasm and irreverence"; he was no more than a poor relation.³⁹

It was possible for Federalists to sneer at Clinton's supporters in New York City as "a few sycophants, whom he has put in Office and their dependents."⁴⁰ They were a remnant of the old popular Whig leadership; McDougall, Sears, and John Morin Scott died in the 1780's; most of the other Liberty Boys had gone over to the Federalists. The anti-Federalists who had not were businessmen, not mechanics, and all they had in common was that they were not connected with the trade with Britain, the backbone of the Federalist mercantile interest.

Some were natives to the city: John Lamb, Marinus Willett, and Henry Rutgers. Lamb, chairman of the Federal Republican Society in 1788, had been secretary of the Sons of Liberty in the 1770's. His father, an English mathematical instrument maker, had been trans-

37. Lynd, *Anti-Federalism in Dutchess County*, ch. 2.
38. Joan Gordon, Kinship and Class: The Livingstons of New York, 1675-1860 (unpubl. Ph.D. diss., Columbia Univ., 1959), 192-202.
39. Dangerfield, *Chancellor Robert R. Livingston*, 229.
40. Samuel B. Webb to Killian K. Van Rensselaer, Mar. 22, 1789, Worthington C. Ford, ed., *Correspondence and Journals of Samuel Blachley Webb*, 3 vols. (N.Y., 1893), I, 126-27.

ported to America in 1724 as an accomplice of a notorious burglar. The son began in his father's original craft but by the 1760's was a well-to-do wine merchant. In the war, he served as an artillery commander and a general, lost an eye, and was imprisoned at Quebec. In 1784 Clinton appointed him Collector of the Port of New York, a lucrative office. He was one of the city's largest purchasers of confiscated land, engaged in the West Indies trade, and lent money on a large scale. In 1797 he pledged his private fortune to make good on an employee's embezzlement from the custom house.[41]

Marinus Willett, a Liberty Boy who was rewarded for bravery by Congress for his many engagements on the New York frontier, was appointed sheriff of New York in 1784. His father had been a tavern keeper in the 1750's; Marinus served as an apprentice to a cabinetmaker, married the boss's daughter, and soon was a master craftsman. After the war his wealth from confiscated estates and other sources enabled him to build an elegant mansion on the outskirts of the city. As a biographer portrays him, Willett was "a plain blunt man, outspoken, perfectly fearless."[42]

Among these native urban Clintonians, Henry Rutgers alone was born to wealth, his principal income coming from the extensive holdings in city real estate he had inherited from his father. Rutgers Street still bears the family name. He also owned a brewery, and dabbled in manufacturing ventures. He was so ardent a member of the Sons of Liberty that the British confiscated his house, marking it with "G.R." for George Rex, a badge he preserved on his doorfront for decades. He gave generously of his fortune to schools, churches, and in later years to the college which was named after him.[43]

Three of the anti-Federalist leaders were postwar migrants to the city: Melancton Smith, Jonathan Lawrence, and David Gelston. All originally were from Long Island; Smith and Lawrence came directly from Dutchess County. Smith was the son of a prosperous yeoman of Jamaica, Long Island, who as already noted began as a clerk in Poughkeepsie and was a merchant of substance by the time of the

41. See Frank E. Ross in *DAB* s.v. "Lamb, John"; Leake, *Memoirs of John Lamb*, 296-98, 352-55; for his financial transactions of the 1790's, see John Lamb Papers, N.-Y. Hist. Soc., *passim*.

42. Daniel Wager, *Col. Marinus Willett: The Hero of Mohawk Valley* (Utica, 1891), 45-48; Howard Thomas, *Marinus Willett, Soldier-Patriot, 1740-1830* (Prospect, N.Y., 1954), 21-23, 165-68, 185-86.

43. See L. Ethan Ellis in *DAB* s.v. "Rutgers, Henry"; Thomas J. Wertenbaker, *Father Knickerbocker Rebels: New York City During the Revolution* (N.Y., 1948), 104.

Revolution.[44]   He served as a militia captain, a commissioner for detecting Loyalist conspiracies, and county sheriff. He was also a purchasing agent for the state government, an aide to the federal commissary-general, and was himself a contractor to the governments he served as agent. He speculated in confiscated land and state securities; when he moved to New York City he immediately joined the Chamber of Commerce. Alone among the anti-federalists, he had connections with William Duer, nibbling around the edges of Duer's large-scale speculations. Although the highest office he held was as member of Congress in the late 1780's, he was considered a close advisor to the Governor, if not the closest. Melancton Smith, as contemporaries knew him, was "a man of rough exterior, powerful in bodily appearance and undaunted in expressing his mind which he did in plain language," a "man of remarkable simplicity and of the most gentle liberal and amiable disposition." He was the "Patrick Henry" of the New York ratifying convention, although he spoke in a style that was "dry, plain and syllogistic" which set him off from the bombastic Virginian.[45]

Jonathan Lawrence continued to be associated with Smith in business in New York City. He shared in the purchase of confiscated estates and presumably took care of the faithful as a Commissioner of the Loan Act in 1786. Also from Queens, he had served as senator from the southern district through the war (appointed by the legislature) and as a member of the Council of Appointment.[46] David Gelston had come to the city from Suffolk, which he had represented in the assembly from 1777 to 1785. Clinton appointed him surrogate of New York County. In the 1790's he engaged in the West Indies trade. Known as a close friend of the Governor, he would become the first president of the Democratic Society of the city and in 1802 Jefferson's appointee as Collector of the Port.[47]

44. Robin Brooks, Melancton Smith: New York Anti-Federalist, 1744-1798 (unpubl. Ph.D. diss., Univ. of Rochester, 1964), chs. 1, 2, and pp. 64-75 for his land speculations. See Julian P. Boyd in DAB s.v. "Smith, Melancton."

45. William Dunlap, History of the New Netherlands, Province of New York and State of New York . . . , 2 vols. (N.Y., 1839-40), II, 260; for other personal recollections along similar lines, see Kent, ed., Memoirs of James Kent, 305-6; William Duer, Reminiscences of an Old Yorker (N.Y., 1867), 7-8; William Duer, New York as It Was During the Latter Part of the Last Century (N.Y., 1849), 44. For his importance to Clinton, see Hammond, Political Parties, I, 25, 61.

46. For speculation by New York City anti-Federalists see below ch. 3, n.21; the pattern of loans under the 1786 loan act, Laws of the State of N.Y., 9th Sess., ch. 40, has never been investigated.

47. For Gelston there is no sketch; for his importance see Gelston to George

In other counties a few anti-federalist leaders varied from the general pattern and even they have been misinterpreted. John Williams, for example, the leading anti-federalist from Washington County on the northeastern frontier, is little understood if characterized as a "physician and lord of vast estates with many tenants."[48] He had the checkered career of a parvenu. English-born and for a time a surgeon's mate on an English man-of-war, he came to the New York frontier on the eve of the Revolution in 1773 and was everything from "a tumbler to a quack doctor," as a foe put it. He began in the Revolutionary militia as a surgeon, ended as a brigadier general. Elected to the first senate, he was expelled for defrauding the militia of pay and for peculation, although this did not prevent Washington County from returning him regularly from 1784 to 1795. He married an heiress and bought confiscated estates which he sold or rented; he was also a country merchant and wholesaler. Undoubtedly the largest landholder of his district, he nonetheless could present himself as a foe of "the manor influence." He pursued one theme consistently from the senate to the Poughkeepsie convention through his later career in Congress—the need to prevent taxes from falling on the pioneer farmers of his district. By 1796 he became a Federalist (chiefly over the issue of Jay's Treaty) and a collaborator of the old established landlords he had previously opposed.

Samuel Jones, to take another seeming exception, was the only former Tory in high Clintonian circles. A member of a prosperous family of Queens landholders and an accomplished lawyer, Jones was

Clinton, Sept. 8, 1794, Clinton Misc. MSS, N.-Y. Hist. Soc., Aaron Burr to Caesar Rodney, June 30, 1801, Burr Manuscripts, N.Y. State Lib. As for other members of the small Federal-Republican Society: Charles Tillinghast, the Secretary, was Lamb's son-in-law and later Deputy Collector of the Port. John McKesson was Clerk of the Assembly for a decade and a sometime business manager of Clinton's properties; see Spaulding, *George Clinton*, 229. Peter Curtenius, former State Auditor, was an iron manufacturer who considered himself the victim of Egbert Benson's malice in his efforts to recover £5000 he loaned the state in the Revolution; see Curtenius to George Clinton, Mar. 2, 1788, Bancroft Transcripts, N.Y. Pub. Lib. Col. Isaac Stoutenburgh, a merchant, was Commissioner of Forfeitures. John Stagg was a leader of the Mechanics Society, the only one who worked with the Clintonians at this time; Ezekial Robbins was a hatter; see Alfred Young, "The Mechanics and the Jeffersonians: New York, 1789-1801," *Labor History*, 5 (1964), 247-48.

48. McDonald, *We the People*, 308; for his economic activities, see John Williams Papers, vols. I, II, and IV, N.Y. State Lib.; for the Revolution, see *Minutes of the Council of Appointment, April 4, 1778-May 3, 1779* (N.-Y. Hist. Soc., *Collections*, New York, 1925), vol. 58, 18-20, 43-44; for his election campaigns, see chs. on congressional elections of 1792, 1794, 1796.

disbarred for Tory sympathies and sat out the war in the British-
occupied southern district. Elected to the assembly in 1786 he sponsored the repeal of anti-Tory legislation. He rose rapidly to become
the "leading and strong man" among "the friends of the Governor."
He was a legal scholar; together with Richard Varick, he codified
the statutes of New York as colony and independent state; later he
was known as "the father of the New York Bar." Very likely he filled
the need among Clintonians in the legislature for a skilled lawyer.
Queens elected Jones to the Poughkeepsie convention as an anti-
Federalist by a narrow margin but when it shifted perceptibly in its
sentiments he became one of the principal shapers of the maneuver for
ratification. Clinton kept him in tow for a while by appointing him
Recorder for the City of New York but by the mid-1790's he went over
to the Federalists; in 1797 Governor Jay appointed him the first
comptroller of the state. "To tell the truth," he explained in later
years when asked for the secret of his political success, "when my
troops won't follow me, I follow them." There was always a place for
an opportunist in the Clintonian party.[49]

IV

Anti-Federalist leaders also differed from their counterparts in
"tone." Historians who have expended so much energy in counting
noses among leaders of both groups as to economic interests, property
holdings, and occupations might well pay attention to this distinction
which eighteenth-century New Yorkers were acutely aware of. The
typical anti-Federalist leader lacked "tone"; that is, he lacked social
status,[50] polish, the experience of command, education, and oratorical
ability.

If one examines the forty-six anti-Federalist delegates at the Poughkeepsie convention—a broader sample than our catalog of major leaders—their lack of "tone" is striking. The leading Federalist delegates
included men long accustomed to wielding political power, men who

49. Hammond, *Political Parties*, 10, 75n.; see Durward V. Sandifer, in *DAB* s.v.
"Jones, Samuel"; Pomerantz, *New York An American City*, 108-9 and *passim*.

50. Thus Melancton Smith was the only New York City anti-Federalist leader
who may be found on Mrs. John Jay's lengthy "dinner and supper list" for 1787-
88, which "seems to indicate the circle of New York Society in that period." Governor and Mrs. Clinton and Justice Robert Yates of the Supreme Court were
included. But while John Watts, a Tory merchant, and William Duer and Lady
Kitty Duer, and all the Livingstons, Schuylers, and Morrises were in, Sheriff Marinus
Willett, Port Collector John Lamb, and the long-established Henry Rutgers were
out. Griswold, *Republican Court*, 98-99.

had held seats in the colonial assembly, a former attorney general, a recorder, and an admiralty judge under the crown. By contrast only three anti-Federalist delegates had been elected to the assembly before the Revolution. Eighteen had sat in the provincial congresses which first met in 1775, nineteen in the postwar legislature. Nine among them had never before seen the inside of a state deliberative body. Most had begun life in respectable families of the middling sort and at least three very likely were sons of tenant farmers. If rank in the army is an indication of the experience of command, then of twenty-five anti-Federalist delegates who can be located in military rosters, ten were of high rank but fifteen were of low rank: eight were privates, two sergeants, three lieutenants, and two captains.[51] Their educational attainments tell a similar story: only three of the forty-six had a college education and only six were lawyers. Nothing suggests their lack of political experience more than the fact that they were "not used to public speaking," as Clinton put it to King. At the convention they bristled when they were ridiculed by a polished orator like Chancellor Livingston.[52]

In his home county, the world of the anti-Federalist leader was that of the county courthouse, the meeting of town supervisors, the militia muster, Sunday meeting, a round of politics and rum at the local tavern, and for some a yearly stay of a month or so at sleepy little Albany or Poughkeepsie or sophisticated New York City at the annual session of the state legislature. The view that most Federalists held of many anti-Federalists was well summed up by Federalist James Kent's appraisal of anti-Federalist Smith Thompson of Poughkeepsie, later a justice of the United States Supreme Court: "He was a plain modest sensible ignorant young man with narrow views and anti-Federalist politics."[53]

Michel Guillaume Jean de Crèvecoeur has left a memorable portrait of the breed in his sketch of Jesse Woodhull, an anti-Federalist dele-

51. I have checked the list of delegates against the members of the various legislative bodies in Werner, comp., *Civil List of N.Y., passim*, and against N.Y. State Comptroller, *New York in the Revolution as Colony and State* (Albany, 1897), a military roster. Lloyd Ultan, Propaganda against the Constitution in New York State, August 1787-July 1788 (unpubl. M.A. thesis, Columbia Univ., 1960), 47-50, finds that of 55 anti-Federalist leaders (including the delegates), 25 held appointive office, 37 were in the state government or knew Clinton, 3 had served in Congress, and 44 had served in the state militia.

52. Jonathan Elliot, ed., *The Debates in the Several State Conventions, on the Adoption of the Federal Constitution . . .* , 5 vols. (Washington, 1854), II, 392, 396, for comments of Thomas Tredwell and John Williams on this point.

53. Kent, ed., *Memoirs of James Kent*, 56.

gate, whom he knew from his long sojourn in Orange County. Wood-hull, county sheriff before the Revolution, served as a state senator and a militia colonel during the war. Crèvecoeur describes an encounter with him at his plough.[54] "How much land do you cultivate," a friend accompanying the Frenchman asked Woodhull. Woodhull replied: "Seven hundred forty-eight acres. That is too much, I know, for one man can scarcely oversee such a big undertaking. But the machinery is in operation; I would not be able to do otherwise. Besides, I have nine children, and if all of them wanted to be farmers like their father, you see that the 1500 acres that I own here would not be enough to make each of them a good plantation. I have attended to that by a considerable purchase which I have just made in the new county of Otsego."

"Since there are no stumps in your field," Crèvecoeur's friend said to him, "this great clearing must have been begun before your time." "No. I myself cut down the first tree thirty-one years ago; I was then eighteen." Woodhull also repaired his own ploughshares, explaining: "It is not for the sake of economy, . . . that I sometimes beat on my anvil, but in order to gain time, which is our whole fortune here. Time is more rapid than the water in my river. How often have I lost whole days of labor while waiting for the neighboring black-smith to do a half-hour's work."

His political chores were also demanding. "Then too as sheriff of the county, I must spend several days at Goshen every time the upper and lower courts come there to hold their sessions; and as colonel of the militia for the same county, I am often obliged to leave my fields because of the four big yearly drills and the frequent inspections. All these extra duties, joined to the urgent care that is required by such a big undertaking and a household of thirty-five people, whom it is necessary to feed and clothe, contribute to make the time more rapid and precious for me than for most others."

Woodhull, the working landholder, the jack-of-all-trades, the bour-geois miser of time, the responsible citizen, Cincinnatus at the plough, was the anti-Federalist leader personified. Crèvecoeur's cameo, for

54. Michel G. Jean de Crèvecoeur, *Eighteenth-Century Travels in Pennsyl-vania and New York*, Percy G. Adams, trans. and ed. (Lexington, Ky., 1961), 18-25. Crèvecoeur, who lived in Orange County before the Revolution and visited after it, writes as if he were describing the post-Revolutionary scene but refers to Woodhull as sheriff, a post he held only until 1777. Woodhull was more wealthy than the typical anti-Federalist; he funded $4887 in continental and $14,960 in state securities; McDonald, *We the People*, 305.

all the romantic proclivities of its author, tells as much about the New York anti-Federalists as a mound of statistics.

V

The politics of the Clintonians—the means by which the Governor and his circle consolidated an "interest"—are best summed up by an apt phrase of George Dangerfield: they represented "the politics of opportunity" as opposed to "the politics of privilege." Clinton stood for what another analyst of his philosophy has called "the middle class democracy of New York State."[55] He was neither a "radical," nor a "pure agrarian," nor a "reformer," although historians have pinned all these labels on him.

Clearly Clinton never stood for "levelling principles." The aim of government, he told the legislature, was to preserve "lives, liberties and estates." "The security of property," he said, "forms one of the strongest bonds of society; too much care cannot be taken to preserve and strengthen it."[56] The virtues he prized were those of the northern states, "where freedom, independence, equality and frugality are natural to the climate and soil." Southern slaveholders, and by implication Hudson Valley estate holders, were men with "a passion for aristocratic distinction" who "know not what it is to acquire property by their own toil, nor to economize with the savings of industry."[57]

There had to be opportunity, according to Clinton, for men whose "manners and fortunes bear a more equal resemblance" to those of the citizenry at large to hold office. Encouraging education therefore was "the peculiar duty of the government of a free state where the highest employments are open to citizens of every rank." For the same reason there also had to be adequate compensation for public officials, "now that a field is open for the display of talents and industry"—the twist in the phrase, avoiding Jefferson's "talents and virtue," was characteristically middle class. Only then would those

55. Dangerfield, *Chancellor Robert R. Livingston*, 88n.; Lynton K. Caldwell, "George Clinton Democratic Administrator," *N.Y. History*, 59 (1951), 134-56.

56. Lincoln, ed., *Messages from the Governors*, II, 255-56 (Jan. 16, 1786).

57. "Letters of Cato," in Ford, ed., *Essays on the Constitution*, 258-59, attributed to Clinton by Ford apparently because the MS. version in John Lamb's handwriting was located in Clinton's Papers. DePauw, *The Eleventh Pillar*, 284-92, questions this attribution; Clinton, however, undoubtedly subscribed to the sentiments.

who "have a prospect of advancing themselves and their families in private life" be able to hold office.[58]

There also had to be opportunity to acquire land, although it must be said that Clintonian policies favored the speculator rather than the settler. Clinton looked forward, he told the legislature, to "a speedy settlement" of the vast interior by pioneers and endorsed the idea of a tax on "large tracts of uncultivated lands" in the hands of "absentees and aliens," which, had it passed the legislature, would have forced one body of land engrossers to disgorge, but he also looked upon the public land as a source of revenue and drew a distinction between the promoter who presumably would sell land quickly and the unproductive land speculator. This approach led him to distribute confiscated Tory land to speculators as well as farmers, to open the state land to speculators in the late 1780's and to distribute in 1791 some 5,000,000 acres on a scale more lavish than that of any royal governor.[59]

Clinton is not understood as a "radical," even if that term is modified to be "no violent radical."[60] His postwar record on the tenant question continued that of the war years. He showed his colors in the acid test of the 1780's, Shays's Rebellion. The uprising in Massachusetts in 1786 immediately across the border from Albany County frightened landlords, especially after fugitives escaped into eastern New York. Clinton excoriated the "horrid and unnatural rebellion," offered a reward for the capture of the leaders, enjoined New Yorkers from aiding them, and ordered three regiments of Dutchess and Columbia militia to eastern New York. He personally made his way up from New York City at three in the morning on a wintry February night to direct the operations that dispersed the refugee rebels and impressed the local tenants with the might of the state. Clinton's followers were at pains to point out they were not "Shaysites."[61]

58. Lincoln, ed., *Messages from the Governors*, II, 183 (July 11, 1782), 199-200 (Jan. 21, 1784).
59. *Ibid.*, 199 (Jan. 21, 1784), 218-19 (Oct. 18, 1784); for 1791 see below ch. 13.
60. Dangerfield, *Chancellor Robert R. Livingston*, 204.
61. Clinton to Maj. Gen. Lincoln [of Mass.], Mar. 15, 1787, Lincoln Papers, Massachusetts Historical Society, Boston; Nathan Dane to Gov. Bowdoin of Mass., Mar. 4, 1787, Dane Papers, *ibid.*; Lincoln, ed., *Messages from the Governors*, II, 269 (Feb. 19, 1787); Mark, *Agrarian Conflicts*, 204-5; Spaulding, *New York in the Critical Period*, 150. Marion Starkey, *A Little Rebellion* (New York, 1955), 153-54, 178-80, claims that the New York government did not respond to the request of the Massachusetts government for action until the latter threatened to march its militia into New York and to ask for federal intervention. Even if true, Clinton acted decisively.

As he was not a "radical" neither did he typify "the pure agrarian" in economics.[62] Characteristically in a formal message to the legislature he took note of the fact that "the toils of the Husbandman have been amply awarded by a fruitful season and a plentiful harvest." But it was not merely a political gesture when he added that "while we are pursuing agriculture as our first object, commerce and manufactures also deserve our attention." Bitter because American trade was being thrown "into the hands of persons styling themselves or acting among us on the disguise of British subjects," he advocated tonnage discrimination by the state against British ships, tariff protection against British imports, and "particular encouragement" for New Yorkers' budding trade with India.[63] To encourage native manufactures, he favored state bounties and, later, loans. He was not opposed on principle to the state's chartering banks—it depended on who was asking for the charter. And he never encouraged an inflationary currency. Clintonians were responsible in 1786 for issuing £200,000 in currency backed by land, which was as stable as the colonial "Land Bank" on whose precedent it was based.[64]

Clinton, furthermore, was only a mild reformer. He advocated public support for education, yet in the 1780's was satisfied with the legislature's formal and parsimonious response to his appeal. Personally, he was anti-slavery; he even served a one-year term as vice-president of the Manumission Society in New York City. Officially, he avoided the issue which would have alienated the small slaveholders of the Hudson Valley who voted for him.[65]

Hamilton's electioneering gibe in 1789—"I do not recollect a single measure of public utility since the peace, for which the state is indebted to its chief magistrate"—was not as damning as he thought.[66] Clinton's program, by design, was essentially negative. The lodestar of his policy was to avoid any measure which might burden his agrarian constituents with taxes; hence Clintonians were indifferent to any program entailing large-scale expenditures, and weighed any new measure by the standard of how much revenue it might bring into state coffers.

Herein lay one of the major sources of the evolution of "Clinton-

62. Lee Benson, *Turner and Beard; American Historical Writing Reconsidered* (Glencoe, Ill., 1960), 216-17, 222.

63. Lincoln, ed., *Messages from the Governors*, II, 251-56 (Jan. 18, 1786).

64. See ch. 3, sec. 6, and ch. 10.

65. See ch. 11.

66. Hamilton, "Letters of H.G.," No. 4, Syrett, ed., *Hamilton Papers*, V, 270.

ianism" into anti-Federalism. During the years of New York's wartime peril, as Federalists reminded them, Clintonians approved nationalist measures.[67] In the closing years of the war and the first years of peace a double process was at work. The popular Whigs became disillusioned with the Confederation government. It failed to support New York in her claim to Vermont lands, which nationalists like Hamilton and Gouverneur Morris were willing to surrender.[68] It was unable to force Britain to evacuate the forts she illegally held, five of which were within New York on Lake Champlain and Lake Erie, allegedly a source of British influence over the Indians and a reason the lucrative fur trade no longer flowed into Albany. Under the same peace treaty, drafted by New York's nationalist John Jay, the Confederation government made a recommendation to restore confiscated Loyalist estates, which was unthinkable to Clintonians who had acquired them.

At the same time the popular Whigs were suspicious of a program for centralization put forward by their political enemies which threatened to reduce the sinews of the state government's power. Nationalists advocated a federal funding of the debt and the transfer of the power to tax imports from the states to the Confederation. The impost yielded more than a third of New York's total revenue. If lost, it could force more than a doubling of the tax on real and personal property, the second source of revenue.[69] "What hath kept the taxes so low in this state," Senator John Williams asked; "the reason is obvious, impost duties . . . Let our imposts and advantages be taken from us, shall we not be obliged to lay as heavy taxes as Connecticut, Boston etc. What hath kept us from those burthens but the privileges, which we must lose, if the present proposed constitution is adopted."[70] Furthermore after 1786 when the state adopted its own funding program, calling in some $2,300,000 in federal securities and reissuing state notes in exchange, the impost was all the more essential to meet the interest payments on the funding operation. Clinton, no

67. *Ibid.*, No. 7, 277-78; Elliot, ed., *Debates*, II, 358-60.
68. "Resolution of the State Legislature, Nov. 19, 1781," in Lincoln, ed., *Messages from the Governors*, II, 174-79; Dixon Ryan Fox, *Yankees and Yorkers* (N.Y., 1940), ch. 6; Spaulding, *George Clinton*, ch. 11.
69. Cochran, *New York in the Confederation*, 159-60, chs. 7-9, and Appendix. It is difficult to agree with Mrs. DePauw, The Eleventh Pillar, 40-56, that the Clintonians were willing to surrender the impost but only wanted to retain state collection. As Cochran points out, "unless the collectors were responsible to Congress there was no reason to suppose that the impost would be paid into the Continental Treasury any better than other requisitions." See Cochran, *ibid.*, 173; see also Spaulding, *New York in the Critical Period*, ch. 8.
70. Cited in DePauw, The Eleventh Pillar, 224.

less than Hamilton, knew that the public creditors would help sustain the government that best protected their interests.[71]

In 1787 after the new Constitution emerged from the Philadelphia convention, Hamilton undoubtedly had New York in mind when he singled out as factors against its success "the disinclination of the people to taxes and of course to strong government" and "the influence of many inconsiderable men in possession of considerable offices under the state governments who will fear a diminution of their consequence, power and emolument by the establishment of the general government and who can hope for nothing there."[72] In New York the "power" of the Clintonians rested on catering to a constituency with a "disinclination to taxes." Their particularism was in good part a product of their fear of what the nationalists would do with more centralized power to undermine them within the state. To understand them fully one must turn to their opposite numbers, whose nationalism was in good part a product of frustration with the Clintonians.

71. McDonald, *We the People*, 289-96; E. James Ferguson, *The Power of the Purse: A History of American Public Finance, 1776-1790* (Chapel Hill, 1961), 180-81, 231-32. It is difficult to agree with McDonald that the Clintonians wanted New York "to go it alone."

72. Hamilton, "Conjectures about the New Constitution," probably Sept. 17-30, 1787, Syrett, ed., *Hamilton Papers*, IV, 275-76.

CHAPTER 3

The Nationalists:

From Conservative Whigs

To Federalists

———•———

In the fall of 1787 when Alexander Hamilton took stock of the "circumstances" in favor of the "success" of the new Constitution drafted in Philadelphia, he enumerated "the good will of most men of property" who want "a government of the union able to protect them against domestic violence and the depredations which the democratic spirit is apt to make on property," "the hopes of the Creditors of the United States that a general government possessing the means of doing it will pay the debt of the Union," and "the good will of the commercial interests" for a government "capable of regulating, protecting and extending the commerce of the Union."[1] In effect he described the interests which New York's conservative Whigs had forged into the Federalist party, led by the "confederacy of the great and opulent families" Clinton spoke of to Rufus King in 1789.

I

Among the gnarled roots of nationalism in New York none is more striking than the fear of "the depredations which the democratic spirit is apt to make on property." By the mid-1780's the anxiety over

1. Hamilton, "Conjectures about the New Constitution," probably Sept. 17-30, 1787, Syrett, ed., *Hamilton Papers*, IV, 275-76.

[59]

the character of the men in the state legislature which Hamilton expressed to Robert Morris in 1782 was chronic. The legislature, Hamilton wrote to Robert Livingston, was dominated by men with principles of "the levelling kind" who were a threat to "the security of property." "The truth is," he wrote, "that the state is now governed by a couple of New England adventurers," naming Assemblymen Jacob Ford and Matthew Adgate from Albany County, "who make tools of the Yates and their associates." The Council of Revision alone had thwarted their attempts "to destroy the rights of private property." "The principal people in the community" and "all those who have anything to lose" had to be active in trying to reverse this "alarming" situation. The lord of the upper manor, sharing these fears, replied that his family had taken steps to unite "the interests of the Rensselaer, Schuyler and our family with other Gentlemen of property in [the] county."[2]

The character of the men in office at the county level was equally alarming. In appealing to Jay to run for governor in 1786, Schuyler complained bitterly of the judges appointed by Clinton: "Not only the lowest but the most unworthy characters are countenanced by him [Clinton], and through his influence placed in office of trust; [a] great part of the magistracy of this [Albany] and the adjacent western [Montgomery] and northern counties [of the upper Hudson] are wretches that would disgrace the most despicable of all governments,—these serve his turn. He abets a faction . . . which wishes to destroy both public and private credit, and whose whole aim is to rise into importance on the ruin of others."[3]

Landlords' anxiety about their tenants remained high. Their success in quelling the tenant rebellions of 1777 was offset by their failure to defeat confiscation and the sale of Loyalist estates. A dangerous precedent had been established: would Whig estates be next? "This state has a strong Democratic Spirit prevailing," Thomas Tillotson sniffed to his brother-in-law, Robert R. Livingston, as the war ended; if the people were "a little more impoverished, they would aim the first stroke at the tenanted estates which the people on the borders of New England have already in contemplation, 'entre nous.'"[4]

As it happened New York's tenants were relatively quiet in the

2. Hamilton to Robert Livingston, Apr. 25, 1785, Livingston to Hamilton, June 13, 1785, *ibid.*, III, 608-9, 614-16.
3. Philip Schuyler to John Jay, May 30, 1785, John Jay Papers, Columbia Univ.
4. Thomas Tillotson to Robert R. Livingston, June 17, 1782, R. R. Livingston Papers, N.-Y. Hist. Soc.

Confederation years. For some the feverish antagonisms of the Revolution were blunted by the acquisition of land, for some by migration, for others by the landlord's relative leniency in exacting overdue rents and generous terms for attracting new tenants. But there were always sources of resentment. In 1785 there was a sharp dispute in the easternmost towns of Albany County—later part of Columbia— between the Livingstons and alleged squatters who claimed the land they settled on belonged to Massachusetts and not New York, a very old issue. After hearing threats to murder one of the "manor lords," Governor Clinton commanded the sheriffs of Albany and Dutchess counties to assist the proprietors in apprehending the "rioters."[5] The county election of 1785 in the eyes of Henry Livingston was "a Tryal between Demo and Aristo."[6] Shays's Rebellion the following year was alarming to landlords precisely because of such combustibles on their side of the New York-Massachusetts border.

Conservatives never ceased to wring their hands about taxes. In 1784 the Council of Revision vetoed, without success, a law which granted the vestrymen of New York City the right to rate and assess taxes "according to the estates *and other circumstances and abilities to pay taxes*," rather than on the basis of property alone. The council feared that "if the assessors are of the richer class of citizens they will overburden the poor [and] if chosen from among the poor they will endeavor to oppress the rich." The following year the council successfully vetoed a bill which would have taken away from the courts the provision for the review of persons unjustly rated and given it to the county supervisors, who like the assessors, were elected and subject to democratic pressures.[7]

In peace, as in war, the lower manor Livingstons whined the loudest about taxes, very likely because the income from their small estate was considerably less than that of other larger landholders. Margaret Beekman Livingston had apparently given up praying for deliverance from the assessors; nothing could be done about them, she told her son. Robert R. Livingston again took his case to Governor Clinton, claiming that his tax of £475 in 1786 (compared to his previous tax of £187) was on an estate "that has never yet averaged me £300 a year" and "was levied by men not indeed being able to read or write."

5. Edwin Brockholst Livingston, *The Livingstons of Livingston Manor* . . . (N.Y., 1910), 313-16.
6. Henry Livingston to Walter Livingston, Apr. 24, 1785, R. R. Livingston Papers, N.-Y. Hist. Soc.
7. Lincoln, ed., *Messages from the Governors*, II, 211-13, 234-36.

Meanwhile, his brother-in-law reported that the legislature had renewed "the old iniquitous tax law" and threatened to pass Abraham Yates's proposal for a tax on uncultivated lands, which could affect a vast Livingston tract in Ulster County.[8] With a combination of landlord and merchant discontent, it is not surprising that Hamilton, when first elected to the assembly from New York City, made a major order of business in the 1787 session the reform of a taxing system which, he said, permitted men to be "dependent on the caprices, the affections or enmities of another."[9]

From a conservative point of view it was apparent that the state constitution was not functioning as it was supposed to. Although the Council of Revision returned more vetoes after than during the Revolution—eight in 1784, and nineteen in 1785—it was often reversed by the legislature. If it succeeded in striking down one tax measure, it was overridden in another; if it struck down a gradual emancipation bill or a charter of incorporation for the General Society of Mechanics and Tradesmen for New York City, it could not hold the dike against numerous anti-Tory laws.[10] The senators, presumably the protectors of property, "are more eager in the pursuit of popularity than the Assembly," a Livingston complained. "The democratical part of the government is always encroaching."[11] This could easily have been the conservative slogan of the 1780's.

II

The "depredations" against property were nowhere more obvious than in the state's disposition of confiscated Loyalist estates. The "Eagle Eyes of speculation," Chancellor Livingston warned Clinton, had already marked out the prizes and "some of these who have fastened on the spoils of the public have a strong interest in the legislature." Hamilton saw the same thing: "schemes to engross public property in the hands of those who have present power."[12] Living-

8. Margaret Beekman Livingston to Robert R. Livingston, July 16, 1782, Morgan Lewis to Robert R. Livingston, Aug. 3, 1782, Robert R. Livingston to George Clinton, Feb. 20, 1787, R. R. Livingston Papers, N.-Y. Hist. Soc.

9. Hamilton, "New York Assembly Remarks . . . Feb. 17, 1787," Robert R. Livingston to Hamilton, Mar. 3, 1787, Syrett, ed., Hamilton Papers, IV, 94-96, 103.

10. Lincoln, ed., Messages from the Governors, II, 202-51, passim.

11. Thomas Tillotson to Robert R. Livingston, Apr. 12, 1783, R. R. Livingston Papers, N.-Y. Hist. Soc.

12. Robert R. Livingston to George Clinton, Feb. 19, Apr. 2, 1783, Hastings, ed., Public Papers of George Clinton, VIII, 77-79, 109-10; Hamilton to Gouverneur Morris, Apr. 7, 1784, Syrett, ed., Hamilton Papers, III, 528-29.

ston's complaint would have been better directed elsewhere. Historians of the land question in New York have focused so long on whether the distribution of Loyalist estates favored the farmer or the land speculator that they have neglected an equally important, related question: who benefited politically? The evidence suggests that, no matter who got the land, the state's policies worked to the disadvantage of the old established landed gentry and to the advantage of the "new men" in politics.

Land confiscation, first of all, took a heavy toll of the largest estate holders of the province. It eliminated one or more major estate holders from each county where landlordism was entrenched. Along the Hudson Valley it removed from Manhattan the Delanceys; from Westchester, the Philipses; from Dutchess, Beverly Robinson and Roger Morris. To the west in Tryon, it removed the Johnsons; to the northeast in Charlotte, the Skenes, the Jessups, and John Tabor Kempe. The great Whig estates of course remained intact. Yet confiscation shook up the social structure, if it did not level it, by removing the Tory wing of the landed aristocracy as well as a segment of the Tory wing of the mercantile aristocracy. The Tories affected came from all classes, but of a total claim for $10,000,000 in property losses filed by New York Loyalists with the British government, $5,353,000 was filed by only thirty-two men.[13]

Secondly, the sale of the estates increased the number of freehold farmers in counties where tenantry previously was predominant. The distribution of the estates, the work of recent scholars suggests, was far broader than the findings of Harry Yoshpe for Westchester led a generation of historians to conclude for the state as a whole.[14] When compiled for all districts, the evidence may well support the hypothesis of Staughton Lynd that on the larger, heavily tenanted estates "the speculators found marginal pickings" while "small, scattered, uninhabited or urban parcels lent themselves to speculative operations." Lynd, investigating Dutchess County, found that 414 lots which formerly belonged to the Robinson and Morris estates were sold to 401 persons, often former tenants.[15] For Philipse Manor in Westchester, Beatrice Reubens found that "the immediate result of the sale by the state was to displace one wealthy and powerful landlord who had

13. Flick, *Loyalism in New York*, ch. 7.
14. Harry B. Yoshpe, *The Disposition of Loyalist Estates in the Southern District of the State of New York* (N.Y., 1939), 113-19, for a summary; for the laws, Cochran, *New York in the Confederation*, 57-65.
15. Lynd, *Anti-Federalism in Dutchess County*, 74-75.

ruled over 50,000 acres and more than 270 tenants, and to install 287 independent owners with an average holding of 174 acres. Moreover, at least 196 of the new owners, or over two-thirds of the total, bought farms which they had worked as tenants or inherited from tenants."[16] In Manhattan, by contrast, "the greater part" of the 200 or so parcels of the Delancey estate in Manhattan "fell to the lot of substantial families" although, as Sidney Pomerantz pointed out, "the fact still remains that property belonging to a single person became the possession of many."[17] In the Mohawk Valley the pattern found by Catherine Crary seems to be more mixed. During the war speculative purchasers were the primary beneficiaries; she could identify two-thirds of 29 purchasers of 41 tracts from 1780 to 1783 as members of prominent families; from 1784 to 1788, however, the 142 purchasers of 34 parcels were evenly divided between speculative purchasers and middling farmers.[18]

Third, wherever speculators were beneficiaries, supporters of the Governor figured prominently among them. This is not to argue that conservative Whig landlords and merchants did not also drink from the public trough. No one could miss the importance of the son-in-law of Pierre Van Cortlandt, the Lieutenant-Governor, buying the Delancey home in Westchester (via his brother-in-law Philip, a Commissioner of Forfeiture) or the exquisite symbolism of Robert R. Livingston's acquiring Oliver Delancey's "large Square" pew at St. Paul's Church in New York City.[19] The legislature made it possible for capital-poor Whigs to pay for estates in depreciated state securities. The Commissioners of Forfeiture, almost without exception, were men who can be identified as leaders in the "Governor's interest" at one time or another.[20] It is not surprising therefore that almost every

16. Beatrice G. Reubens, "Pre-Emptive Rights in the Disposition of a Confiscated Estate: Philipsburgh Manor, New York," *Wm. and Mary Qtly.*, 3d Ser., 22 (1965), 435-56, esp. 445-46.

17. Pomerantz, *New York An American City*, 80-81.

18. Catherine Snell Crary, "Forfeited Loyalist Lands in the Western District of New York: Albany and Tryon Counties," *N.Y. History*, 35 (1954), 239-58.

19. Reubens, "Pre-Emptive Rights," *Wm. and Mary Qtly.*, 3d Ser., 22 (1965), 450; Dangerfield, *Chancellor Robert R. Livingston*, 200-201. It is not clear whether Livingston was able to raise the £6000 credit he sought for a more ambitious venture in confiscated land.

20. Dangerfield, *Chancellor Robert R. Livingston*, 246; Flick, *Loyalism in New York*, ch. 7, *passim*. The commissioners at one time or another were: for the western district, Jeremiah Van Rensselaer and Henry Oothoudt, then Jacob G. Klock and Christopher Yates; for the middle district John Hathorn; for the eastern, Alexander Webster; for the southern, Isaac Stoutenbergh and Philip Van Cortlandt.

man of the small knot of anti-Federalist faithfuls in New York City in 1788 could be found on the roster of purchasers of confiscated estates in the southern district,[21] or that the six chief organizers of the anti-Federalists at Albany in 1788 (who included two Commissioners of Forfeiture) all secured state land in the late 1780's.[22]

The political effects of these economic changes are difficult to calculate. Confiscation of course "was meant to, and did destroy the Delancey interest entirely," as the Tory historian Thomas Jones bitterly observed. More than that, it weakened the hold of the old "Livingston party."[23] In Dutchess it made continued landlord dominance difficult, the chronic complaint of Robert R. Livingston's family. In Westchester it enabled a landlord family like the Van Cortlandts to increase their influence. In Washington (formerly Charlotte) County on the northeastern frontier it permitted a *nouveau-riche* landholder like John Williams to emerge as a potentate. All three of these landholders gravitated into George Clinton's orbit, it may be noted. Everywhere the increased number of freeholders created potential support for Clinton.

One detects in the established landed gentry of New York a note of frustration in dealing with Clinton for public land in general, and not only Tory estates. In 1787, for example, when Philip Schuyler, Gouverneur Morris, Robert Morris, and a handful of other Federalists acquired a large tract known as the St. Lawrence Ten Towns they had to operate behind the scenes through a front man, Alexander Macomb, who for several years kept secret the names of his sponsors; he probably took John Lamb into the syndicate because of Lamb's in-

21. I have checked the members of the Federal Republican Society of 1788 and Governor Clinton's election committee of 1789 against the list of purchasers in Yoshpe, *Disposition of Loyalist Estates*, Appendix 2, and in Flick, *Loyalism in New York*, Appendix.

22. For the principal Albany County leaders, see the list to whom the New York committee sent pamphlets in 1788 and the correspondents, in Lamb Papers, N.-Y. Hist. Soc.; Crary, "Forfeited Loyalist Lands," *N.Y. History*, 25 (1954), 252-53, who has examined the MS records for the western district, enumerates John and Abraham Lansing among the large-scale speculators. I find the following leaders in the *Calendar of New York Colonial Manuscripts, Indorsed Land Papers in the Office of the Secretary of State of New York, 1643-1803* (Albany, 1864), *passim*: Jeremiah Van Rensselaer in 1787-88 alone received 12 certificates of location for 17,000 acres; John Lansing, Jr., received 5 certificates in 1787 for 6900 acres; Henry Oothoudt received 4 certificates in 1786-88 for about 20,000 acres (some jointly held); Peter W. Yates in 1789 received a certificate locating 8000 acres in a joint purchase; Matthew Visher alone received but one small tract. It is not clear, however, from this calendar whether the land granted was Loyalist land.

23. Jones, *History of New York*, I, 291 n.1.

fluence with the Governor.[24] In 1788 Clinton squelched another group of speculators which read like a Who's Who of the Livingstons, Van Rensselaers, and Schuylers of the upper Hudson Valley who had acquired title to a vast tract in western New York by dealing with the Indians directly, a practice forbidden by the state constitution.[25] By contrast the state enabled a group of speculators which reads like a roster of Dutchess County anti-Federalists (with a sprinkling of their Long Island brethren thrown in) to acquire a 43,000-acre tract to the north which became Plattsburgh.[26] Clintonian policies were a bonanza for the "entrepreneurial operators," the men who, as Richard Morris puts it, "considered land as an instrument for speculative gains rather than as a means to preserve or enhance social status"—in short, for Clintonians.[27]

III

Conservative Whigs opposed the "depredations of the democratic spirit" against Loyalists in general. To the popular Whigs, confiscation of Tory land was not enough. Nor was it enough that after the war some 35,000 Loyalists left the state, about 18 per cent of the total prewar population of 192,000, the largest percentage in the country. For every Tory who left, however, two others remained.[28] Hatred of these Loyalists was intense in New York. No other state had had as many battles fought within its borders; no state had as large a section as the southern district occupied by the British for so long; no state

24. The character of this speculation was not revealed until 1792; see ch. 11.
25. See Orsamus Turner, *History of the Pioneer Settlements of Phelps and Gorman's Purchase and Morris' Reserve* (Rochester, 1852), 106-7; the speculators, later compensated by the state, are listed in *Laws of the State of N.Y.*, 16th Sess., ch. 26; for Clinton's report to the legislature, see Lincoln, ed., *Messages from the Governors*, II, 291; for Philip Schuyler's political embarrassment, Schuyler to Stephen Van Rensselaer, Feb. 1788, Schuyler Papers, Lib. Cong.
26. "Jonathan Lawrence's Map of the Town of Plattsburgh," [n.d. but after 1786] which has names of lot owners, Map Room, N.-Y. Hist. Soc. Zephaniah Platt, the Dutchess anti-Federalist, filed a claim in 1785 for 43,000 acres in class and bounty rights and in 1786 was given 20 certificates of location for tracts amounting to this. See *Calendar of New York Land Papers*, 657, 733-35.
27. Morris, "Class Struggle and the American Revolution," *Wm. and Mary Qtly.*, 3rd Ser., 19 (1962), 10.
28. Flick, *Loyalism in New York*, 179-82, for the traditional estimates, undoubtedly high. Robert R. Palmer, *The Age of the Democratic Revolution: A Political History of Europe and America, 1760-1800*, 2 vols. (Princeton, N.J., 1959-64), I, 187-89, for comparison of the proportion of émigrés in the United States with France. Even if the traditional figure given for the émigrés is high, it is likely that the population of New York in 1776 was closer to 170,000 than 190,000.

had as many Tories. Whig farmers were incensed at Tory farmers who had grown wealthy as suppliers of the British; Whig refugees returning to New York City were jealous of the collaborationists who profited under the British. The result was a wave of Toryphobia in which economics gave the added drive to pent-up emotionalism.

Popular Whigs meeting in New York City asked to have Tories excluded from "advantages of trade and commerce" as well as from the vote. Hamilton depicted their arguments: "to the trader they say, you will be overborn by the large capitals of the Tory merchants; to the Mechanic, your business will be less profitable, your wages less considerable by the interference of Tory workmen."[29]

The political motive was equally apparent. A month after the British evacuation of New York the Whig refugees, mechanics for the most part, elected to the assembly a slate of nine former Sons of Liberty including John Lamb, Marinus Willett, Isaac Sears, and Henry Rutgers. Robert R. Livingston discerned three parties in the city: first, "the tories, who still hope for power"; secondly, the "warm and hot headed whigs who are for the expulsion of all tories from the state and who would wish even to render the more moderate whigs suspected in order to preserve in their own hands all the powers of government"; and "the third, are those who wish at present to soften the rigorous laws with respect to the tories by degrees as they see their party broken." Conservative Whigs were the "third" party.[30]

In response to this popular Whig clamor the legislature raised havoc with Tory property by a variety of laws favoring Whig debtors at the expense of Tory creditors and permitting easy suits against Tories for wartime damages. In violation of the peace treaty, they refused to restore confiscated estates to Loyalists and made it impossible for them to return to repurchase their property. They also continued the sweeping wartime disfranchisement, which barred from the polls an estimated nine-tenths of the voters of Queens, two-thirds of New York City, Richmond and Kings, and most of Westchester.[31]

Such policies drove the Tories into the arms of the conservative Whigs who took them into a marriage of political convenience in which love soon bloomed. Two factors lay behind the conservative Whig decision. It was a requirement, first of all, of the "spirit of

29. Hamilton, "A Letter from Phocion," Jan. 1-27, 1784, Syrett, ed., *Hamilton Papers*, III, 493-94.
30. Robert R. Livingston to John Jay, Jan. 25, 1784, to Gouverneur Morris, Dec. 20, 1783, R. R. Livingston Papers, N.-Y. Hist. Soc.
31. Spaulding, *New York in the Critical Period*, ch. 6.

conciliation" toward Great Britain to which the treaty of peace pledged
the United States. The requirements that foreign obligations imposed on domestic policy were always keenly felt by the New York
nationalists who gave the nation its first two secretaries for foreign
affairs, Robert R. Livingston, and his successor, John Jay, a negotiator
of the Treaty of Paris.[32] The economic ties of the New York mercantile interest with Britain further dictated conciliation. Secondly, immediately after the war, conservative Whigs were desperate for political
allies; the large number of Tories in New York City and the southern
district as a whole beckoned.

The conservative leaders bid for Tory support with unmistakable
signals. Hamilton, acting with John Laurance, Morgan Lewis, and
Richard Varick, all Federalists-to-be, served as counsel to a number
of Tories who sought restitution of their confiscated land. Hamilton
as "Phocion" wrote the leading newspaper defense of the policy of
conciliation. Then he made a *cause célèbre* of Rutgers v. Wadding-
ton, in which he argued that the state's Trespass Act violated the
treaty of peace. The Mayor's Court (on which James Duane sat)
handed down a compromise decision that displeased the "warm and
hot headed whigs."[33]

The political scene in New York City shifted with kaleidoscopic
speed. By the spring election of 1784 Livingston could report a defeat
for a party "so jealous of power as to endeavor to exclude property
and abilities from the weight that they must and will have in every
society." Things were "settling down upon their old foundation." By
the spring of '85 Tories apparently were voting. By 1786 conservatives in the legislature restored the rights of citizenship to Tories, if
not their property. In the battle over the Constitution in 1788, the
New York City Federalists ran two prominent Tories on their ticket
and united the city behind them.[34]

Years later, Robert Troup, Hamilton's political lieutenant, continuing Rufus King's political education in New York politics long
after Clinton had begun it, explained quite frankly what had happened after the war: "Soon after we regained possession of New York,

32. Jay to Hamilton, Sept. 28, 1783, Syrett, ed., *Hamilton Papers*, III, 459-60.

33. Alexander Hamilton, *et al.*, to Thomas Mifflin, President of Congress, Dec.
10, 1783, "A Letter from Phocion," Jan. 1-27, 1784, Syrett, ed., *Hamilton Papers*,
III, 478-79, 483-97; for the Rutgers case, see Pomerantz, *New York An American
City*, 84-87.

34. Robert R. Livingston to Charles DeWitt, May 9, 1784, R. R. Livingston
Papers, N.-Y. Hist. Soc.; Lynd, The Revolution and the Common Man, ch. 8.

we permitted the Tories to enlist under our banners; and they have since manfully fought by our side in every important battle we have had with the democracy; some of them in the character of officers, and others in those of common soldiers. And when monies have been necessary to support our cause, many amongst them never scrupled to pay their quota of the general tax. Moreover we ought not to forget their zealous and useful service in our great contest for the constitution."[35]

IV

Among those fearful of the "depredations which the democratic spirit is apt to make on property," the "manor lords" were the most logical recruits for the conservative Whig leaders. Yet there were obstacles to forging the "confederacy of the great and opulent families," and it did not coalesce until about 1787.

At the end of the war Philip Schuyler and his family, for whom Alexander Hamilton was increasingly the spokesman, stood almost alone as premature anti-Clintonians. When Schuyler ran for governor in 1783 he seems to have had no support from other estate holders. Robert R. Livingston backed Clinton. Pierre Van Cortlandt had become Clinton's perennial running mate as lieutenant-governor. Jay was unwilling to be a sacrificial lamb on a Federalist election altar. And it is interesting to note that in 1786 out of six nationalists appointed delegates to the Annapolis convention, only Hamilton and Egbert Benson attended. Rufus King heard that both Duane and Robert R. Livingston, who did not make the trip, were "very little concerned in the politics of the present time."[36]

There was no underlying economic factor keeping the landlords from Federalism. The "manor lords" were not exclusively agrarian, as Beard and others once depicted them.[37] The agriculture of the Hudson Valley was thoroughly commercial. There were landings, Robert R. Livingston pointed out, every two miles along the east bank of the river from Albany southwards (and every ten miles along the west bank) at which river sloops picked up farm produce for the

35. Robert Troup to Rufus King, Apr. 4, 1809, King, ed., *Correspondence of Rufus King*, V, 148-49.
36. Rufus King to Jonathan Jackson, Sept. 3, 1786, Mass. Hist. Soc., *Proceedings*, 59 (1915-16), 89.
37. Charles A. Beard, *An Economic Interpretation of the Constitution of the United States* (N.Y., 1913), 28-29.

New York market and overseas export.[38] Moreover, the leading landed families were themselves engaged in trade. Invariably they had members who devoted themselves exclusively to commerce. And it was hardly for pleasure that Philip Schuyler lived in Albany or that Chancellor Livingston and others in his clan maintained town houses in New York City. The estate holders invested in land for speculation, in bank stock, in securities, in foreign trade.[39] The upper manor Livingstons did a lively trade in iron forged on their estate, and Philip Schuyler at one time employed scores of workmen in a flaxmill and linenworks, besides the sawmills, gristmills, and stores common to all the estates.[40] The "manor lords," in short, were only a shade different from bourgeois entrepreneurs.

Yet, however much they shared a common conservative outlook and common economic interests, the New York estate holders, like the Virginia planters they resembled, were proud aristocrats, often jealous of each other and ambitious for office and prestige. Moreover, Clinton was able to maintain enough of an attraction to delay a few of them although not to prevent them from gravitating into an aggressive Federalism.

James Duane, owner of Duanesburg (36,000 acres and 235 tenants), is a case in point. Duane became so powerful in the Continental Congress by 1781 that he was subjected to personal attack. Sam Adams was amazed at the prospect of a "compleat New York administration." The other nationalist leaders, as Duane's biographer puts it, "may have distrusted Duane but they dared not show it to Clinton." Duane alone among the nationalists vigorously pursued New York's claim to Vermont, as well he might as the largest land claimant in the area.

38. Robert R. Livingston to Hector St. Jean de Crèvecoeur, Dec. 27, 1788, R. R. Livingston Papers, N.-Y. Hist. Soc.; also see the description of Hudson in Thomas Jenkins to Robert R. Livingston, Jan. 10, 1789, ibid.; for Crèvecoeur on this same point, see Crèvecoeur, Eighteenth-Century Travels, trans. and ed., Adams, 1-3, and Brissot de Warville, New Travels, eds., Vamos and Echeverria, 138.

39. For the economy of the upper manor Livingstons, see Gordon, Kinship and Class, 134-48 and Klein, William Livingston, 25-26; the business activities of John and Walter Livingston may be traced in the Robert R. Livingston Papers, N.-Y. Hist. Soc., passim; for the wartime period see Mason, "Adjustment to a War Economy," Business Hist. Rev., 40 (1966), 190-212, and Robert A. East, Business Enterprise in the American Revolutionary Era (N.Y., 1938), ch. 5; for Robert R. Livingston's interest in trade with West Indies, see Livingston to Duane, Mar. 30, Aug. 7, 1784, James Duane Papers, N.-Y. Hist. Soc., cited in Lynd, The Revolution and the Common Man, 171; Robert R. Livingston to Walter Livingston, Feb. 4, 1785, R. R. Livingston Papers, N.-Y. Hist. Soc.; for Gouverneur Morris, see Ferguson, Power of the Purse, 264-65.

40. Gerlach, Philip Schuyler, ch. 2, Pt. I; East, Business Enterprise, ch. 5.

He was suspected of being behind the move by Yates and Scott to remove Robert R. Livingston as chancellor late in the war. In that tiff Clinton backed Robert R. Livingston, but it is hardly unconnected that in 1784 he appointed Duane mayor of New York, a post he held until 1789. The appointment put Duane on the shelf politically for a few years; he was late in joining Hamilton and Schuyler for the crucial battles of 1787-88, and while active in the election campaign and at the Poughkeepsie convention, he never seems to have regained their confidence, if he ever had it. In 1789 Hamilton would block his election to the United States Senate.[41]

The upper manor Livingstons were the most jealous and individualistic of any estate holders. Robert, lord of the upper manor (150,000 acres and some 600 or so tenants), and his sons, Peter R., John, Walter, and Henry, had never recovered from the trauma of losing their "manor seat" in the legislature in 1777. In the Revolution they acquired the lustre neither of Robert's brother William, governor of New Jersey, nor of his brother Philip, a signer of the Declaration, nor of their cousin, Chancellor Robert R. Livingston. The influence that James Duane, Robert's son-in-law, had acquired did not redound to them. In the 1780's a tempestuous feud broke out between the upper and lower manor, over the weighty matter of the Chancellor's claim to build a dam for a gristmill on the Roeliff Jansen Kill whose headwaters began on upper manor land. This poisoned the possibility of political cooperation between the two families.[42] Also jealous of the Schuylers, they did not unite with them on behalf of assembly candidates until 1785 and then were not able to make good on Lord Robert's promise to "Stick Close to Each other."[43]

To increase their own influence, the upper manor clamored to have their section of Albany County set up as a separate county. In 1786 the legislature obliged, creating Columbia County, the Clintonians probably acting in the hope that it might be easier to conquer the landlords if they were divided. Robert R. Livingston of the lower manor was furious. If anything, he had wanted his small estate, Clermont (13,000 acres and perhaps 80 tenants), in the southern part of Columbia put in with Dutchess County immediately to the south, the county which traditionally had returned his father to the provin-

41. Alexander, *James Duane*, 144-50, 168-70, 190-97, 201-2.
42. Dangerfield, *Chancellor Robert R. Livingston*, 75, 192-93, 215-16, and *passim*; Gordon, Kinship and Class, 203-8, 213-16, 295-312.
43. Robert Livingston to Hamilton, June 13, 1785, Syrett, ed., *Hamilton Papers*, III, 614-16.

cial assembly and where his influence would be combined with that of his mother and several brothers-in-law. In Columbia, by contrast, he would have to ride on the upper manor's coattails. He warned Robert of the upper manor of other potential dangers. If the family could not agree with the Schuylers and Van Rensselaers, who would still have influence in Columbia, they could not carry the county; if they did, "your united influence" would throw all the other elements against the landlords.[44] The Chancellor's prediction came true. The new city of Hudson and the anti-landlord towns on the Massachusetts border opposed the upper manor Livingstons. By 1788, in the crucial battle for Poughkeepsie convention delegates, Philip Schuyler found that "all was in confusion," and in desperation he and James Duane traveled through the county attempting to rally the Livingstons to back the Federalist candidates. Partly because of this disunity among the landlords, anti-Federalists carried the county in 1788.[45] In 1789 the upper manor backed Schuyler's candidate for Congress and his candidate against Governor Clinton, but within a year or two they lapsed into their jealousy of Schuyler. Their chief interest in politics, as always, remained the Livingstons.

Robert R. Livingston's rift with the upper manor helped drive him into the arms of Schuyler and Hamilton. In 1783 Livingston backed Clinton; in 1784 he fought Hamilton over banking policy; but in 1786 the creation of Columbia County left him with even less influence locally. Clinton, furthermore, gave no signs of responding to his frantic pleas for intervention on his tax assessment, or of considering him for other public offices. He was interested in "a liberal or honorable appointment," he pointedly informed Hamilton in 1787, "such as would enable me to live as I would wish constantly at New York City," an appointment which he could not "expect from the prevailing party." The implication was obvious; perhaps he could expect something from the rising Schuyler faction. Driven by these needs—for place, for prestige, and for protection for his estate—Livingston became an active Federalist, submerging his differences with

44. Robert R. Livingston to Henry Livingston [n.d., misdated 1789 by the curator but unquestionably 1786], R. R. Livingston Papers, N.-Y. Hist. Soc.; Gordon, Kinship and Class, 309.
45. Henry to Robert R. Livingston, Mar. 13, Seth Jenkins to Robert R. Livingston, Mar. 18, 1787, William Wilson to Robert R. Livingston, Mar. 13, 1788, and Philip Schuyler to Robert R. Livingston, Mar. 29, 1788, R. R. Livingston Papers, N.-Y. Hist. Soc. See also Peter Van Schaack to Robert R. Livingston, Van Schaack Papers, N.Y. State Lib.

Hamilton over banking and finance and with Jay over foreign policy.[46]
In 1788 the nationalists also won over the Van Cortlandts temporarily. Hamilton spoke of the Van Cortlandts and their Westchester
County neighbors, the Morrises, as "zealous advocates" of the Constitution; Philip, the eldest son, was a Federalist convention delegate
and he and Pierre, Jr. (who had read law in Hamilton's office), signed
a Federalist election broadside.[47] Pierre Van Cortlandt, the head of
the family, was not quite a Clintonian even though he had been
Clinton's lieutenant-governor since 1777. He had been elected in '77
with the backing of the conservative Whigs. He was re-elected in 1780
by the Whig coalition that backed Clinton too. Hamilton in his
portrait gallery of 1782 said of him only that he was "an honest man
without pretensions." He owed his high place in the patriot government to the fact that the Van Cortlandts and the Morrises were the
leading patriot landlords in a county in which the largest landlord,
the Philipses, and most of the population was Tory; he had been ar-
dently wooed by Tryon, the last royal governor, but he was wooed by
the patriots as well.[48]

Clinton kept Van Cortlandt on his ticket because it served his
purpose of dividing the "great families." Van Cortlandt, by going
along, won a higher place for himself than as a relatively small estate
holder (fewer than 200 tenants) he could have hoped to have won in
nationalist circles. He had trouble producing votes even in his home
county.[49] Van Cortlandt shifted to the Federalists in the ratification

46. Robert R. Livingston to Hamilton, Mar. 3, 1787, discussing an appointment, follows a lengthy letter from Livingston to Clinton, Feb. 20, 1787, about
taxes, very likely unanswered. Livingston to Philip Schuyler, Mar. 20, May 9, and
Sept. 9, 1788, show his active politicking for the Federalist cause; all in R. R.
Livingston Papers, N.-Y. Hist. Soc. For Livingston's differences with Hamilton
over banking see this ch., sec. VI; with Jay over foreign policy, see ch. 16.

47. Hamilton, "To The Supervisors of the City of Albany," N.Y. Daily Adver-
tiser, Feb. 20, 1789; "Friends and Countrymen . . . Apr. 12, 1788," broadside,
N.-Y. Hist. Soc.; Hamilton to Pierre Van Cortlandt, Feb. 16, 1789, Syrett, ed.,
Hamilton Papers, V, 254; Philip Schuyler to John Jay and Richard Varick, et al.,
Jan. 31, 1789, Schuyler Papers, N.Y. Pub. Lib.

48. Charles H. Brown, Van Cortlandt Manor (Tarrytown, N.Y., 1965), passim,
sums up some of the findings of the research staff at Sleepy Hollow Restorations,
Tarrytown. Other details are in material in their files and in Van Cortlandt
Papers, N.Y. Pub. Lib. and N.-Y. Hist. Soc.; see also John Krout in DAB s.v. "Van
Cortlandt, Pierre, Sr.," and "Van Cortlandt, Philip"; and J. T. Scharf, History of
Westchester County, New York, 2 vols. (Phila., 1886), I, passim. The size of the
estate is not clear; originally a grant of 86,000 acres, it was considerably reduced
by land sales before and after the Revolution.

49. See Appendix, Table 4, for returns for governor, 1789-92, and Table 6 for

contest because Hamilton held out the possibility of support the following year in the gubernatorial election. After 1789 when Federalists endorsed Van Cortlandt only for the second spot, he drifted back to Clinton. He and his sons would become Republicans. Thus the family played a middle role between the two parties, somewhat akin to the lower manor Livingstons.

The Van Cortlandts were a notch lower in social status and wealth than the "great families" to the north. The recently restored family home at Croton suggests more the solid comfort of a Dutch farmhouse than the elegance of Philip Schuyler's stately Georgian mansion at Albany. Years later the Van Cortlandt-Clinton alliance would be sealed by the marriage of Pierre, Jr., to Catherine Clinton, George's daughter.

Whatever the reason, by 1788 every "great family" of the Hudson Valley was directly represented by one or more Federalist delegates at the Poughkeepsie ratifying convention: the Schuyler-Van Rensselaers by Alexander Hamilton (Philip Schuyler's son-in-law, Stephen Van Rensselaer's brother-in-law); the upper manor Livingstons by James Duane (married to a daughter of Robert, lord of the upper manor); the lower manor branch of Columbia and Dutchess by their head, Chancellor Robert R. Livingston (whose brothers John and Edward and brothers-in-law, Morgan Lewis and John Armstrong, were Federalist); and other branches of that prodigious family by John Jay (who had married William Livingston's daughter) and Philip R. Livingston; the Westchester county landlords, the Morrises, by the brothers Lewis and Richard Morris (sons of the lord of the manor and half-brothers to Gouverneur); and the Van Cortlandts by Philip Van Cortlandt (son of Pierre, the lieutenant-governor).

Thus Charles Beard, basing his thesis in 1913 on Orin Libby's ill-researched monograph, could hardly have been more wrong in assigning the "manor lords" of New York to the anti-Federalist camp. In his 1935 preface when he accepted Thomas Cochran's correction, Beard still left the impression that most but not all the landlords were anti-Federalist. On the other hand Forrest McDonald, Beard's most weighty critic, is equally misleading in claiming that the great families were "about evenly divided." Gilbert Livingston and Jeremiah Van Rensselaer on the anti-Federalist side hardly balanced the "confederacy" on the Federalist side. Beard's obiter dictum of 1935—

---

returns for Congress, 1792-96, when Philip Van Cortlandt was the Republican candidate.

"seldom if ever, is there total class-solidarity in historical conflicts" —was particularly inappropriate for the example.[50] There was probably no other point in the second half of the eighteenth century when the great estate holders were more united.

V

However much Beard erred in regard to "the manor lords" of New York, his perception was not misplaced in regard to the public creditors. That "the hopes of the creditors" Hamilton enumerated in 1787 were a powerhouse for nationalism in the middle states has been reasserted by the most authoritative recent student of American public finance[51] and accepted by Beard's severest critic. Of the "economic coalitions" welded together by Robert Morris, writes Forrest McDonald, "the broadest based and best coordinated were public creditors, both original investors and speculators; they had been formed into militant organizations in cities from Baltimore to Boston and were strongest in Philadelphia and New York. They were the greediest, most ruthless, and most insistent in demanding political action on their behalf."[52] In New York almost every major conservative Whig leader could be reckoned in Robert Morris's camp: Gouverneur Morris became the assistant superintendent of finance; Hamilton was appointed by Morris as receiver of taxes for the state; Robert R. Livingston was Secretary for Foreign Affairs while the Great Man was financier; Duer became a member of the Board of Treasury after Morris's resignation; Duane was active in Congress on behalf of the creditors.[53]

As early as 1781 the nationalist leaders in New York began to exert

50. Beard, *An Economic Interpretation of the Constitution*, preface, xv, xvi, 28-29; Cochran, *New York in the Confederation*, 17. Spaulding, *New York in the Critical Period*, ch. 12, also corrected Beard. McDonald, *We the People*, is contradictory. He writes that "the great landlords in the convention were divided about evenly," 309, that "the powerful Livingston and Van Cortlandt families were split," 297, and that both parties "included equal numbers of large and small landholders," 300. Then in analyzing "the Hudson valley patricians," after recognizing their "close identification with mercantile interests," he argues that "there was very little economic reason why they should desire the changes brought about by the Constitution," 368-69, thus seemingly placing them as anti-Federalists.

51. Beard, *An Economic Interpretation of the Constitution*, ch. 3; Ferguson, *Power of the Purse*, ch. 6. See below, ch. 8.

52. Forrest McDonald, *E Pluribus Unum: The Formation of the American Republic, 1776-1790* (Boston, 1965), 34. McDonald insists, however, that this group which functioned in 1783 did not exist in 1787-88.

53. *Ibid.*, ch. 1; Broadus Mitchell, *Alexander Hamilton*, 2 vols. (N.Y., 1957-62), I, ch. 16; Dangerfield, *Chancellor Robert R. Livingston*, Pt. II, chs. 4, 5.

pressure on the legislature on behalf of the public creditors. Hamilton was appointed receiver late in 1781. In the spring of 1782, at the request of a special delegation from Congress, the New York legislature agreed to a resolution introduced by Schuyler and probably drafted by Hamilton calling for an enlargement of Congress' powers of taxation and a general convention to revise the Articles of Confederation. In the fall, a group of public creditors held a meeting at Albany at which Philip Schuyler presided, proposing a state convention of creditors and appointing a committee to bring about a national convention.[54]

At this point the creditors made common cause with the since famous conspiracy of the army officers encamped at Newburgh, New York, who were also seeking a source of national revenue to settle their unmet demands for pay. General Alexander McDougall, the erstwhile Liberty Boy, emerged from the smoky fires at Newburgh a convert to nationalism, the head of a three-man delegation that carried the officers' *cahier* to Philadelphia. Robert Morris, Gouverneur Morris, Duer, and Hamilton all coached the officers in the politics of nationalism. The officers apparently were willing to play the part of the Roundheads who overawed the Rump Parliament in 1653, but when Washington refused to play Cromwell, the cabal collapsed, leaving the public creditors to pursue their ends by the more frustrating game of civilian politics. A year later McDougall appeared as the first president of Hamilton's Bank of New York. His untimely death in 1786 deprived Hamilton of an "aegis" that might have been as "essential" in New York politics as was Washington in national affairs.[55]

In New York, there were heavy holdings of both state and federal debt distributed among two types of creditors: several thousand small holders (both original lenders and speculators) and several hundred large-scale speculators who by the mid-1780's had already acquired hundreds of thousands of dollars in certificates. The state government also became a creditor when it accepted certain types of certificates in payment for confiscated land. In 1786 the Clintonian legislature completed the alienation of the small group of wealthy public creditors

54. Ferguson, *Power of the Purse*, 142-43, 150-51; Mitchell, *Alexander Hamilton*, I, 266-74; Spaulding, *New York in the Critical Period*, 13; Egbert Benson to Robert R. Livingston, July 22, 1782, R. R. Livingston Papers, N.-Y. Hist. Soc.

55. Ferguson, *Power of the Purse*, 162-67, 175-78; Merrill Jensen, *The New Nation: A History of the United States During the Confederation, 1781-1789* (N.Y., 1950), 54-67.

by a double blow: it funded part of the public debt in a way that left them out in the cold and refused once again to surrender the state impost to Congress, thereby effectively killing the effort to establish an independent source of national revenue. The legislature funded the entire state debt and about $1,400,000 of continental debt in a plan by which holders of the latter loaned their certificates to the state government in return for interest. The plan, according to McDonald, "created in effect a list of 5000 pensioners" and also gave a windfall to speculators tipped off as to which securities were likely to rise in the market.[56] At the same time it left unrewarded several hundred holders of $3,600,000 in unfunded federal certificates and wreaked havoc among those speculators who had been buying securities at a low price and using them as payment for confiscated estates. In the assembly William Duer led the opposition to Clinton's program. A critic charged it was "a studied design to divide the interests of the public creditors."[57] The operation left the frustrated public creditors no alternative but to attach their "hopes" to the banners of the Federalist party.

VI

The "good will of the commercial interest" also came naturally to the leaders of nationalism. In 1786 when Hamilton ran for the assembly from New York City, Schuyler said that "the Quakers [former Tories, for the most part] Merchants, and some of the Mechanics are for him, but part of the latter adverse."[58] By the battle of 1788, there was only one prominent merchant, Henry Rutgers, in Clinton's camp; another, John Broome, president of the Chamber of Commerce, a staunch Whig, had a reputation as a "lukewarm" Federalist.[59] Otherwise, it would be hard to locate a merchant from an established family, a leading export-import man, an insurance broker, a wealthy stockholder or director of the Bank of New York—in short, anyone at the apex of wealth and power in the mercantile community—who was not a Federalist.[60] And the vote for delegates—2700 to about 50-150

56. McDonald, *We the People*, 292-96, and "The Anti-Federalists, 1781-1789," *Wisconsin Magazine of History*, 46 (1963), 209-11. McDonald offers no proof that the beneficiaries of this scheme acted accordingly in politics.
57. "Gustavus," *New York Packet*, Apr. 13, 1786.
58. Philip Schuyler to Stephen Van Rensselaer, Apr. 20, 1786, cited in Spaulding, *New York in the Critical Period*, 111.
59. See ch. 6.
60. I have compared bank directors, insurance brokers, and officers of the

for the anti-Federalist candidates—shows how pervasive was "good will" in the commercial center. The conservative espousal of the interests of Loyalists, public creditors, and men of property in general won friends among merchants. So did Hamilton's championing of a commercial bank. Early in 1784 Chancellor Livingston sought a charter from the legislature for a Land Bank, whose capital would be based on mortgages on improved land. It secured considerable support from "the country interest" and at first from some city merchants who remembered the highly successful land bank which the provincial legislature had rechartered in 1771. This threat hastened the gestation of a commercial venture based on specie, known as the Bank of New York. At first Hamilton's concern was to obtain for his brother-in-law, John Barker Church, and his partner, Jeremiah Wadsworth, more power in the Bank of North America at Philadelphia. But when he found he could not lick his potential rivals in the Bank of New York, he joined them, drafting the bank's constitution and rallying political support. By the spring of 1784, Hamilton could boast that "all the mercantile and monied influence" was against the Land Bank.[61]

The personnel of the Bank of New York reflected Hamilton's budding political coalition: William Seton, the cashier, and four members of the Board of Directors were Tories; other directors were conservative Whigs and the president was Alexander McDougall, the one-time popular Whig. Even Melancton Smith, Marinus Willett, and John Lamb signed the bank's plea to the legislature for a charter.[62] There, however, political pressure for each bank canceled the other out; neither got a charter. The state loan act of 1786 which also embodied Clinton's program to fund the debt, satisfied the demand for a land-backed currency by issuing £200,000 in bills of credit against the security of mortgages. The Bank of New York continued to function without a charter of incorporation.[63]

Chambers of Commerce listed in *New York City Directory*, and merchants listed as major business figures in Pomerantz, *New York An American City*, and East, *Business Enterprise*, with lists of known Federalist and anti-Federalist leaders of 1788-1789.

61. "Constitution of the Bank of New York," "Outline of a Charter for the Bank of New York," Hamilton to John B. Church, Mar. 10, 1784, Syrett, ed., *Hamilton Papers*, III, 514-22; Mitchell, *Alexander Hamilton*, I, ch. 21; Pomerantz, *New York An American City*, 185-86; Dangerfield, *Chancellor Robert R. Livingston*, 201-3; McDonald, *E Pluribus Unum*, 41-43.

62. Lynd, The Revolution and the Common Man, 205-15.

63. *Laws of the State of N.Y.*, 10th Sess., ch. 40; see ch. 10 for the continuation of the bank war in the 1790's.

Foreign trade, more than any other single factor, solidified the city behind Federalist leadership. The evidence is weighty that there was a serious imbalance in trade in the mid-1780's as British manufactured goods flooded the city at the same time that Great Britain closed the West Indies to American ships. The prices of the state's agricultural exports dropped sharply, there was a scarcity of cash, the city's shipyards were idle, there were bankruptcies right and left. Throughout 1785 the Chamber of Commerce complained of trade "daily on the Decline" and "languishing under fatal obstructions." In mid-1786, newspapers still spoke of "stagnation in trade." Recovery seems to have been underway by 1787. In 1788, some 75,000 tons of shipping entered the port (compared to 26,000 in 1770-72) of which 55,000 tons was owned by New Yorkers.[64]

By this time Federalists had reaped the political dividends. Tariff duties passed by the state government were an ineffective dike against imports. Moreover, discriminatory duties on British tonnage and goods imported in foreign vessels did not sit well with the "British Interest" in New York City—a phrase commonly used to describe the many Anglo-American firms, American firms trading on British capital, and agents of British merchants. This group would consistently have Federalist support in defeating the same sort of discrimination from 1789 on when Madison and Jefferson would propose it in the national government. Most important, the state, by failing to surrender the impost, deprived the federal government of the revenue by which it might build the national muscle necessary to break down foreign restrictions on American commerce.[65]

Within the Federalist "commercial interest" there were several types of merchants. One was the old-line wealth dominant since provincial days for whom Nicholas Low and Isaac Roosevelt, two merchants on the Federalist delegation to the Poughkeepsie convention, were appropriate representatives. Both had been active conservative patriots before the Revolution, Low serving as chairman of various

64. Minutes of the Chamber of Commerce of New York City, Mar. 3, 1785 (photostat), N.Y. Pub. Lib.; Lynd, The Revolution and the Common Man, 223-37, mobilizes a convincing case for the depression, contra McDonald, We the People, 296, n.139, whose statistics on shipping nonetheless seem valid. See also Spaulding, New York in the Critical Period, ch. 1, and Pomerantz, New York An American City, 147-56.

65. See William F. Zornow, "New York Tariff Policies, 1775-1789," N.Y. History, 37 (1956), 40-63, and Albert Geisecke, American Commercial Legislation before 1789 (Phila., 1910), chs. 2, 3, 4, 6, passim. The British interest is discussed below, ch. 16.

committees organized to counter the radical Whigs. A member of "the important mercantile firm" of Low & Wallace before and after the Revolution, Low was "one of the city's most highly assessed property owners," a director of the Bank of New York, a purchaser of some $8250 of confiscated estates, and a speculator in securities who in the first federal funding operation alone funded $38,729.[66] Roosevelt was a member of an old mercantile family, a leader of the Chamber of Commerce, a sugar refiner, a purchaser of confiscated estates in New York City worth $12,190, and from 1786 on, president of the Bank of New York.[67]

A second type of Federalist merchant was the newly risen speculative operator, of whom William Duer, William Constable, his brother-in-law William Edgar, and Alexander Macomb were outstanding representatives. None were delegates; but neither were they barred from political office. All have been identified as members of the "interstate coalition" of businessmen connected with Robert Morris. Duer had inherited a share of his father's West Indies plantations; when he came to New York in 1768 Schuyler had advised him on investments in land. Macomb, Edgar, and Constable were parvenu Irishmen; at one time or another each served as president of the Society of the Friendly Sons of St. Patrick. All had risen spectacularly during the war, especially as army contractors. Their postwar speculations in public securities, bank stock, and public land were on a breathtaking scale. These men backed the Federalist cause and were on intimate terms with Hamilton from whose plans they would later profit handsomely. Except for Duer, they also were on friendly terms with George Clinton, their fellow Irishman. If they stirred a ripple of resentment among old republicans against "nabobs" and "purse proud aristocrats," they also gave the Federalist party the flavor of the *nouveau riche* which prevented it from being the party of exclusive established wealth.[68]

66. See Richard B. Morris in *DAB* s.v. "Low, Nicholas"; McDonald, *We the People*, 302, Spaulding, *New York in the Critical Period*, 7, 225, 246.

67. Pomerantz, *New York An American City*, 160, 179-80, 186, 196; Spaulding, *New York in the Critical Period*, 7, 141, 246; McDonald, *We the People*, 302.

68. For their speculations in securities, see below, ch. 8; in bank stock, see ch. 10; a picture of the group emerges from East, *Business Enterprise*, ch. 10, 11, 12, and especially from Joseph S. Davis's essay, "William Duer," in his *Essays in the Earlier History of American Corporations*, 2 vols. (Cambridge, Mass., 1917), I, 111-338.

VII

Thus in New York one group of Whig leaders became nationalists not so much because they were, as one theory would have it, "the young men of the revolution" whose personal careers and ambitions were pinned to the success of the central government.[69] It was true of course that the major Federalists had all been schooled in nationalism by their experiences in high national councils during the war. But it is equally demonstrable that they spoke for interests which required nationalist solutions. They pursued careers in the national government because they simply could not gain positions of influence in a state government run by men who suspected them and threatened their interests.

Nationalism in New York was thus a product of frustrated conservatism. When Jay took stock in 1786 of "the insecurity of property" that was driving "the better kind of people" to abandon republican government, he enumerated all the democratic prejudices that New York's conservatives had to contend with for a decade: "a reluctance to taxes, an impatience of government, of rage for property and little regard to the means of acquiring it, together with a desire for equality in all things."[70] When Robert R. Livingston gave the Independence Day address to the New York Society of the Cincinnati in 1787 he presented a summa of the frustrations of his kind with the class that seemed to have taken over in New York. "Can it be believed," he asked the former officers of the New York line,

that an enlightened people think the science of government level to the meanest capacity—That education, experience, application, and genious [are] unnecessary in those who are to frame laws for the government of a State. Is it [not] well known that in some states the competence which afford leisure to attend to the affairs of government even in the hands of men who have risked their all for the establishment of freedom is urged by some as sufficient cause for their not sharing in the administration of their country? Are not abilities and education proscribed by those who want them and supply their place by that cunning which renders them suspected in others? Have you yourselves escaped the general obloquy, are you not calumniated by those you deem unworthy of your society. . . . You are not

69. Stanley Elkins and Eric McKitrick, "The Founding Fathers: Young Men of the Revolution," *Political Science Quarterly*, 76 (1961), 203-6.

70. Schuyler to Jay, May 30, 1785, Jay to Washington, June 27, 1786, Jay to Jefferson, Oct. 27, 1786, Johnston, ed., *Correspondence of John Jay*, III, 151-52, 204-5, 212-13.

formed to follow the lead of those you despise. Men used equally to command and obey are sensible to the value of government and will not easily consent to its debasement.[71]

Hamilton's famous five-hour ultra-conservative Jeremiad at the Philadelphia convention in the context of a decade of experience of New York's Federalist leaders takes on meaning as the thinking not of an exotic West Indian who did not understand his adopted country but of a class who knew their own state all too well. Hamilton, it will be recalled, moved from the premise that "all communities divide themselves . . . into the rich and the well born" and that "the mass of people seldom judge or determine right" to the conclusion that a general government in which the states might be "extinguished" should be ruled by a president and senate elected for life. Jay advocated much the same thing.[72] For the moment the New York conservatives had abandoned the tactic that served them so well from the 1770's on: Robert R. Livingston's tactic of "yielding to the torrent" with the aim of controlling it.

But only for a moment. The final product from the Philadelphia convention—balancing the "democratical" with the "aristocratical" and the powers of the national government and the states—was, after all, in keeping with the conservative, middle-of-the-road constitution Jay and Livingston had shaped for their own state ten years before. Jay and Hamilton quickly joined Madison in *The Federalist*, defending the Constitution on moderate grounds; Chancellor Livingston would join them at the Poughkeepsie convention to form a conciliatory Federalist triumvirate. Thus, to find a following among a democratic-minded electorate and to wean stubborn anti-Federalist politicians from their intransigence, the "pilots" returned to their traditional tactic of "swimming with the stream" to secure a prize they had sought so long.

71. "Draft of an Oration to the Society of the Cincinnati given July 4, 1787," R. R. Livingston Papers, N.-Y. Hist. Soc., published as *An Oration, Delivered Before the Society of the Cincinnati of the State of New York; in Commemoration of the Fourth of July* (N.Y., 1788).

72. Hamilton, "Speech on a Plan of Government," Syrett, ed., *Hamilton Papers*, IV, 178-207. The quotations are from Robert Yates's version of the speech, 200. For a similar proposal from Jay, see Jay to Washington, Jan. 7, 1787, Johnston, ed., *Correspondence of John Jay*, III, 226-29.

CHAPTER 4

The Electorate:

Yeomen, Tenants, and

Mechanics

In New York, who voted Federalist and who voted anti-Federalist? To whom did ordinary citizens—the yeoman and tenant farmers of the countryside and the mechanics, tradesmen, and laborers of New York City and the towns of the Hudson Valley—give their political allegiance? Who, indeed, voted, and under what conditions? In short, what was the stage on which the politics of the Confederation era and later years was played?

I

Measured either in absolute numbers or as a proportion of the adult male population, the electorate in New York State was fairly large, and at the same time clearly restricted by the compromises of the constitution of 1777. The electoral census of 1790 showed a total electorate of 38,824 voters, and not 57,468, as has been reported by several generations of historians who have misread the electoral charts. In 1788 there were probably 5000 fewer voters.[1] In 1790, 19,369 voters, little more than half the total, qualified as owners of freeholds worth £100 or more to vote for governor and senators as well as assemblymen, while 18,859 could vote only for the assembly, 4056 as

1. See Appendix, Tables 1, 2, 3.

freeholders of £20 and 14,674 as 40-shilling renters. In 1790 out of a total population of 340,120 there were approximately 67,000 adult white males over 21, and about 55,000 the census classified as "heads of families." Thus 58 per cent of the adult white males and 70.7 per cent of the heads of families could vote for assembly, but only 28.9 per cent of the adult males could vote for senators and governor.

In the countryside probably all yeoman farmers could vote, most of them very likely in the higher category. At the same time most of the tenants also qualified, a large proportion as £100 freeholders. Tenants with leases of 21 years or more qualified as freeholders, as they did before the Revolution, and landlords had the same stake as before in seeing their property evaluated high enough to qualify their tenants in the £100 category.[2] An even larger group of tenants qualified as 40-shilling renters. In the rural regions probably the most numerous group excluded by the suffrage requirements were the adult sons of yeomen and tenants, exceptionally poor tenants, and the small number of laborers and poor craftsmen. Such tax records as have survived suggest that all taxpayers were probably voters.[3]

In New York City the restrictions of the suffrage requirements were more obvious. Of the approximately 6600 men over 21, about 60 per cent, or 3975 qualified to vote. Less than a third of the total

2. Spaulding, *New York in the Critical Period*, 91-92; David Ellis, *Landlords and Farmers in the Hudson-Mohawk Region, 1790-1850* (Ithaca, 1946), 42-43; Williamson, *American Suffrage*, 28, for example; Williamson finds that on Philip Schuyler's estate at Saratoga, immediately after the Revolution, of 201 tenants, 141 were freeholders. Alexander, *James Duane*, 230, reports that in 1790 of 332 tenants, 48 were counted as £100 freeholders, 280 as £20 freeholders and 4 as 40 s. renters. William B. Fink, Stephen Van Rensselaer: The Last Patroon (unpubl. Ph.D. diss., Teachers College, Columbia Univ., 1950), 28-30, reports that Rensselaerswyck went from about 276 tenant families immediately after the Revolution to about 3000 by 1800 (and 50,000 by 1840). Almost all Stephen Van Rensselaer's leases entitled tenants to vote; for rising land values see, *e.g.*, Vanderkemp, Diary, 11, Vanderkemp Papers, N.-Y. Hist. Soc.

3. The evidence is sparse. Miss Juliet Wolohan, Associate Librarian, has located in N.Y. State Lib. partial assessment rolls for three counties, Orange 1786, Dutchess 1786, and Montgomery 1786 and 1788. In Orange in 3 townships there were 805 taxpayers in 1786, 1303 voters in 1790. In Dutchess in 11 townships there were 1456 taxpayers in 1786 and 3535 voters in 1790. Even allowing for a high rate of population growth in these counties, it is hardly likely that by 1790 the number of taxpayers equalled the number of voters. In frontier Montgomery County, on the other hand, the gap seems less. In four towns which had 1787 taxpayers in 1786 and 2200 in 1788, there were in 1790 2153 voters. The number of taxpayers was at least 2700 the same year, assuming the same rate of population growth. This evidence would seem to support Williamson, *American Suffrage*, 27-28, who found that "a study of eleven tax districts and townships" for "the period of the Revolution," unidentified as to time and place, "among adult male residents, and

electorate, 1209 voters, could vote only for assemblymen and congressmen. Thus, of all the adult white males in the city in 1790, about three out of five could vote, but only slightly more than one out of five could vote for all offices. In municipal elections in which the 40-shilling renters were excluded, the proportion of eligible voters was even less. All merchants and professionals could vote. Of the several strata of mechanics, most of the master craftsmen—property holders and employers—qualified to vote as £100 freeholders. Most, if not all, of the "industrious tradesmen"—petty retailers and crafsmen—qualified as 40-shilling renters. And most of the propertyless, unskilled or semiskilled wage workers—dockworkers, sailors, factory hands, hawkers, and servants—qualified not at all.[4]

The returns in the 1788 convention election when universal male suffrage was permitted for the first and only time in the Revolutionary era give some indication of the number of men who would have voted if given the opportunity. In heavily tenanted Albany there were 7300 convention voters compared to 4900 assembly voters, or 2400 more; in tenanted Columbia on the other hand the vote was 5300 and 4800, only 500 more. In New York City 2700 ballots were cast for convention delegates, about 1450 for assembly candidates, almost twice as many. In the counties of the yeomanry, the gap was smaller: in Orange three of the four delegates had about 300 votes, the assemblymen on the average 200; in Queens the delegate vote averaged 500, the assembly vote about 375. One election of course is not an adequate test, after years of nonvoting, but the gap is hardly without meaning.[5]

Yet the suffrage was sufficiently broad to satisfy the most democratic-minded anti-Federalists. "When we were colonies," Melancton Smith commented in a casual remark in the debate at Poughkeepsie, "our representation was better than any that was then known; since

in some cases among all male taxables, 50 to 80 per cent were freeholders in 1779," and therefore voters. Tenants, it should be pointed out, paid taxes, but not all tenants who paid taxes were qualified to vote. Tax rolls for several New York City wards for 1793 and 1796, N.-Y. Hist. Soc., would permit comparison with the 1795 electoral census.

4. Lynd and Young, "The Mechanics and New York Politics," *Labor History*, 5 (1964), 215-24.

5. For the returns see n.22 below. It is difficult to agree with Mrs. DePauw, *The Eleventh Pillar*, 142-43, that the difference between the two votes was "very small." In New York City Richard Harison, for example, received 2677 votes as a delegate and 1500 as a candidate for the assembly; in Columbia, Matthew Adgate received 1850 votes for the convention, 1486 for the assembly.

the revolution, we had advanced still nearer to perfection."[6] Universal male suffrage in the election of convention delegates in 1788, one suspects, was initiated by Federalists and agreed to by Clintonians reluctantly.[7] It is not surprising that in the closing days of the ratifying convention at Poughkeepsie many anti-Federalists supported a little-noted motion by John Jay to amend the federal Constitution to restrict voting for presidential electors and members of Congress to freeholders.[8]

Anti-Federalists were more concerned with the number of qualified voters who did not appear at the polls than with the number of men not qualified to vote. "Sometimes . . . not 1 in 10 of the people at large vote," Abraham Yates claimed; Greenleaf, the New York City anti-Federalist editor, put it at one in four and occasionally only one in ten.[9] The turnout in the 1780's should have been higher, if only because the electoral arrangements were superior to prewar practices. Elections were annual and at a fixed time, the poll beginning on the last Tuesday of April and continuing for five days at the discretion of local officials. There was a polling place in each town, which meant as many as fourteen in Ulster and twenty-one in Westchester, and one in each city ward, giving New York City seven and Albany three. Even so in frontier Washington and Clinton to the north or vast Montgomery and Ontario counties to the west it must have required a long journey for a pioneer settler to vote. The procedure for registering voters was lenient; a person testified as to the value of his property which qualified him to vote in one category or another and was allowed to vote, it seems, unless challenged.[10]

6. Elliot, ed., *Debates*, II.

7. DePauw, *The Eleventh Pillar*, 141-42, and Spaulding, *New York in the Critical Period*, 199-200, find no debate in the legislature or newspapers and no comment in private correspondence. It is noteworthy, however, that the sole objection to universal male suffrage in the senate came from John Williams, a leading anti-Federalist, and that the defense came from James Duane and John Laurance, both Federalists.

8. Mitchell, *Alexander Hamilton*, I, 462.

9. Abraham Yates, Speech to the Delegates in Continental Congress, 1786-87, Yates Papers, N.Y. Pub. Lib.; *N.-Y. Journal*, Jan. 22, 1789.

10. George D. Luetscher, *Early Political Machinery in the United States* (Phila., 1903), 26; Williamson, *American Suffrage*, 121-22; *Laws of the State of N.Y.*, Sess. 1, ch. 16 (Mar. 27, 1778), revised by Sess. 10, ch. 15 (Feb. 13, 1787). Sess. 11, ch. 63, "An Act for Dividing the Counties of This State into Towns" (Mar. 7, 1788) increased the number of towns and thereby the number of voting places in a few counties. But contrary to several scholars, voting prior to this act was not exclusively at one place in the county. The 1778 law provided that voting was to be "not by counties, but by Boroughs, Towns, Manors, Districts, and Precincts,

The explanations for absenteeism get beyond the legal requirements and the statistics of voter eligibility to the realities of the
political scene in New York. One factor doubtless was the absence of
adequate protection for the voter. The constitution of 1777 established a written ballot only in gubernatorial voting. The legislature
did not extend it to senate and assembly voting until 1787 which
meant that up until then the poorest voters, the £20 freeholders and
the 40-shilling renters voted viva voce, if they voted at all. Not until
the same year did New York adopt a Bill of Rights stating that "all
elections shall be free, and that no person by force of arms nor by
malice or menacing or otherwise pressure presume to disturb or
hinder any citizen of the state to make free election upon pain of fine
and imprisonment and treble damages to the party grieved." Even so
there were loopholes in the election code which made coercion possible.[11]
    A second factor reflected the state of party politics. Absenteeism
was highest, Yates pointed out, "when there is no great opposition,"
which meant a good deal of the time in many counties. Several counties were safely Clintonian, like Ulster or Orange; a number were
safely Federalist, like New York and those of the southern district.
In only a few counties during the 1780's—Dutchess, Columbia, and
Albany—were there hotly fought elections.[12] In the statewide elections
Federalists failed to run a candidate against Clinton in 1786. In 1783
when they put up opposition only in the north the total turnout was
no more than 5000. In 1789 when they fought Clinton tooth and nail
it climbed to 12,000.
    A third factor on which Abraham Yates concurred with Robert R.
Livingston was "the torpor and indifference"[13] of the people to which
a number of conditions contributed. Illiteracy was widespread; "unlettered persons," Hamilton claimed, made up "in some places . . . one
half or one third of the whole district."[14] There was not a public ele-

and by wards in the several cities." Thus for the 1787 election, Abraham Yates
to   ?, June 2, 1787, Yates Papers, N.Y. Pub. Lib., referred to returns from eight
polling places in Columbia County and 11 in Albany County.
    11. Laws of the State of N.Y., Sess. 10, ch. 1 (Jan. 26, 1787). For methods of
coercing tenants, see Sec. III, below.
    12. I base this on an analysis of the changes in the annually elected assembly
for the 8th-11th sessions of the legislature elected 1784-1787; see Werner, Civil
List, passim. See n.21.
    13. Yates in his speech cited in n.9 above noted Robert R. Livingston's use of this
phrase in An Oration Before the Cincinnati.
    14. Alexander Hamilton, New York Assembly: Remarks on an Act for Regulat-

mentary school in the state. Dutch was still spoken in Kingston, Albany, Brooklyn, and elsewhere; in Albany County travelers found Dutch farmers who had never been more than five miles from their homes.[15] In the Mohawk Valley Germans resident for several generations at German Flats, German Town, and Herkimer Town "have chiefly preserved the manners, language, and religion of their ancestors."[16] Voters literate in English could often absorb only the plainest writing; the Albany anti-Federalists had to warn their New York City brethren that a pamphlet they sent up was "in a style too florid and sublime for the common people." To keep political discourse alive outside New York City in 1788 there were only half a dozen papers, at Albany, Lansingburgh, Hudson, and Poughkeepsie, and their editors counted their circulation high when they reached 500 copies of each weekly edition.[17]

Communication was slow; it was a three-day sail on a river sloop from New York to Albany and no other river was navigable. Roads were poor, even in settled regions.[18] Many easterners were isolated; the southern part of Dutchess County was cut off by a range of high hills; men in the hill country of Columbia County on the Massachusetts border or in the Lake Champlain region to the north or along the Mohawk or Susquehanna were out of the swim of things politically. And there were no permanent political organizations to agitate the citizenry; committees were formed at elections, then dissolved until the following year. The Federal Republican Society of New York City and the Constitutional Society of Dutchess County formed in 1788 were the first of their kind since the Revolution.[19]

The over-all New York electorate, one may conclude, was fairly broad, but the proportion of men eligible to vote for all offices and of

---

ing Elections, Jan. 30, 1787, Syrett, ed., *Hamilton Papers*, IV, 31; about a third of the upper manor Livingston tenants made a mark for their signatures; see a petition, 1795, in Edmund B. O'Callaghan, comp., *The Documentary History of the State of New York*, 4 vols. (Albany, 1849-51), III, 499-502.

15. Among many sources, see "The Passing of the Dutch Language," *Olde Ulster*, 10 (1914), 113; Strickland, Journal of a Tour . . . 1794-95, Oct. 8, 19, 1794, and *passim*, N.-Y. Hist. Soc.

16. Francis Adrian Vanderkemp, Journal of a Trip . . . 1792, p. 19, N.-Y. Hist. Soc.

17. Albany Anti-Federal Committee to the New York Committee, Apr. 12, 1788, Lamb Papers, N.-Y. Hist. Soc.; Milton W. Hamilton, *The Country Printer, New York State, 1785-1830* (N.Y., 1936), 211-14 and ch. 3.

18. See below, ch. 11.

19. For the Federal-Republican Society, see Lamb Papers, N.-Y. Hist. Soc.; for the Dutchess group, *Poughkeepsie Country Journal*, Apr. 15, 1788.

qualified voters who actually cast ballots was rather small. Conditions moreover were not all favorable for the growth of democratic
practices in spite of the gains of the Revolutionary era.

II

On what basis did voters in the countryside divide? Philip Schuy-
er in his letter pleading with John Jay to run for governor sketched
the geographic pattern of party loyalty of the mid-1780's. If Schuyler
ran, he explained, he "should carry a majority of at least fifteen hundred votes in this [Albany] and Montgomery County [to the west] and
some in Washington [to the northeast]" but he was "so little known
in the southern part of the state that I should fail there." If Jay ran,
however, he would have Schuyler's northern votes, would run well in
New York City where he stood well "with all classes," would "generally carry" Westchester and Richmond, and might achieve a "ballance"
in the strongly Clintonian counties of the mid-Hudson Valley, Ulster,
Orange, and Dutchess.[20] In the legislature the pattern of division on
major issues was along similar lines. New York City and the surrounding counties, Kings, Queens, and Richmond, were the most reliably
Federalist; depending upon who was elected for the year they might
be joined by Albany, Westchester, and Montgomery. The most consistently Clintonian counties were Ulster, Orange, and Dutchess in the
mid-Hudson and Washington on the northern frontier, often joined
by Montgomery to the west. The major battleground of the contending factions was Albany (and Columbia formed from it in 1786);
lesser ones were Dutchess, Westchester, and Montgomery counties.[21]

In the election of delegates to the convention in 1788 this pattern
varied somewhat, in part because universal suffrage prevailed. Anti-
Federalists won 46 delegates and 9 counties to 19 delegates and 4
counties for the Federalists; the total vote, as well as it can be calculated, was about 14,000 to 10,500. Anti-Federalists took one group of
counties by a near-unanimous vote: Ulster (1372-68), Orange (340-0),
and Suffolk (no opposition). They took a second group by 2 to 1 or
3 to 2 margins: Dutchess (1765-892), Albany (4861-2627), and Colum-

20. Philip Schuyler to John Jay, May 30, 1785, Johnston, ed., *Correspondence
of John Jay*, III, 151-52.
21. Main, *The Antifederalists*, 50, 98-99, and The Upper House in the Revolutionary Era, ch. 5, MS; McDonald, *We the People*, 299; Spaulding, *New York in
the Critical Period*, 103, 180. There are slight variations in the analyses of these
authors.

bia (1863-1498) of the Hudson Valley and on the frontier Montgomery (1209-806) and Washington and Clinton (reported as 2 to 1 anti Federalist without returns). In the southern district by contrast they ran very poorly. They took Queens by a narrow margin (517-416), lost Westchester (399-694), received only a token vote, largely for George Clinton, in New York City (134-2735), and ran no candidates in Kings and Richmond (no returns). Thus about 3500 anti-Federalist votes came from the middle district, half from Ulster and Orange on the west bank of the Hudson, half from Dutchess on the east, 6500 from Albany and Columbia, about 1650 from the frontier west and north east, and from 1500 to 2000 from the southern district, the largest bloc from Suffolk. The Federalist vote came from two areas: the southern district (2700 from the city and about 1500 from the surrounding counties) and from the east bank of the Hudson (about 5000 from Dutchess, Columbia, and Albany) with perhaps 1000 more from the frontier.[22]

Recent explanations of this division all leave something to be desired. To categorize Federalist support as "downstate" and anti-Federalist support as "upstate," or as a division of "south" against "north" as some historians have done,[23] obscures the fact that two-thirds of the total Federalist vote came from their minorities in the *upstate* counties of Columbia, Albany, and Montgomery and that anti-Federalists took the *southern* counties of Suffolk and Queens. To say that the division was between "the commercial interest, including those landowners who were producing for export, opposed to the more isolated upstate farmers" is more fruitful.[24] Yet this hypothesis over-

22. For the vote see N.Y. *Daily Advertiser*, June 3-14, 1788, reprinted with a few errors in Spaulding, *N.Y. in the Critical Period*, 202-3; McDonald, *We the People*, 286. My totals run higher than most historians because I have supplied estimated votes for five counties for which the newspapers did not report returns but reported candidates. My estimate is based on returns in subsequent elections, with due allowance for what is known of the state of political activity in the county in 1788. Thus I have added, on the anti-Federalist side: Suffolk, 500 to 1000, Washington and Clinton together, 400; on the Federalist side: Kings and Richmond together, 500, Washington and Clinton together, 200. In giving the vote for each county I give the highest delegate vote; in most counties there was a variation of only 20 to 30 votes from the highest to the lowest candidate on the ticket.

23. McDonald, *We the People*, 310, refers to Clintonians as supported by "most of the smaller upstate farmers." Spaulding, *New York in the Critical Period*, 220, writes "geographically, the contest was to be of north against south." Benson, *Turner and Beard*, 196, suggests that "the more remote from New York City, the more strongly agrarian communities supported anti-Federalism."

24. Jackson Turner Main, *The Antifederalists*, 240; Cochran, *New York in the*

ooks the fact that farmers in the entire Hudson Valley engaged in commercial agriculture for the export market. River sloops transported the flour, beef, timber, potash, and flax of anti-Federalist farmers of Ulster no less than of Federalist landlords of Columbia.[25] The related hypothesis that Federalists were the "wealthy agrarians" does not take into account the fact that Suffolk, Dutchess, Ulster, and Orange counties, all of which went anti-Federalist, were among the wealthiest in the state,[26] and that Federalist voters included some of the poorest farmers: recent migrants to frontier Montgomery and tenants in Albany and Columbia counties.

An explanation which takes into account social-economic class and the politics of the Revolution along with the type of agriculture shows most promise of resolving these contradictions. Anti-Federalist voters, first of all, were primarily yeomen farmers. Upstate Orange and Ulster, the most consistently Clintonian, anti-Federalist, and then Democratic-Republican counties in the state, were the counties par excellence of the independent yeomanry. Anti-Federalist voting strength lay distinctly in other counties most free of great estates: Suffolk on Long Island, Washington and Clinton to the northeast. Within the counties of the landlords it lay in the areas not under leasehold, such as central Dutchess or southern Dutchess whose former tenants had acquired land in the Revolution or else in an area like eastern Columbia along the Massachusetts border where disputes with the landlords were endemic.

Secondly, anti-Federalist voters, not surprisingly, by and large had been Whigs in the Revolution. The correlation of the areas of rural anti-Federalism with Whiggery and of rural Federalism with Toryism is too striking to be ignored although not completely consistent. The number of signers and non-signers of the General Association authorized by the Continental Congress and promoted with zeal by Whigs

Confederation, 83; Orin G. Libby, *The Geographical Distribution of the Vote of the Thirteen States on the Federal Constitution, 1787-1788* (Madison, Wis., 1894), 18, speaks of "the entire mass of interior counties" as "solidly anti-federal."

25. See ch. 3, n.38.

26. Manning J. Dauer, *The Adams Federalists* (Baltimore, 1953), 24-25, 7, 18. For one example of many, William Strickland, the English visitor, observed that as a result of the war the farmers on Long Island were "now the richest farmers on the continent," many with "large fortunes"; he found central Dutchess with "a respectable yeomanry in good circumstances"; the county has "long been the favorite residence of this state." See Journal of a Tour, Sept. 25, Oct. 9, 1794, N.-Y. Hist. Soc.

in 1775 provides a good index of prewar Whiggery.[27]   In Orange
County in 1775 there were approximately 1550 signers and 250 non
signers; in 1788 the vote was 340 anti-Federalist, with no recorded
votes for the Federalists; in Ulster there were 1770 signers and 80
non-signers; in 1788 the vote was 1372 to 68 in favor of the anti-
Federalists. In Suffolk in 1775 there were 2060 signers and 200 non
signers; in 1788 the anti-Federalist slate was elected without opposition
In Queens, on the other hand, there were 17 signers and 209 non
signers; in 1788 the vote was 517 anti-Federalist, 416 Federalist. In
Dutchess there were 1680 signers and 882 non-signers; in 1788 the
vote was very similar: 1765 anti-Federalist, 892 Federalist.

The typical anti-Federalist voter, at his idyllic best, was the pros
perous yeoman of Orange County limned by Crèvecoeur in his well
known *Letters from an American Farmer.* "The cheerful glass, the
warmth of their county politics," he wrote, "the ruddy faces of their
daughters, the goodness of their houses would give you a more lively
idea of their happiness as men, of their native pride as freeholders
than anything I could tell you."[28]   Crèvecoeur exaggerated, but the
solid stone houses still standing at New Paltz and the bucolic festivi
ties Washington Irving described among Rip Van Winkle's fellow vil
lagers across the Hudson hint at the same rustic comfort. The typical
New York yeoman was a commercial farmer owning two and three times
the land he "can pretend to cultivate." He was a slaveholder—there
were 8500 of them in the state—and a literate man. He very likely
owned government securities, state or federal. Above all he was an
individualist and a jack-of-all-trades; Robert R. Livingston described
him as a man "habituated from early life to rely on himself. He can
mend his plough, erect his walls, thrash his corn, handle his axe, his
hoe, his sithes, his saw, break a colt or drive a team with equal
address."[29]

27. Force, *American Archives*, III, 582-619, which lists the signatories and non
signers of each county; also in N.Y. Secretary of State, *Calendar of Historical Manuscripts*, I, 5-99, *passim*; Becker, *Political Parties in N.Y.*, 215. There are variations
in the totals for each county.

28. Hector St. Jean de Crèvecoeur, *Sketches of Eighteenth Century America*
More Letters from an American Farmer, ed. Henri L. Bourdin *et al.* (New Haven
1925), 97.

29. Vanderkemp, Journal of a Trip . . . 1792, N.-Y. Hist. Soc., 9-10, based on
observations in Ulster County; Robert R. Livingston, "American Agriculture,"
written for the *Edinburgh Encyclopedia*, ca. 1813, cited in Percy W. Bidwell and
John I. Falconer, *History of Agriculture in the Northern United States, 1620-1860*
(Washington, 1925), 131.

A second type of anti-Federalist voter, less numerous than the first, was a notch below the prosperous yeomen. He might live on the less fertile land, for example, in southern Dutchess or eastern Columbia, or on newly opened frontier land in Washington and Clinton counties to the north. He owned less property and probably no slaves, and his distance from market may have made him a non-commercial farmer. More often a resident of the east bank of the Hudson, his attitude to the nearby landlords was akin to that of the poor southern yeomen to the wealthy plantation owner.[30]

It was to the yeomanry that anti-Federalists appealed first and last. "Consider you the common people, the yeomanry of the country, for to such I principally address myself," wrote Melancton Smith as "A Plebeian." "When a tyranny is established there are always masters and slaves; the great and well born are generally the former, and the middling class the latter." "What is your condition?" he asked, "Does not every man sit under his own fig-tree having none to make him afraid? . . . The farmer cultivates his land, and reaps the fruit which the bounty of heaven bestows on his honest toil."[31]

"The safety of the rights and liberties," Abraham Yates intoned, "depended upon the Middle sort of the people . . . the yeomanry of the country . . . the husbandmen and mechanics." "Give the people at large time to consider—as their object is right, they generally determine so; and when they go wrong, it is owing to the over-rich and over-poor who play into each others' hands. The common people like common sense generally hold the balance between the two extremes." "Cato," whether or not he was George Clinton, spoke to those who feared that "the greatest measure of your labor are to be swallowed up in taxes" at the expense of "great landholders" and "men of opulence."[32]

The appeal was avowedly to class and its effectiveness may be judged by Hamilton's enumerating among the "circumstances" against the "success" of the Constitution "the democratical jealousy of the people which may be alarmed at the appearance of institutions that may seem calculated to place the power of the community in few

30. For vivid descriptions of poor Hudson Valley farmers suggesting this type see Strickland, Journal, Oct. 1794, 235-36, 259-60, and passim, N.-Y. Hist. Soc.

31. A Plebeian [Melancton Smith], An Address to the People of the State of New York Showing the Necessity of Making Amendments to the Constitution . . . (N.Y., 1788), in Ford, ed., Essays on the Constitution, 94-96, 109-10.

32. Abraham Yates, Speech to the Delegates in Congress, 1786, Yates Papers, N.Y. Pub. Lib.; [George Clinton?], "Letters of Cato," No. 6, N.-Y. Journal, Dec. 16, 1787.

hands and to raise a few individuals to stations of great preeminence." The anti-Federalists owed their victory in New York, Robert Yates informed George Mason, to the "Spirit and Independency of the Yeomanry."[33]

III

Federalist support in the countryside can be inferred from this analysis of their opposite numbers. Federalist voters were either yeomen farmers oriented by their commercial status, Tories, or tenants. In the southern district they were the first two. In the Hudson Valley they were the second two.

Federalist leaders made distinct appeals based on the economic grievances of agriculturalists. John Jay in his popular pamphlet of the election campaign talked bread-and-butter issues, not the political theory of the *Federalist* essay.[34] In lamenting the loss of foreign markets, he asked whether there was "an English, or a French or a Spanish island or port in the West Indies to which an American vessel can carry a *cargo of flour*"—a principal export of the state's farmers— and answered, "Not one." This loss in foreign trade was especially damaging, he pointed out, to "*our little towns and cities.*" "American stars seldom do more, than shed a few feeble rays about *the humble masts of river sloops and coasting schooners*," he grieved. The farmer was suffering because of the fall in the price of cattle, wheat, corn, and lumber, and he pointed out that "even our houses and lands cannot command money—that law suits and usurous contracts abound— that our farms sell on execution for less than half their value." Locally Federalist compaigners made similar gritty appeals.[35] Farmers in the southern district who voted Federalist undoubtedly had the most commercially developed agriculture, most attuned to the export market. That other commercial farmers of the mid-Hudson Valley remained anti-Federalist may be attributed to a triumph of class feeling over economic grievances.

That the Federalist rural following came from areas that were strongly Tory during the Revolution has already been established.

33. Hamilton, "Conjectures about the New Constitution," probably Sept. 17-30, 1787, Syrett, ed., *Hamilton Papers*, IV, 275-76; Robert Yates to George Mason, June 21, 1788, copy, Lamb Papers, N.-Y. Hist. Soc.

34. John Jay, *An Address to the People of the State of New York on the Constitution* (N.Y., 1788), in Paul Leicester Ford, ed., *Pamphlets on the Constitution of the United States . . . 1787-1788* (Brooklyn, N.Y., 1888), 73-74 (italics added).

35. John Smith to David Gelston, n.d., 1788, John Smith Papers, N.-Y. Hist. Soc.

All strongly Tory counties were also strongly Federalist, except for Queens.[36] The counties surrounding New York City not only voted Loyalist in 1775 but contributed recruits to the British during the war, sold produce to the British army, suffered for their Loyalism at the hands of the Clintonians after the war, and owed their restoration to grace to the Federalists. Past Toryism operated although to a lesser extent among the tenantry of the upper Hudson Valley and the former followers of the Sir William Johnson family in the Mohawk Valley.

That Federalism in the upper Hudson Valley rested primarily on tenants and other farmers subject to the power of the great landlords is established by evidence of various sorts.

First, the broader electorate made up of the 40-shilling renters and £20 freeholders was not protected by a written ballot until 1787. They had scant experience in voting at all. Second, it was common practice for landlords and their agents to electioneer among their dependents. Philip Schuyler armed himself with a copy of the poll list for Albany County obtained at an expense of £10 from the secretary of state; occasionally he visited the voters; more often he seems to have relied on his son, who was a resident at the family's Saratoga estate. Robert Livingston of the upper manor depended on his sons, who, he reported on one occasion, were "out attending the election. They had good success yesterday at Millers, today at Takkanick, tomorrow at Ancram," naming hamlets within the upper manor. James Duane, the mayor of New York City, depended on his son-in-law, Benjamin North, or his overseers to handle the tenants at Duanesburg. Young Stephen Van Rensselaer usually attended the polls himself, but with so vast an estate he made use of Thomas Witbeck, his steward, the same man responsible for dealing with tenants on business matters.[37] It was the same with the lower manor Livingstons: the Chan-

36. Queens which went anti-Federalist by the narrow margin of 517-416 was increasingly Federalist as the convention progressed. Three of its four anti-Federalist delegates were Tories; all four voted to ratify at the end. Samuel Jones who was one of the architects of the anti-Federalist surrender at Poughkeepsie later became a Federalist. The county's political behavior can be attributed in part to his influence. Thus it was not such an exception to the pattern of the counties surrounding New York City.

37. For Schuyler see Robert D. Harpur to Hamilton, Aug. 2, 1786, and Hamilton, "Cash Book," Aug. 3, 1786, in Syrett, ed., *Hamilton Papers*, III, 20, 679-80; Robert Livingston to James Duane, Apr. 30, 1788, John Meyers to James Duane, Apr. 5, June 23, 1788, Duane Papers, N.-Y. Hist. Soc.; William North to Stephen Van Rensselaer and James Fairlie, Apr. 24, 1790, William North Manuscripts, N.Y. State Lib.; for Van Rensselaer, Fink, Stephen Van Rensselaer, 36, 46, 48-49, 51-52; and for Witbeck see succeeding chapters on elections.

cellor left political arrangements to Dr. William Wilson, his agent; his mother, Margaret Beekman Livingston, left these affairs to hers. Thomas Tillotson, her son-in-law, reminded the Chancellor to have "mama" write her agent, William Cockburn, "to go around in her name to the tenants a few days previous to the elections and request them to come out to vote."[38]

Third, neither the written ballot, nor the belated Bill of Rights prevented landlords from influencing their tenants; it only forced them into new ways. Before the Revolution, they seem to have resorted more to bribery, afterwards to bullying. Deference to the landlords of course had not disappeared; "Will anyone say," Melancton Smith asked in 1788, "that there does not exist in this country the pride of family, of wealth, of talents, and that they do not command respect among the common people?"[39] But after the war there is less evidence of hand shaking and treating and more evidence of threats to collect overdue rents or to enforce fines for the alienation of property.[40]

On election days landlords used a variety of techniques to detect their tenants' choice. Van Rensselaer tenants were instructed at one election "to fold up their ballots in a particular manner"; at another the favored ticket was printed on a silk-like paper, enabling a cooperative election inspector to detect each voter's choice by the feel of the ballot in his hand. "Monitor," writing in the anti-Federalist *Albany Register*, mockingly counseled a "manor lord" on a less subtle technique. Make yourself election inspector, he wrote. Have a tenant who is rent free stand at your side to give the ballots to the voters, have the voters hand their ballots to you, pretend to open the ballot, make a hub bub if a voter insists on handing in his own ballot, and take down his name to intimidate others.[41]

38. Thomas Tillotson to Robert R. Livingston, Mar. 23, 1787, R. R. Livingston Papers, N.-Y. Hist. Soc.; Livingston-Wilson correspondence, 1790's, *passim*, William Wilson Papers, William L. Clements Library, Ann Arbor, Mich.

39. Elliot, ed., *Debates*, II, 245-46.

40. Ellis, *Landlords and Farmers*, 37-39; Philip Schuyler was reported to have said, ca. 1776, that the landlords made their money by charging as much as one-fourth of the value of a farm on every transfer; see Alexander, *James Duane*, 66. William Strickland, Journal of a Tour, Oct. 11, 1794, N.-Y. Hist. Soc., recorded that Robert R. Livingston retained the "right of pre-emption at the market price or a fine of about one-tenth of the value on alienation."

41. Jeremiah Van Rensselaer to Benjamin Egbertson, Apr. 20, 1788, Stephen Van Rensselaer Manuscripts, N.Y. State Lib.; Schuyler to Hamilton, Apr. 20, 1789, Syrett, ed., *Hamilton Papers*, V, 339; Elihu Goodrich to Samuel B. Webb, Apr.

It is difficult to measure the effectiveness of tactics such as these in the absence of voting returns by townships for the 1780's. Beginning in 1785, the landlords in Albany County and what became Columbia County began to regain some of the influence over their tenants they had lost in the Revolution, ousting from the assembly the "levelling" Yankees who drove Hamilton to sound a tocsin of alarm. But the task required constant pressure each election. In the crucial battle of 1788 the anti-Federalists took Albany County, 4670-2620, and Columbia, 1850-1490, but the victory was "much greater than we had reason to suspect," Abraham Lansing reported. Judging by fragmentary reports, Federalists in Columbia, where "compulsive measures has been used to lead the tenants," carried the upper and lower manor of the Livingstons.[42] Anti-Federalists took the eastern towns along the Massachusetts border where "the ill fated controversies about their lands" of prewar origin made the election "a contest of Aris et Focis"—for hearth and home. In Albany County we know that James Duane's tenants resisted his agent's pressures and the same must have been true of many on the Schuyler and Van Rensselaer estates. With universal male suffrage prevailing, a written ballot in use, and after an intense campaign which appealed to their class feelings, tenants and poor farmers overcame their fears and poured out to the polls. But the combination of circumstances was unusual and anti-Federalists had no confidence in repeating the feat. If the Poughkeepsie convention were to adjourn and if there were a second election, Abraham Yates was told, "the Baneful Manor interest will be exerted to obtain instructions to the delegates and the poor deluded, yeomanry of our County not having it in their power to follow the dictates of their own conscience will be compelled to sign these instructions to keep well with their masters."[43]

Finally, if more proof be needed that the tenant vote generally responded to Federalist pressures, Clintonians made a persistent effort to curtail it. Anti-Federalists usually referred to tenants as "the

25, 1789, in Ford, ed., *Correspondence of S. B. Webb*, III, 98; "Monitor," *Albany Register*, Apr. 3, 1790.

42. For the over-all vote, see N.Y. *Daily Advertiser*, June 5, 1788; there are no returns by townships; Abraham Yates to ?, June 2, 1787, Abraham Lansing to Yates, May 27, 1788, Yates Papers, N.Y. Pub. Lib., and C. Wynkoop to Peter Van Gaasbeck, May 5, 1788, Van Gaasbeck Papers, F.D.R. Lib.

43. Peter Van Schaack to Philip Schuyler, Apr. 3, 1788, Schuyler Papers, N.Y. Pub. Lib.; Abraham Lansing to Abraham Yates, July 20, 1788, Yates Papers, N.Y. Pub. Lib.; Robert Livingston, Jr., to James Duane, Apr. 30, 1788, Duane Papers, N.-Y. Hist. Soc.; Alexander, *James Duane*, 191-92.

mechanical creatures of the Aristocracy." As early as 1781 they tried to ban leases of more than twenty-one years' duration by a bill "artfully inserted to prevent the landlords influence over tenants," placing themselves at odds with tenants whose interest lay in more secure leases. Anti-Federalists also instructed their election workers to challenge the qualifications of tenants to vote, especially in the £100-freehold category.[44] Neither popular Whigs nor anti-Federalists were comfortable with tenant suffrage in New York.

IV

Nationality had relatively little to do with determining allegiances.[45] Federalists made appeals on the basis of nationality to wean away traditional rural and smalltown support from Clinton. They reprinted the Constitution in Dutch as well as German, but with indifferent results. Three areas of the state where Dutch was spoken all behaved differently at the polls: Ulster (Clinton's home county) was almost solidly anti-Federalist; Brooklyn (a Tory county) was as decidedly Federalist; and Albany (a center of leaders of both factions) was divided. At the Poughkeepsie convention an irritated Federalist dismissed the anti-Federalist delegates as a "set of ignorant Dutchmen" under the "perfect command" of Clinton, Yates, Smith, and Lansing, forgetting that the Federalist chieftains at Albany were Schuyler, Van Rensselaer, Gansevoort, Van Vechten, and Ten Broeck, presumably wise Dutchmen.[46] To appeal to Germans, Federalists also secured an

44. Henry Livingston to Gilbert Livingston, Jan. 1, 1782, Gilbert Livingston Papers, N.Y. Pub. Lib., cited in Lynd, *Anti-Federalism in Dutchess County*, 26; A. G. Lansing to Hendrick Gardiner, Apr. 19, 1786, Yates Papers, N.Y. Pub. Lib.

45. The national origins of New Yorkers calculated on the basis of the nomenclature of heads of families in the 1790 census was as follows: English 52 per cent (163,000); Scottish 7 per cent (22,000); Irish-Ulster 5.1 per cent (16,000); Irish-Free State 3 per cent (9,000); German 8.2 per cent (26,000); Dutch 17.5 per cent (55,000); French 3.8 per cent (12,000); Swedish 0.5 per cent (1,500); unassigned 2.9 per cent (9,000); see American Council of Learned Societies, "Report of Committee on Linguistic and National Stocks in the Population of the United States," American Historical Association, *Annual Report for 1931*, 3 vols. (Washington, 1932), I, 123-35. For nationality characteristics of particular countries and towns I rely on a variety of travel accounts, memoirs, political correspondence, and local histories. For surveys of the colonial period when the population was much smaller see William Smith, *The History of the Late Province of New York from its Discovery to 1762*, N.-Y. Hist. Soc., *Collections*, 2 vols. (N.Y., 1829-30), I, 283-318, *passim*, and Nicholas Varga, New York Government and Politics, *passim*.

46. For Dutch and German reprints of the Constitution see Douglas McMurtrie, *A Check List of Eighteenth Century Albany Imprints* (Albany, 1939), entries 33-35; Samuel B. Webb to Joseph Barrell, July 1, 1788, in Ford, ed., *Correspondence of S. B. Webb*, III, 108-9.

endorsement for their ticket at New York City "at a numerous meeting of Germans" and distributed an address from the German Society upstate. Germans in New York City (a Federalist town anyway) doubtless voted Federalist; but Germans in Columbia County whose ancestors years before had been victimized by the Livingstons seem to have voted anti-Federalist.[47] To counteract George Clinton's natural appeal among his fellow Scotch-Irishmen, Federalists circulated a broadside signed by fifty-five "SCOTSMEN" of New York City, a move apparently initiated by the St. Andrews Society. Its influence outside the city is doubtful; one wag, catching the names of two Van Cortlandts on the list, scrawled across his copy, "a fine set of Scotsmen these."[48]

There was no clear-cut line-up of any of the major national groups of the state. New York, a polyglot city, was almost solidly Federalist; Orange, whose mixture of nationalities prompted Crèvecoeur to make his exaggerated claim for the "new American"—a man whose "grandfather was an Englishman, whose wife was Dutch, whose son was married to a French woman, and whose present four sons have now four wives of different nations," was equally anti-Federalist.[49] There was a similar division among New England migrants. The Yankees in the southern part of Dutchess and the eastern part of Columbia County (both with anti-landlord traditions) seem to have been anti-Federalist. Commercial Hudson, founded by Yankees, was Federalist.[50] Politicians in New York clearly were aware of the political significance of nationality; but the most that can be said is that national loyalties enforced decisions arrived at on the basis of other factors.[51]

47. For the nomination, see N.Y. *Daily Advertiser*, Apr. 28, 1788; for the society, Leonard Gansevoort to Stephen Van Rensselaer, Apr. 6, 1788, cited in DePauw, *The Eleventh Pillar*, 132; for Columbia, see Thomas Hunt, *A Historical Sketch of The Town of Clermont* (Hudson, 1928), who claimed that in the twentieth century, descendants of the Palatine settlers "still revel in the misfortunes of their ancestors."

48. "Friends and Countrymen," broadside, New York City, Apr. 12, 1788, reprinted at Albany, Apr. 21, 1788, endorsed by 15 subscribers, N.-Y. Hist. Soc.

49. Hector St. Jean de Crèvecoeur, *Letters from an American Farmer* (London, 1782, N.Y., 1912), Letter No. 3, 43; Pomerantz, *New York An American City*, 199-209.

50. For southern Dutchess, see Lynd, *Anti-Federalism in Dutchess County*, 44-46, and "Who Should Rule at Home?" *Wm. and Mary Qtly.*, 3rd Ser., 18 (1961), 334-35; for eastern Columbia see the references above.

51. I have thus tested in a schematic way Lee Benson's suggestion in *Turner and Beard*, 154-59. The statistical evidence is not available for the systematic testing of ethnic group voting patterns Benson did in *The Concept of Jacksonian Democracy: New York as a Test Case* (Princeton, N.J., 1961).

V

The mechanics were the last to be harnessed to the Federalist char-iot—and the first to kick over their traces in the 1790's. In the hot flush of Toryphobia after the war the Whig mechanics of New York City were a militant, democratic, class-conscious group. They elected the radical Whig ticket in late 1783, organized the Committee of Mechanics which pressed for Tory exclusion, formed the General Society of Mechanics and Tradesmen and were furious at being denied a charter, nominated and elected several of their own class to the assembly, and espoused such democratic proposals as the popular election of the mayor. In 1785-86, however, a mechanic-merchant alliance was in the making in New York as in other American cities. In '86 a mechanics committee met with a merchants committee to endorse a Federalist as-sembly slate, "some of the mechanics," as Schuyler noted, helping to elect Hamilton. In the spring of 1788, with universal suffrage prevail-ing for the election of delegates to the Poughkeepsie convention, some 2700 New Yorkers voted Federalist; in the summer from 5000 to 6000 marched in the massive parade celebrating ratification, every craft under its own banners. Obviously all but a handful of mechanics had deserted the Clintonians.[52]

If the vote of the yeomanry for the anti-Federalists was a triumph of class feeling over economic interest, the shifting political allegiances of the mechanics represented the reverse. In a commercial center such as New York the interests of most craftsmen inevitably rose or fell with the foreign trade which determined the prosperity of the city as a whole. This certainly was true of craftsmen who built, fitted out, or sailed ships (shipwrights, sailmakers, ropewalk workers, and sail-ors); of the men who prepared, moved, and inspected the merchants' produce (coopers, cartmen, dock workers, weighers, and gaugers), and of the craftsmen-shopkeepers who sold goods in the naturally protected local consumer's market (the butcher, the baker, and the candlestick maker). Mechanics who made goods which competed with British imports (leather workers, hatters, shoemakers, and ironmongers) came over to Federalism in quest of a federal tariff shield to protect them from the British goods that flooded the New York market.[53]

52. Lynd, "The Mechanics and New York Politics," *Labor History*, 5 (1964), 232-41.
53. For analyses of types of mechanics, see McDonald, *We the People*, 374-76, and Richard B. Morris, *Government and Labor in Early America* (N.Y., 1946), especial-ly ch. 3.

Federalists appealed to the economic interests of mechanics, Jay pointing out, for example, that there was so little shipbuilding that "our shipyards have almost ceased to disturb the repose of the neighborhood by the noise of the axe and hammer," and some shipwrights had even departed for alien shores.[54] But mechanics did not require politicians to point out the obvious. The slogans the craft groups carried in the 1788 parade testify to their blend of nationalism and protectionism.[55] The skinners, breeches makers, and glovers carried a "flag of cream colored silk" with their coat of arms and the motto, "Americans, encourage your own manufacturing"; the carpenters carried a portrait of "his excellency George Washington with the motto, 'Freedom's favorite son'" and a frieze with a motto "The love of our country prevails"; the blacksmiths, sailors, and ship joiners held aloft the poem:

> Our merchants may venture to ship without fear
> For pilots of skill shall the Hamilton steer
> This federal ship will our commerce revive
> And merchants and ship wrights and joiners shall thrive

Urban workingmen had been consistently nationalist from 1776 on.

Mechanic postwar radicalism faded as the returned refugees scurried to climb the economic ladder. Many mechanics made good in an era in which mobility was high.[56] Conservatives, moreover, wooed the mechanics, just as they had before the Revolution. While it is true that some newspaper writers derided the "vulgar" notion that mechanics could be Solons, others stressed the mutuality of interests between manufacturing and commerce. In The Federalist, essay No. 35, Hamilton was able to claim that "mechanics and manufacturers will always be inclined with few exceptions, to give their votes to merchants, in preference to persons of their own professions and trades," and indeed in 1788 the mechanics backed a slate of merchants, lawyers, and landlords for the convention. From 1789 on, however, to make sure of the mechanic vote, Federalists always

---

54. Jay, *An Address on the Constitution*, 73-74.
55. "Federal Procession," *N.Y. Packet*, Aug. 5, 1788, reprinted in part in Alfred Young, ed., *The Debate on the Constitution, 1789-1791* (Chicago, 1966), 6-8.
56. For awareness of the economic factor see *Mentor's Reply to Phocion's Letter* (N.Y., 1784), 11; for statistical evidence of mobility among the merchants of the city see Jackson T. Main, *The Social Structure of Revolutionary America* (Princeton, N.J., 1965), 187-91.

found a place on their annual assembly ticket for one or more recognized mechanic leaders.[57]

The alliance between merchant and mechanic, however, as it has been remarked of Charleston, was "not completely natural."[58] It hardly bridged the growing social gulf in the city. Once upon a time, Noah Webster observed, there was a tradition in New York, whereby "the principal families by associating in their public amusement with the middling class of well bred citizens, render their rank subservient to the happiness of society, and prevent that party spirit, which an affectation of superiority in certain families" had produced in Philadelphia. But "several causes have operated to diminish the sociability of the citizens of New York," said Webster, enumerating "the change of inhabitants and loss of property during the ravages of war, and the unfavorable state of business since the establishment of peace."[59]

For several years the return of prosperity papered over this latent antagonism; so too did the temporary mutual interest of manufacturer and import merchant in tariffs which would provide both a national revenue and a mild protection. Once the federal shield wore thin, once the import merchants placed their trade connections with Britain above the national interest, the honeymoon of merchant and mechanic would be over.

In the smaller port towns along the Hudson River the conversion of the "commercial interest" to Federalism was less complete than in New York by 1788. Hudson was solidly Federalist, a new town settled by New Englanders whose ships entered the whaling trade. So was Troy, also settled by Yankees. Albany and Poughkeepsie were divided, as were their counties as a whole. Kingston, set in the midst of a thoroughly anti-Federalist county that was also the home of the Governor's "family" connections, was anti-Federalist in 1788 but began to desert the year after until it became the headquarters of a Federalist junto. Thus the political complexion of the surrounding counties and the strength of Governor Clinton's connections seem to have stemmed the normally Federalist inclinations of the river towns.[60]

57. Jacob Cooke, ed., *The Federalist* (Middletown, Conn., 1961), 219; Young, "The Mechanics and the Jeffersonians," *Labor History*, 5 (1964), 249-50.

58. Richard Walsh, *Charleston's Sons of Liberty: A Study of the Artisans, 1763-1789* (Columbia, S.C., 1959), 123, 135.

59. Noah Webster, "General Description of the City of New York," *American Magazine*, 1 (N.Y., 1787-88), Mar. 1788, 226.

60. For voting patterns of the Hudson Valley towns, see, for Poughkeepsie,

VI

The fact that tenants and mechanics voted Federalist did not make of it a tenant or mechanic party, any more than the fact that George Clinton was a wealthy landholder and Melancton Smith a comfortable merchant made the anti-Federalists the party of the estate holders and merchants. Leaders of both interests knew as much. In the privacy of their political correspondence where they could ill afford to delude each other, anti-Federalists spoke of themselves as representing "the common man," "the common people," or "the yeomanry." Their opponents were "the better sort," Melancton Smith wrote Abraham Yates; "I confess I fear their power." Or they were "the better kind of people," or "the well born."[61] Privately Federalists were as candid. "The Balance of Abilities and Property," Jay reported to Washington, was against the Clintonians. The anti's, another Federalist consoled himself, while more numerous at the Poughkeepsie convention, "cannot boast of a Single great Character" on their side.[62] Hamilton never published the memorandum which set down "the good will of most men of property" and "of the commercial interest" and the "hopes of the creditors" on the Federalist side. In the gubernatorial election of 1789, however, when the alignment was similar, he boasted publicly that the Federalist candidate had the support of "the principal part of the men of the most considerable property."[63]

The debate over the Constitution at the Poughkeepsie convention also suggests the underlying differences in the character of the two interests. Those who have read the proceedings of that dramatic conflict with a knowledge of the background of the dramatis personae can hardly disagree with George Dangerfield that "one feels beneath the constitutional arguments . . . the presence of some older quarrel

Abraham Bancker to Evert Bancker, Jan. 19, 1788, Abraham Bancker Papers, N.-Y. Hist. Soc.; for Hudson and Albany, Abraham Yates to ?, June 2, 1787, Yates Papers, N.Y. Pub. Lib., and C. Wynkoop to Peter Van Gaasbeck, May 5, 1788, Van Gaasbeck Papers, F.D.R. Lib. For the detailed returns by towns for 1789, confirming the Federalist character of the port towns, see ch. 6.

61. Melancton Smith to Abraham Yates, Jan. 28, 1788, Yates Papers, N.Y. Pub. Lib.; Henry Oothoudt to John McKesson, Apr. 3, 1788, McKesson Papers, N.-Y. Hist. Soc.; James Hughes to John Lamb, June 16, 1788, Lamb Papers, N.Y. Hist. Soc.

62. Jay to Washington, Feb. 3, 1787, Johnston, ed., *Correspondence of John Jay*, III, 322; Samuel B. Webb to Joseph Barrell, Apr. 27, 1788, Ford, ed., *Correspondence of S. B. Webb*, III, 99.

63. Hamilton "To The Electors of the State of New York," Syrett, ed., *Hamilton Papers*, V, 317-29.

between the representatives of New York aristocracy and the representatives of those who had suffered under its rule, and who did not wish
this rule to be perpetuated under the new national constitution."[64]

The "quarrel" was epitomized in the debate over Article I, Section
2 of the Constitution that pitted the ideologues of the two parties
against each other: Melancton Smith versus Alexander Hamilton. Was
one congressman adequate representation for 30,000 people? Smith
began with the premise that there was a "natural aristocracy": "Every
society naturally divides itself into classes. The Author of nature has
bestowed on some greater capacities than others; birth, education,
talents, and wealth, create distinctions among men as visible, and of
as much influence, as titles, stars, and garters. In every society, men
of this class will command a superior degree of respect; and if the
government is so constituted as to admit but few to exercise the powers
of it, it will, according to the natural course of things, be in their
hands."

If election districts were large, as would be inevitable with the
ratio of one congressman for 30,000 people, said Smith, "frame your
election laws as you please . . . it is almost certain none but the great
will be chosen, for they easily unite their interests; the common people
will divide, and their division will be promoted by others." As a
result, "a substantial yeoman of sense and discernment will hardly
ever be chosen," and the government will "fall into the hands of the
few and great." His reasoning was frankly environmentalist:

> The circumstances in which men are placed in a great measure
> give a cast to the human character. Those in middling circum-
> stances have less temptation; they are inclined by habit, and the
> company with whom they associate, to set bounds to their pas-
> sions and appetites, If this is not sufficient, the want of means
> to gratify them will be a restraint: they are obliged to employ
> their time in their respective callings; hence the substantial yeo-
> manry of the country are more temperate, of better morals, and
> less ambition, than the great. The latter do not feel for the
> poor and middling class; the reasons are obvious—they are not
> obliged to use the same pains and labor to procure property as
> the other. They feel not the inconveniences arising from the
> payment of small sums. The great consider themselves above
> the common people, entitled to more respect, do not associate
> with them; they fancy themselves to have a right of preemi-
> nence in every thing. In short, they possess the same feelings,
> and are under the influence of the same motives, as an heredi-
> tary nobility.

64. Dangerfield, *Chancellor Robert R. Livingston*, 226.

He would "by no means" exclude the "great" from a share of the legislature. That would be impolitic because "They would be factious, discontented, and constantly disturbing the government. It would also be unjust. A representative body, composed principally of respectable yeomanry, is the best possible security to liberty. When the interest of this part of the community is pursued, the public good is pursued, because the body of every nation consists of this class, and because the interest of both the rich and the poor are involved in that of the middling class." Hence it was crucial that the ratio of representatives be increased to one for every 20,000 persons, a solution, of course, hardly in proportion to the dimension of the problem it was supposed to meet.[65]

Hamilton, in replying for the Federalists, could not restrain himself from mocking Smith's definition of aristocracy: "For my part, I hardly know the meaning of this word, as it is applied. If all we hear be true, this government is really a very bad one. But who are the aristocracy among us? Where do we find men elevated to a perpetual rank above their fellow-citizens, and possessing powers entirely independent of them? The arguments of the gentlemen only go to prove that there are men who are rich, men who are poor, some who are wise, and others who are not; that, indeed, every distinguished man is an aristocrat." "While property continues to be pretty equally divided," he contended, "and a considerable share of information pervades the community, the tendency of the people's suffrages will be to elevate merit even from obscurity."[66]

Smith was tart in his brief rebuttal:[67] "The gentleman, had ridiculed his idea of an aristocracy, and had entered into a definition of the word. (He himself agreed to this definition, but the dispute was not of words, but things.) He was convinced that in every society there were certain men exalted above the rest. These men he did not consider as destitute of morality or virtue. He only insisted that they could not feel sympathetically the wants of the people."

The "dispute" between the "aristocracy" and "the middling classes" was indeed "not of words but [of] things." And in the month that followed this scorching exchange, the conservative Whig nationalists won the contest for ratification, ending the era of unchallenged Clintonian supremacy, and presented Governor Clinton with the predicament that in the spring of 1789 brought him to Rufus King.

65. Elliot, ed., *Debates*, II, 245-51, *passim*.
66. *Ibid.*, 251-59, *passim*.
67. *Ibid.*, 260.

PART II

The Anti-Federalists at Bay
1788-1790

CHAPTER 5

Anti-Federalists Defeated:

Ratification and Its Aftermath

1788

————•—————

In June 1788, as the convention to consider the federal Constitution assembled at Poughkeepsie, the anti-Federalists were at the high water mark of their political career, outnumbering the Federalists 46 to 19. At the end of July, when the convention adjourned after ratifying the Constitution by a vote of 30 to 27, it was apparent that a Federalist era was beginning. In the months that followed the anti-Federalists felt the backlash of opinion that was running strongly against them, and they searched desperately for tactics to force the changes they sought in the Constitution. But they were split asunder between the "adopting" and "non-adopting" factions and ended in the stalemate over the choice of United States senators that eventually brought Governor Clinton to Rufus King.

I

The Poughkeepsie convention compels attention for what it reveals about the tactics and components of the Federalist and anti-Federalist parties and the climate of opinion in New York. The convention caught up all the political forces in New York and bequeathed the heritage of politics for the years ahead.[1]

1. For good summaries, see Spaulding, *New York in the Critical Period*, ch. 14,

A bare recital of the events during the six weeks' convention suggests some of the factors responsible for the outcome. When the delegates assembled on June 17, eight states had ratified the new Constitution and the conventions of New Hampshire and Virginia were also sitting. After Governor Clinton was elected permanent chairman, the convention defeated a motion to adjourn and adopted another to take up the Constitution article by article. At the end of the first week of debate, news arrived that New Hampshire had ratified; a week later, on July 2, there was similar news from Virginia. By July 8 the New York convention had completed debate on the Constitution itself. Thereafter debate revolved around the question of amendments—in essence, whether ratification was to be conditional or not. On July 15 the convention defeated Melancton Smith's motion to ratify "on condition" that a second convention consider the desired amendments in a given number of years. The Federalist victory came July 23 when Samuel Jones' motion to ratify "in full confidence" of revision passed 31 to 29. In the final voting on July 26, the convention ratified "in full confidence" of amendments, 30 to 27. On the deciding votes nineteen Federalists were joined by from eight to a dozen anti-Federalists, a number of others abstaining. The convention also approved two documents, the first a list of thirty-two specific proposals to revise the structure of the proposed government, with a preamble enumerating the liberties to be protected in a Bill of Rights, the second, a circular letter to the state legislatures calling on them to approve a second convention. On July 26 it adjourned.

Four factors influenced the outcome: a rising tide of popular opinion in the state favorable to ratification; a sharp division among the anti-Federalist delegates; skillful tactics by the Federalists in the tradition of the conservative Whig leadership; and the change of circumstances brought about by ratification in New Hampshire and, especially, Virginia, making the union a *fait accompli.*

"The sentiments of the people," Hamilton observed in mid-May, "have been for some time travelling towards the constitution."[2] This was due in part to ratification in May and June by the seventh and eighth states presaging ultimate success for the Constitution, in part to the delayed impact of pamphlets such as John Jay's *An Address to the People of the State of New York,* whose reasonableness and eco-

---

and DePauw, *The Eleventh Pillar,* 183-279, which I read as Ph.D. diss. (Johns Hopkins Univ., 1964) after this account was written.

2. Hamilton to Madison, May 19, 1788, Syrett, ed., *Hamilton Papers,* IV, 649-50.

nomic appeals probably made more converts than the learned *Federalist* essays.[3] Even before the convention this shift of opinion had given pause to the most staunch anti-Federalists, particularly in the southern district. Marinus Willett, it was said, "had become a proselyte, declaring it [the Constitution] might be right—since it appears to be the sense of a vast majority." After the news from New Hampshire and Virginia, "a great change in sentiment had taken place with those who were before opposed to the Constitution." Now there were "but few if any in this city [New York] who do not think it expedient for this state under the present circumstances to become part of the union." Moreover, "this sentiment is general in the southern part of the state."[4] Such opinion would be of special concern to anti-Federalist delegates from Queens, who had been elected by a narrow margin, or to someone like Melancton Smith, whose future political career lay in New York City. On the other hand it was a less immediate threat to delegates from Ulster and Orange counties, elected without opposition, or delegates from Albany and Columbia and the three other northern counties. Yet Dutchess delegates elected by a two-to-one margin might well differ over interpreting the trend within their county.[5]

This changing climate of opinion contributed to the division among anti-Federalists at the convention, shaping their strategy. Throughout the winter of 1787-88 Governor Clinton favored an outright rejection of the Constitution but had delayed New York's convention so that other states might do the dirty work. After the April election, with ratification by nine states looming, he switched to the tactic of forcing amendments to the Constitution. Toward this end the New York City leaders attempted to work out a joint strategy with the Virginia anti-Federalists, a plan which misfired for lack of time, interference in the mails, and other reasons which are still unclear. As the convention opened, Clinton would have preferred a long adjournment—to stall for time in order to mesh gears with Virginia and to avoid the political risks that drastic action might raise within New York. By this time, however, a large number of anti-Federalist

3. John Jay, *An Address*, reprinted in Ford, ed., *Pamphlets on the Constitution*, 69-70, 85; Spaulding, *New York in the Critical Period*, 211-12; Monaghan, *John Jay*, 292.

4. Morgan Lewis to Margaret Beekman Livingston, May 4, 1788, Robert R. Livingston Papers, N.-Y. Hist. Soc.; Ezra L'Hommedieu to John Smith, July 20, 1788, John Smith Papers N.-Y. Hist. Soc.

5. See above, ch. 4, sec. II.

delegates were not prepared either to reject or to adjourn.[6] "It is doubtful," John Jay observed, "whether the leaders will be able to govern the party. Many in opposition are friends to union and mean well."[7]

At a caucus before the convention anti-Federalists agreed to work for "previous and absolute amendments," i.e., "the Constitution will be effectually amended previous to its adoption—or that it will be totally rejected." They appointed a committee with Robert Yates as chairman to correspond with Virginians and to work out the specific amendments. In agreeing to a protracted clause-by-clause debate, some were counting on unfavorable action by Virginia; others on working out the desired amendments, all on avoiding the charge of reckless-ness. This strategy masked the fundamental differences among the delegates, even to George Clinton,[8] but it could not eliminate them. After the news of New Hampshire's ratification arrived, Jay detected two major groups with four distinct proposals among the "minor partisans." "The greater number," he believed, "were adverse to a vote of rejection. Some would be content with recommendatory amendments; others wish for explanatory ones to settle constructions which they think doubtful"; at the other extreme were the proponents of "absolute and previous amendments; and I am mistaken if there not be a few who prefer a separation from the union to any national government whatever."[9]

Federalist strategy, the third factor shaping the outcome, was de-signed from the beginning to exploit the fears among their opponents brought about by the changing circumstances nationally. "Argu-ments," Hamilton knew, "confound, but do not convince. Some of the leaders however appear to be convinced by circumstances and to be desirous of a retreat." Hamilton's goal, therefore, was to shape the circumstances: first, to delay action in New York, in hope that the

6. Spaulding, *New York in the Critical Period*, 258-61; Abraham Lansing to Abraham Yates, June 1, 15, 1788, Yates Papers, N.Y. Pub. Lib.; David Gelston to John Smith, June 25, 1788, John Smith Papers, N.-Y. Hist. Soc.

7. John Jay to George Washington, May 29, 1788, in Johnston, ed., *Correspon-dence of John Jay*, III, 334.

8. Abraham Lansing to Abraham Yates, July 9, 1788, Yates Papers, N.Y. Pub. Lib.; Robert Yates to George Mason, June 25, 1788, Emmet Collection, No. 9528, N.Y. Pub. Lib.; George Clinton to John Lamb, June 21, John Lamb Papers, Box 5, N.-Y. Hist. Soc.; Clinton to Abraham Yates, June 28, 1788, Yates Papers, N.Y. Pub. Lib.

9. Jay to George Washington, June 30, 1788, Johnston, ed., *Correspondence of John Jay*, III, 346.

news from Virginia and New Hampshire (which he arranged to have rushed at breakneck speed) would be favorable; second, to coerce, by the threat of a secession of the southern district; and third, to conciliate, by stressing the liberal features of the Constitution and holding out the prospect of amendments.[10]

The threat that the counties of New York, Kings, Queens, Suffolk, Richmond, and Westchester would secede and join the new union was advanced before the convention and was made pointedly to individuals at Poughkeepsie, while it rose to a crescendo in New York City. It "operates powerful on the Minds of the opposite Party," Jay wrote.[11] It was effective enough for Abraham Yates to write caustically of his brethren that "it is said that they were decided and deceived by fear of convulsions, anarchy and confusion" and "from an invincible reluctance to a separation from our sister states."[12]

With this club of coercion went the carrot of conciliation, the tactic of "yielding to the current" as Chancellor Livingston had put it ten years before. Hamilton, Livingston, and Jay were "continually singling out members of the convention when out of convention." "You would be surprised," Charles Tillinghast told John Lamb, "did you not know him, what an *amazing republican* Hamilton wishes to make himself be considered. *But he is known.*"[13] Jay, who did not bear the incubus of Hamilton's president-for-life proposals at Philadelphia or Livingston's insufferable arrogance, was probably most effective. Granting that the Constitution had its "imperfections," Jay had argued in his pamphlet published in the spring that the issue was "whether it is probable that a better plan can be obtained." In any event, the government "will always be in the hands and power of the people" and "if it should be found defective or incompetent, they may either remedy its defects or substitute another in its room."[14]

10. Hamilton to Madison, May 19, Hamilton to Gouverneur Morris, May 19, 1788, Syrett, ed., *Hamilton Papers*, IV, 649-50. For the unfolding strategy, see Hamilton to Madison, June 8, 19, 21, 27, 1788, *ibid.*, V, 2-4, 10, 35, 91; see also Mitchell, *Alexander Hamilton*, I, ch. 26.

11. Abraham Yates to Abraham Lansing, May 28, 1788, Yates Papers, N.Y. Pub. Lib.; Samuel B. Webb to Miss Hogeboom, July 13, 1788, Ford, ed., *Correspondence of S. B. Webb*, III, 111; Jay to Washington, July 4, 1788, cited in Miner, *Ratification of the Constitution by New York*, 117.

12. "To the Members of the Legislature of State of New York" in "Rough Hewer" notebook, dated Dec. 8, 1788, Yates Papers, N.Y. Pub. Lib.; printed in *N.-Y. Journal*, Dec. 4, 1788.

13. Charles Tillinghast to John Lamb, June 21, 1788, Lamb Papers, Box 5, N.-Y. Hist. Soc.

14. Jay, *An Address*, in Ford, ed., *Pamphlets on the Constitution*, 69-70, 85.

At the convention, an anti-Federalist conceded his "reasoning is weighty as gold, polished as silver, and strong as steel."[15] The triumvirate offered what seemed to be genuine concessions. They did not balk at "recommendatory" amendments or "constructive declarations" and in the final ten days, much to James Madison's dismay, even consented to New York's right to withdraw from the union if a second convention were not called. Actually they had already agreed on the saving strategy: the new Congress and not a convention would take up the amendments and adopt some of them; "this will satisfy the more considerate and honest opposers of the Constitution," wrote Hamilton, "and with the aid of them will break up the party."[16]

The fourth influential factor, the change in circumstances, did not work automatically—anti-Federalists did not break until two weeks after the news arrived of Virginia's ratification.[17] But with the union established, the Federalist threat of secession was more frightening, and anti-Federalist fears of the political consequences of rejection were greater. "Rough Hewer" and "Plebeian" had prepared them for the relatively easy decision of accepting or rejecting the sinful Constitution, not to weigh the dilemma of joining or staying out of a union that would exist whatever they did. Federalist offers of conciliation also increased after they knew that they had won the main race. No wonder, then, that Melancton Smith, in reversing himself, warned his recalcitrant colleagues that rejection might mean "convulsions in the southern part" of the state, "factions and discord in the rest," with the result that their party might be "dispersed like sheep on a mountain."[18]

Under these pressures the anti-Federalist ranks broke. DeWitt Clinton in desperation warned about the "Scylla" of "non conditional adoption" and the "Charybidis" of "a disunion of the opposition," but his uncle was powerless to avoid either.[19] At what seems to have been the final anti-Federalist caucus, a motion to reject the Constitution was defeated over virulent opposition and a motion to ratify "on

15. A letter dated June 26 in *N.-Y. Journal*, July 4, 1788, possibly by DeWitt Clinton; see Dorothie Bobbé, *DeWitt Clinton* (N.Y., 1933), 41-46.
16. Hamilton to Madison, July 8, 19, 1788, in Syrett, ed., *Hamilton Papers*, V, 147-48, 177-78.
17. Mitchell, *Alexander Hamilton*, I, 438-39; DeWitt Clinton to Charles Tillinghast, July 2, 1788, Lamb Papers, N.-Y. Hist. Soc.
18. N.Y. *Daily Advertiser*, July 28, 1788.
19. Clinton to Tillinghast, July 12, 1788, Lamb Papers, N.-Y. Hist. Soc.; Clinton to ?, July 18, 1788, cited in Bobbé, *DeWitt Clinton*, 45; see also Abraham Lansing to Abraham Yates, July 9, 1788, Yates Papers, N.Y. Pub. Lib.

condition" adopted. According to an anti-Federalist privy to the caucus secrets—probably DeWitt Clinton—the intransigents were "much enraged" at Melancton Smith for his offer to compromise; "some detest Smith as much as Hamilton." Governor Clinton and John Lansing also "appear to be against Smith's proposal," but "perhaps this may be political in order to keep in with the violent members."[20] It is unlikely that amidst this acrimony the delegates who changed sides were "selected by design" by the Governor to make the rout appear more orderly, as has been contended.[21] Even after this caucus Hamilton found "so great a diversity of views" among the anti-Federalists that it was "impossible to predict anything."[22] Moreover, harmony was not restored. The breach between what DeWitt Clinton called the "adopting" and "non-adopting antis," as we shall see, racked the party for more than a year, costing Melancton Smith election to the United States Senate, and nearly costing George Clinton re-election as governor.

To account for the delegates who changed sides or absented themselves, scholars have generally focused on the underlying economic factors. Most of the explanations that have been advanced, however, fail to account for the many anti-Federalist delegates who voted *against* the Constitution whose personal backgrounds were similar to those who voted for it. The holding of federal securities—Beard's "personalty interest"—would seem to have been of least importance. Although "about half of the anti-Federalist security holders were among those who changed sides," the largest security holders among the anti-Federalists remained anti-Constitution to the end.[23] The shift-

20. Notes, July [19 or 20], 1788, in DeWitt Clinton Papers, vol. 24, No. 28, Columbia Univ. N.Y.C. DeWitt Clinton was at the convention reporting events to New York anti-Federalists and Greenleaf's paper. These may have been notes for a letter or article. An internal reference, "Judge Platt told my father . . ." probably refers to James Clinton, DeWitt Clinton's father, a delegate from Ulster.

21. McDonald, *We the People*, 288n. McDonald's contention rests on an account of the caucus in Dunlap, *History of New York*, II, 281n. An examination of the note reveals that Dunlap got the information about the caucus from one George F. Hopkins who heard it as a boy, a dubious source compared to the firsthand account cited above in n.20.

22. Hamilton to Madison, July 22, 1788, in Syrett, ed., *Hamilton Papers*, V, 187.

23. According to Main, *The Antifederalists*, 242n., "Of those [delegates] who had $100 or more [in securities] when the convention sat, 7 were Federalists and 14 were anti-Federalists of whom 8 changed sides or did not vote." According to McDonald, *We the People*, 309, twenty-six anti-Federalist delegates held securities of some sort "of whom six voted for ratification and three abstained" leaving seventeen security holders against the Constitution. The data seems to sustain

ers shared some of the over-all economic interests of their Federalist opponents; they were "among the more well-to-do, including one merchant, one large landowner, and three lawyers who were large landowners while four lawyers and a large landowner refrained from voting." Two of the three college graduates on the anti-Federalist side shifted.[24] Yet, it must be pointed out, the leading hold-outs among the anti-Federalists also came from the more prosperous members of the party, for example, Robert Yates, John Lansing, James Clinton, and John Williams. The moderate political leanings of some of the wavering delegates have also been noted. The two architects of the compromise were Samuel Jones, the former Tory, a conservative legal scholar who became a Federalist, and Melancton Smith, regarded by his sometime business partner, William Duer, as "the mildest and most moderate" of the anti-Federalists.[25] Yet, here too the correlation is incomplete; among those voting nay were Robert Yates, who was put up by the Federalists for governor in 1789, and John Williams, who by 1796 became the leading Federalist of the northern frontier.[26]

Emphasis on the constituencies which the delegates represented involves fewer contradictions. Seven of the delegates who shifted were from the southern counties, the four from Queens and three of the four from Suffolk; five were from the middle district, four of the eight from Dutchess (among whom Melancton Smith was from New York City) and one of the four from Orange. A few of the anti-Federalist delegates from the northern counties absented themselves, but no anti-Federalist from the upper Hudson Valley or frontier defected nor, it should be emphasized, did nine of the ten from Orange and Ulster, in the middle district. Thus, adding the anti-Federalist votes of Queens and Suffolk to the Federalist votes from New York, Westchester, Kings, and Richmond, the sectional character of the final vote —south against north—is unmistakable;[27] the four votes from Dutchess and one from Orange were the only non-southern votes in the group.

the skepticism about the importance of security holding entertained by many scholars. See Benson, *Turner and Beard*, 198-200.

24. Main, *The Antifederalists*, 241-42; see also 256-59. Beard, *An Economic Interpretation of the Constitution*, 245-46, 270-71.

25. Duer, *Reminiscences of an Old Yorker* (N.Y., 1867), 7-8; see also James Kent, "Memoirs of Alexander Hamilton," in Kent, ed., *Memoirs of James Kent*, 305-6.

26. Others who later became Federalists but voted against the Constitution in 1788: from Montgomery, John Frey; from Orange, Jesse Woodhull.

27. Spaulding, *New York in the Critical Period*, 267-68; Benson, *Turner and Beard*, 195-97; Hammond, *Political Parties*, ch. 1.

The explanation that the constituents of the switching delegates were engaged in commercial agriculture and were oriented around the export of their surplus crops through New York City while the foes of the Constitution were non-commercial, self-sustaining farmers[28] does not take into account the economic facts of life in the Hudson Valley. Ulster, Orange, Dutchess, Columbia, and Albany were only a shade less commercial in their agriculture than the five farming counties surrounding New York. Yet their delegates voted nay to the end.[29]

An explanation of anti-Federalist voting in rather simple terms of "politics" has merits. Anti-Federalist delegates were sharp country politicians who would have to stand for re-election as assemblymen and senators the following April. They probably were thinking more of their political than their personal fortunes, more of their county's ballot boxes than of the number of hogsheads of flour it exported. In 1789 in the southern district Queens would go Federalist; in Suffolk anti-Federalists would feel constrained to back a moderate Federalist for Congress. Melancton Smith and the leaders from Suffolk, Queens, and New York would have to make their way politically in the southern senatorial district in which the Federalist ice was freezing over. There simply was no future for them as intransigents.

By contrast, the delegates who held out came from areas in the middle and northern counties where opinion was least affected by the Federalist threat of secession and changing circumstances. These areas also harbored the most class feeling against the "manor lords" and "patrician families." Delegates from Orange and Ulster thus could think of themselves as "safe" politically and while delegates from Albany and Columbia, the two landlord centers, had much to worry about, no matter how much they compromised, they may have reasoned that the Schuylers, Van Rensselaers, and Livingstons would not hold out the olive branch to them. These intransigents knew they could go before their constituents with unblemished hands; they had withstood the snares of the mighty and resisted temptation.

As to the Dutchess delegates who divided four and four—the only

28. Main, *The Antifederalists*, 268-81; Libby, *The Distribution of the Vote on the Constitution*, 18-26.

29. See for example a letter from the Chamber of Commerce of New York City to the farmers of New York appealing for better quality wheat for export, in *Poughkeepsie Journal*, June 2, 1791, and Lansingburgh *American Spy*, Nov. 11, 1791, probably reprinted widely; "A Citizen of Dutchess County," *N.-Y. Journal*, Apr. 7, 1792, referred to Ulster as an "ancient, extensive and opulent county" with 3000 farmers, two-thirds of whom were freeholders. See also ch. 3, n. 38, ch. 4, n. 26.

county with so sharp a split—they may well have responded to different constituencies within their county. In April 1788 Dutchess was anti-Federalist by a two-to-one vote; in 1789 it would elect a Federalist congressman by a margin of ten votes out of 1158 cast.[30] The delegates who shifted included the county "bosses," Gilbert Livingston and Zephaniah Platt. They were men who had to think about the fortunes of the party in the county as a whole and who came from the Poughkeepsie area where yeoman farmers predominated. By contrast, two of the hold-outs, Jonathan Akin and Jacobus Swartwout, hailed from the isolated southern part of the county, where since the 1766 rebellion they had been associated with the tenants' battles against the manor lords.[31] Perhaps they simply could not see themselves voting with the Livingstons and Schuylers to the north and the Van Cortlandts and Morrises to the south.

For the anti-Federalist delegates who switched, the Federalist tactic of promising amendments and a second convention made it easier to face the rising tide of pro-Constitution sentiment at home. They could claim that they had not voted for the Constitution which their party had condemned as "aristocratic," "consolidated," and "tyrannical" but for the Constitution as it would become, protecting the states and individual liberties. And before long the anti-Federalists' version of ratification history would be that the issue at Poughkeepsie in 1788 was not "to adopt" or "not to adopt" but simply whether amendments should be added "previous to" or "after" adoption.[32]

As anti-Federalists made their way home, intransigents were bitter at the compromisers, who for their part were eager to disassociate themselves from the "violent men." Governor Clinton, it was true, had salvaged something from the debris. As convention chairman he had been spared a vote, and in his closing speech he paid formal obeisance to the result. The Constitution had not been rejected—that would have been political suicide; instead he had led the fight for amendments. But the blow to his prestige was incalculable; it was his first serious political defeat, and he faced the unenviable task of convincing his opponents that he was not a "disorganizer" and assuring his divided followers that he had not led them into the wilderness.

30. Poughkeepsie *Country Journal*, Apr. 14, 1789.

31. Lynd, *Anti-Federalism in Dutchess County*, ch. 2, 86-88.

32. See appeals in the election of 1789, below, ch. 6, sec. III, and in the vice-presidential election of 1792, "Lucius" [probably Melancton Smith], *N.-Y. Journal*, Nov. 24, 28, 1792.

The political baggage Federalists returned with was lighter. They had the obligation to make good on amendments or at least the prospect of change. They would also have to conduct the new national government so as to convince moderate anti-Federalists that their fears were unjustified. But for the first time since the Revolution, they had a prospect, in Hamilton's phrase, of "break[ing] up the [Clintonian] party." Once again the Federalist political "pilots" had made their way through turbulent waters as they had in the 1770's, by "yielding to the torrent."

II

The surge of popular enthusiasm for the successful Constitution left the anti-Federalists high and dry. There were celebrations for the Constitution in a number of rural strongholds of anti-Federalism. At the festivities the local militia paraded, orators extolled the virtues of the new union, and Federalists offered toasts to "a speedy coalition of parties in pursuit of the public good." In Dutchess, Henry Livingston, in the grand tradition, provided a feast for five hundred country folk complete with barbecued oxen and dancing to the tunes of the local fiddler.[33]

In New York and Albany violence isolated anti-Federalists still further. At Albany on July 4 a clash between Federalist and anti-Federalist paraders had led to "a general battle—with swords, bayonets, clubs, stones etc., which lasted for some time, both parties fighting with the greatest rage, and determined obstinacy." In August when Albany Federalists organized a parade to celebrate ratification, they invited the anti's to join them. The Lansings advised their host to "remain at home on the rejoicing day" and "not to molest them in the least," but a small group of hotheads prepared to greet the Federalist paraders with a discharge of pebbles and refuse. Someone spiked their cannon, and Federalist horsemen came charging down, wielding cutlasses and bayonets. The anti's hurled back paving stones and brickbats. Before the day was over, a Federalist mob attacked Peter Yates, who was lucky to escape alive, and Abraham Lansing, even though he had counseled moderation. The fray had so many comic opera overtones that one Albany wit, "Pilgarlic," produced a mock epic poem, *The Albaniad*, heaping scorn on both sides. The Federalist parade,

33. For notices and accounts of celebrations: N.Y. *Daily Advertiser*, Aug. 13, 15, 17, 29, Sept. 2, 1788; *Hudson Weekly Gazette*, Sept. 2, 1788; Poughkeepsie *Country Journal*, Aug. 12, 19, 26, 1788.

meanwhile, was a festive outpouring of all classes of the city and
countryside led by Philip Schuyler and Stephen Van Rensselaer.
Farmers marched with a banner, "God Speed the Plough," carpenters
with the simple slogan, "United," hatters with a flag, "Success to
American Manufacturers," and ship captains under a streamer, "May
Our Exports Exceed Our Imports."[34]

In New York City Federalist mobs attacked Thomas Greenleaf and
John Lamb. While thousands from every class and craft marched at
the parade on July 23, "the poor anti's generally minded their own
business at home; others who were spectators at an awful distance
looked as sour as the devil." A few days later, when the celebration
was renewed to welcome the final action at Poughkeepsie, "several"
anti-Federalists "drank fully of the Federal Bowl, and declared they
now were perfectly reconciled to the New Constitution." Greenleaf
ran a satirical account of the "Grand Procession" which, he said,
"made a very pompous appearance," but he later apologized.[35] He
was also accused of printing some scurrilous handbills, probably unjustly. Late one night a large mob tried to break down the door of
his print shop, the ax in the hands of Colonel W. S. Livingston, a
Deputy Grand Marshal of the parade. The printer fired at him from
the second story but his pistol failed to go off. With the mob about to
break in, he and his apprentice beat a hasty retreat through the back
door, and the rioters then "threw everything into pi, damaged the
cases, and carried off some of the materials." Greenleaf could not go
to press for days, and to add insult to injury, some sixty New Yorkers
canceled their subscriptions. Undaunted, he hurled defiance at this
attack on "freedom of the press."[36]

Its appetite whetted, the mob then marched to the home of Governor Clinton, but fortunately he was out of town and missed being
hissed at. The mob beat the Rogue's March, and then marched on to
Lamb's house. The old General was better prepared than Greenleaf:
the women had been taken to a place of safety, the doors and windows

34. *Albany Gazette*, Aug. 28, 1788, reprinted in Joel Munsell, ed., *Annals of Albany*, 10 vols. (Albany, 1850-59), I, 229-35; Abraham Lansing to Abraham Yates,
Aug. 3, 1788, Yates Papers, N.Y. Pub. Lib.; Hammond, *Political Parties*, I, 20-21;
"Pilgarlic," [pseud.], *The Albaniad, an Epic Poem, in Three Cantos* (N.Y., 1791); for
violence against anti-Federalists at Hudson, *Hudson Weekly Gazette*, July 8, 1788.
35. *N.-Y. Journal*, July 24, 28, 1788.
36. Leake, *Memoirs of John Lamb*, 332-36; *N.-Y. Journal*, July 31, Aug. 7, 21,
1788; a newspaper clipping from *Morris's National Press Journal for Home*, Sept.
19, 1846, placed in Lamb Papers, N.Y. Pub. Lib.; Mary L. Booth, *History of the
City of New York*, 2 vols. (N.Y., 1867), I, 590-91.

barred, the front hall and stairway barricaded with the dining room furniture, and the lights extinguished. Lamb and three relatives were waiting on the second floor, armed with rifles and side arms. When the shouting marauders arrived, the dark house seemed deserted. The mob soon realized how well defended it was and abandoned the sortie. Conservatives who could remember the attack of the Sons of Liberty in 1775 on the Tory printer, James Rivington, must have savored the irony of the political change.

Actually anti-Federalists did not need the lash of the mob to tame them. A few days after the convention, Robert Yates of Albany—a "non-adopting anti" at Poughkeepsie—said that although he had opposed the Constitution "it was now his and every other man's duty to support it." Jonathan Havens of Suffolk was of like mind: "If my county chooses to adopt the new government, I say we must support it afterwards and every individual citizen of this community must take his chance with the majority."[37] In confidence anti-Federalists admitted to much more. "Our friends," Abraham Lansing wrote to Abraham Yates, Jr., "are much better pleased with [the Constitution] than we had reason to expect. The Bill of Rights which is interwoven with the adoption is considered by the majority of those to whom I have shown it as a security against the encroachments of the General Government." Perhaps the adoption was "best so both in a political and private light" for had the Constitution been changed so that the Confederation Congress "would not accept it—yourself and our Friends would have incurred blame and censure if any serious commotions had ensued." Now the main task was to elect an anti-Federalist to the new federal Congress the following spring to "assist in bringing about the reformation we wish."[38]

But "Rough Hewer" Yates most emphatically did not agree. If he was re-elected as a delegate to the expiring Continental Congress, he was prepared to vote against the ordinance organizing the new government. The delegates "in adopting without express conditional amendments were mistaken both in their expectations and apprehensions."[39] But Yates, though not alone, was not typical. By mid-September John Jay could say "the opponents in this State to the Consti-

37. Hammond, *Political Parties*, I, 30; Jonathan Havens to John Smith, Apr. 5, 1788, John Smith Papers, N.-Y. Hist. Soc.
38. Abraham Lansing to Abraham Yates, Aug. 3, 1788, Yates Papers, N.Y. Pub. Lib.
39. A statement in Yates's hand, Aug. 8, 1788, *ibid.*

tution decrease and grow temperate." By October, Aaron Burr found "political strife still high" at Albany, but this was "the only part of the state where the spirit of party is kept thoroughly alive."[40]

III

By autumn the anti-Federalists were ready to salvage what they could from the debris of Poughkeepsie. Their eyes were on the special session of the legislature which would act on the proposal for a second constitutional convention and choose presidential electors and United States senators.

Whether the anti-Federalist leaders seriously believed a second convention possible or whether, as John Jay thought, they were simply going through the motions, the short and curious history of the Republican Society may testify.[41] On October 30, ten anti-Federalist leaders met at Fraunces Tavern in New York City to form the society "for the purpose of procuring a general convention to revise the Constitution." In effect it was a revival of the Federal Republican Society which had led the battle the previous spring against ratification, although Marinus Willett, rather than John Lamb, was chairman. The two leaders of the "adopting" faction at Poughkeepsie—Samuel Jones and Melancton Smith—were present as were Lamb, Charles Tillinghast, and David Gelston, all anti-Federalist organizers of '88. All were Clintonians, and all save two, Jones and Nathaniel Lawrence of Queens, were from the city.[42] The secretary kept careful minutes, and took attendance, and a committee kept drafts of several stiffly worded letters—all as if for the record.

At the first meeting a committee was appointed to correspond with persons within and outside the state about a second convention. At the second session, only five members attended, but they drafted a letter to the "Republican Committee of Ulster" deploring the division

40. John Jay to George Washington, Sept. 21, 1788, Johnston, ed., *Correspondence of John Jay*, III, 360; Aaron Burr to Theodore Sedgwick, Oct. 10, 1788, Sedgwick Papers, Mass. Hist. Soc.

41. See "Minutes of the Republican Society," Lamb Papers, Box 5, N.-Y. Hist. Soc.; Spaulding, *New York in the Critical Period*, 269-70; Leake, *Memoirs of John Lamb*, 320-26, and for earlier activities, 304-18; for national aspects of this campaign see Edward P. Smith, "The Movement Towards a Second Constitutional Convention in 1788" in J. Franklin Jameson, ed., *Essays in the Constitutional History of the United States in the Formative Period, 1775-1789* (Boston, 1889), 46-116, in particular 94-115.

42. Compare the list of members in the Minutes with Clinton's election committee, N.Y. *Daily Advertiser*, Feb. 27, 1789.

at Poughkeepsie between those who urged conditional and recommendatory amendments. Unity was essential to elect the right candidates to Congress, "the only mode that is now left." At a meeting about a week later, in mid-November, "a sufficient number for business not having met," the society adjourned, the secretary making his last entry in his minute book. A few articles appeared in the papers, doubtless emanating from members, and a letter or two seems to have been dispatched to friends in Pennsylvania. But by the end of 1788 the Republican Society clearly had expired.

In response to this flurry of anti-Federalist activity, Federalists continued their pose of reasonableness. Jay, convinced that the proposal for a convention was a sham, recommended that it be adopted and then delayed for three or four years; Hamilton, convinced that "the rage for amendments" was "rather to be parried by address than encountered with open force," advised delaying altogether; "the mode in which amendments may best be made and twenty other matters" could be used as pretexts. In this vein, an article appeared by "A Federalist Who is for Amendments."[43]

Anti-Federalists recognized the danger but differed as to what to do about it. "A Federal Republican," in all likelihood Melancton Smith, sounded the alarm: the Federalists were going back on their promises; the state would never have ratified without expecting a second convention. But he conceded that "the system is adopted and it is the duty of every true friend of his country to acquiesce"; the only solution was to elect congressmen pledged to revision.[44] On the other hand Abraham Yates, in search of a lever to pry the amendments loose, insisted the state legislature should "inhibit your federal officers" from taking an oath to support the new government until amendments were guaranteed.[45]

Anti-Federalists in the legislature were in no mood for Yates's radical tactics. Clinton, in submitting to the legislature the amend-

43. Jay to Washington, Sept. 21, to Edward Rutledge, Oct. 15, 1788, Johnston, ed., *Correspondence of John Jay*, III, 360-62; Hamilton to Theodore Sedgwick, Nov. 9, 1788, Syrett, ed., *Hamilton Papers*, V, 230-31; N.Y. *Daily Advertiser*, Nov. 22, 1788.

44. "A Federal Republican," Nos. 1, 2, 3, *N.-Y. Journal*, Nov. 27, Dec. 11, 1788, Jan. 1, 1789. The sentences in the last are similar to the development of the argument in Melancton Smith to John Smith, Jan. 10, 1789, John Smith Papers, N.-Y. Hist. Soc.

45. "Sidney," *N.-Y. Journal*, Dec. 4, 1789 (and doubtless in *Albany Register*). A draft is in Yates's "Rough Hewer" notebook, dated Dec. 8, 1789. Other articles on this theme are dated Jan. 5, 18, 26, Feb. 2, 9, 16, 23, Mar. 9, 23, 1789. Yates Papers, N.Y. Pub. Lib.

ments proposed by the Poughkeepsie convention, spoke only of his "duty" to do so. The anti-Federalist assembly set up a committee to draft a letter to Congress requesting a call for a second convention. The Federalist senate, while conceding the Constitution was "susceptible of salutary improvement," demurred, criticizing the Governor for not having called the session earlier. Clinton lashed back, the session turned to other business, and the second convention proposal lay on the table for three months.[46]

IV

The same session was charged with selecting presidential electors and United States senators. With anti-Federalists in control of the assembly and Federalists of the senate, the parties at once were in a wrangle over the method of selection that lasted until they adjourned in February. How was the choice to be made: by a joint ballot of both houses or separate ballots by each? The tradition for the election of delegates to the old Congress had been by joint ballot and in a test of strength on the choice of five delegates to the expiring Congress, Federalists consented to a joint ballot. But with the vote ranging from 36 to 39 for the anti-Federalists against 29 to 33 for the Federalists, they refused to agree to concurrent voting on the new federal offices.[47]

The problem of the anti-Federalists, as Governor Clinton candidly explained to King six months later, was twofold: they had "conscientious scruples concerning the manner of choice," but they also were "not united in their men." The division over men, according to DeWitt Clinton, was between both the "adopting" and "non-adopting antis" and spokesmen for the "northern" and "southern" sections. The rivals were Robert Yates and John Lansing of Albany from the north, and Melancton Smith of New York City and Thomas Tredwell of Suffolk from the south. Of the four, Smith and Yates were the front runners. Lansing, according to George Clinton, would not serve if elected because his income was inadequate. But the trouble with Smith and Yates was that some members of the party were "not convinced that either of them is orthodox," Smith having "disgusted"

46. Hammond, *Political Parties*, I, 36; Lincoln, ed., *Messages from the Governors*, I, 290-94.

47. Assembly proceedings reported in N.Y. *Daily Advertiser*, Dec. 26, 27, 1788; Jan. 10-21, 1789; *Journal of the Senate of the State of New York* (published annually at New York or Albany), 12th Sess., 10-11; 20-22, 25, 43, 49, 50-51.

many by his role at the convention, Yates, probably, by his recent
remarks. DeWitt Clinton thought there was hope of electing both
senators from the anti-Federalist ranks, if only the leaders "are not
divided"; if they were it would be "a calamity."[48]

Anti-Federalist "scruples" about the mode of election reflected the
underlying fear of the Senate. The federal senators, Smith explained
to a legislator, were not elected by the people and were not removable
for a six-year term. If the state senate gained a "veto" in their election the danger of an "aristocracy" would be increased because a few
of "the high minded gentlemen would want to elect one of their own
kind."[49] The Federalists, for their part, were more concerned with
power than principle; by holding out long enough they might split
the prize, one senator to each party.[50]

The question of methods of choosing presidential electors was also
political, rather than principled. Federalists were piqued at Clinton
for calling the session so late; with no prospect of winning in the
legislature Hamilton and others wanted the choice of electors to be
"in the hands of the people." With opinion going their way, they
were willing to risk a popular election, just as they had risked universal male suffrage for the convention the year before. When the
choice of electors devolved on the legislature, Hamilton hoped to play
on the "schism" among the anti's for "some pretty equal compromise."[51] New York was entitled to eight electors; anti-Federalists proposed a joint ballot on all eight; the Federalist senate recommended
that each house select four. A joint conference proved fruitless. Federalists next suggested a compromise: nominations by each house
separately, followed by a joint ballot. This, too, was rejected, as the
"non-adopting" and "adopting" anti-Federalists stood united. December passed with no decision.[52]

Anti-Federalists were content with the stalemate because they had
abandoned their effort to push Clinton for the vice-presidency, if
indeed they had ever been serious about it. Late in the year when the

48. Rufus King, "Memorandum, June 12, 1789," King, ed., *Correspondence of
Rufus King*, I, 354-56; DeWitt Clinton to James Clinton, Nov. 23, 1788, DeWitt
Clinton Papers, Lib. Cong.
49. Melancton Smith to John Smith, Dec. 28, 1788, John Smith Papers, N.-Y.
Hist. Soc.
50. Madison to Jefferson, Dec. 8, 1788, in Julian P. Boyd, ed., *The Papers of
Thomas Jefferson*, 17 vols. (Princeton, N.J., 1950-65), XIV, 339-40.
51. Hamilton to Madison, Nov. 23, 1788, in Syrett, ed., *Hamilton Papers*, V.
335-37.
52. *Journal of the Senate of N.Y.*, 12th Sess., 10-11, 22.

Virginia anti-Federalists talked of Clinton for the post, the Republi
can Society of New York City drafted a few letters to out-of-state
men.[53] But they made no systematic campaign as they could easily
have done, with John Lamb's many contacts. By January David Gel
ston regarded talk of Clinton as a candidate as "a mere piece of
finesse, intrigue, design or whatever you please to call it" spread to
injure him in the gubernatorial campaign then taking shape. When
the day set for presidential voting passed, New York cast no ballot.
Anti-Federalists had no regrets; it was only unfortunate, Melanctor
Smith wrote, that a friend of amendments was not elected to the vice
presidency. Nor was Hamilton overly regretful; "the most we could
hope would be to balance accounts and do no harm."[54]

Meanwhile, in the impasse over the choice of federal senators, com
mittees of the state senate and assembly went through a series of con
ferences to no avail. Anti-Federalist orators expanded on the demo
cratic principle that would be sacrificed if the senate were allowed to
veto the assembly which "will be more obedient to the known voice
of the people."[55] No doubt Federalists wanted to have "a few well
born sensible and judicious" men (they must have great estates) to
elect and choose and legislate.[56] Federalists raised the spectre of the
state going unrepresented in the new Congress and of New York City
losing the site of the capital.

Early in January Hamilton "set out for Albany . . . to be on the
spot in directing his Friends." He asked Samuel Jones, a leader of
the "adopting" anti's, to be "an umpire between the zealots of all
parties," following this up with a letter appealing for "the compro
mise we have talked of."[57] Crèvecoeur, now the French consul at
New York, heard that the arrangement might be Philip Schuyler and

53. Madison to Jefferson, Dec. 8, 1788, in Boyd, ed., *Papers of Thomas Jefferson*
XIV, 339-40; two letters, probably drafts, to nameless persons in other states, Lamb
Papers, N.-Y. Hist. Soc.; Spaulding, *George Clinton*, 185; *N.-Y. Journal*, Jan. 15,
1789, reprinting a letter from Philadelphia *Pennsylvania Packet and Daily Adver
tiser*, Jan. 4, 1789.
54. David Gelston to John Smith, Jan. 9, 1789, Melancton Smith to John
Smith, Jan. 10, 1789, John Smith Papers, N.-Y. Hist. Soc.; Hamilton to Sedgwick
Jan. 29, 1789, Syrett, ed., *Hamilton Papers*, V, 250-51.
55. Debate reported in *N.-Y. Journal*, Jan. 29, Feb. 5, 12, 19, 26, Mar. 5, 1789
"Extract of a Letter from a Gentleman in this city to his friend in New York,
Albany, Jan. 26, 1789, broadside, N.Y. State Lib., Albany, N.Y.
56. David Gelston to John Smith, Jan. 5, 1789, John Smith Papers, N.-Y. Hist
Soc.
57. Hamilton to Samuel Jones, Jan. 21, 1789, Syrett, ed., *Hamilton Papers*, V
244-46.

Robert Yates, "the only one of that party who can be listn'd to with some patience; all the rest being Illiterate and Ignorant."[58] By the end of the month, however, compromise was "impracticable."[59]

The real trouble lay in the inability of the anti-Federalists to close ranks. In vain DeWitt Clinton appealed to the leaders "to be prudent, laying aside every other consideration, to select the senators from the adopting and non-adopting anti's—it will perhaps heal every animosity and cement firmly the friends of amendments."[60] Melancton Smith inquired of his Dutchess associate, Gilbert Livingston, who had joined him in compromise at the convention, whether things had changed: "How stand our old friends towards you. Is former confidence revived, and old grudges forgotten?"[61] Clearly they were not. Anti-Federalists were in no mood to reward Smith or Yates. As a result the state went unrepresented in the Senate until July 1789, four months after it convened.

Both parties capped this fruitless session with a hollow gesture for a second constitutional convention. When the Poughkeepsie resolution was finally taken up, the Federalist senate joined the anti-Federalist assembly in appealing to the new Congress "in a most earnest and solemn manner" for another convention.[62] By then, however, few could have seriously believed there was any prospect for it.

The record of the session was not one anti-Federalists could point to with pride. Their peevishness was an appropriate climax to the intransigence they had shown from the beginning of the battle over the Constitution: from Yates and Lansing's angry departure from the Philadelphia convention in the summer of 1787, to Clinton's stubborn refusal to call a ratifying convention until June 1788, through the impractical goal of the caucus of "previous and absolute amendments," to the refusal in the winter of 1788-89 to compromise over electors or senators. Such decisions may have been personally satisfying to men of "conscientious scruples," but they were not "smart

58. St. Jean de Crèvecoeur to Thomas Jefferson, Jan. 5, 1789, Boyd, ed., *Papers of Thomas Jefferson*, XIV, 415-16.
59. Hamilton to Sedgwick, Jan. 29, 1789, Henry Cabot Lodge, ed., *The Works of Alexander Hamilton*, 12 vols. (N.Y., 1904), VIII, 206.
60. DeWitt Clinton probably to John McKesson, Jan. 18, 1789, DeWitt Clinton Papers, N.Y. State Lib.; John Lansing to John Lamb, Feb. 18, 1789, Lamb Papers, N.-Y. Hist. Soc.
61. Melancton Smith to Gilbert Livingston, Jan. 1, 1789, cited in Mitchell, *Alexander Hamilton*, II, 8.
62. *Journal of the Senate of N.Y.*, 12th Sess., 53; Smith, "The Movement Towards a Second Constitutional Convention in 1788," in Jameson, ed., *Essays*, 94-115.

politics." The anti-Federalists had outfoxed themselves and lost every battle.

As the spring election of 1789 approached, Crèvecoeur caught Clinton's predicament. "Our Govr. who Sees that nothing can stop the Federal Tide is very much Chagrined. He loses dayly some degree of popularity among his Warmest Partisans who [,] perceiving that spite the Idea they had of his abilities as well as of the righteousness of their cause every Thing goes against them [,] begin to Think him less infallible and the new Sistem less obnoxious."[63] As a result, Federalists had good prospects of achieving the goal which Hamilton had espoused at Poughkeepsie: to "break up" the Clintonian party.

63. Crèvecoeur to Jefferson, Jan. 5, 1789, in Boyd, ed., *Papers of Thomas Jefferson*, XIV, 415-16.

CHAPTER 6

Anti-Federalists Dismayed:

The Elections of 1789

———•———

As anti-Federalists turned their thoughts to the spring elections
in 1789, there was a note of despair in their comments. Early in March
six congressmen would be chosen; at the end of April a governor, the
entire assembly, and part of the senate. And the new legislature in
turn would have to choose the two federal senators.[1] But "few, very
few" anti-Federalists, John Lansing reported from Albany to John
Lamb, "have both the inclination and ability to make any advance
to effect the common cause." Surveying the scene from New York
City, DeWitt Clinton was almost as gloomy.[2]

Anti-Federalists even feared for the survival of Greenleaf's *New
York Journal and Patriotic Register.* What the mob had begun, canceled subscriptions might complete. In desperation they launched a
campaign for subscribers, for "the paper must not be permitted to
sink. It is of too much consequence to the common cause to permit."
In the state legislature they tried unsuccessfully to make Greenleaf
the official state printer.[3] Meanwhile, the *Albany Register,* launched

1. New York's first two congressional elections in 1789 and 1790 took place in
March. New York's regular annual election began on the last Tuesday in April,
lasting for five days. Beginning with the elections for the third Congress, 1793,
the congressional poll was taken on the fourth Tuesday in January.

2. DeWitt Clinton [probably to John McKesson], Jan. 18, 1789, DeWitt Clinton
Papers, N.Y. State Lib.; John Lansing to John Lamb, Feb. 8, 1789, Lamb Papers,
N.-Y. Hist. Soc.

3. Cornelius Schoonmaker to Peter Van Gaasbeck, Jan. 14, 1789, Van Gaasbeck

[129]

by Clintonians earlier in the year, was barely on its feet.[4] In Orange County there was a new weekly, the *Goshen Repository*, but a paper in the most safely Clintonian county in the state was hardly necessary.[5] As the first political battle under the new federal Constitution approached, the anti-Federalist weapons were not enough and the warriors were disheartened.

I

Although voting for congressmen would take place first, attention focused on the nomination of candidates for governor; in fact, Federalists had begun their search for a candidate several months earlier. It was taken for granted by both "interests" that Clinton would again be a candidate to succeed himself, and for the Federalists, the four-time winner was still a formidable foe, despite the declining fortunes of his party. Hamilton and Schuyler, rightfully calculating that it would not be possible to win with a candidate strongly identified with Federalism, decided on the tactic of divide and conquer; their candidate would be Robert Yates, the anti-Federalist associate justice of the supreme court who had recently told a grand jury of "everyone's duty" to uphold the Constitution.

Among less flexible Federalists the first talk was of running Richard Morris, chief justice of the supreme court, or Egbert Benson, state attorney-general, tested conservatives prominent in the ratification campaign.[6] Pierre Van Cortlandt, Clinton's lieutenant-governor, entered the picture by an unusual announcement in the papers that he had been "requested by a number of my friends in the several counties to offer myself [as] a candidate for Governor" and was ready to "serve." Schuyler, acting for the Albany Federalists, appealed to him not to run but Van Cortlandt insisted. "He thinks himself too far engaged to recede," Schuyler reported to New York leaders, "a circumstance which has given us great pain, not only on account of his

Papers, F.D.R. Lib.; John Lansing to John Lamb, Feb. 18, 1789, Lamb Papers, N.-Y. Hist. Soc.; *N.-Y. Journal*, Jan. 29, 1789; N.Y. *Daily Advertiser*, Jan. 8, Feb 7, 1789, reporting the proceedings of the assembly.

4. Abraham Lansing to Abraham Yates, Mar. 2, Aug. 3, 1788, to William Barber, Aug. 31, 1788, Yates Papers, N.Y. Pub. Lib.

5. Clarence S. Brigham, comp., *History and Bibliography of American Newspapers, 1690-1820*, 2 vols. (Worcester, Mass., 1947), I, "New York—Goshen Repository," 577.

6. DeWitt Clinton to James Clinton, Nov. 25, 1788, DeWitt Clinton Papers, Lib. Cong.

personal merits, but also from the persuasion that every division among the Federalists must be attended with the utmost danger."[7]

In New York City on February 11 Hamilton presided over a Federalist meeting which nominated Yates for governor and Van Cortlandt for lieutenant-governor. On February 17 a caucus of Federalist state senators at Albany repeated the nomination. Yates accepted, and a few days later Morris issued a statement that he would not run, leaving his followers grumbling about the "junto" that had thwarted him. Hamilton wrote to Van Cortlandt to smooth his ruffled feathers (he would be "more happy if circumstances permitted me to be a channel of a very different application") and to ask him to "withdraw from a competition" which injured the prospects for "the removal of the present Governor."[8]

Given the tactic of dividing the Clintonians, the Yates-Van Cortlandt ticket was astute. In nominating Van Cortlandt, who had offended no one as lieutenant-governor, the Federalists made Clinton the target. In nominating Yates they put forward a moderate anti-Federalist to contrast with Clinton's intransigence. Yates's political strength lay precisely in his impeccable anti-Federalist record as the delegate who had quit the Philadelphia convention in a huff, the chairman of the anti-Federalist caucus at Poughkeepsie who had voted against ratification to the end. But for Federalists he had many saving graces: his recent conciliatory speech on the Constitution, his court record of reasonableness to Tories; and perhaps most important, his extensive "family connections" in Albany County.[9] Like conservative Whigs, Federalists were ever "solicitous to remove talents" from their opposition, as one of them put it.[10]

Clintonians had no other choice but to endorse the Governor for a fifth term. On February 3 a caucus of about forty Clintonian members of the legislature met at Albany and unanimously nominated Clinton for governor and Van Cortlandt for lieutenant-governor, ringing the alarm bell about Federalist efforts to "divide us." Nomina-

7. A letter by Van Cortlandt, dated Jan. 28, 1789, in N.Y. *Daily Advertiser*, Feb. 2, 1789; a draft of a letter from the Albany Committee of Correspondence to John Jay and Richard Varick, Jan. 31, 1789, Philip Schuyler Papers, N.Y. Pub. Lib.

8. Hammond, *Political Parties*, I, 38-41; John Lamb to John Smith, Feb. 11, 1789, John Smith Papers, N.-Y. Hist. Soc.; Hamilton to Van Cortlandt, Feb. 16, 1789, Syrett, ed., *Hamilton Papers*, V, 254-55.

9. See above, ch. 2, sec. III.

10. James Watson to Alexander Hamilton, Feb. 2, 1792, in John C. Hamilton, ed., *The Works of Alexander Hamilton*, 7 vols. (N.Y., 1850-51), V, 496. The reference was to Aaron Burr but the principle was applied to others.

tions then followed rapidly in local meetings in New York City and throughout the state.[11] That Van Cortlandt was nominated by both "interests" was testimony not to his personal popularity but to the symbol of nonpartisanship he gave to them both. As for Clinton, his personal popularity outran the waning support for anti-Federalism; in Ulster, his home county, the local leaders considered his candidacy essential to bring out the full vote.[12] Furthermore, he had retained a following, although a small one, in the Federalist commercial centers, New York and Albany. And he alone could heal the schism between the "adopting" and the "non-adopting" wings of his party. In short he was the only man for his followers as he faced the first serious challenge to election since 1777.

II

With the gubernatorial candidates set by mid-February, attention focused for the next few weeks on the congressional elections which ran concurrently with the state contest. New York was entitled to six federal representatives. In the state legislature Federalists pushed for election of the six at large, obviously hopeful of more success in a state-wide poll. Anti-Federalists argued for separate districts; familiarity was necessary for a wise choice, otherwise voters might be forced to choose from candidates they did not even know. After a warm exchange the legislators decided on electoral districts, but rejected by one vote another anti-Federalist proposal requiring candidates to reside in the district. Such a measure was unconstitutional, John Lansing conceded, and might best be left to the good sense of the voters.[13] The districts drawn by the legislature gave some advantages to the anti-Federalists by consolidating their strong areas and more or less isolating Federalist centers. Voters would choose congressmen from Long Island and Richmond (potentially anti-Federalist); New York City and lower Westchester (inevitably Federalist); Dutchess and northern Westchester (potentially anti-Federalist); Ulster and Orange (inevitably anti-Federalist); Columbia, eastern Albany, Clinton, and

11. Broadside, Albany, Feb. 19, 1789, N.-Y. Hist. Soc.; N.Y. *Daily Advertiser,* Feb. 27, 1789; *N.-Y. Journal,* Feb. 26, 1789; Abraham Bancker to Peter Van Gaasbeck, Jan. 30, 1789, Van Gaasbeck Papers, F.D.R. Lib.

12. Peter Van Gaasbeck, Mar. 31, 1788, Van Gaasbeck Papers, Senate House Museum and Library, Kingston, N.Y.

13. Reported in N.Y. *Daily Advertiser,* Dec. 31, 1788, Jan. 30, 1789.

Washington; and western Albany and Montgomery (the latter two hopefully anti-Federalist).[14]

   In two districts anti-Federalists were unopposed. In Ulster-Orange their candidate was John Hathorn, a "non-adopting" anti of 1788, after some squabbling for the nomination from this safe district.[15] On Long Island there was unity on behalf of General William Floyd, a signer of the Declaration of Independence and a Clintonian senator who seems to have favored the Constitution in 1788 and Clinton for governor in 1789; he would take a stand as an anti-Federalist in the first Congress.[16]

   In three upstate districts the election pitted men clearly identified as anti-Federalists in '88 and Clintonians in '89 against Federalists of '88 and Yates supporters of '89. In the Dutchess-northern Westchester district Theodorus Bailey, brother-in-law of the anti-Federalist chieftain Gilbert Livingston, faced Egbert Benson, long a kingpin of the conservative Whigs and a warm Federalist.[17] In the Columbia County-eastern district Matthew Adgate, an anti-Federalist delegate and senator, ran against Peter Sylvester, who was backed by Philip Schuyler and the upper and lower manor Livingstons.[18] In the Albany-western district Jeremiah Van Rensselaer, chairman of the anti-Federalist committee in '88 and Clinton's committee in '89, opposed Abraham Ten Broeck, an unsuccessful Federalist candidate the year before and a relative of Schuyler.[19] The issue to the anti-Federalists

14. Werner, comp., *Civil List of New York*, 552.
15. Cornelius Schoonmaker to Peter Van Gaasbeck, Jan. 3, 1789, and Abraham Bancker to Van Gaasbeck, Jan. 30, 1789, Van Gaasbeck Papers, F.D.R. Lib.; John Bogert to Van Gaasbeck, Jan. 21, 1789, and Christopher Tappen to Van Gaasbeck, Feb. 27, 1789, Van Gaasbeck Papers, Kingston Senate House; *N.-Y. Journal*, Apr. 9, 1789; Poughkeepsie *Country Journal*, Apr. 14, 1789.
16. John Smith, draft of a letter [1789], John Smith Papers, N.-Y. Hist. Soc.; Richard Morris in *DAB* s.v. "Floyd, William"; Madison to Washington, Mar. 19, 1789, in Gaillard Hunt, ed., *The Writings of James Madison*, 9 vols. (N.Y., 1900-1910), V, 329-30.
17. For biographical details on New York congressmen, see *Biographical Directory of the American Congresses, 1774-1927*; and Billy Bob Lightfoot, State Delegations to the Congress of the United States, 1789-1800 (unpubl. Ph.D. diss., Univ. of Texas, 1958), ch. 8. For Benson and the Livingstons, see Thomas Tillotson to Henry Livingston, Apr. 14, 1789, Robert Livingston Papers, F.D.R. Lib.; and Staughton Lynd, "Who Should Rule at Home?" *Wm. and Mary Qtly.*, 3d Ser., 18 (1961), 350-51.
18. *N.Y. Daily Advertiser*, Feb. 27, 1789; *Hudson Weekly Gazette*, Apr. 17, 1788, Apr. 21, 1789; Spaulding, *New York in the Critical Period*, 239.
19. *N.Y. Daily Advertiser*, June 8, 1788; Lansingburgh *Federal Herald*, Mar. 2, 1789; Spaulding, *New York in the Critical Period*, 222.

in these three districts was "the election of persons as were for obtaining amendments to the Constitution."[20]

By contrast in the New York City bastion of Federalism the anti-Federalists took a leaf from Hamilton, camouflaging themselves behind a moderate Federalist. Hamilton's candidate was John Laurance, in many ways the complete Federalist: English-born, an aide-de-camp of General Washington, an early nationalist with the added political appeal of having married the daughter of the radical Whig Alexander McDougall, a lawyer, a member of Trinity Church and a trustee at Columbia College, a man "of handsome dignified presence."[21] Laurance was nominated at a meeting that repeated the Federalist endorsement of Yates. The anti-Federalists were artful. After caucusing at John Lamb's house, they published a notice announcing a meeting at the Coffee House of all those interested in nominating a merchant for Congress. The next day they announced the chairman, General William Malcolm, who had presided at Clinton's nominating meeting ten days before. On the morning of the meeting an unsigned notice in the papers suggested the candidate: John Broome, "a gentleman of great mercantile knowledge, sound judgment, and firmly attached to the Constitution—altho' a merchant, he is a Man of Letters, and well acquainted with law."[22] Broome was a strong candidate: an alderman and city chamberlain (the treasurer) since 1784, president of the Chamber of Commerce since 1785, he had been a warm Whig in the Revolution, a colonel in the army, and a member of the Continental Congress and the state convention.[23]

Forewarned of this strategy, Hamilton placed a notice in the same day's paper urging his following to attend the meeting; as a result the turnout was so large that the meeting had to be adjourned until the next night and to a larger hall. With Malcolm presiding, Robert Troup, Hamilton's lieutenant, nominated Laurance; Melancton Smith and Marinus Willett "spoke repeatedly and largely" against him but to no avail. The meeting endorsed Laurance and Yates with no more

20. Statement by the Albany election committee, N.Y. *Daily Advertiser*, Feb. 27, 1789.

21. Charles Spencer in *DAB* s.v. "Laurance, John." His name is occassionally spelled Lawrance or Lawrence. Spaulding, *New York in the Critical Period*, 160-61.

22. John Lamb to John Smith, Feb. 11, 1789, John Smith Papers, N.-Y. Hist. Soc.; N.Y. *Daily Advertiser*, Feb. 24, 26, 1789.

23. Walter Barrett [pseud. of Joseph Scoville], *The Old Merchants of New York City*, 5 vols. (N.Y., 1863-70), III, 213-15, 232-36; New York State, Division of Archives and History, *The American Revolution in New York*, 79, 83; N.Y. *Daily Advertiser*, Mar. 3, 1789.

than forty "nays" in the crowd. The Federalists had stolen the show.[24]

Broome's supporters, instead of calling their own nominating meeting, simply proceeded to campaign for him, attempting to remove the Federalist–anti-Federalist issue from debate. Both candidates, argued "A Federal Shopkeeper," are and have been equally federal. It was true that Clinton's supporters backed Broome, but did this make him an anti-Federalist? The real question was whether a merchant or a lawyer should represent the district. The major qualification for a candidate, wrote "Mercator," echoing Hamilton's remarks at Poughkeepsie, was that he "should possess mercantile information." "The commerce of the union is placed under the direction of the general government; on its success the interest of the farmers, the mechanic and every other order of men of this district are connected."[25] To Federalists, Broome was an anti-Federalist Trojan horse. Here was an attempt, Hamilton warned, "to destroy or weaken the national government." A man of an "early and decided attachment" to the Constitution was needed; Broome's support was "tardy and equivocal." The fact that Laurance was a lawyer was irrelevant because he had the overwhelming support of the merchants and a knowledge of commerce. Federalists mocked their opponents with a satire on "the wickedness of these wicked lawyers . . . Beware, beware, beware of Lawyers."[26]

The election returns—a three-to-three split of the six seats—were a blow to the anti-Federalists.[27] Federalists took the New York City district by 2342 to 373, all but repeating the Federalist sweep for convention delegates the year before. This was no surprise, but they also took the Dutchess-northern Westchester district by 584 to 574 and the Columbia district by 1628 to 1501. In Columbia, Schuyler and both branches of the Livingston family got out their tenants, while in Dutchess, Margaret Beekman Livingston, the Chancellor's mother, boasted that "I have been the means of geting in Benson by

24. Alexander Hamilton, "To the Independent Electors of the State of New York" in N.Y. *Daily Advertiser*, Apr. 2, 1789, reprinted in Syrett, ed., *Hamilton Papers*, V, 310-15, reviews the events; see notices, *ibid.*, Feb. 27, 28, 1789.

25. "A Federal Shopkeeper," and "Mercator," N.Y. *Daily Advertiser*, Mar. 3, 1789.

26. *Ibid.*: Alexander Hamilton's "Address," Mar. 3; "Extract of a Letter from Albany," Mar. 2; "Lynceus," Mar. 2; "A Federal Shopkeeper," Mar. 5, and "Brutus," Mar. 2, 1789; "Beware of Lawyers," Mar. 4, 1789, mistakenly treated in Pomerantz, *New York An American City*, 395-96, as an anti-Federalist document.

27. For the returns see: *N.-Y. Journal*, Apr. 4, 1789; N.Y. *Daily Advertiser*, Apr. 4, 1789.

my exertions."[28] Anti-Federalists won only Long Island and Ulster-Orange where they were unopposed, and the Albany-western district where Jeremiah Van Rensselaer's margin was low, 1456 to 1215 votes. Anti-Federalist party leaders blamed their poor showing on insufficient campaigning;[29] actually their trouble lay deeper, as the number of anti-Federalists who stayed away from the polls suggested. It was a harbinger of the trouble that lay ahead for Clinton a month later.

III

In the gubernatorial campaign Federalists retained the full array of the "interests" they had in their camp the year before in the battle for the Constitution: in the upper Hudson, the major landlords; at New York City, old established merchants and new speculative operators like Duer, Richard Platt, and William Constable, the chairman of Yates's committee.[30] Robert R. Livingston's brother-in-law, Morgan Lewis and Thomas Tillotson, were active, although the Chancellor did not exert himself for Yates. Hamilton had to write to him twice to verify a simple factual point for an article against Clinton.[31] In New York City, the mechanics, a bulwark of the party since 1786, were also loyal. Hamilton met with a joint committee of mechanics and merchants to set the assembly nominations, and Clintonians grumbled that the Federalist "electioneering corps" was composed of "the masons, stonecutters, the carpenters and the mortar carriers" employed in refurbishing Federal Hall for the new Congress.[32] Hamilton was a dynamo for his party. He organized the nominating meetings and ward organization in New York City, wrote the official party appeals, traveled to Albany where he also wrote the

28. Margaret Beekman Livingston to Robert R. Livingston, Apr. 1789, R. R. Livingston Papers, N.-Y. Hist. Soc.

29. Peter Yates and Richard Lush to Jonathan Lawrence, Apr. 19, 1789, Lamb Papers, N.-Y. Hist. Soc.

30. N.Y. Daily Advertiser, Feb. 20, 1789; for the upper manor in Columbia County, Hudson Weekly Gazette, Apr. 21, 1789.

31. For Morgan Lewis as candidate in New York City, see N.Y. Daily Advertiser, May 27, 1789; for election activity, Thomas Tillotson to Henry Livingston, Apr. 14, 1789, Livingston Family Papers, F.D.R. Lib.; Brockholst Livingston to William Livingston, William Livingston Papers, Mass. Hist. Soc.; Hamilton to Robert R. Livingston, Mar. 18, Mar. 22, 1789, R. R. Livingston Papers, N.-Y. Hist. Soc. There is no evidence of an answer by Livingston.

32. Notes on a Nominating Meeting, Apr. 20 [?], 1789, Hamilton Papers, N.-Y. Hist. Soc.; "Civis," N.-Y. Journal, Apr. 9, 1789; for nominations, N.Y. Daily Advertiser, Apr. 8, Apr. 30, 1789.

official party statement, did a series of sixteen articles as "H.G." raking Clinton fore and aft, and supervised the poll watchers.[33]

For the Clintonians the old anti-Federalist stalwarts, John Lamb's committee at New York City and Jeremiah Van Rensselaer's committee at Albany were the principal organizers. In Albany Yates's candidacy produced no visible defections among the numerous tribe of Yateses and Lansings; in New York City the only non-Federalist on Yates's committee was Aaron Burr, a personal friend who had been a mild opponent of ratification the year before. Here and there in other counties, however, anti-Federalists drifted into Yates's committees.[34]

Election practices were similar in both groups.[35] As the nominating procedure suggests, political custom dictated that both "interests" avoid the appearance of party; Clinton's New York City supporters, for example, called themselves "The Federal Republican Committee." Elsewhere it was more typical that nominating committees first identified themselves as "a respectable body of freeholders" or "a respectable gathering" and then called themselves "the supporters of Mr. Clinton" or the "friends of Mr. Yates." The usual practice was for the qualified electors in each town, and occasionally a county, to meet and nominate one of the two gubernatorial candidates already nominated at Albany or New York, at the same time nominating local candidates for the senate and assembly. Usually, two separate meetings were held in each town, one organized by each party. On occasion, however, one party might claim that its nomination represented the choice of the entire town. Then there might be a counter-meeting and the local newspaper might resound with long-winded charges and countercharges as to who really was the town's candidate.[36]

The campaign was directed by the election committees at New

33. Mitchell, *Alexander Hamilton*, II, 8-10; see memoranda and poll lists used in the 1789 election in Hamilton Papers, N.-Y. Hist. Soc., not reprinted in Syrett, ed., *Hamilton Papers*; the articles are cited below.

34. For the 1788 leaders and election committee of Apr. 25, 1789, see Lamb Papers, Box 5, N.-Y. Hist. Soc.; for another 1789 committee see *N.-Y. Journal*, Apr. 2, 1789; for the 1788 leaders, see a letter without salutation dated Albany, Feb. 27, 1788, Emmett Coll., N.Y. Pub. Lib.; for the 1789 election committee, see N.Y. *Daily Advertiser*, Feb. 27, 1789; Hammond, *Political Parties*, I, 40-41; at Albany, Abraham I, Abraham, Jr., Christopher P., and Peter W. Yates were active for Clinton as were Abraham, Jacob, Jacob, Jr., and Gerritt Lansing, Jr.

35. For an over-all survey, see George D. Luetscher, *Early Political Machinery in the United States* (Phila., 1903), 72-75, 114-16.

36. For a controversy at Rhinebeck, Dutchess County, see Poughkeepsie *Country Journal*, Mar. 17, 24, 31, Apr. 7, 21, 1789.

York and Albany, in touch both with each other and with local county and township committees.[37] The Clintonian committee at New York was composed of thirty-six men chosen at a public meeting of about one hundred. Drawn from the seven wards of the city, they in turn chose a committee of correspondence. Hamilton also organized ward committees in the city which canvassed the voters, reported back to election headquarters, and brought out the voters.

Campaign literature featured official statements by the election committees which were published in the papers and often republished as broadsides. Most of the newspaper electioneering was carried out by correspondents under sobriquets or classical pseudonyms not only to mask the author but to strike the desired pose. Members of election committees often wrote such articles and broadsides and arranged for their distribution.[38] Local leaders campaigned in the countryside to spread the gospel at well-frequented taverns, militia musters, and town meetings, and state leaders like Jeremiah Van Rensselaer of Albany and Hamilton traveled to other cities.[39]

The Federalist campaign, its tone set by Hamilton, was a shrill three-pronged attack against Clinton.[40] The first theme was his anti-Federalism. Not only had the Governor been "obstinate and haughty" in opposing ratification, but he was still "an enemy of American union." The latest proof was his alleged "want of a decent republican hospitality" to Congress. The state had to have a governor "free from all temptation wantonly to perplex or embarrass the National Government." Second, Clinton "instead of being the impartial head of a state" had become the zealous head of a party. The state should have "disinterested, discreet and temperate rulers" who would "promote conciliation, not dissension." Yates was the man to do this. Although formerly a foe of the Constitution, he was esteemed by all as a judge, a man of moderation, and a "man likely to compose the differences

37. Southhampton Election Committee to David Gelston, Mar. 25, 1789, Peter W. Yates and Richard Lush to Jonathan Lawrence, Apr. 19, 1789, Lamb Papers, Box 5, N.-Y. Hist. Soc.; Jeremiah Van Rensselaer to the Republican Comm. of Kingston, Apr. 23, 1789, Van Rensselaer MSS, N.Y. State Lib.

38. Lamb Papers, Box 5, N.-Y. Hist. Soc., contains a 1789 manuscript signed "Brutus" and marked "T.T. of Suffolk," doubtless Thomas Tredwell. Another manuscript signed "A Customer" is clearly in the hand of Charles Tillinghast of the New York election committee.

39. Peter W. Yates and Richard Lush to Jonathan Lawrence, Apr. 19, 1789, Lamb Papers, Box 5, N.-Y. Hist. Soc.

40. Hamilton, "To the supervisors of . . . Albany," Feb. 18, "To the Election of the State of New York," Apr. 9, 1789, in Syrett, ed., Hamilton Papers, V, 255-61, 317-29.

of the state." Third, Clinton had held power too long, creating an "undue and dangerous influence" and a large personal fortune. To "perpetuate himself" in office, he had used his extensive patronage powers and influence in the Council of Appointment. "As no man has a right to office or reelection in virtue of long possession" he should be turned out; "rotation" was necessary./

The Federalists also made rank class appeals. Conservatives were told of Clinton's "scandalous appointments" of men "destitute of capacity" from the "scum of society"—long the complaint of conservative Whigs.[41] Clinton was also accused of sympathy with Daniel Shays. Some time after "Shay's rebellion," it was claimed, Clinton saw Shays in an Albany tavern, walked across the room, and greeted him.[42] Tenants, on the other hand, were reminded that Clinton had not made good a promise to his own tenants on his recently acquired Dutchess estate of remitting their wartime rents.[43]

Hamilton's contribution as "H.G." was a personal attack on Clinton, devastating in its innuendos. Clinton "stood fair on the test of probity" but was "a very artful man." As a general, while vigorous and courageous, he did not merit the claims of his "panegyrists"; at Fort Montgomery he led a "well-timed retreat"; at the burning of Esopus he was "culpably deficient." Others deserved more credit than he for his measures as wartime governor. Since the peace he had made no innovations. He was guilty of siding with "the most heated" in persecuting Tories.[44] Clinton was a mediocrity and a demagogue—this was the only conclusion the reader could draw. "Abuse both in prose and verse is current at every corner of the streets," one of the old Liberty Boys lamented. "Even poor Mrs. Clinton is sacrificed on the altar of party—the kitchen and pantry have been critically examined in order to shew that she does not keep cooks capable of suiting the palate of everybody but consults the taste of his own family only."[45]

Experienced political warriors, Clintonians tried to define the con-

41. "Cato," Poughkeepsie *Country Journal*, Apr. 14, 1789, in answer to "Junius," Mar. 31, followed by "Junius," Apr. 28, and "Cato," May 12. This possibly was by a member of the lower manor Livingston family; "Cato" was a pseudonym used by Robert R. Livingston.

42. A letter in Lansingburgh *Federal Herald*, Mar. 23, 1789.

43. Clinton to Peter Tappen, Apr. 1, 1789, Clinton Papers, N.-Y. Hist. Soc.

44. "Letters of H.G." in N.Y. *Daily Advertiser*, Feb. 20-Apr. 9, 1789, in Syrett, ed., *Hamilton Papers*, V, 262-330.

45. James Hughes [from New York City] to John Smith, Feb. 11, 1789, John Smith Papers, N.-Y. Hist. Soc.

test in familiar terms of class. Anti-Federalism was not the issue, wrote "A Freeholder of the Southern District"; it was a "political Rawhead and Bloody Bones like the hue and cry about Popery in England." Nor was Yates the issue. He was not a principal, but "the mere puppet of the show," a "dupe," a "wholly ambitious man," and a "deserter." The real conflict was between "the plebeian interest" and the "patrician families." Behind Yates stood "the proud and aristocratic families" whose pride was hurt by a governor whose "virtues are not attached to entails nor are they comprehended with patents of land. . . . Their manners are haughty, and their estates and those of their connections are immense, and beyond all proportion to a popular government and therefore dangerous." Clinton's followers, by contrast, were "the old-fashioned Whigs of the Revolution . . . natives and fixtures of the soil and representatives of the yeomanry of the counties." They were not "desperate debtors or persons in embarrassed circumstances" but possessed "that republican mediocrity of estate" which "will give them nerves and constitutions for the field and a sympathy for the distresses of the moderate class of mankind." "Friend of the People," "A Yeoman," "A Mechanic," "Junius," and "Brutus" followed along similar lines. Marinus Willett as "William Tell" lashed out at Hamilton as head of "an expecting band of sycophants, a train of ambitious relations and a few rich men" backing Yates.[46]

Federalists were quick to answer this "indiscriminate cry against men of property." Hamilton in a committee statement conceded that Federalists did indeed have the backing of "the principal part of the men of the most considerable property." But "will it follow that it must be wrong because men of property concur in it?" he asked. Yates himself was not rich; there was a "sinister design" to the anti-Federalist outcry "because by destroying the confidence of the body of the people in men of property it makes a cooperation between them for the defense of their common privilege and interests more difficult." As a result it would be easier "for aspiring men in possession of power . . . to prosecute schemes of personal aggrandizement and usurpation."[47]

46. "A Freeholder of the Southern District," *N.-Y. Journal*, Mar. 19, 1789. The article was refused by the N.Y. *Daily Advertiser* and "read with avidity" by the Albany anti-Federalist committee; "A Yeoman," Mar. 26, "A Friend to the People," Apr. 23, "Brutus," Apr. 16, "To The Electors of Ulster County" by "Junius," Apr. 2, 1789, all in *N.-Y. Journal*; "William Tell" [Marinus Willett] in answer to "Letters of H.G." [Hamilton], N.Y. *Daily Advertiser*, Mar. 21, 23, 1789.

47. "To the Election of State of New York . . . Address of the Federal Election

The New York Clintonian committee rebutted: "We have raised no cry against men of property, nor is it our design to do it. We are persuaded that the merit of no man is to be depreciated because he is rich." But, they added, turning the tables, "nor are any to be despised because they are poor." "We neither wish to see men of dangerous wealth or dependent poverty in office," wrote "A Friend to the People." "The governor possesses just that degree of property which will be a security for his independence of sentiment."[48]

Despite this aggressive stance, Clintonians were forced onto the defensive to answer the three specific political accusations against the Governor—his extreme anti-Federalism, his partisanship, and his "overgrown power." Their answers reveal some of the ambiguities of their position. On the anti-Federalism issue they rode two horses. In New York City, they tried to finesse the issue, as the name "Federal Republican Committee" and the campaign for John Broome suggested. The principal issue of 1788, they insisted, had been only whether amendments should "precede or follow adoption."[49] Upstate, however, they warned of an insidious campaign to depreciate amendments by "generally the rich, the powerful, the great, the well-born and the upstart."[50]

Their reply to the charge of partisanship was ambivalent. They acknowledged the common aversion to the spirit of party which "seeks private emolument or private honor" but also defended the idea of a party. Where did the danger stem from, asked the New York committee. "Men of family, wealth and of eminence and of grandeur" were most likely to be "men of ambition and to form parties to promote their own views." Clinton was forced to form a party because

---

Committee," Alexander Hamilton, chairman, *N.-Y. Journal*, Apr. 9, 1789, in Syrett, ed., *Hamilton Papers*, V, 317-29.

48. "To the Independent Electors . . ." from a Committee, Jonathan Lawrence, Chairman, *N.-Y. Journal*, "Extraordinary" [extra page], Apr. 23, 1789; for the committee's earlier plea, also conservative, see "To the Unbiased and Independent Electors," N.Y. *Daily Advertiser*, Apr. 14, 1789; "A Friend to the People," *N.-Y. Journal*, Apr. 23, 1789.

49. "A Friend to Union and the New Constitution," broadside, Apr. 30, 1789, and N.Y. Federal Republican Committee, Apr. 23, Apr. 28, 1789, broadsides, N.-Y. Hist. Soc.

50. *Albany Register*, Mar. 2, 1789, reprinted in *N.-Y. Journal*, Mar. 19, 1789, and Poughkeepsie *Country Journal*: "Cassius," Mar. 3, "Junius," Mar. 31, and Apr. 28, 1789. See also "Extract of a letter from Dutchess County," *N.-Y. Journal*, Apr. 2, 1789.

he lacked an extensive family of this sort, but its aim was not to further his personal interests.[51]

As to Clinton's alleged abuse of the patronage to build his own power, it was simply denied. The Governor's appointments, a member of the Council of Appointment wrote, were made "with candour and impartiality," many Federalists having been appointed. In fact, said another, too many jobs, far from going to "court favorites," went to opponents.[52] Rotation in office was a good principle, but did not apply when the government was sound. A majority of "unbiased freemen" elected Clinton; that was the "Republican criterion" of good government. The principle of rotation applied to the powerful presidency at all times, but Clinton's twelve years of service to the state was proof of his fitness for office, not of the need to turn him out. Admittedly, Clinton had accumulated a fortune in office but, explained Thomas Tredwell, writing as "Brutus," this was the product of frugality, not corruption. The Governor had saved his salary and invested it prudently and could be blamed neither for possessing property nor the manner of acquiring it. He was from a "family, always reputable, holding a middle rank in the community" and could not be charged with an extravagant manner of living.[53]

As this heated exchange—personal, political, and principled—drew to a close, Federalists were blessed by the most spectacular campaign windup in American history: the arrival and inaugural ceremonies of George Washington. The President-elect made his triumphal entry into New York City in the last week of electioneering and actually was inaugurated while the polls were open.[54] With the city wildly enthusiastic over the new President, last-minute Federalist broadsides claimed that Clinton wanted to get rid of the national capital; the voters therefore had to "remove every source of embarrassment" to the national government, "rooting out anti-Federalism" and "removing its GREAT HEAD."[55] Clintonians, in desperation at the band-

51. N.Y. Federal Republican Committee, *N.-Y. Journal*, Apr. 23, 1789, "A Friend to the People," Apr. 23, "A Yeoman," Mar. 26, 1789.

52. David Hopkins and "An Independent Elector" in *Hudson Weekly Gazette*, Feb. 21, Mar. 6, 1789, reprinted in *Goshen Repository*, Mar. 31, 1789; "Brutus," *N.-Y. Journal*, Apr. 16, 1789. The New York committee makes the same point in *N.-Y. Journal*, Apr. 23, 1789. "Junius," Poughkeepsie *Country Journal*, Apr. 28, 1789.

53. "Brutus," *N.-Y. Journal*, Apr. 16, 1789; "A Friend to the People," Apr. 23, and "No Party Man from Westchester County," Apr. 12, 1789, *ibid.*

54. See ch. 7, sec. I.

55. "To the Inhabitants of the Southern District," Apr. 25, "A Tried Friend

wagon psychology, tried to neutralize the anti-Federalist issue. "Has not Judge Yates been as much opposed to the new government as Governor Clinton?" And if Yates were elected, the *state* capital would be moved to Albany to appease "the most powerful men" in his camp.[56] "The struggle has been very hard indeed," wrote David Gelston, but he predicted Clinton's election by a 1500 vote majority.[57]

IV

Clinton won, but by his narrowest margin since 1777. When the ballots were canvassed in June, a month after the voting, the vote was 6391 to 5962, and the majority of 429 votes was less than 3.5 per cent of those cast.[58] Had the Westchester votes that were "lost" because of irregularities in reporting been counted, Clinton's margin would have been even less. The total vote, 12,353, was about 70 per cent of the 18,000 or so eligible voters in the £100 category—a high percentage and more than two and a half times the vote in any previous gubernatorial election.[59] Observing the voting from New York City, William Grayson, senator from Virginia, believed that "almost all the gentlemen as well as all the merchants and mechanics combined together to turn [Clinton] out" while the "honest yeomanry" alone gave him support.[60] There was much truth but also some error in this analysis. Clinton's greatest strength continued to come from

---

to the Federalists of New York," Apr. 29, "A Federalist," Apr. 30, 1789, broadsides, N.Y. Pub. Lib.

56. "To the Electors of the City and County of New York" from Jonathan Lawrence, Chairman, Apr. 28, "To the Freeholders of the Southern District" by "An Independent Elector," Apr. 29, "A Friend to Union and the New Constitution," Apr. 30, 1789, broadsides, N.-Y. Hist. Soc.

57. David Gelston to John Smith, Apr. 27, May 7, 1789, John Smith Papers, N.-Y. Hist. Soc.; Melancton Smith *et al.*, draft of a letter, Apr. 18, 1789, Jeremiah Van Rensselaer to the Republican Committee of Kingston, Apr. 23, 1789, Lamb Papers, N.Y. Hist. Soc.

58. See Appendix, Table No. 4; N.Y. *Daily Advertiser*, May 27, 28, 29, 30, June 1, 2; N.-Y. *Journal*, June 4; *Albany Register*, June 8, 1789. Election returns for the 1780's and 1790's may be found only in newspapers, which published the returns given them by the official Committee of Canvassers a month after the election in several consecutive issues. The New York City papers usually published the returns for every county, broken down by townships and wards.

59. The electoral census taken after March 1790 revealed 19,369 voters in the £100 and over category. Allowing for some increase in a state whose population was growing there would have been about 18,000 qualified voters in 1789. See Appendix, Table 1.

60. William Grayson to Patrick Henry, June 12, 1789, W. W. Henry, ed., *Patrick Henry: Life, Correspondence and Speeches*, 3 vols. (N.Y., 1891), III, 389-95.

the agricultural areas most free of landlordism. His bastions were Orange and Ulster counties, which he carried by a five-to-one majority. His other safe areas were the southern counties of Long Island and Richmond, and Clinton and Washington on the northern frontier, where his margins ran two to one and more.

Yates's most solid support, in contrast, came from the areas where the merchants and landlords predominated. The cities were Federalist: New York (833–385), Poughkeepsie (64–54), Hudson (177–17), Albany (153–55), Schenectady (132–71), all save Kingston (17–261), which would swing over in another year. The landlords delivered to Yates the tenants in the three counties of their greatest influence: Albany, Columbia, and Dutchess. Anti-Federalists charged coercion[61] when they saw the returns from Stephen Van Rensselaer's Stephentown (173–21) and Rensselaerswyck (188–23); from Philip Schuyler's Saratoga (67–14) and Watervliet (294–50); and from Livingston Manor (270–5) belonging to the upper manor. The Clermont Livingstons did well for Yates in Rhinebeck, northern Dutchess, Margaret Beekman's home (237–7), but not on the lower manor (43–29). Robert R. Livingston was away in the city; the tenants, his mother told him, were for Clinton; she would not risk "going among them" and was content with letting the steward do what he could.[62] James Duane's small estate, Duanesburgh, was even more in favor of Clinton, 14–9. In Columbia, the eastern townships with a long heritage of battle with the "manor lords" voted for Clinton (Hillsdale, 218–64 and Canaan, 338–142) although similar towns in southern Dutchess were not as consistent.[63]

No class, it was clear, was totally aligned on either side. Clinton's New York City vote among the £100 electorate—385 out of 1218 cast, compared to John Broome's 373 out of 2715 in the poorer congressional electorate—showed that in the city Clintonians had more support among the well-to-do than the poor. On the other hand, Yates's minority vote in Montgomery, a frontier county, and in Ulster showed

61. For Van Rensselaer's answer to charges, see "To the Inhabitants of . . . Rensselaerswyck," broadside, Apr. 27, 1789, N.Y. State Lib.; for charges against the upper manor Livingstons, see Elihu Goodrich to Samuel B. Webb, May 25, 1789, Ford, ed., *Correspondence of S. B. Webb*, III, 130-33.
62. Margaret Beekman Livingston to Robert R. Livingston, Apr. 1789, R. R. Livingston Papers, N.-Y. Hist. Soc.
63. In three Dutchess towns made up of yeomen who formerly were tenants, the vote in favor of Clinton was Frederickstown (40—71), Southeast (1—61), and Philipstown (25—3).

that it was possible for Federalists to win votes among the Clintonian ✓ yeomanry.

There was no secret to the Federalist near-victory. The tactic of nominating a moderate anti-Federalist and of making essentially democratic appeals against Clinton almost worked. So, too, did the unity of Federalist landlords and merchants. George Clinton, toasted as "The Favorite of the People,"[64] was re-elected because of his personal popularity and the continuing suspicions of "the patricians" among the yeomanry. But if he was to survive the battle ahead, he would have to find some new allies.

V

Despite Clinton's victory, Federalists kept control of the state senate and took the assembly, sweeping Dutchess, Columbia, Albany, and Montgomery counties which had elected anti-Federalist delegates the year before.[65] At a special session of the legislature in July, Federalists reaped the fruits of this victory: the election of two United States senators.[66] Now, however, it was they who were plagued by personal rivalries and the need to balance northern and southern interests, as well as an added obligation to take care of their defeated candidate, Robert Yates. Philip Schuyler, James Duane of New York, Richard Morris and Lewis Morris of Westchester, and Ezra L'Hommedieu of Long Island all sought the Federalist nominations. With the tables turned—Federalists divided and anti-Federalists a minority in the assembly—Governor Clinton was in a position to influence the outcome.

At first, Federalist politicking for the Senate seats was overshadowed by their obligation to Robert Yates. The upstate Federalists felt duty bound to support Yates "in order to convince the public that our only object in pushing him for the government was not merely the removal of Mr. Clinton." An alternate strategy proposed by Morgan Lewis was to choose "the old chief," Richard Morris, chief justice of the state supreme court, in order to push Yates, an associate justice, upstairs.[67] When the Federalist legislators caucused, their first

64. *N.-Y. Journal*, June 4, 1792.
65. Hammond, *Political Parties*, I, 41-42.
66. Spaulding, *George Clinton*, 190-91; Hammond, *Political Parties*, I, 44; Alexander, *James Duane*, 198-201.
67. Morgan Lewis to Alexander Hamilton, June 24, 1789, Syrett, ed., *Hamilton Papers*, V, 344-45.

step was to offer Yates the nomination as United States senator; when he refused, Philip Schuyler "waited upon him and begged him to accept an appointment," but Yates still said no, releasing the Federalists to turn to one of their own.[68]

With Yates eliminated the principal contenders were Schuyler, Duane, and King. Schuyler's record and power gave him unquestioned priority and without debate he became the unanimous first choice of the caucus. Duane as both mayor of New York and landlord near Albany had support from the northern district and southern Federalists who preferred him out of "delicacy . . . as an old inhabitant." For the second place King had support from Hamilton, New York City, and the southern district as a whole. "Our King," Robert Troup reported to Hamilton from Albany, "is as much followed and attended to by all parties as ever a new light preacher was by his congregation. . . . He is happy in his manner—his language [,] his reasoning and choice of subjects to speak upon."[69] Hamilton did his Machiavellian best for King in New York City, reporting that he "set about circulating an idea that it would be injurious to the city to have Duane elected—as the probability was, that some very unfit character would be his successor."[70] But the caucus voted 24 to 20 for Duane, and King "instantly declined all opposition to Duane—said he was ashamed of being opposed to him etc. and the matter was settled." But it was not. Two Federalist senators, Ezra L'Hommedieu of Long Island and Lewis Morris of Westchester, "both extremely anxious for their own appointment," announced they would not abide by the decision of the caucus.[71]

In the legislature the old problem of how to vote—the two houses separately or concurrently—led to another wrangle and the adoption of a new Federalist scheme which was vetoed by the Council of Revision; finally a compromise solution was worked out.[72] In the voting for senator, Schuyler was elected at once over Clintonian opposition. Then true to his offer, Clinton mobilized his supporters for King.

In his interview with King, Clinton made clear his political purpose: in effect to keep the "great families" from having a "monopoly"

68. Robert Troup to Alexander Hamilton, July 12, 1789, *ibid.*, 359-61.
69. *Ibid.*
70. Hamilton to King, July 15, 1789, *ibid.*, 362-63.
71. Troup to Hamilton, July 12, 1789, *ibid.*, 359-61.
72. Hammond, *Political Parties*, I, 43-44; Lincoln, ed., *Messages from the Governors*, II, 303 (Council veto).

of the federal offices.[73] Clinton realized that the election of two Fed-eralists, Schuyler one of them, was inevitable. The state elections demonstrated his need for new allies, especially in mercantile circles. With Federalists divided, he had a chance to get the lesser evil or at the best to throw out a line to a potential ally. To swing his followers behind an inveterate foe would have been impossible, but King, a newcomer, had made no enemies. Before serving as a Massachusetts delegate to the Constitutional Convention of 1787, King had married the daughter of John Alsop of New York City, whom he described as "a very respectable and eminent merchant." Now he had just moved to the city permanently. He had been elected to the assembly the month before near the top of the Federalist ticket and had already attracted attention as a man of uncommon abilities. Brissot de War-ville on his visit in 1788 said he "passed for the most eloquent man in the United States" yet in "his modesty he appeared ignorant of his own worth."[74] Clinton may also have known via Lansing or Yates that King's Federalism was a shade more moderate than Hamilton's; at the Philadelphia convention he had, for example, argued for the right of the states to instruct senators and against property qualifica-tions for suffrage.[75] King was therefore worth a gamble.

What Clinton could not have known was that King already had or would soon get Hamilton's support for the Senate. Hamilton had worked with King before in national affairs and had backed him for the New York assembly. When King told him of Clinton's offer, as he must have, Hamilton had even more reason to support him, for King was a sure winner.[76] That King made an agreement with Clin-ton was unlikely. He did not have to; there is no subsequent evidence of any *quid pro quo*. King was cordial—that is clear from the inter-view—but he must have realized that Clinton's predicament permitted

73. Rufus King, "Substance of a Conversation with Governor Clinton, 12 June 1789," Rufus King Papers, N.-Y. Hist. Soc. Also in King, ed., *Correspondence of Rufus King*, I, 354-56.

74. King, ed., *Correspondence of Rufus King*, I, 132; Brissot de Warville, *New Travels*, trans. and ed., Vamos and Echeverria, 146; Richard E. Welch, Jr., "Rufus King of Newburyport: The Formative Years (1767-1788)," Essex Institute *Historical Collections*, 96 (1960), 241-76.

75. King, ed., *Correspondence of Rufus King*, I, ch. 16; Jane Butzner, ed., *Constitutional Chaff—Rejected Suggestions at the Constitutional Convention of 1787, with Explanatory Argument* (N.Y., 1941), 27, 86, 114, 154.

76. For Hamilton's participation in the meetings at which King was nominated to the assembly see footnote 33 above; for Hamilton and King at the Constitutional Convention at Philadelphia, see Mitchell, *Alexander Hamilton*, I, 407, 409, 411.

the Governor no alternative; all King had to do was accept the support when it came.

In the state assembly the motion for King was introduced by Cornelius Schoonmaker of Ulster, a Clintonian lieutenant, and the anti-Federalist bloc voted for him. On the first ballot King was defeated. Schoonmaker then nominated Lewis Morris, the dissident Federalist senator, a lesser landlord of Westchester, who presumably might perform the same function that Clinton envisioned for King. Morris failed and after two whole days of balloting, King was finally chosen by a coalition of Federalists and anti-Federalists.[77]

If Clinton's goal was only minimal, to prevent the Livingstons and Schuylers from cornering the two Senate seats, he had succeeded. If he expected King to deviate from orthodox Federalism, however, he must have been disappointed, for in his years in the Senate King performed as a thorough-going Hamiltonian. In any case, Clinton's maneuver revealed in a flash the desperate plight of the Governor and his party. They had retreated from one defeat to another since the summer of 1788: from the debacle at Poughkeepsie, to the collapse of the movement for a second convention, to a stalemate over presidential electors, to a poor showing in the congressional elections, to a near defeat in the gubernatorial elections. In July 1789 they were backed into a corner where they had to choose among rival Federalists for the Senate. And with the national government already underway at New York City the threats to the anti-Federalist future had only begun.

77. *Journal of the Assembly of the State of New York*, 13th Sess. (special meeting), 22-25; *Journal of the Senate of N.Y.*, 13th Sess. (special meeting), 15-16.

CHAPTER 7

Anti-Federalists Disarmed:

The New Government

1789-1790

On the defensive, divided, almost defeated, the New York anti-Federalists were all but disarmed by the operations of the new federal government in its first year. Their predictions about the new colossus had been dire; Federalists not only failed to fulfill them but went far to appease and undermine anti-Federalist opinion. As a result, when the first test of Federalist policies came in the congressional elections of the spring of 1790, Hamilton was close to his goal of "breaking up" the anti-Federalist party.

I

The new ship of state slid down the ways on a sea of good will from New Yorkers. As the President-elect's barge moved across the Hudson from New Jersey to the city, "the claps—the shouts—the huzzas from the surrounding thousands exceeded all descriptions. I declare to you," David Gelston wrote an anti-Federalist friend in Suffolk, "I never felt such strong emotions upon any public occasion."[1] Only a few iconoclasts resisted the hero worship of George Washington. According to General John Armstrong, someone drew "a caricature . . .

1. David Gelston to John Smith, Apr. 27, 1789, John Smith Papers, N.-Y. Hist. Soc.

called 'The Entry,' full of very disloyal and profane illusions. It represents the General mounted on an ass, and in the arms of his man Billy—Humphreys leading the Jack and chanting hosannas and birthday odes."² But such irreverence was not typical of the anti-Federalists.

At the inaugural, the enormous crowd swelled by country folk from Westchester and Long Island stood hushed as Chancellor Livingston delivered the oath. When Livingston stepped forward to shout "Long live George Washington, President of the United States, . . . all the bells in the city rang out a peal of joy, and the assembled multitude set forth a universal shout."³ Greenleaf reported the momentous events with enthusiasm,⁴ and Governor Clinton, contrary to Hamilton's accusation, was conspicuous in his hospitality to Washington, his old comrade in arms. He helped plan the city's welcome, was there to escort Washington through the streets when his barge landed, entertained him at dinner that evening, offered him his house —which Washington politely declined, attended the inaugural, and in the months ahead appeared with him on many occasions, public and private.⁵

Others who were fighting the Federalists at the polls followed Clinton's lead. In the inaugural parade Marinus Willett, the city's Clintonian sheriff, was conspicuous, and General William Malcolm, chairman of Clinton's nominating committee, marched at the head of his militia brigade, followed by such Clintonian militia captains as Henry Rutgers and John Lamb. For such staunch Whigs, honoring their former commander-in-chief was an act of genuine homage. Lamb avowed that Washington was the only man he would trust with the extensive powers of the presidency.⁶ To David Gelston he was "the great farmer—the great statesman—the great general—the President General—in short the greatest man in the world."⁷ And could George Clinton's feelings have been much different? Had he not named a son

2. General John Armstrong to Horatio Gates, n.d., cited in Griswold, *The Republican Court*, 122-23.

3. Cited from contemporaries by Thomas E. V. Smith, *The City of New York in the Year of Washington's Inauguration, 1789* (N.Y., 1889), 221-32.

4. *N.-Y. Journal*, Apr. 23, 30, May 7, 14, 1789.

5. Spaulding, *George Clinton*, 194-95; Stokes, *Iconography of Manhattan Island*, 1239-41, 1245-46, 1248, 1255.

6. Smith, *City of New York*, 66, 225; Leake, *Memoirs of John Lamb*, 331.

7. Gelston to Smith, Apr. 27, 1789, John Smith Papers, N.-Y. Hist. Soc.; Spaulding, *George Clinton*, 101.

George Washington Clinton in '78 and a daughter Martha Washington Clinton in '83?

II

The ship of state thus afloat, Washington proceeded to reward his leading Federalist supporters in New York generously by his appointments.[8] Hamilton would be Secretary of the Treasury and through Hamilton's influence William Duer, one of the city's leading speculators in securities, would be the Assistant Secretary, the appointment being justified presumably for his past services on the old Board of Treasury. Other appointments in New York also showed Hamilton's hand: James Duane, the disappointed senatorial choice of the Federalist caucus, became a federal judge; Robert Troup, Hamilton's occasional law partner, became clerk of the federal court; and Richard Harison, associate justice of the state supreme court, became District Attorney.[9] By mid-September 1789, only two prominent New York Federalists had not been recognized—John Jay and Chancellor Livingston —and there was only one major vacancy which might attract either, Chief Justice of the United States. Gouverneur Morris, another of their conservative comrades of the Revolution, at the moment in France on behalf of Robert Morris, later would be appointed to a diplomatic mission to England.[10]

Washington also faintly appeased the Clintonians. One of the President's criteria for appointments was to avoid arbitrary removals. Over the objections of the New York Federalists Washington continued John Lamb as Collector of the Port of New York, a post he had held from the state government since 1784. Retention of Lamb offered an opportunity to demonstrate nonpartisanship, reward a well-known patriot, and undermine anti-Federalist fears. He remained in his lucrative post—his fees in 1792 alone were $8424, the highest of any collector in the country—through the decade, his politics un-

8. See Dexter Perkins, "New York and the Federal Government" in Flick, ed., *History of the State of New York*, VI, 89-90. *American State Papers: Documents, Legislative and Executive, of the Congress of the United States*, 38 vols. (Washington, 1832-61), *Miscellany*, I, 57-68.
9. Mitchell, *Alexander Hamilton*, II, 210-24, 156-57.
10. Samuel F. Bemis, *Jay's Treaty, A Study in Commerce and Diplomacy*, 2d ed. rev. (New Haven, 1962), 65. Morris, after Clintonians failed to return him to Congress in the 1780's, remained in Philadelphia but returned to New York to purchase the family home at Morrisania, in Westchester. He remained close to the New York Federalists, who on his return from Europe in 1800, elected him to the U.S. Senate.

changed but his public activity lessened by recurrent attacks of gout.[11] Washington was sensitive to the quest for status. After he rejected Sheriff Marinus Willett's petition to be United States marshal, he found a temporary position of prestige for him as commissioner to receive a visiting delegation of Indian chieftains.[12] Other Clintonians who applied for federal jobs seem to have been turned down, but at least none were turned out.

Federalists also tried to appease anti-Federalists by the passage of constitutional amendments. The strategy worked out by Madison with Washington refined the methods Jay and Hamilton had discussed to placate the New York anti-Federalists. Congress would sift the amendments proposed by the ratifying conventions, and submit them to the states, thus short-circuiting the movement for a second convention. And the amendments would be only of the libertarian sort, leaving the "structure and stamina"—Washington's phrase—of the federal government intact. The strategy was designed, as William Grayson, Virginia's anti-Federalist senator, charged, to be "an anodyne to the discontented."[13]

Congress received the New York legislature's petition for a second convention and buried it, settling down to a protracted debate on Madison's amendments lasting from May through September.[14] New York's anti-Federalists were inactive in the debate but took every opportunity to vote for the proposals their brethren had offered at Poughkeepsie the year before, for example, to curb congressional intervention in state elections and to limit direct taxation.[15] Some Fed-

11. Leake, *Memoirs of John Lamb*, 336-37; *American State Papers, Miscellany*, I, 57-58, 60-62.

12. Gaillard Hunt, *Calendar of Applications and Recommendations for Office During the Presidency of George Washington* (Washington, 1901) for applications of Clintonians arranged alphabetically: see Abraham Bancker, John Lamb, Nathanial Lawrence, Jr., Marinus Willett; Marinus Willett to James Duane, July 11, 1789, Duane Papers, N.-Y. Hist. Soc.; for Willett and Indians, see *N.-Y. Journal*, July 23, 30, Aug. 3, 17, 1790; for retention of Sebastian Bauman as postmaster, see Leonard White, *The Federalists: A Study in Administrative History* (N.Y., 1948), 182, 261.

13. Washington to Madison, [May ?] 1789, John C. Fitzpatrick, ed., *The Writings of George Washington*, 39 vols. (Washington, 1931-44), XXX, 341-42; William Grayson to Patrick Henry, June 12, 1789, W. W. Henry, ed., *Patrick Henry*, III, 391.

14. For the legislative history, Edward Dumbauld, *The Bill of Rights and What It Means Today* (Norman, Okla., 1957), 35-50; Robert Rutland, *The Birth of the Bill of Rights, 1776-1791* (Chapel Hill, N.C., 1955), ch. 9.

15. Joseph Gales and W. W. Seaton, eds., *The Debates and Proceedings in the Congress of the United States, 1789-1824*, 42 vols. (Washington, 1834-56), hereinafter cited as *Annals*, 1st Cong., 1st Sess. For Laurance's motions and opinions, see

eralists wanted to make no concessions to the opposition; Congressman John Laurance sneered at "speculative amendments" while editor John Fenno found Madison's proposals "dangerous in the experiment." In the middle was Congressman Egbert Benson of Dutchess, a member of the committee which prepared the House's final proposals and a conservative Whig long skilled in placating radicals in the state government.[16]

During this debate anti-Federalist polemicists throughout New York were quiet. In the city Greenleaf recorded the discussion in Congress without comment; from May to September he ran only one letter defending Madison from his critics. The old anti-Federalist pamphlets of 1787-88 which he continued to advertise presumably served the same purpose.[17]

At Albany Abraham Yates prepared a lengthy opus elaborating a conspiracy thesis about the origins of the Constitution.[18] In his prolix style Yates tried to show that the Tories had "joined the Whigs . . . under the [name] of federal Men" and schemed "to get the Power out of the Hands of the People"; that the Superintendent of Finance under the Articles of Confederation had plotted "with such art and secrecy with Members of Congress" to centralize finance and thereby centralize government; that there was "a Combination" between the army officers and congressmen to fund the debt and get half pay for the army; that Congress had become "a center of Intrigue and cabal . . . progressively to enlarge the powers of Congress at the express of the Liberties of the People"; that at Philadelphia the centralizers "turned a Convention into a Conspiracy and under the epithet Federal . . . destroyed the Confederation"; and that the "American Rulers, if not worse than British, are every way as likely to abuse their powers, to act the wolf in sheep's cloathing." All this led to the

363, 733, 740, 754, 774-75. For votes, Aug. 18, 21, 22, 24. On five recorded votes on specific proposals the New York delegation divided. For Fenno, see N.Y. *Gazette of the United States*, June 3, July 22, Aug. 1, 1789.

16. Dumbauld, *The Bill of Rights*, 30, 26-30, 189-98.

17. *N.-Y. Journal*, June 18, 25, July 30, Aug. 20, Sept. 10, 17. For articles in the N.Y. *Daily Advertiser* in support of amendments, see "L.," July 14 and two letters Aug. 17, 18, 1789.

18. In "Essays on Various Political Subjects," Abraham Yates Papers, N.Y. Pub. Lib., edited by Staughton Lynd as "Abraham Yates's History of the Movement for the United States Constitution," *Wm. and Mary Qtly.*, 3d Ser., 20 (1963), 223-45. I find no evidence that this appeared in pamphlet or serialized form in the *Albany Register*, the most likely newspaper or *N.-Y. Journal*. Nor is it marked with a date as are the published articles in Yates's "Rough Hewer" notebook.

conclusion that "we [should] leave not a stone unturned to obtain the Necessary amendments to the new System, to avert the curse (Next to that of Adam) which we will Entail upon our Descendants without amendments." But after considerable labor searching the journals of the Continental Congress, the Bible, and the writings of Raynal and Montesquieu, Yates seems to have put his tract on the shelf—unpublished.

When the House's seventeen amendments emerged from the Senate reduced to twelve, they were a far cry from what the Poughkeepsie circular letter had proposed. New York's suggestions were, as Edward Dumbauld observed, "perhaps the least influential of any states." Federalists were relieved, recognizing, as "Pacificus" wrote, that they "can do little good or hurt as to the merits of the Constitution." Even Fenno came around; the "concession" was granted, he wrote.[19] Greenleaf published the amendments in 12-point type, an unusually large print. When the legislature convened in January 1790, Governor Clinton transmitted them without comment.[20] Abraham Yates, however, was wrathful; he condemned the guarantees of individual liberty as "unimportant and trivial" when compared with the other proposals of the ratifying convention which had been "intended either to explain or to restrict certain dangerous powers expressly or impliedly lodged in Congress" concerning elections, the militia, the laying of poll taxes, direct taxes, and excises. Where were these restrictions? Even the amendment on salaries would still allow "the enormous wages of six dollars a day" already voted by congressmen.[21] But Yates seemed almost alone in his protest. The state senate adopted unanimously a favorable report from a committee chaired by John Williams, a "non-adopting anti" at Poughkeepsie; the assembly followed suit, also with little debate. New York passed eleven of the twelve amendments, rejecting the congressional restriction on salaries, probably as an inadequate measure.[22] There was no rejoicing among the Clintonians. The leaders knew that the Federalists had disposed of what the New York anti-Federalists had proposed, but they were

19. *N.-Y. Journal*, Sept. 1789; N.Y. *Gazette of the United States*, Dec. 23, 1789; "Pacificus," N.Y. *Daily Advertiser*, Aug. 17, 1789.
20. Lincoln, ed., *Messages from the Governors*, II, 304.
21. "Rough Hewer" notebook drafts of two articles, dated Mar. 15, Mar. 22, 1790 but possibly published earlier in *Albany Register*, Yates Papers, N.Y. Pub. Lib.
22. *Journal of the Senate of N.Y.*, 13th Sess., 9; *Journal of the Assembly of N.Y.*, 13th Sess., 19; *Laws of State of N.Y.*, 13th Sess., ch. 15 (Feb. 27, 1790).

unwilling to parade their defeat publicly. They had been out-maneuvered.

The "tone" set by the new administration for its public image also reflected the lessons of moderation which New York's "aristos" had learned from New York's "demos," contrary to the impressions of the salty Pennsylvania democrat Senator William Maclay.[23] Federalists, Hamilton confided, wanted "a pretty high tone" yet "not so high as in the abstract might be desirable"; "the notions of equality" in the country were "too general and too strong" for that.[24] Robert R. Livingston, in a paper on etiquette, also warned the President against keeping the "utmost distance" from the people—he should mingle and converse at dinners so that he might have access to many sources of information. And for a title, "Supreme Magistrate and President of the United States" was better than "His Most Christian Majesty."[25]

The amalgam of measures adopted blended the aristocratic and democratic. The simple title "President of the United States," the choice of the House, won out, but in the Senate's chamber in the newly remodeled "Federal Hall" the president's chair was "elevated three feet above the floor and [placed] under a rich canopy of crimson damask. The curtains of the windows and coverings of the chairs of the senators [were] of the same color." President Washington held levees and official dinners marked by a chilling formality but also by a relative public absence of pomp. Yet the levees "were numerously attended by all that was fashionable, elegant and refined in society. . . . None were admitted . . . but those who had either a right by official station to be there, or were entitled to the privilege by established merit and character; and full dress was required of all."[26] John Fenno, publisher of the new *Gazette of the United States,* began reporting the women present at Martha Washington's reception as Lady Kitty Duer, Lady Sterling, Mrs. Livingston of Clermont, and The Lady of his Excellency the Governor.[27] When the President appeared in

23. William Maclay, *The Journal of William Maclay* (N.Y., 1927), 2-27, *passim.*
24. Hamilton to Washington, May 5, 1789, Syrett, ed., *Hamilton Papers,* V, 335-37.
25. Robert R. Livingston to George Washington, May 2, 1789, an eight-page letter marked unsent but with reference to a continuing conversation on the subject with Washington; "On the Title Proper to be Given to the President," 2-pp. MS draft, R. R. Livingston Papers, N.-Y. Hist. Soc.
26. A Col. Stone cited in Griswold, *The Republican Court,* 165n.; for the Senate chamber, see *ibid.,* 119-22.
27. *Gazette of the United States,* May 30, June 3, 1789.

public, he might board his canary-colored carriage led by four or six white stallions, complete with postillion and livery. Yet he could also be seen strolling through city streets almost alone. The residence he chose, Samuel Osgood's house, could hardly be distinguished from neighboring dwellings, and the President astonished foreign visitors because he had but a handful of footmen and servants.[28]

Understandably the reaction to the "tone" of the new government depended upon what part of the elephant one chose to see. From Albany, "A Republican" suggested that we "leave to the sons and daughters of corrupted Europe their levees, Drawing Rooms, Routs, Drums and Tornedos." And "Pro Republica" reminded Fenno that the Constitution forbade titles. An Orange County citizen sniffed at the influence of the Cincinnati, a self-conceived "nobility" who might "riot in luxuries—build FEDERAL CITIES in every state on this side of the Allegheny mountains, and mimick the splendour of European courts."[29] Washington, on the other hand, went unassailed. The President's lack of pomp led a fledgling New York City poet to sing the praises of

> The worthy patriot [who] shunn'd a vast parade
> And unattended, sought the silent shade.

It prompted the city's playwright producer, William Dunlap, to have a character in one of his plays say of Washington: "Poor men love him just as he were poor."[30] A scribe in the anti-Federalist *Albany Register* believed the government was "the landholder's government" because at its head stood "one of the most distinguished landholders and cultivators," "the farmer of Mount Vernon."[31]

In any case what influenced public opinion was laws, not levees. Here, too, as Congress settled down to measures necessary to keep the new ship of state afloat, Federalists showed their skill at keeping things on a balanced keel. The revenue measures were remarkable for accommodating the interests of both merchant and mechanic sup-

28. Bernard Faÿ, *George Washington, Republican Aristocrat* (Boston, 1931), 248, 254-55.
29. "A Republican," *Albany Register*, June 8, 1789; "Pro Republica," *ibid.*, June 6; *Goshen Repository*, Dec. 22, 1789.
30. N.-Y. *Daily Advertiser*, Nov. 13, 1789, cited in Smith, *City of New York*, 243; Dunlap, cited in Martha Lamb, *History of the City of New York: Its Origin, rise, and Progress*, 3 vols. (N.Y., 1877-96), II, 352.
31. An unsigned paragraph, *Albany Register*, Feb. 22, 1790.

porters of Federalism in New York.[32] The mechanic interest raised the demand for protective tariffs in the celebrations for the Constitution, at public meetings, and in a special petition to Congress sent by the General Society of Mechanics and Tradesmen of New York, probably the first of its kind.[33] The merchant supporters of Federalism as importers of British manufactured goods were hostile to protection, but as public creditors wanted to assure an adequate revenue to the treasury in order to fund the national debt.[34] Moreover, as a group closely tied to British interests, they were anxious to defeat James Madison's dangerous proposal to discriminate against British shipping.[35] By contrast, the New York anti-Federalists for many years had favored just such discrimination against British bottoms when Governor Clinton sponsored it.[36] But they showed relatively little interest in protection for manufactures.[37]

In Congress, New York City Federalist John Laurance accomplished the feat of speaking for all the diverse interests of his constituency. He pleaded for lower duties on rum, Madeira wine, and molasses (imports of the city's West Indies merchants) and for higher duties on beer, candles, hemp, and cordage (all manufactured by New York artisans). He argued for lower duties on behalf of the poor, "that part of the community who are least able to bear it," and argued against tonnage discrimination as a device that "will destroy agriculture itself." The state's three anti-Federalist representatives, all from rural areas, were silent on the question of tariffs and divided

32. For the legislative history, see Edward Channing, *A History of the United States*, 6 vols. (N.Y., 1905-25), IV, 60-64.

33. For the petition, see *American State Papers: Finance*, I, 8-9; see N.-Y. *Daily Advertiser*, Aug. 2, 1788, for protectionist slogans in the 1788 celebration; Poughkeepsie *Country Journal*, Sept. 16, 1788, for an address on manufactures to the Constitutional Society of Poughkeepsie; Frank Monaghan and Marvin Lowenthal, *This Was New York: The Nation's Capital in 1789* (Garden City, N.Y., 1943), 76, for a resolution of the Peruke Makers Society; Smith, *City of New York*, 115, for a resolution of the German Society.

34. For analysis of this factor, see Charles Maurice de Talleyrand, "Observations on Speculation in Land in the United States of America" in Hans Huth and William Pugh, trans. and ed., *Talleyrand in America as a Financial Promoter, 1794-1796: Unpublished Letters and Memoirs* (American Historical Association, Annual Report for the Year 1941 [Washington, 1942]), III, 151.

35. Irving Brant, *James Madison: Father of the Constitution, 1787-1800* (Indianapolis, 1941), ch. 19.

36. Lincoln, ed., *Messages from the Governors*, II, 251-56.

37. For a comment by Hamilton on this in 1794, see a published MS fragment in Charles A. Beard, *Economic Origins of Jeffersonian Democracy* (N.Y., 1915), 246-47.

on tonnage discrimination.[38] The revenue bills that emerged were a compromise: a mildly protective tariff on some imports, others free, and tonnage discrimination defeated. Thus did Congressman Laurance demonstrate one of the secrets of Federalist success in maintaining the coalition of merchant and mechanic in New York City.

This is not to suggest that Federalist national policies removed all the issues of 1787-88 from New York politics; a number of minor matters kept them alive. All had to do with setting precedents for the operation of the federal ship of state. How much power, for example, did the president have? Did he have the authority to remove officials in the executive department? If he did, was it by virtue of a constitutional or legislative grant? Federalists advocated an "energetic" executive and "confidence" in the president while anti-Federalists were suspicious of a broad delegation of authority.[39] Congressman Benson helped to draft the bills establishing the executive department which he, Laurance, and Peter Sylvester defended and Hathorn and Van Rensselaer opposed.[40] In whose name should federal judicial writs be issued, in the name of the president or of the United States of America? Federalists favored the former; anti-Federalists, the latter. Although "apparently unimportant," DeWitt Clinton wrote his uncle, it "smells strongly of monarchy . . . a federal process beginning with George Washington by the grace of God will make the American President as important in law forms as the British King." Again the New York congressmen divided three and three.[41] How high should congressional salaries be, and should senators and representatives receive equal pay? Federalists wanted salaries which would attract men of talents and elevate the select Senate; anti-Federalists championed "republican simplicity" and equality for the "democratical" branch with the Senate. The New Yorkers voted more or less as might be expected.[42]

Each of the policies set by Federalists in the spring and summer of 1789—titles, presidential etiquette, revenue, amendments, the forms

38. *Annals*, 1st Cong., 1st Sess., Apr. 14, 1789, 131, 133-35, 150, 153; Apr. 24, 205-6.
39. For analysis, see White, *The Federalists*, 20-25, 88-96; for the debate, see *Annals*, 1st Cong., 1st Sess., I, 473-608 *passim*. For conflicting positions see Maclay, *Journal*, 101, 107-10, and Fisher Ames to G. Minot, June 23, 1789, Seth Ames, ed., *Works of Fisher Ames*, 2 vols. (Boston, 1854), I, 54-55.
40. *Annals*, 1st Cong., 1st Sess., I, 412, 779-84.
41. DeWitt to Dr. Charles Clinton, Feb. 8, 1790, DeWitt Clinton Papers, N.-Y. Hist. Soc.; *Annals*, 1st Cong., 1st Sess., 949, 951.
42. *Annals*, 1st Cong., 1st Sess., 715, 923-24.

ɔf government, salaries—involved questions of principle. Yet the equal division in the New York delegation in Congress was not reflected in New York public opinion. DeWitt Clinton expressed alarm and Abraham Yates snorted, but when the chips were down, the state legislature stood by the pledge it had made to President Washington in July 1789: "to afford you our united aid and support."[43] Anti-Federalists voted with Federalists to turn over the state-operated lighthouse at Sandyhook to the federal government, to authorize sheriffs to receive prisoners accused of federal crimes in county prisons, and even to make a $5000 appropriation to improve Federal Hall in New York City in order to keep the national capital in the state.[44] Madison's report to Jefferson in France that the work of the new government was "extinguishing the honest fears which considered the system as dangerous to republicanism" could easily apply to New York.[45]

III

In 1789 Washington and Hamilton sowed but one real tare in New York. Earlier in the year Chancellor Robert R. Livingston and his brothers Edward and John, all of the lower manor, and four members of the upper manor branch of the family formally solicited federal appointments from Washington.[46] The Chancellor would have been satisfied to become Chief Justice, Secretary of State, or Secretary of Treasury, probably in that order of preference. At the end of May the President prepared him for a rejection; in June he confided to Livingston's sister, Janet Montgomery—wife of the Revolutionary general—his "fear of making so many appointments for this state." On September 26 when he nominated John Jay as Chief Justice, it was clear that neither Robert nor his brothers from the lower manor would be recognized.[47] On the other hand, the upper manor clan

43. *Journal of the Senate of N.Y.*, 13th Sess., 1st meeting, July 14, 1789, 11-12. See also N.Y. *Daily Advertiser*, Aug. 5, 1789.

44. *Laws of the State of N.Y.*, 13th Sess., chs. 3, 15, 25.

45. James Madison to Thomas Jefferson, May 27, 1789, in Boyd, ed., *Papers of Jefferson*, XV, 153.

46. See Hunt, *Calendar of Applications*, 76, for applications of John, Henry B., and Walter Livingston of the upper manor and John R. Livingston of the lower manor; for correspondence on job seeking, see Robert R. Livingston to Oliver Ellsworth, Oct. 21, 1788, John to Robert R. Livingston, Feb. 3, 1789 (both *in re* John's desire to be secretary of the Senate), Edward to Robert R. Livingston, June 7, Nov. 12, 1789 (*in re* Edward's application for Undersecretary of State), R. R. Livingston Papers, N.-Y. Hist. Soc.

47. Robert R. Livingston to Washington, Oct. 21, 1788, May 2, 1789, Washington to Livingston, May 31, 1789 (indicating a letter of application from Livingston May 15), Janet Montgomery to Livingston, June and July, 1789, R. R. Livingston

was rewarded, not through the immediate members who applied, but through Jay, Samuel Osgood, and James Duane, all of whom had married Livingstons.

The Chancellor, although a man of uncommon pride, was within the bounds of justifiable egotism in believing that his services to the country—and party—entitled him to high office as much as any other New Yorker.[48] Washington could hardly have believed that in appointing Jay and Duane, he was recognizing the Clermont branch; during the Revolution he had visited Clermont, and the jealousy between the upper and lower manor could hardly have been lost on a Virginia planter.[49] Nor was the reason given, the political danger of giving all the plums to one state, relevant; a place might have been found for the Chancellor earlier. In truth, Livingston was neither as able nor as "sound" in finance as Hamilton; in foreign affairs, his experience as Secretary was no match for Jefferson's after his years in Europe. As Livingston suspected, Hamilton had blocked him for high office, a fact that the Secretary of the Treasury unwittingly admitted two years later when he explained to the Chancellor's brother-in-law that in 1789 he had tried to get Livingston appointed either as Minister to Britain or loan agent.[50]

The Chancellor was the last man in the state of New York to be asked to swallow so bitter a pill. He was shocked. In the opening months of the new government, he had administered the oath to Washington, dined with him frequently, and been close enough to offer advice.[51] His pride was hurt. The other members of the Federalist triumvirate of the Poughkeepsie convention, Jay and Hamilton, had been recognized; so too had the other leading estate holders of the Hudson: Schuyler, Duane, Gouverneur Morris. Even the upstart merchant, William Duer, had been appointed, and all on the advice of a West Indian of illegitimate birth, a New Yorker for less than fifteen years, a parvenu who had married into the gentry. Hamil-

Papers, N.-Y. Hist. Soc. Madison heard that Livingston wanted the Treasury position; see Madison to Jefferson, May 27, 1789, in Boyd, ed., Papers of Jefferson, XV, 153.

48. Dangerfield, Chancellor Robert R. Livingston, 243-47.

49. For Washington's criteria of appointments, see James Hart, The American Presidency in Action, 1789 (N.Y., 1948), 112-22; for his visit, see Dangerfield, Chancellor Robert R. Livingston, 194.

50. White, The Federalists, 263; Morgan Lewis to Robert R. Livingston, Jan. 24, 1791, Livingston to Lewis, Jan. 27, 1791, R. R. Livingston Papers, N.-Y. Hist. Soc.

51. Duer, Reminiscences of an Old Yorker, 68-69; Leake, Memoirs of John Lamb, II, 371.

on knew how much a lucrative appointment meant to Livingston; he Chancellor had confessed as much when he joined Hamilton in 787, bidding adieu to Clinton. Worst of all, perhaps, was Livingston's jealousy of Jay, his friend since college days at King's, his ormer law partner, and his successor as Secretary of Foreign Affairs. Livingston considered Jay his inferior in every respect; now Jay was elevated to a judicial post higher than his own.[52] Within six months of Jay's appointment in September 1789 the Chancellor was finding ault with Hamilton's policies.

The vacancies created in state offices by federal appointments and elections gave Governor Clinton an opportunity to build his own political fences.[53] In May 1789 he replaced Attorney General Egbert Benson, elected to Congress, with Richard Varick whom he had appointed recorder of New York after the war. Varick, while a leading Federalist, was a prominent lawyer from a middling Dutch New Jersey family.[54] In September Clinton moved in Varick as mayor, and as attorney general appointed Aaron Burr, the mild anti-Federalist of 788 who had supported Yates in '89; Burr was regarded by some Federalists as "the most rising young man in the state."[55] Varick's former job as recorder went to Samuel Jones, a leader of the "adopting" faction at Poughkeepsie with ties to Hamilton that would ultimately make him a Federalist. At the same time Clinton appointed John Lansing mayor of Albany. His major moves of the year as a whole were to his "right." Clinton was trying to attach to his interest outright Federalists (Rufus King and Varick), middle-of-the-roaders (Burr), and conservative "adopting" anti-Federalists (Jones). At the same time he was reassuring his loyal followers (Lansing). What the Governor would do when Chancellor Livingston's personal pique found political expression remained to be seen; for the time being, there was no reason to make any gestures in the direction of Clermont.

IV

Late in 1789, from his vantage point at New York City, Washington observed that "the opposition is either no more or hides its

52. Monaghan, *John Jay*, 304-5; "To Timothy Tickler" by "Aristedes" [Robert R. Livingston], *N.-Y. Journal*, Apr. 4, 1792, discussed below, ch. 13, sec. IV.
53. Hammond, *Political Parties*, I, 42-43.
54. Pomerantz, *New York an American City*, 43-44; letter from Albany Federal Committee, probably by Philip Schuyler to John Jay and Richard Varick, Jan. 31, 789, Schuyler Papers, N.Y. Pub. Lib.
55. Parton, *Aaron Burr*, I, 134.

head."[56] In April 1790, when the opposition showed its head in th
second congressional elections, Federalists all but cut it off.[57] The
not only re-elected their three incumbents, but also defeated two o
the three anti-Federalists and came within hailing distance of takin
the Ulster-Orange district, the Clintonian stronghold.[58]

The three Federalist incumbents all won by wider margins tha
in 1789. In the Dutchess-northern Westchester district, Egbert Benso
stretched a lead of a scant ten votes to 256 with strong support fron
townships influenced by the Clermont Livingstons and the Wes
chester Van Cortlandts.[59] In the Columbia-eastern district, Peter Sy
vester widened his plurality from one hundred to five hundred vote
In New York City no one even challenged John Laurance. The Fed
eralist accusation that the anti-Federalists would again run Joh
Broome "under an affected zeal for the mercantile interest" prove
baseless. Although "mechanic" and "merchant" factions of the part
split over assembly nominations after holding "meeting after mee
ing," they had no trouble uniting behind Laurance. The "old stand
ing committee" of the anti-Federalists—Gelston, Lamb, Smith, Jone
Jonathan Lawrence—caucused but decided to concentrate on electin
Jones and Gelston to the state senate from the southern district as
whole. They endorsed a ticket headed by Laurance and Federalis
candidates for the assembly on both "mechanic" and "merchant"
tickets.[60] Laurance, as a result, ended up with 691 votes to 11 fo
Melancton Smith who was not even talked about in the campaign.[6]

In the three districts that had returned anti-Federalists in 178
the party was plagued by dissension and desertion. On Long Islan

56. Washington to Gouverneur Morris, sometime before Dec. 1789, cited i
Hart, *The American Presidency*, 442-43.

57. The elections were held in April, after Hamilton introduced his Report o
Public Credit (Jan. 9, 1790) and after Madison's proposal for discrimination i
funding was defeated (Feb. 22) but before assumption was defeated on its fir
test (Apr. 12). It was too early for much news of these financial measures to b
circulated and much too early for their meaning to be clear. The election there
fore is not a test of Hamilton's financial policies, with the possible exception c
New York City where Congress was located. Newspapers indicate that financi
issues were not featured in the campaign.

58. For returns, see Appendix, Table 5.

59. *Poughkeepsie Journal*, May 29, 1790; N.Y. *Daily Advertiser*, May 21, 1790.

60. David Gelston to John Smith, Apr. 17 (with internal additions dated Ap
19, 20), Apr. 21, 1790, John Smith Papers, N.-Y. Hist. Soc.

61. For notice of nominations, see N.Y. *Daily Advertiser*, Apr. 17, 1790; fc
election appeals, see three broadsides: "A Federal Elector," Mar. 4, 1790, "On
and All," Mar. 4, 1790, and "A Fast Friend," Apr. 20, 29, 1790, N.Y. Pub. Lib
for returns, see *N.-Y. Journal*, May 25, 1790.

where General William Floyd won without opposition in 1789 there were at least two anti-Federalists among the five candidates for the office. James Townshend, a Federalist (perhaps a former anti-Federalist), won with 592 votes; Floyd had 319; Thomas Tredwell, an anti-Federalist leader at the Poughkeepsie convention, 284. The latter two split Suffolk, the anti-Federalist stronghold. Neither party showed any unity.[62] In the western Albany-frontier district the anti-Federalist incumbent, Jeremiah Van Rensselaer, lost to James Gordon by a three-to-two margin. Gordon of Saratoga County owed his victory to the influence of Philip Schuyler and the growing power of Federalist land proprietors on the frontier.[63] In the Ulster-Orange district, where the vote in 1789 had been unanimously anti-Federalist, Peter Van Gaasbeck, a wealthy Kingston merchant and budding Federalist, challenged Cornelius Schoonmaker, a firm Clintonian. Schoonmaker won, 898-753, only because Orange and southern Ulster stood by him, but two-thirds of Ulster, in particular the north near the port of Kingston, backed Van Gaasbeck.[64] Two years later Van Gaasbeck would win as a full-fledged Federalist.

The only thorn in the Federalist side was in Columbia County where the customary rivalry of the upper manor Livingstons with Schuyler reappeared. In 1789 the upper manor, lower manor, and Schuyler interest had maintained an uneasy alliance, electing Peter Sylvester, Schuyler's candidate, over Matthew Adgate, an arch anti-Federalist. In 1790 John Livingston of the upper manor insisted on the Federalist nomination; he had been nursing a grudge against Schuyler since their bitter wrangle over county nominations in 1788.[65] The Schuyler interest and commercial Hudson stood by Sylvester. Chancellor Livingston, however, was in no mood to back an upper manor cousin. The Chancellor had serious reservations about Hamil-

62. *N.-Y. Journal*, May 21, 1790; N.Y. *Daily Advertiser*, May 19, 20, 1790; Townshend was defeated for election to the Poughkeepsie convention in 1788 by an anti-Federalist slate and identified as a Federalist; see Spaulding, *New York in the Critical Period*, 225; Hammond, *Political Parties*, I, 38, identifies him as an anti-Federalist in 1789. The fact that both Floyd, who voted anti-Federalist in Congress, and Tredwell, a strong anti-Federalist leader, ran against Townshend suggests that in 1790 he was a Federalist. He died in 1790 before taking office; Tredwell was elected in 1791.

63. *N.-Y. Journal*, May 25, 1790; N.Y. *Daily Advertiser*, May 22, 26, 1790.

64. Conrad E. Elmendorph to Cornelius Schoonmaker, Apr. 12, 1790, Van Gaasbeck Papers, Kingston Senate House; *Poughkeepsie Journal*, May 29, 1790; *N.-Y. Journal*, May 25, 1790.

65. Philip Schuyler to Robert R. Livingston, Mar. 29, 1788, R. R. Livingston Papers, N-Y. Hist. Soc.

ton's "funding system" then before Congress, but he had not yet broken with Hamilton or Schuyler. He was at the peak of his feud with the upper manor over Roeliff Jansen Kill. The two families were not on speaking terms. "The ties of friendship are now broken between us (except as relates to the old Gent)," Robert, lord of the manor, the Chancellor wrote, and "I am perfectly indifferent about their renewal."[66]

The anti-Federalists did not put up a man of their own. Sylvester as a result defeated Livingston more easily in 1790 (1712-1218) than he had defeated his anti-Federalist opponent the year before (1628-1501). He carried Columbia County by a narrow margin (914-855).[67] Livingston had the upper manor in his pocket (374-37) but lost the lower manor (6-37) and the anti-landlord town of Hillsdale (68-151), which seems to have preferred a Federalist lawyer to a Federalist landlord. Sylvester built his margin on the basis of the dependent vote Schuyler and Van Rensselaer gave him in Albany (562-58) and a minority in Washington (236-305). Philip Schuyler, despite the victory of his candidate, was enraged at the upper manor Livingstons, completely puzzled that "people in a station in life which should put them far above what is mean low and unworthy should suffer themselves to be made the instruments of by a set who only despise them."[68] But he had no bone to pick with the Chancellor or his clan.[69]

In the six districts of the state as a whole the anti-Federalist vote plummeted. In the 1789 congressional race, out of a total vote of about 12,000, the anti-Federalists had about 6000, the Federalists slightly fewer. In 1790, of about 9200 votes cast, Federalists had 6000, anti-Federalists, by the most generous estimate, 3200. In New York City voters had no choice; on Long Island they had a confused choice; in Columbia they could choose between two Federalists. Elsewhere, in the Dutchess, Ulster-Orange, and the Albany-western districts the anti-Federalist candidates stood for their discredited platform of 1788.

66. Robert R. Livingston to Peter Van Schaack, Jan. 20, 1790, Margaret Beekman Livingston to Robert R. Livingston, Dec. 15, 1790, *ibid.*; Dangerfield, *Chancellor Robert R. Livingston*, 215-18, 240-41, 249-50.
67. *N.-Y. Journal*, May 25, 31, 1790; N.Y. *Daily Advertiser*, May 25, 26, 1790.
68. Philip Schuyler to Stephen Van Rensselaer, May 29, 1790, Schuyler Papers, N.Y. State Lib.
69. For continuing close relationship to Hamilton, see Morgan Lewis to Hamilton, July 26, Aug. 9, Oct. 10, 1790, Brockholst Livingston to Hamilton, Apr. 4, Syrett, ed., *Hamilton Papers*, VI, 347-48, 511, 553, VII, 106-7; for Brockholst Livingston as Fedralist senatorial candidate, see *N.-Y. Journal*, Apr. 22, June 4, 1790.

Anti-Federalist voters either stayed at home or switched their allegiance. The conclusion is inescapable that insofar as New York opinion is concerned, historians have exaggerated the impact of the allegedly "aristocratic" policies of the Federalists' first year in national office. In New York anti-Federalist supporters turned increasingly from their frustrated leaders to Federalist candidates. If it was true, as Jefferson recalled twenty years later, that on his arrival in New York City early in 1790 "politics was the chief topic of conversation and a preference for a kingly over a republican government evidently the favorite subject,"[70] such talk must have been confined to private dinner tables, not the public coffee houses, country taverns, or newspapers. If Federalists were enlarging the powers of the executive, it was by such means as judicial writs which DeWitt Clinton conceded were "apparently unimportant." And though Congressman Laurance might sneer at "speculative amendments" Federalists did come up with the Bill of Rights.

The political frustration of the old anti-Federalists was epitomized by the petulance of Abraham Yates. Yates's polemic against the proposed amendments was abortive; a diatribe against Hamiltonian finance in the spring of 1790 was feeble. In the election of 1790 he decided not to run for the seat in the state senate he had held since 1777—the Federalist tide in the new western district would have swept him under. Instead, he reverted to his old tactic of refusing to take an oath to support the federal government demanded of him by the election inspectors. He had refused in the 1789 election, been denied the vote, and publicly acknowledged his mistake.[71] In 1790 two Federalist inspectors again demanded that he take an oath upholding the Constitution. He again refused and again was not allowed to vote. This time he instituted a lawsuit against the inspectors, retaining Aaron Burr as counsel. The inspectors then apologized, the suit was withdrawn, and the following year Yates voted.[72] It was an act of personal integrity reflecting political isolation.

70. Jefferson to Martin Van Buren, June 29, 1824, cited in Bernard Mayo, ed., *Jefferson Himself: The Personal Narrative of a Many-Sided American* (Boston, 1942), 156; Jefferson, "The Anas" in Paul L. Ford, ed., *The Writings of Thomas Jefferson*, 10 vols. (N.Y., 1892-99), I, 159-160.

71. For the 1786 phase, see Yates to Abraham Lansing, Mar. 1, 1786, Samuel Osgood *et al.* to Yates, Mar. 28, 1786, and for 1789, see "Grotius," *Albany Gazette*, Sept. 10, 1789, in "Rough Hewer" notebook, Yates Papers, N.Y. Pub. Lib.

72. Burr to Yates, June 13, 1790, Yates to Burr, Apr. 24, 1791, certificate by Dirck Ten Broeck, June 16, July 27, 1791, by Enoch Leonard, July 26, 1791, *ibid.*

Federalist success forced George Clinton to attempt to consolidate his dwindling following through his power of appointment. When Richard Morris, the conservative Federalist, resigned as chief justice of the state supreme court, Clinton in September 1790 elevated Associate Justice Robert Yates, his erstwhile foe of 1789. To fill Yates's vacancy on the court he successfully fought for John Lansing over Congressman Egbert Benson. Finally, to fill the position of mayor of Albany, which Lansing had held for only a year, he appointed Abraham Yates.[73] Clinton had not deserted his "left" (Abraham Yates and Lansing), but his prime problem was still the sagging "center" (Robert Yates) and "right."

The appointment of Abraham Yates, the crusty 66-year-old radical Whig despised by Schuyler and Hamilton during the Revolution as the "cobbler" turned lawmaker, to his new post of honor marked the end of his career as "Rough Hewer," the polemicist. He would lift up his pen several times again in the six years before his death in 1796.[74] But he recognized, as he confessed, that "the temper of the times" had changed. After one year on the political seas, the federal ship of state had taken the wind out of the anti-Federalist sails. It would be several years before the political winds would blow the other way.

73. Hammond, *Political Parties*, I, 47-48; DeWitt to James Clinton, Oct. 1, 1790, Van Cortlandt Mansion Papers, N.-Y. Hist. Soc.

74. In "Rough Hewer" notebook, containing drafts of Yates's newspaper articles, the last entries for 1790 are Apr. 2 and Apr. 12. The next piece is dated July 18, 1793, on canals, the next on national policy, on Jay's Treaty, Dec. 18, 25, 1795, a suggestive pattern, Yates Papers, N.Y. Pub. Lib.; see also Spiegelberg, Abraham Yates, ch. 7.

PART III

The "Republican Interest" Emerges

1790-1792

CHAPTER 8

New York and

Hamiltonian Finance

1790-1791

———•·•———

For New York, "Mr. Hamilton's funding system" taken up in the
spring and summer of 1790 in the second session of the first Congress
was the first divisive issue of the Federalist era. And yet provocative
as it was, it operated differently on opinion within the state than has
been supposed. New York's anti-Federalists supported funding of the
federal debt and opposed Madison's proposals to discriminate in favor
of original holders. They opposed assumption of the state debts but
seem to have approved the understanding about the accompanying
settlement of Revolutionary War accounts between the states and the
federal government. They did not, however, mount much of a public
offensive against those parts of the Hamiltonian program that anti-
Federalist congressmen voted against. Once the measures were passed,
discontent rose, in particular in response to speculation, but even
then, New York late in 1790 was not like Virginia: there was no
seething protest against Hamiltonian finance. Indeed, perhaps the
chief political consequence of "the funding system" in the state was
to provide Chancellor Livingston with the occasion of his first public
opposition to Hamilton's policies.

To understand these reactions—and lack of reaction—one must

turn to the array of interests in New York, public and private, that were affected by funding, assumption, and the settlement of accounts.

I

On the surface of things New York's anti-Federalists might have been expected to challenge funding of the federal debt. The proposal was drafted by Hamilton with the collaboration of Philip Schuyler and William Duer—three men they had learned to distrust. It had the support, as Congressman Laurance boasted with speculators jamming the galleries of the House, of "the general opinion of men of property."[1] If adopted, it would make inevitable an excise tax, the anti-Federalist *bête noire* of the ratification controversy. And the orgy of speculation before, during, and after the plan was before Congress gave evidence of "the few" profiting at the expense of "the many."

The concentration of security holdings was especially pronounced in New York. Eventually $4,949,253 in federal securities or about one-sixth of the $32,000,000 was funded by New Yorkers, an amount second only to Massachusetts. About $2,300,000 of this was held by the state government—a fact of major political importance.[2] But of the amount in private hands there is no reason to believe that its distribution differed from the general pattern found in the country as a whole by James Ferguson, the most recent student of the subject; there was "an enormous concentration in a very few hands."[3] New York City, "heavily populated by speculators and securities brokers," was "the national center of speculation." The scope of the speculators' operations is suggested by a sample set of treasury records examined by Ferguson recording subscriptions of $2,486,507 for 254 persons. Among the New Yorkers listed were John Delafield ($321,620), Theodosius Fowler & Co. ($202,387), and Watson and Greenleaf ($125,954). And actually these men were not the biggest operators. On a larger scale were William Constable, who had several arrangements with Robert Morris, Gouverneur Morris, and Daniel Parker; the firm of Herman LeRoy and William Bayard, who "were probably the foremost agents of Dutch capitalists investing in the American debt"; and William Duer and his associates, who included some of the men already named.[4] Thus there is a good deal of evi-

1. *Annals*, 1st Cong., 2nd Sess., 1134.
2. *Ibid.*, 2nd Cong., Appendix, 1071, "Statement of the Debt of the United States Funded from the 1st of October to the 30th of September, 1791."
3. Ferguson, *The Power of the Purse*, ch. 12 at 284, 273, 279.
4. *Ibid.*, 258.

dence to support the contemporary accusation accepted by Madison that most of the continental securities were held by about forty men in New York City, together with forty in Philadelphia, thirty in Boston, two to twelve in Baltimore, and six in Charleston.[5]

The large operators with one or two exceptions were Federalists, and the biggest were close to the centers of political power. William Constable was chairman of New York's Federalist election committee in 1789 and a frequent companion of Hamilton. Duer was Under-Secretary of the Treasury and an active party worker. Nicholas Low, a leading city merchant and banker, was a delegate at the Poughkeepsie convention.[6]

New York's chief federal officeholders also profited personally from the laws they wrought. Hamilton, we know, was disinterested, but Senator Schuyler, his father-in-law, redeemed $67,000 in securities and his brother-in-law, John B. Church, even more.[7] Senator King entered into the giant syndicate organized by Duer and Constable while Gouverneur Morris doubled as American agent and speculators' agent in England.[8] Congressman Laurance of the city was put down by Jefferson's informants as a "paper man," as were Judge James Duane and Richard Harison, the District Attorney.[9]

In addition, it is now known with certainty that the New York Federalists in high office leaked secrets that became a source of tremendous profit to speculators. Duer was the main informant, a fact not unconnected with his resignation from the Treasury in April 1790. But "it may be," as Hamilton's sympathetic biographer puts it, "that Hamilton in the intimacy of his home disclosed too much to a friend who had a pressing ulterior motive," namely to William Constable. To Constable, as to the whole tribe of New York speculators, Hamilton was "our Pitt."[10] Thus there were the makings of a first-rate political issue replete with corruption, malfeasance in office, and a resignation under dubious circumstances.

5. Brant, *James Madison*, II, 302; Dumas Malone, *Jefferson and His Time* (Boston, 1948—), II, 290-91. The charge originally appeared in N.Y. *Daily Gazette,* Feb. 10, 1790.

6. See above, ch. 3, sec. VI. Of a list of leading brokers in Ferguson, *The Power of the Purse*, 258, almost everyone can be identified as a Federalist.

7. McDonald, *We The People*, 48-49; Beard, *An Economic Interpretation of the Constitution*, 270-71.

8. Brant, *James Madison*, II, 302; Ferguson, *Power of the Purse*, 265.

9. Beard, *An Economic Interpretation of the Constitution*, 107, 109, 110, 114.

10. Mitchell, *Alexander Hamilton*, II, 163; Constable to Jno. Inglis, Jan. 4, 1790, cited *ibid.*, 164.

Two factors, however, stayed the hands of the anti-Federalist leaders: the stake of the state government in funding the federal debt and the personal stake of anti-Federalists—constituents and leaders—in funding. The state government had assumed some $2,300,000 in federal securities in 1786, and if anyone had to be reminded of the fact, the "Statement of the Auditor" listing "Continental Securities Now in the Treasury of the State of New York" filled several columns of the *Daily Advertiser* the same week that Hamilton's funding plan was released.[11] The state assumption of 1786, accompanied by a paper emission act reserving part of the issue to pay some of the interest on the federal securities, had been passed by a coalition of creditors and paper money spokesmen and had drawn general political support from the several thousand holders of certificates. The Clintonians' interest in avoiding congressional taxation also acted in favor of the state's taking care of the federal creditors. Under the scheme the state took a major portion of the debt out of private hands and paid only a fraction of the interest due.[12] Thus in 1790 the state government of New York stood to gain from the funding of the federal debt; after the plan was adopted the auditor's report the following year listed state holdings of $898,847 in "six per cents," $680,681 in "three per cents," and $520,668 in "deferred stock" on which there was interest due January 1, 1792, of $71,007.[13]

Of the securities that remained in private hands or were acquired by secondary holders after 1786, a good number, of course, had *not* passed into the clutches of the giant operators.[14] Greenleaf, the anti-Federalist editor, underscored this fact in justifying his publication of the prices current on securities in the New York market, to which some had taken exception. All the debt had not been transferred to a few wealthy men; Bancker's notes were appreciated, he warned his readers, referring to an issue of 1786 named after the state auditor; "Part not with them on easy terms, . . . take notice ye Citizens of New York."[15]

11. N.Y. *Daily Advertiser*, Jan. 18, 1791.
12. Ferguson, *Power of the Purse*, and Ferguson, "State Assumption of the Federal Debt During the Confederation," *Mississippi Valley Historical Review*, 38 (1951), 318, 321-24.
13. "An Account of the Continental Stock in the Treasury of the State of New York on December 31, 1791 by Gerard Bancker, Treasurer," Philip Schuyler Papers, Miscellany, N.Y. Pub. Lib.
14. Ferguson, *Power of the Purse*, 255.
15. N.-Y. *Journal*, Feb. 17, 1791.

"An Original Holder" also pointed out that the state act of 1786 had permitted men to pay for state land with federal securities.[16]

Among these small-scale holders of the federal debt were a good many anti-Federalist leaders. If one takes the delegates at Pough-keepsie as a sample of leadership, the most recent and most precise in-vestigation of the treasury records shows 22 of the 46 delegates to be security holders. Most of the amounts were small: 11 were below $500, 3 between $500 and $1000, 3 between $1000 and $2000, and only 5 above that, the maximum being $7311. Yet prominent leaders redeemed significant sums: Governor Clinton, $1288 (perhaps more); his brother James, perhaps $6895; John Lansing, $7311; Jesse Woodhull of Orange, $4887.[17] Other key leaders also stood to gain, among them Melancton Smith, General William Malcolm, and Jeremiah Van Rensselaer.[18] Peter Van Gaasbeck, the Kingston merchant-politician, had agents scouring the Hudson Valley; when he proposed to "send out a man" in Dutchess, Abraham Lansing, the Albany anti-Federalist, pleaded with him to make purchases for him, too. Van Gaasbeck's anti-Federalism waned as his speculation grew.[19] Thus the interest of the state government in funding and the prospect of personal profit dulled the reflexes of political leaders who otherwise might have taken to the hustings about the machinations of the wealthy.

It is not surprising that Madison's proposal to discriminate in favor of original holders produced only a few ineffectual squibs in Green-leaf's paper.[20] An incident in the Society of Cincinnati was a good index of opinion. The New York Society, far from being exclusively Federalist, included a host of anti-Federalists; John Lamb had almost won the presidency in 1783, George Clinton had been vice-president, and would actually capture the presidency in 1792. In 1790, a group of ex-army officers circulated a petition on behalf of discrimina-tion. Immediately the Society was under pressure to disavow it. When the members convened, after considerable discussion, they voted al-most unanimously to disclaim the petition. The report was released

16. N.Y. *Daily Advertiser*, Feb. 18, 1791.

17. McDonald, *We the People*, 304-8; cf. to Beard, *An Economic Interpretation of the Constitution*, 123, 270.

18. McDonald, *We the People*, 304-8; Spaulding, *New York in the Critical Period*, 158.

19. Van Gaasbeck to Abraham Lansing, Sept. 27, 1790, [a copy] Van Gaasbeck Papers, F.D.R. Lib.; Lansing to Van Gaasbeck, Aug. 23, 29, Sept. 15, 1790, Feb. 2, 1791, Abraham Lansing MSS, N.Y. State Lib.

20. See footnotes 42, 43, 44 below.

to the public by John Stagg, popular Whig and member of Clinton's election committee the year before.[21] The Clintonians, the incident suggests, were not interested in discrimination; nor is there evidence of concern for any of the more realistic measures to scale down the debt, proposed for example by Senator Maclay of Pennsylvania.

In the House, the New York Federalists, Benson and Laurance, were warm opponents of Madison's plan, claiming that all the sacred rights of property and contract were at stake in funding at face value. So were Schuyler and King in the Senate. Of New York's anti-Federalist congressmen, none rose on behalf of Madison's proposal. When the House voted on discrimination, Madison mustered a scant thirteen yeas to be drowned out by thirty-six nays. His support was almost exclusively southern; New York's three anti-Federalist congressmen voted with their Federalist colleagues.[22]

II

Assumption was a different matter. The interests of each state on this part of the funding were so clearly defined that each state's congressional delegation voted as a bloc.[23] Not so New York's congressmen. Schuyler and King in the Senate and Benson and Laurance in the House were in the forefront of the battle for assumption, while the state's three anti-Federalists voted with the opposition, helping to kill the measure in April; they continued to hold out against it when it was passed late in July.[24] New Yorkers divided in part because "the middle states were not vitally affected"[25] and in part because there were a variety of interests within the state touched by assumption and a variety of ways in which those interests could be interpreted. Political leaders had to weigh four factors to come to a decision on the issue.

First were the gains and losses to the state's fiscal position. The state owed its creditors about $1,200,000. This was less than one-

21. N.Y. *Daily Advertiser*, Feb. 3, 22, 1790; "Cincinnatus," *N.-Y. Journal*, Feb. 11, 1790; for anti-Federalists in the Society of Cincinnati, see ch. 14, n. 37.

22. *Annals*, 1st Cong., 2nd Sess., for Laurance's speeches, Feb. 9, 18, 1790, 1191-93, 1333-36; for Benson's, Feb. 16, 1790, 1272-73. For the vote which was not by roll call, 1675; for a table of votes in the first Congress, see Orin G. Libby, "Political Factions in Washington's Administration," *University of North Dakota Quarterly Journal*, 3 (1913), 293-318.

23. Ferguson, *Power of the Purse*, ch. 14; Whitney K. Bates, The Assumption of State Debts, 1783-1793 (unpubl. Ph.D. diss., University of Wisconsin, 1951), chs. 5 and 8, which revise Beard, *Economic Origins of Jeffersonian Democracy*, chs. 5, 6.

24. *Annals*, 1st Cong., 2nd Sess., 1753, 1755.

25. Ferguson, *Power of the Purse*, 309.

fourth the $5,000,000 or so owed by Massachusetts and South Carolina, who clamored for assumption, and six times that of the smallest debtor states who would not gain from assumption. The amount was not overwhelming or at least so it could be argued in relation to the resources within the state that could be tapped to discharge this debt. As a prominent Republican of later years explained, "The state had paid its troops better, and defrayed the expense of the war within its borders in a better currency than those of most of the other states. . . . In the sale of its unsettled land, the state had the means of payment within itself. It had then lately and before the ratification of the Constitution by nine states, issued a large emission of state currency which was as good as gold and silver."[26] Moreover, if the federal government assumed the large debts of the other states, the ultimate burden to New Yorkers in the form of federal taxes would be much more than if the state were left with only its own obligations. On the other hand, New York's debt was substantial enough to make the prospect of the federal government's taking it over an appealing one.

Second to be calculated was New York's interest in regard to the settlement of wartime accounts between the states and the federal government. To New York this question was of more importance than to any other state.[27] The exact amount of money due to or from the United States was in itself a subject of dispute, but according to the reckoning completed in 1793, six states owed $3,500,000 to the United States and of this New York owed about $2,000,000; five states had a balance due them, two close to $1,250,000 each. New York thus owed four times as much as any other debtor state, and if forced to pay, might have to saddle her citizens with an unprecedented tax burden. Throughout the Confederation period New York's spokesmen laid down a barrage of arguments challenging the size and validity of the debt, even suggesting that a balance was due *from* the central government. The state, it was claimed, had supplied war material at lower prices than other states, and was partially occupied and therefore unable to make the same contribution as other states.[28]

The settlement question was part of the debate in Congress on

26. Erastus Root, "Appendix, Note M," in Hammond, *Political Parties*, I, 577.

27. For general background, Jensen, *The New Nation*, ch. 19, and Bates, Assumption of State Debts, ch. 7.

28. Cochran, *New York in the Confederation*, 116-22, 152-54; Spaulding, *New York in the Critical Period*, 168-69.

assumption; the issue passed into the arena of bargaining and became as important a part of the final compromise as the famous deal on the location of the capital. After assumption failed its first test, a settlement plan was adopted which eased the way for passage of assumption. New York congressmen disagreed as to what population base to use in apportioning state war debts, insisting that the time of the Revolution was fairer than the 1790 census, but they approved the general pattern of settlement. The task of calculating the settlement was turned over to a commission; creditor states would be given public securities; about the debtor states nothing was said.[29] A debate in Congress in 1796 gives every indication that in 1790 New York's leaders of both parties understood that the debtor states would not be required to make good their obligations. And with New York Federalists so influential in shaping early fiscal policy this was very likely the case. As it happened the settlement commission in its 1793 report presented New York with a bill for $2,074,896, much to the shock and indignation of both parties,[30] who fought the demand bitterly in a debate in the fourth Congress. In 1790, however, the common understanding about the settlement made assumption a less bitter pill for New Yorkers to swallow.

The third factor to be weighed was the direct economic interests of holders of state and federal securities as they were affected by assumption. The holders of certificates of the New York debt would be paid, one way or the other, by either the state or the federal government, and knew it; there seems to have been no demand from the New York state creditors for federal assumption.[31] There were, however, two other powerful interest groups tugging against each other.

On the one hand were the men engaged in an orgy of speculation in the securities of other states who naturally stood to make a killing if assumption passed. Beginning late in 1789 on the basis of the tips leaked to them, a small band of New Yorkers were in the forefront buying up state debts, in particular in three southern states. Fifteen New Yorkers bought $149,850 of the Virginia debt; 32 acquired $819,028 of the North Carolina debt; 51 acquired $747,876 of the South Carolina debt. These New Yorkers, 78 men all told, bought

29. Ferguson, *Power of the Purse*, 322.
30. "Balances Due to and From the Several States," *American State Papers, Miscellany*, I, 69. The debate in Congress in 1796-97 is discussed below, ch. 25, sec. II.
31. An opinion of Robert R. Livingston in the work cited in footnote 51 below.

up $2,717,754 of the certificates of these states, or about 31 per cent of their total debt, and 60 per cent of the amount acquired by non-residents. Eight New Yorkers bought up more than $1,500,000 of this sum. The biggest men included the firm of LeRoy and Bayard ($584,845); Richard Platt ($209,544) and Walter Livingston ($99,046), the latter two associates of William Duer; two brothers of the Chancellor, Edward and John Livingston ($75,808), and his cousin Brockholst Livingston ($47,180).[32]

On the other hand were the federal creditors—although often the same men, and yet a distinct group—who were fearful that if assumption were tacked on to the funding measure, the taxing resources of the federal government would not be adequate to meet the demands of both funding and assumption and that the promised interest on the federal debt might be further reduced. In the Federalist *Daily Advertiser* there was a running stream of articles hostile to assumption written from the point of view of those who favored funding, reflecting the interests of this group.[33]

Lastly, among the factors influencing the division of opinion among New Yorkers was the political issue raised by assumption, the question of "consolidation." Hamilton's plan was avowedly political: by giving the state creditors "the same interests as the federal creditors," he argued, it would "unite them in support of the fiscal arrangements of the government."[34] As soon as assumption was proposed, Senator King heard that the Clintonian leaders in order to forestall federal action were talking of meeting whatever demands the state creditors made. "They think that the advantages to be derived to the state from the retention of the debt are so great and important," he was told, "that they stand ready to accede to any terms which the creditors may propose."[35] In his message to the legislature, January 13, with Hamilton's plan in the offing, Clinton spoke of "the necessity of a permanent arrangement for the support of government and the

32. Bates, Assumption of State Debts, 244-48; and "Northern Speculators and Southern State Debts: 1790," *Wm. and Mary Qtly.*, 3d Ser., 19 (1962), 30-38.

33. N.Y. *Daily Advertiser*, "Honestus," Feb. 3, 16, "A Merchant," Feb. 5, 12, 22, Mar. 30, and an unsigned article, Mar. 10, 1790; see also Bates, Assumption of State Debts, 182-85, 188, 251-54.

34. Hamilton, "Report on the Public Credit," Jan. 9, 1790, Syrett, ed., *Hamilton Papers*, VI, 51-110.

35. C. Gore to R. King, Jan. 24, 1790, in King, ed., *Correspondence of Rufus King*, I, 385. Essentially about the Massachusetts anti-Federalists, this may be applied to the New Yorkers as well.

maintenance of public credit."[36] Whatever proposals were made, however, did not come to fruition in legislation.[37]

Thus, arrayed on behalf of assumption in New York were the Federalist political aim of centralization, the belief that the state government would gain by having its debt burden lightened, the understanding about the settlement of accounts, and the interests of men with large speculations in state debts. Arrayed in opposition were the anti-Federalist political fear of "consolidation," the belief that the state government would have less of a burden if it funded its own debt, and the fear of large holders of federal securities that their payments would be jeopardized by assumption.

The fact that the six New York representatives divided along familiar party lines suggests that, given the possibility of a varied interpretation of the state's fundamental economic interests, the political issue was of major importance. And the fact that there were so many compromises in the final measure suggests that Federalist leaders were mindful of the need to take care of fretful New Yorkers. There was not only the understanding implicit in the settlement of state accounts, but an extra allowance of $200,000 was added to the amount of New York debt to be assumed. As Ferguson writes, "Under the grand compromise by which the state debts were assumed, the capital located on the Potomac and the settlement of accounts brought to completion, the material interests of all the states were in some degree propitiated."[38] And this may explain why, although assumption aroused opposition in New York, it did not become an issue of major proportions.

III

Although there was a general malaise with "the funding system"— a term contemporaries used to apply both to funding and assumption— it must be said that critical comment on Hamiltonian finance in New York was neither very widespread nor sustained. Governor Clinton was rumored to be the author of an anti-Hamiltonian article,[39] and Abraham Yates took up his pen again. But the discussion was not up to the level of intensity anti-Federalists could arouse when they threw

36. Lincoln, ed., *Messages from the Governors*, II, 304-5.
37. I find no evidence of discussion of the issue in *Journal of the Assembly of N.Y.*
38. Ferguson, *Power of the Purse*, 325.
39. Maclay, *Journal*, 194.

themselves into a fight. While the measures were before Congress the *New York Journal* ran only two ineffective series of articles together with a cluster of short letters, the *Albany Register* probably no more.[40] The *Daily Advertiser* was a vehicle primarily for public creditors dissatisfied either with assumption or Hamilton's failure to give them a uniform 6 per cent on all federal certificates. There was only one pamphlet—an important one—from a New Yorker, and no meetings or petitions save the protest squelched in the Cincinnati.

Part of the problem was that few could fathom funding. If after the third reading Henry Van Schaack, an educated Federalist, found Hamilton's report "obscure" and "complicated and difficult to understand," small-town rustics may well have given up on the first. Understandably as the months went by, the very obscurity of the system became a mark against it; it was a "mystery," "abstruse, intricate and perplexing."[41]

The orthodox anti-Federalist writers who took up the funding system seldom offered more than traditional agrarian and economy-minded prejudices. In a series of short pieces "X" made a special appeal for frugality to reduce expenses—why were there so many officials "who bask and spread their peacock plumage in the sunshine of a salary and civil offices?" What would come next: an army to police taxes, magnificent circuits of national judges and royal courts to ape Europe and detract from the state governments? He especially questioned the ability of the country to pay all the debts Hamilton wanted to assume.[42] Another writer of a series indulged in anti-Semitism, castigating speculators for their "Israelitish avarice" that made them worse than Shylock.[43] And of course anti-Federalists came down heavily on the political dangers of assumption; they were opposed to "the twin bastards of consolidation and assumption";[44] assumption was "the wooden horse which would have ruined the political existence of the states."[45]

40. Very few issues of the *Albany Register*, 1788-1791, are extant. See, interestingly, a paragraph favoring assumption, Aug. 2, 1790.
41. Henry Van Schaack to Theodore Sedgwick, Feb. 2, 1790, cited in Nathan Schachner, *Alexander Hamilton* (N.Y., 1946), 252-53; a paragraph in *N.Y. Journal*, Aug. 13, 1790.
42. Signed "L.X.," "X," or "Z," but probably all by one person, *N.-Y. Journal*, Apr. 1, 15, May 18, 28, July 20, 1790; in the same vein, "Manlius," *ibid*.
43. Seemingly a series signed by "C," Apr. 22, "A.B.," Apr. 29 and May 11, "B.C.," June 8, "M," June 15 and July 2, and "N.P.G.," Sept. 9, 1790, all in *N.-Y. Journal*.
44. An unsigned article, N.Y. *Daily Advertiser*, Mar. 10, 1790.
45. "C," *N.-Y. Journal*, Apr. 22, 1790.

The contribution of Abraham Yates to the funding debate may perhaps typify the seeming inability of anti-Federalists to come to grips with the enemy on the field of high finance. Yates had been fighting centralized finance since the 1780's in a running battle with Robert Morris that had produced a spate of articles and pamphlets.[46] In 1789 he warned about the dangerous plan to establish a treasury department and perpetuate the national debt.[47] Then in April 1790 he drafted two articles against Hamilton's funding plan. In the first he decried the talk of the "rage for trade." In the second he listed the pros and cons of funding in his familiar style, quoting at length from authorities: on the pro side, "Postelwroth" (Postlethwayt) and Gale; on the con, Blackstone, Montesquieu, Low, and again Postlethwayt. But he trailed off, without a conclusion of his own, and the series apparently was over. It was as if he was overwhelmed by the "pernicious system" he was examining.[48]

Of more moment was a line of criticism sympathetic to funding yet critical of assumption and some of Hamilton's underlying principles. The argument was best expressed in *Considerations on the Nature of a Funded Debt*, written by an anonymous author who can now be identified as Robert R. Livingston.[49] Livingston, in New York City attending sessions of his chancery court while Hamilton's proposals were being debated, looked with a jaundiced eye on the effects of speculation as early as January 1790. "The only evil here," he informed his sister, "is that money continues as scarce as ever and that no property or credit can raise a shilling. This is principally owing to the rise of our funds and the spirit of stock Jobbing which has invaded all ranks of people." The speculation in state debts, which involved even his own family, drew his special attention.[50]

46. Rough Hewer, Jr. [Abraham Yates, Jr.], *Political Papers Addressed to the Advocates for a Congressional Revenue in the State of New York* (Albany, 1786); *Resolutions and Extracts from the Journal of the Honorable the Congress relative to the Continental Loan Offices in the Several States; and Certain Letters Passed between Robert Morris, Esq., Superintendent of Finance—the Board of Treasury of the United States, and Abraham Yates, Jun., Esq., late Commissioner of the Continental Loan Office of the State of New York* (Albany, 1786).

47. "Rough Hewer" notebook, draft of an article late 1789 by "Sidney" possibly published in *Albany Gazette*, Yates Papers, N.Y. Pub. Lib.

48. *Ibid.*, drafts of articles marked published Apr. 2, Apr. 12, 1790. No copies of the *Albany Register* or *Albany Gazette* were found for this month.

49. [Anon], *Considerations on the Nature of a Funded Debt* . . . (N.Y., 1790), listed in Charles Evans, *American Bibliography* . . . , 14 vols. (Chicago, 1903-59), No. 22432.

50. Robert R. Livingston to Janet Montgomery, Jan. 15, 1790, Livingston to John Armstrong, Jan. 2, 1790, R. R. Livingston Papers, N.-Y. Hist. Soc.

Sometime in February or March he wrote two long essays reviewing the entire Federalist financial program—his first sustained political writing since 1788. The first was published anonymously at New York without so much as a printer's imprint on the pamphlet; the second he completed but, it seems, did not allow to see the light of day.[51]

The theme of the pamphlet was expressed in the subtitle: *"tending to show that it* [a funded debt] *can never be considered as a circulating medium, and that the interest of the United States renders it essentially necessary to fund it agreeably to terms of the original contract at this time and not to adopt the debts of the respective states."* Livingston first disposed of Hamilton's political argument for funding, perhaps the only New York writer even to argue the question. He agreed that a national debt "may serve to cement a government composed of distinct members since it is evident that those who hold property dependent upon the revenues of the union will zealously advocate that union." But how important were the "stockjobbers?" "The number of holders is to the number of people as one to four thousand." If heavy taxes were the result, "the many must pay the few," and if "the murmurs of the many will drown the voices of the few, this supposed cement will appear to consist of untempered mortar." He then settled down to rebut the argument that "a large debt would facilitate loans, promote manufactures, add to the value of lands and encourage agriculture." Granting some validity to this, his thesis was that "the *debt itself* can never be a substitute for *money*." "When we are creating a commodity which is to be *sold for money*," we must not think, he insisted, "that we are creating a circulating medium which is to operate as money." Actually because the value of the public debt would fluctuate it would "increase the evils our agriculture and manufactures labor under, render loans more difficult and depreciate the value of land." After developing his economic reasoning, Livingston hastened to reassure his reader he should not "number me with those who are for applying a spung [sponge?] to the

51. "On Funding Debts and Assumption of State Debts" [Livingston's title], R. R. Livingston Papers, N.-Y. Hist. Soc., Box 17, labeled by the Curator "Reflections on the Funding of the Debt." This manuscript has two separate "letters," the first of which, aside from a different beginning and ending is the same as the pamphlet, *Considerations*. The second could not be located either as a pamphlet or series of articles in the New York City papers. The essays showed a careful weighing of Hamilton's *Report on Credit* issued Jan. 9 and of the public discussion yet clearly were written before assumption was defeated in April.

debt." "No sir, I not only think that the *debt should be funded* but that it should be funded on the best possible terms for the creditor." By this he meant "on such terms as will transfer a considerable portion of our debt to foreigners; in return for which we shall receive money, that spring which can alone give force and vigour to our agriculture and manufactures." If this were done "money will flow in from abroad to facilitate every opportunity of finance, to reduce interest, to create new capitals, and to convert those waste lands . . . into an effective fund for sinking the debt."

In the manuscript draft of his unpublished "letter," Livingston argued that assumption would deal a "fatal" blow to the public credit, jeopardize funding, and necessitate new taxes the political consequences of which might be even more disastrous. Reviewing at length the classes of debts owed by the states and weighing their validity, Livingston emphasized the lack of legal grounds for creditors' demanding that the federal government assume these debts. He was not indifferent to the problems of particular states, but he was "convinced that the debts should be paid by the states, nay I would *after we had satisfied the legal demands* upon the union set in to the aid of such states as were too heavily burthened, but I would be just before I was generous." The problem was who would pay for funding eighty as opposed to fifty-six millions of debt? "Does it not instantly compel us to seek for objects of taxation which might with the debt be safely left to the states?" The excise tax would prove inadequate; therefore direct taxation and increased duties would be necessary. On the other hand the states themselves had enough "back lands and other objects to absorb the debt. All of them are able to lessen the weight of direct taxation by collecting a part of it in the paper which constitutes the debt itself." If a direct federal tax were adopted, one would "not need the spirit of prophecy" to show "the heartburning that this system will occasion and the odium in which it will involve the Federal government."

Cogent, sustained, reflecting an economic philosophy developed years before, Livingston's essays grappled with the heart of Hamilton's argument, especially on money, with a competence in economic matters unmatched by Hamilton's other New York critics.[52] The argument—whether from Livingston or others—was not without influence. "Publicola" in the *Daily Advertiser* developed a similar line on the

52. Curtis Nettels, *The Emergence of a National Economy, 1775-1815* (N.Y., 1962), 112-13, for the relation of the funding plan to currency in Hamilton's mind.

unproductive effects of the public debt on the economy, while DeWitt Clinton picked out the inevitable consequences of high taxes to sustain funding of so large a debt as his principal reason for being critical of Hamilton's plan.[53] The essays were most important, however, for what they revealed of the Chancellor's point of view and state of unrest, a matter of no little consequence for future developments in New York politics.

IV

Even the loss of the federal capital to Philadelphia stirred little more than a ripple. The removal of the capital, of course, left New York holding the bag—in this case Federal Hall overdecorated at a cost of $50,000. The "seat of government" question, as it was known, was nothing less than "a despicable grog shop contest" even before it was thrown in with the bargaining over assumption.[54] It was a foregone conclusion that the capital would have to move farther south; but how far south, how soon, and where the temporary capital would be until then were all grist for the mill. Without hope of retaining the capital permanently, New York's Federalist leaders, Rufus King at their head, hoped they might keep it for perhaps another five years and accordingly were in the thick of the trading, offering their support for various permanent sites in return for prolonging a temporary stay in the city.[55]

Their cause had what later generations would call "bipartisan" support. Federalists, of course, wanted George Washington's beneficent glow to continue to melt New York's anti-Federalist chill. The "interests" had ample proof of the value of being close to the center of influence. To the city as a whole the capital was a mixed blessing. But if its presence raised rents and inflated prices, it unquestionably augured future prosperity. And the social advantages for the "aristocracy" were inestimable; the ladies who crowded the galleries during the residence debate smiling only on those who spoke favorably for the city were, a congressman complained, "a severe trial for susceptible

53. "Publicola," N.Y. *Daily Advertiser*, Feb. 22, 1790; "Publicola" may well have been Livingston; DeWitt Clinton to George Clinton, Feb. 18, 1790, Clinton Papers, N.-Y. Hist. Soc.

54. Fisher Ames cited in Claude G. Bowers, *Jefferson and Hamilton; the Struggle for Democracy in America* (Boston and N.Y., 1925), 65.

55. See the memoranda left by King, June-Sept., 1789 in King, ed., *Correspondence of Rufus King*, I, 302-3, 372-75, 383-85.

minds."[56] As for the anti-Federalists, if they had not abandoned their fears of the "federal city" they at least knew better than to express them in public. The state legislature in fact made provision for land for "the residence and accommodation" of the president.[57]

After the unexpected defeat of assumption in April, the New York Federalists split over the capital question. To Hamilton his financial program was "the primary object; all subordinate points which oppose it must be sacrificed," and he brought pressure to bear on Senator King, who at this point was holding out for a combination of New York City and Baltimore.[58] A letter from Philip Schuyler faintly hints that Federalists also approached New York's anti-Federalist congressmen to switch their votes on assumption.[59] But if the effort was made it did no good, for while the anti-Federalists maintained a solid phalanx with their Federalist colleagues on every vote on the capital, they held out against assumption to the end.[60]

The bargain trading away the capital led to caustic comment Philip Freneau, the *Daily Advertiser's* poet-printer, bade farewell to the parting government in biting doggerel:

> New chaplain now, shall ope their jaws,
> New salaries grease unworthy paws
> Some reverend man that turtle carves
> Shall fatten, while the soldier starves.[61]

Others were savage. When assumption was first defeated a satirist poked fun at the birth and death of "the baby assumption," the "bastard of Eastern speculators who have lost their Puritanic manners," duly baptized "Al--ex--der Assumption." But the metaphor was occasionally switched. "Spotless Miss Assumption" was really "a prude and a prostitute" who had been seduced by "Mr. Residence" and had given birth to two illegitimate children, "Potowmacus" and "Philadelphia."[62]

56. Cited in John C. Miller, *Alexander Hamilton: Portrait in Paradox* (N.Y., 1959), 251.
57. *Journal of the Assembly of N.Y.*, 13th Sess. (1790), 64; *Laws of the State of N.Y.*, 13th Sess., ch. 25.
58. King, ed., *Correspondence of Rufus King*, 383-85.
59. Philip Schuyler to Stephen Van Rensselaer, May 16, 1790, Schuyler Mansion Papers, N.Y. State Lib.
60. *Annals*, 1st Cong., 2nd Sess., Aug. 1790, *passim*.
61. Philip Freneau, *Poems Written Between the Years 1768 and 1794* (Monmouth, N.J., 1795), 419-20; see also 414-15.
62. *N.-Y. Journal*, June 11, Aug. 31, 1790; for other criticism see *ibid.*, "A Citizen of New York," July 13, "Connecticut," July 6, "A Citizen," July 20, and

Actually anti-Federalists were not inclined to make an issue out of losing the capital. "I can not say I am much agitated about it," wrote Theodorus Bailey, Dutchess County's outgoing congressman. "The child" would flourish better in its native city and would grow "into a Giant under the auspices of its immaculate Godfathers, Wils-n and M-r-s [James Wilson and Robert Morris] which I believe is the object with many of the Federal Gentry."[63] In short, "good riddance."

V

Congress adjourned in August 1790. Through the remainder of the year resentment of the funding system grew, probably as a reaction to the new wave of speculation which it set off. The charges against it were steeped in the prejudices of country farmers and city mechanics against their traditional enemies, speculators and moneylenders. Speculation would "cause the whole people of America to become slaves to less than one hundred men." It was "a fact well attested," wrote an Albanyite, that "NINE-TENTHS of the assumed debt of this state are owned by a few speculators in the city of New York." "A Dutchess County Farmer" believed that nine-tenths of the original debt certificates were now in the hands of "brokers, speculators, Jews, members of Congress and foreigners." "Square Toes" had his own variation; those getting rich were "British riders, Amsterdam Jews, American Tories, speculating lawyers, doctors and parsons."[64] Philip Freneau in his doggerel poems lashed out at "The Travelling Speculator," "A Theological Scripmonger," and especially at the *nouveaux riches* created by speculation:

> On coaches now, gay coats of arm are wore
> By *some* who hardly wore a coat before:
> Silk gowns instead of homespun now are seen,
> And sirs, 'tis true ('twixt me and you)
> That some have grown prodigious fat,
> And some prodigious lean![65]

shorter articles July 23, July 27. See in the N.Y. *Daily Advertiser*, an unsigned article, June 3, "A Friend to Good Government," June 25, and "A Federalist," June 3, 1790.

63. Theodorus Bailey to Nathaniel Lawrence, July 24, 1789, Emmet Collection, No. 11268, N.Y. Pub. Lib.

64. "Extract," Aug. 13, "A Dialogue," Sept. 10, 1790, in *N.-Y. Journal*; "Dutchess County Farmer," *Poughkeepsie Journal*, Jan. 9, 1793; "Square Toes," widely reprinted in many papers, cited in Donald Stewart, Jeffersonian Journalism: Newspaper Propaganda and the Development of the Democratic-Republican Party, 1789-1801 (unpubl. Ph.D. diss., Columbia Univ., 1950), 103.

65. Freneau, *Poems*, 429-30, 430-31, 402. These appeared in the newspapers in 1790.

Despite such carping, it was clear that the federal administration in general and Washington in particular retained a reservoir of good will among many New York anti-Federalists and future Republicans. In August when Washington made a trip to Rhode Island to celebrate her entry into the union he and Jefferson were accompanied by Governor Clinton—who could not have been unaware that he was a symbol to Rhode Islanders that their fears of the central government had been overdrawn.[66] The same month, the Society of Tammany served as the government's unofficial host, and Marinus Willett, the anti-Federalist sheriff, did not object to serving as official federal representative for a visiting delegation of Indian chieftains.[67] Solomon Simpson, head of the city's Jewish congregation and a few years later president of the Democratic Society, joined in a fulsome message of congratulations sent by his coreligionists of other cities to the President who had initiated "the reign of freedom" in the new world.[68]

Late in 1790 New York was put to the test. In November the Virginia House of Delegates adopted a "Protest and Remonstrance" asking other state legislatures to join her in condemning assumption as unconstitutional and the creator of a "large monied interest" which would lead to "the prostration of agriculture at the feet of commerce."[69] Chancellor Livingston's prophecy about the "odium" assumption would bring on the federal government was being fulfilled. On December 27, 1790, at the St. John's Day dinner of the Masons he brought his opposition out into the open. Dr. James Tillary reported breathlessly to Hamilton that Livingston "declared himself to me without any stipulation of secrecy that he was not only opposed to your Funding system but that Robert Morris and several other well informed influential characters viewed it as a system of public injustice."[70] What the Chancellor would do, what the response of the New York legislators to the challenge from Virginia would be—these were the imponderables of New York politics at the end of 1790.

66. Nathan Schachner, *The Founding Fathers* (N.Y., 1954), 123.
67. N.Y. *Daily Advertiser*, July 22, Aug. 4, 1790; *N.-Y. Journal*, Aug. 3, 10, 1790.
68. "The Address of the Hebrew Congregations in the Cities of Philadelphia, New York, Charleston and Richmond, Dec. 13, 1790," in Morris U. Schappes, ed., *A Documentary History of the Jews in the United States, 1654-1875* (N.Y., 1950), 82-83.
69. Commager, ed., *Documents of American History*, No. 92.
70. Dr. James Tillary to Hamilton, Jan. [probably 20], 1791, Syrett, ed., *Hamilton Papers*, 614-16.

CHAPTER 9

Preparations for Republicanism

1791

———•———

Politically, 1791 was a year of omens and portents which some Federalists read with foreboding. The first jolt for Hamilton's party came when Chancellor Livingston joined Governor Clinton in lining up support to reject Philip Schuyler for a second term in the United States Senate and replace him with Aaron Burr. The second came in the spring when Thomas Jefferson and James Madison visited Livingston and Burr on their famous journey through New York betokening the founding of an alliance with the Virginians. A third was in the spring elections which marked the return of Melancton Smith to the assembly and to influence. In New York City there were still other signs that the mechanics were nearing the end of their honeymoon with Federalist merchants. More ominously, an alarming incident in the heart of the landlord country raised the specter of a new wave of tenant restiveness. In short, some of the ground on which Federalists had built their party in New York was eroding.

I

The election of Burr to the Senate in January 1791 was the Federalists' first setback after welding their successful coalition in 1788, and it was all the more unnerving because it was so unexpected. The warning signs were there had the Federalists but read them properly.

Both the assembly and the senate which had been elected the previous spring were Federalist by slight majorities, yet early in the against assumption. Governor Clinton had the language of the Virginia against assumption. Governor Clinton had the language of the Virginia Resolution toned down and saw it through the legislature over the opposition of what he called "the aristocratic faction among us supported by host of stock-jobbers and speculators who have suddenly amassed great wealth and consequently possess a considerable degree of influence."[1] The legislature also sided with Virginia in protesting against the practice of the upper house's sitting in secret session behind closed doors, a symbol of "high toned" Federalism. By moving "to instruct" New York's senators to oppose this practice, anti-Federalists also asserted their old contention that senators were agents of the state government. In the assembly the vote was 25 to 25, the Federalist speaker breaking the tie by voting against it. Two days later Philip Schuyler was defeated for the Senate. Twelve days later when the motion to instruct was raised again, it passed 44 to 10 and when Senators Schuyler and King acknowledged the legislature's memorial, they wisely "yielded to the torrent," concurring in its recommendation.[2]

In the legislature a vague discontent with Philip Schuyler eased his removal. It had been expected that Schuyler, the venerable patriot general, would lead the New York delegation in Congress, yet, Chancellor Livingston observed, he "is supposed to be led by the Treasury"; in Senator William Maclay's pungent phrase he was "the supple jack" of his son-in-law Hamilton. "The idea had not been very honorable to the state," wrote Livingston, "and they begin to think it has not been promotive of their interest."[3] Schuyler, moreover, had overstepped himself with the state legislators. The year before, they had passed a ban on dual office-holding which deprived not only Schuyler but Senator King, Judge Duane, and Congressmen Laurance and Hathorn of their seats in the state assembly or senate. All accepted the decision except Schuyler who refused to resign from the Council of Appointment to which he had been elected as representative of the

1. George Clinton to James Monroe, Feb. 16, 1791, Monroe Papers, Lib. Cong. See also James Kent to Theodorus Bailey, Jan. 27, 1791, James Kent Papers, I, Lib. Cong.

2. *Journal of the Assembly of N.Y.*, 14th Sess., 22, 34, 48; *Journal of the Senate of N.Y.*, 14th Sess., 10, 17. *N.-Y. Journal*, Mar. 3, 1791.

3. R. R. Livingston to Morgan Lewis, Jan. 27, 1791, R. R. Livingston Papers, N.-Y. Hist. Soc.; William Maclay, *Journal*, 389-90.

western senatorial district. Although challenged, he continued to attend sessions of the council, regularly voting against Governor Clinton's nominations.[4]

To bridge the gap between Clinton and Livingston and to detach wavering Federalists, Aaron Burr was an ideal candidate: in 1788 he had been a member of "the medium party," in Jabez Hammond's phrase, a mild foe of ratification; in 1789 he had been a partisan of Yates; then Clinton's appointee as attorney general. As a lawyer his clients ranged from the Livingstons to Abraham Yates.[5] Hamiltonian Federalists were suspicious of him; Assemblyman James Kent reported Burr as "a character then who has always been regarded as unfriendly to the government and its administration."[6] At the same time he had a reputation for independence which fascinated substantial men of both parties. Intellectually, he was a man of the Enlightenment who might already have shocked Hamilton with his "rank Godwinism" and enthusiasm for the French Revolution.[7] On the national issue on which Congress would soon act, chartering a national bank, he had reservations, a position that would stand well with both the Chancellor and the Governor.[8]

Burr's election, as one of Hamilton's correspondents put it, was "the fruit of the Chancellor's coalition with the Governor" or, in the astute observation of another, was "a coalition of interests from different principles,"[9] among which we may set down Clinton's hawk-like search for a chance to strike at Federalism, Burr's soaring ambition, and the Chancellor's desire to settle scores with Hamilton and Schuyler.

The Chancellor, critical of assumption and "stockjobbing" from the spring of 1790, probably made his decision to challenge Schuyler late in 1790 when he came down to the city from Clermont, and as likely as not he made it alone. There was no in-gathering of the clan—at least not at this point.[10] Thomas Tillotson, a state senator,

4. Hammond, *Political Parties*, I, 46-47.
5. *Ibid.*, I, 50; Nathan Schachner, *Aaron Burr; A Biography* (N.Y., 1937), 100.
6. Kent to Bailey, Jan. 27, 1791, Kent Papers, I, Lib. Cong.
7. Parton, *Aaron Burr*, I, ch. 4 and pp. 106-11.
8. Burr to Theodore Sedgwick, Jan. 20, Feb. 17, 1791, Sedgwick Papers, Mass. Hist. Soc.
9. William Duer to Hamilton, Jan. 19, 1791, Meyers Collection, No. 402, N.Y. Pub. Lib.; Dr. James Tillary to Hamilton [about Jan. 20], 1791, Syrett, ed., *Hamilton Papers*, VII, 614-16.
10. For the traditional account, see Hammond, *Political Parties*, I, 107; for a modern corrective, see Dangerfield, *Chancellor Robert R. Livingston*, 243-49. For

was the Chancellor's spokesman in the legislature, but to Morgan
Lewis, another brother-in-law, who was close to Hamilton, the action
was as "unexpected" as it was "undesired." And brothers John R. and
Edward, who had between them taken in $75,808 of the South Caro-
lina debt at no more than twenty cents on the dollar, would hardly
have been predisposed to a political protest against assumption. As
Morgan Lewis said of them, his relatives in town were "so absorbed
in speculations that I cannot prevail upon them even to answer my
letters." As for the upper manor branch of the family, even though they
had a long-standing vendetta with Schuyler, they were not on speaking terms with the Clermont branch and therefore not in on the plot
to dump him. When Robert, the old lord of the upper manor, died
in December 1790, the Clermont men did not even attend his
funeral.[11]

When the legislature convened, the wheels had been oiled. Tillotson was elected to the Council of Appointment and probably was the
go-between with the Governor. The Chancellor had chance enough
to chat with Burr, who was pleading cases in the chancery court which
met in the Chancellor's town house in New York City.[12] Burr was
active, wining and dining a few likely converts among the assemblymen, so much so that Schuyler had the impression that he "was the
principal in the business."[13] The maneuver required delicate management. The Clintonians had to stay united, a few Federalists had
to be won over, and a few others had to absent themselves. "The
twistings, combinations and maneuvers," Robert Troup told Hamil-

the timing of the Chancellor's decision: The legislature convened Jan. 1791 at
New York City. The Chancellor came down from his customary summer retreat
at Clermont in Sept., returned briefly in Oct., was in the city probably in Nov.,
definitely by Dec. 8. See Minutes of the Court of Chancery, 1789-1793, entries for
Aug.-Dec. 1790, Hall of Records, County Clerk's Office, N.Y. County Court House,
N.Y.C. News of the Virginia protest, confirming the Chancellor's predictions about
assumption, arrived in the city in late Nov. The first public utterance of the
Chancellor against Hamilton may be dated from the Masons' St. John's Day dinner,
probably Dec. 27; see Tillary to Hamilton [probably Jan. 20], 1791, Syrett, ed.,
Hamilton Papers, VII. This activity beginning at the latest in November would
confirm the impression of William Seton that "the other party has been undermin-
ing for months," Seton to Hamilton, Feb. 3, 1791, ibid., VIII, 4-5.

   11. Morgan Lewis to R. R. Livingston, Jan. 24, 1791, Margaret Beekman
Livingston to R. R. Livingston, Dec. 15, 1790, R. R. Livingston Papers, N.-Y. Hist.
Soc.; Lewis to Hamilton, Oct. 10, 1790, Syrett, ed., Hamilton Papers, VII, 106-7.

   12. Minutes of the Court of Chancery, 1789-1793, entry for Dec. 21, 1790, N.Y
County Court House.

   13. Philip Schuyler to Hamilton, Jan. 29, 1792, Syrett, ed., Hamilton Papers, X,
579-81.

ton, were "incredible." "It would take a quire of paper to give you a minute detail." Clinton, as might be expected, wielded patronage as a whip; a new Council of Appointment was chosen "by a bargain" and as "many who were Federalists were sucked into his Excellency's vortex, the Chancellor's family became one of the principal satellites of this noxious planet."[14]

In the assembly Schuyler was nominated and rejected by a vote of 32 to 27. Burr then was elected by the same vote. In a last-minute maneuver, Federalists offered as a substitute Congressman Egbert Benson, (years before close to both the Chancellor and the Governor) but were defeated, 35 to 24. The vote, James Kent felt, was "in some measure a question of Northern and Southern interests," the latter with Schuyler, the former with Burr.[15] In the senate Burr was nominated by David Gelston, Clinton's friend, and out of twenty-four members, the vote for Burr was 14 to 4. Of Burr's supporters, twelve were anti-Federalists, one a moderate Federalist, and the other Tillotson. Among Schuyler's handful of supporters were his son-in-law, Stephen Van Rensselaer, and Philip Livingston of Westchester. About five or six Federalists stayed away, including Schuyler's nephew Peter, and such stalwart merchant Federalists as Nicholas Low and Isaac Roosevelt. Had the voting been delayed, William Duer thought, "several who united with the anti-Federalists," could have been won back.[16]

Presiding in court when he heard the news of Burr's election, the Chancellor was "singularly happy." Although Burr was properly reserved, Clinton was jubilant, reporting to James Monroe that "the removal of one of our Senators affords some Evidence of a declension of Influence of a certain faction."[17] He had bet on the wrong horse in 1789 in backing Rufus King; Burr was a much better gamble.

Federalists were panic stricken, Hamilton's correspondents outdoing each other in prophesying doom. "We are going headlong into the bitterest opposition to the general government," Troup wrote. The political situation "has a most gloomy aspect," William Duer claimed. There was "so much rottenness" in the state legislature

14. Robert Troup to Hamilton, Jan. 19, 1791, *ibid.*, VII, 445.

15. *Journal of the Assembly of N.Y.*, 14th Sess., 23; James Kent to Theodorus Bailey, Jan. 16, 27, 1791; Kent Papers, I, Lib. Cong.

16. *Journal of the Senate of N.Y.*, 14th Sess., 12. Duer to Hamilton, Jan. 19, 1791, Syrett, ed., *Hamilton Papers*, VII, 442-43.

17. Troup to Hamilton, Jan. 19, 1791, Syrett, ed., *Hamilton Papers*, VII, 445; Burr to Theodore Sedgwick, Jan. 20, 1791, Sedgwick Papers, Mass. Hist. Soc.; Clinton to James Monroe, Feb. 16, 1791, Monroe Papers, Lib. Cong.

"that I know not whom to trust." What was worse, there was not "a person on the Federal side capable of taking the lead." Unless help was forthcoming "to rally a broken party," there was danger of "utter destruction." Who would be the leader, Dr. Tillary asked Hamilton; Duer could "never prop the good old cause" because he was "unfit as a leader, and unpopular as a man." Perhaps General Schuyler on his return from the Senate "would revive a drooping party."[18] As for Schuyler, he was more than ready for revenge: "I hope however the day will come when I shall be able to retaliate on Mr. Clinton and his tools."[19]

Actually, insofar as Livingston was concerned, the entire operation portended less than Federalists feared. As he was at pains to explain to Morgan Lewis, the report of a coalition with Clinton was true only as to ousting Schuyler; it was "unfounded if carried beyond that object." "I feel myself too independent to draw with any party farther than I think the public interest may require." In other words, he had made no longterm alliance with Clinton; nor had he closed the door to a continued relationship with Federalist leaders. He simply wanted to make it clear that he "knew how to make adequate return in kind for political injuries though offered by private friends." Defeating Schuyler was a gesture of personal retribution. At the same time it was an act of opposition to Hamilton's policies; "I have disapproved of one of his political measures," presumably assumption, he wrote. "I can esteem both him [Hamilton] and Schuyler while I disapprove their politics."[20] Thus, as Livingston's able biographer has written, in his action there was a "mixture of motives."

II

The April elections showed just how far the coalition had gone. In New York, Edward, the Chancellor's younger brother, ran for the assembly for the first time, nominated by the "mechanics" on a ticket that included Federalists and leaders of the Mechanics Society. He ran against the "merchant" nominations which in effect were the "regular" Federalist slate. Although half the mechanic slate got in, Edward, the

18. Troup to Hamilton, Jan. 19, 1791, Tillary to Hamilton [probably Jan. 20], 1791, Duer to Hamilton, Jan. 19, 1791, Syrett, ed., *Hamilton Papers*, VII, 442-45, 614-16.

19. Philip to John B. Schuyler, Jan. 26, 1791, Schuyler Papers, Family Miscellany, N.Y. Pub. Lib.

20. R. R. Livingston to Morgan Lewis, Jan. 27, 1791, R. R. Livingston Papers, N.-Y. Hist. Soc.

ow man with 574 votes, did not. Anti-Federalists ran no ticket but concentrated on getting Melancton Smith elected.[21] Apparently a deal was made, for Smith was elected with 674 votes, running sixth among he eight victors. The winners were a mixed bag—"our motley city representatives," Robert Troup called them. Troup was "mortally disgusted with the weakness of some of our associates and in the treachery of others of them." Moreover, John Laurance did not intend to run again for Congress in 1792, and Troup feared that Smith was after the office; "we are," he lamented, "without materials to make a proper successor."[22]

Chancellor Livingston fumed only at Edward's defeat, "another example of the influence of one who has always directed our politics" —obviously Hamilton.[23] In the mid-Hudson the new coalition worked somewhat better for the Livingstons. Thomas Tillotson was re-elected to the state senate, defeating Theodorus Bailey, the anti-Federalist war horse. Both were from Dutchess, where the vote was split, but Tillotson won support from the Clintonian counties of Ulster and Orange across the river where Bailey got almost none. In the assembly election for Dutchess, Morgan Lewis was elected, although apparently without anti-Federalist votes.[24]

In the southern district a number of anti-Federalists made comebacks besides Melancton Smith. On Long Island, in a congressional by-election made necessary by the death of the Federalist incumbent, a "non-adopting" anti-Federalist delegate, Thomas Tredwell, won out in a field of six candidates. The year before he had run fourth in a five-man race, but with twice as many voters at the polls in 1791, Tredwell doubled his vote.[25] The southern senatorial district also returned Samuel Jones to the senate, and Suffolk restored Jonathan Havens to the assembly.

Despite the re-emergence of several anti-Federalist stalwarts, Federalists held their own in the state as a whole. Philip Schuyler re-

21. For Smith's nomination, *N.-Y. Journal*, Mar. 30, 1791; N.Y. *Daily Advertiser*, Apr. 22, 1791.

22. Robert Troup to Hamilton, June 15, 1791, Syrett, ed., *Hamilton Papers*, VIII, 478-79.

23. For the nominations, N.Y. *Daily Advertiser*, Apr. 13, 20, 1791; for electioneering, *N.-Y. Journal*, Mar. 30, Apr. 9; for returns, N.Y. *Daily Advertiser*, June 2; R. R. to Edward Livingston, June 5, 1791, R. R. Livingston Papers, N.-Y. Hist. Soc.

24. For returns, N.Y. *Daily Advertiser*, June 7, 1791. Tillotson received 317 votes in Dutchess, 471 in Ulster, and 217 in Orange, while Bailey got 329 in Dutchess, and only 90 in Ulster and 40 in Orange.

25. *N.-Y. Journal*, May 25, June 4, 1791.

entered state politics, winning handily as a state senatorial candidate
from the western district and throwing his weight behind other
candidates.[26] Thus the elections of 1791 showed a certain fluidity in
New York politics but not a great amount of dissatisfaction with
national policies.

III

While the Governor, the Chancellor, and the Senator-elect were
redrawing New York's political lines, the three moved closer to the
Virginia leaders of the emerging "republican interest." The New
Yorkers had different contacts with the Virginians. Clinton shared
his exultation over his triumphs of the winter with James Monroe, a
fellow anti-Federalist of the battle of 1787-88.[27] Although he knew
Madison and Jefferson neither had ever been a co-worker. He had
spent a week with Jefferson, the summer before on Washington's tour
of Rhode Island. But Madison was a former foe of '88; Clinton's other
Virginia friend, in fact, was Patrick Henry, Madison's arch-enemy.

Robert R. Livingston, by contrast, was an old political friend of
Madison with whom he had collaborated closely in the Continental
Congress. In fact, late in the war, the two shared the same Philadelphia lodging house as well as the same nationalist pro-French principles.[28] Livingston and Jefferson were less well acquainted. Jefferson
knew him as "a gentleman with whom I acted in the earlier stages of
this contest," i.e., the Revolution, whose "discernment and candour"
he respected.[29] More important, Livingston as the first Secretary for
Foreign Affairs and Jefferson as Minister to France might well be
called fellow "Gallicans." In 1790 when Jefferson came to New York
to assume his new duties as Secretary of State, there was much the
two experienced diplomats could talk about.[30] As scientific farmers

26. Philip to John Schuyler, Apr. 14, 1791, Schuyler Papers, N.Y. Pub. Lib. For
returns, N.Y. *Daily Advertiser*, June 4, 6, 1791.

27. George Clinton to James Monroe, Feb. 16, 1791, Monroe Papers, Lib. Cong.

28. Dangerfield, *Chancellor Robert R. Livingston*, 127; Brant, *James Madison*
II, 122-24. Ralph L. Ketcham, formerly editor of The Madison Papers, informs
me there is additional evidence verifying this close relationship.

29. Jefferson to Livingston, Nov. 26, 1782, in Boyd, ed., *Papers of Jefferson*, V.
206; see the other routine correspondence from Livingston as Secretary of Foreign
Affairs to Jefferson as abortive minister to the peace negotiations, *ibid.*, 202, 204,
228-29, 238-40, 250-51, 257-60, and Malone, *Jefferson and His Time*, I, 398-400.

30. For a discussion of the foreign policy views of Livingston and Jefferson
see ch. 16, sec. I, below. For their cordial relationship, see Jefferson to Livingston,
Oct. 6, 1787, and Livingston to Jefferson, Mar. 3, 1788, in Boyd, ed., *Papers of*

and philosophical inquirers they had other things in common. When Jefferson returned to Virginia in the summer of 1790, the two warmed quickly to a correspondence about an experiment the Chancellor had been conducting to reduce friction in mill machinery. Jefferson, "finding that you amuse yourself mathematically," sent him a copy of his recent report to Congress on weights and measures. In October, Livingston again wrote about his mill; in December he asked the Secretary of State about a patent for his invention.[31] On February 4, 1791, Jefferson replied from Philadelphia, all apologies for the pressures of work which had delayed his answer. He appreciated Livingston's reactions to his weights and measures study—"I shall always be glad to hear from you and have your ideas which are always valuable." Moreover, he had submitted Livingston's sketches to the patent board which asked for more complete drawings and a model. Then, abruptly, a political iceberg jutted through the still waters of this scientific calm: "Are the people in your quarter as well contented with the proceeding of our government as their representatives say they are? There is a vast mass of discontent gathered in the south and how and when it will break God knows."[32]

Jefferson did not have to wait long for his answer. On February 20 Livingston wrote, enclosing his article, "Thoughts on Coinage and the Establishment of a Mint," criticizing Hamilton's latest proposal; it appeared only the day before in the *Daily Advertiser*. He moved on to Jefferson's query quickly: "Our delegates deceive themselves if they believe their constituents are satisfied with all the Measures of government." There were "many instances in which their interest has been neglected or misunderstood," and he supposed (modestly) that "the removal of General Schuyler by a majority of 16 to 4 in the Senate was in some sort evincive of this." Even so, he could not ignore the fact "that such is the unbounded prosperity of this state doubling its population in 12 years, possessing an extensive trade and fruitful Lands increasing in wealth, and feeling no taxes, that they scarce consider as a serious evil anything so remote as the measures of the federal government"; "in this disposition their ill humour

---

Jefferson, XII, 213, 640. That they were on a visiting relationship in 1790 is intimated clearly in the letters from Livingston in the following footnote.

31. R. R. Livingston to Jefferson, Aug. 1, Oct. 1, Dec. 9, 10, 1790, drafts, R. R. Livingston Papers, N.-Y. Hist. Soc.; Jefferson to Livingston, Aug. 8, 1790, transcript, Jefferson Papers, Princeton Univ. Lib., Princeton, N.J.

32. Jefferson to Livingston, Feb. 4, 1791, Jefferson Papers (microfilm), Lib. Cong.

evaporates." He ended with a jibe the Virginian would appreciate. "In this city [New York] hundreds have made fortunes by speculating in the funds and look forward to a great increase in them by the establishment of a bank."[33] Livingston's answer to Jefferson's question clearly established political rapport between the New Yorker and the Virginian.

On the same day, Livingston clipped another copy of his article on coinage, pasted it on a piece of stationery, and mailed it off to "James Madison, Esq., Congressman at Philadelphia."[34] The political message to the Virginians would be doubly clear. Sometime late in April, Madison came up from Philadelphia to induce Philip Freneau, his former Princeton classmate, to leave the *Daily Advertiser* and set up a Republican paper in the new capital.[35] With politics uppermost in his mind, Madison could not have avoided visiting Livingston without being rude. Moreover, there were questions Livingston could answer; did he share Madison's enthusiasm for Freneau? What did he, as a contributor to the *Advertiser*, think?

A month later, on May 20, Madison returned to New York with Jefferson on the first leg of a projected tour of the eastern states.[36] A notice in the *Daily Advertiser* recorded their arrival: "Yesterday arrived in this city from Philadelphia, the Honorable Thomas Jefferson, Esq., Secretary of State, on a tour to the northward, accompanied by the Honorable Mr. Madison from Virginia."[37] The next day, the

33. Livingston to Jefferson, Feb. 20, 1791, draft, R. R. Livingston Papers, N.-Y. Hist. Soc.; Jefferson's copy kindly checked against the transcript in the Jefferson Papers, Princeton Univ. Lib., by Julian Boyd. The enclosure may be inferred from the evidence in footnote 34.

34. In the Broadside Collection, Portfolio 112, No. 4, Lib. Cong., a clipping, "For the Daily Advertiser, Thoughts on Coinage and the Establishment of a Mint" pasted on a piece of paper on the back of which is the salutation to Madison. The article appeared in the paper Feb. 19, 1791. The original MS with the same title, dated Feb. 1791, is in R. R. Livingston Papers, N.-Y. Hist. Soc., Box 18. A second manuscript, "Reflections on Coinage" dated 1793, is in Box 24.

35. Lewis Leary, *That Rascal Freneau: A Study in Literary Failure* (New Brunswick, N.J., 1941), 166-92; Brant, *James Madison*, II, 334-46; Malone, *Jefferson and His Time*, II, 351, 423-26; Samuel Forman, *The Political Activities of Philip Freneau* (Baltimore, 1902), 28-29.

36. For the traditional Federalist interpretation of the trip implying sinister politicking, see John C. Hamilton, *History of the Republic of the United States of America . . .* , 7 vols. (N.Y., 1857-64), IV, 506, based on the letter of Troup in footnote 22. For recent versions minimizing the political character of the trip, see Malone, *Jefferson and His Time*, II, 359-63; Brant, *James Madison*, II, 336-40; and Philip Marsh, "The Jefferson-Madison Vacation," *Pennsylvania Magazine of History and Biography*, 71 (1947), 70-72.

37. N.Y. *Daily Advertiser*, May 21, 1791. There was no notice in the anti-

two boarded a sloop and sailed up the Hudson, stopping in Pough-keepsie where their arrival was noted in the *Poughkeepsie Journal*.[38] On May 26 the travelers arrived at Albany. A correspondent reported that "on thursday last this city was honored by the presence of Mr. Jefferson, Secretary of State, accompanied by the Charles Fox of Amer-ica, the celebrated Mr. Madison. We are informed they intended going North, as far as Lake Champlain, and from thence across the 15th constellation, East of the Connecticut River."[39]

These were the scant public notices of a trip since celebrated by historians as marking the birth of the Virginia-New York axis of the Democratic party. About a month after Jefferson and Madison left the city, Robert Troup sent a short letter to Hamilton which to this day remains the sole authority for the political character of the stop-over in the city. "There was every appearance," he wrote his chief, "of a pasionate courtship between the Chancellor, Burr, Jefferson and Madison when the two latter were in town. Delenda est Carthago [Carthage must be destroyed] I suppose is the maxim adopted with respect to you."[40] None of the four principals left a written record of the visit or commented on it. Jefferson's only relevant comment was made a year later when he was defending himself against charges of conspiring with Freneau. He said that he saw Freneau "but once, and that was at a public table, at a breakfast at Mrs. Ellsworth's, as I passed through New York last year."[41]

In light of the contacts between Livingston and the Virginians in the preceding months, it is difficult to conceive of Madison and Jeffer-son not meeting with Livingston, if not with Burr, despite the paucity of evidence. Troup was often alarmist as to the implications of events

Federalist *N.-Y. Journal*, May 21 or May 25, 1791. Confirmation of the date of arrival is in a letter from Jefferson to Dr. Joseph Willard, New York, May 20, 1791, Jefferson Papers (microfilm), Lib. Cong.

38. *Poughkeepsie Journal*, May 26, 1791, kindly located for me by Mrs. Wil-helmina B. Powers, Librarian, Adriance Memorial Library, Poughkeepsie, N.Y.

39. Phila. *Gazette of the U.S.*, June 8, 1791, with a brief item headed Albany, May 30. A search of the *Albany Gazette* and *Albany Register* failed to locate local notices of the trip.

40. Robert Troup to Alexander Hamilton, June 15, 1791, Syrett, ed., *Hamilton Papers*, VIII, 478-79.

41. Jefferson to George Washington, Sept. 9, 1792, in Ford, ed., *Writings of Jefferson*, VI, 106-7; see also Noble E. Cunningham, Jr., *The Jeffersonian Republi-cans: The Formation of Party Organization, 1789-1801* (Chapel Hill, N.C., 1957), 14-15.

but he was usually reliable as to simple fact.[42] Livingston was in the city attending sessions of the chancery court which did not end until May 23. So was Burr, who pleaded a case before him two days before the Virginians arrived.[43] Governor Clinton may or may not have been in town,[44] but we may be reasonably sure he did not share the interview; if he had, Troup would surely have picked up that juicy morsel. Besides, conversation with Livingston in Clinton's presence might still have been a shade awkward.

What might two inquiring Virginians and two knowledgeable New Yorkers have talked about the evening of Friday, May 20, in New York City? Between Jefferson and Livingston the fascinating matter of reducing friction in mill machinery might easily have opened the conversation. The Chancellor's interesting "Thoughts on the Coinage" might have come next. And from this it was only a short jump to the state of New York opinion. Congress had approved the Bank of the United States and an excise tax since Livingston had answered Jefferson's question. What was the likely reaction in New York? Could Colonel Burr add anything from his plentiful stock of political intelligence? If they wanted to be practical about politics it would have been easy to take up the proposal for a national Republican newspaper. Could they count on subscribers in the state? (Burr would become one.) Doubtless the Virginians wanted to take the measure of New York's young senator-elect; he would be in Philadelphia for legislative business in the fall. Thus, laying aside Robert Troup's hysterics—who was courting whom?—the first leg of the Jefferson-Madison trip unquestionably was political.

The rest very likely was not. On their leisurely journey up the

42. For an accurate factual letter see Troup to Hamilton, Mar. 19, 1792, Syrett, ed., *Hamilton Papers*, XI, 155-58.

43. Minutes of the Court of Chancery, 1789-1793, N.Y. County Court House, N.Y.C., entries for May 17, 18, 23, showing that Livingston presided over the court at New York City, and June 15, the next entry, showing that he was at Clermont. A letter from Livingston to Lord Ranelagh is dated New York City, May 24, 1791; a letter on June 5 to Edward Livingston is from Clermont, R. R. Livingston Papers, N.-Y. Hist. Soc. Dangerfield, *Chancellor Robert R. Livingston*, 254-55, and others are thus in error in implying a meeting between the Chancellor and the Virginians *at Clermont*.

44. On May 9 Clinton attended the first session of the state land commissioners, who did not meet again until June 22. See *Journal of the Assembly of N.Y.*, 15th Sess. (1792), 183-200; he attended Tammany's anniversary dinner, May 12; see "Tammanial Dinner," *N.-Y. Journal*, May 14, 1791. But some receipts he paid in May for house rent and some for lumber are ambiguous as to his whereabouts May 20-21 and suggest he may have been preparing to go up to his regular home in Ulster; see Clinton Papers, N.-Y. Hist. Soc.

Hudson Valley the Virginians had plenty of opportunities at their numerous stops to test the New Yorkers' observations on the state of opinion. But they made no other political visits.[45] At their Albany stopover they were the guests of Philip Schuyler who went out of his way to make sure his son at Saratoga would extend them the same hospitality. "I have intreated Mr. Jefferson and Mr. Madison to take beds with you on their way to Lake Champlain," he wrote; his son should also "be so good as to accompany them" on a tour of the Revolutionary War battle sites. "On their return the Gentlemen will proceed from your house to Bennington, pray give them the road."[46] After a week of sightseeing in the Lake Champlain-Lake George region, the two made their way down through Massachusetts and Connecticut. They spent four uneventful days crossing Long Island—they did stop at the home of General Floyd, signer of the Declaration of Independence and a fellow congressman and supporter of Madison—and passed through New York City, June 15, on their way home to Philadelphia. Thus the longest part of their month-long journey was pretty much what it pretended to be—a vacation excursion.

For the Chancellor the prospect of collaborating with the Virginians nationally was an added stimulus to aggressive action within New York. In June, back at his Clermont estate, he planned his next move—an attempt to move in Edward, who had been defeated in the assembly elections, as state attorney-general to replace Burr. He suggested that Edward "speak candidly and fully to Col. Burr to know his views and to see how far you may depend upon his support and do the same with the G[overnor]."[47]

Clinton was ready to cooperate, displaying the same knack for building new political fences that he had shown in mending old ones in the two years gone by. In fact, by the fall of 1791 the Governor was driven further toward the Chancellor by the first sign

45. Edward Dumbauld, *Thomas Jefferson, American Tourist* (Norman, Okla., 1946), Appendix, "Tour Through New England in 1791," 237-38, to which Julian P. Boyd has added information of additional stops from Jefferson's account book and other records. None of these sources indicates a stop at the home of a Republican personage. A comparison of their itinerary with the maps in Christopher Colles, *A Survey of the Roads of the United States of America, 1789*, ed. Walter W. Ristow (Cambridge, Mass., 1961), 141-45 (Plates 21-25), suggests that they stuck to the main road.

46. Philip Schuyler to John B. Schuyler, May 26, 1791, in Schuyler Papers, Box 38, N.Y. Pub. Lib.

47. R.R. to Edward Livingston, June 5, 1791, R. R. Livingston Papers, N.-Y. Hist. Soc.

that Burr, their joint creation as senator, was out to build an "interest" of his own. Clinton was willing to appoint Edward Livingston attorney-general but Burr, according to Hamilton's informant, "wants to put it in Nat Lawrence's hands," a young admirer of Burr from Queens who had been a member of the short-lived Federal Republican Club of 1788. To force the appointment Burr threatened to continue to hold the state job in addition to the Senate seat. "Clinton is staggered," Troup reported; "he is afraid to turn Burr out [as attorney-general] and Burr won't resign" until a new Council of Appointment was chosen. There was also a dispute over naming the New York City sheriff: Clinton wanted to reappoint Marinus Willett; "Nat" Lawrence and, according to Hamilton's informant, Melancton Smith favored Miles Hughes, nephew of James Hughes, the old Liberty Boy and anti-Federalist.[48] It is not clear just how much of a clash there was, but it was the first sign of disagreement between Clinton and Smith. The result was a Clinton-Livingston victory, as might be expected with Thomas Tillotson on the Council of Appointment. As a compromise between Edward Livingston and Lawrence, they settled on Morgan Lewis, the Chancellor's brother-in-law, for attorney-general, and Marinus Willett retained his post as sheriff.

For the time being there were no other outward signs of the alliance between the New Yorkers and the Virginians. Privately the friendship was secure. When the Federalist Nathanial Hazard wrote Burr for some indication of his pending role in the Senate, Burr reassured him that there would be nothing more than "casual differences of opinion" between himself and the administration but added: "I shall not renounce my acquaintance with M[adison] and J[efferson] as Men of Science."[49] In December when the Chancellor wrote Jefferson to introduce his brother who was traveling to Philadelphia, he thanked Jefferson for his "late acts of friendship." A while later

48. Nathanial Hazard to Hamilton, Sept. 30, 1791, Syrett, ed., *Hamilton Papers*, IX, 246-47. Hazard also wrote of Lawrence, Smith, and Miles Hughes that "all three dislike Clinton." In view of Smith's close association with Clinton in the election campaigns of the spring of 1792 this seems overstated. On the other hand, Smith clearly was working for Burr in the vice-presidential campaign late in 1792. It is interesting that Hamilton wrote to Smith, Dec. 27, 1791, accepting his proposal to furnish rations at West Point, a contract that may well have had political overtones on Hamilton's part in view of his knowledge that Smith was thinking of running for Congress. See an exchange in Syrett, ed., *Hamilton Papers*, X, 394-95, 404-5, 470.

49. Nathanial Hazard to Alexander Hamilton, Nov. 25, 1791, Syrett, ed., *Hamilton Papers*, IX, 529-37.

Jefferson assumed the same note of familiarity in introducing the sculptor Ceracchi to Livingston.[50] The events of 1791, political and personal, had brought them together.

IV

While leaders of the republican interest politicked over the loaves and fishes, a ferment among the mechanics of New York City and the tenants and poor farmers in the landlord country prepared a potential new following for them. In the city the showing made by Melancton Smith and Edward Livingston in the 1791 assembly election reflected a new wave of mechanic consciousness. New craft organizations were also emerging in the Hudson Valley—the carpenters at Albany and Lansingburgh, the mechanics as a whole in Catskill and Albany[51]— but it was in the city that they grew most rapidly. The General Society of Mechanics and Tradesmen, organized in 1785, included about 400 members by 1791.[52] The society itself was not political in the partisan sense, as anniversary toasts to George Washington and George Clinton suggest, but it was bròadly republican.[53] The spasm of class feeling engendered in 1786 by the legislature's rejection of their petition for incorporation had been submerged by the common interest of mechanics and merchants in a stronger national government. In 1791 the society again applied for a charter, but to their shock the assembly again turned them down. "Mechanics—what became of your petition to be incorporated," asked "A Friend to Equal Rights." "While the bank business was treated with every attention, hasn't your wish to be incorporated been treated with contempt or neglect? . . . Those who assume the airs of 'the well born' should be made to know that the *mechanics* of the city have *equal rights* to the merchants, and that they are as important a set of men as any in the community."[54] It was

50. Livingston to Jefferson, Dec. 28, 1791; transcript, Jefferson Papers, Princeton Univ. Lib.; Jefferson to Livingston, Mar. 6, 1792, Jefferson Papers (microfilm), Lib. Cong.

51. See a broadside, "Rules and Regulations of the United Society of House Carpenters and Joiners of Lansingburgh and Troy," June 19, 1790, N.Y. State Lib.; an address to an unnamed mechanics society at Hudson, *Hudson Gazette*, Mar. 15, 1792. The General Society of Mechanics at Albany was organized early in 1793, see Munsell, ed., *Annals of Albany*, III, 97, VII, 240-41.

52. *Charter of the General Society of Mechanics and Tradesmen* (N.Y., 1798), 19-24, for about 500 charter members by 1792.

53. N.Y. *Daily Advertiser*, Jan. 5, 1791.

54. "A Friend to Equal Rights," *N.-Y. Journal*, Mar. 30, 1791.

this spirit which lay behind the mechanics' running a separate assembly ticket in 1791 and electing four of their candidates.[55]

Although the mechanic charter finally passed in 1792,[56] it was
clear that the fight had pushed the mechanics into questioning their
well-to-do political allies. "Unwarrantable combinations," wrote
"Leonidas," "should be checked" but a mechanics society

> would create a bulwark, formed of the middle order of citi-
> zens, against the undue influence which large associations, of
> overgrown monied importance and ambition would produce
> among us. . . . Who will deny that a republican government
> is founded on democratic principles? If it is, then, whatever
> assists in preserving this basis of equal liberty, should be
> kindly fostered by the legislature. That the manufacturing
> interest from its nature, is and ever will remain, of the demo-
> cratic denomination, none can deny. Why then incorporate
> large monied interests, and not democratic ones? Should we
> not have a counterpart to the ravings of unbounded affluence.
> Should we not have a wholesome check to the baneful growth
> of aristocratic weeds among us?[57]

The Tammany Society embodied a similar republican spirit, even
though it was neither political nor run by anti-Federalists in its early
years. Founded in 1786, Tammany had few recruits until 1789. By
the fall of 1791, it boasted of more than 300 recent members and
there was talk of constructing its own building. Its chief founder
was John Pintard, a partner of William Duer who was elected to the
assembly in 1790 as a Federalist. Yet the society was, as Pintard himself described it, "a political institution founded on a strong republican basis whose democratic principles will serve in some measure to
correct the aristocracy of our city."[58] Its aims, as Dr. William Pitt
Smith of the Columbia medical faculty explained, were "to cherish
. . . the great principles of civil liberty . . . to cultivate political information . . . to give exercise to the divine emotions of charity—and
finally . . . to enjoy without restraint the generous effusions of national enthusiasm." With membership open to any citizen able to
meet the low initiation fee of from $2 to $8 and quarterly dues of

55. *N.-Y. Journal*, Apr. 13, 16, 1791.
56. *Laws of the State of N.Y.*, 15th Sess., ch. 26.
57. "Leonidas," *N.-Y. Journal*, Feb. 22, 1792.
58. Reports in *Goshen Repository*, Sept. 13, Oct. 1, 1791; for background, Edwin
P. Kilroe, *Saint Tammany and the Origin of the Society of Tammany or Columbian Order in the City of New York* (N.Y., 1913), chs. 1-3; John Pintard to Jeremy
Belknap, Oct. 11, 1790, cited in *ibid.*, 136-37.

twenty-four cents, Smith could truly claim that it united "in one patriotic band, the opulent and industrious—the learned and the unlearned, the dignified servants of the people and the respectable plebeian, however distinguished by name, by sentiment or by occupation." Mechanics were most numerous among the rank and file, merchants and professionals among the leadership. But the "Grand Sachem" was William Mooney, upholsterer, paperhanger, and dealer in furniture, and the "sachems" included three or four officers of the mechanics society.[59]

Tammany met once a month, held public celebrations on its anniversary each May and on July Fourth, and marked Washington's Birthday and later Columbus Day and Evacuation Day, the latter observing the departure of the British troops from New York in 1783. Every observance was an excuse for a parade followed by a collation with a minimum of thirteen toasts. In a more sober vein, the society could boast of a library and reading room and the city's first historic and scientific museum.[60]

However Tammany's members voted in public elections, they chose Thomas Greenleaf, the anti-Federalist printer, and Melancton Smith, the city's leading anti-Federalist politician, among their "sachems," and young DeWitt Clinton as their "scribe." At their anniversary celebration in May 1791, their honored guest was Governor Clinton.[61] For the first time since the end of the Revolution anti-Federalists were not *persona non grata* in New York City.

Tenants and poor farmers in the Hudson Valley put Clintonian politicians to a more difficult test than did urban mechanics. Essentially quiescent in the Confederation period, tenants became restive early in the 1790's when landlords attempted to collect arrearages in rent under the threat of prosecutions[62] and when Philip Schuyler in particular attempted to evict alleged "squatters" in the eastern part

59. William Pitt Smith, "An Oration Before the Tammany Society, May 12, 1790," *New York Magazine or Literary Repository*, 1 (1790), 290-95; for an analysis of the membership, see Peter Paulson, "The Tammany Society and the Jeffersonian Movement in New York City, 1795-1800," *New York History*, 34 (1953), 50. Taking a sample of 74 members in 1789, Paulson found that of those whose occupations he could trace, 11 were merchants or brokers, 15 professionals, 11 small tradesmen and 37 mechanics. Of 98 officers in the period 1789-1795, 38 were mechanics and 8 small tradesmen, somewhat less than half the total.

60. N.Y. *Daily Advertiser*, Jan. 16, Feb. 24, May 21, 1791; Kilroe, *Saint Tammany*, 173-77; *New York Magazine*, 1 (1790), 312.

61. *N.-Y. Journal*, May 14, 25, 1791.

62. See legal notices, *Poughkeepsie Journal*, Dec. 1790, ff.

of Columbia County. Poor farmers burdened with debt were also aroused at the methods used by county officials in forced sales. According to the legislature "collusions between sheriffs and purchasers sometimes happen" with farms "often sold at a very small sum in proportion to their value." To curb such abuses, the legislature in 1790 prohibited sheriffs or their deputies from buying land in execution and required due notice of a public sale.[63]

In 1791 there was no rebellion as in 1766 or 1777, only a "Jacquerie" confined to the eastern part of Columbia in Hillsdale and Noblestown where Yankee migrants eked out a poor living on "a gravelly loam and clay" among "ranges of high hills."[64] It was the same area where in 1788 "the ill fated controversies about their lands" turned the ratification controversy into a class conflict;[65] it was next door to the upper manor Livingston estate, scene of the abortive tenant uprising of 1777. Philip Schuyler now was the chief protagonist. According to Schuyler, there were a great many squatters on his land as well as tenants who had not paid rent for as long as seven years. Schuyler's advisers on the scene warned him that while "many people to the eastwards appear anxious for a final settlement," it was "almost impossible to do anything with the Noblestown people" unless suits were pressed.[66] Schuyler followed two policies. To "leasees and other occupants" he sent a broadside letter offering all a chance to buy their own farms at 18 shillings an acre with a five-year mortgage and the cancellation of back rent. To those who preferred to rent, he was willing to cancel all obligations on the payment of one year's rent. To those who refused these liberal "concessions," he issued a threat "to institute suits for the recovery of his property."[67]

The flare-up occurred in October 1791 when Jonathan Arnold of the hamlet of Noblestown was faced with an execution by the county sheriff. On the day of the sale, "the Noblestown people assembled and with threats deterred the deputy from proceeding with the ven-

63. Laws of the State of N.Y., 13th Sess., ch. 57.

64. John H. French, Gazetteer of the State of New York, 8th ed. (Syracuse, 1860), entry for "Hillsdale."

65. Peter Van Schaack to Philip Schuyler, Apr. 3, 1788, Schuyler Papers, N.Y. Pub. Lib.

66. A. Rutsen Rensselaer to Schuyler, Sept. 20, 1790, Philip to John Schuyler, Oct. 10, 1790, Schuyler Papers, N.Y. Pub. Lib.

67. Hudson Weekly Gazette, Nov. 18, 1790; a somewhat different version as broadside, Dec. 14, 1790; a manuscript copy, Schuyler Land Papers, N.Y. Pub. Lib. Schuyler was administrator of the land in question which belonged to his wife Catherine, daughter of John Van Rensselaer.

due."[68] A few days later, Cornelius Hogeboom, the county sheriff, appeared with the county judge, Stephen Hogeboom, and a deputy. After waiting all afternoon for another deputy to arrive with the necessary papers, and after "a number of people having assembled in a riotous manner," they began to leave. At this point Arnold fired a pistol "at which signal seventeen men painted and in Indian dress sallied forth from the barn, fired and marched after them, keeping up a constant firing." The Indian garb would become standard disguise in the "downrent" wars of the nineteenth century. At the first shots Sheriff Hogeboom said, "They only mean to frighten us." Then one of the "Indians," accompanied by Arnold rode up to him, fired at Hogeboom and killed him instantly. The "Indians" fled, the deputies retreated to Federalist Hudson where they organized a posse. Some four of the desperate farmers set out for New London, Connecticut, from which, it was said, they hoped to sail for Nova Scotia. Arnold hid out for several weeks, but was finally captured. Eventually thirteen men were put under heavy guard in the Claverack jail. Nearby on the upper manor, the landlords were "much distressed"; Henry Livingston had a "fear of revolt," if, following Schuyler's lead, he tried to use the law to force tenants to meet their obligations.[69]

The political alignment on the incident in one sense was familiar. Schuyler and the Hogebooms and the upper manor Livingstons were Federalists; the area townships, Hillsdale and Clavarack, generally voted anti-Federalist or divided.[70] The anti-Federalist leaders outside the county, like the popular Whigs in the rebellions of 1766, 1777, and 1786, condemned the tenants. Clintonian papers at New York and Albany ran hostile accounts, the *Goshen Repository* in the home of the Orange County yeomanry scorned Columbia's "ruffian gang," and the Governor's nephew, Charles, sneered at the "villains."[71] Clinton made

68. A letter, *Albany Gazette*, Oct. 31, 1791.

69. Franklin Ellis, *The History of Columbia County, New York* (Phila., 1878), 62, 236; *Albany Register*, Oct. 24, 1791, reprinted in *N.-Y. Journal*, Nov. 2, 1791, an exaggerated account; Henry to Walter Livingston, Oct. 24, 1791, R. R. Livingston Papers, N.-Y. Hist. Soc.; Henry Livingston to Samuel B. Webb, Mar. 29, 1791 in Ford, ed., *Correspondence of S. B. Webb*, III, 172.

70. C. Wynkoop, Jr. to Peter Van Gaasbeck, May 5, 1788, Van Gaasbeck Papers, F.D.R. Lib., for the election of 1788; in 1789 Hillsdale voted for Clinton, 218–64; in 1792, 325–27; in the congressional election of 1789 it voted anti-Federalist 174–125, in 1792, 216–230; see relevant chapters on these elections.

71. *Albany Register*, Oct. 24, 1791, also reprinted in *Poughkeepsie Journal*, Nov. 3, 1791. *N.-Y. Journal*, Nov. 2, 1791, *Goshen Repository*, Nov. 1, 1791; George Clinton, Jr., to Charles Clinton, Nov. 17, 1791, George Clinton, Sr., Papers, N.-Y. Hist. Soc.

the incident the first subject of his message to the legislature in January 1792, branding it as "a daring outrage against the laws and authority of government." Although it was an "unhappy affair," he praised "the judicious and spirited exertions" of the local magistrates and thanked the governors of "our sister states" for their "friendly and effective cooperation"[72] in apprehending the criminals.

Within the county, however, Clintonians behaved differently. The judges included leading anti-Federalists of the county. When the accused were brought to trial in February 1792, "contrary to the general expectation not ONE was found guilty of the charge."[73] John Livingston of the upper manor was disgusted; Peter Van Ness was "the only judge" who "had behaved well in the case of the prisoners."[74] Others criticized the tactics of the prosecution or asked why Clinton had been slow "to create officers that the Hillsdalers might be brought to trial."[75] In short, from the landlords' point of view, the court had not protected property interests.

At the end of the year the Columbia farmers shifted their battle to the legislature with a petition demanding an investigation of the Schuyler-Van Rensselaer title to land in Hillsdale, Canaan, Claverack, and Kinderhook. Their support was considerable—even Peter Van Ness, in the midst of his campaign for Congress, signed their petition. In the legislature the Clintonian chairman of the committee to whom their petition was referred, Jonathan Havens of Suffolk, reported that it was "necessary to quiet the disturbances" and settle the disputes "for a long time." Although he urged full consideration at the next session, no action seems to have been taken.[76]

By the summer of 1792, Stephen Van Rensselaer's tenants at Phillipstown in Albany County seemed ready to emulate their Columbia

72. Lincoln, ed., *Messages from the Governors*, II, 319.
73. *Poughkeepsie Journal*, Feb. 16, 1792.
74. John to Walter Livingston, Feb. 16, 1792, R. R. Livingston Papers, N.-Y. Hist. Soc.; Ellis, *Columbia County*, 62, lists the judges of the court of oyer and terminer at this trial as John Lansing, of the state supreme court, the well-known anti-Federalist; Matthew Adgate, anti-Federalist delegate and congressional candidate; Philip Frisbie, in 1794 chairman of the Democratic Society of Columbia County; William Whiting, known as a Clinton supporter in 1795. Other judges were Peter Van Schaack of a well-known Federalist family; Israel Spencer, a Federalist leader in 1789, David Pratt, who cannot be readily identified, and Peter R. Livingston of the upper manor and congressional candidate later in 1792.
75. "Extract of a Letter from ———————— in Hillsdale," *Poughkeepsie Journal*, Feb. 23, 1792; see also "One of the People," *N.-Y. Journal*, Apr. 4, 1792. It is not clear what the charge was.
76. *Journal of the Assembly of N.Y.*, 16th Sess., 54, 83, 179, 219-20.

brethren. The patroon wanted arrearages paid but the tenants objected, organizing a committee which made counter proposals. Thomas Witbeck, the patroon's agent, reported there was "more uneasiness than you can be aware of." Shortly afterward Van Rensselaer tenants also challenged the patroon's legal title to his land.[77] Tenants of the upper Hudson Valley were at the beginning of a new wave of unrest, the political implications of which were not clear.[78]

V

There was a general quickening of the political pulse in New York in 1791. The debate over the French Revolution between John Adams and Edmund Burke on the one hand and Thomas Paine on the other aroused considerable interest. New York printers brought the controversy to the state in pamphlet reprints[79] and newspaper articles.[80] There was a veritable Paine revival, and the Albany Federalist printer issued new editions of all his writings. Greenleaf, the New York anti-Federalist, approved: "Every American should be possessed of Paine's works."[81] To Tammany he was already "the scourge of aristocracy."[82]

A few New Yorkers were so inspired by the debate that they wrote

77. Thomas Witbeck to Stephen Van Rensselaer, Aug. 4, 1792, cited in William B. Fink, Stephen Van Rensselaer: The Last Patroon (unpubl. Ph.D. diss., Columbia Univ., 1950), 43-44.

78. See below, ch. 24, sec. IV.

79. The ex-Tory Hugh Gaine brought out Edmund Burke, *Reflections on the Revolution in France* (N.Y., 1791), and *A Letter from Mr. Burke to a Member of the National Assembly* . . . (N.Y., 1791). The Federalists Childs and Swain brought out Burke, *An Appeal from the New to the Old Whigs* . . . (N.Y., 1791). Gaine also reprinted Joseph Priestley, *Letters to the Rt. Hon. Edmund Burke Occasioned by His Reflections on the Revolution in France* etc. (N.Y., 1791).

80. For examples of reprints of Adams' *Discourses* and John Quincy Adams' defense of it as "Publicola," see *Albany Gazette*, May 9, 1791; N.Y. *Daily Advertiser*, May-Aug. 1791.

81. *N.-Y. Journal*, July 27, 1791. The pamphlet editions of Paine did not appear until 1792. In New York City Berry Rogers and Hugh Gaine each brought out editions of *The Rights of Man*. Samuel Loudon brought out Paine's *Letter to Mr. Secretary Dundas*. At Albany, Charles and George Webster, Federalists, brought out three editions of the *Writings of Thomas Paine*, two separate editions of *Rights of Man*, and five other essays by Paine which were also included in the *Writings*. Greenleaf, who did not publish any Paine, brought out a reprint of Joel Barlow, *A Letter to the National Convention of France* . . . (N.Y., 1791).

82. William Linn, D.D., *Blessings of America. A Sermon Preached in the Middle Dutch Church on Fourth of July, Being the Anniversary of the Independence of America: at the request of the Tammany Society or Columbian Order* (N.Y., 1791), 34; *N.-Y. Journal*, July 13, 1791; see also [Philip Freneau], "Lines Occasioned by Reading Mr. Paine's *Rights of Man*," N.Y. *Daily Advertiser*, May 27, 1791.

learned political disquisitions of their own, among them "Philodemos" and "Brutus" from New York City and an anonymous writer at Poughkeepsie.[83] Chancellor Livingston, his ire aroused by "Publicola" (John Quincy Adams), whom he considered a "panegyrist of the British constitution," began a long manuscript condemning the "new order of advocates of monarchy" which had arisen in America.[84]

Enthusiasm for the French Revolution mounted. There was more news in the papers about events in Europe, and more books and pamphlets were imported from France. A young orator at Columbia chose "the late Revolution in France" as his theme. At its annual birthday celebration, Tammany carried the French cap of liberty at the head of its procession. And at its Independence Day observance, the Reverend Mr. Linn could hardly find words to express his feelings for France: "The Revolution in France is great—is astonishing—is glorious."[85]

Although early in the 1790's this enthusiasm was bipartisan,[86] Republicans-to-be saw the implications of the upheaval for American politics. "The Revolution of France," an upstate man hoped, "will reverberate its glorious effects" and "inspire the sons of America with a determination to perfect the work they have so notably begun by purifying it from all extraneous and noxious principles."[87] The rising level of political interest was epitomized in New York City by the newly formed Uranian Society, a nonpartisan group which resolved "that the treasurer purchase all productions relative to the French Revolution." Composed of about thirty young men, many of them Columbia graduates, the society met once a week to debate a wide range of questions. "Is a public education more advantageous than a private education?" "Whether the council of appointment is the best medium of appointment." "Should foreign commerce be encouraged?" DeWitt and George Clinton, Jr., the Governor's nephews,

83. "Philodemos," six numbers, June 21-Aug. 12, "Brutus," four numbers, June 28-July 16, N.Y. *Daily Advertiser*; a letter reprinted from *Poughkeepsie Journal* without signature, *N.-Y. Journal*, July 2, 13, 1791.

84. "Reflections on Monarchy," R. R. Livingston Papers, Box 24, N.-Y. Hist. Soc. dated 1793 by the manuscripts curator and 1792 by Dangerfield, *Chancellor Robert R. Livingston*, 265, but by internal evidence, this was in response to "Publicola" whose final articles appeared in the N.Y. *Daily Advertiser*, Aug. 1791, *passim*.

85. *N.-Y. Journal*, May 7, 14, July 13, Nov. 30, 1791; Linn, *Blessings of Liberty*, 31.

86. Kurt Beermann, The Reception of the French Revolution in the New York State Press: 1788-1791 (unpubl. Ph.D. diss., N.Y. Univ., 1960).

87. "An Ulster County Gentleman," *N.-Y. Journal*, Dec. 28, 1791.

were among its officers. The questions posed were enlightened, and judging by the vote recorded after each debate, so were the opinions.[88]

Political interest throughout the state could also be measured in the support given to what would soon be called "the republican press." Although Philip Freneau moved to Philadelphia, his peppery *National Gazette* found its way back to the state, especially in excerpts lifted by New York printers.[89] Republicans also gained a new paper at Sag Harbor on the tip of Long Island, where *Frothingham's Long Island Herald* was published by a poor young Yankee who kept it going until 1798, no mean feat.[90] Most important, Greenleaf could boast in the *Journal and Patriotic Register* early in 1792 that he had never been so well supported.[91] The *Albany Register* would soon do the same after Solomon Southwick, another energetic Yankee, joined John Barber as co-publisher.[92]

The formation of a loose alliance among Clinton, Chancellor Livingston, and Burr, their identification with their Virginia counterparts, and Melancton Smith's success in breaking out of political isolation—this was the New York "republican interest" in gestation. The general quickening of political interest, the ferment among the "respectable mechanics and tradesmen" and land-hungry farmers— these were signs of a potential Republican following. But in 1791 leaders and following had not yet molded potential into power. Nor would leaders find it easy to convert social and economic discontent into opposition to the national Federalist administration.

Washington had wide support. The anti-Federalist *Albany Register* spoke of the federal government's being run on "liberal, just, independent and successful principles." Hamilton's prestige was still high. On his return to the city, the Chamber of Commerce gave him "a superb entertainment" and commissioned a portrait by John Trumbull.[93] Chancellor Livingston's report to Jefferson in February 1791

88. Minutes of the Uranian Society, Mar. 15, 1791-June 25, 1793, *passim*, N.-Y. Hist. Soc.
89. Leary, *That Rascal Freneau*, 195-96; Matthew Davis, *Memoirs of Aaron Burr*, 2 vols. (N.Y., 1836-37), I, 305.
90. Hamilton, *The Country Printer*, 55, 274; Douglas McMurtrie, *A Check List of the Imprints of Sag Harbor, L.I., 1791-1820* (Historical Records Survey, W.P.A., American Imprints Series, No. 12 [Chicago, 1939]), Introduction.
91. N.-Y. *Journal*, Feb. 2, 1792.
92. *Albany Register*, June 2, 1794.
93. Stokes, *Iconography of Manhattan*, V, July 20, 1791; Mitchell, *Hamilton*, II, 153; *Albany Register*, July 18, 1791.

still held: prosperity and the remoteness of the federal government evaporated the "ill humour" of New Yorkers. Hamilton was right in December when he confirmed Jay's view that "accounts from all quarters bespeak the same content which you mention as prevailing in the country."[94] Actually it remained for the threat of the Bank of the United States, the wave of speculation, and the panic of 1792 to shatter the Federalist sense of security as the administration entered the last year of Washington's first term.

94. Hamilton to Jay, Dec. 5, 1791, Jay Papers, Columbia Univ.

CHAPTER 10

Federalists Divide:

The Battle of the Banks

1791-1792

In January 1791, when William Duer reported the disastrous news of Aaron Burr's election, he suggested to Hamilton that nothing could save the New York Federalists from "utter destruction" except Philip Schuyler's residence in the city and the establishment of a branch of the Bank of the United States.[1] At the end of February, President Washington signed the bill establishing the bank; in July the subscription books were opened, by the fall a Board of Directors had been chosen, and by the end of the year, over Hamilton's objections, a branch was planned for the city.[2] The bank precipitated a frenzied movement for a new state bank, and in the aftermath of the battle of the banks a sizable body of Federalists led by the Livingstons went over to George Clinton in the spring election of 1792.

I

One root of the bank war of the early 1790's lay in the conflict of 1784 between Chancellor Livingston's "land bank" and Alexander

1. William Duer to Alexander Hamilton, Jan. 19, 1791, Syrett, ed., *Hamilton Papers*, VII, 442-43.
2. For general background on banking, see Bray Hammond, *Banks and Politics in America from the Revolution to the Civil War* (Princeton, 1957), ch. 3; Mitchell, *Alexander Hamilton*, I, ch. 21. See above, ch. 1, sec. VI.

Hamilton's commercial venture, the Bank of New York. That battle ended in a stalemate; neither bank received a charter; the loan act of 1786 satisfied the demand for a land-backed currency, the state issuing $500,000, $375,000 of which was to be loaned against mortgages in sums from £20 to £300 at 5 per cent interest for 14 years;[3] while the Bank of New York continued to do business without a charter of incorporation. The array of interests of the 1780's toward banking was still present: enthusiastic support from "all the mercantile and moneyed influence,"[4] backed by the Federalists on behalf of commercial banking; support from the "country interest," including the Clintonians, for land-backed currency. Clintonian businessmen like Smith, Lamb, and Willett, however, were not the least bit opposed to banks,[5] and even Robert R. Livingston, promoter of the "land bank," was not opposed to commercial banks per se.

The 1784 fight gave Robert R. Livingston the opportunity to expound his philosophy of banking. As Livingston viewed the scene from his rural vantage point, "a Bank is advantageous to a commercial City, as it affords a secure deposit for money; as it introduces punctuality in payments, and as it extends credit:—It is disadvantageous as it facilitates the exportation of specie, when the balance is against a country, as it is liable to be the subject of speculation; and as it turns the attention of Merchants from Commerce to Stock-jobbing." A bank "whose whole capital is money" would be "liable to more shocks." If run by active merchants it might not have the reputation needed to attract all sources of credit and might best be managed by "established merchants who have retired from business." The land bank he proposed would eliminate many of these evils. It would have a capital of "at least one third money, and the remainder in houses or improved lands," it would be "exclusively established, yet should always be open to new subscriptions," and it would receive public money. It would circulate no more than its capital—a criterion of good banking—and prevent the "dangers and mischiefs" of "a competition of Banks." Conservatism, stability, the encouragement of productive capital and investment by foreigners—these were the values that guided Livington's approach to banking.[6]

3. Ferguson, *Power of the Purse*, 6, 13-18; McDonald, *We the People*, 231-32.
4. Hamilton to John B. Church, Mar. 10, 1784, Syrett, ed., *Hamilton Papers*, III, 520-22.
5. Papers of the Bank of New York, Box 9, Bank of New York, cited in Lynd, *Farm Tenants and Artisans in New York Politics*, 294, n.134.
6. "To the Citizens of New York" by "A Citizen," No. I and No. II, N.Y.

After its defeat in the first battle of the banks in 1784, the Bank of New York did not apply for a charter again until 1789 and did not mount a major effort for one until 1790, by which time it was undergoing significant internal changes.[7] As late as 1789 its capital was no more than $75,000; by the spring of 1791 it was more than $300,000. More important, there was a "consolidating influence" on the ownership of its stock. Although the number of shares increased about 40 per cent, the number of stockholders dropped from 227 to 193. Almost half the stock, about three hundred shares, was in the hands of only two dozen men, inevitably some of the wealthiest merchants of the city.[8] Politically the bank was run by Hamiltonian Federalists, its directors including Senator King, Isaac Roosevelt, and Nicholas Low. Three or four anti-Federalists were small shareholders from 1784 on, the largest on the 1791 list being David Gelston with four shares.[9] Anti-Federalists could also be found on "A List of Customers on the First Ledger, 1787-88,"[10] and there were two members of the board of directors—Daniel McCormick and Thomas Randall, each with fifteen shares—who in the spring election of 1792 became supporters of Governor Clinton. But, essentially, the bank was a Federalist institution.

The bank asked for a charter in 1790 on an avowedly Federalist basis: incorporation would be "an indispensable step towards enabling

---

Independent Journal: or, the General Advertiser, Mar. 13, 17, 1784. The drafts in the R. R. Livingston Papers, N.-Y. Hist. Soc., Box 13, are called "Thoughts on the Establishment of a Bank" and "Observations on the Proposed Establishment of a Bank."

7. Pomerantz, *New York, an American City*, 185-86.

8. See East, *Business Enterprise*, Appendix A, 327-29, for a list of "New York Bank Stockholders, 1784 or 1785" and Henry Domett, *History of the Bank of New York, 1784-1884* (N.Y., 1884), Appendix, 132-35, for "A list of Stockholders of the Bank of New York at the Time of Its Incorporation in 1791." In 1784 there were fourteen large shareholders: four owners held from 14 to 20 shares each, ten owned from 6 to 10 shares. In 1791, however, there were twenty-five large shareholders: one held 34 shares, another 25, nine held from 12 to 16 shares; fourteen others held from 8 to 10 shares.

9. In 1784 there were 227 stockholders in the bank. Of a group of 21 anti-Federalist leaders in 1788-89, 4 may be found among these stockholders. Of 193 stockholders in 1791, 9 can be identified as supporters of Governor Clinton in 1792, including Daniel McCormick, Michael Price, and Thomas Randall, large shareholders each of whom had about 15 shares. McCormick and Randall were members of the Board.

10. Papers of the Bank of New York, Box 11, Bank of New York, reported to me by Staughton Lynd. I assume customer meant borrower, not depositor. Of 15 members of Governor Clinton's election committee of 1789, 7 were "customers."

it to give any material aid to the government of the United States."
The plea was without effect; in the senate, a tie vote was broken by
the speaker against the bank. The entire favorable vote was cast by
Federalists, while the anti-Federalists were unanimously opposed,
joined by one Federalist.[11] The case against the bank, however, was
not political. The bank, "Censor" charged in the papers, was a "corporation of usurers," lending money for 30 days at a rate of 30 to 60
per cent interest a year; the directors, "by issuing their own notes . . .
had depreciated the State paper medium" by more than 10 per cent;
they were "a company of wealthy men"—no more than 250 men with a
stock of $500,000 "formed for private emolument injurious to the
public welfare." Even "Publicola" in defending the bank from the
charge of usury opposed a charter if it were for "no other purpose
than to secure the private fortunes of the partners"—an echo of Chancellor Livingston's philosophy.[12]

Thus stood the banking situation in 1790: one conservatively managed but rapidly expanding bank, charterless; arrayed against it a
residual agrarian hostility to commercial banks and the grumbling of
"impatient, risk-loving" businessmen impatient with the "cautious
and conservative" bankers in charge.[13] In December, Alexander Hamilton dropped among these volatile elements his proposal for a national bank to be chartered by the federal government.

II

The Bank of the United States, drafted into law in the Senate with
Schuyler's aid, had the enthusiastic support of New York's Federalist
delegation. It was a measure that promised rich returns for stockholders and an extra bonus to security holders who would be allowed
to offer funded certificates in partial payment for bank stock.

Some anti-Federalists had qualms about the proposal. In the legislature there was a move to "instruct" the United States senators
against the bank, but it did not come to a vote.[14] Aaron Burr, who

11. The petition is in N.Y. *Daily Advertiser*, Jan. 19, 1790. *Journal of the
Senate of N.Y.*, 13th Sess., 2d meeting, 23.

12. "Censor," *New-York Packet*, Jan. 16, 19, 23, 1790; "Publicola," *ibid.*, Jan.
21, 1790. This may have been by Robert R. Livingston, advancing an argument
resembling his in 1784. "Publicola" was the signature of a piece on funding in
N.Y. *Daily Advertiser*, Feb. 22, 1790, which also was possibly by Livingston.

13. Hammond, *Banks and Politics*, 71-76; Channing, *History of the United States*,
IV, 83-88; Mitchell, *Alexander Hamilton*, II, ch. 5.

14. James Kent to [Theodorus Bailey], Jan. 27, 1791, Kent Papers, I, Lib. Cong.

was not yet in the Senate, would have preferred to delay incorporation, arguing that "a charter granted cannot be revoked" and that
the "promised advantages of a bank appeared problematical."[15] The
New York Journal reported that "it is expected the Bank Bill will
receive but little opposition," and little there was.[16] The vote was
39-20 in favor of the bank, with New York's three anti-Federalists
recorded with the majority. Madison's argument that the bank was
unconstitutional, a monopoly, and partial to commerce found no echo
in New York.[17]

Their actions in the state legislature in 1791 suggest that the
Clintonians, assuming that the bank would be chartered, were already
thinking of two other objectives: a state bank to serve as a counterweight to the national bank and state investment in bank stock as a
means of producing revenue. Whatever Clintonians thought about the
merits of the national bank, the threat of its passage alone was enough
to force them into a dramatic about-face on the Bank of New York
which they had refused to charter the year before. "The Governor and
his adherents," a Federalist assemblyman reported, "are as eager for it
as they have formerly been against it."[18] In the state senate, the charter
was reported favorably by a committee headed by Senator Cantine,
who the year before had voted against incorporation, and it passed
without opposition.[19] In the assembly anti-Federalists from the mid-

---

No record of a debate or vote on such a motion was found in either the assembly
or senate.

15. Aaron Burr to Theodore Sedgwick, Feb. 3, 1791, Sedgwick Papers, Mass.
Hist. Soc.

16. *N.-Y. Journal*, Jan. 31, 1791. The paper was devoid of discussion of the
bank. An issue of *Albany Register*, Feb. 14, 1790, reporting the debate reprints an
item from a Philadelphia paper challenging the constitutionality of the bank.

17. Brant, *James Madison*, II, ch. 26; *N.-Y. Journal*, Feb. 8, 1791, recorded the
favorable vote of the New York anti-Federalists in Congress without comment.
Jabez Hammond, who in an early edition of his book reported the New York
"republicans" as anti-bank, admitted an error in a later edition and ran an
appendix by Erastus Root, a Democratic politician, explaining that Republicans
"saw the necessity of a national currency equally good in every state." See Hammond, *Political Parties*, I, 577-78.

18. James Watson to James Wadsworth, Jan. 16, 1791, Wadsworth Papers, Conn.
Hist. Soc. The Bank of the United States passed the Senate Jan. 20 and the House
Feb. 8, 1791. On Feb. 9 a charter for the Bank of New York was reported favorably
by a committee in the New York Assembly. Debate began two weeks later, Feb.
24, a day before the President signed the bill creating the Bank of the United
States. It is apparent from Watson's letter of Jan. 16 that the Clintonians had
decided to pass the Bank of New York charter even before passage of the national
bank was completely assured.

19. *Journal of the Senate of N.Y.*, 14th Sess., 50, 53.

dle Hudson Valley voted for Matthew Adgate's motion to reject the charter, but with many other anti-Federalists siding with the bank the proposal lost, 29 to 20.[20] Behind this switch lay an anti-Federalist political principle which drew support from moderate Federalists. As James Kent, then a young Dutchess County assemblyman, explained, "it is as requisite to have a state bank to control the influence of a national bank as for a state government to control the influence of a general government." Even a Federalist Bank of New York, the Clintonians must have reasoned, would be compelled to compete with a Federalist Bank of the United States. As a result any number of senators and assemblymen who, as Kent put it, were "in general opposed to the thing in the abstract" voted to charter the Bank of New York.[21]

A second and subordinate reason for the reversal was an outgrowth of Clintonian concern for sources of revenue for the state government, narrowed by the loss of the impost to the federal government. A report of a legislative committee laid down a principle that was already operational: the state should augment its annual income "by converting a proportion of its revenue into productive capital."[22] In chartering the Bank of New York the legislature reserved the option to buy 100 shares worth $50,000, which it took up the following year.[23] No sooner was the national bank in existence than the legislature voted unanimously to buy 190 shares in it too, and by the end of the year the people of the state of New York were the owners of 152 shares of the Bank of the United States purchased for $60,000.[24] The legislators, it would appear, felt safe in betting on two horses at once.

On July 4, 1791, when subscriptions were opened to the national bank in New York City, the stock was oversubscribed in a few hours, triggering a new wave of speculation in bank stock and securities. "Stockjobbing drowns out every other subject," Madison observed.

20. *Journal of the Assembly of N.Y.*, 14th Sess., 78, 95. Other efforts to curb the powers of the Bank of New York failed. Jonathan Havens, an anti-Federalist leader from Long Island, proposed amendments on the method of voting for director and to reduce the director's term of office from two years to one. The first lost by a vote of 29 to 27, the second by 31 to 25, *ibid.*, 94, 99, 109; see *N.-Y. Journal*, Feb. 28, 1791.

21. James Kent to Theodorus Bailey, Feb. 27, 1791. Kent Papers, I, Lib. Cong. and Kent, ed., *Memoirs of James Kent*, 41-42. For similar opinions in Massachusetts see Christopher Gore to Rufus King, Aug. 7, 1791, King, ed., *Correspondence of Rufus King*, I, 400-401.

22. *Journal of the Assembly of N.Y.*, 15th Sess. (1792), 45-46.

23. *Laws of the State of N.Y.*, 14th Sess., ch. 37; 15th Sess., ch. 1.

24. *Ibid.*, 14th Sess., ch. 49; *Journal of the Assembly of N.Y.*, 14th Sess., 121.

"The Coffee House is an eternal buzz with the gamblers."[25] What was new was the degree of involvement: "mechanicks, deserting their shops, shop-keepers sending their goods to auction, and not a few of our merchants neglecting the regular and profitable commerce of the City."[26] In August the market broke temporarily. Hamilton scolded William Duer for creating "a South Sea bubble." In September the New York Stock Exchange was formally organized.[27] Meanwhile, Hamilton helped launch the Society for Useful Manufactures, offering a new field for New York speculators, with the Duer group foremost among them.[28] The *Journal* jibed constantly at "scripomania," "scripophobia," "speculative mania," "stock-jobbing," and "stock gambling."[29] On Long Island, the complaint was of the "rage for speculation"; in Orange County, of "an association of sharpers."[30] "Rusticus, Jr." tried to point out the political lesson: "No news stirring but that of the national bank; alias the speculators Bubble;—alias the aristocratical engine; squirting money into our pockets as plenty as dirt, which is an argument used by our war word speculators to guild the bait of an oppressive land tax, to pay the interest of notes at 20 shillings which were extorted from the poor soldiers at 2 shillings 6 pence."[31]

The reaction that counted, however, was not among the people at large but in a select circle of New York City businessmen. By the late fall a new and frenzied round in the battle of the banks began in response to the entirely unprecedented banking situation in the state: one large institution, the Bank of New York, was now incorporated; one national bank was very likely to establish a branch in the city, and there was the prospect of either collaboration of the two or competition with each other.

25. Madison to Jefferson, July 10, 13, Aug. 8, 1791, cited in Brant, *James Madison*, II, 341-42; N.Y. *Daily Advertiser*, Aug. 9, 1791.
26. Rufus King to Hamilton, Aug. 15, 1791, Syrett, ed., *Hamilton Papers*, IX, 59-61.
27. Hamilton to Duer, Aug. 17, Hamilton to King, Aug. 17, 1791, *ibid.*, 74-76; broadside, "At a Meeting of the Dealers in Public Funds . . . September 21, 1791," N.Y. Pub. Lib.
28. For background, Davis, *Essays in History of Corporations*, I, 349-518, and for the role of New Yorkers, 370-409. For a newspaper attack, *N.-Y. Journal*, Aug. 31, 1791.
29. See articles Aug. 10, 13, 17, 20, 31, *N.-Y. Journal*.
30. Sag Harbor, *Frothingham's Long-Island Herald*, Sept. 13, 1791; *Goshen Repository*, Oct. 25, 1791.
31. "Rusticus, Jr.," *N.-Y. Journal*, Aug. 10, 1791.

III

The first question to be decided was who would control the new national bank. Some large-scale New York operators had trouble buying shares in the new bank. After the subscription was closed at Philadelphia in July 1791, William Constable complained bitterly to William Duer that he had "not got a single share in the Bank . . . for myself or my friends." When Walter Livingston complained on behalf of himself and Constable of the "partiality" of opening day sales, Thomas Willing, the new president, blamed it on "the hurry of the day."[32] Constable, Livingston, and a few others who can be counted in William Duer's speculator circle picked up only a few crumbs; as a result, when elections for Board of Directors were held in October, they were frozen out. At first the New York stockholders worked together "to form a junction" with a Boston group to prevent exclusive control by Philadelphians. Then rival factions of New Yorkers campaigned for seven seats on the board apparently set aside for the city. All the contestants were Federalists but the victors were unmistakably Hamiltonian. They included Senator King, Congressman Laurance, Nicholas Low, Philip Livingston (who had voted for Schuyler against Burr in the state senate), and James Watson and John Watts, both later Federalist congressional candidates. The losers included Walter and John R. Livingston of the upper manor, Alexander Macomb, and a number of people close to William Duer.[33] Brockholst Livingston presided over a meeting of the losing slate.[34] Thus by the fall it was clear that an aggressive circle of New York financial operators was excluded from a voice in the new national bank, men who aside from Alexander Macomb were also excluded from control of the Bank of New York.

The second question to be decided was the relationship of the national and state banks. There were interlocking directorates of the two banks. King and Low were directors in both, and two other large

32. William Constable to William Duer, July 5, 1791; Thomas Willing to Walter Livingston, Oct. 18, 26, 1791; Constable to Livingston, Oct. 31, Nov. 12, 1791; Duer to Livingston, Jan. 10, 1792 [misdated 1791], R. R. Livingston Papers, N.-Y. Hist. Soc.

33. LeRoy and Bayard to Hamilton, Sept. 1, 1791, Syrett, ed., *Hamilton Papers*, IX, 157. For general background, see James O. Wettereau, "New Light on the First Bank of the United States," *Pa. Mag. of Hist. and Biog.*, 71 (1937), 263-85, and Wettereau, "Branches of the First Bank of the United States," *Supplement to the Journal of Economic History*, 2 (1942), 66-100. Also East, *Business Enterprise*, 297-99.

34. *N.-Y. Journal*, Oct. 5, 1791.

national bank stockholders were Bank of New York directors.[35] As for ownership, "one half of the original owners of the branch bank of the United States were small stockholders in the Bank of New York." However, the big investors had far more at stake in the national than the state bank.[36] Thus the Bank of New York was not secure, and even if the New Yorkers on the board of the national bank wanted to protect the Bank of New York, they were only seven among twenty-seven directors.

On the national board there were sharp differences as to policy toward the banks in New York, Boston, and Philadelphia. Some directors, out of fear of the anti-Federalist potential of state banks, sought "the annihilation of all" of them, favoring branches of the Bank of the United States.[37] Hamilton, fearful of going too far and ever solicitous of his god-child, the Bank of New York, at first opposed the creation of branches, favoring cooperation with state banks.[38] The fearful directors of the Bank of New York, "hoping to prevent the establishment of a branch," offered the national bank 300 shares of their stock "so as to create a kind of partnership."[39] When the Bank of the United States turned this down and voted to establish branches, William Seton, treasurer of the Bank of New York, warned Hamilton that "a wish on their part to destroy us would revive State Politicks to the prejudice of the General Government and give a handle to

35. East, *Business Enterprise*, 299. The New York City Directors of the Bank of the United States with the number of shares they held in the Bank of New York were: Rufus King (12 plus 4 held by his father-in-law, John Alsop), Nicholas Low (8), James Watson (4 plus 2 as Watson and Greenleaf), Herman LeRoy (1), Philip Livingston (1), and John Laurance (1). The stockholders in the Bank of New York for 1791 are listed in Domett, *History of the Bank of New York*, Appendix, 132-35.
36. For example, the following big stockholders in the Bank of the United States had one share or less in the Bank of New York early in 1791: William Clark, William Duer, John Delafield, Richard Harison, Josiah Hoffman, Brockholst Livingston, John R. Livingston, and Cornelius Ray. The following large stockholders in the Bank of the United States owned no stock at all in the Bank of New York early in 1791: Andrew Craigie, Alexander Macomb. The names of stockholders in the Bank of the United States were taken from a list of deputies elected by the stockholders in New York City to vote for directors of the bank, *N.-Y. Journal*, Oct. 9, 1791.
37. Fisher Ames to Hamilton, July 31, 1791, Syrett, ed., *Hamilton Papers*, VIII, 589-91.
38. Mitchell, *Alexander Hamilton*, II, 173.
39. Fisher Ames to Hamilton, Aug. 15, 1791, Syrett, ed., *Hamilton Papers*, IX, 55-59; Christopher Gore to Rufus King, Aug. 7, 1791, King, ed., *Correspondence of Rufus King*, I, 400-401.

party."[40] Hamilton, sharing Seton's anxieties, wrote to Nicholas Low about the need for the "avoiding of political parties which will naturally grow up in the monied interest from rival banks under Federal and State Authorities." Accepting the idea of branches, he proposed that each have its own board of directors, all to be appointed by and under the supervision of the national board, a compromise which was adopted. "The whole affair of the branches," Hamilton claimed, "was *begun, continued,* and *ended,* not only without my participation, but *against my judgment.*"[41]

Against this background—with a branch on the way and with the prospect of cooperation between the two banks still alive—new banking schemes burst on the scene in January 1792, and the city was seized with "a bancomania." Within one week, no fewer than three separate banks were projected: the "Million Bank" to be capitalized at $1,000,000 and oversubscribed to the extent of $10,000,000, the "Merchants Bank" to be capitalized at $1,000,000, and the "Tammany Bank" to be capitalized at $2,000,000. At the end of a week of feverish promotion, the three ventures were consolidated and a united request presented to the legislature to charter a bank capitalized at $1,800,000, referred to at first as the "Million Bank" and later as the "State Bank."[42]

The promoters of the new venture, according to Alexander Macomb who was close to them, were "the disappointed in the direction of the existing banks."[43] Actually there were two separate but overlapping circles of businessmen with dissimilar purposes who soon split. One group centering around William Duer was at the height of its speculative activity.[44] Duer's "fertile genius" was "always suggesting new speculations," as Macomb wrote to their associate in England, William Constable; in a single letter Macomb reported news of the new banking venture, reviewed their on-going speculation in the debt, sketched a plan to buy 3000 shares of the new Society for Useful Manufactures, outlined a scheme to build bridges in New Jersey with Nicholas Roosevelt as a front, and pushed a plan to buy the

40. William Seton to Hamilton, Nov. 21, 1791, Syrett, ed., *Hamilton Papers,* IX, 518-20.

41. Hamilton to Seton, Nov. 25, 1791, *ibid.,* 538-39; Hamilton to Nicholas Low, Dec. 21, 1791, *ibid.,* X, 398-400.

42. For the best over-all summary, Davis, *Essays in History of Corporations,* II, 81-90; for newspaper reports, see N.Y. *Daily Advertiser,* Jan. 17-24, 1792.

43. Macomb to Constable, Feb. 21, 1792, Constable Papers, N.Y. Pub. Lib.

44. The best discussion of Duer is in Davis, *Essays in History of Corporations,* II.

ship *America* for a voyage to India.[45] The most favored members of the group were Macomb, Constable, John Dewhurst, Benjamin Walker, and Royal Flint. A dozen others were cut in on one scheme or another; John Pintard acted as Duer's agent. The interest of the Duer group in the new bank scheme marked an ulterior objective. On December 29, 1791, Duer and Macomb formally drew up an agreement "for speculations in the debt of the United States and in the Stock of the Bank of the United States and Bank of New York"; others were let into what became known as the "Six Per Cent Club."[46] Of about 700 shares of the Bank of New York in existence, Macomb bought 290, then went up to 400; in the frenzied buying later on, it was said that he and Duer somehow committed themselves for more shares than the total capitalization of the bank.[47] At the same time they bought national bank stock, and Macomb was approached about becoming a director of the newly proposed branch board.[48]

The purpose of the Duer group, as well as it can be made out, was twofold: to force a coalition of the Bank of New York and the Bank of the United States and thereby bid up the price of stock for both; and secondly, to gain control of the Bank of New York and have an instrument to finance their other speculations. They were hostile at first to establishing a branch of the Bank of the United States. On January 1, Alexander Macomb reported to Constable that "a coalition is in contemplation. I think it will have a happy material effect and will especially benefit the stock of our bank [which] upon strength of this has risen and should the junction be effected it will be very high."[49]

The new bank scheme alarmed the Duer group. "I can't think Col. Duer interested in this business," Seth Johnson reported, "as he is interested in the contracts for almost the whole of the stock of the Present Bank, and at a high price." A new bank therefore might ruin him. Macomb and John Pintard, Duer's agent, promptly joined the venture with a view to controlling it. Pintard, Johnson wrote, "has appeared to advocate the business, and subscribed, largely from a view to counteract it."[50] Very likely the Duer group wanted to do

45. Macomb to William Constable, Jan. 1, 1792, Constable Papers, N.Y. Pub. Lib.
46. Duer Papers, N.-Y. Hist. Soc., cited in Mitchell, *Alexander Hamilton*, II, 171.
47. *Ibid.*, citing Macomb to Duer, Jan. 1, 1792, Duer Papers, N.-Y. Hist. Soc., and Macomb to Constable, Jan. 11, 1792, Constable Papers, N.Y. Pub. Lib.
48. Macomb to Constable, Dec. 7, 1791, Constable Papers, N.Y. Pub. Lib.
49. Jan. 1, 1792, *ibid.*
50. Seth Johnson to Andrew Craigie, Jan. 22, 1792, Craigie Papers, III, Amer.

no more than use the threat of the new bank to force the coalition of the national and Bank of New York. There seems to have been a struggle for control among the promoters, the Duer group lost, and within a few weeks Macomb washed his hands of the whole thing, denouncing it as "a child of darkness." At about the same time he was publicly proposed as a director of the new branch of the Bank of the United States whose appearance Duer had informed him was inevitable.[51]

When the Duer group's spokesmen left, the second group of promoters who retained control of the new bank project was identified by Macomb as "all the Livingstons except English Phil," i.e., Philip Livingston who had been successfully elected to the board of the national bank and proposed for the branch board. Making the same observation, Seth Johnson named as "warm advocates" of the new bank Brockholst and Walter Livingston, and John R. and Edward Livingston, the Chancellor's two brothers. Among the others were Richard Platt and Theodosius Fowler & Co.[52] In the assembly Morgan Lewis was active for their bill, making the lower manor's public support almost complete.[53] The Chancellor was not directly involved but his subsequent reaction on the Council of Revision implied that he too looked sympathetically at the measure.

The aim of the Livingston-led group, like their rivals, was also twofold. They, too, wanted a bank within their control to finance their own ventures. Secondly, they wanted to depress the market because they were selling bank stock and securities to the Duer group for future delivery. The Livingstons thus were the bears, Duer's group the bulls. In order to keep the price of securities low, according to John C. Miller, the Livingstons "cornered all the gold and silver in New York; then drawing the specie from the banks, they forced down the price of securities, prevented the banks from discounting and obliged them to call in their loans. Duer and his associates having gone heavily in debt to the banks, were caught in the

Antiq. Soc.; David Sterling, New York Patriarch: A Life of John Pintard, 1759-1844 (unpubl. Ph.D. diss., New York Univ., 1958), 131-36, 148-50.

51. Macomb to Constable, Jan. 11, 21, Feb. 21, 1792, Constable Papers, N.Y. Pub. Lib.; for the nominations of branch directors see N.Y. Daily Advertiser, Jan. 21, 1792.

52. Seth Johnson to Andrew Craigie, Jan. 22, 1792, Craigie Papers, III, No. 71, Amer. Antiq. Soc.

53. Troup to Hamilton, Mar. 19, 1792, Syrett, ed., Hamilton Papers, XI, 155-58.

middle of a ruinous credit squeeze."[54] Duer personally tried to hedge, secretly ordering Walter Livingston to sell short 100 shares of the Bank of New York stock he held on his own. Walter Livingston, it would appear, kept a foot in both camps, or at least was Duer's "principal dupe,"[55] and eventually was pulled down with him by the weight of $203,875 in notes he endorsed for him.

From the beginning an anti-Federalist political potential was implicit in the third bank scheme, and within a month after the Livingstons won control it was explicit. At the inception of the plan, Seth Johnson felt he had to tell Andrew Craigie that its origin was "not from anti-federalism but from speculation." A week later, Schuyler, writing to Hamilton for arguments to fight the charter in the legislature, also saw no politics in it; neither did Macomb in pulling out. By mid-February, however, the nominations for the gubernatorial election were underway, and the reports changed. "Electioneering and banking line—the only objects which at present agitate the public mind," Macomb wrote Constable; then news of the banking situation in a postscript: "The Chancellor and family have declared for Clinton at the ensuing election."[56] By early March Hamilton heard that "the Bank mania rages violently in this city and is made an engine to help the governor's election." In mid-March the panic was on. Robert Troup, remorseful over being taken in on the third bank scheme, thought he saw it all clearly in retrospect: "mingled with the motives of some of the leaders of the association" of would-be bankers, he told Hamilton, was "a large portion of personal enmity to you and of rooted hatred of the government."[57]

The role of Clintonian leaders in promoting the new bank is obscure enough to suggest it was minimal. Melancton Smith, according to Seth Johnson, "has had no hand in the origins of the New Banks." He joined a committee to draw up its charter, then in the assembly served on a committee of five to consider and revise its constitution; he also worked against a rival Albany bank whose application for a charter appeared at the last minute. Thus it may be inferred that he

54. Miller, *Alexander Hamilton*, 305.

55. Mitchell, *Alexander Hamilton*, II, 175; Duer to Walter Livingston, R. R. Livingston Papers, N-Y. Hist. Soc.

56. Johnson to Craigie, Jan. 22, 1792, Craigie Papers, III, No. 71, Amer. Antiq. Soc.; Schuyler to Hamilton, Jan. 29, 1792, Syrett, ed., *Hamilton Papers*, X, 579-81; Macomb to Constable, Feb. 1, 21, 1792, Constable Papers, N.Y. Pub. Lib.

57. Dr. James Tillary to Hamilton, Mar. 1, 1792, Robert Troup to Hamilton, Mar. 19, 1792, Syrett, ed., *Hamilton Papers*, XI, 109-10, 155-58.

favored the "State Bank."[58] On the other hand David Gelston of New
York City, an equally prominent Clintonian, seems to have opposed
the new bank in the senate. Gelston was a stockholder in the Bank
of New York and later was proposed as a director of the new branch
of the Bank of the United States, possibly as a political reward.[59] In
the panic Smith was stuck with about $20,000 in endorsements for
Duer from which his friends bailed him out.

The charter proposed by the sponsors of the "State Bank," as they
liked to call it, shows a conscious effort to appease a number of
interests pressuring the legislature at the same time.[60] The bankers
proposed that 500 shares at $500 each be reserved for the state govern-
ment and that 6 per cent interest be paid on state funds deposited
with the bank—both enticements to revenue-oriented legislators. They
offered to make loans on mortgage security—the pattern of the 1786
loan act favored by "the country interest" then up for renewal. To
meet the demand for local banking facilities, they would establish
branches in Albany and other cities. And finally, their charter would
allow them to build canals—matching a proposal for separate companies then up for consideration.

The sponsors attempted to win public support by appealing to
legitimate business motives. "Men of all classes," it was claimed when
subscriptions were opened, "flocked to share the advantages which
were held up to view." In a long speech to the subscribers Edward
Livingston enumerated the reasons.[61] First, "the injury non-subscrib-
ers in the national bank and N.Y. Bank sustain by a monopoly of
the stock"; secondly, "a partial administration of the latter," i.e.,
favoritism in the lending policy of the Bank of New York; and thirdly,
the need to meet "the demand for money,—the large sums of which
will be wanted for opening canals, settling the new lands etc." Almost daily articles in the *Daily Advertiser* followed up each of these
themes: "the pride and partiality" of the Bank of New York, "improper influence" at elections, the high interest rate of 8 per cent, the
need for loans "in the remote parts of the state." New sources of
credit, it was claimed, would enable "persons of small capital and

58. N.Y. *Daily Advertiser*, Jan. 18, 1792; Seth Johnson to Andrew Craigie, Jan.
22, 1792, Craigie Papers, III, No. 71; Johnson to Craigie, Jan. 23, 1792, Craigie
Papers, Box 9, Amer. Antiq. Soc.
59. For nominations of directors, see N.Y. *Daily Advertiser*, Jan. 21, 1792.
60. Printed in N.Y. *Daily Advertiser*, Feb. 13, 1792.
61. Johnson to Craigie, Jan. 22, 1792, Craigie Papers, III, No. 71, Amer. Antiq.
Soc.

good character to pursue such common or other objects as would without this aid be embraced only by those few with greater means."[62]

The promoters did not hesitate to ring up old anti-Federalist battle slogans on their banners. "Decius"—probably Brockholst Livingston—offered the efforts by Hamilton and his "minions" to frustrate the new bank as proof of the necessity of "some establishment which may check the increasing influence of the general government and its encroachments upon that of the state."[63] The Secretary of the Treasury, he claimed, wrote "letters upon letters" in order to "dissuade his friends" from supporting the venture. "Brutus" linked up funding, assumption, the plans to support manufactures, and the national bank as means to attract support to the "general government" and give it an "undue balance." Now the national bank was about to "branch out in every trading city of the union," its local directors appointed by the general directors and all under the control of the Secretary of the Treasury. "Yet, not content with this, a scheme is set on foot, for consolidating the different state banks with this general bank, and thus to concentrate the whole monied interest of the community in a few hands."[64]

The Bank of New York, of course, was in a dilemma. Which way should it turn: toward the new "State Bank" or the forthcoming but ominous branch of the national bank? Hamilton was alarmed lest its directors "listen to a coalition with the newly engendered monster" and held out the prospect of "a better alliance."[65] Apparently calmed by this reassurance, even though Hamilton had failed to block the creation of branch banks as he promised, the board brought financial pressure against the new bank promoters and went before the legislature to head off its charter. Greatly relieved, Hamilton promised Seton that "General Schuyler will do everything in his power" in the state senate against the "mad scheme." To him it was by now an out-and-out political battle: "The enemies to Banks and the credit are

62. In N.Y. *Daily Advertiser*, "A Fair Dealer," Jan. 22, "Agricola," Feb. 7, "A Citizen," Jan. 23, "Plain Truth," Jan. 25, "A Speculator," Feb. 7, "Curiosity," Feb. 18, "Curtius," Feb. 23, "Aristotle," Feb. 29, 1792.

63. "Decius," *N.-Y. Journal*, Feb. 15, reprinted in N.Y. *Daily Advertiser*, Feb. 17, 1792.

64. "Brutus," *N.-Y. Journal*, Jan. 21, 1792. "Decius" and "Brutus" were the only contributions to the *Journal* on the bank question.

65. Hamilton to Seton, Jan. 18, 24, 1792, Syrett, ed., *Hamilton Papers*, X, 525, 562-63.

in a fair way of having their utmost malignity gratified."[66] In the papers the hard-put defenders of the banking status quo attacked the new bank mercilessly as the work of speculators and disappointed anti-Federalists;[67] William Duer joined the chorus under the pseudonym of "Gracchus"—the man had a sense of humor.[68] With the lines thus tautly drawn the bank battle shifted to the legislature.

IV

In the legislature the hassle was complicated by the demand for bank charters from Albany and nearby Hudson. Unlike the New York City venture, both the Bank of Albany and the Bank of Columbia, as they were called, were rooted firmly in legitimate business needs.[69] The sponsors of the Albany bank represented a variety of interests—land speculation, manufacturing, trading, canal promotion—and their orientation was toward productive rather than speculative ventures. In both banks the sponsors also were smaller businessmen than any of the New York City promoters, the Albany bank being capitalized at only $75,000 in $150 shares and the Columbia venture at $60,000.[70]

Politically, the Albany bank was very likely a diversion by Schuyler to pull Hamilton's chestnuts out of the fire. The prime organizer of the venture was Elkanah Watson, an energetic promoter and a close associate of Schuyler. Schuyler was its chief lobbyist and Stephen Van Rensselaer, his son-in-law, the first president of its board.[71] Interestingly enough, however, they secured support from the area's anti-Federalists. Congressman Jeremiah Van Rensselaer was chairman of the

66. Seton to Hamilton, Feb. 6, Hamilton to Seton, Feb. 10, 1792, *ibid.*, XI, 17-18, 27-29.

67. In the N.Y. *Daily Advertiser,* "A Merchant," Jan. 20, "A Citizen," Jan. 20, "Banco," Jan. 25, "Aristedes," Feb. 3, "A Citizen," Feb. 11, "A Friend to Useful Institutions," Feb. 21, "Zeno," Feb. 28, 1792.

68. "Gracchus," *ibid.*, Feb. 15, 1792. Alexander Macomb to William Constable, June 15, 1792, Constable Papers, N.Y. Pub. Lib., identifies Duer as the author of another anti-Clinton broadside in June.

69. East, *Business Enterprise,* 302-3; Munsell, ed., *Annals of Albany,* I, 288-92; *N.-Y. Journal,* Feb. 22, 29, 1792.

70. For the directors, *N.-Y. Journal,* Mar. 14, June 12, 1792. Directors who had significant investments in manufactures were James Caldwell, John Stevenson, Jeremiah Van Rensselaer, and Elkanah Watson.

71. Winslow C. Watson, ed., *Men and Times of the Revolution; or Memoirs of Elkanah Watson, Including His Journals of Travels in Europe and America* (N.Y., 1856), 389; Elkanah Watson, Journal D, p. 42, Watson Papers, Box 2, vol. 8, N.Y. State Lib.; Watson, "Commonplacebook," cited in Hugh Flick, Elkanah Watson, Gentleman-Promoter, 1758-1842 (unpubl. Ph.D. diss., Columbia Univ., 1958), 114-15, 117.

organizational meeting, a director, and a later president. And the anti-Federalist *Albany Register* was "happy" to report that stock was rapidly subscribed for this "independent northern bank" which would be the "most effectual barrier we could raise against the exclusive monopoly of New York."[72] The Hudson bank which drew support from Columbia County was similarly bipartisan. Its president was Thomas Jenkins, the Federalist founder of the city of Hudson. Two upper manor Livingstons, John and Henry, were on the board, while such anti-Federalist county stalwarts as Matthew Adgate and Peter Van Ness gave it support.[73]

In the senate Schuyler never seems to have been worried about having the votes to block the "State Bank." A committee of the assembly at first reported favorably on their petition. The Bank of New York entered the fray offering 7 per cent interest on state funds to better the new bank's offer. The promoters countered with a petition claiming widespread support in the city's mercantile community.[74] On March 7 it was common knowledge that Albany's assemblymen were instructed "to vote against the one for this city [the State Bank] as it has a power of making branches in the state and opening the roads and canalls which they think should be done by the state and not for the benefit of companies or individuals."[75]

The panic of 1792 gave the *coup de grâce* to the "State Bank." On March 10 William Duer stopped payments, pulling down with him not only his entire group but his creditors, the Livingstons, as well. To country assemblymen critical of "stock-jobbers" this was dramatic proof of the speculative side of the entire scheme.[76] With understandable caution the legislature let the "State Bank" die. It never came to a vote, and the legislative record is so sparse as to prevent an analysis of its partisans and detractors. But with remarkable speed the legislators moved to meet the legitimate aspirations of those to whom the bank appealed. On March 14 they renewed the successful loan act of

72. *Albany Register*, Feb. 13, 20, 1792; for Van Rensselaer, see N.Y. *Daily Advertiser*, Feb. 15, referring to meeting of Feb. 3.

73. *Hudson Gazette*, Mar. 15, 1792; Ellis, *Columbia County*, 50. Henry Livingston to Samuel B. Webb, Mar. 24, Apr. 2, 1794, Ford, ed., *Correspondence of S. B. Webb*, III, 178-79.

74. Schuyler to Hamilton, Jan. 29, 1792, Syrett, ed., *Hamilton Papers*, X, 579-81; *Journal of the Assembly of N.Y.*, 15th Sess., 31, 49, 64; reports by "Gracchus," Feb. 15, "Curiosity," Feb. 18, "Curtius," Feb. 23, N.Y. *Daily Advertiser*.

75. Daniel McCormick to William Constable, Mar. 7, 1792, Constable Papers, N.Y. Pub. Lib.

76. For an account of the panic, see ch. 13, sec. VI.

1786, which again made credit available in small sums on mortgage security throughout the state. On March 21 the assembly rejected a motion to table the Albany bank, and its charter passed the assembly on March 26 and the senate on April 2. On March 30 two canal companies, also fathered by Schuyler and Elkanah Watson, were chartered. The Bank of Columbia, introduced too late for action, was tabled until the following session, when it passed easily. Then, as if to rebuke the instigators of the panic, the lawmakers approved a measure "to prevent the pernicious practise of stock jobbing."[77]

The Albany bank charter passed the legislature, according to Elkanah Watson, because Schuyler "by the most vigorous efforts forced it through." Both parties were split. While anti-Federalists of the northern part of the state favored it, the two New York City anti-Federalists, Melancton Smith in the assembly and David Gelston in the senate, moved to table it.[78] A reasonable assumption is that Smith opposed it as a partisan of the new "State Bank" while Gelston opposed it as a partisan of the branch Bank of the United States.

Over the legislative hurdle, the Albany bank then came before the Council of Revision where it put to the test Governor Clinton, Robert R. Livingston, and John Sloss Hobart, a conservative Federalist justice. Both Hobart and Livingston at first were opposed and Watson has left a vivid account of his eleventh-hour efforts to save his project in the council. Clinton probably favored it, since Watson does not mention him as an obstacle. Watson had the good fortune to be Hobart's nephew. With only two days left of the ten-day period within which the council had to act, as he tells the story, "I labored hard to a late hour of that night with my Uncle . . . and succeeded to satisfy him, especially as there was not then a single bank in the State outside of the City of New York." The next day Watson was introduced to Livingston at the latter's house and talked to him at length. The following day "about noon, . . . I was in the Senate Chamber of the old City Hall when the Chancellor tapped me on the shoulder with the bill in his hand, saying 'Your Bank is incorporated.' "[79]

Why Livingston endorsed the Albany bank may only be conjectured. It did not meet all of the criteria he set down in 1784 as philosopher of the land bank. Yet it was to be conservatively run and

77. *Laws of the State of N.Y.*, 15th Sess., chs. 25, 40, 60, 61, 16th Sess., ch. 38.
78. *Journal of the Assembly of N.Y.*, 15th Sess., 127-28, 136, 150; *Journal of the Senate of N.Y.*, 15th Sess., 69-70.
79. Watson, ed., *Memoirs of Elkanah Watson*, 390-91.

oriented toward productive rather than speculative capital. Livingston probably would have supported the new "State Bank" had it passed the legislature; now that it was doomed and a new branch of the Bank of the United States was on the way he probably saw the desirability of new banks as a counterweight, even when they were sponsored by his rival, General Schuyler. The next year he would let the Bank of Columbia pass the council, and in 1799 he would support the Bank of Manhattan, successor to the ill-fated "State Bank" of 1792.

In the wake of the panic, the movement for the "State Bank" collapsed, and the Bank of New York and branch of the Bank of the United States closed ranks. Hamilton assured Seton that "it will be enjoined" upon the branch to cooperate; if not "I will decidedly aid your institution so as to preserve it from harm."[80] When the two boards met in March, Alexander Macomb was beyond joy in reporting to Constable on the "mutual harmony and free communication" pledged. The same day he added another shocked note: dealers were refusing to endorse his notes because he was so deeply involved with Duer, who was in jail, and Alexander Whippo, who had fled. A few days later he felt reassured; the Bank of New York was attempting to steady things and the Secretary of the Treasury was continuing his efforts to buoy up the market. Early in April, however, Macomb joined his partner in jail, grim at "my ruin." "I curse myself for my credulity in believing in Duer." To him the panic was the result of the extravagance of Duer's schemes and the "attempts to injure the Bank of New York by the Million Bank which first caused a stop to credit."[81]

As a result of the bank war of 1790-1792, the state granted charters to the Bank of New York, which it had long held at arm's length, and to two others, the Bank of Albany and the Bank of Columbia; it rejected a charter for the "State Bank"; the Bank of the United States established a branch in New York City under control of its national Board of Directors; and the state invested in all four banks and revived the loan act of 1786. When the panic subsided and a new boom began, the Bank of New York and the branch of the Bank of the United States drew apart, the smaller bank fearful of the desire of the branch to "preponderate." A year later their relations were "toler-

80. Hamilton to Seton, Mar. 19, 1792, Seton to Hamilton, Mar. 21, Syrett, ed., *Hamilton Papers*, XI, 154-55, 163-64.
81. Macomb to Constable, Mar. 24, 28, Apr. 7, 11, May 9, 1792, Constable Papers, N.Y. Pub. Lib.

ably smooth"; thereafter, they had a feverish quality, now up, now down.[82] Both continued to show "partiality" in their lending poli-cies.[83] As a result, interest in a third bank stimulated by the scheme of 1792 remained an undercurrent in New York business life, finally coming to the surface in 1799 in support of Aaron Burr's Bank of Manhattan.

The immediate political effects of the turmoil were even greater than the economic expansion of banking facilities. In the spring elec-tion of 1792 a segment of the mercantile community left the Federal-ists to give Clinton the best showing he ever made in New York City. The Livingstons, baptized as leaders of a popular cause, were ready to wreak vengeance on their enemies for their financial losses. In the popular mind the Hamiltonian Federalists were stigmatized as pro-ponents of privilege and Hamilton's former assistant, the "prince of speculators" William Duer, was marked as the first villain of the era. In short, popular support for the emerging "republican interest" was enlarged.

82. Davis, *Essays in History of Corporations*, II, 91-95.
83. Leake, *Memoirs of John Lamb*, 338-39; Davis, *Memoirs of Aaron Burr*, I, 417.

CHAPTER 11

Clintonians, Federalists, and the

State Government

1789-1792

If there was a Hamiltonian system in the national government, there was a Clintonian system in the government of New York, the full shape of which emerged by the end of Clinton's fifth term as governor in the spring of 1792. Contrary to the opinions of historians who have reduced George Clinton's policies simply to "agrarianism" or "radicalism,"[1] Clinton and his party supported charters for banks, extravagant grants to land speculators, generous, if selective, support for manufacturers, and aid for publicly built roads and privately built canals. They also stood for the cautious expenditure of state money for schools and a near indifference to reform, whether it was the plight of the tenant farmer, Negro slave, or imprisoned debtor. Their guiding principles lay in encouraging aspiring entrepreneurs whatever their field, avoiding taxes that would fall on the yeomanry by the prudent investment of state revenue in income-producing capital, and disbursing all this largesse for maximum political advantages.

1. For a discussion of Clinton's philosophy, see above, ch. 2, sec. V. For a study of the relation of the state government and the economy touching on the Clintonian outlook, see Beatrice G. Reubens, State Financing of Private Enterprise in Early New York (unpubl. Ph.D. diss., Columbia Univ., 1960).

I

In Clinton's fifth term from 1789 to 1792, New York was at an impasse in its public land policy. A vast reservoir of undeveloped land lay in the hands of speculators as a result of the lavish grants of the royal governors before the Revolution. Every program that had been adopted after the Revolution had the same result, delivering more land into the hands of speculators than to actual settlers. The disposition of confiscated Loyalist estates, while relatively democratic in the lower Hudson Valley, was of advantage primarily to speculators on the frontier areas.[2]

The military bounty plan designed to reward soldiers of the New York Line was a fiasco. The Indian title to a tract set aside in the Finger Lakes district in 1782 was not extinguished until 1789. Meanwhile, an alternate area in the extreme north known as the "Old Military Tract" proved undesirable. Some veterans as a result squatted on Indian land, others sold their claims to speculators.[3] In April 1790, with the title clear to 1,680,000 acres in western New York, the legislature provided for twenty-eight 60,000-acre towns with 100 lots in each, banning any but original grantees from balloting for the lots. The Council of Revision overruled the bill which had to be rewritten. When the land was allotted it was found that of about 1900 parcels in the first batch, no more than half were in the hands of original owners.[4] Albany merchants had brought up claims by the dozens, a few by the hundreds. The legislature soon was inundated with appeals from squatters already on the land and from veterans and their heirs who had neglected to make a claim or were not covered by the letter of the law. A legislative commission was appointed in 1792 but did not unravel the confusion until 1800. Throughout this period the "great uncertainty" of titles thwarted settlement.[5]

The disposition of land in the westernmost part of the state was even worse. In the dispute over ownership of the region between New

2. See above, ch. 3, sec. II.
3. See Jeanette Sherwood, "The Military Tract," New York State Historical Association, *Quarterly Journal*, 7 (1926), 169-80; Cochran, *New York in the Confederation*, 108-9; Ruth Higgins, *Expansion in New York, with Especial Reference to the Eighteenth Century* (Columbus, 1931), ch. 9.
4. *Laws of the State of N.Y.*, 12th Sess., ch. 44 (1789), 13th Sess., ch. 59 (1790); Lincoln, ed., *Messages from the Governors*, II, 309-10.
5. *Laws of the State of N.Y.*, 15th Sess., ch. 53; Davis, ed., *Memoirs of Aaron Burr*, I, 319-27, reprints Burr's report as commissioner. Theodore Sedgwick to Rufus King, July 26, 1799, King, ed., *Correspondence of Rufus King*, III, 71.

York and Massachusetts, New York retained political jurisdiction
while her neighbor got title to the land. Massachusetts granted
3,000,000 acres to a syndicate headed by Oliver Phelps and Nathanial
Gorham who by 1790 were selling land in entire townships, introducing a galaxy of satellite land promoters to Ontario County. A major
part of their land which reverted to Massachusetts in default of payment had been resold to Robert Morris who in 1791-92 disposed of
one vast tract to the Pulteney Associates of England and another
1,500,000 tract to the Holland Land Company, keeping a large tract,
"Morris' Reserve," for himself. Morris' son, Thomas, had already arrived in the Genesee country; Charles Williamson, the Pulteney agent,
would begin operations in 1792-93 to be followed shortly by Dutch
agents.[6]

   In 1789 the state still held about 7,000,000 of the 29,000,000 acres
within New York. Under the land policy adopted in 1786 requiring
sale at auction of either 64,000-acre townships or 640-acre lots with
full payment in 60 days, little land moved. The only significant sale
was in 1787 to a syndicate headed by Alexander Macomb of a 500,000-
acre tract known as the St. Lawrence Ten Towns, or the Ogden Purchase.[7] In 1789 the legislature gave the land commissioners authority
to pursue a more flexible policy. In one area to be surveyed as the
Twenty Townships, the commissioners could fix a reasonable price
above a minimum of three shillings an acre and accept written applications. If the land did not sell they could reduce the price although
not below the minimum. A quarter of the purchase price was still
required as down payment but credit was extended to six months. In
1790 the receipts of the land office were a paltry $3000.[8]

   Finally in March 1791, apparently without either discussion or discernible opposition, the legislature granted the commissioners authority to "sell and dispose of any of the waste and unappropriated lands
in this state in such parcels on such terms and in such manner as they
shall judge most conducive to the interests of the state."[9] With this
broad discretionary power, the commissioners, consisting of Governor

6. See Higgins, *Expansion in New York*, ch. 10; Turner, *History of Phelps and Gorham's Purchase*, chs. 1, 2.
7. *Laws of the State of N.Y.*, 9th Sess., ch. 67 (1786); 7th Sess., ch. 60 (1784); 8th Sess., ch. 66 (1785); Channing, *A History of the United States*, IV, 96.
8. *Laws of the State of N.Y.*, 12th Sess. (1789), ch. 32; Don Sowers, *The Financial History of New York State from 1789-1912* (N.Y., 1914), Appendix I, 302-4.
9. *Laws of the State of N.Y.*, 14th Sess., ch. 42.

Clinton, Attorney-General Burr,[10] and the secretary of state, treasurer, and auditor—all Clintonians—proceeded to dispose of land on a scale that might have made the most generous royal governor of the province blush.

A number of factors shaped their decision, the first of which was the pressure of speculators. Speculation in federal and state debts and in bank stock rose to a crescendo between 1790 and 1792. In New York there was no less a "rage for speculation" in land; it would be hard to find an important merchant, lawyer, or politician who did not have a finger in some speculative pie.[11] Anti-Federalist leaders figured as prominently in speculation as their resources permitted. Their names may be found on the official records of confiscated estates,[12] soldier's bounty claims,[13] and tracts of the public domain.[14] The well-known speculations of Clinton, the head of the party, have been detailed.[15] Melancton Smith, democratic ideologue, had what his recent biographer calls an "appetite for land" that led to purchases in almost every part of the state. By 1793 he was recommended to a would-be investor in land as a man "acquainted with almost every person of consequence," i.e., every land dealer, in western New York.[16] There was hardly a blue-nosed anti-speculator in a carload of Clintonian leaders; Robert and Abraham Yates may be the exceptions.

10. For attempts to absolve Burr of responsibility, see Davis, ed., *Memoirs of Aaron Burr*, I, 327-30, and Schachner, *Aaron Burr*, 98; for the opposite view, see Hammond, *Political Parties*, 59. Burr was absent from most of the commissioners' sessions; it is beyond credibility that he was ignorant of an operation so fraught with politics.

11. Francis Adrian Vanderkemp, "Extracts from the Vanderkemp Papers," Buffalo Hist. Soc., *Publications*, 2 (1880), 42, 45; Huth and Pugh, trans. and ed., *Talleyrand in America*, II, 137, 173; entry of Oct. 22, 1794, William Strickland Diary, 314, N.-Y. Hist. Soc.

12. See above, ch. 3, sec. II.

13. See Secretary of the State of New York, *A List of the Names of Persons to Whom Military Patents Have Issued Out of the Secretary's Office and to Whom Delivered* (N.Y., 1793). This pamphlet lists about 1900 patents and includes the original grantee and the person to whom he sold it. The names of several dozen Clintonians are recognizable among the purchasers, including Jeremiah Van Rensselaer of Albany, James Clinton and Moses and John DeWitt of Ulster County, Melancton Smith, Michael Connally, and John Quackenboss of New York City.

14. See e.g., "Jonathan Lawrence's Map of the Town of Plattsburgh," n.d. but after 1785, N.-Y. Hist. Soc.

15. See ch. 2, sec. I. For the speculations of the Governor's brother, James Clinton, see a broadside (1789) in N.-Y. Hist. Soc., advertising 20,000 acres for sale in various tracts.

16. Brooks, Melancton Smith, 64-75, citing a comment in Bossenger Foster to Andrew Craigie, July 26, 1793, Craigie Papers, Amer. Antiq. Soc.

Second in importance in shaping Clintonian land policy were the pressures of politics. The anti-Federalist leaders had watched the magnetic effects of the Hamiltonian system on political allegiances. By 1791 it was clear they had lost the state to the Federalists in national elections. By then it was also clear that the new, growing frontier counties were adding reserves to Federalism under the guidance of land proprietors like William Cooper, Oliver Phelps, and Thomas Morris working hand in glove with Philip Schuyler.[17] Clintonians could have calculated that a judicious disposal of the public domain might kill several birds at once: attach some substantial interests to Governor Clinton in state politics, plant a few potentially loyal land proprietors among the Federalists in the western wilderness, and feather their own nests.

Public opinion was no obstacle. Outside of landlord circles it was commonly accepted that it would be preferable social policy to create a yeomanry in the interior. "What an asylum for the oppressed," exclaimed a young Republican editor of Long Island, if land was "divided on agrarian principles, what multitudes may here find freedom and support." Land, therefore, had to be kept from "the grasp of unprincipled land jobbers."[18] When it came to practical politics, however, there was no articulate group in the state demanding direct sales in small tracts to settlers, rather than to "jobbers." The principal would-be migrants to the interior were New Englanders without power to shape New York's policy. New settlers on the frontier were few in number and the large landholders already there were beginning to dominate its politics. Tenants of the Hudson Valley were without spokesmen in high circles.

Most important, the voice of the eastern yeomanry hostile to land engrossment was stilled by an economic philosophy which made the avoidance of taxes the *sine qua non* of state policy.[19] The public domain, Thomas Paine instructed Americans in *Common Sense,* was a means "not only to the discharge of the present debt, but to the constant support of government."[20] Governor Clinton from the time

17. See ch. 12 for the politics of the west.

18. Sag Harbor, *Frothingham's Long Island Herald,* Oct. 25 and Dec. 13, 1791; see also an oration of Samuel L. Mitchill, in *Transactions of the Society for the Encouragement of Agriculture, Manufactures and the Useful Arts* (N.Y., 1792), 3-7.

19. For a brief discussion of this question, see Sowers, *Financial History of N.Y.,* 42.

20. Philip Foner, ed., *The Complete Writings of Thomas Paine,* 2 vols. (N.Y., 1945), I, 36, 42-43.

he first broached land policy to the legislature did so in the context
of discharging the public debt; the public lands were "among the
means that present themselves for this provision beyond direct taxation." Secondly, he hoped that "the land office, will . . . be so regulated as while it is rendered an object of revenue it will at the same
time afford the utmost encouragement to the speedy settlement of
the country."[21] The ordering of these goals was crucial.

Years later, Jabez Hammond, the Jeffersonian politician-historian,
argued with justification that "the wants of the state were surely not
so pressing but that if the commissioners had confined their sales to
from one hundred to ten thousand acres to each purchaser, enough
funds might have been raised to meet all the public exigencies."
"Land agents on the part of the state," he pointed out, "might have
been created, whose sole business should have been to make sales of
lands to actual settlers."[22] Yet this was the voice of the next generation. In 1791, if the state disposed of its land in small lots directly to
settlers, it would have had to extend long-term credit and to be resigned to a long, uncertain wait for returns. But if it sold large tracts
to eastern businessmen, it could expect both an immediate revenue
and returns over a period of years.

The revenue-to-avoid-taxes philosophy was one key with which
politicians unlocked the public domain to large purchasers. Another
was the distinction Governor Clinton and other contemporaries drew
between the "land jobber," the speculator pure and simple who bought
land with no other purpose than to hold on to it for the profit that
would automatically accrue, and the land promoter, who sold land
quickly and invested in developing his area.[23] In public Clinton excoriated the absentee and alien owners "of large tracts of uncultivated
lands" who "contribute nothing to the exigencies of government,"
who "retard the progress of improvements while their estates continue
to increase in value by the labor and industry of the citizens who
settled and cultivate adjacent lands." Without success anti-Federalists had tried in the 1780's to pass a tax on such land to force it into
circulation.[24] Clinton also would have no truck with overzealous

21. Lincoln, ed., *Messages from the Governors*, II, 199.

22. Hammond, *Political Parties*, I, 59.

23. Clinton to Louis Cook, Nov. 13, 1791 [copy], Pickering Papers, Mass. Hist.
Soc.; Seth Johnson to Andrew Craigie, Mar. 4, 1792, Craigie Papers, Amer. Antiq.
Soc., for a land speculator's impatience with Clinton's methods.

24. Lincoln, ed., *Messages from the Governors*, II, 218-19; see a remark by Cong.
John Williams in a debate on national land policy, *Annals*, 4th Cong., 1st Sess., 408.

speculators who dealt with the Indian tribes for land in violation of the state's constitution and laws, especially when they were from "the great families."[25] But he never objected to large sales to men who could bring about "speedy settlement," a fact well known to land-buyers.[26]

From May through September 1791, the land commissioners, sitting at New York in sixteen sessions, faced an inevitable dilemma. The choice before them in 201 applications (a good many of them duplicates or by the same men with different partners) was not between settlers and speculators, but only among speculators. A handful of applications were for tracts of less than one thousand acres; all the rest ran into the tens of thousands or millions.[27] By the end of the summer the commissioners, with Governor Clinton presiding, had approved thirty-five grants covering 5,542,170 acres with a total sale price of $1,030,433, most of it payable in installments. Ninety per cent of the land was awarded in extremely large tracts, the largest of which became the most famous: the Macomb sale of 3,635,200 acres. Five other grantees received tracts totaling 1,198,000 acres; another eleven received a total of 574,000 acres in parcels of from 40,000 to 67,000 acres. The seventeen remaining grantees got tracts of from 5,000 to 10,000 acres. The prices varied widely, presumably with the quality and availability of the land.

In the following election, in April 1792, Federalists charged that the land was "lavishly dealt out to the friends and partisans of Governor Clinton." A broadside, probably written by Philip Schuyler, named sixteen specific grantees with some type of connection with the Governor,[28] an accusation that objective analysis generally confirms not only for the sixteen but for the entire list. Putting aside for the moment the Macomb sale, the grantees might be put into one of several categories. There were "old faithfuls" like Melancton Smith (2000 acres), Marinus Willett (6000 with Smith), Clinton's brother James (1000), and his erstwhile business manager and clerk of the

25. See his handling of the N.Y. Genesee Land Company in Turner, *History of Phelps and Gorham's Purchase*, 106-7.

26. See footnote 39.

27. The records of the commission, which include applications for land as well as awards, are in *Journal of the Assembly of N.Y.*, 15th Sess., 182-200.

28. "To the Free and Independent Electors" [n.d., n.p., misdated, by the curator, 1791], broadside, N.-Y. Hist. Soc. For a discussion of the political context see ch. 13. For a list of Clinton's New York City supporters in the election to which the grantees can be compared, see *N.-Y. Journal*, Feb. 25, Mar. 21, 1792, and for a post-election list, July 18, 1792.

assembly, John McKesson (3000). There were the "party regulars," Senators John Williams, Alexander Webster, and Edward Savage of the north country (for the three: 25,000), Assemblyman Matthew Adgate of Columbia, *bête-noire* of the landlords in 1785 (45,000, 40,000, and 1400), and Jonathan Lawrence, chairman of the New York City election committee (50,000). There were, thirdly, "rewards for services rendered," for example to Senator Nicholas Roosevelt, who had conveniently absented himself from the state senate when Aaron Burr needed votes to defeat Schuyler (Nicholas and John Roosevelt: 500,000). There were, lastly, favors for "new converts": Leonard Cutting (50,000 and 25,000) and Thomas Ludlow (50,000), men who would appear for the first time on Clinton's election committee in 1792, and Robert C. Livingston of the upper manor, who according to the Federalist broadside had "recently become a friend and advocate" of the Governor. As if to confirm the political character of the winners, a number of Clinton's prominent opponents were flatly turned away, among them William Cooper and Jacob Morris of frontier Otsego, Nicholas Low, the Hamiltonian banker of New York City, and Peter Van Gaasbeck, the renegade anti-Federalist from Kingston.[29]

On the other hand much can be said in justice to the commissioners. First, they rejected a great many applications, noting "price too low" on bid after bid; many of the men ultimately favored had to raise their offers or scale down the amount requested. Secondly, they did not oblige every friend or potential friend; for example, Brockholst Livingston and John R. Livingston went unrewarded in four bids. Third and most important, a good number of Federalists were given grants. Nicholas Roosevelt's bid, for example, was taken instead of one by Jonathan Lawrence, the party "chairman" in New York City. The largest grants in fact went to Federalists: to Macomb, to the two Roosevelts, to John Watkins and Royal Flint (the latter a close associate of William Duer), and to James Caldwell of Albany. Lastly, the Governor's closest friends, Smith and Willett, received some of the smallest grants—although it is possible, as Federalists claimed, that they were secret partners in other tracts. Given the broad discretionary power vested in the commissioners, it might even be argued that they made an effort to distribute the spoils in a fairly bipartisan fashion. This perhaps was the purpose. Federalist leaders such as

29. The final grants may be compared with the applications in *Journal of the Assembly of N.Y.*, 15th Sess., 182-200.

Schuyler might better have been worried about the number of influential Federalists they might lose as a result of Clinton's shrewdness.

II

The Macomb purchase was in a class by itself, rich with political
implications overlooked by historians. Alexander Macomb made the
application for the land; not until the following year did he reveal
publicly that William Constable and Daniel McCormick were associated with him. He had carried out his purchase of the St. Lawrence
Ten Towns in 1787 in the same way, fronting for a larger group which
then included the Federalists Schuyler, Hamilton, Henry Knox, Robert Morris, Gouverneur Morris, some Albany men, and John Lamb,
perhaps the only anti-Federalist among them.[30]

Macomb was known as one of the richest and most splendidly
housed "merchant princes" of the city—it was in his house that Washington stayed for a while in 1789. He was a business associate of
William Duer, with whom he was deeply involved in speculation in
bank stock. Duer was not party, however, to this New York land
speculation; in the spring of 1791 he was pulling off his own giant
speculation in 2,000,000 acres in Maine.[31] Constable was also a leading speculator, in a "strategic position" as "a contact man or go-between for a circle of eight or ten, in America and Europe."[32] Mc-
Cormick, although a wealthy man, a speculator, and like Constable, a
director of the Bank of New York, operated on a less grandiose scale
than either Duer or Constable.

In politics Macomb and Constable were both well-known Federalists; Macomb was a successful candidate on their 1788 assembly slate;
Constable was chairman of Robert Yates's election committee in 1789.
Macomb, however, seems to have drifted from the party; he failed to
be re-elected in 1791. Constable was especially close to Hamilton.[33]

30. Revealed by Daniel McCormick in an affidavit, May 4, 1792, in the *N.-Y.
Journal*, June 16, 1792. Seth Johnson in a letter to Andrew Craigie, Apr. 15, 1792,
cited in Davis, *Essays in History of Corporations*, I, 302, referred to "the great land
speculation owned by Macomb, McCormick and Constable."
    31. For his wealth, Pomerantz, *New York An American City*, 292, and James
Kent to Theodorus Bailey, Feb. 27, 1791, Kent Papers, I, Lib. Cong.; for economic
background, Davis, *Essays in History of Corporations*, I, 279-80, 395-96, and East,
Business Enterprise, 191-94.
    32. Mitchell, *Alexander Hamilton*, II, 162-63.
    33. For Constable, N.Y. *Daily Advertiser*, Feb. 17, 1789; for Macomb as an
assembly candidate, *N.-Y. Journal*, Apr. 22, 1790, Apr. 20, 1791; N.Y. *Daily Advertiser*, June 2, 1791.

Daniel McCormick, on the other hand, was a close friend of the Governor,[34] even though he was a former Tory. In the confidential correspondence of the three men, Macomb referred to Clinton as "our old friend" and he too expressed pleasure at Clinton's re-election in 1792, whether out of gratitude for the grant or from traditional support is not clear.[35] All three businessmen were in turn presidents of the Society of the Friendly Sons of St. Patrick of which George and DeWitt Clinton were also members.[36]

Macomb's application was one of the first received by the commissioners and the second to be granted. The Ten Towns tract he purchased in 1787 fronted on fifty miles of the St. Lawrence and extended twenty miles inland. He first requested "all the vacant land between Lake Champlain and the river St. Lawrence and North of Totten-Crossfield's purchase." The commissioners rejected this "on account of its extent and because it contained lands joining old patents and fronts too great a proportion of water communication." Macomb then scaled down his request, excluding the area to the east fronting on Lake Champlain, but adding an area to the southwest on Lake Ontario. The commissioners then noted after his application, "accepted, the quantity being reduced."

The tract, on a modern map of the state, covers all of Lewis County, part of Oswego, and almost all of St. Lawrence, Franklin, and Jefferson counties. There probably were no more than a handful of squatters in the entire region. Most of it was relatively good farm land although its reputation was poor; its location on and near the St. Lawrence and Lake Ontario gave it highly desirable water transportation.[37] The commissioners agreed to Macomb's offer of eight cents an acre and his proposal for payment: no down payment, one-sixth in a year, and the rest in five annual installments. They also exempted Macomb from the requirement of having a stated number of settlers on his land within a given time.

In the election of 1792 Federalists charged that Governor Clinton stood to profit from the transaction via his friend McCormick who,

34. "Independent Elector," N.Y. *Daily Advertiser*, Apr. 29, 1789; *N.-Y. Journal*, July 18, 1792.
35. See the letters cited in footnotes 40-43.
36. Murphy and Mannion, *The History of the Sons of Saint Patrick*, 155-59. McCormick was president, 1784-1788, Constable, 1789-90, Macomb, 1791, and McCormick, again, 1793-1827. Between 1784 and 1795 the society had about 100 members; *ibid.*, 535-37.
37. *Journal of the Assembly of N.Y.*, 15th Sess., 184-86.

it was alleged as Macomb's secret partner, was holding a third of the tract, a part of which he planned to transfer to Clinton.[38] Weighing the accusation on its own merit and putting aside its politically suspect origins, testimony of the speculators themselves on the whole absolves Clinton of a personal motive in the sale. Late in 1791 Constable set off to Europe to try to dispose of large tracts of the purchase. Meanwhile, Macomb contracted with Colonel William Smith, John Adams' son-in-law, who would also leave New York for Europe soon, to dispose of 1,000,000 acres. In one of his first letters to Constable, Macomb made clear Clinton's attitude: "I informed our friend G[eorge] C[linton] of the contract I had enter'd into with Col. Smith. He was much pleased with it and wishes it may be compleated—a speedy sale and settlement will best serve his interest, and for his part he would have no objections that the whole was disposed of at the same rate—Our friend Daniel [McCormick] is of the same sentiment and I confess such sale would make the speculation a good one."[39] Early in February 1792, Macomb reported that "we have great electioneering talk— the anti-Clintonians wish to injure him by blaming him for the sale made to me—but I believe that [it] will end well, and George be again returned."[40] In May, with Macomb in the debtors' jail following Duer's collapse, McCormick reported to Constable that Macomb "was obliged to let his creditors know that you and I were equally interested in the land"; this information "General Schuyler made a great handle of against the Governor as being the person who held this reserved share." McCormick was unequivocal in denying the accusation. "Mr. M[acomb] and myself have made oath that the Governor never was interested in any agreement or promise whatever. Which the Governor requested and said as honest men we could not refuse. As he had declared to us both that he never would be concerned in any land he as governor was the granter of and I hope he will have it in his power to make S[chuyler] and his informant Mr. N[icholas] Low appear as they deserve."[41]

In June after the election Clinton published the affidavits he had solicited from the grantees. Macomb swore that "he doth not know

38. The charges are presented fully in the account of the election of 1792 in ch. 13, sec. V.

39. Macomb to Constable, Nov. 3, 1791, also Dec. 3, 1791, Constable Pierrepont Papers, N.Y. Pub. Lib.

40. Macomb to Constable, Feb. 5, 1792, *ibid.*

41. McCormick to Constable, May 10, 1792, Macomb to Constable, May 9, 1792, *ibid.*

nor has he any reason to believe" that Clinton "was either directly or indirectly concerned in the said purchase; or that he was to have ever had, or now hath any shares, part or interest in the said tract of land." Nor was there any "agreement or promise" of land for the future. McCormick's affidavit was similar. Macomb also swore that Clinton had no interest in the 1787 purchase of the Ten Towns, revealing for the first time the names of the prominent Federalists involved in that purchase.[42] When Macomb resumed his correspondence with Constable he was "glad the old Governor is re-elected. I rejoice at the end" and "as I know your sentiments you will be pleased with this election."[43]

In spite of the affidavits and the letters, the possibility that Clinton was bribed cannot be completely ruled out. Macomb, while he was denying under oath that Clinton had profited from the land sale, also was advising Constable that in order to get the state to remove the Indian tribes from the St. Lawrence River area he was willing to reward Clinton if necessary. He was confident, however, that friends of the Governor could manage the affair, presumably without any inducement. Samuel Ogden and John Lamb, both of whom had a share of the original tract, pressed Clinton to remove the Indians, and the Governor agreed, an action, however, that was consistent with his established policy wherever the Indian claim had been extinguished.[44]

If there was an understanding that Clinton would be paid off, no evidence has come to light that he acquired land in the Macomb purchase. After Macomb failed, his land was divided among his partners and creditors; in the 1790's it was sold and resold. DeWitt Clinton, the Governor's nephew, acquired Macomb land. So did Aaron Burr, who as land commissioner had conveniently absented himself from the sessions at which Macomb got his grant.[45] Their purchases might be regarded as normal business deals or as arrangements among men who had an understanding with each other.

42. *N.-Y. Journal*, June 16, 1792.
43. Macomb to Constable, June 15, 1792, Constable Pierrepont Papers, N.Y. Pub. Lib.
44. Macomb to Constable, Sept. 6, 1792, *ibid.*
45. For evidence of DeWitt Clinton's holdings as a "trustee" and of Melancton Smith's purchase of Macomb land from him, apparently as a blind for Oliver Phelps, see Melancton Smith to Oliver Phelps, Nov. 7, 9, 19, Dec. 5, 1796, Oliver Phelps Papers, Box 23, N.Y. State Lib. For Burr, see letters, Jan. 20, 1793, Sept. 22, and Nov. 23, 24, 1794, Constable-Macomb Land Papers, N.Y. Pub. Lib., indicating that Burr bought a tract of 200,000 acres from Samuel Ward and had other dealings with Constable.

Perhaps Alexander Hamilton can be allowed to give the final word on George Clinton. Late in 1792, Hamilton had occasion to discuss Clinton in connection with the vice-presidential contest then underway. To his fellow Federalists whom he was counseling not to vote for Aaron Burr, Hamilton was candid. The Governor was "a man of narrow and perverse politics. Still Mr. Clinton is a man of property, and in private life, as far as I know, of probity."[46] Thus it could be argued that Hamilton in effect absolved Clinton from the accusations his party made in the heat of the election, just as he would absolve Jefferson from wild Federalist charges when he again sought Burr's defeat in the presidential election of 1800.

The following year, 1793, when Clinton brought a private damage suit for libel against his detractors, asking $50,000 in damages, the jury gave him the verdict, although it reduced the reward to $1000. As the years went by, Federalists, who never tired of raking over the coals of the "scandal of '91," gradually softened their accusation against Clinton from personal interest simply to bad policy.[47] This too would seem a reasonable judgment by posterity. Looking at the land grants of 1791 as a whole, they are more suggestive of Clinton's quest for political support than personal profit.

III

The revenue received and anticipated from land sales, combined with the bright prospects of income from other "productive" investments, set the stage for the state's embarkation on a program of unprecedented expenditures in a variety of fields. The state's income leaped ahead spectacularly to $256,000 in 1791 and $559,500 in 1792 and even when it leveled off in the mid-1790's was at a point higher than it had ever been.[48]

In his annual message to the legislature in 1792 Governor Clinton could make the American politician's most cherished claim: "it appears that our treasury will receive an augmentation sufficient under prudent management, to produce an annual revenue exceeding the ordinary expenses of government." It was still advisable to "render

46. Hamilton to ?, Sept. 21, 1792, Lodge, ed., *Works of Hamilton*, VIII, 289.
47. "To the Independent Electors of the State of New York" by Samuel Stringer, Chairman of the Federal Republican [Federalist] Committee, Albany, 1801 and "Remarks of the Federal Committee" by Stringer, broadsides, DeWitt Clinton Collection, Albany Institute of History and Art.
48. See Appendix, Tables 7 and 8.

it [the revenue] productive"; for this reason he urged "giving this capital an extensive circulation," i.e., renewing the loan act of 1786. But he endorsed a report he had received recommending state aid to build a canal, "especially as the resources of the state will prove adequate to these and other useful improvements without the aid of taxes." In closing his message he also renewed his old plea to make "our seminaries of learning" among "the first objects of your care and patronage."[49] The message had all the lineaments of the Clintonian welfare state.

In recognition of the new condition of the state treasury the legislature loosened its hold on the purse strings. In 1791-92 the state invested heavily in bank stock; it also passed a new loan act of $554,600 in 1792. It appropriated other money on a lavish scale in support of roads, canals, and manufactures, and on a smaller scale to aid education and a hospital.

The most novel expenditure for the state was on transportation, the most pressing internal problem. "The present road system," Elkanah Watson commented, was "a disgrace to this fine state and cried loudly for change." Routes to the west were the foremost need; pioneers and land promoters were clamorous for action.[50] The natural waterways into the district were all inadequate. The Mohawk River route required frequent portages; the rivers running north and south, the Delaware, Susquehanna and Genesee, although navigable, were plagued with rapids and heavy overgrowth.

In the 1780's, as before the Revolution, building roads was a function of the counties; the legislature only approved their location and the levying of local taxes. In 1789 the state did no more to encourage roadbuilding than to set aside 50,000 acres of land to be granted as an incentive to individuals who opened roads at their own expense.[51] But this hardly built roads. Regional rivalry was also a road block. In 1790, for example, Clintonians wanted a road to the Delaware River through Ulster County, their stronghold, while Philip Schuyler wanted a route along the Mohawk into Ontario County which might become a Federalist constituency and was closer to his own land interests. Ulster won, Clinton himself admitting that the location was "governed by interested motives."[52]

49. Lincoln, ed., *Messages from the Governors*, I, 319-21.
50. Watson, *History of the Western Canals*, 26; William Cooper to Aaron Burr, Apr. 9, 1790, Burr Papers, N.-Y. Hist. Soc.
51. *Laws of the State of N.Y.*, 12th Sess., ch. 33.
52. *Journal of the Assembly of N.Y.*, 13th Sess., 33-34; *Laws of the State of N.Y.*,

In 1791, for the first time, Governor Clinton asked for a policy "to facilitate the means of communication" with "our frontier settlements," especially "to prevent the produce of those fertile districts from being diverted to other markets."[53] The legislature did not respond and western pressure continued; some twenty petitions reached the assembly in 1792,[54] finally forcing the adoption of a major new policy under which state commissioners would supervise the expenditure of state money. Some £17,600 was appropriated, all earmarked for specific projects in the four senatorial districts. Specifications were laid down and several routes chosen with an eye to paving the way for both Clintonian and Federalist politicians.[55]

In contrast to the use of public enterprise to build roads was the decision to charter two private corporations to build canals, one to the west, the second to the north.[56] The idea of a canal to improve and link the existing natural waterways of the Mohawk route, dormant since the mid-1780's, was revived early in the '90's by eastern land speculators who saw it as a means of enhancing the value of their western investment.[57] The promoters of the western canal were Elkanah Watson and Philip Schuyler. Watson was the canal's leading publicist while Schuyler pushed it through the legislature and then became president of the board, chief engineer, manager, and director.[58]

From the beginning anti-Federalists backed the canal. The commission appointed in 1791 to survey the route included Watson,

13th Sess., ch. 25; Clinton to Peter Tappen, June 15, 1791, Clinton Miscellaneous Manuscripts, N.-Y. Hist. Soc.

53. Lincoln, ed., *Messages from the Governors*, II, 311-13.

54. *Journal of the Assembly of N.Y.*, 15th Sess., 12, 24, 30, 35, 38, 43, 44, 50.

55. *Laws of the State of N.Y.*, 15th Sess., ch. 60.

56. Noble Whitford, *History of the Canal System of the State of New York . . .*, 2 vols. (Albany, 1906), I, ch. 1.

57. A list of subscribers dated Apr. 4, 1793, is in Philip Schuyler's Canal Papers, N.Y. Pub. Lib.; see Nathan Miller, *The Enterprise of a Free People: Aspects of Economic Development in New York State During the Canal Period, 1792-1838* (Ithaca, N.Y., 1962), 24-26; Davis, *Essays in History of Corporations*, II, 158-64; East, *Business Enterprise*, 158-64.

58. For the minor controversy over who deserved credit as the originator of the New York canal system, see Robert Troup, *Vindication of the Claim of Elkanah Watson to the Merit of Projecting the Lake Canal Policy and also a vindication of the claim of the Late General Schuyler . . .* (Geneva, 1821), printed at the back of Elkanah Watson, *History of the Rise, Progress and Existing Condition of the Western Canals . . .* (Albany, 1820). Watson further presents his own role in Watson, ed., *Memoirs of Elkanah Watson*, 263-65, 280-81, 313-15. For a scholarly summary of Watson's role, see Flick, *Elkanah Watson*, ch. 4, 146-67.

Jeremiah Van Rensselaer, the Albany anti-Federalist chieftain, and Philip Van Cortlandt, son of the lieutenant-governor and a civil engineer. Governor Clinton recommended action on their favorable report,[59] and the anti-Federalist papers in New York and Albany ran nothing but sympathetic articles.[60] Clintonians were not prepared, however, to give Schuyler everything he wanted; the first draft of a canal bill drawn up by a committee headed by John Williams, the leading anti-Federalist of the north country, was "so exceptionable" to Schuyler that he had to draw up an entirely new bill and sell it to the committee.[61] There was also a "want of faith" among skeptics who had to be convinced that the project was not "a half century too soon," as well as a touch of economic rivalry from the Hudson River port towns.[62]

In his newspaper article promoting the canal Watson painted a vivid picture of the project as potentially "more precious than the mines of Potosi." It would draw migrants from Europe and the east, "tend to erect a strong frontier barrier," and increase the value of land held by the Indians. It was not premature; it should precede and not follow settlement. "In return it will inevitably follow that a vast wilderness will as it were, by magic arise into instant cultivation."[63] Another writer in Greenleaf's paper expanded on the advantages of the canal to each interest: the "landed," "agricultural," "manufacturing," "commercial," and "monied classes."[64]

The question of who should build the canal—the state or a private company—aroused discussion. Watson left the question open, arguing that in either case the state had nothing to lose. If the state invested its money, it would easily receive a ten-fold return, perhaps 12 or 15 per cent a year. If individuals undertook it, there would be no cost at all to the public. Privately Watson indicated he wanted to see the state do it "out of its own ample means" because a toll "ought not

59. Lincoln, ed., *Messages from the Governors*, II, 319-21.

60. *N.-Y. Journal*, May 2, 1792; *Albany Register*, July 16, Dec. 31, 1792.

61. Schuyler to Watson, Mar. 4, 1792, in Watson, ed., *Memoirs of Elkanah Watson*, 364-66; *Journal of the Assembly of N.Y.*, 15th Sess., 49.

62. Watson to Philip Schuyler, Feb. 1792, in the appendix to Troup, *Vindication*, 16-17. The opposition from the river towns may be deduced from motions in the assembly and from Robert R. Livingston to Tench Coxe, Mar. 4, 1788, R. R. Livingston Papers, N.-Y. Hist. Soc.

63. "American Citizen," *N.-Y. Journal*, Jan. 28, 1792, which is identified in Watson Papers, Box 3, Vol. 11, N.Y. State Lib.; see also "An Inland Navigator," *N.-Y. Journal*, Mar. 17, 1792, very likely the "Navigator" referred to by Watson as his own.

64. "Argus," *N.-Y. Journal*, Jan. 28, 1792.

to exist in a land of liberty where the intercourse should be as free as the air we breathe."[65] Governor Clinton's message also implied public construction[66] and opinion at Albany seems to have run along these lines.[67] But in the legislature the traditional sentiment for a revenue-producing investment won out. Why after all should the state risk its valuable surplus when private entrepreneurs were willing to do it? A canal sponsored by the proposed "State Bank" was rejected. The only serious questions seem to have been how far the western canal should extend and what powers should be given to its directors. At the end of debate both the western and northern companies got their charters by voice vote without opposition.[68]

The charters hedged in the powers of the canal corporations. The legislature provided a list from which the first directors had to be chosen—including many legislators—and laid down exact regulations about conducting business. The company was prohibited from establishing a bank or owning bank shares, securities, or any lands other than those it needed for the construction of the canal. The size of the canal boats, maximum tolls, and a maximum rate of profit were also established. The western company was given five years to build a canal linking the Mohawk and Lake Oneida and fifteen years to reach Lake Ontario and Lake Seneca or forfeit its charter.[69] The Northern Inland Navigation Company was chartered to build a canal between the upper Hudson and Lake Champlain. It seems to have come in on the political coattails of its western brother; indeed, it may well have been designed to placate John Williams, the leading landholder of the north country who was chairman of the senate's canal committee.[70]

When subscriptions to the new corporations were opened at Albany and New York in the summer of 1792, anti-Federalist editors warmly recommended support on the basis of "the respectability of the characters who have already subscribed."[71] Anti-Federalists became stockholders as well as members of the boards of directors over

65. Watson, History of the Western Canals, 99-100.
66. Lincoln, ed., Messages from the Governors, II, 321.
67. Daniel McCormick to William Constable, Mar. 7, 1792, Constable Papers, N.Y. Pub. Lib.
68. Schuyler to Watson, Mar. 4, 1792, in Watson, ed., Memoirs of Elkanah Watson, 364-66; Journal of the Assembly of N.Y., 15th Sess., 49.
69. Laws of the State of N.Y., 15th Sess., ch. 40; Reubens, State Financing of Private Enterprise, 93-101.
70. A List of Subscribers of the Northern Inland Navigation Company, June 29, 1792, Schuyler Canal Papers, N.Y. Pub. Lib.
71. N.-Y. Journal, May 2, 1792; Albany Register, Dec. 31, 1792.

both of which Philip Schuyler presided. In the spring of 1792, Clintonians and Federalists alike were enthusiastic sponsors of the state's first venture in canal building, the little-known forerunner of DeWitt Clinton's more famous enterprise.

IV

State money also supported manufacturing, a policy which had the backing of "agrarian" anti-Federalists no less than Hamiltonian Federalists. "Part of the farmer's wealth," Crèvecoeur explained to his visitor to the mid-Hudson farmlands, "goes to pay for . . . foreign products and that is why public opinion is so strong for building up local manufactures." Factories were already scattered throughout the state in Clintonian Poughkeepsie as well as Federalist Hudson.[72] Iron furnaces founded in colonial days thrived in anti-Federalist Orange County[73] and under the auspices of the Federalist upper manor Livingstons in Columbia.[74] Greenleaf, the anti-Federalist editor, described the Hartford-made suit George Washington wore at his inaugural and reported the appearance of new "manufactories" with no less approval than his Federalist rivals. The Society for the Promotion of Agriculture, Manufactures, and Useful Arts, which applauded an oration praising government encouragement of manufactures, was composed of gentlemen of both parties.[75]

There was, moreover, a distinct manufacturing interest among anti-Federalists. In almost every local circle of anti-Federalist leaders there were a few manufacturers or would-be manufacturers.[76] There was also a leaning toward manufacturing among the handful of businessmen who would be prominent in the Republican movement of the mid-1790's, for example, all three presidents of the Democratic Society of New York City,[77] and Elkanah Watson of Albany.[78] The foremost

72. Thomas Jenkins to Robert R. Livingston, Jan. 10, 1789, R. R. Livingston Papers, N.-Y. Hist. Soc.; *Goshen Repository*, 1789-1793, *passim*, advertisements for manufactures.

73. Crèvecoeur, *Eighteenth-Century Travels in Pennsylvania and New York*, trans. and ed. Adams, 3, 10.

74. Gipson, *The British Empire Before the American Revolution*, III, 210; and Henry Livingston to Walter Livingston, Nov. 13, 1791, and *passim*, R. R. Livington Papers, N.-Y. Hist. Soc.

75. *Transaction of the Society for the Promotion of Agriculture . . .* , 10.

76. See ch. 2, sec. III.

77. For Henry Rutgers' ownership of a "bleach-field and thread manufactory" see N.Y. *Daily Advertiser*, May 12, 1791; for Solomon Simpson's interest in the New York Iron Manufacturing Corporation see Davis, *Essays in History of Corporations*, I, 274; and for his interest in a lead mine see Jacob F. Marcus, "Light on

company organized in New York City early in the 1790's, the New York
Society for the Encouragement of Manufacturing, was as much an
anti-Federalist venture at its inception as Hamilton's Society for Useful Manufactures was a Federalist affair. Melancton Smith was its
first president, James Nicholson its second, and the low price of its
stock enabled several dozen anti-Federalists to become shareholders.
Even after Federalist businessmen took over, four anti-Federalists remained on its board.[79]

In practice the legislature was generous, in response to specific requests. In the years from 1788 to 1792 it granted one charter of incorporation and turned down another, made loans to three manufacturers, rejecting half a dozen others, purchased stock in one company,
issued one patent (on a steam engine), and granted bounties to growers
of hemp and mulberry trees.[84] Doubtless political favoritism came

Governor Clinton advocated state support for manufactures as early
as 1786. When he first raised the question, he felt he had to justify
such aid in agrarian terms. By 1791 he could say that "the promotion
of manufactures, is at all times highly worthy the attention of government,"[80] provided, of course, a manufacturer's product was "of public
utility" or "connected with the public weal," phrases used by a Clintonian assembly committee.[81] Clinton recommended support for the
manufacture of iron and gunpowder on military grounds and support for maple sugar to reduce importation from abroad.[82] In its
petition to the legislature the New York Society for the Encouragement of Manufacturing argued that its textile factory would "give
constant employment to the poorer class of citizens," train apprentices,
provide a market for flax produced by the state's farmers, and reduce
the money sent abroad to import linen.[83]

Early Connecticut Jewry," *American Jewish Archives*, 1 (1949), 18; for James
Nicholson's chairmanship of the New York Manufacturing Society see 1790 *New
York City Directory*, 119-20.

78. For Watson's glass factory, see Flick, *Elkanah Watson*, 133-36; for his maple
sugar venture, see Watson, ed., *Memoirs of Elkanah Watson*, 391.

79. For the subscribers, see N.Y. *Daily Advertiser*, Mar. 17, 1789; for officers,
1790 *New York Directory* (N.Y., 1789), 119-20.

80. Lincoln, ed., *Messages from the Governors*, II, 251-56, 311-13.

81. The chairman was Matthew Adgate, a leading Clintonian, *Journal of the
Assembly of N.Y.*, 16th Sess., 175, 182.

82. Lincoln, ed., *Messages from the Governors*, II, 251-56, 311-13.

83. N.Y. *Daily Advertiser*, Feb. 16, 1790; *Laws of the State of N.Y.*, 13th Sess.,
ch. 90.

84. *Laws of the State of N.Y.*, 13th Sess., chs. 26, 33, 56, 14th Sess., ch. 51, 15th
Sess., ch. 64, 16th Sess., ch. 47.

into play. The legislature besides granting the New York Society the only charter of incorporation, bought 100 shares of stock at $25 a share. Influential sponsorship alone, however, was not enough. The legislature refused, for example, to encourage a plan for large-scale maple sugar production even though it had the backing of Albany anti-Federalists, the Governor and the Chancellor; it was "a visionary piece of business."[85] And legislative support of course could not make for economic success; the New York Society failed by 1793.[86]

The legislature was also liberal in chartering non-profit associations to encourage manufacturing. The General Society of Mechanics and Tradesmen of New York City whose charter was vetoed by the Council of Revision in 1786 was incorporated in 1792 as a benefit society, in response to mechanic pressure. The state also chartered the Society for the Promotion of Agriculture, Manufactures, and the Useful Arts whose roster read like a Who's Who of gentlemen farmers of New York but which also included men like Chancellor Livingston and Dr. Samuel L. Mitchill of the Columbia faculty whose interests ranged broadly in the mechanic arts.[87] The state government could thus appear before the people as a patron of manufacturing and its friends in all social strata.

V

In the 1780's the legislature's response to Clinton's warm plea for the "encouragement of seminaries of learning" was meager. It established a Board of Regents to found "schools and colleges" but held on to the purse strings. Within the board and legislature there was strong sentiment among the country members against Columbia College as a result of which the state's only college got but one small appropriation in 1785.[88] In 1789 the educational scene was bleak: one college, much in need of nourishment, a handful of private academies providing secondary education to the middling sort, and for primary education, schools sponsored by churches, landlords, or private asso-

85. *Journal of the Assembly of N.Y.*, 15th Sess., 104; Robert R. Livingston to Elkanah Watson, Feb. 16, 1793, Watson, ed., *Memoirs of Elkanah Watson*, 391.

86. Reubens, State Financing of Private Enterprise, 86.

87. Ulysses P. Hedrick, *A History of Agriculture in the State of New York* (Albany, 1933), 112-17; for other charters to non-profit groups, see *Laws of the State of N.Y.*, 19th Sess., chs. 13, 26; 16th Sess., ch. 59.

88. Lincoln, ed., *Messages from the Governors*, II, 183, 200; *Laws of the State of N.Y.*, 7th Sess., ch. 51; 8th Sess., ch 15; and 10th Sess., ch. 82; Alexander, *James Duane*, 181-84.

ciations. "There is scarcely a respectable school from New York to Albany," it was held, and on the frontier conditions were worse.[89]

Early in the 1790's sentiment for state assistance to education was still limited. Yankee migrants to the Hudson Valley were shocked at the state's backwardness.[90] In New York City there were a few democratic appeals for "improvements of the understanding of the middling and lower classes of the people" as the "only sure barrier against the wealth and power of the rich."[91] But anti-Federalist leaders were primarily concerned with the academies, of which a number of them were directors,[92] and with Columbia, to which country merchants and well-to-do farmers aspired to send their sons.[93]

Gradually the legislators loosened the purse strings. In 1790 the state provided £1000 and the income from a tract of land near Lake George for the academies and Columbia. Ulster County Clintonians backed the measure over the opposition of an economy-minded anti-Federalist bloc led by Senator Williams.[94] In 1791 the legislature authorized the Regents to establish a medical school but did not vote money for it.[95] In 1792 Clinton renewed his plea for aid to "our seminaries of learning," and the Regents asked for money for Columbia and the medical school, and to establish "small libraries in distant parts of the state."[96] The legislators voted a five-year grant for the academies and Columbia which amounted to $19,250 in 1792 and a few thousand a year for the next four years. They voted no money,

89. An unsigned article, Poughkeepsie *Country Journal*, Jan. 12, 1789. For a description of Columbia, see "Atticus," *New York Magazine*, 3 (1792), 179-80.
90. "Northern Centinel" No. 7 (1791), in MS form in Elkanah Watson, Commonplacebook, Box 8, Vol. 12, Watson Papers, N.Y. State Lib.; "Public Schools," Oct. 13, 1789, "Philomathes," Dec. 6, 1790, *Albany Register; Poughkeepsie Journal*, Oct. 13, 1789; "Portius," *Hudson Weekly Gazette*, Oct. 28, 1790.
91. See "A Correspondent," Jan. 4, 1790, "A Federalist," Jan. 16, 1790, "A Proposal," Jan. 27, 1791, N.Y. *Daily Advertiser;* "A Friend to the Rising Generation," *N.-Y. Journal*, July 30, 1791.
92. *Poughkeepsie Journal*, Oct. 13, 1789; for other support from small towns, see "Portius," *Hudson Weekly Gazette*, Oct. 28, 1790, and an address by Abraham Skinner at the opening of Union Hall Academy, Jamaica, Long Island, *N.-Y. Journal*, May 9, 1792; Eugene P. Link, *Democratic Republican Societies, 1790-1800* (N.Y., 1942), 169; *Poughkeepsie Journal*, May 24, 1792.
93. Among the Hudson Valley young men studying at Columbia were DeWitt and George Clinton, Jr., of Ulster and John and William Van Ness of Columbia, all of anti-Federalist families; see Scrapbook, Columbiana Collection, Columbia Univ.
94. *Journal of the Senate of N.Y.*, 13th Sess., 2d meeting, 29; *Journal of the Assembly of N.Y.*, 13th Sess., 2d meeting, 91-93.
95. *Laws of the State of N.Y.*, 14th Sess., ch. 45.
96. Reprinted in *N.-Y. Journal*, Jan. 22, 1792.

however, for the medical school or libraries, although they were willing to charter private library associations.[97] As for aid to elementary education, people were "astonishingly indifferent," an advocate of education at Poughkeepsie observed.[98]

VI

The Clintonian solicitude for the speculator, canal promoter, and manufacturer was not matched by a concern for the tenant, slave, or debtor. "Every institution or act which has humanity as its moving principle was welcome," Greenleaf, the anti-Federalist editor, wrote. But in New York City, Melancton Smith was one of the few anti-Federalists active in humanitarian causes, serving as vice-president of the Manumission Society, committeeman in the Society for the Relief of Distressed Debtors, and founder of the New York Dispensary.[99] In the city, the Manumission and the Debtors' societies were in the hands of Christian ministers and conservative merchants, especially Quakers, and Tammany and the Mechanics Societies were as yet indifferent to reform. In the countryside hardly a voice was heard to champion the distressed, save that of the tenants who spoke for themselves. It was typical of the low ebb of humanitarianism early in the 1790's that the Uranian Society, composed of a handful of educated young men, was the only group in New York City that even debated such issues.[100] Governor Clinton gave no leadership to reform except for education, which he thought of in terms of opportunity for the middling classes.

The abolition of slavery failed early in the 1790's because of the opposition of Clintonians. New York had about 21,000 slaves owned by about 8500 families. About one family in seven was a slaveholder. Of these families, about 6700 owned one, two, or three slaves, while a scant 700 owned more than six.[101] The largest owners were landlords like Chancellor Livingston and Philip Schuyler, and New

97. *Laws of the State of N.Y.*, 15th Sess., ch. 69; 13th Sess., ch. 41, ch. 13.

98. An unsigned article, Poughkeepsie *Country Journal*, Jan. 12, 1789.

99. *N.-Y. Journal*, Oct. 26, 1790; for Smith see notices N.Y. *Daily Advertiser*, Jan. 1, 4, 1791, and 1792 *New York City Directory*, 233, 235.

100. Minutes of the Uranian Society of New York, Nov. 15, 1791, N.-Y. Hist. Soc.

101. The best analysis of slavery is in Edwin Olson, Negro Slavery in New York, 1626-1827 (unpubl. Ph.D. diss., New York Univ., 1938); Edwin Olson, "Social Aspects of the Slave in New York," *Journal of Negro History*, 26 (1941), 66-78. Olson gives the following breakdown of ownership: slaveholders owning one slave, 3858; two, 1758; three, 1055; four, 633; five, 436; six, 267; seven, 164; eight, 99; nine, 62; ten or more, 112. The average was 2.4 slaves per owner.

York City and Albany merchants. But slaves were well distributed among the yeomanry in Clintonian strongholds[102] and among leaders of the party, and were not confined to leaders of the Federalists, as Dixon Ryan Fox once claimed. The Clintons, Lansings, Yateses, Schoonmakers, and Wynkoops, John Lamb, and David Gelston all were slaveholders.[103] In Clintonian Ulster, where "a great majority" of the country's "Dutch inhabitants" owned "many slaves," slaveholders petitioned the legislature to strengthen the laws against runaways.[104]

In New York City most of the leading anti-Federalists were anti-slavery—Smith, Lamb, and Willett. But because abolition met with "great opposition from the country members" of the legislature, "who are in general owners of a large number of slaves,"[105] neither city nor rural anti-Federalists took up the cause of abolition. The successive presidents of the Manumission Society, Jay, Hamilton, and Matthew Clarkson, were Federalists, as were the New York City assemblymen who introduced its bills.[106] George Clinton was vice-president for one year but was conspicuously silent about the issue in his official capacity as governor.[107]

In the first flush of humanitarianism after the Revolution, Clintonians and nationalists backed a gradual emancipation bill, which was blocked by the Council of Revision. In the 1780's the Clintonian legislature banned the importation of slaves and the purchase of slaves for sale outside the state; it also liberalized the conditions of individual manumission. At the same time, however, it re-enacted a severe slave code.[108] In 1790 when the Manumission Society pushed a conservative bill for the gradual emancipation of slave children, Governor

102. For the distribution of slaves per county, see *New York State Census for 1855*, ix. The counties with the largest number of slaves were Albany, 3924; Ulster, 2906; Queens, 2309; New York, 2369; Dutchess, 1856.

103. Arthur Alexander, "Federal Officeholders in New York State as Slaveholders, 1789-1805," *Jour. of Negro Hist.*, 28 (1943), 326-27; Dixon Ryan Fox, "The Negro Vote in Old New York," *Political Science Quarterly*, 32 (1917), 252-75.

104. John Wynkoop to Peter Van Schaack, Feb. 23, 1792, Van Schaack Papers, Lib. Cong.; Brissot de Warville, *New Travels*, 151, makes a similar comment; A Petition to the State Legislature, Jan. 24, 1792 (photostat), N.Y. Pub. Lib.

105. Charles Tillinghast to Col. Hughes, Feb. 26, 1785, Lamb Papers, N.-Y. Hist. Soc.; a petition against the sale of slaves for export, *N.-Y. Packet*, Mar. 13, 1786.

106. See Minutes of the New York Society for Promoting the Manumission of Slaves and for Protecting Such of Them as Have Been or May Be Liberated, N.-Y. Hist. Soc.; Mary S. Locke, *Anti-Slavery in America . . . 1819-1908* (Boston, 1901), ch. 4; and Pomerantz, *New York An American City*, 221-24.

107. See for example, Lincoln, ed., *Messages from the Governors*, II, 7-357.

108. Edgar McManus, Negro Slavery in New York (unpubl. Ph.D. diss., Columbia Univ., 1959), ch. 11.

Clinton was silent. "It was a lame bill," DeWitt Clinton claimed, because it failed to provide for the support of the freed Negro children or for "the protection of their rights."[109] Republican printers, although they published an occasional poem or article sympathetic to the Negro,[110] carried nothing in favor of the measure. In fact, the sole contribution of Greenleaf's *Journal* to the debate was a vitriolic attack on the Quakers, defending slavery.[111]

In the assembly the Ulster Clintonian, Cornelius Schoonmaker, made the motion to bottle up the emancipation bill in committee, succeeding over the opposition of the Federalist delegation from New York, 28 to 27. The next day when Assemblyman Matthew Clarkson of New York made a motion to reconsider, the house tied 27 to 27— some Clintonians in favor, most against—and the speaker, Gulian Verplanck, a Federalist, broke the tie in favor of Clarkson's motion. But later in the session when the bill came up a third time, it was rejected,[112] and abolition lay dormant until 1796.

Imprisoned debtors fared somewhat better. In New York City in 1787 and 1788 almost 1200 debtors had been sent to jail, more than half for sums recoverable before a justice of the peace and many for debts of less than £1. Anti-Federalists were sensitive to their plight. "The wretchedness" in the prison, Sheriff Willett wrote DeWitt Clinton, "is past my power to attempt a description—If distress ever claimed legislative assistance . . . the confined debtors in this place demand attention."[113] The New York Society for the Relief of Distressed

109. DeWitt to Charles Clinton, Feb. 8, 1790, DeWitt Clinton Papers, N.-Y. Hist. Soc.

110. The anti-slavery publications of Republican printers up to 1792 were as follows: Thomas Greenleaf published a poem "in honor of the sable race" in his *Almanac for 1793* (N.Y., 1792); William Durrell published *Gustavus Varra, the African; A Slave Narrative* (N.Y., 1792); Philip Freneau published, among other things, the poem "The Island Free Negro," N.Y. *Daily Advertiser*, Feb. 1, 1791; David Frothingham published an anti-slavery article, "An Inhabitant of Queens" in Sag Harbor *Frothingham's Long Island Herald*, Nov. 22, 1791; *Goshen Repository* reprinted Benjamin Franklin's "Address to the Abolitionist Society of Pennsylvania Together With A Plan for Improving the Condition of Free Blacks," Dec. 22, 1789.

111. "A Citizen of the Union," N.-Y. *Journal*, Mar. 18, 1790; a few answers appeared in the N.Y. *Daily Advertiser*: "E——," Mar. 23, "An Extract," Mar. 29, and "Rusticus," Mar. 30, 1790.

112. *Journal of the Assembly of N.Y.*, 13th Sess., 15; the debate in N.Y. *Daily Advertiser*, Jan. 22, 23, 1790.

113. For background see David M. Schneider, *The History of Public Welfare in New York State, 1609-1866* (Chicago, 1938), I, 42-43; Marinus Willett to DeWitt Clinton, Mar. 11, 1790, DeWitt Clinton Papers, No. 15, Columbia Univ.

Prisoners was organized in 1787 in an attempt to dispense charity to prisoners and "to provide liberation of such as were confined for small sums, and were of meritorious conduct, by discharging their debts."[114] Occasionally Tammany, the Mechanics Society, or a militia company sent donations. Letters in the *Journal* attacked the "savage barbarities" of the system and "the miseries of the imprisoned." And individual debtors themselves regularly sent the assembly petitions praying for "legislative interposition."[115] In 1789 in response to a memorial from the Relief Society, the legislature amended the debtors' laws to make it possible for a man owing £10 or less to be discharged after thirty days in jail and for someone owing £200 or less to free himself by surrendering all his property to his creditors. In 1791 it permitted freedom to debtors owing from £200 to £1000, if they had been in jail a year or more and if three-fourths of their creditors agreed.[116] The essential problem of the debtor remained, however, leaving debtors high and low, from Duer and Macomb to the shoemaker and the cartman, to molder away in New York's debtors' prisons though the 1790's.

The legislature was not completely deaf to the "cause of humanity." It voted a five-year grant of £2000 to the Society of the Hospital of the City of New York, a charitable venture organized in 1790.[117] But it obviously was in no mood early in the 1790's to tamper with the social-economic status quo. The same could be said of the political status quo. By a vote of 51 to 3 the assembly rejected, with scarcely a debate, a proposal to require election rather than appointment of the mayor of New York City.[118] There was a bit more grumbling about the Council of Appointment, "the rotten part of our constitution," but as long as Clintonians controlled the legislature and governorship the time was hardly ripe for change.[119]

114. George P. Bauer, The Movement Against Imprisonment for Debt in the United States (unpubl. Ph.D. diss., Harvard Univ., 1935), 89-95; Pomerantz, *New York An American City*, 89-95; for the officers, see *New York City Directory*, 1788-1792, *passim*.

115. "A Friend to Liberty," *N.-Y. Journal*, Aug. 28, 1788, and an unsigned article, *ibid.*, Nov. 1, 1790. *Journal of the Assembly of N.Y.*, 14th Sess., 52, 58, 65, 71, 79, 92, 80, 83 for typical petitions.

116. *Laws of the State of N.Y.*, 13th Sess., chs. 10, 24; 14th Sess., ch. 29.

117. *Ibid.*, 15th Sess., ch. 67.

118. *Journal of the Assembly of N.Y.*, 15th Sess., 151; "Attitude," *N.-Y. Journal*, Apr. 7, 1792.

119. "Mentor," Dec. 6, 1791, "The Tattler," July 28, 1792, "Julius," Feb. 18, 1792, N.Y. *Daily Advertiser*; Minutes of the Uranian Society, May 17, 1791, N.-Y. Hist. Soc.

During Clinton's fifth term there was something in the state grab bag for everyone, except for the propertyless. Tenants who protested landlordism by Shaysite means received little sympathy from the Governor and most of his party. But for land speculators there were lavish grants which Clintonians hoped would be resold quickly to would-be pioneers; for westerners, roads and canals, of equal advantage to land promoters and pioneers; for Albany and New York businessmen, bank charters; for small entrepreneurs of all sorts, a new loan act which would also provide a stable currency; for a handful of manufacturers, loans and bounties; for sons of "the middling sort," financial aid for the academies and Columbia College; for New York City mechanics, a long-sought charter. And for one and all there was the prospect of a near taxless paradise made possible by income from land sales, the funded debt, and investments in banks and canals. Small wonder, then, that New Yorkers could grow rapturous in describing the advantages of the state to foreigners: "Unencumbered with debts—what is more a creditor of the United States, . . . New York can advance to its industrious citizens thousands of pounds . . . nevertheless it posesses an immense surplus to bestow on its dayley expenditures, on the digging of canals, clearing of creeks and erecting sluices without burdening its inhabitants with taxes—triffling ones except for the benefit of individual counties."[120]

By no means could George Clinton and his party claim exclusive credit for these policies. Clintonian policy in its broad outlines had the support of Federalists. Some policies were initiated by Clintonians with Federalist approval, for example land sales in large tracts. Others, like canal chartering, were pushed by the Federalist chieftain Philip Schuyler with Clintonian backing. Support for some measures, such as aid to manufacturing and the academies, crossed party lines. From a political point of view, however, it was inevitable that a governor who advocated so many of these measures should get the credit and the blame. The state's achievement was an enviable suit of armor for the Governor to don as he entered the election battle of 1792. Politically it had but one Achilles' heel. On the basis of the operations of the land office Federalists were counting on ousting the chief architect of the Clintonian system from office.

120. Vanderkemp, Journal, 4, N.-Y. Hist. Soc.

CHAPTER 12

The Rise of

Frontier Federalism

1788-1792

Despite Governor Clinton's concern for "our frontier settlements,"
despite the prospect of roads and canals, New York's west went Federalist in 1792. A western issue, the land sales, dominated the campaign; the results turned on the ballots of three interior counties, and
when their votes were ruled out on a technicality, the state was con-
sumed for months with a political fire stoked by its frontier Federalists. The gubernatorial election of 1792 thus marked the debut of
the New York west as an influence on the statewide political scene.

In 1788 the sparsely settled interior was an undeveloped wilderness
whose little political influence was Clintonian. It sent six silent anti-
Federalist delegates to the ratifying convention, and in 1789 cast a
scant 450 votes for governor, most of them for Clinton. By 1792 "the
Western parts of this State . . . now generally considered, as its richest
and most valuable part,"[1] cast 3000 predominantly Federalist votes.
Just at the time when eastern merchants and landlords who led that
party saw the first signs of a loss of their traditional strength in New
York City, Federalism bloomed on the frontier. In the mid-1790's, as
the number of Republicans rose further in the east, so the Federalists

1. Vanderkemp, "Vanderkemp Papers," Buffalo Hist. Soc., *Publications*, 2 (1880),
42.

[257]

increased on the frontier, the replacements at one end of the state more than offsetting the desertions at the other. Not only did westerners "go Federalist," but they put into office eastern landlords like Philip Schuyler and Stephen Van Rensselaer and resident land proprietors like William Cooper and Thomas Morris. To appreciate this behavior, allegedly so "strange" for an American frontier, one can turn with profit to three principal factors that shaped western politics: the backgrounds of its migrants; a unique social-economic system which fixed the land proprietor in a status of power and prestige; and the political needs of the district vis-à-vis the state and federal governments.[2]

I

The migration into the New York interior that began after the Revolution struck New Yorkers as something of epic proportions. "Emigrants are swarming into these fertile regions in shoals, like the ancient Israelites seeking the land of promise," wrote Elkanah Watson, the Albany Yankee. "The beehive of New England is opened," said Francis Adrian Vanderkemp, who moved from Ulster County to the frontier.[3] The west had a "stupendously increasing population."[4] The 1790 census showed that of the two far western counties Montgomery had 29,000 people and Ontario some 3000 more.[5] By 1794 westerners boasted of 84,000 inhabitants in the entire district. In 1788 there were a scant 1700 eligible voters; in 1792 more than 3000 votes were actually cast in the congressional election; in 1795 the electoral census showed about 14,500 eligible voters.[6]

2. For a traditional interpretation with which the following account differs, see Homer C. Hockett, *Western Influences on Political Parties to 1825: An Essay in Historical Interpretation* (Ohio State University Bulletin, XXII, No. 3, Columbus, 1917), 62-65. Hockett attributed the Federalism of New York's frontier solely to the New England background of the settlers.

3. Watson, ed., *Memoirs of Elkanah Watson*, 292-311; for an over-all summary, see David M. Ellis, "The Yankee Invasion of New York, 1783-1850," *New York History*, 32 (1951), 1-17; Vanderkemp, "Vanderkemp Papers," Buffalo Hist. Soc., *Publications*, 2 (1880), 35.

4. See the following brief reports of migration in *N.-Y. Journal*: from Cooperstown, July 2, 1789; from Albany, Mar. 10, 1791; from Lansingburgh, June 25, 1791, and Feb. 18, 1792; see also *Albany Gazette*, Sept. 20, 1790; a report from Albany, N.Y. *Daily Advertiser*, Mar. 13, 1792.

5. United States [Census Office], *Return of the Whole Numbers of Persons within the Several Districts of the United States* (Phila., 1791).

6. For detailed electoral statistics, N.Y. *Daily Advertiser*, Jan. 15, 1791, Jan. 27, 1796. See Appendix, Tables 1-4.

The new migrants pushed west along the already settled Mohawk
Valley, went down the upper Susquehanna Valley into Otsego County,
Judge Cooper's domain, and leaped over the military bounty lands
into the distant Genesee country where Oliver Phelps, Nathaniel Gorham, and others were offering land on easy terms.[7] Everywhere
pioneers were "making a pitch." "Everywhere one hears the axe,"
reported a traveler, "everyone is busy felling trees."[8] Overnight tiny
towns shot up in the wilderness. In Otsego, Cooperstown had "twenty
dwelling houses, six of which are two-story houses, besides a snug court
house and gaol under one roof," all built within one year.[9] On the
Mohawk were Fort Schuyler (shortly called Utica), Fort Stanwix (soon
called Rome) where "the ear is tingling from the bustle of business,"[10]
and Whitestown with a population of 300, a good gristmill, a large
store, and a pearl ashery, giving "the appearance of becoming a place
of note being situated in a fast improving country."[11] To the far west in
the Genesee country, there were Canandaigua, with "two small frame
houses and a few huts surrounded by woods,"[12] and Geneva, a "small
unhealthy village containing about fifteen houses, all log except three
. . . about twenty families," and enough fleas to make life miserable.[13]
Yet as these travelers' vivid descriptions attest, the towns were no more
than crossroads hamlets. In 1792, none supported a newspaper, and in
the entire district the schools and churches could probably be counted
on the fingers of two hands.

A handful of migrants came from Pennsylvania and New Jersey
making their way north over clogged rivers into south-central New
York and the Genesee country; a somewhat larger number came from
eastern New York; a few were from Europe. The overwhelming majority, however, were from New England, poor farmers driven by land

7. For an over-all survey of the New York frontier at this time, see Higgins,
Expansion in New York, and Flick, ed., *History of the State of New York*, V, chs.
4, 5.

8. John Lincklaen, *Travels in the Years 1791 and 1792 in Pennsylvania, New
York and Vermont* (N.Y., 1897), 103.

9. Edward P. Alexander, ed., "Judge Kent's 'Jaunt' to Cooperstown, 1792," *New
York History*, 22 (1941), 455; James F. Cooper, *The Chronicles of Cooperstown*
(Cooperstown, 1838), *passim*.

10. John Horton, ed., "The Mohawk Valley in 1791 [Excerpts from James Kent's
Diary]," *New York History*, 22 (1941), 210-11.

11. Entry of May 15, 1793, William Hartshorne, Diary of a Journey from New
York to Detroit, 1793 (photostat), N.Y. Pub. Lib.

12. Charles Williamson, *Description of the Settlement of the Genesee Country* . . . (N.Y., 1799), 6.

13. Watson, ed., *Memoirs of Elkanah Watson*, 306.

hunger and drawn by the dream of new life.[14] As a writer in a Hudson Valley paper envisioned it, in New York's west "an industrious
youth may in a few years acquire property enough to make him respectable; and such as have little property with families in old settlements may render themselves independent and lay a foundation for
making old age comfortable."[15]

Of the early settlers, an overwhelming proportion were in "extreme poverty"; in Otsego, for example, not one in twenty owned a
horse.[16] The average pioneer could load all his worldly possessions on
a sleigh: "an axe, a plow, a wheel, a frying pan, kettle, bed and pillow
with a scanty provision of flower, potatoes and salt pork."[17] Sprinkled
among the poor were an important minority "in tolerable circumstances . . . with every article of necessary household furniture, farming utensil, stock etc.," migrants whom the land proprietors made
every effort to attract.[18]

The background of the migrants predisposed them to support the
Federalist party. Until late in the 1790's the New England countryside, Connecticut in particular, was under the sway of Federalism and
the conservative Congregational church. The farmers of that section
were the last in the country to be converted to the Republican creed.
Although the migrants included a sprinkling of "Shaysites" and a
larger number of religious dissenters, on the whole their political and
religious creed was conservative.[19] Socially, however, they were democratic in spirit. As a young aristocratic lady had observed of the breed
in the colonial era, the old settlers of New York, who presumably
knew their place, were being "succeeded by Obadiah, or Zephaniah
from Hampshire or Connecticut, who came in without knocking; sat
down without invitation; and lighted their pipe without ceremony;

14. For the background of migration, see Lois K. Matthews Rosenberry, *The
Expansion of New England . . . 1620-1865* (Boston, 1909), ch. 6; Rosenberry, *Migration from Connecticut Prior to 1800* (New Haven, 1934), 25; Lewis Stilwell,
"Emigration from Vermont (1776-1860)," Vermont Historical Society, *Proceedings*,
New Ser., 5 (1937), 84-88, 94-95.
15. *Goshen Repository*, Aug. 11, 1789.
16. William Cooper, *A Guide in the Wilderness; or the History of the First
Settlements in the Western Counties of New York . . .* (Dublin, 1810, Rochester,
1897), 9-10.
17. Vanderkemp, "Vanderkemp Papers," Buffalo Hist. Soc., *Publications*, 2
(1880), 67; see also "Reminiscences of James Sperry," in Turner, *History of Phelps
and Gorham's Purchase*, 191-94.
18. An unsigned paragraph, *N.-Y. Journal*, Feb. 18, 1792.
19. William A. Robinson, *Jeffersonian Democracy in New England* (New Haven,
1916), ch. 1; Rosenberry, *Migration from Connecticut*, 29.

then talked of buying land; and finally began a discourse on politics, which would have done honour to Praise God Bare-Bones, or any of the members of his Parliament."[20]   They also stuck together. The fact that most of them were from New England fortified the sense of cohesion natural to new settlers in an early stage of frontier life— especially in the face of antipathy from the older Dutch and German settlers.[21] New York's pioneers were thus poor, individualistic, equalitarian, and essentially democratic in their outlook, but it would be some time before they would seek their natural level in the politics of the state.

II

As migrants made their way into the interior they fell into an economy in which the large proprietor was already assured a dominant place by virtue of the land policies of the colonial, Revolutionary, and postwar governments. The names of many of the first towns of western New York bear testimony to the owners of the "patent" who founded them: in Otsego County, Cooperstown (for William Cooper), Harpersfield (for Alexander Harper), Harpursville (for Robert Harpur); in what became Herkimer County, Whitestown (after Hugh White), and Sangersfield (for Jedidiah Sanger); in what became Oneida County, Steuben (after the famous baron); in Steuben County, Wadsworth (for James and William Wadsworth) and Lindley (for Eleazer Lindsley); and in Ontario, Phelps (for Oliver Phelps).[22] In the mid-1790's the names of the agents of the English and Dutch companies would grace other towns.

In the late 1780's and early 1790's few soldiers moved onto their bounty land and almost no settlers bought their land directly from the state. As Gouverneur Morris later explained, it was "absurd to suppose a person with scarce a second shirt to his back can go two or three hundred miles to look out a farm, have it surveyed, travel back again to the office for a patent, etc., clear the land, cut a road, make a settlement, and build a house and barn and then an owner under

20. Anne Grant, *Memoirs of an American Lady* . . . , 2 vols. (London, 1808), II, 232.
21. Fox, *Yankees and Yorkers*, 199-223; Watson, ed., *Memoirs of Elkanah Watson*, 292-93.
22. These names can still be located on any detailed modern road map. For a contemporary map see Appendix, p. 595. Lindley's name was more commonly spelled Lindsley.

a prior grant may come forward and take possession."[23] More than a few pioneers squatted on either state or private land, but for most there were enough inducements to deal with the proprietor. The private land dealer charged more than the state, but provided everything that the state government failed to provide: a small tract, a site the settler could see in advance and choose for himself, and liberal credit in exchange for a long-term mortgage. And often he built or helped to build the roads, sawmills, and gristmills crucial to the pioneer.[24]

Competition for settlers forced the proprietor to be liberal. William Cooper, doubtless the most successful of them all, later set down the lessons in his *Guide in the Wilderness*, actually a guide to would-be land promoters. If an owner pursued restrictive policies, "he will have the mortification to find some neighboring spot with fewer natural advantages outstrips him in prosperity and cast[s] him entirely in the shade." On the other hand "a moderate price, long credit, a deed in fee, and a friendly landlord" were "infallible inducements to a numerous settlement and where there is much people, there will be trade, and where there is trade there will be money, and where there is money, the landlord will succeed."[25]

Cooper's term, "landlord," was misleading. As an economic type, the western proprietor was a far cry from the Hudson Valley landlord. The latter was essentially a "rent collector" who lived off income assured by his tenants and usually had a retinue of slaves as servants. He might be a gentleman farmer who dabbled in agricultural experiments to increase the yield of his land. The western landowner was essentially an entrepreneur and property manager. As a result of the shortage of labor, he often did physical work himself as did his wife who was reduced to one or two servants. He was constantly active, traveling over his property, interviewing new settlers, supervising improvements, in the thick of every new community venture.

Not all proprietors, of course, were models—the very fact that

23. Gouverneur Morris to Randolph Harrison, May 3, 1816, cited in Dixon Ryan Fox, *The Decline of the Aristocracy in the Politics of New York* (N.Y., 1919), 126.

24. For the policies of the proprietors, in particular Cooper, see James Frost, *Life in the Upper Susquehanna, 1783-1860* (N.Y., 1951); for Charles Williamson's policies which began about 1793 but throw much light on the general process, see Helen Cowan, *Charles Williamson, Genesee Promoter, Friend of Anglo-American Rapprochement* (Rochester, 1941).

25. Cooper, *Guide in the Wilderness*, 17, 6-8.

Cooper had to warn that "nothing is more discouraging" to the settler than "any appearance of views distinct from the prosperity of the whole" speaks for itself. Not all owners were "ever in the midst of the settlers aiding and promoting every beneficial enterprise." More than a few withheld choice tracts of land in the heart of settled territory in order to bring higher prices a few years later.[26] Some landholders, moreover, transplanted tenantry to the frontier. The electoral census of 1790 showed some 1600 40-shilling renters; the 1795 census, 4000. But instead of a small number of large tenanted estates—the pattern of the Hudson Valley—the west seems to have had a large number of small estates. Sometimes they were owned by resident landlords like Baron Von Steuben; more often they belonged to absentees who were either landlords like Philip Schuyler and the Livingstons, Britishers like George Clarke, New York City merchants such as Dominick Lynch, or anti-Federalist leaders.[27] The terms of tenantry in the west were liberalized by the competition of land sellers, yet the system rested on the attraction it held for migrants in dire poverty who hoped to accumulate enough capital while renting to move on to greener pastures.[28]

In the early 1790's there was little criticism of the land proprietors. Francis Adrian Vanderkemp, a Dutch political refugee who moved to Oneida County, voiced shock at "a few great landholders owning more acres of land than many princes and dukes in Germany" and "regretted" that a "few individuals . . . as soon as they have made some flourishing establishments, . . . are enabled to encrease the price of the remainder arbitrarily." But he held that these were outnumbered by "the prudent" landholders who built roads and mills, made "liberal advances to the honest industrious settlers and make the payments easy."[29] Thus he drew the same distinction between the two types of large landholders that Governor Clinton made. Presumably a proprietor like William Cooper fulfilled Clinton's goals of encouraging "speedy settlement and sale." In any case it is not surprising that resident landholders, like the father of James Fenimore Cooper, were

26. *Ibid.*, 37.
27. Ellis, *Landlords and Farmers*, 46-48; Frost, *Life in the Upper Susquehanna*, 18-19, 133; Edith Fox, *Land Speculation in the Mohawk Country* (Ithaca, N.Y., 1949), x-xi.
28. For an example, John M. Palmer, *General Von Steuben* (New Haven, 1937), 343-67, *passim*.
29. Vanderkemp, "Vanderkemp Papers," Buffalo Hist. Soc., *Publications*, 2 (1880), 42-43.

toasted as "the poor man's benefactor and the widow's support—the Father of his County"[30] and heroes who "tamed the howling wilderness."

Even the pioneer's debtor status did not alter his feelings toward the proprietor. He came west with boundless optimism. "The influence of hope is very apparent," observed a minister of the settlers in one poor, isolated town. "There is no complaining of hard times; but everyone is cheerful and contented—for they all foresee that in a few years they will have great plenty of worldly goods in a common course of events."[31] There was, moreover, a "safety valve" to remove the discontented. Many of the settlers, Talleyrand observed in his stay on the New York frontier, "brought by inconstancy" to one point "are led away by the same mobility."[32]

More important, the pioneer could stay put and expect to rise. The most spectacular successes were those proprietors who began as no more than middle-class men. William Cooper, at one time a wheelwright and then co-owner of a store in New Jersey, was worth $700,000 on his death in 1809.[33] Hugh White came to the Mohawk Valley in 1786 and bought a large tract of land. In his first year he built a log house and barn; in 1788, a sawmill and gristmill; in 1790, a "genteel frame house," a new barn, and a store. By 1796, he was "a kind of patriarch, having seen the land advance from a rude wilderness to a well cultivated and productive country."[34] Augustus Porter began as a surveyor for Phelps and Gorham, then was a land agent, and finally a proprietor in his own right.[35] There were any number of variations on this theme; if the industrious farmer could scrape together enough capital or secure credit from the local proprietor, he too might make a speculation in land and climb the ladder.

In the early years distinctions between classes were either hard to define or else were concealed. While the gentry built their "genteel

30. "A Ploughjogger [Jedediah Peck]," *Whitestown Gazette* (New Hartford, N.Y.), Dec. 13, 1796.

31. Reverend John Taylor, "Journal of a Missionary Tour Through the Mohawk and Black River Countries in 1802," ed., Edmund B. O'Callaghan, *Documentary History of the State of New York*, 4 vols. (Albany, 1849-51), III, 1149.

32. Huth and Pugh, trans. and ed., *Talleyrand in America*, III, 90.

33. Lyman Butterfield, "Judge William Cooper (1754-1809): A Sketch of His Character and Accomplishment," *New York History*, 30 (1949), 386.

34. Jeremy Belknap, *Journal of a Tour from Boston to Oneida, June, 1796* (Cambridge, Mass., 1882), 14.

35. "Reminiscences of Augustus Porter," Orsamus Turner, *Pioneer History of the Holland Purchase of Western New York* (Buffalo, 1849), 370-74.

frame houses" as soon as possible, William Cooper's ungainly home was as much an object of ridicule as of envy. Even "Otsego Hall" which he built later was hardly Philip Schuyler's beautifully proportioned Georgian mansion.[36] With roads poor and freight expensive, how much fancy furniture could be imported from the east? And even if "the Squire," as Cooper was called, had more creature comforts than the pioneer, they had gone through so many trials together as to forge a common bond. "I had not funds of my own for the opening of new roads," Cooper recalled, "but I collected the people at convenient seasons and by joint efforts we were able to throw bridges over the deep streams, and to make in the cheapest manner, such roads as suited our then humble purposes." And who had not heard of the "starving time" of 1789 when famine struck the Mohawk Valley and Otsego area? With "two hundred families about me and not a morsel of bread," Cooper led the settlers in catching fish, then organized the distribution of corn which the state government sent.[37] As one pioneer fondly recalled of the early years, "all were friendly; mutual dependence made us so; and struggling with the hardships of pioneer life, there was a fellow feeling, a sympathy with each other's misfortunes."[38] Even squatters, though "rude and uncouth both in manners and appearance," were not social outcasts; proprietors hoped that they would buy land rather than move on.[39] And not surprisingly, even slaves, the few that there were, fared better on the frontier.[40]

Most important for its political repercussions, the frontier forced democratic ways on the proprietor. It was said of William Wadsworth, one of the large landholders of the Genesee country, that "the backwoodsmen called him 'old Bill' " and that "at a log house raising, a 'bee,' or a rude frolic 'he was one of them.' "[41] Another first settler told Oliver Phelps that "the times you entered our homes, encouraged us under our difficulties and took a condescending notice of us and our

36. See the description of his father's house in James Fenimore Cooper, *The Pioneers, or the Sources of the Susquehanna: A Descriptive Tale* (1823, N.Y., 1959 ed., intro. by Leon Howard), and the model and painting on display at the Fenimore House, New York State Historical Association, Cooperstown, N.Y.

37. Cooper, *Guide in the Wilderness*, 10-11.

38. "Reminiscences of Stephen Durfee" in Turner, *History of Phelps and Gorham's Purchase*, 383.

39. Watson, ed., *Memoirs of Elkanah Watson*, 353.

40. See, for example, Levi Beardsley, *Reminiscences . . . [of the] Early Settlement of Otsego County* (N.Y., 1852), 20, and James Fenimore Cooper, *The Legends and Traditions of the Northern Country* (N.Y., 1921), 99.

41. Turner, *History of Phelps and Gorham's Purchase*, 330.

children . . . will never be forgot."[42] In New York's "far west," a well-to-do merchant thought nothing of going to a dance attended by the man who was his hired hand a few years before, now "a handsome young playhouse gentleman."[43]

William Cooper epitomized this new social type, a curious blend of "silk hose and leather stocking."[44] The eastern landlord was aloof from his "inferiors"; Cooper, Moss Kent recalled from the years he lived in his house, was "always facetious and trifling," a manner that helped build a bridge of pleasantry between himself and the pioneer.[45] James Fenimore Cooper also remembered how his father "used to lighten the way with anecdote and fun" and in his novel, *The Pioneers*, portrayed his father as "Marmaduke Temple," moving easily among settlers at tavern refreshment, "turkey shoot," and church meeting.[46] A vigorous man, Cooper had a standing offer of 100 acres of land to the man who could throw him in wrestling; only once did he have to make good on it. Yet if he did not demand the deference eastern landlords got, he expected compliance. As his son also makes clear in *The Pioneers* he was jealous of his rights as a landholder and stern as the first judge of the county. Nothing was done in Otsego without the approval of "the Squire."

In politics Cooper's blend was similar. On the one hand he was a master, if not the originator of democratic tactics usually associated with the Whigs of 1840: "Reports say," Philip Schuyler wrote in admiration, "that you was civil to the young and handsome of the [opposite] sex, that you flattered the old and ugly—and even embraced the toothless and decrepit, in order to obtain votes—When will you write a treatise on Electioneering."[47] But he was also capable of bullying lowly farmers and jailing his opponents. He defined politics as "the art of Hook and Snivery."[48]

What did not come to the proprietors naturally could be won by sheer economic power. The degree of dependence on men of wealth was greater in the isolated, self-contained frontier communities than

42. Catoneen Rice to Oliver Phelps, June 13, 1792, Phelps Papers, N.Y. State Lib.
43. Samuel Forman, Diary, 88-89, N.Y. Pub. Lib.
44. James M. Lee, in *DAB* s.v. "Cooper, William."
45. Moss to James Kent, June 22, 1796, Kent Papers, II, Lib. Cong.
46. Cited in Butterfield, "William Cooper," *New York History*, 30 (1949), 396.
47. Philip Schuyler to William Cooper, May 7, 1792, in James F. Cooper, *Legends and Traditions*, 142-43.
48. William Cooper to Benjamin Walker, Jan. 6, 1802, *ibid.*, 175; for Cooper's tactics in the 1792 election, see below, chs. 13, 14.

in the cities and landlord counties of the east. The proprietor was creditor, mortgage holder, and often storekeeper to the farmer. He very likely set up the miller, the innkeeper, and in time the printer, and was the chief patron of the lawyer and local artisans. Would-be officeholders naturally gravitated to him, and this budding middle class formed the nucleus of his active political workers for nominating meetings and the like.[49] Small wonder then that the young lawyer Moss Kent had to reassure his brother, James, that he had not become "a tool" of Judge Cooper,[50] his client.

The proprietors, with a few exceptions, were Federalists, by virtue of their previous political allegiances and the natural gravitation of men of wealth to the conservative party. By 1792 a natural alliance was implicit in the relationship of a William Cooper and a Philip Schuyler, or a Thomas Morris and a Stephen Van Rensselaer.[51] Western proprietors served as land agents and land scouts for eastern businessmen; eastern Federalists served as lawyers for the westerners. William Cooper was an agent for Philip Schuyler; Alexander Hamilton was Cooper's lawyer. Equally important, western proprietors saw the interests of themselves and the region best served by policies pursued by Federalists in both the federal and state governments.

III

New York's frontiersmen, like their counterparts in other regions in the early stage of growth, had three crying political needs: defense, transportation, and representation. Of the three, defense was the most pressing and did the most to rivet western loyalties to the Federalist-controlled national government.

Until mid-1796 western and northern New York was haunted by the specter of Indian war. The remnants of the once powerful Six

49. At Otsego, Cooper's center, the first sheriff, Richard Smith, was a merchant; the second assemblyman, Jacob Morris, was a large landholder. The first few lawyers of the county, Abraham Ten Broeck, Jacob Fonda and Moss Kent, were active Federalists. John Williams, another active Federalist, was storekeeper. For occupations, see Cooperstown Otsego Herald, 1795-97, advertisements, passim, and Ralph Birdsall, The Story of Cooperstown (Cooperstown, 1917), 25-45, passim.

50. Moss to James Kent, Dec. 25, 1794, Kent Papers, II, Lib. Cong.

51. William Cooper to Stephen Van Rensselaer, Jan. 19, 1792, Cooper Papers, N.Y. State Hist. Assoc.; Van Rensselaer to Cooper, June 28, 1792, Cooper Transcripts, N.-Y. Hist. Soc.; Schuyler to Cooper, May 7, 1792, in James F. Cooper, Legends and Traditions, 142-43; Thomas Morris to Stephen Van Rensselaer, Nov. 19, 1792, Apr. 19, June 30, Nov. 13, 1793, MS Nos. 799, 864, 1950, 1951, N.Y. State Lib.

Nations, reduced to a population of six thousand by the ravages of war, rum, and disease, were no longer the power they had been in colonial days when they terrorized the New York frontier.[52] But they were feared as a potential danger, because their brother tribes in the Northwest Territory had taken to the warpath and because there was British influence among them, facilitated by England's retention of forts on American soil in violation of the peace treaty. Of the seven forts, five were in the state; two on Lake Ontario, one on the St. Lawrence to the west, and two on Lake Champlain in the east. The warfare across the Great Lakes was only a short distance from the Genesee country, and the British forts were considered a point of launching for invasion. Understandably in 1790 and 1791 when the American army under Generals Harmar and St. Clair suffered stunning defeats in the Northwest Territory, tension mounted throughout western New York.[53]

The plight of the Six Nations was worsened by the inevitable rifts among them in face of insistent white pressure for land.[54] The practices of unscrupulous speculators who bribed dissident chieftains to secure land titles especially rankled. And the occasional wanton murder of Indians by settlers only rubbed salt in open wounds.[55] Some Indian leaders were willing to adjust to the reservations offered by the state; others succumbed to the deals of individual speculators without the consent of their brothers; still a third group was bitterly irreconcilable, so that land cessions were made which did not have the united support of the tribes. The British and a few American speculators fanned such smoldering discontent for their own purposes. As a result, when the tribes of the Old Northwest took to the warpath, some of the Six Nations' leaders were anxious to make common cause with them.

In Indian affairs New Yorkers sought three goals: pacification of the Indians of New York and the Northwest by diplomacy or armed strength; evacuation of the British-held forts; and acquisition of the remaining land within the state still held by the Six Nations. The western attitude toward the Indians was shaped by land hunger, racial

52. For the background of the New York Indians, see Flick, ed., *History of the State of N.Y.*, II, ch. 6, IV, ch. 6.

53. Bemis, *Jay's Treaty*, ch. 1; Schachner, *Founding Fathers*, 64-66, 70-72, 144-45, 192-95.

54. Turner, *History of Phelps and Gorham's Purchase*, 135-49.

55. Oliver Phelps to Nathaniel Gorham, Aug. 7, 1790, in Turner, *Holland Purchase*, 332.

prejudice, and the green memories of the massacres that had devastated the frontier in the Revolution,[56] leaving hundreds of burnt out cabins along the Mohawk Valley. Only a handful on the frontier would have agreed with the missionary long among them, Reverend Samuel Kirkland, that "there is land enough for us both. Why need we be knocking one another on the head for a little piece of disputed ground or mistaken idea of claim?"[57]

Governor Clinton and the federal government clashed in the attempt to meet the Indian problem and inevitably the federal government won out.[58] The state constitution vested the Governor with authority to negotiate with Indians for the acquisition of land titles. Clinton pursued this goal vigorously and for this purpose was engaged in constant diplomacy with chieftains of the Six Nations, especially the famous Joseph Brant.[59] Clinton's first conflict with the federal government was over tactics. Henry Knox, the Secretary of War, was anxious to stave off an alliance of the Six Nations with the warring tribes of the Northwest, and in 1791 he called a meeting of the New York chieftains to assure their neutrality. When he asked Clinton to use his influence with Joseph Brant, the Governor refused, fearful of the consequences of bringing the tribes together.[60] As a result, Knox turned to the Reverend Mr. Kirkland, who carried on Knox's negotiations and produced a treaty in the spring of 1792.[61] In the wake of this, a United States Commissioner for Indian Affairs was appointed in the Genesee country, a symbol of the federal government's supremacy in Indian affairs. Israel Chapin, a Federalist assemblyman and a landholder associate of Oliver Phelps, got the post.[62]

Clinton next found his authority challenged over a typical frontier incident involving the murder of an Onondaga chieftain by some white settlers. It was feared that this was "a premeditated thing by some enemies of our infant Western country—perhaps by the British government in order to breed a war between us and the Six Nations

56. Horton, ed., "The Mohawk Valley in 1791," *New York History*, 22 (1941), 213; Watson, ed., *Memoirs of Elkanah Watson*, 312.

57. Rev. Samuel Kirkland to Israel Chapin, May 31, 1792, O'Reilly Collection, VIII, No. 18, N.-Y. Hist. Soc.

58. Spaulding, *George Clinton*, 148-53.

59. See above, ch. 3, sec. II, n. 25.

60. Spaulding, *George Clinton*, 152-53.

61. Joseph D. Ibbotson, "Samuel Kirkland, the Treaty of 1792 and the Indian Barrier State," *New York History*, 19 (1938), 374-91.

62. Cowan, *Charles Williamson*, 50; Turner, *History of Phelps and Gorham's Purchase*, 166, 169, 172, 291-92.

of Indians."[63] To pacify the irate Indians, settlers turned to the resident federal commissioner.[64] But Clinton intervened and resolved the difficulty, reporting to the legislature a few months later that peace was preserved and the confidence of the Indians in the justice of the state government retained.[65]

On military defense Clinton was least successful of all. At every opportunity he pushed his proposal for improving and equipping the western militia but got little response from the legislature.[66] In 1791 the state appropriated a few thousand pounds "to prevent incursions on the frontier" but as late as 1794 the district remained "totally destitute of arms."[67] Thus on all matters of Indian policy—diplomacy, minor disputes, defense—Clinton took action, but it was obvious that as long as the Indian menace remained across the Great Lakes, pioneers would look to federal and not state military power as their shield. As for the forts, even Clinton had to admit that the means for the recovery "lay in our federal capacity."[68]

The congressmen elected from the western district gave proof of the primacy of defense, each in his own way. James Gordon, the first, broke from his consistently Federalist voting record only when it was a matter of additional military appropriations.[69] Silas Talbot, the second, resigned from Congress in the 1794 crisis with Great Britain to rejoin the navy. William Cooper, the third, rose to prominence in the House only once, in a fanatic appeal to put John Jay's treaty in operation to recover the British-held forts.[70]

For transportation and representation the district of necessity had to turn to the state government. Improved land and water transportation was the *sine qua non* of western prosperity. Without roads the farmer could not market his crops or the proprietor expect a return on his investment. The legislature, as we have seen, by 1792 provided for

63. Moses DeWitt to DeWitt Clinton, Aug. 12, 1792, DeWitt Clinton Papers, No. 21, Columbia Univ.

64. Asa Danforth to Israel Chapin, July 7, 1792, Chapin to Danforth, Aug. 10, 1792, O'Reilly Collection, VIII, Nos. 30, 39, N.-Y. Hist. Soc.

65. Lincoln, ed., *Messages from the Governors*, II, 324.

66. *Ibid.*, 220, 255.

67. Nathaniel Taylor and Phineas Pierce to Governor Clinton, May 5, 1794, O'Reilly Collection, X, No. 23, N.-Y. Hist. Soc.

68. Lincoln, ed., *Messages from the Governors*, II, 252-53.

69. See the votes of James Gordon charted in Libby, "Political Factions in Washington's Administration," *Univ. of North Dakota Qtly. Journ.*, 3 (1913), 293-318.

70. See below, ch. 21, sec. IV.

several roads and a canal to the west. But from the westerner's point of view, there still were not enough roads; they were not built fast enough, and whatever he got he had to fight for. Proprietors like Cooper kept up the demand, and as new land agents like Charles Williamson made their way into the Genesee country, they were loud in complaining that there was "not a road within one hundred miles . . . that will admit of any sort of conveyance otherwise than on horseback or on sled."[71] Roads thus remained a political issue.

In their third need, political representation, frontier spokesmen had several objectives: more assemblymen and senators in the state legislature, a congressional district of their own, and division of the two large western counties into smaller ones. The last demand was especially important to settlers who had to travel fifty or a hundred miles to file a deed at a county seat; proprietors were also anxious to have the force of "law and order" closer at hand and to have districts that would be more manageable politically.[72]

Although there was some grumbling about eastern reluctance to redistrict,[73] the area actually obtained its new counties and increased representation quickly. The state constitution required an electoral census and reapportionment "once in every seven years," and Governor Clinton dutifully reminded the legislature of its obligation.[74] After the returns from the 1790 census were in, bills went through the legislative mill in 1791 without discernible opposition. Out of Montgomery and Ontario four new counties were created—Saratoga, Otsego, Herkimer, and Tioga—making a total of six western counties and increasing the area's representation in the assembly from six to thirteen seats. All six counties continued to be attached to Albany County in the east as a senatorial district.[75] Such political changes only whetted the appetite for more. In 1792 there was another wave

71. Charles Williamson to Patrick Colloquon cited in Turner, *History of Phelps and Gorham's Purchase*, 252; see also Charles Williamson, *Observations on the Proposed State Road . . .* (N.Y., 1800), 6-7.

72. See for example an undated petition from about 150 residents of Clinton County requesting the creation of St. Lawrence County, Assembly Papers, V, N.Y. State Lib.; William Cooper to Leonard Gansevoort, Dec. 23, 1790, Cooper Papers, N.Y. State Hist. Assoc.; William Hanna to Jacob Morris, Dec. 15, 1794, cited in Frost, *Life in the Upper Susquehanna*, 12.

73. An unsigned letter from Montgomery County, *Albany Gazette*, Apr. 14, 1791.

74. Lincoln, ed., *Messages from the Governors*, II, 271-72, 311-13.

75. Hammond, *Political Parties*, I, 52-53; *Journal of the Assembly of N.Y.*, 14th Sess., 26-27; *Laws of the State of N.Y.*, 14th Sess., chs. 4, 10. Montgomery was apportioned five assemblymen, Saratoga four, and the other four, one each.

of petitions for new counties from western Ulster, southern Otsego, Montgomery, and Tioga—all of which the legislature either shelved or rejected as "inexpedient."[76] In December 1792, however, the state was assigned four additional representatives in Congress, and the western counties were given a congressman of their own.[77]

Measured against the treatment received by other frontier regions from eastern legislators, New York's westerners got most of what they wanted with remarkable speed. Yet they remained dissatisfied. The legislature did not anticipate their need for roads. Nor did it apportion representatives fast enough; as a result they considered themselves chronically under-represented. As for Indian policy, as long as the tribes of the Northwest were undefeated and the British retained the forts, western New York was not at ease. Hence the district, like most frontier regions, grew up with a "chip on its shoulder." Governor Clinton was attentive to their interests but when the legislature did not keep pace with their demands, sectional feeling increased and Clinton, rightly or wrongly, bore the onus for the lag.

As a result western sectionalism, instead of being turned against eastern "aristocrats," as happened in other states, was taken in tow by them. Federalists like John Jay of Westchester and James Kent, a circuit-riding judge from Dutchess and New York, displayed some of that mixture of trepidation and contempt for the westerner usually ascribed to eastern Federalists.[78] But Federalists of the Albany region knew better. The arrangement that from 1777 placed the sparsely populated frontier counties in the same senatorial district with Albany gave the Albany Federalists the opportunity to court and serve a western constituency. Westerners could not bypass Philip Schuyler and Stephen Van Rensselaer even if they wanted to. And Schuyler's personal interests in western land and in canal building gave him, like other upstate Federalists, a common stake with westerners. Moreover, exploiting western grievances with the status quo was easy as long as George Clinton was governor. Hence, it is not surprising that eastern landlords and merchants forged an alliance with western land proprietors that covered state as well as national politics.

76. *Journal of the Assembly of N.Y.*, 15th Sess., 64, 70, 74, 99, 105.
77. *Laws of the State of N.Y.*, 16th Sess., ch. 5.
78. See John Jay to William Bingham, May 31, 1785, and to Thomas Jefferson, Apr. 24, 1787, Johnston, ed., *Correspondence of John Jay*, III, 153-54, 245; John Horton, *James Kent, A Study in Conservatism, 1763-1847* (N.Y., 1939), 126-27.

IV

It was not that Clintonians did not try to nurture an "interest" in the western country. Clinton tried to use his appointing power to build the party. The leaders of the anti-Federalists in Montgomery County in '88 were John Winn, the sheriff, and Christopher P. Yates, of the Yates family of Albany, clerk, first judge, and sometime assemblyman. Jonas Platt, son of Zephaniah Platt, the Dutchess anti-Federalist, was made clerk of Herkimer as soon as he arrived.[79] When William Floyd went from Suffolk to Oneida in the mid-1790's, he was taken up as candidate before his land was cleared.[80] But only a few of the old Clintonians moved to the interior. The Governor doubtless had this scarcity of supporters in mind when the land commissioners pondered the bids before them in 1791, yet even so none of the eastern Clintonians who received grants became residents of the west.

Clinton, true to his political tactic of making do with what he had, tried to woo proprietors already in the west, even when they were Federalist. Melancton Smith helped Oliver Phelps with a bill to organize the county of Ontario; other Clintonians were ready with other legislative favors.[81] The Council of Appointment made Phelps first judge of the new county, and William Cooper first judge in Otsego, positions of great influence. Conceivably such appointments might attach them to the Governor's "interest" in state affairs, or at least show that the door was open.[82]

But despite Clintonian efforts—or perhaps because of them—by 1792 they had lost the region to the Federalist proprietors. The Federalist base lay in the two counties dominated by large proprietors, Otsego and Ontario. In the former by 1792 Judge Cooper had already earned a reputation as the "Bashaw of Otsego"—a Turkish pasha.[83] Cooper's

79. For 1788 leaders see list of correspondents in John Lamb Papers, N.-Y. Hist. Soc., and list of elected delegates to convention. For county officials and dates of appointment, see Werner, comp., *Civil List of New York*, *passim*. Platt who migrated in 1791 was appointed clerk Feb. 17, 1791.

80. In 1795 Floyd was the Republican candidate for lieutenant-governor, *N.Y. Journal*, Feb. 6, 11, 1795; Richard Morris in *DAB* s.v. "Floyd, William."

81. Oliver Phelps to Melancton Smith, Sept. 11, 1791, Phelps Papers, N.Y. State Lib.; for another request from Chenango, see Benjamin Hovey to John McKesson, Mar. 6, 1793, McKesson Papers, N.-Y. Hist. Soc.

82. Phelps was appointed judge May 5, 1789, Cooper Feb. 17, 1791. The Council of Appointment of 1791 was elected in the bargaining that preceded the election of Burr to the Senate and may be assumed to be under Clinton's control.

83. Thomas Jefferson to James Monroe, June 23, 1792, Monroe Papers, N.Y. Pub. Lib.

relative, Richard Smith, with whom he was associated as merchant, was sheriff, and Jacob Morris, probably the second largest landholder in the area, was county clerk, assemblyman for three terms, and later senator.[84] In Ontario Oliver Phelps, first judge of the county, was later a senator, while his partner's son, Nathaniel Gorham, Jr., was first clerk. Thomas Morris, son of Robert Morris, owner of another great tract, became in turn assemblyman, senator, and in 1800 a member of Congress. The first assemblyman of the county was Eleazer Lindsley, sub-purchaser from Phelps-Gorham of a 23,000-acre township, while the second was Israel Chapin, a Phelps associate, the man appointed United States Indian Commissioner. All were Federalists.[85]

In the other counties Federalist dominance was less complete. Local Clintonian leaders usually were also men of substance. In the section of Montgomery that became Herkimer County, the four major political leaders, Michael Myers, Jedidiah Sanger, Jonas Platt, and Hugh White, were large landholders; the first two were Federalists, the latter two Clintonians.[86] In Saratoga Beriah Palmer, a Clintonian elected to the assembly, was known as "a very wealthy person."[87]

But with a firm base in Otsego and Ontario, Federalist strength in the district as a whole began to jell. In the first congressional election in 1789, the sparse frontier vote helped send Jeremiah Van Rensselaer, the Albany anti-Federalist, to Congress in preference to an Albany Federalist.[88] Against him in the second contest in 1790 the Federalists ran James Gordon of Saratoga who described himself as "a farmer" acquainted "with the country interest." Nominated not by a small caucus but by delegates from the entire county, a democratic innovation, Gordon defeated Van Rensselaer 1465 to 1007. His votes came from his home county, Saratoga, Judge Cooper's domain in Otsego, and the Schuyler and Van Rensselaer tenantry in Albany County.[89] The following year, 1791, when Philip Schuyler ran for the

84. For Morris, see Frost, *Life on the Upper Susquehanna*; Fox, *Decline of the Aristocracy*, 135; for Smith see the character "Richard Jones" in James F. Cooper, *The Pioneers*, and see below ch. 14 on the election dispute of 1792.

85. Turner, *History of Phelps and Gorham's Purchase*, 149-52, 170-71, 172-74, 291-92; Lincklaen, *Travels*, 59-60; Cowan, *Charles Williamson*, 50.

86. *Journal of the Assembly of N.Y.*, 15th Sess., 183-200 (the records of the land sales of 1791); Vanderkemp, "Vanderkemp Papers," Buffalo Hist. Soc., *Publications*, 2 (1880), 54-55; James Kent to Moss Kent, Mar. 12, 1796, Kent Papers, II, Lib. Cong.

87. Moss Kent to James Kent, Oct. 14, 1790, Kent Papers, I, Lib. Cong.

88. See ch. 6, sec. II.

89. James Gordon to John Porteous, Mar. 7, 1790, MS No. 9691, N.Y. State Lib.; for returns, N.Y. *Daily Advertiser*, May 22, 24, 1790.

state senate from the Albany-western district, a third of his vote came from the new counties of Otsego and Herkimer, giving him an easy victory in the district.[90]

By 1792 the Clintonians were already reduced to pockets of strength within a few counties: in Saratoga, on the Hudson, the easternmost county in the district; Herkimer on the Mohawk; and Tioga, a thinly settled county to the south.[91] Their support came from a variety of sources: a few non-Federalist proprietors, probably the older Dutch and German settlers along the Mohawk who resented Yankee intruders; settlers not enmeshed in the dependence on Federalist proprietors; perhaps religious dissenters like the Baptists.[92] Local issues, too, like the location of a courthouse, could swing voters.[93] Anti-Federalists could still win assembly seats and Governor Clinton could command a following, but in the mid-1790's as tens of thousands of additional settlers poured into the district the Clintonians became more and more isolated as political islands in the wilderness. The congressional election of December 1792 would be fought out principally between rival Federalists, William Cooper and Silas Talbot, with John Winn, the Clintonian, running third.

Frontier politics had a free-wheeling, sometimes explosive quality. Westerners fought their political battles hard; the losers in the first elections in three newly created counties challenged the results for fraud in the state legislature.[94] The large land proprietors also were an individualistic breed. For example, in 1791 although Oliver Phelps was the biggest owner in Ontario, Eleazer Lindsley, a smaller proprietor, "collected a few backwoodsmen, held an election, got a few votes for himself"—actually forty-two—"carried them to New York, and was admitted to the legislature."[95] Phelps ousted him a year later.

Western proprietors were also unwilling to be junior partners to their Albany brethren. No sooner did the district receive additional

90. N.Y. *Daily Advertiser*, June 4, 1791. The vote was Schuyler 1392, Volkert Veeder 568.

91. Based on an analysis of gubernatorial returns for 1792, *N.-Y. Journal*, June 13, 1792; of the congressional election of 1792, *ibid.*, Feb. 27, 1793, and the senatorial election of 1793, Lansingburgh *American Spy*, June 18, 1793.

92. Beriah Palmer, for example, was an active Baptist layman; see Moss Kent to James Kent, Oct. 14, 1790, Kent Papers, I, Lib. Cong.

93. Vanderkemp, "Vanderkemp Papers," Buffalo Hist. Soc., *Publications*, 2 (1880), 50.

94. *Journal of the Assembly of N.Y.*, 15th Sess., 4-5, 9-10, 23-25, 39-40, 84-85.

95. Turner, *History of Phelps and Gorham's Purchase*, 172; *Journal of the Assembly of N.Y.*, 15th Sess., 26-27.

representation in the senate in 1792 than William Cooper wrote Stephan Van Rensselaer: "I claim the privilege of nominating our Senator and ask your aid."[96] As long as eastern landlord acquiesced in western choices, and as long as the western proprietor had his following under control there were no complaints about this collaboration.

On the eve of the gubernatorial elections of 1792 Chancellor Livington rightly feared Philip Schuyler because of his "powerful influence in the western and northern counties" and his "close and intimate connections with an extensive back country."[97] Schuyler on the other hand was optimistic, counting on the west to accomplish what heretofore was impossible: to oust Clinton and bring Federalists into control of the state government.

96. Cooper to Van Rensselaer, Jan. 19, 1792, Cooper Papers, N.Y. State Lib.
97. Robert R. Livingston, "Political Essay on Elections," [1792], draft, R. R. Livingston Papers, N.-Y. Hist. Soc.

CHAPTER 13

"The Republican Interest" Emerges:

The Gubernatorial Election

1792

———•———

The state elections in the spring of 1792 brought to a focus in New York the issues of George Washington's first administration and George Clinton's fifth. For the budding "republican interest" it was not only a test of Clinton's record. It was also a test of how well the coalition of Livingston, Clinton, and Burr would function on the state level and of what use they could make of the bubbling discontent with the national government. For the Federalists it was something more than a test of the record of their gubernatorial candidate; it was also a test of the alliance between eastern merchants and landlords and their new-found friends in the western district and in Ulster County. But more particularly it was a test of Hamilton's record at Philadelphia and Philip Schuyler's in the state legislature. National issues —assumption, the Bank of the United States, the panic, "consolidation"—joggled state issues—the land scandals, the "bank mania," abolition. All were mixed with charges and countercharges of "aristocracy," "landed interest," "monied interest," and "overgrown influence" to create a scene tense with political excitement.

I

In 1789 Federalists came within a hair's breadth of defeating Clinton by sponsoring the moderate anti-Federalist, Judge Robert

Yates. The vote was 6391 to 5962. Three years later the Federalist strategy of "divide and conquer" still had adherents. At Albany Philip Schuyler pressed Yates to accept the nomination again. Yates declined, offering as a reason the financial loss he would suffer if elected; he was also under pressure not to run from Aaron Burr who had backed him three years before. Yates's refusal sent a wave of panic through the Federalists, for it brought into the open the fact that Burr was making a play for the nomination from both parties, sustained by dissidents within both who were counting on the fluidity of party lines in state politics and the sentiment for a candidate who was above partisanship.[1]

Burr's brief record in the Senate since October 1791 was republican. He counted himself a "warm admirer" of the new French constitution and an enthusiastic reader of Freneau's National Gazette.[2] In relation to the other Republican leaders of New York, however, he remained independent. He fought with Clinton over patronage in 1791 and never seems to have moved close to Chancellor Livingston. A Federalist leader spoke of the "cautious distance observed by this gentleman towards all parties," while his supporters claimed that he "did not belong to either party."[3]

Burr had already drawn to himself a curious assortment of supporters: Melancton Smith, Marinus Willett, perhaps David Gelston, all of New York City and all normally Clintonians;[4] Peter Van Gaasbeck, Kingston merchant, renegade anti-Federalist, and Burr's principal creditor;[5] Thomas Witbeck, Stephen Van Rensselaer's steward and

1. Schuyler and Hamilton, Jan. 29, 1792, Hamilton, ed., Works of Hamilton, V, 492-94; Hammond, Political Parties, I, 54-55; Henry Livingston to Samuel B. Webb, Feb. 10, William Livingston to Webb, Feb. 12, 1792, Ford, ed., Correspondence of S. B. Webb, III, 175-76; a letter from a New York City correspondent to Albany Gazette reprinted in N.-Y. Journal, Feb. 22, 1792.

2. Schachner, Aaron Burr, 107-10; Parton, Aaron Burr, I, 195-96; Burr to Mrs. Burr, Nov. 14, Dec. 15, 1791, in Davis, ed., Memoirs of Aaron Burr, I, 306, 312.

3. James Watson to Hamilton, Feb. 2, 1792, Hamilton, ed., Works of Hamilton, V, 495-96; "A Farmer," Albany Gazette, Feb. 27, 1792, cited in Hammond, Political Parties, I, 55.

4. See ch. 15, sec. I, below for the activities of Smith and Willett on Burr's behalf in the vice-presidential campaign. I am assuming they were active earlier in the year. For Smith's political cooperation with Burr and coolness to Clinton in 1791, see Troup to Hamilton, June 15, 1791, Syrett, ed., Hamilton Papers, VIII, 478-79; for Smith's personal relationship, see Burr to Mrs. Burr, Nov. 14, 1791, in Davis, ed., Memoirs of Aaron Burr, I, 306. On the other hand James Cheetham's claim in A View of the Political Conduct of Aaron Burr . . . (N.Y., 1802), 16-17, that Burr's "little band" was already in existence seems overstated.

5. Peter Van Gaasbeck to Aaron Burr, Mar. 28, 1792, Van Gaasbeck Papers,

political agent;[6] and Dr. Isaac Ledyard of Queens, all three Federalists.[7] Even Robert Troup, Hamilton's New York City lieutenant and long Burr's personal friend, flirted with him politically.[8] Van Gaasbeck as the would-be potentate of Ulster had a pressing political need for a candidate with a Republican aura who could cut into the heart of Clinton's stronghold. Burr, he was convinced, could carry three-fourths, if not four-fifths of the county.[9] Fundamentally this is why others sought him: Burr was a potential winner, just as Yates had been.

Even to orthodox Federalists Burr had fascinating attraction. As James Watson, a prominent Federalist merchant, argued with Hamilton, the party should always be "solicitous to remove talents, perseverance and address as far from the opposition as possible."[10] Suppose, he wrote, the Federalist nomination were denied Burr but he was elected governor anyway: "will it not make him an enemy, if he is not one now?" Secondly, in the event "he is refused this support and fails, will he not return to the Senate of the United States, embittered against the government and its ablest advocates?" On the other hand, should Federalists give him the nomination, even if he lost, "will it not serve to moderate his conduct, or rather to bind him by the ties of interest and gratitude to his supporters?" Fourth, if he were elected and did not support the Federalists, "would not the ingratitude and atrocity of the act diminish his power of doing harm and make all future opposition to him equally just and popular?"

One roadblock to Federalist support for Burr was uncertainty about his convictions on national policy. Accordingly, Ledyard interviewed him "to procure from him an artless declaration with respect to the Union" and Federalist fiscal policies, and wrote enthusiastically to Hamilton that Burr had expressed "an entire confidence in the wisdom and integrity of your designs and a real personal friendship."[11]

Kingston Senate House; see also Burr to Jacob Delamater, June 15, 1792, in Davis, ed., *Memoirs of Aaron Burr*, I, 355-56. The evidence that Van Gaasbeck was lending money to Burr appears in the Van Gaasbeck Papers, 1794-1796.

6. James Fairlie to Stephan Van Rensselaer, Feb. 13, 1792, Fairlie Papers, N.-Y. Hist. Soc.

7. See footnotes 11 and 16.

8. See footnote 19.

9. Van Gaasbeck to Burr, Mar. 28, 1792, Van Gaasbeck Papers, Kingston Senate House.

10. Watson to Hamilton, Feb. 2, 1792, Hamilton, ed., *Works of Hamilton*, V, 495-96.

11. Isaac Ledyard to Hamilton, Feb. 1, 1792, *ibid.*, 494-95.

Early in February, Philip Schuyler scurried down to Philadelphia to consult with his son-in-law, carrying Ledyard's letter with him. Federalist susceptibility to Burr's charms spurred the party regulars to block his candidacy.[12] In mid-February, upstate members of the legislature met in New York City. After Yates publicly declined to run, John Jay was nominated, and Yates announced he was "in honor bound" to support the ticket "as well as in inclination." A few days later the Albany Federalists followed suit. Stephen Van Rensselaer was chosen as Jay's running mate.[13]

Greenleaf's *Journal* now reported three candidates in the field: Jay, Clinton, and Burr. "*Parties* in this great business seem not all yet to be formed and the minds of many (famed electioneering individuals) are yet in suspense, undetermined which STANDARD to support." Clinton's renomination never seems to have been in doubt, however, for about a week after Jay was put up, a caucus of Clintonian legislators at New York nominated the Governor and his perennial running mate, Pierre Van Cortlandt.[14] Van Cortlandt, "roil'd" because Federalists had nominated Van Rensselaer and not him, again accepted the Clintonian nomination[15] and this time, unlike 1789, Hamilton made no effort to neutralize him.

Burr's supporters would not give up, nursing the hope of a three-way race. Ledyard pleaded with Hamilton to give Burr covert support or at least not oppose him.[16] Not until the end of March did Van Gaasbeck write that they had given him up in Ulster "with the greatest reluctance."[17] Burr withdrew, releasing a following which clearly was not enough to challenge Jay and Clinton. In the electioneering that followed, he took no part himself; his Republican supporters in New York City worked for Clinton while his Federalist admirers beat the bushes for Jay.[18]

Federalists were caught off balance. Troup, who at about the

12. Mitchell, *Alexander Hamilton*, II, 201-3; "Z.A."[Robert R. Livingston], Apr. 3, 1792, N.Y. *Daily Advertiser*.

13. *N.-Y. Journal*, Feb. 22, 25, 29, 1792; for Yates, *Albany Gazette*, Mar. 26, 1792.

14. *N.-Y. Journal*, Feb. 15, 18.

15. William Livingston to Webb, Feb. 12, 1792, in Ford, ed., *Correspondence of S. B. Webb*, III, 170.

16. Ledyard to Hamilton, Feb. 17, 28, 1792, Syrett, ed., *Hamilton Papers*, XI, 37-38, 54.

17. Van Gaasbeck to Burr, Mar. 28, 1792, and Van Gaasbeck to Robert Lennox, Apr. 7, 1792, Van Gaasbeck Papers, Kingston Senate House.

18. Davis, ed., *Memoirs of Aaron Burr*, I, 331-32; Burr to Jacob Delamater, June 15, 1792, *ibid.*, 355-57.

same time had been taken in by the "State Bank" scheme, wrote sheepishly to Hamilton, "I have reason to suspect we have both been abused."[19] Excitable Federalists like Dr. James Tillary were in a tizzy. "To confound and distract the city," he wrote Hamilton, there was "Judge Yates' sudden and unexpected resignation, or rather declination—Judge Jay's sudden and unexpected acceptation—the obstinacy of Governor Clinton—the interference of Burr and the tergiversation of the Chancellor." What was more, "the bank mania rages violently in the city"; obviously, "the malignant spirit of anti-Federalism" was "hovering over our land."[20]

Although the Federalists could not get Yates and did not want Burr, the nomination of Jay did not mean a reversion to "high flying" Federalism. On the contrary, of all their public figures in New York, John Jay was the consistent symbol of middle-of-the-road conservatism, from the time he had drafted the New York constitution of 1777 through his moderation in the ratification debate in 1788. Although fully committed to Hamiltonian policies, as Chief Justice he was not identified with either the partisanship or personal profit with which they were associated in the public mind. The fact that he had already enunciated a doctrine of judicial review of both congressional and state legislation was not appreciated,[21] and in any case would not have been a source of objection by New Yorkers who accepted the same thing in their own Council of Revision. The fact that he had not committed himself on the issues of state government was a decided asset. He was, it was true, thoroughly aristocratic in his concept of leadership; he regarded it as "improper . . . to make any effort to obtain suffrages," and throughout the campaign remained on his Westchester estate tending to agriculture and reading the classics.[22] Federalists had been trying to get him to run since 1786; he had a natural appeal to the "great families"; his mother was a Van Cortlandt, his father "a rich and reputable colonial merchant," his wife the daughter of the late Governor William Livingston; James Duane of the upper manor Livingstons was confident the year before that he would have

19. Robert Troup to Hamilton, Mar. 19, 1792, Syrett, ed., *Hamilton Papers*, XI, 155-58.

20. James Tillary to Hamilton, Mar. 6, 1792, *ibid.*, XI, 109-11.

21. Schachner, *Founding Fathers*, 127-29; Monaghan, *John Jay*, 307-8, 314.

22. Jay to J. C. Dongan, Feb. 27, 1792, Johnston, ed., *Correspondence of John Jay*, III, 413-14; see also Jay to Mrs. Jay, June 18, 1792, *ibid.*, 434-35; Monaghan, *John Jay*, 327-33.

the support of his "family and friends."[23] Of the conservative Whig leaders of New York there was not another who could match his record of service to the nation as a leading member of Congress, negotiator of the successful peace treaty, Secretary of Foreign Affairs, and then Chief Justice. His only political liabilities were his past presidency of the Manumission Society and the fact that he had not been connected with state affairs for many years.[24]

On the other hand the nomination of Stephen Van Rensselaer, eighth lord of Rensselaerswyck, by the 1790's the largest estate owner of the Hudson Valley, the son-in-law of Schuyler and brother-in-law of Hamilton, was a bold identification of the Federalists with land-lordism and Hamiltonianism. At the age of twenty-eight the young patroon had served two undistinguished years in the state senate. Nonetheless, he added strength to the ticket: as a "northerner" he balanced Jay of the southern district; he was well known in the rising western district which had elected him handily in 1790; and it was expected that he would bring out perhaps 1500 of his own tenants to the polls.[25] He claimed to be generous to his tenants and was beginning to bestow his largesse in such a way as to gain a reputation for philanthropy.

II

By 1792 Governor Clinton had changed in his appeal from the candidate of 1789. Three years before he had been the doughty warrior against "consolidation," easily branded as a foe of the new government. Since then he had dissipated such accusations by his cordiality to Washington and the federal government while they had been in New York City. On the other hand, as an opponent of assumption he could attract the opposition to the Federalists that had been aroused on this score. Most important, as leader of the state government he had established the remarkable record which came to a climax in the session of early 1792.

The "gentlemen in Mr. Clinton's interest"—the party term was still avoided—showed that disenchantment with national policies and the attraction of state policies had indeed produced new support for the

23. Samuel F. Bemis in *DAB* s.v. "Jay, John"; James Duane to Walter Livingston, Jan. 8, 1791, abstract, Jay Papers, Columbia Univ.

24. See letters cited in footnote 53.

25. William Livingston to Samuel B. Webb, Feb. 12, 1792, Ford, ed., *Correspondence of S. B. Webb*, III, 170; James Fairlie to Stephen Van Rensselaer, Feb. 13, 1792, Fairlie Papers, N.-Y. Hist. Soc.

Governor. Among the lower manor Clermont Livingstons, Clinton could count in his camp the Chancellor, his brothers Edward and John (in the thick of their fight for the "State Bank"), Morgan Lewis (made attorney-general by Clinton the previous fall), and no doubt Senator Thomas Tillotson—in short, all but John Armstrong. Edward Livingston and Morgan Lewis ran for the assembly in New York (although still not on the Clintonian ticket), and Morgan Lewis also ran in Dutchess, while the Chancellor campaigned actively for Clinton.[26] "The Livingstons have all joined the Clintonians against Jay," a shocked Federalist reported from New York City. Even Brockholst Livingston, John Jay's brother-in-law, seems to have been active.[27]

But the real catch for the Governor was the upper manor, the sons of Robert Livingston, who had died in 1790: John, now ostensibly the head of the family in politics, Walter, Henry, indeed all save the maverick Peter R., the eldest, who was feuding with his brothers. John planned to run for the state senate from the eastern district for which he would require Clintonian support. Defeated by Schuyler's candidate for Congress in 1790, he was completely at odds with the Schuylers. He was also ripe for the attraction of Clinton's magnet of land. He wanted the Governor to extinguish the Indian title on a tract of land apparently promised the New York Genesee Land Company when Clinton abrogated their illegally obtained title to a vast tract in western New York.

The negotiations between the upper manor and the Governor were hardly subtle. In November 1791, "the Governor on his way up to Albany," John confided to Walter, "did me the *honor* to stop and breakfast and on his return staid and supped. In the course of conversation," Livingston broached the question of the land. Clinton insisted that the area was still in possession of Indian tribes. To Livingston this was a feeble excuse; Britain had conquered the territory from France, the United States from Britain; title therefore was with New York, not the Indians. The Governor, while adamant, did not

26. See John C. Wynkoop to Peter Van Schaack, Feb. 23, 1792, Van Schaack Papers, Lib. Cong.; for the candidates, see nominations and "Atticus," *N.-Y. Journal,* Apr. 18, 1792.

27. Sarah Jay to John Jay, June 10, 1792, John Jay Transcripts, Columbia Univ., mentions Brockholst, Edward, William S., and Maturin Livingston as active on behalf of Clinton in the post-election ballots controversy. William S. Livingston was pro-Jay early in the campaign; see William S. Livingston to S. B. Webb, Feb. 12, 1792, Ford, ed., *Correspondence of S. B. Webb,* III, 176, but it is reasonable to assume that men who were so frenzied defending the canvassers' post-election decision were also Clinton's partisans prior to the election.

close the door. "Perhaps," wrote John, "the approaching election may do as much for us in this business as anything whatever"; Clinton "cannot play off and on."[28]

In February 1792 as the candidates were being chosen, John reported to Walter that the Schuyler interest was making overtures to him, but that he was determined . . . not to swallow Toads nor Skittle-pots for any of the party." The time was ripe to strike a bargain with the Governor—"If Clinton will take you up [Walter] for Lieutenant Governor and will do as he ought to do I have no objection to support him to the utmost. Perhaps it will be well to push the land business at this moment." Perhaps brother Henry "could ask Clinton in a way that would not give offence but not pledge himself in such a way that Clinton can have any hold on him." The diplomacy was successful. A month later John wrote that he was "clearly in his interest [i.e., Governor Clinton] and were not the Chancellor in his favor I should be very warm for Clinton. I love to retaliate and no better opportunity can offer." Walter did not get the second place on the ticket, but John seems to have gotten his land and support for the state senate.[29] By April 1, Peter R. Livingston reported that "all my brothers" were "using their utmost for Clinton" and "will carry considerable" in Columbia County.[30] At the end of the year he, too, seems to have drifted away from the Federalists.[31] The Livingstons' neighbor, Peter Van Schaack, observing the collaboration of both manors with Clinton, was amazed at the "forced and unnatural coalition" which he considered "not less unnatural than that of North and Fox in 1783." "People cannot be brought to believe that there is some concealed Quid pro Quo in this bargain."[32]

28. John to Walter Livingston, Nov. 13, 1791, R. R. Livingston Papers, N.-Y. Hist. Soc.

29. John to Walter Livingston, Feb. 16, Mar. 1, Mar. 7, 1792, ibid. Later, Clinton extinguished title to land in the Niagara area; John also received a large grant of land as one of the participants in the N.Y. Genesee Land Company; see Laws of the State of N.Y., 16th Sess., ch. 26. The grantees also included Henry and Peter R. of the upper manor and Henry G. and Henry B. Livingston, among several dozen other speculators.

30. Peter R. Livingston to Peter Van Schaack, Apr. 1, 1792, Van Schaack Papers, Lib. Cong.

31. Late in 1792, Peter failed to receive Federalist support when he ran unsuccessfully for Congress from the Columbia County district. Early in 1793 Hamilton tried to get federal appointments for him and John Armstrong, the only member of the Chancellor's family that had not deserted in 1792; see Hamilton to John Armstrong, Apr. 1, 1793, Peter R. Livingston to Hamilton, Aug. 13, 1793 (indicating an earlier letter from Hamilton), Hamilton Papers, Lib. Cong.

32. Van Schaack to Van Gaasbeck, Apr. 12, 1792, Van Gaasbeck Papers, Kingston Senate House.

In the cities there were other desertions from Federalism. At Albany Elkanah Watson refused Schuyler's plea to join Jay's electioneering committee, and as he tells the story, was read out of the Federalist party.[33] In New York City Clinton's two election committees had about fifty members, half of whom were men of substantial property.[34] They included Joseph Hallett, one of the wealthiest property holders in the city;[35] Leonard Cutting and Thomas Ludlow, recipients of 50,000-acre land grants; Thomas Randall, a large stockholder in the Bank of New York;[36] and two merchants who had been prominently identified with the Federalists, Commodore James Nicholson, the naval hero who had commanded the mock ship "Hamilton" in the constitution parade of 1788, and Samuel Osgood of Massachusetts who had recently resigned as Washington's postmaster general and taken up residence in the city. There were also at least ten artisans on the committee, although none were leaders of the Mechanics Society.[37]

Federalists, in contrast, had lost a number of their stalwarts in New York City—William Duer and Richard Platt deliberately hung back. Pointing to federal officeholders who were pro-Jay, Platt felt "as they are all Federal men and loaded with the honors of the Government, let them work, as they have the watch."[38] In trouble in the city, Federalists were counting on their new allies in Ulster County and in the west. In Ulster, the Clintonian stronghold, Peter Van Gaasbeck, after his defeat for Congress in 1790, organized the first Federalist machine in the county, perhaps in the state. Under his direction as

33. Flick, Elkanah Watson, 201, citing a letter of Watson to Judge Hobart. At Albany 3 or 4 members of the election committee of 13 were newcomers; see N.-Y. Journal, Mar. 17, 1792. For the 1789 committee, see Munsell, ed., Annals of Albany, IV, 327.

34. The Clintonians first announced a committee of 30, only 6 of whom were active in 1789, then announced a committee of 25, all of whom were new to the cause; see N.-Y. Journal, Feb. 25, Mar. 21, 1792. A check of the two committees against the New York City Directory for 1791 and 1792 reveals the following occupations: 26 merchants (or otherwise identifiable as such), 6 petty shopkeepers, 4 lawyers, 1 doctor, 10 artisans.

35. "Assessment of the Real and Personal Property of the East Ward, City of New York, June 24, 1791," New York Historical Society, Collections, 44 (1912). On this tax assessment roll for only one of the city's seven wards, 11 members of the Clinton committee were found. Of these, 7 were listed as worth from £1440 to £5900. Hallett owned a wharf, two stores, and other property worth £5900.

36. Five other men held 14½ shares of stock between them, a small amount; see Domett, History of the Bank of New York, 132-35.

37. For officers see N.Y. City Directory for 1791 and 1792.

38. Richard Platt to Samuel B. Webb, Mar. 4, 1792, Ford, ed., Correspondence of S. B. Webb, III, 177.

chairman of the Kingston election committee, party workers wrote articles for the papers at Kingston and Goshen, circulated handbills from New York, and visited voters throughout the county. Clintonians charged that "the Kingston junto" was supported only by Ulster farmers who owed debts to Van Gaasbeck and his partner.[39] In frontier Otsego Judge Cooper practiced all the arts of "Hook and Snivery," as an inquiry by the legislature later brought out. If Jay won, he was prepared to "Illuminate as well the town as the lake on which we shall raise Bonfires on Platforms, cannonading, musick, Hornes and conche shells." If Clinton won, "I must hang up my fiddle."[40] In distant Ontario, Thomas Morris urged James Wadsworth to bend every effort for Jay's election "as one of the most important objects that can interest the back settlers of our state."[41] A Federalist victory depended on how well their new allies could deliver their constituencies.

III

The Federalist campaign, directed as it had been in 1789 to wooing Clinton's anti-Federalist following away from him, was marked by flexibility, energy, and cunning. Schuyler took to the road "to converse with the people," as he put it.[42] An Ulster Federalist boasted how he had planted an article under the pen name "A Clintonian" while others posed as "A True-Blue Clintonian" and "A True Republican" to appear as Clintonians who had seen the light.[43] A Van Rensselaer advised the Lansingburgh committee that if they could not win over Clintonians for Jay, then they should at least get their votes for local candidates.[44] "Personal animadversions" had to be avoided,

39. S. Sleght to Van Gaasbeck, Apr. 1792, Ebenezer Foote to Van Gaasbeck, [probably Apr.] 1792, Sylvanus Miller to Van Gaasbeck, Apr. 15, 1792, S. Sleght to Van Gaasbeck, Apr. 9, 1792, Van Gaasbeck Papers, Kingston Senate House; Josiah Hoffman to Ebenezer Foote, Apr. 20, 1792, Foote Papers, Lib. Cong.

40. Cooper to Stephen Van Rensselaer, May 2, 1792, Schuyler to Cooper, May 7, 1792, in James F. Cooper, *Legends and Traditions*, 137-38, 143-44.

41. Thomas Morris to James Wadsworth, Mar. 8, 1792, MS No. 3992, N.Y. State Lib.; Amos Hall to Oliver Phelps, Apr. 9, 1792, Oliver Phelps Papers, N.Y. State Lib.

42. Philip to John Schuyler, Mar. 11, Apr. 23, 1792, Philip Schuyler Family Papers, N.Y. Pub. Lib.

43. "A Clintonian," *Poughkeepsie Journal*, Apr. 26, 1792; Sleght to Van Gaasbeck, Apr. 9, 1792, Van Gaasbeck Papers, Kingston Senate House; *N.-Y. Journal*, Mar. 14, 1792; The Albany Federalist Committee to the Kingston Committee [n.d., 1792], Van Gaasbeck Papers, F.D.R. Lib.

44. John Van Rensselaer and six others to Peter Van Schaack, Apr. 15, 1792, Van Schaack Papers, Lib. Cong.

counseled Ambrose Spencer of Hudson, and attacks against Jay should be left unanswered.[45]

The appeal of the official statement circulated by the state-wide Federalist committee was moderate. "Granting to Mr. Clinton upon the score of merit, all that the most zealous of his friends contend for," they wrote, he should not be re-elected because it was "improper to give any man . . . perpetuity in the chief magistracy." "Frequent change in government" was indispensable to destroy undue influence, corrupt connections, and factions. They based their appeal for Jay on his services to the nation and the state and on his unimpeachable character.[46] But while they took this moderate tack, they also laced into Clinton on his vulnerable flanks—the land office scandals and the Livingstons.

The essential appeal of the Clintonians was conservative: return Clinton and Van Cortlandt, the "old, tried and faithful servants of the public." They dilated on the flourishing condition of the state with its boundaries established, debts discharged, and population doubled since the Revolution; on the record of the state government with appropriations for schools, roads, and canals, matched by revenue from state-owned "property in money, funded debts, bank shares, and land which will preclude taxation."[47] What was there Governor Clinton could not do?

Federalists responded derisively:

> The Hessian fly Clinton can kill
> Our floods with fish and oysters fill
> Can bid our rivers ebb and flow
> Can call down rain, or dew, or snow;
> Can legislate our wives with child;
> Can make dame fortune harsh or mild;
> Can take the Congress by the nose,
> If, as they may, become our foes;

45. Ambrose Spencer and John Thurston to Peter Van Gaasbeck, Mar. 29, 1792, Van Gaasbeck Papers, Kingston Senate House.

46. "To the Independent Electors," *N.-Y. Journal,* Mar. 24, 1792; see also "A Clintonian" and "Democritus," *Poughkeepsie Journal,* Apr. 18, 26, 1792; "An Orange County Farmer," *Goshen Repository,* Mar. 20, 1792; in the *N.-Y. Journal:* "A Friend to the Liberties of His Country," Feb. 24, "A True Republican," Feb. 29, and "A Letter from a Farmer . . . ," Mar. 21, 1792.

47. "Circular" by the New York Election Committee, *N.-Y. Journal,* Apr. 21, 1792; see especially "An Independent Citizen," *ibid.,* Feb. 25, 1792, and "To the Independent Electors of the County of Columbia," by "An Elector," *ibid.,* Apr. 14, 1792.

Can feed us, clothe us, give us drink,
Can talk for us and for us think.[48]

In addition to the Governor's record, Clintonians stressed his personal qualities. Why was the Governor attacked—because "he is too plain a man" was the answer; "he has not visited the European courts" —like Jay. What were the requirements of a man for governor, asked "Cato." He had to have "political integrity; the love of the people at heart; he must be generous; brave; well versed in the military art; not reserved; [and] accessible to every member of the community." Clinton had all these virtues. With a candidate and record such as this, why "change merely for the sake of changing?"[49]

When the Clintonians took the offensive they condemned Jay and Van Rensselaer for their class status and aristocratic attitudes. They questioned Jay's devotion to republican principles. He had been abroad five years and had absorbed too many aristocratic ideas; his "language and deportment" smacked of aristocracy; he was not accessible to the common man. It was rumored that he once said "that there ought to be in America but two sorts of people, the one very rich and the other very poor." Furthermore, he was not enough of a New Yorker because he had been out of the state ever since his return from Europe. There was also something suspicious about a man already drawing $4000 a year as a judge who wanted to be governor.[50]

Van Rensselaer, of course, was an even better target. In an article aimed at the Ulster yeomanry, the Clintonians dismissed him as "a young lord of a manor in Albany" nominated because "as he already knew [how] to lord over his tenants and cast up his rents, he could very easy lord over everybody else, and draw up tax laws." He was a "young man of 25 without any other pretensions than those which his estate and his relation to the Secretary [Hamilton] gave him"; he was put forth "in conformity to the fashionable tenets of advancing the rich and the well born."[51]

48. "A Friend to Freedom," N.Y. *Daily Advertiser*, cited in Monaghan, *John Jay*, 331-32.
49. "Independent Citizen," N.Y. *Daily Advertiser*, Mar. 7, 1792; *Poughkeepsie Journal*, Apr. 19, 1792, extra page; see also "To the Independent Electors of . . . Columbia," *N.-Y. Journal*, Apr. 14, 1792; see the series "The Guardian" by "Tammany," *N.-Y. Journal*, Mar. 17, 21, 28, 1792.
50. N.Y. *Daily Advertiser*, cited in Monaghan, *John Jay*, 331-32; in *N.-Y. Journal*, an unsigned article, Mar. 31; "To the Public," a notice by Joshua Purdy, *et al.* of Westchester County, *ibid.*
51. "A Dialogue . . . Ulster County," *N.-Y. Journal*, Apr. 21, 1792; N.Y. *Daily Advertiser*, Mar. 1, 1792; "To the Independent Electors of . . . Columbia," *N.-Y.*

The aristocrats Jay and Van Rensselaer were a danger above all because of their ties to the federal government. The Dutchess County committee pointed out that the state had much to fear, because the assumption of state debts had consolidated the public debtors behind the national government, and the national bank had further attached the moneyed interest and created "a real monopoly against all other banks." Jay and Van Rensselaer were spokesmen for the federal government—their connections with Hamilton and Schuyler were proof—and if elected they would not resist its encroachments on the state.[52]

And finally among the minor themes, true to Federalist predictions, Clintonians played on the small slaveholder's fears about Jay's intentions on slavery. When asked, Jay acknowledged his abolitionism but stressed his gradualism; other Federalist leaders similarly refused to compromise. As a result, Van Gaasbeck gloomily reported "many difficulties" from Ulster. Late in the campaign, however, he helped Ulsterites to discover that Clinton was "at least as much for manumitting the slaves as his competitor" which he felt enabled Federalists to recoup their losses. Only in New York City did a few Clintonians take exception to their party's pro-slavery stance.[53]

IV

Chancellor Livingston began the campaign as participant and ended as an issue. Livingston's frame of mind on the eve of the election is not difficult to fathom. As he wrote of himself, "The Chancellor . . . has openly declared against those measures of the federal government which tend to introduce a moneyed aristocracy and to annihilate the state governments."[54] Secondly, Philip Schuyler, whom he had knocked out of the national Senate, had emerged "at the head

Journal, Apr. 14, 1792; "Extract of a letter from New York," Lansingburgh *American Spy*, Apr. 30, reprinted in *N.-Y. Journal*, Apr. 14, 1792.

52. "To the Electors of the County of Dutchess," *ibid.*, Apr. 14, 1792; see also "Many," Apr. 11, 1792.

53. John Jay to J.C. Dongan, Feb. 27, 1792, in Johnston, ed., *Correspondence of John Jay*, III, 413-15; Peter Van Schaack to John Wynkoop, Mar. 13, 1792, Wynkoop to Van Schaack, Apr. 17, 1792, Van Schaack Papers, Lib. Cong.; Peter Van Gaasbeck to Aaron Burr, Mar. 28, 1792, Van Gaasbeck Papers, Kingston Senate House. See the interesting debate over racial differences, *N.-Y. Journal*: "Africanus," Feb. 4, Mar. 3; "Americanus," Feb. 11, May 10; "Consistency," May 2, 1792.

54. Political Essay on Elections [1792], R. R. Livingston Papers, N.Y. Hist. Soc.; Dangerfield, *Chancellor Robert R. Livingston*, 253-54. Like Dangerfield I have been unable to locate a printed version of this incomplete MS in the papers and agree that it was "too revealing to see the light of day."

of the aristocratic party in this state." Livingston correctly analyzed the sources of Schuyler's growing strength: the largest tenant vote in the state (his own, his son-in-law Stephen Van Rensselaer's, James Duane's); "his close and intimate connections with an extensive back country"; and the "extensive patronage" of the federal government through his other son-in-law, Hamilton. The extension of Schuyler's influence in the state government would end the possibility of additional appointments such as Morgan Lewis' or the progress of such measures as the third bank favored by Edward and John. Moreover, the prospect of John Jay as governor, an office a notch higher than chancellor, made him livid with jealousy. Finally, the Chancellor once again felt close to the Governor—in fact on March 1 he wrote a letter to Clinton asking for a land grant,[55] his first request for a favor in five years. All these factors weighed on the Chancellor as he gave Clinton his first support since 1783. Self-consciously he saw his family in the image he had of its role of the late colonial era when "a close union of the Livingston family with the democratic interests of the state" blocked the aristocratic party.[56]

Livingston's contributions to the campaign were heavy handed. He spent one fine spring day, for example, visiting Assemblyman David Van Ness of Columbia, a Yates supporter who felt it would be "inconsistent" to switch to Clinton. As Van Ness told the story, Livingston said he "had had a conversation with the governor" about the next appointment as Columbia County sheriff and that "he had no doubt but what I as an old Inhabitant of the county could get that office or any other he had." Van Ness said he was uninterested; later he came out for Jay.[57]

The Chancellor's appearance in the newspapers on Clinton's behalf was marked by an envenomed personal attack on Jay and an immodest defense of himself. In his first article Livingston stuck to political issues.[58] He questioned Jay's republicanism, deprecated his perform-

55. Robert R. Livingston to Clinton, Mar. 4, 1792, R. R. Livingston Papers, N.-Y. Hist. Soc.

56. [Robert R. Livingston], Political Essay on Elections [1792], R. R. Livingston Papers, N.-Y. Hist. Soc.

57. David Van Ness to William Wilson, Oct. 20, 1794, and R. R. Livingston to Wilson, Sept. 10, 1794, William Wilson Papers, Clements Library, Ann Arbor, Mich.

58. "To —— M ——, Esquire, Representative of —— County," N.Y. Daily Advertiser, Feb. 27, 1797; N.-Y. Journal, Mar. 24 and "Extraordinary," Mar. 31, 1792; in MS form "To Mr. M, Representative from M County," R. R. Livingston Papers, N.-Y. Hist. Soc.; see in same vein "Cato," N.-Y. Journal, Mar. 31, Apr. 1, 2, 3, 4, 1792. No MS draft of this is in the Livingston Papers, but "Cato" is a pseud-

ance as peace negotiator and drafter of New York's constitution—(for its "distinguishing features," the Council of Revision and senate based on the landed interest, "it was indebted I have often heard to Mr. Chancellor Livingston"). His principal concern was the encroachments by the federal government. He asked:

Can you see the father-in-law of the Secretary of the Treasury, the most active partisan of Mr. Jay—can you see his brother-in-law, at an age when he can have no pretentions to such dignities, endeavoring to divest an old servant of the people of the honors which he has richly earned by the labors and hazards he has undergone—can you see the Chief Justice of the United States, stepping forward to add to his present emoluments, those of Governor of this state—can you see him supported by district judges, attorneys, clerks, and every officer of the United States?—can you see his arrangement take place, while General S———R is at Philadelphia in the house of the S———y of the T———y?—can you see the powerful landed interest of Mr. Van Rensselaer combining itself with that force which is derived from the weight of administration, and the new made monied men that it has created; and can you be free from all apprehensions of corrupt influence? Do you not tremble for the independence of the states, so essential, as well as to the preservation of our domestic, as of our federal government? Who shall set bounds to this power? Do we not daily see the most ingenious devices to justify the profuse expenditure of public money, to prevent the diminution of the national debt, and to contrive pretexts for the accumulation of taxes, and the multiplication of armies and tax-gatherers.

Federalists were quick to ridicule Clinton's aristocratic critic of aristocracy. To whom has the Governor resorted for "friendship and alliance," a broadside asked. "To the family of Livingstons—Is there a more aristocratic family in the state . . . who hold the honest yeomanry of the country in more sovereign contempt? Are they not notorious for their pride, their ambition and their avarice? For grasping at all the officers of the state?" Federalists were also quick to deflate the Chancellor's pretentions to personal influence. "My dear friend," wrote "Tempora Mutantur," "I know thou art a wag, and readest merry books—thou rememberest it is written in Rabelais, that when Pantagruel f--ted, he shook the earth three leagues around. Does thou

onym that can be identified as Livingston in a series in July 1792, and which he used frequently thereafter.

seriously believe that the C———r's influence will extend over as many acres in any county?"[59]

The defenders of Livingston—or the Chancellor himself—only made him vulnerable to further attack. "John Old Castle," deriding "that nasty blackguard book, Rabelais," claimed that the Chancellor "through the whole of a very active life [had] never been charged with a single political error." "Aristogiton" thought it would be extraordinary if a man of his position, property, and family connections "whose character is unspotted" and patriotism "unimpeached" did not have influence.[60]

"Timothy Tickler" promptly accused Livingston of writing both "Old Castle" and "Aristogiton," deriding him for his vanity and labeling him "an apostatizing zealot." Livingston's current views on aristocracy, rotation, and the state governments were "a bundle of inconsistencies," compared to his views of 1788. They were too much from "an infallible statesman—a Pope in politics." His change of outlook, "Tickler" charged, could be ascribed not to principle but to the President's rejection of him for high office in 1789.[61]

Livingston lashed back in two different styles. Writing as "Z.A.," he explained that political changes accounted for his alleged "inconsistencies."[62] In 1788, he pointed out, "each state possessed a considerable debt which attracted the *state creditors* to the *state* governments, while the United States had another set of creditors dependent upon them. This divided the monied interest but by 'the precipitate assumption of this debt the monied interest' were taught to look up to the federal government." "This measure in turn was the parent of a general excise," a deplorable measure. Continuing his catalog: "No man who agreed to the federal Constitution ever contemplated a Na-

59. "To the Electors . . ." [1792], broadside, N.Y. State Lib.; "A Farmer," N.Y. *Daily Advertiser*, Feb. 28, 1792; "The Following Extract, with the Annexed Observations and Answers," N.Y. *Daily Advertiser*, Mar. 1, 1792; *N.-Y. Journal*, Mar. 31, 1792.

60. "John Old Castle," N.Y. *Daily Advertiser*, Mar. 23, 1792 and *N.-Y. Journal*, Mar. 24, 1792; "Aristogiton," N.Y. *Daily Advertiser*, Mar. 1, 1792 and *N.-Y. Journal*, Mar. 31, 1792 with "The Following Extract" cited in the above footnote. "Timothy Tickler," cited below claimed Livingston wrote both of these; Livingston as "Aristedes" and "Z.A." cited below said they were not written by the same man, leaving open the possibility that he wrote "Aristogiton."

61. "Timothy Tickler," N.Y. *Daily Advertiser*, Mar. 31 and *N.-Y. Journal*, Mar. 31, 1792. Dangerfield's suggestion that the author was John Armstrong, Livingston's still Federalist brother-in-law, is reasonable. See footnote 31 above.

62. "Z.A.," N.Y. *Daily Advertiser*, Apr. 3, 1792, in MS as "To the Printer," R. R. Livingston Papers, N.-Y. Hist. Soc.

tional Bank, and an attempt to consolidate the whole monied interest of the continent into a few hands." In addition "we see a standing army of 5000 men raised and new taxes contemplated." With all of these measures "may we not reasonably say that a variety of circumstances have concurred to reduce the weight of the state governments in the general scale and will it be inconsistent with the sentiments professed by the firmest federalists to guard against further encroachments?" In short, "changes in our circumstances" "called for changes in our measures."

Assuming "Timothy Tickler" to be John Jay, Livingston also wrote a hot-tempered blast at his former friend.[63] Jay was friendless—the "companions of your youth . . . These you have sacrificed to a mere jealousy of their superior abilities, to an overwhelming ambition, which made you dread them as your rivals." Jay was cold—"Your cold heart graduated like a thermometer finds the freezing point nearest the bulb." Jay was obnoxious—"You travel through life, as fretful men do in a stagecoach disgusted with and disgusting those that you are compelled to be near." Jay was talentless—"but, sir, you of all should have been cautious of provoking an investigation into the extent of your talents. You who are in every walk of science and polite literature, are very far beyond your compeers."

A few days after this splenetic performance John Jay sent a brief note to the papers denying that he was the author of any electioneering articles.[64] In blind rage the Chancellor had blasted the wrong target. "Timothy Tickler" chortled that "every genuine republican will in his heart either despise or abhor" the "combination of the Livingstons with the Governor." The Clintonians, he claimed, "while they approve the treason, despise the traitor." In New York City after the election the Chancellor sensed an "indifference" to him among the Governor's friends which he could not quite grasp.[65] To Clintonians the entire spectacle would have been amusing were it not so embarrassing.

V

Federalists also handled the land scandal with aplomb. The first criticism of the commissioners had circulated widely in the summer

63. "Aristedes," *N.-Y. Journal* and N.Y. *Daily Advertiser*, Apr. 4, 1792; in MS as John Jay Exposed for What he is, R. R. Livingston Papers, N.-Y. Hist. Soc.
64. *N.-Y. Journal*, Apr. 7, 1792.
65. "A Real Republican," *Poughkeepsie Journal*, Apr. 26, 1792; Robert to Edward Livingston, July 20, 1792, R. R. Livingston Papers, N.-Y. Hist. Soc.

of 1791 in the form of a two-part article by "A Northern Centinel," the work of Elkanah Watson.[66] Although a Federalist of '88 and an associate of Schuyler in the Albany bank and western canal in 1791-92, Watson insisted he did the articles on his own.[67] He did not repeat the charges against Clinton in the election of 1792 in which he refused to support Jay.

In his first article the "Northern Centinel" established himself as a partisan of "northern" interests (a term that included the west) and a proponent of roads and canals, opposed to spending lavish funds, for example, on a "palace" for the governor at New York City. In his second he attacked the entire proceeding of the land commissioners from the point of view of "the honest farmer." In putting the public domain up for sale, the commissioners received bids only from New York City residents. How, therefore, was the pioneer to acquire land? He first had to explore land on the frontier, next place a bid at the southern end of the state, and then wait six months for a decision. Under such an arrangement everyone knew "who will milk the cow for the sake of the cream. Possibly some buttermilk may finally be sold out to some indigent people in this quarter." As for the Macomb sale, it was obnoxious on every ground: five-sixths of the land was good and well watered; higher prices were possible; why then was there such haste? A single man was listed as the purchaser but who were the "associates behind the curtain?" What, too, were the results? One-tenth of the entire state now was "the sport of speculating landjobbers, probably rich foreigners, to whom future settlers must become tributary." "Enormous patents" were a "curse" and a "scourge to a free country."

There were a few ineffectual retorts to this firecracker, but after the fall no more was heard of the land issue until the gubernatorial campaign.[68] Late in January 1792, Federalist leaders approached Philip Schuyler to draw up a resolution for the legislature censuring Clinton.[69] According to Watson, Schuyler was sympathetic, yet hesi-

66. The first article appeared originally in the *Albany Gazette*, and was reprinted in the *Albany Register*, June 27, 1791, and in the *N.-Y. Journal*, July 6, 27, Aug. 24; in the *Poughkeepsie Journal*, July 21, Aug. 25, and in other papers.

67. Elkanah Watson, Journal D, p. 438, Watson Papers, Box 2, vol. 8, N.Y. State Lib.

68. "Impartial Spectator," No. 1, Aug. 23, 1791, "A Northern Farmer," No. 1, Oct. 26, 1791, reprinted from *Albany Gazette*, and No. 2, Nov. 19, 1791, all in *N.-Y. Journal*.

69. Alexander Macomb to William Constable, Feb. 5, 1792, Constable Papers, N.Y. Pub. Lib.

tated; the issue, to use Schuyler's own phrase, was "a two edged sword."
Macomb was a well-known Federalist; Schuyler himself was a leading speculator, who it might be revealed was a secret partner in Macomb's earlier St. Lawrence Ten Towns speculation. Thus in accusing
the Governor, Schuyler might end up in the dock. Judging by events,
Schuyler advised that the question be postponed until late in the
campaign when a charge would be difficult to answer.[70]

On April 9, three weeks before the voting, Silas Talbot, a Federalist
assemblyman from Montgomery, a western county, introduced a motion of censure which was probably Schuyler's handiwork.[71] Although
it singled out the Macomb sale, it stressed the general policy of "extravagant large tracts." The intent of the legislature, it was claimed,
was that land be sold in small parcels because "too great an accumulation of real estate in the hands of one, or a few wealthy individuals"
was "incompatible with the spirit of the government and the true
interests of the people." Had it passed, Talbot's resolution would
have required that Macomb make full payment on his purchase at
once—which would have forced its reversion to the state—and that the
remainder of the public domain be disposed of in townships no greater
than 25,000 acres with preference to purchasers of tracts of 250 acres.
The following day Assemblyman Melancton Smith countered with a
resolution endorsing the land commissioners, which passed the anti-
Federalist assembly promptly by a party vote, 35-20. The resolution
condemned the previous policy for not yielding a revenue, pointed out
that the legislature had granted discretionary power to the land commissioners, and brazenly praised the commissioners for their "judicious sales."[72]

The Federalist resolution clearly avoided the radical overtones of
"A Northern Centinel" and any hint of personal corruption. On
April 14 "Decius"—undoubtedly Philip Schuyler—appeared in a devas-
tating article that party workers rushed to the countryside.[73] "Decius"

70. Schuyler to Hamilton, Jan. 29, 1792, Hamilton, ed., *Works of Hamilton*, V,
493; Watson, ed., *Memoirs of Elkanah Watson*, 332.
71. "From a Correspondent," *N.Y. Journal*, Apr. 11, 1792.
72. *Journal of the Assembly of N.Y.*, 15th Sess., 200-203.
73. "Decius," N.Y. *Daily Advertiser*, Apr. 14, 1792; for distribution of this article
to Ulster County, see Schuyler to Van Gaasbeck, Apr. 16, 1792, Van Gaasbeck Papers,
Kingston Senate House; Josiah Hoffman to Ebenezer Foote, Apr. 20, 1792, Foote
Papers, Lib. Cong. "Lucius" cited below named Schuyler as the author and
"Decius" in his third piece, Apr. 23, 1792, announced he had to end the debate
to leave for upstate. No one was as knowledgeable of the entire land operation
and legislative history as Schuyler.

took his stand with the "middling farmer who constitute the strength of our country"; "The principle of a republic is a principle of equality"; land therefore should be distributed in 500-acre lots and every fourth town in 250-acre lots. Why had Governor Clinton, who had frequently "animadverted upon the pernicious policy of the colonial government" of bestowing large tracts, sanctioned a grant larger than the state of Connecticut? There was no need for revenue because the two million invested in funded debt was producing $55,820 a year, which would double in four years' time. There was no need for immediate income because the money appropriated for roads, canal companies, the loan act, and schools did not have to be disbursed at once. "Decius" claimed a plot—a meeting in the City Tavern in New York in which Clinton's friends suggested the revision in the land law. As for Smith's resolution, it was no more than a cover-up arranged by the "leading characters" who had themselves profited.

"Lucius"—probably Melancton Smith—provided an answer that went off in several directions.[74] In principle, sales in large tracts were undesirable; but "in a country where industry and enterprise are suffered to reap the fruits of their labor, some will acquire large property, and the man who has the ability and inclination"—he made no mention of connections—"to obtain great landed wealth will hold it whether he purchases it in tracts of five hundred or five millions of acres." In any case, the landed interest was not the real danger. "By the establishment of the funding system and of the national Bank the monied interest of the country is so concentrated and united that there is infinitely more to fear from its influence than there is from the landed interest, especially as by our laws, entails and the rights of primogeniture are abolished." Furthermore, it was not the legislature's intention to sell in small tracts; revenue was the aim and previous laws had been unproductive. The tavern meeting was "idle fiction." "Lucius" defended the Macomb sale as the best proposal for the tract, pointing out that the price offered was good, part of the request was rejected, and the land granted was not even especially fertile. An *ad hominem* attack wound up the article: was not "Decius"

74. "Lucius," N.Y. *Daily Advertiser*, Apr. 18, 1792. Smith handled the Clintonian defense in the assembly; he therefore was best equipped to write this article. Moreover, the pseudonym "Lucius" was used for two articles advancing Clinton for the vice-presidency which very likely were by Smith (see ch. 15, n. 24) and for an article defending Clinton in the election dispute (see n.86) when Smith was also an insider.

the surveyor-general—i.e., Schuyler—who had profited from land himself?

Schuyler now let go full blast at Clinton himself in a second "Decius" article, a broadside, and private letters.[75] Was the Governor "a principal or an accomplice?" Tracts went to "particular freinds and trustees of themselves and the Governor"; benefits would go "perhaps to the Governor himself." "Decius" listed some nine friends of Clinton who received grants. The broadside, whose accusations were noted earlier in discussing the sales, hinted darkly that "Macomb has a partner in this business—Who this partner is time, the discloser of all things, will show." Privately Schuyler passed on the word that the "partner" was Daniel McCormick, Clinton's "devoted friend," who secretly owned one third of the grant and had agreed to cut Clinton in for a future share. After the election Schuyler repeated the charge in an affidavit published in the papers.[76] Clintonians were sucked into the debate. Marinus Willett tried to prove "Decius" a "lying rascal" for a charge about Willett's interest in a particular grant, only to have "Decius" reply with allegations about his interest in six other tracts. Jonathan Lawrence, the Clintonian election chairman in the city, exchanged sallies with William Willcocks about the grant he had received.[77] Elsewhere Clintonians did the best they could with the millstone round their necks, denouncing the attack as "a mere electioneering trick." They claimed that the advantages to the yeomanry from the revenue from the land sales were incalculable. Jay's associates, they said, were also beneficiaries. The attack came from frustrated speculators like Peter Van Gaasbeck of Kingston, whose application for a 50,000-acre grant was turned down. In the north country Senator Williams even spread the rumor that Jay would quit the race because the assembly's report on the commissioners was so favorable to the commissioners. Any defense only called attention to the accusations; the result, as Daniel McCormick observed, was that

75. "Decius," N.Y. *Daily Advertiser*, Apr. 20, 1792; "To the Free and Independent Electors," broadside, N.-Y. Hist. Soc. [misdated 1791]; Philip Schuyler to Peter Van Gaasbeck, Apr. 16, 1792, Van Gaasbeck Papers, Kingston Senate House.

76. Affidavits of Philip Schuyler and Josiah Pomeroy, *N.-Y. Journal*, June 16, 1792. Another charge spread by Schuyler for which there is even less evidence is that Clinton was a member of, and Macomb was the agent for a group of Canadian speculators who were trying to buy the St. Lawrence area land with a view to attaching the territory to Canada. See affidavit of Josiah Pomeroy, Apr. 20, 1792, in broadside (n.d., n.p.), DeWitt Clinton Collection, Albany Institute.

77. Marinus Willett, Apr. 21, "Decius," Apr. 23, Willett, Apr. 24, 1792, in N.Y. *Daily Advertiser*; Willcocks, Mar. 10, Lawrence, Mar. 14, Willcocks, Mar. 16, *ibid.*

the charges were "the occasion of his [Clinton] losing many votes in the country."[78] Schuyler's "two edged sword" cut only one way.

VI

Three years earlier Washington's triumphal inaugural had been the finale for the Federalist campaign against Clinton. In New York City, the last weeks of the 1792 election campaign were played out amidst the wreckage of the panic, giving Clintonians even more of a handle on the Hamiltonians than they had early in March when the "bank mania" was made "an engine to help the Governor's reelection." On March 10 William Duer's speculative bubble burst. On March 23 he was carted off to jail while Walter Livingston, John Pintard, and other associates fled the city. On April 11 Alexander Macomb followed Duer to jail. Meanwhile, Richard Harison, the federal District Attorney, entered a long overdue prosecution against Duer for the tens of thousands he had owed the government from his unbalanced accounts as a member of the Board of Treasury in the '80's.[79]

As a result of Duer's collapse, "everything is afloat and confidence is destroyed," Seth Johnson reported. "The town here has rec'd a shock which it will not get over in many years. . . . Men look as if some general calamity has taken place."[80] In the business community, the chief victims were the Livingstons—the bears in the market. Brockholst Livingston, said Johnson, "must be nearly ruined, as well as the rest of the Livingstons," among whom he mentioned Edward and John, all promoters of the "State Bank." Edward brought the suit that sent Macomb to jail; John, at a meeting of Macomb's creditors, was "disposed to be violent at least in language."[81] Walter Livingston

78. Broadside by the Albany Federalist Committee, Apr. 18, 1792, and the draft of a reply by Williams in John Williams Letterbook, No. 3, N.Y. State Lib.; see also "To John Williams," Lansingburgh *American Spy*, June 15, 1792; "An Ulster County Farmer," "Cincinnatus" and "Alpha," Apr. 18, "A Dialogue of an Ulster County Farmer," Apr. 21, *N.-Y. Journal*, 1792; "To the Independent Electors" by "Plain Truth," Apr. 11, 1792, broadside, N.Y. Pub. Lib.; Daniel McCormick to William Constable, May 10, 1792, Constable Pierrepont Papers, N.Y. Pub. Lib.

79. James Tillary to Hamilton, Mar. 1, 1792, Syrett, ed., *Hamilton Papers*, XI, 109-11; for the suit and Hamilton's reactions, Mitchell, *Alexander Hamilton*, II, 174-80.

80. Seth Johnson to Andrew Craigie, Mar. 25, Apr. 1, Apr. 11, 15, 18, 22, 1792, Craigie Papers, III, Nos. 73-77, Amer. Antiq. Soc.; see also Alexander Macomb to William Constable, Apr. 7, and May 9, 1792, Constable Papers, N.Y. Pub. Lib.

81. Johnson to Craigie, Apr. 15, Apr. 22, Craigie Papers, III, 75, 77, Amer. Antiq. Soc.; and especially Macomb to Constable, May 9, Oct. 11, Nov. 3, 7, Dec. 3, 1792, Constable Papers, N.Y. Pub. Lib.

of the upper manor was hit even harder. There also were a legion of sufferers among common folk from whom Duer had borrowed: "shopkeepers, widows, orphans, butchers, car[t]men, gardners, market women and even the noted bawd, Mrs. McCarty." Construction was halted on a large number of houses in the city and as a result "the mechanics now begin to feel the effect of the failures." Cartmen suffered because "vessels were laying at the wharves without anyone to receive their cargoes." And many farmers who brought their produce to the city returned home, unable to find buyers.[82]

With distress such as this, there was a lynch atmosphere against the leading bankrupts. There was talk of breaking open the jail "to take [Duer] out and tear him piecemeal, and to hang every indorser of his notes if everything is not shortly settled." About two weeks before the voting a mob of "about 4 or 5 hund'd in number assembled round the jail . . . threw Stones etc. and broke some of the prison Windows and Lamps—but were soon dispersed"—apparently by rain. The next day, after Macomb was jailed, "a large collection of People" again assembled "but they appeared to have neither leader nor system" and broke up. One observer was convinced that "a little irritation or a small riot when they are thus convened . . . would burst into such a general flame as would consume the prison and D--r and M'Comb with it." Alarmed, the city officials equipped the jailers with small arms and cannon.[83]

The panic put the election in doubt. Federalists who thought they had the perfect issue in Clinton's questionable relationship to Macomb and McCormick now lamented "the bitter use" which Hamilton's enemies "make of his [Hamilton's] attachment to Col. Duer." As another Federalist put it, "the enemies to [the government] and to Hamilton and his system have now an ample field to give scope to their abuse."[84] How the voters would respond to this welter of charges and countercharges was anyone's guess.

As the campaign drew to a close Federalists were gloomy about

82. Johnson to Craigie, Mar. 25, 1792, Craigie Papers, III, 73, Amer. Antiq. Soc.
83. In addition to the letters of Johnson and Macomb see H.M. Colden to James Wadsworth, Apr. 18, and Col. Talmadge to Wadsworth, Apr. 19, 1792, in Wadsworth Papers, Conn. Hist. Soc.; see also the fragment of a letter without date, signature, or salutation which describes one of these incidents in Miscellaneous Manuscripts—New York City, Box 14, N.-Y. Hist. Soc.
84. James Watson to James Wadsworth, Apr. 3, 1792, Wadsworth Papers, Conn. Hist. Soc.; Johnson to Craigie, Apr. 15, 1792, Craigie Papers, III, 75, Amer. Antiq. Soc.

New York City but optimistic about their prospects upstate, especially in the west.[85] Both sides, probably because they knew how close the vote might be, were zealous in turning out their economic dependents, east and west. Stephen Van Rensselaer served as an election inspector in his own bailiwick and, according to Chancellor Livingston, "his ballots were written on silken paper (probably furnished by the bank) so as to enable him to know with certainty whether his tenants had acted conformably to his wishes." At the same time the Federalist James Kent was convinced that "the Livingston faction" had "forced out the tenants as sheep to the slaughter." Even the Chancellor, the pot who called the kettle black, had to admit that the votes given at Livingston Manor and Clermont were by electors "acting in some measure under the influence of their landlords."[86]

In Otsego William Cooper was as subtle as a frontier wrestler. According to sworn testimony taken later by the assembly,[87] he threatened to put one Clintonian voter in the stocks, to jail a rival election inspector, to foreclose on some debtors, and to sue a wealthy Clintonian leader; he literally "dragged" one voter to the polls and tried to exclude another by demanding a special oath. As young James Moore, a poor farmer, related his experience, Judge Cooper met him on the way to the polls and even though he was eligible to vote only for assembly candidates, urged him to vote for governor, pressing a ballot into his hands. "I opened it," said Moore, "and looked at the name that was in it and made answer in a laughing manner, 'Judge Cooper, I can not vote so, for if I do vote for Governor, I would wish to vote clearly for my own inclinations, as I do not mean to be dictated to by any person at that time.' Judge Cooper appeared in a joking manner, and in good humour until that time. He then took the ballot out of my hand, which he had given me, and appeared to be in a passion. Judge Cooper then said to me, 'What, then, young man, you will not vote as I would have you—you are a fool, young man, for you can not know how to vote as well as I can direct you, for I am a

85. Philip to John Schuyler, Apr. 30, May 5, 1792, Schuyler Family Papers, N.Y. Pub. Lib.; Van Gaasbeck to Robert Lennox, Apr. 7, 1792, Van Gaasbeck Papers, Kingston Senate House; John Wynkoop to Peter Van Schaack, Apr. 17, 1792, Van Schaack Papers, Lib. Cong.; William Cooper to Stephen Van Rensselaer, Apr. 10, 1792, Cooper Manuscripts, N.Y. State Lib.

86. "Cato" No. 1 [Robert R. Livingston], N.Y. *Daily Advertiser*, July 25, 1792; and for the same charge by "Lucius" [probably Melancton Smith], *ibid.*, June 30, 1792; James Kent to Moss Kent, May 2, 1792, Kent Papers, I, Lib. Cong.

87. *Journal of the Assembly of N.Y.*, 16th Sess., 188-200.

man in public office.' He then walked away and seemed to be in a passion." A day or so later when Moore came back to town to cast a ballot in the assembly election, Cooper again approached him and said, "You are a rascal, and owe me a sum of money and if you do not immediately pay me, I will put you in gaol." Moore denied it, insisting he had never dealt with him. Cooper then cursed him, the young Clintonian replied in kind, and Cooper threatened to jail him for using abusive language.[88]

When the unofficial returns began to trickle in, Federalists counted on a victory by the narrowest of margins—perhaps 250 votes; the Clintonians, Robert Troup reported, were "extremely uneasy."[89] According to law, a committee of canvassers appointed by the legislature was charged with counting the ballots and reporting a month after the election, which meant in the first week of June. Normally a routine affair, the counting this time turned up a number of irregularities in three frontier counties, Otsego, a Federalist stronghold, and Tioga to the west and Clinton to the north—both normally Clintonian. The ballots had been cast legally, but the procedure specified by law for getting them to the secretary of state had not been followed. After much *"sturm und drang"* the canvassers disqualified the votes of all three counties and declared Clinton the victor, 8440 to 8332, a margin of 108 votes. The decision produced an uproar. It was not reversed, however, and from what is known of the official returns and can be conjectured about the uncounted ballots, it is possible to analyze the returns.

One striking fact was the size of the vote in the gubernatorial election. From 1789 to 1792 the total vote cast increased from 12,400 to at least 18,000, if one includes the uncounted votes. About 70 per cent of the 25,000 or so voters qualified to vote for governor cast ballots.[90] A second striking fact was the closeness of the vote. Giving to each side all the ballots they claimed, in the three disputed coun-

88. *Ibid.*

89. Robert Troup to John Jay, May 6, 1792, in Johnston, ed., *Correspondence of John Jay*, III, 422-23.

90. *N.-Y. Journal*, June 2-13, 1792; for the 1789 returns, *ibid.*, June 4, 1789. According to the electoral census of 1790 there were 19,369 voters qualified in the £100 category; in 1795 there were 36,338. If this increase were divided evenly at 3394 for each year there would have been 27,157 qualified voters in 1792. However the rate of population growth was higher in the mid-1790's than the early 1790's; hence it is reasonable to assume only about 5000-6000 new voters, or a total electorate of about 25,000 in 1792.

ties and in other towns where votes were dropped, neither side could claim a majority of more than a few hundred ballots.[91] About half of the 5000 to 6000 new voters went to each party.

In the assembly elections the Clintonians won by a safe margin. The division on presidential electors late in 1792 would be 36 to 38 Republicans to 28 to 30 Federalists.[92] Clintonian gains in the legislature were uneven, however. In New York City Assemblyman Melancton Smith was defeated; the lower manor Livingstons, Edward Livingston and Morgan Lewis, ran even worse. The upper manor fared well: John Livingston was elected senator from the eastern district with Clintonian support. And in New York City William S. Livingston was elected to the assembly as one of the top vote-getters.[93]

In the gubernatorial voting, the Clintonians continued to run strongest in the counties of the yeomanry, on Long Island, Dutchess, Orange, and Ulster along the Hudson, Washington and Clinton to the north. To this traditional following they added significant urban support. In New York City the vote was 739 for Jay, 603 for Clinton, compared to a vote three years before of 833 for Yates, 385 for Clinton, the Governor's vote increasing in all wards, including the wealthy Wall Street area. In Albany the electorate was "pretty evenly divided," it was said, although "the Jay interest" was "the most powerful as it respects wealth and personal influence."[94] In Columbia County both branches of the Livingston family as well as the anti-landlord eastern townships came through for Clinton. The township of the upper manor Livingstons shifted from a vote of 313 to 3 against Clinton to 270 to 5 in his favor. The lower manor, Clermont, went from 29-43 against Clinton to 71 to 2 for him. In Hillsdale, to the east, scene of the anti-Schuyler "Indian" incident, the Clinton vote climbed from 218-64 to 325-27, although 150 men who voted for Clinton refused to vote for John Livingston for state senator.

Federalist strength rested as usual on the commercial and landlord centers of the Hudson Valley. New York, Albany, Kingston, Hudson—all the towns but Poughkeepsie—were Federalist. So were the townships of the Schuyler-Van Rensselaer tenantry: Rensselaerville (296-15), Stephentown (214-8), Watervliet (421-31). But Federalists also made their first strong showing among the yeomanry. In 1789 Clin-

91. See ch. 14, sec. I. See Appendix, Table 4.
92. *Journal of the Assembly of N.Y.*, 16th Sess., 15-20, 132.
93. *N.-Y. Journal*, June 2, 1792.
94. B. Foster to Andrew Craigie, June 26, 1792, Craigie Papers, Amer. Antiq. Soc.

tonians romped away with Ulster County, 1039 to 206; in 1792 their margin was 947 to 654. Most of the Federalist gains were in the northern part of Ulster near Kingston, while the Clintonians attracted more of "the poor" and the "lower class" who in Federalist eyes "intertained . . . a hope that the administration of Clinton will soon bring us on a level."[95] On the western frontier Jay took every county but sparsely settled Tioga, his margin increasing as one moved out into the interior. In Otsego it was greatest of all, somewhere between 550 and 800 to about 150 for Clinton.

Clintonians stressed the dependent character of the Federalist vote. Robert R. Livingston saw it resting on coerced tenants in the east and uninformed newcomers in the west, "new settlers little acquainted with the characters of the parties or the politics of the state" who in Otsego "may be supposed to act under the influence of a man [Cooper], to whom as agent for absent proprietors they are generally indebted for their lands, and as shopkeeper for every other necessary which new settlers may be supposed to want."[96] Other Clintonians were more coarse: Jay's vote rested on "ambiguous freeholders" (men unqualified to vote as £100 freeholders), "the refuse of the neighboring states" (poor New England migrants), and "the mechanical creatures of the landed aristocracy" (the tenantry).[97]

Actually Clintonians could not afford to recognize the most striking aspect of the Federalist campaign, its democratic appeal to the very voters they considered their own. However aristocratic Jay, Van Rensselaer, and Schuyler were, the Federalist themes were rotation in office, the influence of the aristocratic Livingstons, and favoritism to the wealthy by the land commissioners. "The principle of a republic is the principle of equality," Schuyler wrote as "Decius," demonstrating it himself as he went out to "converse with the people." In the furor that followed over the disputed election returns, Federalists exploited democratic sentiment even further, producing a little appreciated chapter in the political history of the state.

95. Cornelius T. Jansen to Peter Van Gaasbeck, Apr. 11, 1792, Van Gaasbeck Papers, Kingston Senate House.
96. "Cato" [Robert R. Livingston] No. 1, N.Y. *Daily Advertiser*, July 25, 1792, reprinted from *Albany Gazette*. See ch. 14, n.40 for attribution to Livingston.
97. "Respondent," *N.-Y. Journal*, Aug. 1, 1792.

CHAPTER 14

Federalists as Democrats:

The Election Dispute

of 1792

———— •—— ————

No event in New York since the Revolution, according to the editor, Thomas Greenleaf, aroused more interest than the dispute over the election of 1792. From mid-June, when the canvassers reported their decision, through the summer Federalists fumed and fretted, rallied and resolved, and threatened "a popular convention." Clintonians replied in kind. From both sides manifestos, pamphlets, broadsides, legal disquisitions, learned and unlearned, poured from the presses. In the fall petitions descended on the legislature, an official inquiry began, and witnesses paraded before the assembly. From November 1792 through March 1793 the state was "eaten up with a tedious and stormy political campaign" fraught with unforeseen consequences for Federalists and Republicans alike.[1]

The basic issue at the beginning of the dispute was simply whether the officials of three counties had observed the letter of the law in returning the election ballots to the secretary of state at New York City. Historians, reflecting a pro-Federalist bias, have assumed that the official committee of canvassers, a majority of whom were Clintonians, were guilty of stealing the election as they were accused at the

1. *N.-Y. Journal*, May 30, 1792; James Kent to Moss Kent, Mar. 22, 1793, Kent Papers, I, Lib. Cong.

time, and have usually dismissed their side of the argument.[2] Unquestionably if the "rights of suffrage" are the *sine qua non* of a democratic political system, the Clintonians were in the wrong. Yet there was another side to the dispute. Republicans believed that election laws had to be strictly observed lest precedents dangerous to free elections be established. In their eyes Federalists had sinned, and they pointed to the coercive methods of Stephen Van Rensselaer and William Cooper, contending that Federalist ballots were the product of "fraud and corruption." New York's Bill of Rights guaranteed that "all elections shall be free" and that "no person . . . by malice or menacing" shall presume "to disturb or hinder any citizen of this state to make free election."[3] Thus to match the Federalist cry of the "rights of suffrage" Clintonians countered with a plea for "freedom of elections" and "the letter of the law."

I

The technicalities of the controversy were the sort in which eighteenth-century Americans delighted. The election statute of 1787 spelled out in great detail the procedures for taking and reporting ballots.[4] A paper ticket folded so "as to conceal the writing thereon" had to be deposited in a locked box with a small hole at one end. At the closing of the polls the box had to be "bound with tape and sealed in such manner as to prevent its being opened without discovery." The poll clerks in each town had to bring the ballots to the county sheriff who in turn had to bring them to the secretary of state who presented them to a committee composed of six senators and six assemblymen elected by their respective bodies. They were to count ballots for governor, lieutenant-governor, and senators (county supervisors counted the assembly ballots) and to destroy them when done. All the officials concerned had to swear to an oath prescribed by the legislature and severe penalties were laid down for corruption, neglect, or bribery, as well as for interfering with a citizen's rights of free election.

2. Monaghan, *John Jay*, ch. 16 entitled "Clinton Filches the Governorship." Henry Cabot Lodge called the decision of the canvassers a steal "based on the most flimsy and technical grounds"; see Lodge, ed., *Works of Hamilton*, VIII, 272n. Schachner, *Aaron Burr*, 110-14, also treats the episode cynically. Spaulding, *George Clinton*, 202-6, is less harsh but has not explored Clinton's side of the controversy.

3. *Laws of the State of N.Y.*, 10th Sess., ch. 1.

4. *Laws of the State of N.Y.*, 10th Sess., ch. 15.

There was not much question as to what had happened in the three disputed counties.[5] All three were on the frontier, a journey of many days to the secretary of state in New York City. In Tioga the sheriff gave the ballot box to a deputy who was taken sick on his journey; in turn he gave the box to a clerk who made the delivery. In Clinton the sheriff gave the box to an individual who had no deputation whatever to deliver it. Otsego was more complicated. The sheriff there, Richard Smith, deputized another man to deliver the ballots; there was a question, however, whether Smith was legally sheriff. His one-year term had expired and the Council of Appointment had chosen Benjamin Gilbert in his place. Senator Stephen Van Rensselaer of the council had given the commission to William Cooper, first judge of the county, but Cooper failed to deliver it to Gilbert until after the ballots were sent off.[6] "If he [Smith] was not the sheriff," the canvassers asked, "can the votes sent by him be legally canvassed?" Secondly, only part of the ballots from Otsego were delivered in the required box while the rest were sent in a sealed bundle outside the box; thus there was a question as to whether they had been tampered with and could be legally counted.

From the beginning, Schuyler, aware of "much foul play in the returning officers," feared for the worst from the canvassers, only three of whom he counted as "friends."[7] The majority included Melancton Smith and David Gelston, who, while they had a foot in Burr's camp, had campaigned for the Governor; Thomas Tillotson, the Chancellor's brother-in-law; and Pierre Van Cortlandt, son of the lieutenant-governor. Schuyler counseled with a Federalist canvasser Leonard

5. Hammond, *Political Parties*, I, 62-70. The best summary of the facts is in the statement submitted by the canvassers to Senators Burr and King for their opinions, available in *ibid.*

6. The sequence of events was as follows. The appointment of Richard Smith, the sheriff, ran only until Feb. 18, 1792. A month before, he had announced he did not wish to be reappointed. On Mar. 30, the Council of Appointment appointed Benjamin Gilbert. Early in April, Smith was elected supervisor of the town of Otsego and took office May 1, the last day of the voting. Gilbert's commission of office was handed to Stephen Van Rensselaer by a member of the Council of Appointment about Apr. 13. Van Rensselaer gave it to William Cooper, when, it is not clear, and Cooper did not deliver it until May 11, ten days after the election. Meanwhile the election inspectors had delivered the ballots to Smith who in turn gave them to a deputy who was duly authorized by him to deliver the ballots. The canvassers questioned whether Smith "was sheriff of the county when he received and forwarded the ballots by his special deputy"; see canvassers' statement, *ibid.*, 63-66.

7. Schuyler to Hamilton, May 9, 1792, Syrett, ed., *Hamilton Papers*, XI, 378-79; Schuyler to ?, May 19, 1792, draft, Schuyler Papers, Lib. Cong.

Gansevoort, Tillotson sought advice from his brothers-in-law and cousins,[8] and Smith doubtless consorted with Clinton and with Burr, who came up from Philadelphia for the occasion.

The Livingstons, it would seem, took the initiative. About the middle of May in New York City the lawyers of the family drew up a written opinion asserting the illegality of the returns, which Edward Livingston tried out on Robert Troup, Hamilton's lieutenant. Troup, convinced two weeks before that "the election is ours," was furious. "I gave it to Ned [Edward] plumply against him," he told Jay, "and the opinion threw the party into a consternation." Then "a cabinet council of the Governor, the Chancellor, Ned, Brockholst, etc., was immediately called" and "soon afterwards Brockholst went about almost like a madman vociferating against the legality of the Otsego returns." They were "rummaging through all the law books." Clinton and the Livingstons, Troup said, "seem now to be driven to despair."[9] Cooperating with the Clermont family were Brockholst, William S., and Maturin Livingston.[10] John Livingston of the upper manor, whose seat in the senate rested in part on returns from disputed Clinton County, had no choice but to side with the Governor.[11]

Meanwhile, Federalist leaders went to work. Prominent lawyers drew up an opinion in favor of the legality of the returns.[12] Philip Schuyler dispatched an urgent appeal to Otsego to have both sheriffs sent down to the city to be on hand for questioning.[13]

The canvassers, as might be imagined, spent more than a few meetings struggling with the problem. Clintonian and Jay-ite alike knew the unofficial, if not the official, vote in the contested counties. If they counted the votes from all three, in all likelihood Jay would have won by a small margin. Clinton and Tioga were both Clintonian. Clinton in 1789 voted 42 to 3 for Clinton and in the January 1793 congressional contest voted 214 to 32 for a Republican. The score there in the gubernatorial election was perhaps 75 to 25.[14] In Tioga,

8. See Thomas Tillotson to Robert R. Livingston, June 3, 1792, R. R. Livingston Papers, N.-Y. Hist. Soc.

9. Robert Troup to John Jay, May 6, 20, 1792, in Johnston, ed., *Correspondence of John Jay*, III, 422-27.

10. Sarah Jay to John Jay, June 10, 1792, John Jay Transcripts, Columbia Univ.

11. See footnote 61.

12. *Reasons in Support of An Opinion Offered to the Public Respecting the Votes of Otsego County on June 7, 1792* (N.Y., 1792).

13. Schuyler to ?, May 19, 1792, Schuyler Papers, Lib. Cong.

14. *N.-Y. Journal*, June 4, 1789, Feb. 27, 1793; M. T. Woolsey to John Williams, Dec. 21, 1792, Williams Papers, III, No. 119, N.Y. State Lib. This Republican

whose citizens were voting as a county unit for the first time and where there were perhaps 200 eligible voters, the vote may have been 100 to 50 in Clinton's favor.[15] But even if these two thinly settled counties together gave the Governor a 100-vote majority—the most claimed by Clintonians—they would have been offset by heavily Federalist Otsego. The largest claim for Clintonian votes in Otsego was 150. Federalists claimed from about 700 to as many as 1200; Clintonians insisted the Federalist vote was no more than 550. The evidence is ambiguous but the vote Jefferson heard in Philadelphia—850 to 150—seems realistic.[16] Even if the Federalist majority in Otsego were only 400, Clinton's majority of 100 from Clinton and Tioga, added to his 108 majority in the rest of the state, would not have been enough to overcome Jay's Otsego lead. Jay would have won by 200 or more votes.

Legal precedent, insofar as it can be disentangled from the presentation by partisan lawyers, favored the Federalists. On the question of the authority of holdover sheriffs at dispute in Otsego, "the settled usage and practice had long been that the old sheriff held office until the new one actually took possession of the office." Usage also suggested a liberal interpretation of the power of sheriffs to deputize.[17] On the other hand the common practice of election inspectors and sheriffs in rejecting ballots for irregularities favored the Clintonians. It was a rare election that some township did not see its votes lost on a technicality. In the 1789 gubernatorial election in Westchester returns from three entire townships—830 votes in all, or more than the rest of the county put together—were "lost" for "irregularities." These might well have swung the election to Yates. In 1792, according to newspaper reports, returns from towns in four different counties were

claims 46 votes for Clinton at Plattsburgh, 16 for Jay at Champlain, and makes no mention of three other towns. These 64 voters were probably half the total number.

15. *N.-Y. Journal*, Mar. 2, 1793. The Tioga congressional vote was split 217–18–12, for Silas Talbot, a Federalist, William Cooper, and John Winn, an anti-Federalist, in that order. It was usually Clintonian.

16. For the Clintonian claim, "Veritas," *N.-Y. Journal*, July 4, 1792; for the extravagant claim of 1200, a resolution from Otsego, *ibid.*, June 30, 1792; for the claim of 700 Jay votes, Cooper to Van Schaack, Oct. 1, 1792, Cooper Papers, N.Y. State Hist. Assoc.; for Jefferson's understanding, Jefferson to Monroe, June 23, 1792, Monroe Papers, N.Y. Pub. Lib.; for Otsego elections in the fall, see footnotes 51, 52; for the congressional election, *N.-Y. Journal*, Mar. 2, 1793. In a broader electorate the vote for Congress was Cooper 790, Winn, a Clintonian, 212.

17. Hammond, *Political Parties*, I, 68, and see especially the testimony brought out in the assembly hearings cited in footnote 69.

not counted—New Cornwall in Orange, Genesee in Ontario (because
the election inspector did not sign the poll lists), and towns in Westchester and Richmond ("for want of legality") —and probably would
have gone without comment had not the larger dispute called attention to them.[18] Thus it could be said if "the letter of the law" was
observed, there was justification in either legal precedent or usage for
canvassers to move toward whatever conclusions their political pre-
dilections led them.

To get themselves off the hook—or perhaps to swing more weight
for positions already arrived at—the canvassers asked New York's two
United States senators to render a judgment. The opinion of Rufus
King was predictable; not so Burr, who after failing to win either
nomination had sat out the election. The two solons were closeted
together for two days and Burr, according to his amanuensis, Matthew
Davis, attempted to persuade his colleague that neither of them should
issue an opinion. King refused, announcing he would report in favor
of counting the votes. Burr, then reluctantly, according to Davis, released his opinion: he would count Clinton and rule out Tioga and
Otsego. Aware that "some pretend, indeed, but none can believe that
I am prejudiced" in Clinton's favor, he pointed out to an Ulster friend
that "it would indeed be the extreme of weakness in me to expect
friendship from Mr. Clinton. I have too many reasons to believe that
he regards me with jealousy and malevolence. . . . I have not even
seen or spoken to him since January last."[19] Despite this personal
friction, Burr had to go along with the "republican interest" for his
political future.

The canvassers by a vote of seven to four rejected the ballots from
all three counties.[20] The majority disposed of Tioga and Clinton
briefly and took up Otsego at length. The Otsego sheriff, they claimed,
"had no authority by appointment, by commission, by the constitution
or by any law to hold or exercise the office of sheriff" on the day he
received the ballots; therefore he was guilty of a "usurpation of authority" that was "wanton and unnecessary." In their summation, the

18. N.Y. *Daily Advertiser*, May 5, 1789, and June 2, 1792. *N.-Y. Journal*, June
13, 1792. "Veritas," *N.-Y. Journal*, July 14, 1792, discusses these other missing
towns.

19. Burr to Jacob delaMater, June 15, 1792, in Davis, ed., *Memoirs of Aaron
Burr*, I, 358; the opinions of Burr and King are in *ibid.*, 358ff.; Robert Troup to
John Jay, June 10, 1792, in Johnston, ed., *Correspondence of John Jay*, III, 427.

20. The majority report is in pamphlet form, *An Impartial Statement Respecting the Decision of the Late Committee of Canvassers* (N.Y., 1792) and also in
Journal of the Assembly of N.Y., 16th Sess., 90-93.

majority pointed out that in the past they had rejected the returns of townships when the defect was a minor one in form alone; here, they claimed, the defect was substantial. The custody of the ballots was "a trust of high import." Greater irregularities might occur if this was allowed to pass—it might even be possible for a sheriff to exclude a majority of votes. The great principle at stake was "the freedom of elections and security against frauds."

The Federalist minority[21] wanted to accept the Clinton and Tioga votes on the grounds that the deputation by the sheriff was adequate. On Otsego they took the position that only a court of law could decide whether the ballots had been legally transmitted. The canvassers, they insisted, did not have the right to examine the authority of a sheriff; only the courts could. A holdover of sheriffs was established by precedent. As a broad principle, they maintained that "in all doubtful cases the committee ought to decide in favor of the votes given by the citizens lest by too nice and critical an exposition of the law, the right of suffrage be rendered nugatory." The practical consequence of the Federalist solution would have been to delay the decision further and, if the state's conservative supreme court could be counted on, give the election to Jay. Otherwise George Clinton was slated to be sworn in for his sixth term on July 1.

II

When the official decision was announced, the storm broke. Philip Schuyler, a Clintonian canvasser reported, was "in a most violent passion and is going to overset the state and turn the governor out of office on the first of July."[22] In New York City a Federalist meeting issued a manifesto damning the "invasion of the sovereignty of the people" and the "wanton attack" on the "freedom of the people"; a committee of correspondence of forty was formed which issued an appeal to the counties to apply to the legislature for a redress of the decision; letters followed urging the formation of similar local committees.[23] A broadside, ominously signed "Gracchus"—by no less a plebeian than William Duer, whose partisanship could not be damp-

21. The minority report is in *Reasons in Support of an Opinion . . . June 7, 1792* and also *N.-Y. Journal*, June 16, 1792.
22. Jonathan Havens to John Smith, June 18, 1792, Smith Papers, N.-Y. Hist. Soc.
23. *N.-Y. Journal*, June 20, 1792; Josiah Hoffman to Ebenezer Foote, June 26, 1792, Foote Papers, Lib. Cong.

ened by the walls of the debtor's prison—demanded a special convention elected by the people to resist "the yoke of tyranny."[24]

Upstate Federalists breathed fire. "The die is cast," wrote Ebenezer Foote, Van Gaasbeck's Ulster lieutenant. "Clinton must quit the chair or blood must and will be shed—and if no innocent blood was to flow, I would not care how soon it began."[25] From Albany, Stephen Van Rensselaer, reporting that Federalists had organized a meeting of deputies from the entire county, urged William Cooper to organize a convention for Otsego to be broadened into "a general convention from the counties of the Western District."[26] Cooper had beaten him to the punch with a declaration signed by several hundred men calling for "immediate legal or legislative interference," and claiming that twelve hundred voters were deprived of suffrage "by an unfeeling, chosen and hardy few." "We cannot submit" to such tyranny, they proclaimed, threatening to march to New York to lay their petition before the legislature.[27]

When Jay heard the news of the dispute he was riding circuit for the federal court in New England. "Equanimity and self respect and moderation must be preserved," he wrote his son. As he made his way down from Vermont, he was greeted at the Hudson Valley towns by tremendous turnouts of Federalists demanding action. By the time he reached New York City on July 4 the temper there too had soared to new heights. One Federalist could not recall a larger assemblage to greet the returning Chief Justice. Huge banners proclaimed "Jay Governor by Voice of the People" and "Jay and Liberty," cannons were shot off, church bells rang, and the demonstrators went out of their way to stop menacingly before Governor Clinton's house. Demands were voiced that Clinton resign, including one from the Mechanics Society.[28]

Federalists were not quite certain how they should direct this mounting indignation. Hamilton was cautious. The party, he wrote

24. "To the Free Electors" by "Gracchus," broadside, N.Y.C., June 1792, N.Y. State Lib.; Alexander Macomb to William Constable, June 15, 1792, Constable Papers, N.Y. Pub. Lib., identifies "Gracchus" as Duer, his jailmate.

25. Ebenezer Foote to ?, June 27, 1792, in Katherine Foote, Ebenezer Foote, The Founder (Delhi, N.Y., 1927), 44.

26. Stephen Van Rensselaer to William Cooper, June 28, 1792, Cooper Transcripts, N.-Y. Hist. Soc.

27. N.-Y. Journal, June 30, 1792.

28. John to Peter Augustus Jay, May 17, 1792, abstract, John Jay Papers, Columbia Univ.; Seth Johnson to Andrew Craigie, July 10, 1792, Craigie Papers, Amer. Antiq. Soc.; N.-Y. Journal, July 10, 14, 1792; N.Y. Daily Advertiser, July 11, 1792.

Senator King from Philadelphia,[29] had to "beware of extremes." There was a danger in talk of "the convention and the bayonet." After all, Federalists were "the real friends to order and good government" and could hardly afford to set a dangerous precedent. Public indignation should be kept alive. As for the decision of the canvassers, however, the election law should be amended and the canvassers impeached, but no more. The decision itself, wrote Hamilton, had to stand.

Jay's public response to his admirers was also conservative. He told his Lansingburgh audience that he regretted "any event that tends to introduce discord and complaint." To the Albany committee he counseled "conciliation, benevolence and good neighborhood." At New York he was firm against the course other countries pursued where the people "have often too precipitously recurred to violence and emotion." Jay was not willing, however, to let the decision go unchallenged; he "has an idea," King reported, "of a convention for the sole purpose of canvassing the canvassers and their decision." Others were flirting with the idea of a convention to do more: redress the decision and amend the constitution at the same time, eliminating the Council of Appointment. King was sure only that he wanted a lawful remedy, for "should he [Clinton] persist, and the sword be drawn he must go to the wall—but this my dear Sir, is a dreadful alternative."[30]

The frontier Federalists wanted no eastern counsel of moderation. Judge Cooper, confessing that the canvassers' decision was "admittedly a wrong without a remedy," proposed to Stephen Van Rensselaer that a new election be held in the three disputed counties and that the Council of Appointment refuse to meet with Clinton to avoid lending sanction to his election.[31] In Herkimer County, a mass meeting couched its protest in nothing less than the form of the Declaration of Independence, advancing by eight sections from proof that Clinton lacked a majority of the legal votes through a conclusion that the decision was not binding on the people to a pledge to remove Clinton by "every laudable exertion within the verge of our strength and ability."[32]

29. Hamilton to King, June 28, 1792, Lodge, ed., *Works of Hamilton*, VIII, 269.
30. For the addresses to Jay and his replies, Johnston, ed., *Correspondence of John Jay*, III, 435-44; Morgan Lewis to Robert R. Livingston, July 4, 1792, R. R. Livingston Papers, N.-Y. Hist. Soc.; King to Hamilton, July 10, 1792, Rufus King Papers, N.-Y. Hist. Soc.
31. Cooper to Van Rensselaer, July 22, 1792, Cooper MSS, N.Y. State Lib.
32. Cited in Monaghan, *John Jay*, 340.

This was precisely the spirit that Hamilton feared. At the end of July he sent another admonition to King; "a . . . spirit of dissatisfaction, within proper bounds, should be kept up." But "a resort to first principles in any shape, is decidedly against my judgment." A convention to rejudge the canvassers had "too much the appearance of reversing the sentence of a court by legislative decree." With an eye on the long view, he observed that "the precedent may suit us today but tomorrow we may see its abuse." Moreover, such a convention might undertake other revisions of the state constitution. "Such weapons are not to be played with." The agitation had gone far enough. "Men's minds are too much unsettled, everywhere. . . . Let us endeavor to settle them, and not to set them more afloat."[33]

In response to this pressure from left and right, as it were, King and Jay worked out a strategy that would appease their own hotheads yet stay within the borders of legality. The tactic, King replied to Hamilton, would be to "induce the legislature to call a convention to revise the decision." A majority of the assembly very likely was Clintonian and would not agree to a convention; "should this be the case, the business will there terminate." On this basis they continued the agitation to lay the ground for a contest in the legislature in the fall. Robert Troup reassured Hamilton that he always knew there was no likelihood of a redress; "my object has been to make a strong impression upon the public mind of the corruption of Clinton and his party and thus to render him odious." By the end of the summer he could claim they had "pretty well succeeded."[34]

III

In the first phase of the dispute more than one Clintonian had misgivings about the canvassers' decision. "I confess," Chancellor Livingston wrote, "I would have wished that all the votes had been counted whatever might have been the event." Clinton was "sacrificing the interests of his party to his personal interests." "I wish," said Jonathan Havens, one of the canvassers, that Clinton "would offer to submit again to the people at the next general election." Otherwise, "we must not think of ever holding up Clinton again at another election." In the Hudson Valley, too, "many moderate men" among his followers thought "that Clinton ought to resign."[35]

33. Hamilton to King, July 25, 1792, Lodge, ed., *Works of Hamilton*, VIII, 270-72.
34. King to Hamilton, July 29, 1792, Hamilton, ed., *Works of Hamilton*, V, 516-17; Troup to Hamilton, Aug. 24, 1792, Hamilton Papers, Lib. Cong.
35. Robert R. to Edward Livingston, June 19, 1792, R. R. Livingston Papers,

Publicly Clinton's supporters silenced their consciences by a frenzy of activity. Not to act, Edward Livingston explained, would be interpreted as "consciousness of wrong." Beginning in mid-July the "Republicans"—Edward Livingston now used the term interchangeably with "Clintonian"—formed a committee in New York City to defend the canvassers, composed of seventy lawyers, businessmen, and substantial citizens, only half of whom had been active supporters of the Governor in the election. They sent a page-long public address to the upstate citizenry to form similar committees, held a public dinner in the Governor's honor at which toasts were lifted to him, Chancellor Livingston, and Thomas Jefferson, drew up plans for their own petition to the legislature in the fall, and flooded the newspapers with articles.[36] In New York City, Clintonians even managed to take a meeting of the Society of Cincinnati by surprise and elect Clinton, their tarnished hero, president, and John Lamb, vice-president.[37]

His brother's plans found Chancellor Livingston enthusiastic. More stress had to be placed on answering the Federalists in articles which should be placed not just in Greenleaf's paper, "which is read by only one party"; he would soon have a series of his own in the Federalist *Albany Gazette.* "Whether the canvassers were right or wrong is no longer a question of any moment," said Livingston; "their determination is conclusive, nor do I know of any constitutional mode of revising the question." The Federalist aim, he believed, was merely to keep up a political attack; Schuyler would not go through with a convention. But they may discover that it is "easier to set a house on fire than to say where the flames shall stop."[38]

Over the summer, meetings were held throughout the state, many in towns where Clintonian political activity was unusual. In Columbia County three companies of militia at usually Federalist Kinderhook damned "the menaces of the aristocrats and the impotent vulgar

N.-Y. Hist. Soc.; Havens to John Smith, June 18, 1792, John Smith Papers, N.-Y. Hist. Soc.; Peter Van Schaack to Theodore Sedgwick, June 15, 1792, Sedgwick Papers, Mass. Hist. Soc.; see also Anthony Hoffman to Peter Van Gaasbeck, Aug. 14, 1792, Van Gaasbeck Papers, Kingston Senate House.

36. Edward to Robert R. Livingston, July 14, 1792, Morgan Lewis to Robert R. Livingston, July 4, 1792, R. R. Livingston Papers, N.-Y. Hist. Soc.; *N.-Y. Journal,* July 18, 26, Aug. 11, 1792.

37. *N.-Y. Journal,* July 7, 1792; a letter of complaint, *ibid.,* July 7; an advertisement from army officers, *ibid.,* July 25; "Candidus" No. 1 and 2, *ibid.,* Aug. 4, 18, 1792.

38. Robert R. to Edward Livingston, July 20, 1792, R. R. Livingston Papers, N.-Y. Hist. Soc.

threats of a western braggadocio judge." Even the Clintonian minority in Otsego risked a meeting.[39]

At these defense meetings and in their articles the Clintonians argued along three lines.[40] First, the decision of the majority of the canvassers was "just and legal," "lawful and constitutional," and "final and conclusive." The canvassers, they stressed, had no discretionary power; the ballots had not been transmitted according to law, and the canvassers could not place themselves above the law; by law their decision was binding and therefore could not be overruled. The Jay-ites therefore were "sowers of anarchy and confusion," raising "unnessary tumults" and fanning "the flames of sedition." They, the Clintonians, were the "friends of good order and tranquility." Greenleaf even referred to "Cooper and his Shayite clan."

Secondly, the canvassers' decision was justified by precedent and practice. Clintonians, taking their stand on "the letter of the law," emphasized the other towns whose ballots had been rejected, reviewed similar actions in past elections, and dwelt on the dangers of allowing sheriffs to function without legal authority.

Thirdly, they cast doubt on the claim that Jay had a majority of votes. By counting the votes that had been dropped in townships in four other counties as well as in the three disputed counties, they insisted Clinton would have won anyway.[41] But recognizing implicitly that Jay would have won had only the votes of the three disputed counties been accepted, they tried to shift attention to the coerced character of Federalist votes. Even before the canvassers made their decision public, Greenleaf filled a page of the *Journal* with about a dozen affidavits attesting to intimidation by Cooper. These were proof of "undue influence towards the weak, threats to the debtor and im-

39. See Moses DeWitt to DeWitt Clinton, Aug. 12, 1792, DeWitt Clinton Papers, No. 21, Columbia Univ.; for Ulster: *N.-Y. Journal*, Aug. 29, Sept. 26; for Orange: *N.-Y. Journal*, Sept. 1; for Staten Island: *N.-Y. Journal*, Aug. 4; for Columbia: *N.-Y. Journal*, July 4, *Hudson Gazette*, Aug. 16, *Catskill Packet*, Aug. 20, *N.-Y. Journal*, Aug. 29; for Dutchess: *Albany Gazette*, Aug. 20, *N.-Y. Journal*, Sept. 29; for Herkimer: *Albany Gazette*, Aug. 20, 1792.

40. "To Abraham Ten Broeck, Esq. . . . Chairman of the Albany Committee" by "Cato," reprinted from *Albany Gazette*, in N.Y. *Daily Advertiser*, No. 1, July 25, No. 2, July 28, No. 3, Aug. 4, No. 4, Aug. 22, 1792. The MS draft of No. 3 is in R. R. Livingston's hand in R. R. Livingston Papers, N.-Y. Hist. Soc., mistakenly filed with another series by "Cato" on foreign policy written 1793-94. The 1792 "Cato" series also ran in *Hudson Gazette*. Livingston's short "Squib on Canvassers" defending the decision may also have appeared in an upstate paper.

41. See especially "Veritas," *N.-Y. Journal*, July 4; a rebuttal by "B," *ibid.*, July 14, and an answer by "Veritas," *ibid.*, July 25, 1792.

positions upon the ignorant."[42] The Otsego votes therefore had "met the fate they justly merited." Toward the same end, they publicized Stephen Van Rensselaer's tactics, lamenting the fate of the "dependent creatures of the landed interest."[43] They also charged Federalist inspectors in Ulster with fraud.[44] To counter the image of Clinton "the usurper," they thus offered the impression of an election "influenced by great landlords and managed with fraud."

To the Federalist threat of an "appeal to the people" there was a republican philosophical answer. Tammany—many of whose members refused to drink their customary Independence Day toast to the Governor of the State of New York[45]—conducted a debate on the question: "Can a convention of the people of a country be assembled without the consent or contrary to the will of the government without destroying that government?" For the negative, the only side on which we are informed, Dr. William Pitt Smith of the Columbia faculty, a Tammany member and assemblyman, and soon a Republican,[46] explored the social contract theory. There were five types of government under which the question of a self-appointed convention could arise.[47] Under a "despotic government" such as France had before her revolution, the answer was no—such a convention destroyed the government and was completely justified. Second, under a "republic once free but at length grown radically corrupt" such as England the answer also was no. Smith was hopeful that the people would be "ever successful in . . . the overturning [of] such existing governments." Under the third type, a "well-constructed and free republic," there was no occasion to raise such an issue. A convention could only be the work of a small faction, not the people as a whole. The fourth case, "a free republic found by experience to be inconvenient in some of its constitutional forms," was also no problem. Such a government would not oppose a convention to correct errors. The real problem was in "a free republic grown in some small measure corrupt," his fifth cate-

42. See "Candidus," *N.-Y. Journal*, June 16, 1792.

43. "Lucius" [probably Melancton Smith], *ibid.*, June 30, 1792; "A.B.," *ibid.*, May 30, June 2, 1792; "Respondent," No. 3, *ibid.*, Aug. 15, 1792; "Columbianus," *Hudson Gazette*, Sept. 13, 1792.

44. "Old Whig" from the *Albany Gazette* in *N.-Y. Journal*, Aug. 22, 1792; a correspondent, *ibid.*, Aug. 19.

45. *N.-Y. Journal*, July 7, 1792.

46. See the discussion of the Tammany Society, ch. 9, sec. IV; for Smith's support of Genêt, see ch. 16, sec. III.

47. [William Pitt Smith], *Observations on Conventions Made in a Tammanical Debate* (N.Y., 1793).

gory. The best solution here was to have recourse to "the first subsequent election." "Let the wise and the virtuous keep alive in the public mind the spirit of liberty, but at the same time restrain the impetuous and licentious." There was, of course, a right of revolution, but only when "a remedy is not to be rationally expected from patient waiting for a new rotation." "A convention of the nation in arms" actually was for those peoples "just emerging from a state of nature." Thus did a republican-minded thinker retain the Lockean justification of revolution while denying its applicability to the immediate situation.[48]

The torrent of Republican words helped stem the Federalist tide. It also had an effect outside the state, possibly a purpose from the outset. Jefferson, Madison, and Monroe had given thought to Clinton as a candidate to oppose Adams for the vice-presidency. When Jefferson got his first reports from New York in June, he was angry at Clinton's stand. Since it "seems probable," he wrote, that Jay had a majority, Clinton "would have honored himself by declining to accept and agreeing to take another fair start" in a new election which he would probably win anyway. He was afraid that "the cause of republicanism will suffer and its votaries be thrown into schism by embarking it in support of this man and for what? To draw over anti-Federalists, who are not numerous enough to be worth drawing over." No babe in the woods, Jefferson also knew of Cooper's tactics—the "Bashaw of Otsego" he called him—and how Federalist cries had "silenced all clamor about their bankruptcies." Madison, who was impressed with the Clintonian distinction between legal and coerced ballots, and the number and respectability of Clinton's supporters, was not as negative. Neither was James Monroe who despite his reservations about Clinton's "extreme parsimony," thought he might have to be supported as "a center of union to the republican party in that state."[49] In October when the question was raised of dropping Clinton and running Burr, Madison and Monroe reacted immediately in favor of Clinton.[50] Thus the Clintonians by their campaign saved not only a governor but a vice-presidential candidate as well.

48. Debaters in the Uranian Society voted 8-2 that in a "representative system" there was "a right to appeal from the decisions of the representatives to a majority of the represented." Minutes of the Uranian Society, June 26, 1792, N.-Y. Hist. Soc.

49. Jefferson to Madison, June 21, 1792, Jefferson to Monroe, June 23, 1792, Ford, ed., *Writings of Jefferson*, VI, 89-91, 93-94; Brant, *James Madison*, III, 359; Monroe to Jefferson, July 17, 1792, Hamilton, ed., *Writings of James Monroe*, I, 237-38; Madison to Jefferson, June 29, 1792, Madison Papers, XV, Lib. Cong.

50. See ch. 15.

IV

By the fall, Federalists had retreated further: they would ask the legislature not for a convention, but only for a legislative inquiry into the canvassers. To create pressure, Federalist committees at New York and Albany suggested that petitions and deputations be sent to the senators and assemblymen from every county. "Rouse the inhabitants of your county," read the committees' circular. In Otsego Cooper had his back up; there must be no "shameful compromises"; the legislature should be forced to call a convention. "I can not nor will I ever submit" to the canvassers' decision. "You must have a committee," he wrote Van Schaack of Columbia County, "and they must join us and go from Hudson in a sloop together to [New] York where we must every day meet and march together to the city hall."[51] To select deputies Cooper sponsored a private election at which six or seven hundred Otsego supporters voted, collected 530 affidavits from voters who alleged they cast ballots for Jay in the spring, and erected "a liberty pole at Cooperstown before the court house."[52] Elsewhere preparations were less flamboyant. When the assembly opened in November some eighty deputies from various counties quietly presented a memorial soliciting "a legislative remedy for the late outrage."[53]

To hold the fort for the Governor the Clintonians threw up further bulwarks. After a new series of articles in the papers,[54] they collected petitions from a dozen counties—including the west—which objected to Federalist petitions claiming to speak for their area.[55] Early in November Aaron Burr had ready a forty-six page pamphlet[56] replete

51. The appeal, dated Sept. 17, 1792, appears in *N.-Y. Journal*, Nov. 7, 1792; Cooper to Peter Van Schaack, Oct. 1, 1792, Cooper MSS, N.Y. State Hist. Assoc.

52. "An Elector," *Poughkeepsie Journal*, Oct. 24, 1792; "Victor," *ibid.*, Oct. 21; *N.-Y. Journal*, Oct. 27, 1792; Alexander, ed., "Judge Kent's 'Jaunt' to Cooperstown," *New York History*, 22 (1941), 455.

53. *Journal of the Assembly of N.Y.*, 16th Sess., Nov. 13, 1792; Hammond, *Political Parties*, I, 76.

54. "The Republican," No. 1-No. 5, *N.-Y. Journal*, Aug. 25, Sept. 1, 8, 15, 26, 1792; "Columbianus," No. 1-4, *ibid.*, late Aug. through Sept. 13, 20, 1792.

55. *Journal of the Assembly of N.Y.*, 16th Sess., 60, 63, 66, 68, 75, 78, 81, 116, for receipt of the petitions. See *N.-Y. Journal*, Dec. 1 and Dec. 15, 1792, for additional petitions. The number of petitions per county was as follows: 8 from Columbia, 9 from Ulster, 10 from Saratoga, 3 from Otsego, 4 from Westchester, 1 from Dutchess, 2 from Albany, 1 from Rensselaer, 1 from Richmond, 1 from New York, and several each from Orange, Suffolk, and Montgomery.

56. *An Impartial Statement Respecting the Decision of the Late Committee of Canvassers.* The Federalists countered with *An Appendix to the Impartial Statement . . .* (N.Y., 1792) containing several opinions allegedly submitted to Burr which he did not print.

with the basic documents and opinions of such prominent lawyers as Edmund Randolph and Pierpont Edwards which he, Melancton Smith, and David Gelston had solicited from outside the state. "It can not be expected that the public will reason on law points," Burr explained; therefore, "the authority of great names" was essential.[57] In addition, Clintonians were preparing a counter-strategy to blunt the effect of any investigation of the canvassers' decision: a legislative inquiry into Judge Cooper's "improper influence." In Otsego, Clintonians collected further proof of his actions at the polls in the spring and held three meetings at which they condemned anyone "who forces and influences the good citizens of the county to vote contrary to their opinion or assumes the power of swaying the county as he pleases with misrepresentations, raising liberty poles, inciting insurrections, etc."[58]

Actually Clintonians did not have much to fear in the assembly which, although it elected a Federalist as speaker, would soon choose Republican presidential electors. Clintonians acquiesced in the inquiry without a fight; they could hardly have turned down the delegations with their petitions, and besides, they would have the last word with their inquiry into Cooper's pressure on frontier voters. Federalists had obviously calmed down. Melancton Smith reported that "the Jayite party from a fear of a majority against them have publicly declared their waiver of all farther disputes as to Governor."[59] Hamilton was pressing his colleagues to play things down because his attention was fixed on blocking Burr's unexpected bid for the vice-presidency against Clinton; to criticize Clinton further at this point would only boost Burr. Moreover, "all was over and nothing could be done."[60]

Before the assembly began its inquiry, the Federalists challenged the legality of John Livingston's election to the senate. Should not his

57. Burr to Sedgwick, Oct. 14, 1792, Sedgwick Papers, Mass. Hist. Soc.; Burr to Monroe, Sept. 10, 1792, Monroe Papers, Lib. Cong.; Melancton Smith and David Gelston to Pierpont Edwards, Aug. 20, 1792, Smith Papers, N.Y. State Lib. See also Schachner, *Aaron Burr*, 113-14.

58. For the meetings in Otsego, see *N.-Y. Journal*, Sept. 19, Oct. 13, Nov. 21, 1792; *Poughkeepsie Journal*, Sept. 26, 1792; *Catskill Packet*, Oct. 1, 1792. See also *N.-Y. Journal*, Sept. 5, 1792, reprinting a report from *Albany Gazette*, and *Goshen Repository*, Sept. 23, 1792.

59. John Beckley to James Madison, Oct. 17, 1792, Madison Papers, N.Y. Pub. Lib.

60. Peter Van Schaack to Theodore Sedgwick, Nov. 20, 1792, Sedgwick Papers, Mass. Hist. Soc. See below, ch. 15.

formal admission, based on returns from a disputed county, Clinton, be held up? In the first test, Clintonians were able to seat him, 12 to 11, but the final vote had to wait until the assembly inquiry was over.[61] Federalists were easily ruffled. Senator Stephen Van Rensselaer called Senator Thomas Tillotson, one of the canvassers, "a rascal"; Tillotson challenged him to a duel, Senator Philip Van Cortlandt tried to conciliate them, and only a last-minute apology averted a showdown.[62]

The hearings, which were conducted by the assembly as a whole and not assigned to a committee, dragged out over six weeks into January 1793, at about a dozen sessions in all. Josiah Hoffman of New York City and young James Kent of Poughkeepsie were the managers, assuring an inquiry under the control of eastern Federalists. The secretary of state, his deputy, and his clerk were called as the major witnesses, as were one of the Otsego sheriffs and a few others from that county. None of the principals, however, either from the canvassers' committee or from Otsego was asked to testify.[63]

The Federalists brought out successfully that such a rejection of ballots was unprecedented and that similar irregularities had been allowed in the past. To lend weight to the charge of partisanship, they dwelt on the fact that the canvassers had burnt the controversial ballots, thus making a review of the vote impossible, although this was a normal procedure. On the question of the Otsego sheriff's authority, they got onto the record the fact that the holdover sheriff was "generally reputed" to be the county's sheriff and established that there were sheriffs in three other counties who had delivered ballots even though they had not received their commissions. Even Governor Clinton, they showed, had once rendered an opinion that holdover sheriffs remained in office until their successors were duly sworn in. The Clintonians in their turn at questioning labored two points: first, the fact that Otsego's holdover sheriff was neither sheriff *de facto* nor *de jure* and second, that numerous precedents existed for rejecting

61. On the final vote in January, Livingston won 11 to 6, provoking Schuyler's anger at absentee Federalists. See *Journal of the Senate of N.Y.*, 16th Sess., 48-51, 78-81; Schuyler to Jacobus Van Schoonhaven, Feb. 20, 1793, Schuyler Papers, Lib. Cong.

62. "Narrative," a memorandum by Philip Van Cortlandt, Nov. 1792, in Van Cortlandt Papers, Sleepy Hollow Restorations, Tarrytown.

63. *Journal of the Assembly of N.Y.*, 16th Sess., Nov. 23, 1792-Jan. 3, 1793, *passim.*

ballots on much smaller irregularities. Of the two, the Federalists established by far the better case.

At the end of the inquiry, the Clintonians introduced a resolution to absolve the canvassers of "any mal or corrupt practise" and declare their decision irreversible.[64] Faced with defeat, Federalists cleverly retreated to a position also advanced by the Clintonians: in a counter-resolution they argued that the legislature had no right to review the canvassers' decision, contending that the conduct of the canvassers lay solely within the jurisdiction of the courts. Hence any legislative findings would be "extra-judicial."[65] Clintonians defeated the Federalist motion and offered a substitute declaring that the canvassers had not "conducted themselves with any impropriety," which passed, 32-28. Then they adopted, 33-20, a resolution absolving the canvassers of corruption. Taking cognizance of the Federalist "extra-judicial" allegation, the resolution explained that notwithstanding the fact that the courts had jurisdiction, the legislature had conducted an investigation because of the demands of the citizens for clarification. "After a full and fair examination," the legislators found that the canvassers were not guilty of "any mal or corrupt practise." By law the decision of the canvassers was "binding and conclusive," and the legislature "can not annul or make void" any such decision. The assembly was unwilling, however, to amend the election laws to make the canvassers' decision "absolutely final and conclusive" in every instance of a disputed election.[66]

The first inquiry ended in mid-January 1793. Late in February the Clintonians took over with their investigation of Judge Cooper directed to two questions: whether he was guilty of "mal and corrupt conduct" during the elections and whether he had "conducted himself with good behavior" as required by the constitution of the first judge of a county.[67] In the month allowed for the preparation of witnesses, Federalists countered with petitions from every town in Otsego demanding the dismissal of the charges; the local grand jury, the petitioners reported, had already considered them and found them inadequate to return an indictment.[68] Disregarding the request, Clintonians began five days of hearings managed by David Gelston. Five witnesses from Otsego recounted in vivid detail the threats and intimidation used

64. *Ibid.*, 107; Van Schaack to Sedgwick, Dec. 12, 1792, Jan. 2, 1793, Sedgwick Papers, Mass. Hist. Soc.
65. *Journal of the Assembly of N.Y.*, 16th Sess., 130, 132.
66. *Ibid.*, 14, 121, 134-35, 173.
67. *Ibid.*, 69-70.
68. *Ibid.*, 186-87.

by Cooper and Jacob Morris. In Cooper's defense Federalists called up the election inspectors, the foreman of the grand jury, and several others. They flatly denied a few of the accusations and tried to explain away some of Cooper's acts or threats. On this round, it must be said, it was the Clintonians who made the more convincing case. Even the defense witnesses—most of whom were obligated to Cooper politically—unintentionally lent weight to the charges against him.[69]

Although the evidence was insufficient to warrant a charge of impeachment as judge, Clintonians, hot for the kill, brought in a resolution censuring Cooper for "very improper conduct." To forestall the condemnation, Federalists again took a safe constitutional position. Cooper himself had not been called to testify; consequently, it would be "unconstitutional and unjust and an invasion of the rights of our fellow citizens," to pass a judgment "injurious to [his] character." Accepting this libertarian contention, Clintonians shelved their motion and passed three others; the first asserted the authority of the legislature to issue findings on persons in public office; the second postponed a decision on Cooper until he could be heard at the next session; and the third required publication of the results of the hearings in the newspapers.[70]

There things rested for a few weeks. In the spring elections of 1793 Federalists made hay with the "fraudulent vote" issue, especially in the frontier counties, and Clintonians lost the assembly, for a number of reasons.[71] At the next session Federalists, with an almost two-to-one majority in the assembly, would be able to call the tune. Meanwhile, Clinton brought a suit against Cooper for slander. The trial took place in New York, and the jury deliberated an hour and a half, deciding in the Governor's favor and awarding him £1000 in damages.[72]

In the new legislature the epilogue to this long tragi-comedy was short. Cooper's Otsego accusers submitted a petition renewing the charges against him, and Cooper himself asked for a decision. Without any inquiry Federalists dismissed the petition as "frivolous and vexatious," pronouncing the evidence against Cooper insufficient to

69. *Ibid.*, 188-204, *passim.* My conclusion differs from Frost, *Life on the Upper Susquehanna*, 44-45, and is closer to Hammond, *Political Parties*, I, 76.

70. *Journal of the Assembly of N.Y.*, 240-47.

71. See below, ch. 15.

72. For brief notices of the trial, *N.-Y. Journal*, Nov. 16, 1793; N.Y. *Columbian Gazetteer*, Nov. 18, 1793; and *Albany Register*, Nov. 25, 1793.

support the charges. And with this the curtain came down on the great election dispute of 1792.[73]

The entire controversy, on its Federalist as well as its Republican side, was a subtle preparation for the creation of a broad Republican movement in the next two years. If Federalists refurbished the principles of Locke, some even sanctioning the people's taking matters into their own hands, it was understandable that Democratic societies would soon champion popular vigilance against government. If Federalists huzzahed the "rights of suffrage," common folk could hardly be blamed if they came out to vote in ensuing elections in greater numbers than before. And if Federalists held county meetings, circulated petitions, and erected liberty poles, it would not be long before Republicans would turn the same tactics against Federalists in national politics. Hamilton was right: such weapons were "not to be played with." Where Federalists had sowed, Republicans would reap.

73. *Journal of the Assembly of N.Y.*, 17th Sess., 74-75; the resolution passed by a vote of 40 to 17; Hammond, *Political Parties*, I, 82-83.

CHAPTER 15

The "Republican Interest" on the National Scene:

The Presidential and Congressional Elections

1792-1793

———•———

For the first nine months of 1792, from the spring elections through the furious battle of the ballots of the summer and fall, it was clear that a new coalition led by Clinton, the Livingstons, and Burr was a fact of political life in New York. In the presidential politicking that began in September and ran through November the coalition dissolved into a rivalry of Clinton and Burr for the Republican vice-presidential nomination. There was no question that the New York "republican interest" was a major factor on the national scene but their unity was questionable. So was their effectiveness as a political party. The congressional elections of December 1792-January 1793 suggested that after four years of the Washington administration the Federalists still ruled the roost as far as national politics went in New York.

I

From the spring on, Jefferson and Hamilton were at loggerheads in the cabinet while their defenders took the issues to the public. Late in the summer, frontier Pennsylvania erupted in the first rebellion against the hated excise tax on whiskey; by the fall Madison was promulgating a Republican party platform in Freneau's *National*

Gazette.[1] In New York Greenleaf's readers were told that "there are two parties at present in the United States." The distinction was no longer Federalist and anti-Federalist but between the "Aristocrats," who were "endeavoring to lay the foundations of monarchical government," and "the real supporters of independence, friends to equal rights and warm advocates of a free elective government"—the "Republicans."[2] The term Republican now came into common usage.

By the fall it was also clear that the vice-presidency would be the focus of contention. Washington would stand for a second term, with the approval of Jefferson and Madison and the New York Republicans, no less than of Hamilton, but John Adams would be unacceptable to the Republicans for a second term as vice-president. The spring elections in New York left no doubt that the legislature would choose a majority of Republican electors, but how many the party could swing and for whom was open to question. In 1789 when the legislature had deadlocked over the method of choosing electors, the New York anti-Federalists had let the election pass without serious effort for George Clinton. In 1792 the New Yorkers, by virtue of their spring victory, geographic position, and large bloc of electoral votes—a dozen after the awarding of four new seats in the House of Representatives—were in a key position. Their achievement paved the way for the consummation of a three-state alliance with Virginia and Pennsylvania.

The alliance was not the product of an entente made during the Jefferson-Madison trip of May 1791 or any other single meeting. The leaders of the three states shared an antagonism to Hamiltonian measures, and the fact that theirs were the only states with potential electoral strength against the Federalists led them to work together. Aaron Burr, in Philadelphia since October 1791 as a member of the Senate, helped smooth things along as did John Beckley, clerk of the House of Representatives, a national party chairman in embryo who kept an eye on New York politics for his Virginia sponsors.[3] By the

1. For national politics: Cunningham, *The Jeffersonian Republicans, 1789-1801*, ch. 2; Brant, *James Madison*, II, ch. 28; Malone, *Jefferson and his Time*, II, ch. 27; Schachner, *Founding Fathers*, 223-29; Douglas Southall Freeman, *George Washington, A Biography*, 7 vols. (N.Y., 1948-57), VI, 378-84.

2. "Columbus," *N.-Y. Journal*, Oct. 3, 1792.

3. John Beckley to James Madison, Aug. 1, 1792, Madison Papers, Lib. Cong.; Noble E. Cunningham, Jr., "John Beckley: An Early American Party Manager," *Wm. and Mary Qtly.*, 3d Ser., 13 (1956), 40-52; Philip Marsh, "John Beckley—Mystery Man of the Early Jeffersonians," *Pa. Mag. of Hist. and Biog.*, 72 (1948), 54-69.

summer of 1792, the Virginia leaders followed the ballots controversy with a partisan anxiety for Clinton, and the New York leaders knew what they were doing when they toasted Washington and Jefferson at a dinner tendered to rally support for the beleaguered Governor.[4]

It seems to have been taken for granted by all that the Republican vice-presidential candidate would be a New Yorker. Jefferson, a member of Washington's cabinet, was unwilling to run against Adams, his old friend and "senior" in service; besides, the electors could not be asked to vote for Washington and another Virginian. A New Yorker had some chance of picking up votes in Federalist New England. The Virginians seem to have been counting on Clinton as the candidate, when out of nowhere Burr appeared, maneuvering so skillfully for himself that he could easily beat a retreat to Clinton if he had to.[5]

Burr was "industrious in his canvass"—Hamilton's phrase—early in September. From the fragmentary evidence that survives a picture emerges of Burr in correspondence with Federalist friends (receiving a coded political rundown of New England from Theodore Sedgwick), of Burr traveling to Philadelphia to consult with Pennsylvania Republicans, of Alexander Dallas coming up to New York, after which the Pennsylvanians began their activities for Burr. However, when Beckley came scurrying up from Philadelphia to New York to find out precisely what was happening, Burr gave him "assurance . . . that he would cheerfully support the measure of removing Mr. A[dams] and lend every aid in his power to C[linton]'s election."[6] At this time, in fact, Burr was in the midst of canvassing influential men for publishable legal opinions on Clinton's behalf in the ballots controversy. To James Monroe, for example, he sent a long letter outlining his "authority of great names" strategy, saving to the end a casual question: "Are you talking of elections . . . the Republican interest will be predominant and united both in Pennsylvania and New York."[7]

4. N.-Y. Journal, July 17, 1792; for correspondence of Madison, Monroe and Jefferson, see ch. 14 above.

5. Schachner, Aaron Burr, ch. 10; Parton, Life of Aaron Burr, I, ch. 12.

6. Theodore Sedgwick to Burr, Sept. 1791 [1792?], Sedgwick Papers, Mass. Hist. Soc.; Alexander Hamilton to the President of the U.S., Sept. 23, 1792, Rufus King to Hamilton, Sept. 17, 1792, Hamilton Papers, Lib. Cong.; Benjamin Rush to Aaron Burr, Sept. 24, 1792, Burr Papers, Amer. Antiq. Soc.; Raymond Walters, "Origins of the Jeffersonian Party in Pennsylvania," Pa. Mag. of Hist. and Biog., 66 (1942), 456-57; John Beckley to James Madison, Sept. 2, Sept. 10, Oct. 17, 1792, Madison Papers, N.Y. Pub. Lib.

7. Burr to Monroe, Sept. 10, 1792, Monroe Papers, Lib. Cong.

With Burr thus artfully covered, Melancton Smith and Marinus Willett, claiming to speak for "the republican interest" of New York, wrote to Madison and Monroe asking Virginia to drop Clinton and substitute Burr. A letter of September 30 was sent by a special messenger who stopped at Philadelphia to pick up a similar message from John Nicholson on behalf of the Pennsylvanians asking "our southern brethren" for their opinion.[8] A week later Smith himself set off for Philadelphia to be on hand for negotiations when the answers would arrive; in his pocket was a letter from Burr to Nicholson introducing him as "the representative of the republicans of this state and the man of the first influence in that interest. Any arrangement he may make with you will be entirely satisfactory to those in this state with whom you wish to unite."[9]

Smith and Willett made a forceful plea. Clinton and Burr "and no other to our knowledge have been thought of—So far as our knowledge of the sentiments of the republicans of this state extends, it appears to us that Col. Burr would be preferred considering the men in themselves, their characters, their years and their habits of life." To assure the Virginians that they were unbiased, they pointed to "our knowledge and decided attachment to Gov. Clinton, our general acquaintance with the leading characters in the republican interest in this state, and our long and intimate acquaintance with both gentlemen."

"Two circumstances," they contended, "had removed all hesitation." "1st, Gov. Clinton does not wish to be a candidate—on this head we have had repeated conversations with him both together and apart and he has explicitly expressed his wishes that the republicans would unite in some other person. 2nd. The office of the Governor in this state is in our opinion of more importance to the republican Interest than that of vice President." Clinton, they need not have reminded the Virginians, "has after a great struggle been re-elected"; if he were removed, Burr would be chosen to succeed him as governor, but for obvious reasons it was "highly improper to hazard another election at this juncture." Brushing aside an objection that only Clinton had been "generally considered" in the south, they argued

8. Marinus Willett and Melancton Smith to Madison and Monroe, Sept. 30, 1792, Monroe Papers, Lib. Cong., kindly called to my attention by Donald Dewey, formerly of the Madison Papers; Willett and Smith to Madison and Monroe, Oct. 7, 1792, *ibid.*, cited in Brant, *James Madison*, II, 364; Nicholson to Madison, Oct. 3, 1792, Madison Papers, Lib. Cong.

9. Burr to John Nicholson, Oct. 7, 1792, Burr Papers, N.Y. Pub. Lib.

that in states north of Pennsylvania Burr was "the only person in view" and would run much better in New Jersey and New England. The closing was diplomatic: while hoping that the Virginians would concur, they asked for their "candid sentiments," for "it is not particular men but a general measure we wish to pursue." Clinton and Burr were "not competitors—the Gov's. friends are the friends of Col. Burr. They have fully conversed on the subject." Smith and Willett would "concur in either of the candidates which shall appear to command the most interest."[10]

That Smith and Willett presented the views of their friend Clinton accurately is open to question. Nicholson's more ambiguous letter added a note the New Yorkers omitted: "Although Clinton wishes to decline in favor of Burr, he does not absolutely refuse to serve if elected."[11] It is unlikely that Clinton would have closed the door to the vice-presidency at a moment when it looked as if he could never run again as governor with the albatross of the land scandal and the "stolen" election around his neck. Whatever he had said earlier to Smith and Willett, Clinton now acted with unmistakable intent. Burr's maneuvers were common knowledge in New York by September 17; on October 2 Clinton broke a tie vote in the Council of Appointment to appoint Burr associate justice of the state supreme court, a position that could run for life and might induce Burr to resign from the Senate. To the Federalist James Kent, as doubtless to others, this seemed to be the payoff to Burr for services rendered in the election dispute gone by.[12] In the context of the battle at hand, however, it was more a move to shelve a rival.

Not only Clinton was alarmed by Burr. It was at this juncture that Hamilton showed the first symptoms of what became an almost pathological hatred of Burr. After Burr's performance in the ballots controversy the New York Federalists were "determined to rip him up," Robert Troup said.[13] Hamilton now considered him the "embryo Caesar" whose "aim it is to mount at all costs to the full honors of the state." To puncture Burr's balloon Hamilton, as pointed out

10. Willett and Smith to Madison and Monroe, Sept. 30, 1792, Monroe Papers, Lib. Cong.

11. Nicholson to Madison, Oct. 3, 1792, Madison Papers, Lib. Cong.

12. James to Moss Kent, Oct. 15, 1792, Kent Papers, Lib. Cong.; for public reports, *N.-Y. Journal*, Oct. 6, 1792.

13. Robert Troup to John Jay, June 10, 1792, in Johnston, ed., *Correspondence of John Jay*, III, 427-30; also Peter Van Schaack to Theodore Sedgwick, June 19, 1792, Sedgwick Papers, Mass. Hist. Soc.

in connection with the land scandal, had to give the lie to countless accusations he had sanctioned against Clinton in the two election campaigns gone by: it was true that the Governor was "an enemy of national principles" and "a man of narrow and perverse politics," but still he was "a man of property in private life, [and] as far as I know of probity." He was infinitely preferable to Burr.[14]

It is necessary to recall Burr's reputation in the 1790's to understand the appeal he had for as many outside New York as within. As John Adams reminded others in later years, Burr was "connected by blood with many respectable families in New England." He was "the son of one president, and grandson of another president of . . . Princeton," a fact meaningful to Presbyterians the country over. "He had served in the army, and came out of it with the character of a knight, without fear and an able officer."[15] Republicans thought of Burr as one of their own—"your friends look to you to take an active part in removing the monarchical rubbish of our government," Benjamin Rush wrote to him.[16] And while Clinton was known as a tough, democratic, parochial "Old Irishman," Burr was an aristocratic, urbane moderate who did not have Clinton's anti-Federalist past to live down and had already demonstrated his drawing power to Federalists.

The Virginia Republicans never had any doubt about their preference.[17] Clinton met the two criteria they set down for a candidate: long "service" and "sound principles." He was one of the patriarchs of the Revolution: a "tested whig," a general, a war governor who had devoted almost two decades of his life to his country. Burr would not do; he could not be elected; he was too young in political experience if not in years, and by implication he had not "given unequivocal proofs of what his principles really were." James Monroe found the proposal from Smith and Willett "highly injudicious and improper." The Virginia response, he counseled Madison, had to be diplomatic, giving the "most smooth assurances of esteemed confidence" in Burr, whose youth would be stressed. Madison concurred and the two wrote an unequivocal answer to Smith and Willett: "things should be left

14. Hamilton to ?, Sept. 23, to Rufus King, Sept. 23, to ?, Sept. 26, to C. C. Pinckney, Oct. 10, to John Steele, Oct. 15, and John Jay, Dec. 18, 1792, Lodge, ed., *Works of Hamilton*, X, 19-30.

15. John Adams to James Lloyd, Feb. 17, 1815, cited in Parton, *Life of Aaron Burr*, I, 235.

16. Rush to Burr, Sept. 24, 1792, Burr Papers, Amer. Antiq. Soc.

17. Monroe to Madison, Oct. 9, 1792, in Hamilton, ed., *Writings of James Monroe*, I, 242-45; Madison to Monroe, Oct. 11, 1792, Madison Papers, Lib. Cong.

to the course which they have in a manner spontaneously taken. The gentleman of republican character first contemplated . . . from the circumstances of his being more known, and particularly warmly supported by sundry influential characters" should still be backed. Any change "would hazard more on one side than could be hoped on the other."[18]

A Republican caucus in Philadelphia October 16 wrapped up the matter. Attending the meeting, according to Beckley, were "Melancton Smith on the part of the republican interest of N.Y. (specially deputed) and the principal movers of the same interest" from Pennsylvania, including Beckley, and Pierce Butler of South Carolina. Their decision was "unanimously to exert every endeavor for Mr. Clinton and drop all thought of Mr. Burr." Smith now retreated from Burr and asked Beckley to report to Monroe and Madison that he "pledged himself for those he represented" to campaign for Clinton. He was *"positively certain"* of obtaining the electoral votes of Vermont and Rhode Island and would "immediately set out *himself,* and doubts not of making a considerable diversion" in Connecticut and Massachusetts. Smith also asked if Monroe would write to Patrick Henry "to influence him to interest his friends in North Carolina"—the old anti-Federalists knew their connections. As for New York's electoral vote at this point he counted it as eight for Clinton to four for Adams but hoped to swing it all for Clinton.[19]

How much Smith did in the campaign is hard to say; he wrote articles for Clinton and he remained in contact with Beckley; that Republican votes did not materialize in New England is no reflection on him.[20] Burr completed his pamphlet defending the canvassers' decision on Clinton in time for the opening of the New York legislature in November and did no more. He had carried out his personal campaign with such finesse that even Hamilton wondered whether it was "anything more than a diversion in favour of Mr. Clinton."[21]

Although Burr was no longer a threat, Clinton still had the Livingstons to contend with. Chancellor Livingston sat out the election, chafing at the Clintonians for their failure to appreciate his services

18. Madison and Monroe to Smith and Willett, Oct. 19, 1792, Monroe Papers, Lib. Cong.

19. Beckley to Madison, Oct. 17, 1792, Madison Papers, N.Y. Pub. Lib.

20. For the articles see footnote 24 below; Jefferson, *Anas,* entry for Nov. 19, 1792, in Ford, ed., *Writings of Jefferson,* I, 209.

21. Hamilton to President of the U.S., Sept. 23, 1792, Hamilton Papers, Hist. Soc. of Pa.; Schachner, *Aaron Burr,* 116.

in the gubernatorial and ballots campaign, peeved at the Governor for not having appointed Edward to state office. Edward pleaded with Robert to come down from Clermont to New York City and lend a hand politically. "I am totally indifferent," the Chancellor replied, commiserating with his younger brother over Clinton's ingratitude; "as you advance in life you will be more and more convinced that great obligations are seldom repaid." The race for the vice-presidency did not interest him particularly: "if the choice is to fall upon a man I like better, I will support him, if not the little weight I have will be thrown into A's [Adams'] scale."[22]

At the end of November the assembly by a vote of 36 to 28 chose Clintonian electors dubbed by Greenleaf "twelve of the staunchest friends of true republicanism." None were Burr-ites or Livingstons. Most of them were old anti-Federalist wheelhorses like Abraham Yates; only Samuel Osgood, Washington's former postmaster, was a newcomer.[23] Nonetheless the election campaign marked a stage in the transformation of the old anti-Federalist critics of the Constitution into defenders of strict construction. In Republican eyes the contest for the vice-presidency was between Adams, an advocate of government by "kings, lords and commons," and Clinton, an upholder of the Constitution. In two articles by "Lucius," probably Melancton Smith,[24] it was only necessary to reprint large excerpts from Adams' *Discourses on Davila*, to prove that Adams differed "radically" from the principle of the American Constitution. Clinton was presented in new constitutional garb. It was true that he had opposed the Constitution in 1788 but his dissenting views "ranged within the Republican theory." "The question about the Constitution involved only a modification of this principle." Second, it could be presumed that "many of his objections have been done away with by amendments." And lastly, once the Constitution was adopted, his opposition ceased. Now his election as vice-president was essential if citizens wanted to "preserve their government as at present."

In December when the ballots were cast, New York's twelve electors

22. R. R. to Edward Livingston, Oct. 4, 1792, Livingston Papers, N.-Y. Hist. Soc.
23. *N.-Y. Journal*, Nov. 21, 1792.
24. "Lucius," *N.-Y. Journal*, Nov. 24, 28, 1792, reprinted from Phila. *American Daily Advertiser*. The pseudonym "Lucius" was used by Clinton's principal defender on the land sales in the spring election of 1792 and very likely was Melancton Smith who led Clinton's defense in the assembly. Smith was in Philadelphia for the Republican caucus Oct. 16 and could have placed the article in the Philadelphia paper.

voted unanimously for Washington and Clinton. Forty-one electors from southern states and one from Pennsylvania gave Clinton a total of 54 votes against 77 for Adams and one for Burr. Had the Pennsylvania Republicans upheld their end of the axis, the vote would have stood Clinton 68 and Adams 63 and the New York Republicans would have contributed the second vice-president to the nation.[25]

The election over, Clinton moved with customary acumen to patch up his shaky alliance within the state. When Burr turned down the vacancy on the state supreme court which Clinton had offered him in October, Clinton appointed Morgan Lewis, the Chancellor's brother-in-law. Then to replace Lewis as attorney-general he appointed "Nat" Lawrence, whom Burr and Melancton Smith had unsuccessfully urged on him the year before.[26] Clinton's *modus operandi* was to placate rather than punish wavering allies.

For the New York Republicans the presidential election of 1792 was a benchmark of their rise to prominence as a major component of a national party. The old issues were fading; the old anti-Federalists transformed into Republicans would be in a much stronger position politically. Federalists had cause to be alarmed; the election of Adams was, as John Jay wrote, "a great point gained, but the unceasing industry and arts of the Antis render perseverance, union and constant efforts necessary."[27]

II

Despite the unanimous electoral vote of New York for Clinton, the "republican interest" suffered a stunning setback in the congressional election in January 1793. In April 1790, Federalists had taken five of the six seats, a majority anti-Federalists reduced by one in a by-election in 1791. Congressional reapportionment had subsequently increased New York's seats from six to ten. Republicans should have done well, if only because a Clintonian legislature redesigned the congressional districts, adding the four new seats so as to maximize their own potential and isolate Federalist centers of strength.[28] Instead,

25. Schachner, *Aaron Burr*, 119-20.
26. Hammond, *Political Parties*, I, 73-74; Burr to Governor Clinton, Dec. 3, 1792, in Lincoln, ed., *Messages from the Governors*, I, 327-28; *N.-Y. Journal*, Dec. 20, 1792. See above, ch. 9, sec. III.
27. John Jay to Hamilton, Dec. 29, 1792, Johnston, ed., *Correspondence of John Jay*, III, 452-53.
28. *Laws of State of N.Y.*, 16th Sess., ch. 5; *Journal of the Assembly of N.Y.*, 16th Sess., *passim*, late Nov. to Dec. 18; Republicans failed in an attempt to attach Richmond to New York City; Federalists failed in an attempt to attach several Ulster towns to Columbia, *ibid.*, 29, 30, 51-52.

Federalists won seven out of the ten seats, even taking Ulster-Orange, the old Clintonian stronghold.

The campaign of 1793 was cut short by the reapportioning process. The legislature did not make the districts final until mid-December, nominations were made in late December or early January, and the election was held on the fourth Tuesday in January, separate from the spring elections for the state government.[29] Since there was little time to develop issues in the newspapers and since it was difficult to get around in the dead of winter, the voter's reaction probably depended on the way in which the candidate was identified by his past performance or connections.

In the three southern districts, Republicans retained Long Island, took Westchester-Richmond, and lost New York City. On Long Island, Thomas Tredwell, the anti-Federalist incumbent elected the year before, defeated Joshua Sands, a Federalist member of the canvassers' committee. With the near unanimous support of the Yankee yeomanry of Suffolk County, Tredwell ran twice as well as in his by-election.[30] In a new district made up of populous Westchester County and tiny Richmond County—a district very likely created to accommodate the Van Cortlandt family which by 1792 had cut its ties to the Federalists—Philip Van Cortlandt defeated the Federalist, Richard Hatfield, clerk of the county. Philip, the older son of Pierre, Clinton's lieutenant-governor, had been a general in the Revolution, a Commissioner of Forfeiture afterwards, and a Federalist delegate in 1788. In the spring of 1792 Philip had been loyal to Clinton on the committee of canvassers.[31] Westchester had a strong Federalist voting record; in the spring of 1792 Pierre Van Cortlandt could get no more than an even split among the 150 voters in his own manor town, Cortlandt. His son ran much better on the manor (252–2) as well as in the northern towns, carrying the county (880–704) and the district (1003–804).[32]

In New York City, Federalists faced their first serious challenge

29. The first Congress met in three sessions from Mar. 4, 1789, to Mar. 3, 1791. Representatives elected in Mar. 1790 served in the second Congress which met from Oct. 24, 1791, until Mar. 3, 1793. Hence, a three-year gap in New York between the two elections.

30. N.-Y. Journal, Jan. 23, 1793. For returns, see Appendix, Table No. 6.

31. For discussion of the Van Cortlandt family see ch. 3, sec IV; for biographical data on Philip Van Cortlandt and others elected to Congress, see Lightfoot, State Delegations in Congress, 1789-1801, ch. 8.

32. N.-Y. Journal, Feb. 20, 23, 1793.

from a candidate Republicans were unwilling to endorse. To replace Congressman John Laurance who retired, Federalists nominated John Watts, a merchant, the speaker of the assembly, a former recorder under the Crown who had been at best neutral during the war.[33] Watts' challenger was Col. William S. Livingston, who had deserted the Federalists in 1792 to work with his Clermont cousins first in the bank war, then in the ballots controversy.[34] For two years Col. Livingston had been top votegetter in the assembly elections, nominated by the Federalists but winning with Clintonian support.[35] In the legislature he made himself conspicuous defending a charter for the Mechanics Society and his own bill to give New York City residents the right to elect their own mayor, in past years another demand of the mechanic interest.

Although Hamiltonians scored Livingston as "that whore in politics,"[36] Republicans did not embrace him. Neither did they run their own candidate. Melancton Smith who Troup feared would run announced he would not, as did John Broome for whom a few trial balloons were also floated.[37] Writers in Greenleaf's paper threw as much mud against Livingston as against Watts. Condemning Watts as a Tory, they called him "insidious, crafty, selfish, mean, self sufficient, and forward." Livingston, on the other hand, was a pickpocket, a defender of a bawdy house, and "void of virtue and void of talents."[38] The General Society of Mechanics and Tradesmen denied Livingston's request for an endorsement. Denying his claim that they owed their charter to him, they called him "an improper person" to receive their support; furthermore it was "repugnant to their objects" to participate in elections.[39]

In 1789, the last contested election, John Laurance had defeated

33. Lightfoot, State Delegations in Congress, 1789-1801, 390.
34. William S. was a son of Robert James Livingston, descended from Robert Livingston, "The Nephew," a line distinct from but intermarried with the upper and lower manor Livingstons. See Livingston, The Livingstons, 254-58, 275-76, 525. For assistance in identifying him, I am indebted to Mary-Jo Kline and Milton Klein. For his politics in 1792 see ch. 13, n.27.
35. N.Y. Daily Advertiser, June 2, 1791; N.-Y. Journal, June 2, 1792.
36. James Tillary to Hamilton, Jan. 14, 1793, Hamilton Papers, Lib. Cong.
37. Robert Troup to Alexander Hamilton, June 15, 1791, Syrett, ed., Hamilton Papers, VIII, 478-79. For letters on Broome and Smith and notices by them, see N.-Y. Journal, Jan. 12, 16, 19, 1793.
38. N.-Y. Journal: "A L-----s--n," Jan. 23; "Plain Truth," Jan. 12; "A Citizen," Jan. 19, 1793. Livingston very likely was the same "Col. W. S. Livingston" who led the mob that ransacked Thomas Greenleaf's printing shop in 1788.
39. Ibid., Jan. 12, 1793.

John Broome, 2542-372. In 1793 Watts's victory was less decisive, 1872–702. Many Clintonians must have voted for Livingston, yet his vote was less than the 1140 votes which elected him to the assembly eight months before. Federalists still held the allegiance of the city's merchants and most of the mechanics.[40]

In the two districts of the middle Hudson Valley, the anti-Federalists finally took Dutchess but lost Ulster-Orange. In Dutchess, now a district in itself separated from northern Westchester, Theodorus Bailey, the young anti-Federalist lawyer twice edged out by Egbert Benson, ran against James Kent, a rising young lawyer who had achieved prominence in the assembly as manager of the Federalist inquiry into the canvassers' decision.[41] Republicans made Hamiltonian finance an issue. "Government is calculated to benefit the few and not the many," wrote "A Dutchess County Farmer." As proof there was the funding system which delivered nine-tenths of the public securities into the hands of "brokers, speculators, Jews, M[embers] of C[ongress] and foreigners" and taxed the farmers to pay the costs. For further proof there was the Bank of the United States which was "swallowing" the state banks, destroying competition, and benefiting "the monied rich and not the poor."[42] Secondly, Republicans invoked class feeling against Kent as a "loquacious lawyer" responsible for "spinning out" the assembly's hearings to increase the per diem wages of the legislators. "Officials think little how dearly money comes to those who must earn it by hard labor," one alleged farmer wrote, "digging it in the earth by the sweat of their brows; out of us it must finally come."[43] Bailey, doubling his previous vote, defeated Kent, 979–854. Kent, disgusted at the personal abuse and prejudices of the district, moved to New York City where his legal and political career blossomed.

Across the Hudson in Ulster-Orange where Republicans struck the

40. *Ibid.*, Feb. 20, 1793. Livingston ran best in the fifth, sixth, and seventh wards, the same ones which later would give strong support to Edward Livingston. Republicans refused to endorse Livingston in the 1793 assembly elections; see Philip Ten Eyck to John B. Schuyler, Apr. 3, 1793, Schuyler Papers, Miscellany, N.Y. Pub. Lib.

41. See above, ch. 14, sec. IV.

42. "A Dutchess County Farmer," *Poughkeepsie Journal*, Jan. 8, 1793. See the resolution passed at the meeting at which Bailey was nominated; *ibid.*, Nov. 14, 1792.

43. James Kent to Moss Kent, Mar. 4, Mar. 22, 1793, Kent Papers, I, Lib. Cong.; *Poughkeepsie Journal*: "A Farmer," Jan. 2, "A Citizen" and "Moderatus," Jan. 16, 1793.

same notes as in Dutchess they could blame their unprecedented loss on disunity and Peter Van Gaasbeck. Van Gaasbeck, as La Rochefoucauld-Liancourt found him, was "a shopkeeper" and "a good kind of man"; he was "in principle a federalist," but was "very tolerant in his politics." In the last congressional election he had lost to Cornelius Schoonmaker by a few hundred votes. Since then as head of "the Kingston junto" he had organized a county machine which in the spring gubernatorial election had given Federalists their first inroads in the county. In 1792, Van Gaasbeck ran again; the Republican nomination reverted, probably by arrangement, to an Orange County leader, John Hathorn, who had been elected to the first Congress. Either some supporters of Schoonmaker were miffed or Federalists sponsored a diversion but in Orange 54 votes were cast for Schoonmaker and 139 for three other men. Hathorn carried his home county, Orange, but Van Gaasbeck swept Ulster and squeaked through in the district (1464–1448).[44]

The reshuffling of the two vast congressional districts embracing the upper Hudson Valley and the northern and western frontier gave Republicans a chance to get at the Schuyler-Van Rensselaer influence more easily. Previously half of thickly populated Albany County east of the Hudson was in a district embracing Columbia to the south and frontier Clinton to the north, while the half of Albany County west of the Hudson was in a district with the five western counties. The Schuyler-Van Rensselaer influence thus had radiated in all directions. In the reapportionment the landlords' tentacles were cut. The five western counties were put on their own. A new county, Rensselaer, was formed within Albany embracing the patroon's domain and was placed in a district with anti-Federalist Clinton. Saratoga, a Schuyler-influenced county, was placed with anti-Federalist Washington of the northern frontier, formerly with Columbia. Columbia County was given its own congressman, probably on the theory that the Livingstons, both upper and lower manor, might travel further on the road away from the Schuylers if alone, or else might be more easily overcome by anti-Federalists within the county. All this left a much reduced Albany County as a district in itself, but surrendering one sure seat there to Schuyler and Van Rensselaer, Clintonians must have

44. F. A. F. de La Rochefoucauld-Liancourt, *Travels Through the United States of North America . . . in the Years 1795, 1796, 1797 . . .* , 2 vols. (London, 1799), II, 230-31; for election appeals, *Goshen Repository*, Dec. 18, 1792, Jan. 15, 1793; for returns, *N.-Y. Journal*, Feb. 23, 1793.

reasoned, was a reasonable price to pay for the possibility of weaning four others away from them.

In the three districts of the upper Hudson—Albany, Rensselaer-Clinton, and Columbia—Republican progress was uneven. In Albany the Federalists ran Henry Glen against Jeremiah Van Rensselaer, the anti-Federalist chairman of 1788 who had been defeated after one term in Congress. Glen, a merchant, was supported by Schuyler after Elkanah Watson had turned down the Federalist offer.[45] Federalists charged that Van Rensselaer had cut a poor figure in Congress and that he was still an anti-Federalist, pointing to the chairman of his election committee, the unregenerate Abraham Yates. Federalists won, 927–526.[46]

In the Rensselaer-Clinton district Federalists ran scared. Stephen Van Rensselaer's "manor influence" sponsored John Van Allen, a large landholder and country storekeeper, against Henry Van Rensselaer, an assemblyman who was a cousin of both the anti-Federalist Jeremiah and the Federalist Stephen. Thomas Witbeck, the patroon's bailiff, scurried around the district, traveling even to distant Plattsburgh. Even so, half the tenants on Rensselaerswyck voted against Van Allen. His over-all margin was safe (1165–870) but might have been lower had the count been above suspicion.[47] In several towns Federalist election inspectors refused to count all the votes, and in Van Allen's home town ballots were illegally left overnight in the candidate's house before they were sent off. Republicans charged fraud; at the next session of Congress a special committee conducted an inquiry but found that the evidence of "partial corruption" was "not of sufficient magnitude" to invalidate the election.[48]

In Columbia the Livingstons forced a three-cornered race. In 1790 the incumbent, Peter Sylvester, a Schuyler Federalist, defeated John Livingston of the upper manor and the anti-Federalists did not run a candidate. In 1793 Federalists put up Ezekiel Gilbert, a Schuyler man,

45. Flick, Elkanah Watson, 201, citing Watson's Journal, 439. Schuyler may have made the proposal to Watson during the spring election of 1792 to induce Watson to endorse Jay for governor.

46. For the Republican campaign, Albany Register, Jan. 14, 21, 28, Feb. 4, 1793; for returns, ibid., Mar. 4, 1793, N.-Y. Journal, Feb. 27, 1793.

47. For the campaign, Thomas Witbeck to John Van Allen, Nov. 29, Dec. 14, 17, 19, 22, 27, 1792, Jan. 2, 1793; Jan. 2, 1794, Van Allen Papers, Albany Institute of History and Art; M. T. Woolsey to John Williams, Jan. 30, 1793, Williams Papers, III, 141, N.Y. State Lib.; for returns, N.-Y. Journal, Feb. 27, 1793.

48. Annals, 3rd Cong., 1st Sess., 139-40, 145-48; and American State Papers, Miscellany, I, 70-74.

a Yankee lawyer, and a founder of the town of Hudson;[49] the upper
manor ran Peter R. Livingston; and this time the Clintonians ran a
candidate, Peter Van Ness. Van Ness was the county judge whose
performance at the trial of the "Indians" had satisfied conservatives,
yet he had also signed a petition to the legislature challenging the
upper manor's title to their land. Peter R. Livingston was perhaps
the most eccentric figure of his clan, described as "tempestuous, un-
stable, competitive and egocentric."[50] Although he was the eldest
son, the will of his father Robert denied him his rightful inheritance
for incompetence. Understandably he was jealous not only of Schuyler
but of his brothers. He was still nursing his fury against his younger
brother Walter who had insisted on the state senate nomination the
year before.[51] He alone among his brothers had refused to endorse
Clinton in 1792. Doubtless because his brothers were feuding with
the lower manor, he remained on speaking terms with Robert R. Livingston. Hence it is not strange that for the congressional race he
asked the Chancellor for the "support of our family and their connections and interests," nor is it strange in light of the Chancellor's pique
with Clinton, that he got it. Peter R. Livingston spent more than
$600 on the election—"shameful have been the means used to obtain
votes"—but he lost anyway.[52] The returns were Gilbert, 977; Livingston, 948; and Van Ness, 856. Two thirds of Livingston's vote came
from his own manor and Clermont. Van Ness got a large vote in
anti-landlord Hillsdale (Van Ness 216; Gilbert, 230; Livingston, 16),
but Gilbert won with support in the commercial center of Hudson
and the towns influenced by the Schuylers and Van Rensselaers.[53]

In the two frontier districts the pattern was different. In the district
that included Washington, a pioneering county in the north, and
Saratoga, a populous long-settled area, the Federalist incumbent, James
Gordon of Saratoga, faced John Williams, the largest landholder in
Washington, long an influential Clintonian senator. At the last minute, Judge John Thompson of Saratoga, a Republican-to-be, and two
lesser men in Washington decided to make the race. Williams seems

49. See Gilbert to Schuyler, Feb. 6, Mar. 3, 1786, Acc. 2089, N.Y. State Lib.
50. Joan Gordon, Kinship and Class, 296-303; Dangerfield, *Chancellor Robert
R. Livingston*, 249.
51. Peter R. Livingston to Peter Van Schaack, Apr. 2, 1791, R. R. Livingston
Papers, N.-Y. Hist. Soc. The nomination in 1792 went to his brother John who
was elected.
52. Peter R. to Robert R. Livingston, Nov. 26, 1792, William Wilson to Robert
R. Livingston, Feb. 16, 1793, *ibid.*
53. *Hudson Gazette*, Feb. 28, 1793.

to have persuaded the men in his own county to withdraw but not Thompson, who drew off 355 votes, giving Gordon the victory, 1278–1146.[54] In the western district, anti-Federalists were reduced to a poor third in a three-man contest for the newly created seat. The winning Federalist with 1206 votes was Silas Talbot, a former shipmaster and naval hero of the Revolution who had acquired the Sir William Johnson home on that confiscated Tory estate; the second Federalist with 960 votes was William Cooper, rampaging martyr of the canvassers' decision; the anti-Federalist with 650 votes was John Winn, an anti-Federalist delegate of 1788 and now Montgomery County sheriff. Talbot's votes came mostly from his home county, Montgomery; Cooper's from Otsego; Winn's from Montgomery and the beleaguered Otsego minority. The non-Federalist vote was less than a quarter of the total.[55]

If Republicans examined the returns of this third congressional election they could find some bright spots. Political interest in national affairs had revived; about 24,000 voters turned out, compared to 10,800 at the previous congressional election in 1790. Although the Federalist vote ran about 12,200, the Republican vote of about 9600 (with 2400 going to third candidates) was three times their previous total.[56] A shift of a handful of voters in three districts would have reduced the number of Federalist victors from seven to four out of ten. Yet there was a serious weakness in the Republican showing. Federalists were attracting more support from the poorer electorate than Republicans. The Republican vote in the congressional electorate which included the 40-shilling renters was only 1500 more than the 8000 votes for Clinton among the £100 freeholders; the Federalist congressional vote by contrast was 4000 more than for Jay. Why, after four years of the Federalist administration, were Republicans not doing better in New York?

First of all, they were divided. Party lines were still not tightly drawn. The extra candidates who siphoned off Republican votes gave Federalists their victory in Orange-Ulster and Washington-Saratoga. In Columbia as in New York City the cooperation of Livingstons and Clintonians in the gubernatorial election was not extended to national

54. See David Thomas to John Williams, Jan. 20, 29, 1793, John Williams Papers, III, 124-38, N.Y. State Lib.; for the returns, *N.-Y. Journal*, Feb. 27, 1793.
55. For Winn's nomination, *Albany Register*, Dec. 31, 1792; for the returns, *N.-Y. Journal*, Mar. 2, 1793.
56. My computation on the basis of the published returns cited in the above footnotes; for 1790, see *N.-Y. Journal*, May 25, 1790.

politics. The upper manor insisted on their own congressman and Chancellor Livingston wanted someone in power he could influence. Second, Republicans suffered because their candidates were still identified with the old anti-Federalism. This was not a handicap on Long Island and in Dutchess but in Ulster-Orange and Albany someone other than an anti-Federalist would have fared better, as the vote for Van Cortlandt in Westchester and William S. Livingston in New York City indicates. Third, despite redistricting, the Schuyler-Van Rensselaer influence over their dependents remained a formidable obstacle. Albany County was on the way to becoming the landlords' pocket borough; Henry Glen would be returned without opposition.[57]

Finally and most important, Federalists were simply not very vulnerable in so far as their national policies were concerned. The question of Hamiltonian finance struck fire only in the old anti-Federalist bailiwicks, Dutchess and Orange-Ulster. Assumption as an issue was dormant; the worst of the speculation was over; the Bank of the United States was on good terms with the Bank of New York, and two upstate banks placated the northern interest; the excise on whiskey did not seriously affect New York farmers; a mildly protective tariff for the time being satisfied the mechanics; the most recent issues of Hamiltonian finance, the mint and the sinking fund, raised no fears. High prices for the farmers' wheat, timber, and beef produced a prosperity which wafted away the uneasiness over the national bank, speculation, and corruption registered the previous spring in the vote for Clinton. Republicans might consider the conflict one of "Whigs" against "aristocrats," but Federalists had not done enough to alienate their large following among prosperous farmers, mechanics, and merchants.

After almost four years of Federalist administration under the Constitution, a "Republican interest" had appeared in New York State but it was not yet as broadly based or as cohesive as the Federalist movement. It consisted of a loose coalition of former anti-Federalists connected to Governor Clinton, a smaller group of former Federalists grouped around the lower manor Livingstons headed by the Chancellor, and men of various stripes who followed Aaron Burr. These men had lashed back at the Hamiltonians on assumption, electing Burr to the Senate; they had also aroused some popular uneasiness about speculation, but they had been unsuccessful when they chal-

57. M. T. Woolsey to John Williams, Jan. 30, 1793, John Williams Papers, III, 141, N.Y. State Lib.

lenged the Federalists in the "Battle of the Banks." Even Governor Clinton with new support from the Livingstons and the interests to whom he had dispensed the state's largesse, had barely held on to the reins of power in the state government. The "Republican interest" had elected a United States senator, and it had delivered the state's twelve electoral votes in the presidential contest. But it had done so without having won over public opinion against Hamiltonian policy. As a result it failed to persuade New York voters to reject the Federalists in the congressional elections early in 1793. There was a "Republican interest"; as yet there was no Republican movement.

PART IV

The Battle Joined

1793-1797

————•————

CHAPTER 16

"The Spirit of 1776 Rekindling":

New York and the French Revolution

1793

In New York Hamiltonian finance did not create the Republican movement. Neither did the French Revolution. But beginning in 1793 with the events precipitated by the French Revolution, Federalists began to expose themselves at their most vulnerable spot: their pro-British foreign policy. As a result the "Republican interest," which made only sporadic headway in the first Washington administration, had found a following by 1794 that enabled them to challenge the Federalist tide that set in in 1788 during the contest over the Constitution. But even so Republicans in New York, as elsewhere, frequently bungled, permitting Federalists to recoup their political losses and keep their foreign policy intact.

I

Foreign policy became an issue from 1793 on because New Yorkers, like other Americans, were already predisposed to side with Britain or France because of their economic interests, political experiences in the American Revolution, or cultural background. Throughout the United States the Federalist mercantile community as a whole had strong commercial ties with England.[1] New York City very likely was,

1. Channing, *History of the United States*, IV, 167; Bemis, *Jay's Treaty*, 44-45,

as the French consul claimed, "the town of the United States in which
Aristocracy and what is here called the British *influence* most prevails."[2] Detailed investigation would probably sustain the taunt of
the city's Democratic Society that "all the agents from Great Britain
are on the other side by which means you in great degree direct our
commerce and command our purses."[3] The import trade was almost
completely dependent on Britain, responsible for 95 per cent of the
imported manufactured goods, British capital financed New York merchants, Britishers were partners in Anglo-American firms, and British
agents were indeed present in the port. Clintonian tariff and tonnage
laws of the Confederation period discriminating against the British
had had little effect.[4] New York's export trade, on the other hand,
was more diverse. New Yorkers pioneered in opening new markets in
the Orient after the Revolution; there was also a growing trade with
France, particularly the French West Indies. Yet New York merchants
hankered most for the full restoration of their former British West
Indies trade. Although the trade had been legally closed since the
peace treaty, a brisk quasi-legal trade continued.[5]

A second root of the division of New Yorkers toward France and
England lay in the little appreciated politics of the Franco-American
alliance of 1777. On the surface of things, the alliance was an article
of faith among all parties; in 1788 at the city's feast celebrating ratification, the dome on top of the pavilion displayed "a roll of parch-
ment in which were inscriptions in large characters referring to the
Declaration of Independence, the Alliance with France and the Definitive Treaty of Peace." As late as 1790 New Yorkers of all political
complexions attended the reception in honor of the alliance tendered

---

104-5; Alexander DeConde, *Entangling Alliance, Politics and Diplomacy under
George Washington* (Durham, N.C., 1958), 151-52; Bradford Perkins, *The First
Rapprochement: England and the United States, 1795-1805* (Phila., 1955), 7, 10, 14.

2. Alexander Comte D'Hauterive to Edmund Genêt, June 4, June 14, Aug. 2,
1793, in Roger L. Williams, ed., "Three Papers Pertaining to the Genêt Affair,"
N.-Y. Hist. Soc. *Qtly. Jour.*, 33 (1949), 91, 94.

3. Broadside, "Address to the Republican Citizens of the United States . . ." by
the Democratic Society of the City of New York, *N.-Y. Journal* supplement, May
28, 1794. Cf. George Clinton to Monroe, Apr. 14, 1796, Monroe Papers, IV, Lib.
Cong. Jay's treaty, he wrote, was favored by "aristocrats and the agents and
adherents to this nation [Britain] who you know forms an inconsiderable party in
our city and even in our councils."

4. William F. Zornow, "New York Tariff Policies, 1775-1789," *N.Y. History*, 37
(1956), 48-51; Lincoln, ed., *Messages from the Governors*, II, 251-56.

5. Robert G. Albion, "New York Port in the New Republic, 1783-1793," *N.Y.
History*, 21 (1940), 388-403, and Albion, *The Rise of New York Port, 1815-1860*
(N.Y., 1939), ch. 1; Pomerantz, *New York An American City*, 147-59.

by the French chargé d'affaires.[6] Below the surface, however, the division still existed between the "Gallican" faction, which trusted France and accepted her intervention in American councils in the Revolution, and the "anti-Gallicans," who distrusted her and resented her interference.[7]

Robert R. Livingston and John Jay—New York's ranking spokesmen on foreign policy—in some ways epitomize this division, suggesting its subtle sources. Livingston owed his election as first Secretary for Foreign Affairs to Luzerne, the French minister, and had the reputation of being a "Gallican" secretary who took French advice. During the Revolution he shared the French interest in creating a stronger national government, moved comfortably in the sophisticated circles of the French minister in Philadelphia, and looked sympathetically on France as the home of the Enlightenment.[8] By contrast John Jay as peace negotiator at Paris broke with the French to write a separate treaty with the English, violating Livingston's instructions. Jay held deep suspicions of the French, shaped by a Huguenot heritage, a pious, ascetic character and a mind little touched by the Enlightenment. Considering his experiences as negotiator and subsequently as Secretary for Foreign Affairs, it is not surprising that when the French minister called on him in 1788 Jay asked whether the Franco-American alliance was still in effect.[9]

The cultural heritage of New Yorkers also conditioned them in their attitudes toward Britain and France. If New York City was not quite "the sink of British manners and politics" that Philadelphia's Benjamin Rush claimed,[10] its tone was still distinctly English. "You will find more Englishmen and English manners in this place than in any other on the continent," an English traveler wrote in 1796.[11] Although France enjoyed no such influence she still retained in the formerly patriot parts of the state a large reservoir of gratitude for her aid in

6. Griswold, *Republican Court*, 104, 217.

7. Ralph L. Ketcham, "France and American Politics, 1763-1793," *Pol. Sci. Qtly.*, 78 (1963), 198-223.

8. Dangerfield, *Chancellor Robert R. Livingston*, Part Two, chs. 5, 6.

9. Julian P. Boyd, "Two Diplomats Between Revolutions: John Jay and Thomas Jefferson," *Virginia Magazine of History and Biography*, 66 (1958), 131-46; DeConde, *Entangling Alliance*, 8-16, Bemis, *Jay's Treaty*, 279-86.

10. Benjamin Rush to John Adams, June 3, 1789, Benjamin Rush, *Letters*, ed. Lyman Butterfield (Princeton, 1951), I, 513.

11. Entry of Mar. 15, 1796, Francis Baily, *Journal of a Tour in Unsettled Parts of North America, in 1796 and 1797* (London, 1861), 120-23, cited in Stokes, *Iconography of Manhattan*, V; see too William Strickland, Journal, Oct. 28, 1794, N.-Y. Hist. Soc.

the Revolution. As late as 1795, La Rochefoucauld-Liancourt, the French traveler, found that pioneers in the Mohawk Valley had a "strong attachment to France and most earnestly wish her success. They hate England, confide in their President and speak of DeLafayette with tears in their eyes."[12] Such streams of gratitude prepared the soil for a sympathetic reaction to things French.

Considering the deep roots of the economic, political, and cultural division, it is not surprising that as early as October 1790, Hamilton in analyzing the "two parties with us" spoke of "the gentlemen who think we ought to be connected with France on the most intimate terms" and "others who are at least as numerous and influential who evidently prefer an English connection." British officials were in no doubt that among New Yorkers, Hamilton, Schuyler, Jay, and King were "friends to the British interest" and that Governor Clinton was "an inveterate foe."[13] This was two and a half years before the French Revolution became a partisan issue in American politics.

Hamilton's fiscal program intensified the latent British-French division. In the first Congress when Madison proposed tonnage and tariff discrimination against nations which discriminated against the United States, New York's Federalists fought the measure with an animus that prompted Madison to refer to "the spirit of this city which is steeped in Anglicanism."[14] Clintonians on the other hand favored it as a program they had long experimented with in the state legislature.[15] Once Federalists adopted Hamilton's funding system, depending on revenue from imports, they were even more zealous in guarding the ramparts of the import trade, whose connection to the funding system and in turn the Bank of the United States they well understood.[16]

The schism between "Anglomen" and "Gallicans" did not become a public issue during the first Washington administration, at least not in New York. In 1791 and 1792, enthusiasm for the French Revolution mounted.[17] The pamphlet war between Burke and Paine and their American partisans helped dramatize the issues in terms

12. La Rochefoucauld-Liancourt, *Travels Through the United States*, II, 365-66.
13. Bemis, *Jay's Treaty*, 107, see also, 52, 61-62, 65, 89-90, 142; Mitchell, *Alexander Hamilton*, II, 296-307.
14. Madison to Jefferson, May 9, 1789, Boyd, ed., *Papers of Jefferson*, XV, 114-15; Brant, *James Madison*, III, ch. 19.
15. See above, n.4.
16. See ch. 17, sec. I.
17. See ch. 9, sec. V.

Americans could grasp. But even so, the debate was not narrowly partisan—a complete edition of Paine's works was brought out by a Federalist printer with the blessings of the anti-Federalists. And the reports on the French Revolution in the New York newspapers were "universally sympathetic" to France from 1789 at least through 1791. Editors, Federalist and anti-Federalist, "did not as yet take sides with regard to French events; they all favored the progress of the Revolution as it was described in their pages."[18]

In 1793 all this changed, and the French Revolution became a political issue for New York as for the nation. The execution of King Louis XVI, the launching of the republic, and the outbreak of war with England in 1792 posed a stark question of monarchy versus republicanism. The war and Washington's prompt Proclamation of Neutrality in 1793 brought into the open the dormant question of honoring or abandoning the French alliance. France's complete opening of the French West Indies to American commerce raised the prospect of profits for the city's merchants. And when France's new minister, Citizen Genêt, arrived in the United States, making New York his headquarters after August 1793, he was a personal catalyst few could ignore. The result was "to cast into sharp focus *already existing differences*."[19] The French Revolution, the French alliance, and the "British connection" thus moved into the center of the New York political stage.

II

Early in 1793 a more strident enthusiasm for the French Revolution was evident in New York. At a militia muster in Ulster County volunteers "fired twenty platoons at each of which a toast was drunk . . . and at every fifth platoon the men under arms fired a *feu de joie* and drank a glass to the cause of France."[20] Republican editors grabbed up every morsel of news from the Continent, filling column after column with what Thomas Greenleaf called "THE GLORIOUS SUCCESSES of the French REVOLUTION."[21] At New York, a new paper, the *Columbian Gazetteer*, appeared, devoted almost exclusively to news from abroad, with a French slogan, "Écoutez tout le monde,

18. Beermann, Reception of the French Revolution in the New York State Press, 720, 725.

19. DeConde, *Entangling Alliance*, 87.

20. *N.-Y. Journal*, Feb. 2, 1793; for another pro-French meeting at Newburgh, *Goshen Repository*, Jan. 15, 1793; *Hudson Gazette*, Feb. 28, 1793.

21. See *N.-Y. Journal*, Jan. 9, 1793.

Croyez peu de gens," blazoned on its masthead.[22] In time printers brought out editions of the new French Constitution,[23] Condorcet,[24] Robespierre,[25] and more of Thomas Paine. John Fellows, a Republican book dealer, stocked his new circulating library with such works,[26] as did the New York Society Library.[27]

The news of the execution of the King provided a major divisive issue. When Federalists expressed horror, "A Republican" asked, what was his death, compared to "the millions that have suffered under the cruel yoke of despotism?" Had the King succeeded, an Ulsterite pointed out, eleven thousand revolutionists would have been executed —and without trial at that.[28]

Republicans groped for a way to help France. Greenleaf first suggested that citizens in their " individual and private capacity" contribute money. Then he called on his country readers to raise their production of wheat "to assist those who first assisted us."[29]

In May 1793, Tammany converted its annual anniversary observance into a celebration of the French Revolution, and Governor Clinton ordered the colors displayed at the Battery for the occasion. Four hundred members paraded with the French liberty cap held aloft, side by side with the society's banner and the American flag. At the evening dinner a toast was offered, "Success to the armies of France and wisdom, concord, and firmness to the convention." But "the first sentence of the toast was hardly articulated when AS ONE the whole company arose and gave three cheers, continued by roars of applause for several minutes—the toast was then given in whole and the applause reiterated."[30]

22. The N.Y. *Columbian Gazetteer*, which ran from Aug. 22, 1793 to Nov. 13, 1794.

23. *Constitution of the Republic of France* . . . (N.Y., 1793).

24. Marquis de Condorcet, *A Letter . . . to a Magistrate in Switzerland . . . with a letter from Thomas Paine to the People of France* . . . (N.Y., 1793).

25. Robespierre is in *Political Miscellany* (N.Y., 1793).

26. An advertisement, *N.-Y. Journal*, June 22, 1793; N.Y. *American Minerva*, Apr. 25, 1794.

27. *Charter and By-Laws and Names of the Members of the New York Society Library . . . with a catalog of the books* . . . (N.Y., 1793); *A Supplementary Catalog* . . . (N.Y., 1800).

28. "A Republican," *N.-Y. Journal*, Apr. 6, 1793; Kingston *Farmer's Register*, May 11, 1793; see also, *N.-Y. Journal*, Oct. 10, 1792, and Apr. 4, 1793, both reprinting an anonymous article from Philadelphia *General Advertiser*.

29. *N.-Y. Journal*, Apr. 3, reprinted from Phila. *General Advertiser*, and Apr. 20, 1793.

30. *Ibid.*, May 15, 1793; Clinton to Sebastian Bauman, May 4, 1793, Bauman MSS, N.-Y. Hist. Soc.

Republicans were squaring off for a scrap with the detractors of France. The French were being "villified in our streets and on our wharves, nay in our elegant new coffee house," Tontine's. British sailors were especially to blame. "An Oneida Chief" threatened that if the "Tories" did not cease, the "Mohawks, Oneidas and Senecas"—the Tammany tribes—would act.[31]

Few Republicans, however, were prepared to violate Washington's Proclamation of Neutrality. Governor Clinton issued his own proclamation which in effect endorsed the President's warning. He alerted port wardens to report to him the arrival of ships of war and prize vessels of any belligerent.[32] He also practiced what he preached. When the French tried to outfit the vessel *Polly* as a privateer, he ordered out the militia to detain her and a week later ordered her delivered to the United States marshal. Hauterive, the French consul, protested; Genêt protested; the President considered the matter and ordered the vessel turned over to the courts. For his action the Governor got the backing of the Republican *New York Journal*.[33] A few days later he took similar action against a British privateer, the *Catherine*, earning a round of protest from the British minister.[34]

The sober segments of Republican opinion acquiesced in Washington's policy. America's treaty with France was binding, one writer explained, but there was no obligation to take an active part with France in actual war. The country should help France, but the best way to do this was to grant a preference in trade, and no more. Even the liberal young debaters in the Uranian Society did not believe that the United States was bound to intervene in the war.[35] The pro-French hotheads, on the other hand, were furious at Washington's request to be neutral in spirit toward the two belligerents. How could Americans be "friendly and impartial" to England, with whom they had waged a bitter war for independence?[36]

The arrival of the French naval vessel *L'Embuscade* gave Republicans a chance to vent their pent-up enthusiasms. "Some hundreds of

31. *N.-Y. Journal*, May 29, 1793.

32. *Ibid.*, May 11, 1793.

33. Clinton to Sebastian Bauman, June 8, 15, 1793, Bauman MSS, N.-Y. Hist. Soc.; *N.-Y. Journal*, June 12, 1793.

34. Clinton to Sir John Temple, June 10 and 14, 1793, Temple Papers, Mass. Hist. Soc. Carroll and Ashworth, *George Washington*, VII, 89.

35. "Cursory Thoughts on French Affairs," No. 2, *N.-Y. Journal*, June 19, 1793; Minutes of the Uranian Society, May 14, 1793, N.-Y. Hist. Soc.

36. *N.-Y. Journal*: "Freedom or Death" and "No Dissembler," July 3, "The People," July 24, 1793.

the Republicans" met at Tontine's Coffee House, where, according to Edward Livingston, a cap of liberty was put up "over the bar and several enormous bowls of punch drank to its support—Tho it must have been a 'bitter beer' to the taste of many to whom it was offered yet no one dared refuse the draught." General John Lamb also wined and dined the ship's officers at his home. Tammany tendered a dinner at which Hauterive and the French commander were the guests of honor. The Grand Sachem said the society looked on them as part "of the same family as themselves, even as the sons of freedom."[37]

Political tension mounted. Republicans put another cap of liberty in front of Tontine's—a "beautiful crimson adorned by a white torsel" —so beautiful that some purists would have preferred a cap "spun out of our own wool and woven on our own looms." When conservatives tried to remove it, "The Real Whigs" issued a warning; it would come down only at the risk of a battle.[38] For the merchants who regularly transacted business at Tontine's the coffeehouse was a bedlam. "Wherever two or three people are gathered together," one visitor observed, "there is expected to be a quarrel, and they crowd around, hence other squabbles arise."[39]

The Fourth of July celebration measured the rapid transformation of city opinion. In past years Independence Day had not been much of an occasion. Greenleaf, after calling for a full turnout, was delighted with the "ardor." At nine in the morning Tammany and the militia officers ("the greater part of whom are members") assembled at their hall and the Mechanics Society at Mechanics Hall. Both groups then marched to the Old Presbyterian Church where they were joined by a "numerous body" of men and women who filled the church to overflowing.[40] The observance began with the Grand Sachem reading the Declaration of Independence. The Reverend Samuel Miller, the junior Presbyterian minister, then delivered a sermon which defended the French Revolution against accusations that it "may appear to be sullied by irreligion and vice." In spite of

37. Edward to Robert R. Livingston, May 15, 1793, R. R. Livingston Papers, N.-Y. Hist. Soc.; N.-Y. Journal, June 19, 1793; Leake, Memoirs of John Lamb, 347-48.

38. "Cursory Thoughts on French Affairs," No. 7, N.-Y. Journal, July 5, 1793; ibid., June 15, 1793.

39. Entry of June 13, 1793, Alexander Anderson, Diarium Commentarium Vitae Alexander Anderson, 1793-1799, Columbia Univ.; John Drayton, Letters Written During a Tour Through the Northern and Eastern States of America (Charleston, 1794), in Warren S. Tryon, ed., A Mirror for Americans, 3 vols. (Chicago, 1952), I, 4.

40. N.-Y. Journal, July 6, 1793; July 4, 1793, Anderson, Diary, Columbia Univ.

"violence and inhumanity of the most atrocious and unnecessary kind," he believed the "great pillars of this Revolution rest upon the natural rights of man." "Chase then! ye shortsighted sons of ambition who would oppose this important work." In the evening more than twenty groups held private dinner celebrations; besides Tammany, the militia officers, a body of mechanics, "the patriotic merchants," and "a number of the Sons of Liberty" met. Even the Society of Cincinnati toasted the French.[41] Ten days later Tammany observed Bastille Day at a large banquet for the officers of *L'Embuscade* in its flag-bedecked wigwam. "Citizen Frenchmen," wrote one of them, "believe me, Americans love you—Americans are your brethren—Americans are ready to mingle their most precious blood with yours."[42]

In small towns the Independence Day celebrations also gave clear signs of enthusiasm for the French Revolution. At Poughkeepsie one hundred citizens celebrated under a bower of French and American flags marked "In Honor of the Tree of Liberty in France."[43] At Kingston the French Constitution based on "equal liberty . . . and no king" was toasted. Even in Federalist Hudson, Citizen Genêt was praised.[44] At Albany, the militia paraded, there was a fifteen-gun salute, three cheers for the day, "three cheers for the Republic of France," then a round of dinners in the evening.[45] And on New York's far-flung frontier France kindled a few sparks here and there. At Painted Post, for example, in distant Ontario, the Fourth of July celebration was attended by seventy people whose toasts endorsed the French Revolution and the progress of liberalism through Europe. To the first judge of Ontario County, a Yankee migrant, the French Revolution was lit by "the spark of liberty kindled in Boston in 1775" and he wished it success over the "minions of despots."[46]

41. Reverend Samuel Miller, *A Sermon Preached in New York, July 4, 1793 . . . at the Request of the Tammany Society . . .* (N.Y., 1793), 30-34; *N.-Y. Journal,* July 6, 10, 1793.

42. *N.-Y. Journal,* July 18, 21, 31, 1793.

43. *Poughkeepsie Journal,* July 10, 1793; Kingston *Farmer's Register,* July 13, 1793.

44. Kingston *Farmer's Register,* July 6, 1793; *Poughkeepsie Journal,* July 17, 1793; for other celebrations, *Goshen Repository,* July 9, 1793, and *Albany Register,* July 15, 1793.

45. *N.-Y. Journal,* July 20, 1793.

46. *Catskill Packet,* July 29, 1793; Timothy Hosmer to James Wadsworth cited in Turner, *History of the Phelps and Gorham's Purchase,* 234.

III

In New York City, by the summer the stage had been set for the arrival of Citizen Genêt. They would soon see, as Hauterive wrote, "whether New York be an English or an American city."[47] The French had paved their way in the city, as elsewhere, with economic cement. For the merchants as a whole there was the new trade with the West Indies which mounted steadily through 1793, especially in the grains and meats of the middle states which flowed out through the ports of Philadelphia and New York.[48] For a few merchants there was a more direct profit as French agents. Early in 1793 Colonel William S. Smith had returned from France authorized to buy munitions and receive loan payments from the United States on behalf of France. The son-in-law of John Adams, a successful land agent for Macomb and Constable in England in 1791-92, and a former federal marshal of the New York district, Smith was a leading personage in the city. At a dinner in Philadelphia Jefferson found him among the advocates of "the warmest Jacobinism."[49] In August 1793, Hauterive, the French consul at New York, signed a contract with two other prominent New York merchants, Ebenezer Stevens and Commodore James Nicholson —the naval leader of the Revolution, a Federalist in 1788, a Clintonian in 1792. The two agreed to arrange loans to provision the French fleet in New York at a commission beginning at 2 per cent. They signed a contract the day before Citizen Genêt arrived in the city.[50]

A week before Genêt's arrival a naval battle in the New York harbor between *L'Embuscade* and a British vessel, the *Boston*, provided a dramatic prelude to his visit. Only a week earlier the French vessel had been the victim of a ruse by the *Boston*. To satisfy French honor Captain Courtney of the *Boston* posted a challenge in Tontine's

47. See footnote 2 above.

48. For the national picture, Edmund Buron, "Statistics on Franco-American Trade, 1778-1806," *Journal of Economic and Business History*, 4 (1932), 571-80, based on data from French sources; Adam Seybert, comp., *Statistical Annals . . . Founded on Official Documents . . . 1789-1818* (Phila., 1818), 132-33, based on data from American sources; for New York exports, *ibid.*, 142, and for tonnage data, 320-24.

49. Katherine M. Roof, *Colonel William Smith and Lady* (Boston, 1929), 210-12, 219-20; Bemis, *Jay's Treaty*, 118-19, 201; Carroll and Ashworth, *George Washington*, VII, 29-30, 31-32, n.140. Jefferson to Madison, Mar. [24], 1793, in Ford, ed., *Writings of Jefferson*, VI, 192-93.

50. See a contract signed by the three men dated Aug. 6, 1793, in Ebenezer Stevens Papers, N.-Y. Hist. Soc. Stevens was nominated as a member of the Chamber of Commerce the same day, see Minutes of the Chamber of Commerce of New York, Aug. 6, Sept. 3, 1793, photostat, N.Y. Pub. Lib.

Coffee House to meet the French off Sandy Hook, and Captain Bompard of *L'Embuscade* accepted. Tension mounted as New Yorkers chose sides; fist fights broke out between "Whig" and "Tory" cartmen. On the day of the duel, New Yorkers lined the shore or sailed out, some nine boatloads of them, to watch the cannons boom for almost two hours. Both ships suffered badly but *L'Embuscade* claimed the victory. A day later she sailed back into the harbor together with the entire French fleet of fifteen ships that had been making its way north out of Santo Domingo. Thousands cheered from the Battery; the French admiral waited on Governor Clinton; the officers of *L'Embuscade* presented her flag to Tammany "as a token of respect . . . from their republican brethren in France"; and the city's women supplied old linen to bind the wounds of French sailors taken to the New York Hospital.[51]

The arrival of the fleet brought Genêt scurrying up from Philadelphia to cope with a host of problems: mutinous sailors, refugees in flight from Santo Domingo's Negro revolution, and British and royalist agents stirring up this brew. At the same time he would have his first try at winning New York opinion. His visit put the budding "Republican interest" of New York to a sharp test. His violations of American neutrality had reached the point where the entire cabinet, Jefferson included, recommended his recall. Genêt had just armed the captured British merchant vessel *Little Sarah* and sent her to sea as a French privateer, violating a pledge to Jefferson, and then made a thinly veiled threat to appeal to the people to reverse the administration's neutrality policies. Just before he reached New York, Senator King and Chief Justice Jay slipped into the city to spread this report. Even before this, Jefferson and Madison were counseling Republicans to abandon the Frenchman. Senator Burr was also apprehensive; he heard rumors in Philadelphia that Genêt "goes about visiting the mechanics and the lower orders of the people, leaving cards at their houses when they are not at home!"[52]

Republican leaders, headed by Melancton Smith, Brockholst Livingston, and Samuel Osgood, organized a meeting to plan the reception for Genêt; Greenleaf claimed 1000 attended, the Federalists 300.

51. DeConde, *Entangling Alliance*, 269-70; July 31, 1793, Anderson, Diary, Columbia Univ.; N.Y. *Daily Advertiser*, Aug. 2, 3, 1793.

52. Aaron Burr to John Nicholson, July 16, 1793, Burr Papers, Hist. Soc. of Pa.; Malone, *Jefferson and his Time*, III, chs. 6, 7; DeConde, *Entangling Alliance*, 271-79.

In any case there were many mechanics and a number of faces new to the Republican cause. The meeting was disrupted when John Jay's nephew and another young man harangued the crowd about Genêt's "appeal to the people," but on a motion to prepare a greeting for Genêt there was a chorus of huzzas. A welcoming committee of forty was appointed, styling itself "the Republicans of New York and Friends of France." The secretary was White Matlack, a well-to-do brewer, iron manufacturer, and leader of the mechanics;[53] the chairman was Commodore Nicholson, the ink scarcely dry on his contract with Hauterive.

The Federalists promptly retaliated. The Chamber of Commerce condemned "any attempt" by a foreign government to outfit privateers or recruit sailors in America or "to communicate with this country upon national objects otherways than through" the President.[54] Meanwhile, Senator King took the initiative in organizing a public meeting to support Washington.

On August 8 at eleven the church bells signaled that Genêt's barge was on its way from New Jersey. At noon he landed at the Battery to the sound of a salute from the fort. The committee, together with a group of French refugees, escorted him to the porch at Tontine's where welcoming messages were delivered by Nicholson and William Pitt Smith of Tammany and the Columbia faculty. "We tender to you our hearts and through you to your nation, our warm and undisguised affection," ran their statement. To Genêt went expressions of "high esteem for your person and character." The President's proclamation, they granted, imposed obligations as to conduct; but "as the question related to sentiment and principles there is no neutrality." At the same time they were "ready and willing" to render assistance only if "consistent with our reciprocal welfare and with the duty we owe our country." In his reply Genêt came close to making the very "appeal to the people" he had been accused of. France did not ask America to join her in war; she "had preferred enjoying the spectacle of your prosperity and calling on you to partake of all the riches of her commerce to involving you with her in a common danger"—there was bait. Still she expected "faithful and punctual observance" of the treaty.

53. *N.-Y. Journal*, Aug. 3, 7, 10, "A Flatterer," Aug. 31, 1793; Rufus King to Alexander Hamilton, Aug. 3, 1793, King, ed., *Correspondence of Rufus King*, I, 493; Anderson, Diary, Aug. 8, 1793, Columbia Univ.
54. *N.-Y. Journal*, Aug. 10, 1793.

There was "too much reason to fear" that the United States was "involved in the general conspiracy of tyrants against liberty."[55]

After the reception, the committee of forty met and with one dissent made more explicit that "while ready . . . to express their unfeigned attachment to the Republic of France" they "are deeply impressed with the importance of the United States observing a strict neutrality between the belligerent powers of Europe." Therefore, they recommended that their followers join the Federalist-sponsored meeting scheduled for the same day "in expressing their sincere, warm, and unabated attachment for the person and character of the President of the United States" for his neutrality proclamation.[56]

The Federalist meeting in front of Trinity Church may well have been the "most respectable for numbers—character—and property," even if it was not, as they claimed, the greatest meeting in New York since the Stamp Act. Nicholas Cruger, Hamilton's one-time merchant patron, presided, and resolutions were adopted which praised the President for his proclamation and—slyly—Clinton for endorsing it. Any measures which might interfere with neutrality must be avoided. Unperturbed by the maneuver, Governor Clinton replied, expressing pleasure at the "approbation" of his fellow citizens.[57]

Within a few days Federalists brought up their heavy guns for the onslaught against Genêt. To verify the rumor about the minister's threat to "appeal to the people," King and Jay published a brief paragraph certifying that the accusation was correctly attributed to them. Hamilton primed them further; other articles followed, including a vitriolic series by Hamilton as "No Jacobin." From the Federalist point of view the issue was posed perfectly: Genêt or Washington.[58]

From August through the fall of 1793 a debate raged in the New York papers. Republicans demanded chapter and verse in proof of the accusations against Genêt. The whole tempest, they charged, was

55. *Ibid.*, Aug. 10, 14, 1793; Anderson, Diary, Aug. 8, 1793, Columbia Univ.; Maude Woodfin, Citizen Genêt and his Mission (unpubl. Ph.D. diss., Univ. of Chicago, 1928), 329-34.
56. Phila., *Dunlap's American Daily Advertiser*, Aug. 10, 1793.
57. Robert Troup to Hamilton, Aug. 8, John Bard to Hamilton, Aug. 24, 1793, Hamilton Papers, Lib. Cong.; *N.-Y. Journal*, Aug. 10, 1793; Troup to James Duane, Aug. 14, 1793, cited in Mitchell, *Alexander Hamilton*, II, 227-28.
58. *N.-Y. Journal*, Aug. 12, 1793, and other papers; Mitchell, *Alexander Hamilton*, II, 237-39; Hamilton to King, Aug. 13, 23, 1793, Lodge, ed., *Works of Hamilton*, X, 50-53. For the interstate character of the anti-Genêt campaign, see Harry Ammon, "The Genêt Mission and the Development of American Political Parties," *Journal of American History*, 52 (1965), 725-41.

a plot to embitter French-American relations. Furthermore, in a republic, they asked, what was so criminal about "an appeal to the people." Rapidly they broadened the issue to encompass a criticism of all American foreign policy.[59]

While these political missiles exploded around him, Genêt fared poorly on the projects that had brought him to New York. For his plan to invade Canada he recruited a handful of French refugees and sixty-three Irish immigrants (derided by the sanguine Hauterive as "a band of Irishmen and malcontents"), drilled and equipped them, only to have the scheme collapse in November.[60] To quell his "squadron in insurrection," he seems to have gotten help from city authorities only in keeping order among shore parties of sailors. But he got nowhere with the federal government in his request for advances against loan payments, necessary to solve the underlying financial problems.[61]

Actually Genêt got a great deal in the way of political support from the New York Republicans, especially the Livingstons, even though "the mass of the republican interest" elsewhere, as Jefferson put it, were opposed to "intermeddling by a foreigner."[62] Through the spring the Chancellor had been deeply disturbed by the drift of the administration's foreign policy; in July he had urged Jefferson not to resign as secretary. In August, alarmed at "the strong disadvantages impressed upon the public mind" by King and Jay's "certificates" about Genêt, he implored Edward to take "some efficient measures to refute it."[63] He himself, reviving his old pseudonym "Cato," launched a series of articles scorching Federalist policies, at the same time that Jefferson, without his knowledge, was suggesting him to Washington as his successor.[64] Late in the year Edward and Brockholst Livingston became Genêt's legal counsel in his libel suit against Jay and King. They considered the Federalist accusations "an offense not only against the local law of this country, but against the law of nations." The suit alarmed the President as it did Jay and King, but it was not

59. In *N.-Y. Journal* see: "One of the People," Aug. 21; "Observer," Aug. 24; "A Flatterer," Aug. 28, 30, 31, Sept. 7, 1793.

60. Frances S. Childs, "The Hauterive Journal," N.Y. Hist. Soc., *Qtly. Jour.*, 33 (1949), 72, 79.

61. Woodfin, *Citizen Genêt*, ch. 12; DeConde, *Entangling Alliance*, 278-83.

62. Jefferson to Madison, Aug. 25, 1793, Ford, ed., *Writings of Jefferson*, VI, 397-98.

63. R. R. Livingston to Jefferson, July 1793, draft, R. R. to Edward Livingston, Aug. 19, 1793, R. R. Livingston Papers, N.Y. Hist. Soc.

64. Carroll and Ashworth, *George Washington*, VII, 114.

dropped until Fauchet, Genêt's successor, forced him to withdraw it months later.[65] Genêt's New York fiscal agents were also undeterred in their labors. Colonel Smith arranged purchases and Commodore Nicholson and Ebenezer Stevens arranged loans, including a few from substantial Federalist merchants. For both Nicholson, who late in 1793 was probably involved in founding the Democratic Society, and Stevens, who invited Genêt to a Republican dinner, it was obviously a labor combining political love and profit.[66]

Governor Clinton also expressed political support for Genêt even while enforcing the neutrality laws.[67] In a celebration marking the tenth anniversary of Evacuation Day in November, Genêt headed a committee which offered the Governor "a tribute of gratitude." Clinton received it graciously, going out of his way to express praise for "the orderly behavior" of the French sailors in the city and a warm interest in the minister's personal "prosperity."[68]

The interest of the Governor's older daughter, Cornelia, in Genêt was even warmer. Cornelia was "as smart and sensible a girl as I knew," John Adams' daughter had written, but was "a zealous politician and a high anti-Federalist." She was also a romantic; in fact a few months before she met Genêt she had gone through a romance which she broke off in face of her father's threat to renounce her, promising not to marry without his approval.[69]

As a diplomat Edmund Genêt was headstrong and arrogant; but the young man of thirty, the son of a highly placed French family, was handsome, cultured (a master of six languages besides his own),

65. A letter by these lawyers to Genêt, Dec. 23, 1793, cited in Meade Minnegerode, *Jefferson, Friend of France, 1793: The Career of Edmund Charles Genêt . . . 1763-1834* (N.Y., 1928); Brockholst Livingston to Genêt, Dec. 31, 1793, Genêt Papers, Lib. Cong.; for public notices, *N.-Y. Journal*, Nov. 23, Dec. 4, 1793; for background, DeConde, *Entangling Alliance*, 292-96.

66. Hauterive to Stevens, [Nov. or Dec., 1793], and Dec. 3, 1793, Ebenezer Stevens Papers, N.-Y. Hist. Soc.; Childs, "The Hauterive Journal," N.-Y. Hist. Soc., *Qtly. Jour.*, 33 (1949), 81-82; for Smith, Carroll and Ashworth, *George Washington*, VII, 140n. For Udney Hay, a New York land dealer and former business associate of Melancton Smith who collaborated with Genêt in the Canadian invasion scheme, see Link, *Democratic Republican Societies*, 143-44.

67. Carroll and Ashworth, *George Washington*, VII, 130, reporting a letter from Clinton to Washington, Sept. 14, and Washington's letter to Knox, Sept. 16, ordering the Secretary of War to take action against Genêt.

68. *N.-Y. Journal*, Nov. 30, 1793.

69. Roof, *Colonel William Smith and Lady*, 197; George to Cornelia Clinton, Mar. 10, 1793, Genêt Papers, N.Y. Pub. Lib.; Maria to Cornelia Clinton, May 13, 1783, Genêt Papers, N.-Y. Hist. Soc.; see also two MS fragments by Cornelia Clinton for her adolescent love moods, Clinton Family Papers, N.Y. Pub. Lib.

and a man of the world.[70] Some time in August he met Cornelia; in September he rechristened *La Petite Democrat*, a French vessel, *Cornelia*; by the end of October tongues were wagging that they would be married. "I hope the story is true," a Federalist wrote Hamilton. "The Result, I think would be in a Year or two have a favorable influence on the politics of the state." Crestfallen he had to add a postscript, "since writing the above I learn Mr. Genêt is a married man having two children." Therefore, "the great attention he pays to Govr. Clinton's daughter" was "for the sake of gaining anti-federalist Interest."[71]

By the end of November Genêt was on the verge of being recalled. "The question of the marriage is put off," Hauterive wrote, and he added, "Poor Cornelia."[72] Cornelia, however, remained steadfast. "If I am with your enemies," she wrote to Genêt in Philadelphia, "they abuse you in order to hurt my feelings . . . and I generally treat them with silent contempt." She was defiant—"your enemies I consider mine." "Those democratic principles serve but to endear you to me," she wrote, "for notwithstanding your worth, I do not think I could have been attached to you had you been anything but a Republican."[73]

When Genêt's recall became official he faced the prospect of execution if he returned to France for a new regime had disowned him and his party. From Philadelphia he wrote Cornelia that he hoped her father might use his influence to secure him asylum, but he gallantly refused to agree to marriage or even to see her "until such time as I shall know what will be my lot."[74] Cornelia's father commiserated with Genêt, unaware of his daughter's secret engagement; he hoped Genêt "will find a happy asylum in this country . . . for himself and family." When finally they broke the news of their engagement to him, the Governor seems to have insisted that they postpone their marriage

70. Woodfin in *DAB* s.v. "Genêt, Edmond"; and Woodfin, *Citizen Genêt*, ch. 15.
71. Hugh Williamson to Hamilton, Oct. 24, 1793, Hamilton Papers, Lib. Cong.
72. Childs, "The Hauterive Journal," N.-Y. Hist. Soc., *Qtly. Jour.*, 33 (1949), 82, citing an entry for Nov. 24, 1793.
73. Cornelia Clinton to Genêt, Dec. 18, 1793, Jan. 5, 1794, Genêt Papers, N.-Y. Hist. Soc.; Minnegerode, *Jefferson, Friend of France*, 346, cites a letter from Cornelia Clinton to Genêt without exact reference indicating they were secretly engaged.
74. Genêt to Cornelia Clinton, Dec. 29, 1793, Cornelia to Genêt, Jan. 10, Genêt to Cornelia, Valentine's Day, Feb. 1794, Genêt Papers, Lib. Cong., reprinted in Woodfin, Citizen Genêt, 533-46; see also Cornelia to DeWitt Clinton, Jan. [?], 1794, Genêt Papers, N.-Y. Hist. Soc.

until he checked the false report that Genêt already had a wife in France.[75] Genêt was granted asylum, took an oath of allegiance to the United States government, and bought a farm at Jamaica, Long Island. In July 1794, the marriage was still held up—one rumor had it that the Governor would not give his answer until after the 1795 gubernatorial election—but in November 1794 at a private ceremony at the Governor's house the two were married with Clinton's blessings and a £2000 dowry.[76]

The announcement early in 1794 of Genêt's recall came amidst preparations by the city Republicans for a dinner in his honor. The morning of the affair, Genêt rushed off for Philadelphia. The dinner was held but "the chiefs were absent," including the Chancellor, John Jay gloated. "Genêt is completely on his back," Robert Troup reported from the city, "and I cannot now hear of any person who attempts seriously to defend him." At Albany, too, according to Philip Schuyler, the anti-Federalists "stand abashed."[77]

New York's Republicans retained a sentimental attachment for Genêt, however, for years. In welcoming Fauchet, his successor, they paid Genêt tribute. When he and Hauterive needed advice they got it from James Nicholson and perhaps from other Republicans. The Governor was close to his son-in-law and soon adored his new grandson. And for years Republican groups invited Genêt to be their guest of honor at their festivities.[78]

Publicly in reviewing the New York episode of *l'affaire Genêt*, Chancellor Livingston insisted that the attack on the Frenchman was merely an effort "to wound France through the side of her minister," which had been especially designed for New York City as "the center of British and Treasury politics." It had failed, he insisted, and instead "the enemies of France and freedom have been dragged from their hiding places."[79] Privately Livingston knew better. "So far as the Republican interest is connected with those of France," he told

75. George to Cornelia Clinton, Feb. 2, 1794, Genêt Papers, N.Y. Pub. Lib.; Spaulding, *George Clinton*, 210.

76. Cornelia Clinton to Genêt, July 14, 1794, Genêt Papers, Lib. Cong., cited in Woodfin, *Citizen Genêt*, 540-41.

77. Robert Troup to Hamilton, Dec. 25, Schuyler to Hamilton, Dec. 15, 1793, Hamilton Papers, Lib. Cong. Jay to King, Dec. 12, 1793, King Papers, N.-Y. Hist. Soc.

78. *N.-Y. Journal*, Mar. 12, June 18, 1794; James Nicholson to Albert Gallatin, Apr. 14, 1794, Hauterive to Gallatin, Apr. 14, 1793, Gallatin Papers, N.-Y. Hist. Soc.; Woodfin, *Citizen Genêt*, 551.

79. "Cato," No. 1, and No. 5, *N.-Y. Journal*, Dec. 11, 1793, Jan. 5, 1794.

Edward, "so far is it . . . injured by the intemperate warmth of a minister whether he is right or wrong in his principles."[80]

IV

Citizen Genêt aside, the French Revolution was stirring up libertarian and equalitarian currents in New York, especially among young people. In the spring commencement orations at Columbia College, almost all the graduates took up liberal themes: "the inhumanity of the slave trade," "the impropriety of capital punishments," and "the dignity of man."[81] A stripling student like Daniel Tompkins, a future governor, filled his essay book with similar sentiments.[82] Another, George Clinton, Jr., the Governor's nephew, declared "if France should be not successful, he will go crazy—his heart is rapt in the cause of liberty."[83] Among young women, there were others like Cornelia Clinton. In November 1793, Hannah Nicholson married Albert Gallatin, the Swiss-born Republican senator-elect from western Pennsylvania. Gallatin pronounced the Commodore's younger daughter, a friend of Thomas Paine, "a tolerable democrat and at the same time a moderate one."[84] A political criterion in matchmaking was in vogue. At Albany, "A Fair Correspondent" suggested that Republican bachelors wear French and American cockades to enable the fair sex "to distinguish between *Friends* and *Enemies* of the RIGHTS OF MAN."[85]

The "literati" of the city had a more restrained response. The *New York Magazine*, a journal previously indifferent to liberalism, now published articles by Joseph Priestley, Mary Wollstonecraft, William Godwin, and Thomas Erskine.[86] The gentlemen's literary and discussion clubs took up issues of the Enlightenment. Margaretta Faugeres, a young poetess who usually expressed herself on such prosaic subjects as the "Hudson River," now voiced joy "On Seeing a Print

80. R. R. to Edward Livingston, Nov. 11, 1793, R. R. Livingston Papers, N.-Y. Hist. Soc.

81. *N.-Y. Journal*, May 4, 1793, and Columbia University "Commencements" [Scrapbook Collection of Photostats from New York Newspapers], Columbiana Coll., Columbia Univ.

82. Ray W. Irwin and Edna L. Jacobsen, eds., *A Columbia College Student in the Eighteenth Century. Essays by Daniel D. Tompkins* (N.Y., 1940), *passim*.

83. Cornelia Clinton to Edmund Genêt, Dec. 18, 1793, Genêt Papers, N.-Y. Hist. Soc.

84. Raymond Walters, *Albert Gallatin, Jeffersonian Financier and Diplomat* (N.Y., 1957), 58 and 52-58.

85. *Albany Register*, Mar. 17, 1794.

86. *New York Magazine*, 4 (1793), Jan., June, Aug., *passim*.

Exhibiting the Ruins of the Bastile," while Julia Hatton composed an ode "On the Retaking of Toulon" and an opera on the patriotic Tammany theme.[87]

The French refugees in New York also contributed to the democratic drift. The poor among them became a militant anti-British influence among the city's working classes. "The lowest class of citizens who almost to a man are Frenchmen," Peter R. Livingston reported with exaggeration, rejoiced at French military victories. A young liberal doctor "heard a dram shop full of Frenchmen singing Carmagnole" as he walked through the poor east side section. "The next shop I came upon, some person was singing 'God Bless Great George' etc., which immediately procur'd a parcel of hearty curses upon his majesty from the rest of the company."[88] The middling and better sort among the French refugees, while a mixed bag politically, helped to counteract the British tone of the city by becoming teachers and restaurateurs and entering the service trades.[89] They also contributed to a mild vogue for the French language—even at upstate Lansingburgh the local paper urged the citizenry to patronize the new French language tutor.[90]

There was a heightened sensitivity to the petty symbols of aristocracy. The Common Council obliged a demand to change the names of King, Queens, Princess, and Duke streets, rechristening them Pine, Cedar, Beaver, and Stone. When Republicans met in Belvedere House they dubbed it "Liberty Hall." Edward Livingston had already named the streets of a contemplated frontier town Liberty, Equality, etc.[91] It was about this time, too, that dress, common speech, and everyday habits were subject to similar alterations. Silk stockings, hair powder, pigtails, and shoe buckles began to give way to short hair or small queues and less aristocratic garb. English financial terms were gradual-

87. *The Posthumous Works of Ann E. Bleecker to which Is Added a Collection of Essays by Margaretta Faugeres* (N.Y., 1793), 329-32; Julia Hatton, *The Songs of T-A-M-M-A-N-Y or the Indian Chief. A Serious Opera* (N.Y., 1794).

88. Peter R. to Robert R. Livingston, Jan. 26, 1794, R. R. Livingston Papers, N.-Y. Hist. Soc.; Anderson, Diary, Jan. 9, 1794, Columbia Univ.

89. Frances S. Childs, *French Refugee Life in the United States, 1790-1800: An American Chapter of the French Revolution* (Baltimore, 1940), chs. 2-4, *passim*.

90. *N.-Y. Journal*, July 20, 1793; Lansingburgh *Tiffany's Recorder*, May 27, 1794.

91. *N.Y. American Minerva*, Dec. 30, 1793, Feb. 11, Apr. 19, 1794; Arthur Everett Peterson, ed., *Minutes of the Common Council of the City of New York, 1794-1831,* 21 vols. (N.Y., 1917), II, 73-74 (Apr. 21, 1794); *N.-Y. Journal*, July 10, 1793; for Livingston's street names Francis P. Kimball, *The Capital Region of New York State, Crossroads of Empire*, 3 vols. (N.Y., 1942), I, 451-52; for another land promoter's egalitarian names see "Map of Tivoli," DePeyster Coll., F.D.R. Lib.

ly replaced. "I would not give a penny for it" was the genteel way of putting it; "I would not give a cent for it" was the plebeian counterpart.[92]

It was now common for displays either of anti-French or "aristocratic" sentiment to stir up a hornet's nest. At the performance of a play "the pit took offense at those parts in which the French are held up to ridicule" and made the manager alter the lines.[93] When a fire damaged Albany and a few New York merchants suggested that the state legislature levy a tax on New York City residents to provide relief for the Albany victims, there was a howl. What right did "the Lords of the Tontine Coffee House" and a few "merchants, speculators, land and stock jobbers" have to speak for the city?[94] Federalists in the assembly confirmed the equalitarian state of opinion when they attempted to eliminate the long ceremonial title of the Governor, "Commander in Chief of the Militia and Admiral of the Navy." Lengthy titles, they explained, were "inconsistent with the plainness and real dignity of Republican manners."[95]

Things had reached the point, at least in New York City, where political opinions became a criterion for social relations. "Go into the private families and dinner and evening visits," wrote Noah Webster, the Federalist editor, and "there you will find none but people of the same party." "I am to sup with a set of Jacobins," the merchant Herman LeRoy wrote Senator King, "and I would also as leave be whipped as go."[96]

By the end of 1793 the French Revolution, broadly conceived, had an unmistakable economic and political impact on New York. The export trade to the French West Indies, which totaled $7,000,000 for the country as a whole, second only to the $8,400,000 trade to Britain and her dependencies, was heavy with grains and salt meats shipped by the merchants of the middle states. Imports from the West Indies also mounted. As a result, while there was not a distinct "French interest" in New York City comparable to the "British interest"—the same men often imported from Britain and exported to the French

92. Parton, *Life of Aaron Burr*, I, 222-23.

93. Duer, *Reminiscences*, 91; "Harlequin," *N.-Y. Journal*, Feb. 23, 1793.

94. *N.-Y. Journal*, Nov. 27, "Rights," Nov. 30, "A Hint," Nov. 30, and "Columbia," Dec. 21, 1793.

95. *Journal of the Assembly of N.Y.*, 17th Sess., 12-14.

96. N.Y. *American Minerva*, Dec. 21, 1793, cited in Bowers, *Jefferson and Hamilton*, 232; Herman LeRoy to Rufus King, Feb. 23, 1794, King Papers, N.-Y. Hist. Soc.

islands—there was a sizable body of merchants who would react with alarm if the British threatened to destroy their lucrative new trade.

Politically, the events of 1793 had a mixed effect on "the republican interest." The New York Republicans emerged as a radical wing of the national party on foreign policy: they fit Jefferson's description of "the furious republicans" who embraced Genêt after his warning to abandon him as "a sinking wreck." Chancellor Livingston himself recognized the disadvantage of the party's being wedded to the intemperate Frenchman. On the other hand, if it was not quite true of New York, as Jefferson said of the country as a whole, that "all the old spirit of 1776 is rekindling,"[97] a fire had indeed been lit which British policy and Federalist policy would build higher.

97. Jefferson to James Monroe, May 5, 1793, Ford, ed., *Writings of Jefferson*, VI, 238-39.

CHAPTER 17

"The Spirit of 1776" in Action:

The Crusade Against Britain

January-May 1794

Just when Genêt's extremism led the New York Republicans up a blind alley, the British ministry provoked a crisis that enabled them to whip a patriotic wave of Anglophobia to a frenzy and put Federalists on the defensive. In the spring of 1794 Republicans seized the political initiative both in Congress and New York, the Livingstons emerged as leaders of a popular cause, and the Democratic societies were born and baptized in political fire.

I

The crisis unfolded in stages between January and April 1794, as the news arrived of successive British actions on the seas and on the frontier, affecting a variety of New York interests. To prevent the French from profiting from neutral shipping the British in a series of Orders in Council defined contraband to include food and asserted the right to take enemy-owned contraband from neutral ships. The result was virtually to ban American trade with the French West Indies. In January the city heard of the seizure of some 150 American ships late in 1793.[1] New York-owned ships were seized, a small num-

1. Bemis, *Jay's Treaty*, 215 and in general, chs. 7 and 8; for another general account, DeConde, *Entangling Alliance*, ch. 3.

ber in the first wave, a larger number in the second, news of which did not reach the city until March 1794.² But even without all the reports in it was clear by January to one city merchant that "trade, at least navigation [was] deranged," and the prospect of further shipping to the French West Indies destroyed.³

On the frontier, British activities affected New York more directly than any other state. Five of the eight forts on American soil which the British had occupied since 1783 were on New York land, bordering Lakes Champlain, Erie, and Ontario. Early in 1794 news arrived of incidents in the vicinity of the forts, along with vague rumors of British activities stirring up the Indians. As a result of Britain's holding the forts, Governor Clinton told the legislature in January, "our settlements are greatly impeded, our agriculture obstructed, and our citizens entirely excluded from a very valuable trade to which their situation would naturally have invited them." The forts were also known as a center for British influence among New York State Indians.⁴ Settlers were anxious to be rid of this menace, promoters wanted to remove a deterrent to migration that kept land values down,⁵ and Albany merchants had visions of recovering the once lucrative fur trade, unrealistic as they may have been.⁶

In reality the British ministry in London had abandoned its long-cherished plan for an Indian barrier state in the northwest and was preparing to surrender the forts. But on the scene in Canada Lieutenant-Governor John Graves Simcoe, who supervised British operations from his headquarters at Fort Niagara, harbored thoughts of a preventive war with the United States. He was already infamous to New Yorkers both for his military activities within the state during the Revolution and his subsequent intrigues with Vermont separatists.⁷

Fears for the frontier were heightened by a scheme to form a separate state out of western New York instigated by some of the

2. See the discussion of evidence below at footnotes 33-38.
3. Samuel Ward to William Constable, Jan. 19, 1794, Constable Pierrepont Papers, N.Y. Pub. Lib.
4. Lincoln, ed., *Messages from the Governors*, II, 333-34. See 1796 map, p. 595.
5. See n.17.
6. See "Cato" [Robert Livingston] No. 2, *N.-Y. Journal*, Dec. 18, 1794; William Strickland, Journal, Oct. 21, 1794, N.-Y. Hist. Soc.; Belknap, *Journal of a Tour*, 30.
7. Bemis, *Jay's Treaty*, 168-75, 229-33, 237-44; A. L. Burt, *The United States, Great Britain and British North America from the Revolution to the Establishment of Peace After the War of 1812* (New Haven, 1940), 115-32.

disgruntled speculators of the New York Genesee Land Company.[8] Their apparent aim was to annul the Phelps-Gorham land title by inducing Ontario, Otsego, Tioga, and Herkimer counties to secede, a plan which would have detached all of New York south of the Mohawk River and west of the Susquehanna River valley. To secure support the separatists made utopian promises to pioneers late in 1793 of freedom from taxation, cancellation of mortgage debt, and, apparently, of land distribution. The legal land magnates of Ontario and the local officials—virtually one and the same—organized anti-secession activity, branding the separatists as "turbulent characters" and outsiders from Vermont, and claimed that they had been "crushed."[9] As late as February 1794, however, there was still "great talk" of the scheme in the state legislature. "I almost think it will take," one man reported.[10] Although there does not seem to be evidence that the British were involved, there was no telling what might happen if war broke out.

In New York and other cities along the Hudson the "manufacturing interest" was ripe for action against Britain for still other reasons. By 1794 the protection of Federalist tariff laws was wearing thin. Once again craftsmen, including manufacturers of hats, nails, and hand-bellows at New York City, dispatched petitions to Congress requesting protection.[11] In this they had the support of opinion in the Mechanics Society, Tammany, and the new Democratic Society.[12]

The initial response of the top Republicans in Philadelphia and New York to this crisis was relatively mild. At Philadelphia, James Madison revived the proposals for discriminatory tonnage duties and restrictions on British trade that Federalists had squelched in 1789. His "commercial resolutions," he claimed in speeches reprinted for New Yorkers, would force Britain to mend her ways, break the British monopoly of the import trade, and encourage American manufactures

8. Julian P. Boyd, "Attempts to Form New States in New York and Pennsylvania in 1786-1796," N.Y. State Hist. Assoc. Qtly. Jour., 12 (1931), 257-70, and Cowan, Charles Williamson, 180-81.

9. "Proceedings of a Meeting at Canandaigua, Nov. 8, 1793," [anti-secession], Oliver Phelps Papers, N.Y. State Lib. and in O'Reilly Coll., IX, N.-Y. Hist. Soc.; Thomas Morris to Stephen Van Rensselaer, Nov. 13, 1793, No. 1951, N.Y. State Lib.

10. Michael Connolly to Peter Van Gaasbeck, Feb. 14, 1794, Van Gaasbeck Papers, F.D.R. Lib.

11. Annals, 3d Cong., 1st Sess., 417, 458, 478-79. There were also petitions from craft groups in other cities. For demands for protection from New York in 1792 see Annals, 2d Cong., 1st Sess., 25, 30, 401.

12. July 1, 1795, Minutes of the General Society of Mechanics and Tradesmen (typescript) at the Society's office, N.Y.C.; N.-Y. Journal, Nov. 14, 1794; N.Y. Argus, Nov. 10, 12, 27, 1795.

and ship building.[13] In New York, Governor Clinton proposed a state program of military defense: arms and equipment for the militia and fortifications for both the frontier and port of New York. He was aware that some believed that military protection "is more immediately within the province of the general government." But, he said, he would be derelict in his duty if he did not remind the legislators of "the naked and exposed conditions of our principal seaport" and of "certain complaints" from harassed landholders on the frontier.[14]

These Republican proposals anticipated commercial warfare against Britain and the possibility of a shooting war, both of which were anathema to New York's Federalists. First, the trade of New York City merchants, despite its diversification, was still overwhelmingly with Britain, and a "British interest" was very much a reality. Secondly, Federalists knew that either commercial war or armed hostilities could destroy the Hamiltonian financial system. Philip Schuyler's mind ran to this immediately when he warned Senator King that war would result in "ruin [to] the funding system and a prostration of American credit."[15] Talleyrand spelled out the reasoning of Federalists from his vantage point among them: the funded debt depended on tax revenues, "four fifths of these taxes come from the proceeds of the customs, these customs depend on external commerce on importation and exportation, commerce depends upon peace, and every war with a maritime power of Europe would derange this chain." The Bank of the United States, whose stock was based on the funded debt, would also be upset.[16] Thirdly, Federalist land speculators and land promoters faced disaster because "in the event of war land will fall much for a time," as Samuel Ward, a part-owner of the St. Lawrence Ten Towns tract, informed Constable in London.[17] William Cooper could not have been more blunt in his plea to Senator King: "I feel particularly interested in preserving our neutrality as on that my whole

13. James Madison, *Speech in the House of Representatives . . . January 14, 1794 In Support of His Propositions for the Promotion of the Commerce of the United States . . .* (N.Y., 1794); Brant, *James Madison,* II, 389-93; Malone, *Jefferson and His Time,* III, 155-60.

14. Lincoln, ed., *Messages from the Governors,* II, 333-34.

15. Schuyler to King, Mar. 2, 1794, King Papers, N.-Y. Hist. Soc.

16. Talleyrand, "Observations on Speculation in Land in the United States of America" in Huth and Pugh, trans. and ed., *Talleyrand in America,* III, 151.

17. Seth Johnson to Andrew Craigie, Mar. 3, 1794, Craigie Papers, Box 9, Amer. Antiq. Soc.; Thomas Tredwell to Richard Varick, Mar. 1, 1795, MS 6508, N.Y. State Lib.; Samuel Ward to William Constable, Mar. 3, 1794, Constable Pierrepont Papers, N.Y. Pub. Lib.

fortune which I have obtained by the dint of industry depends." War, wrote the magnate of Otsego, "would at once destroy the countys of Otsego, Herkimer, Onondaga, Tioga and Clinton."[18]

While all Federalists shared a desire to avoid war, they split as to tactics. One group believed that "something must be done," as ex-Congressman Laurance of New York City confided to King; "England has acted a very pitiful part towards us." This group included a segment of the merchants in the city and especially the Federalist interest at Albany. Philip Schuyler already maintained that the port of New York should be fortified; he was not yet convinced there was any menace on the frontier.[19] Another group, which included city merchants with British connections, followed the lead of Assemblyman James Watson, a wealthy merchant who was speaker of the assembly. They were procrastinators, reluctant to endorse any action that would lend credence to the Republican campaign against Britain. Clinton offered his defense proposals the first week of January; a month went by before debate began. In March Clinton complained to Mayor Richard Varick of New York of the "very learned debates" on the constitutional niceties of state versus federal jurisdiction in building fortifications. Even his proposal to equip the militia moldered in committee.[20]

In Congress too the New York Federalists were negative, putting themselves firmly against Madison's proposals for commercial discrimination. Ezekiel Gilbert condemned those who looked at Britain "as a wolf and lion." There was a "general prosperity," he said; commerce and agriculture should be left to "regulate themselves." When the first test came early in February on a Republican motion to postpone debate in order to "learn the sense of their constituents," New York's three Republicans voted for it, the seven Federalists against it.[21] The postponement carried nonetheless and was precisely what Republicans needed. Before debate would resume in mid-March there would be time to kindle the fires of patriotism against the ancient foe.

18. William Cooper to King, Apr. 17, 1794, King Papers, N.-Y. Hist. Soc.

19. John Laurance to King, Jan. 12, Schuyler to King, Jan. 31, Robert Troup to King, Feb. 4, 1794, *ibid.*

20. Clinton to Richard Varick, Mar. 8, 1794, Clinton MSS, N.Y. State Lib.; see James Watson to King, Jan. 20, Feb. [?], 1794, King Papers, N.-Y. Hist. Soc.; Hammond, *Political Parties*, I, 78-82.

21. *Annals*, 3d Cong., 1st Sess., 323-24, 431-32.

II

The Livingstons took a stand on the crisis to the left of Madison and Jefferson, just as they had on the Genêt issue, and asserted their leadership among the New York Republicans more strongly than they had on any previous issue. Foreign policy was, after all, the "province" of Robert R. Livingston, the first Secretary for Foreign Affairs.

The Chancellor confided to Madison his dissatisfaction with the concept of neutral rights that Jefferson had broached in his final reports as Secretary of State late in 1793. Based on classical sources and not "the modern law of nations," it was "totally indefensible." Livingston also told Senator James Monroe of his dissatisfaction with Madison's proposals for commercial retaliation. At first he favored them, but as the crisis deepened, he believed they were not bold enough. "I have laid it down long since," he wrote Monroe, explaining his alternate strategy, "that if war was to be avoided at all it would be by pursuing measures that would convince the world that you neither dreaded nor was unprepared for the event and that in every case it would be important to strike the first blow which often decided the fate of nations."[22] In Monroe, whose enthusiasm for Genêt and whose radical solutions to the immediate crisis set him a shade apart from his fellow Virginians, the Chancellor found an ally.

In a series of articles Livingston led New Yorkers to the conclusion that war with Britain was unavoidable and desirable.[23] In his opening piece in December 1793, he coaxed his readers out of the prevailing anti-Genêt mood by contrasting French conduct with a long catalog of heinous British abuses since 1783. After a scholarly analysis of the laws and precedents of neutral rights (his answer to Jefferson), he launched an assault on the "suppineness" and "Christian meekness" of Federalists to Britain, attributing this to the influence of "tories and foreign emissaries" and a "new phalanx" of "British merchants and American loyalists."

22. Robert R. Livingston to James Monroe, Jan. 4, Mar. 13, Apr. 8, 1794, Monroe Papers, II, Lib. Cong., the drafts of which are in Bancroft Transcripts, N.Y. Pub. Lib., and R. R. Livingston Papers, N.-Y. Hist. Soc.; Livingston to James Martin [Madison?], Jan. 21, 1794, R. R. Livingston Papers, N.-Y. Hist. Soc.; Dangerfield, *Chancellor Robert R. Livingston*, 266-69; for Jefferson's position, which Livingston did not interpret accurately, see "Opinion on Neutral Trade, Dec. 20, 1793," in Ford, ed., *Writings of Jefferson*, VI, 485-88 and Bemis, *Jay's Treaty*, 185, 192.

23. "Cato," *N.-Y. Journal*, Dec. 11, 18, 28, 1793, Jan. 8, 18, 29, Feb. 1, 15, 1794. The MS drafts of two of these articles in R. R. Livingston Papers, N.-Y. Hist. Soc., are in Livingston's hand; misfiled with another Livingston series as "Cato" against Jay's Treaty in 1795.

By his seventh piece Livingston was considering "the advantages and disadvantages" of war. He mocked the "timid language" of the "tories" against any anti-British measures: "Our cities are unfortified —Our funds will be shaken—The Indians are upon our backs etc. etc. etc." It was not possible for Britain to send an army to America, he insisted; her navy was weakened and American ports could be protected. As to the claim that trade would be ruined, what was the sense of crying "peace, peace, peace, where no peace is." In his eighth article Livingston listed half a dozen reasons why "the present moment . . . is the most favorable for commencing a war" with Britain. Her navy was fully employed; she could not defend Canada and the western forts; a war would strengthen France and secure French aid once it was over; a stoppage of American imports would open the eyes of British manufacturers to American power. Unlike her condition before the Revolution, America now had everything necessary for military success—a stable government, arms, manufactures, and unity.

In his final article, February 15, Livingston rejected proposals current in Congress for merely "annoying the enemy." Building frigates was the program of "the ministerial party"; they would not be ready in time to do any good anyway. An embargo was bad because it would halt revenue and disrupt payments on the national debt. His own proposal was to grant letters of marque to American vessels and seize English ships in reprisal for American losses. War would follow. But "can anything be more dreadful than the ignominious situation in which we now are?"—trade devastated, the supply of seamen diminished by impressments, the back settlements soon to be broken up. "If we wish for peace," he concluded, "let us begin by war . . . it is the easiest and the only way to obtain it."

The Republican crescendo rose with the Chancellor. The Clintons clearly shared his views. DeWitt Clinton helped to place his articles in the papers. He and his brother, George Clinton, Jr., helped to draft resolutions for the new Republican Society of Ulster arguing that British ship seizures "call loudly" for action. In the newspapers, "A Native of Columbia" wrote that if the American demand to restore the forts "is not immediately complied with," then "let us take them by force." "A Dutchess County Militiaman" asked that the militia be put in a state of readiness. Others came forward with plans to fortify New York's harbor. In New York City the Mechanics So-

ciety was a shade more sober, toasting preparations for war only for
self-defense.[24]

In February the Democratic Society of New York City made its
public appearance, essentially a response to the foreign policy crisis.
By the end of the month Republicans turned to the device of a "Town
Meeting" to organize public protest. They placed a notice in Greenleaf's paper calling for a meeting at noon the following day to pass
resolutions "instructive to our representatives in Congress respecting
the insults, embarassments and injuries offered to the commerce of our
country by Britain and her savage allies." Nine-tenths of the "persons
who supported and hatched" the meeting, according to a Federalist,
were "the very men who met in the fields and agreed to address Mr.
Genêt" in 1793 and were "members of the Democratic Society."[25]

Scheduled for a room at Tontine's, the meeting had to be adjourned
to the assembly chamber at Federal Hall and ended up out of doors.
Greenleaf claimed an audience of 1500; Federalists said it was closer
to 500; in any case more showed up than for Genêt and most of them
were mechanics. "Where was the mercantile interest?" one Federalist
mocked. "None of the merchants attended," Senator King was reassured.[26] The Livingstons were major speakers and the tone of the
meeting, as much as can be made out from fragmentary reports, was
inflammatory. Peter R. Livingston charged there was a deficiency of
millions in the treasury as a result of the Indian wars instigated by
the British. White Matlack argued that "payment of British debts
ought immediately be suspended and the Western posts taken possession of by force." After Edward Livingston and James Nicholson
spoke, "a discussion took place."

A committee of twenty was named to draw up resolutions, publish
them, and submit them to a second meeting a week later. In that way
the people "might then be able to criticize, approve, or reject them."
Half the committee was made of well-known Republicans, others were
newcomers, like Dr. Samuel L. Mitchill of the Columbia faculty and
General Horatio Gates. Of the ten or so merchants on the committee,
one, Isaac Clason, had had his ship seized. Five men, Federalists

24. DeWitt Clinton to R. R. Livingston, Jan. 10, 1794, R. R. Livingston Papers,
N.-Y. Hist. Soc.; *N.-Y. Journal*, Jan. 15, 18, Feb. 15, 19, 26, 1794.

25. *N.-Y. Journal*, Feb. 17, Mar. 1, 1794; N.Y. *Daily Gazette*, Mar. 4, 1794.

26. Herman LeRoy to King, Feb. 28, 1794, King Papers, N.-Y. Hist. Soc.; for a
Republican account, *N.-Y. Journal*, Mar. 1, 1794; for Federalist accounts, in N.Y.
American Minerva: "Cassius," Mar. 1, "A.B.," Mar. 3, 1794.

charged, had been put on the committee without their permission "for colouring," among them Colonel William Smith and Nicholas Cruger, Hamilton's old patron. In Cruger's case Republicans may have been counting on the fact that he had not yet learned of the fate of one of his ships in the West Indies trade; among those named, however, he alone refused to serve.[27]

Despite vituperative abuse, the second meeting at Federal Hall—a "Town Meeting" it was called—drew 2000 citizens "on a moderate estimate," according to the *Diary*. But Republicans paid a price for taking men into their Resolutions Committee "for colouring." The resolutions, a Federalist rejoiced, were "different from the set expected and were produced by some moderate men attached to the general government." Edward Livingston agreed. "Our resolutions (contrary to my opinion) said nothing." Cleverly they straddled the key issue, defending both the right to remain neutral and the principle of fulfilling treaty obligations. The criticism of British depredations was softened by condemning captures by both belligerents. The resolutions also praised the federal government for attempting to secure redress for commercial losses and criticized it for delaying action. Britain was condemned for keeping the forts but only one specific demand was made, to fortify the coastal ports. Not a word of support for Madison's commercial resolutions, much less Chancellor Livingston's more bellicose proposals.[28]

Undaunted by this setback, Republicans continued their effort to rally opinion in the city. When the news arrived of the French recapture of Toulon, the city's church bells were rung, and Greenleaf, running the story under the heading "Extraordinary," appealed to "all true Republicans" to celebrate the event. Two days later there was a parade organized by the Democratic Society. At ten in the morning, the militia and a group of "citizens" proceeded to the house of the French consul where they were joined by French officers and residents "who each of them took an American Brother by the arm." At twelve,

27. "A.B.," N.Y. *American Minerva*, Mar. 3, 1794; *N.-Y. Journal*, Mar. 8, 1794. Of other members, James Alner and Thomas Nixon became members of the Republican election committee for governor in 1795; see *N.-Y. Journal*, Mar. 11, 1795; Isaac Clason and Thomas Farmer were members of the election committee in 1801; see N.Y. *Republican Watch-Tower*, Mar. 4, 1801.

28. N.Y. *Diary; or Evening Register*, Mar. 4, 5, 6, 1794; *N.-Y. Journal*, Mar. 8, 1794; John Laurance to King, Mar. 8, Nicholas Low to King, Mar. 7, 1794, King Papers, N.-Y. Hist. Soc.; Edward Livingston to DeWitt Clinton, Mar. 13, 1794, Clinton Papers, No. 25, Columbia Univ.

when the city halted work for the noonday meal, the parade began. The marchers, numbering about eight hundred, stretched out three-quarters of a mile and the streets "were lined with republicans." At the "collation" at Corré's Hotel the toasts expressed what the committee resolutions two days before had failed to. Success to the French armies and fleet—nine cheers. The destruction of "the venal and corrupt" government of Britain—nine cheers. The alliance of France and the United States, the Governor of New York, and Citizen Genêt—six cheers each. The recapture of Toulon—thirteen cheers! In the evening at Tontine's, Republicans and Frenchmen sang the Marseillaise and danced the Carmagnole.[29]

In the Hudson Valley there were signs of similar enthusiasm. In Ulster on the west bank and in Columbia on the east Democratic societies appeared. In Westchester a group of Republicans tried to put up a liberty cap at the tavern of "a staunch Tory." When he refused they returned, threatening him with "a sweet coat of tar and feathers"; only when he secured peace warrants did they abandon their plan.[30] At Albany, church bells pealed at the news of Toulon's recapture and the artillery company paraded, as the Republican *Register* gloried in the victory of "The Liberty Boys of France."[31] The patriotic fires were burning.

III

In the second week of March the news arrived that the British had seized another hundred American ships in the West Indies. It was "a terrible slam," especially in New England, Madison wrote.[32] By the end of July 1794, a total of 307 American ships had been taken by the British.[33] Of these, about 25 to 30 were

29. Anderson, Diary, Mar. 10, 1794, Columbia Univ.; *N.-Y. Journal*, Mar. 12, 15, 1794.

30. Gerard Beekman to Philip Van Cortlandt, Feb. 11, 1794, Van Cortlandt Papers, N.Y. Pub. Lib.

31. John Glen to Henry Glen, Mar. 16, 1794, Glen Papers, N.Y. State Hist. Assoc.; *Albany Register*, Mar. 17, 1794.

32. Madison to Jefferson, May 12, 1794, cited in Brant, *James Madison*, III, 394.

33. See "A List of the American Vessels, taken by British Crusiers . . ." issued by the Department of State, July 31, 1794, published in *Philadelphia Gazette*, Sept. 1, 1794. I have examined the copy enclosed by the British minister George Hammond in a dispatch to Lord Grenville, Sept. 5, 1794, in P.R.O., 5/5, 280-81. The list unfortunately contains only the name of the vessel seized, the name of the master and "Names of Owners, or parties interested," without identifying the city of ownership.

owned by New Yorkers, perhaps more. About a dozen were taken in the summer and fall of 1793, another dozen in December and the early months of 1794, the news trickling into the city in fits and starts. Three ships out of the port of Hudson and two owned by Long Islanders were also taken.[34] The number of New York City seizures, however, seems to have been considerably less than the total in other leading American ports and a minority share of the almost 72,000 tons of "registered tonnage" engaged in foreign trade sailing out of New York in 1794.[35] The proportion is of some importance in understanding the relatively restrained reaction to the crisis in the mercantile community. The Chamber of Commerce sat on its hands through the fall and winter. And through the spring of 1794 Rufus King's correspondents who kept the Senator posted on city news never made much of losses to the city's merchants.[36]

The captures of course hit home, no matter how few men were

34. My analysis is based on Jay Treaty Records, Record Group 76, National Archives, Washington, D.C., as follows: (1) Records of the Claims Commission under Article VII: List of Claims . . . Received from Mr. Samuel Bayard on May 18, 1797, by Rufus King; (2) List of 341 Cases In Which The Parties Have Not Appeared to Prosecute Their Claim. These lists report the name of the vessel, master, owner, city, date of seizure for most but not all vessels, and the disposition of the case. The list does not include all the vessels in the Department of State list referred to in n.33; I assume, therefore, that some owners recovered their ships or for one reason or another did not file claims. It is extremely difficult to track down residents of any one city on the Department of State list not only because the residence of the owners is not given but because the names listed for identifiable vessels do no correspond to the names of owners later making claims. Because it was a common practice for many merchants to invest in a particular voyage we can also assume that more men were interested than the owners listed. On the claims list I found 71 claims filed by New Yorkers. Nine are completely undated (but within the period 1793-96). The known dates of capture are as follows: 1793, 17 (3 undated, 11 before Oct., 3 in Dec.); 1794, 17 (9 before Apr., 8 after); 1795, 27 (17 in June or later, 10 undated, but all listed as seized under a British Order in Council of May 1795); and 1796, 1.

35. Based on an impression of the Records of the Claims Commission under Article VII, a MS record worthy of further analysis, and newspaper reports. Philadelphia *General Advertiser*, Apr. 30, 1794, carried a list of about 40 vessels condemned at Martinique with no New York owners; N.Y. *Diary*, Mar. 24, 27, 1794, reported only 3 out of 24 ships taken to St. Kitts and 2 out of 60 taken to Santo Domingo to be owned by New Yorkers. For tonnage see Pomerantz, *New York An American City*, 159.

36. See John Laurance, Robert Troup, John Alsop, Herman LeRoy, and Nicholas Low to King, Jan.-May, 1794, *passim.*, Rufus King Papers, N.-Y. Hist. Soc. The worst report is by Alsop, an insurance broker, Apr. 27: "I have already paid out two losses on vessels captured." See also the letters from Daniel McCormick, Alexander McComb, and Samuel Ward to William Constable, Mar.-Apr., 1794, *passim.*, Constable Pierrepont Papers, N.Y. Pub. Lib., which do not enumerate losses.

affected. They hit such bulwarks of the mercantile community as the Quakers Robert Bowne and the Murray family, the latter very hard. They touched John R. Livingston, David Gelston, and Henry Allmand of Suffolk whose vessel was named *Jefferson*, all already predisposed to Republicanism. But of necessity they affected a much larger number of Federalists from Henry Hocking, who called his ship *Jay*, to the patriarch Nicholas Cruger and the parvenu William Constable.[37] It was possible for the editor of the *Diary*, a moderate mercantile sort of paper, to claim that "all American property" was now "exposed to inevitable seizure and confiscation." Ships were not only being taken but some were being condemned falsely and some were allowed to rot away—Cruger's *Eliza* was one of four vessels tied up for six months in a West Indies port, "their bottoms eat out with worms." Moreover American seamen were being impressed or brutally treated in West Indies prisons. "That accursed nation," the loyal Federalist merchant Seth Johnson said of England.[38]

Republican leaders were now "clear for war," as a Federalist reported of the Livingstons. "I think we should have nothing to fear but everything to hope from a war," the Chancellor goaded Monroe. He was for "doing something decisive" like suspending all debts to the British or capturing the western forts. Edward Livingston was overjoyed: we soon "shall be in a state we ought to have been six months ago—at war with Britain." John Livingston of the upper manor was for war and profits, "buying up all the Salt he can lay his hands on" in a speculation.[39]

The patriot Federalists now moved quickly to escape from their predicament. Hamilton, Jay, Schuyler, and King all favored putting the country in what Hamilton called "a respectable military posture," which meant fortifying ports, expanding the army, and passing a temporary embargo on all exports. At the same time they launched

37. A few of these men are listed on the State Department list in n.33 as having lost vessels before July 31, 1794, but appear on the Claims Records cited in n.34 for losses at later dates.

38. N.-Y. *Diary*, Mar. 15, 24, 1794; for a vivid summary of British actions see John B. McMaster, *A History of the People of the United States . . .* , 8 vols. (N.Y., 1883-1913), II, 166-70; Seth Johnson to Andrew Craigie, Mar. 14, 1794, Craigie Papers, III, No. 68, Amer. Antiq. Soc.

39. Herman LeRoy to King, Mar. 19, 1794, King Papers, N.-Y. Hist. Soc.; R. R. Livingston to James Monroe, Mar. 10, Apr. 8, 1794, R. R. Livingston Papers, N.-Y. Hist. Soc.; Edward Livingston to DeWitt Clinton, Mar. 13, 1794, Clinton Papers, No. 25, Columbia Univ.

maneuvers to send a mission to England to negotiate a settlement.[40] In Congress when the first test came on a Federalist proposal to build six frigates, the New York delegation divided along usual lines, seven Federalists pro to three Republicans con. But ten days later when a bill to fortify the ports came to a vote, the ten New Yorkers were unanimously for it. [41]

At the same time in the state legislature sitting at Albany since January, Federalists continued to drag their feet. James Watson, the speaker, still opposed state construction of a fort for the city "upon constitutional grounds," while his fellow New York City assembly-man, William Willcocks, still believed that the country was "not in imminent danger."[42] There was also opposition to a fort from "rural members,"[43] who presumably balked at the expense involved. As the legislature approached adjournment, it had passed a sum of $75,000 for the militia, but it had failed to make appropriations for forts for the city or frontier or for sorely needed artillery. This delay at Albany and the Federalist proposal at Philadelphia to enlarge the standing army were precisely what Republicans needed. "All the good that can be selected from so much evil," Edward Livingston told DeWitt Clinton, "will be very carefully done by the good republicans here." He was even convinced that "the English party is apparently annihilated here."[44] Republicans fixed on the goal of pressuring the state legislature to supplement Congress' inadequate appropriation for a fort for the New York harbor. A notice in the *Journal* calling patriots to gather in front of Tontine's produced an audience smaller than the first two meetings. A committee of five was appointed to prepare a petition but this time Republicans took no chances: General James Alner was chairman and the members were Chancellor Livingston, Edward Livingston, John Broome, president of the Chamber of Commerce, and only one Federalist, Richard Harison. After circulating a petition that evening for signatures, they sent it off to Albany at noon the following day by express. Harison refused to sign; perhaps he

40. Hamilton to Washington, Mar. 8, 1794, Lodge, ed., *Works of Hamilton*, VIII, 316-18; Mitchell, *Alexander Hamilton*, II, 331-37.

41. *Annals*, 3d Cong., 1st Sess., 497-98; Schachner, *Founding Fathers*, 299-305.

42. Watson to King, Mar. 15, Willcocks to King, Mar. 16, Watson to King, Mar. 22, 1794, King Papers, N.-Y. Hist. Soc.

43. A remark by Jonathan Havens, *Annals*, 4th Cong., 2d Sess., 1370.

44. Edward Livingston to DeWitt Clinton, Mar. 13, 1794, Clinton Papers, No. 25, Columbia Univ.

knew that an appointment to a federal judgeship was less than a month away.[45]

When the petition reached Albany three days later, it was superfluous. Governor Clinton had already laid before the legislature the news that Lord Dorchester had virtually incited delegates from the Indian tribes of the Northwest Territory to war against the United States.[46] The news sent a tremor of alarm through all parts of the state. An upstate Federalist was convinced that the posts "will be taken by our western citizens if in this session of Congress something effectually is not done."[47] Republicans at Albany circulated 500 copies of an article, "The Ghost of Montgomery," by Elkanah Watson, warning Dorchester that an attack would not only find New Yorkers ready but would lead to the liberation of Canada and "a speedy downfall of the British throne."[48] In Westchester a schoolmaster fervently pleaded with his listeners to "join heart and hand with France." In New York City, Tammany horrified Federalists by exhibiting in its museum a guillotine with a beheaded wax figure kneeling before its blade—useful to take care of traitors, a Republican explained, in the event of war.[49] Not surprisingly Federalist opinion in the city also shifted; "those who were very pacific are now differently disposed," Laurance informed King.[50]

In the state legislature Federalists now had no choice. Schuyler, after first dismissing the Indian report as "a fabrication by some land jobbers," changed his mind, raged at "the folly and imprudence" of the British, and pondered the most suitable military strategy against them. Baron Von Steuben, also a Federalist, prepared an "Opinion on a Proper System of defense of the City and Harbour of New York."[51] In the legislature the Federalists managed to pare down an appropria-

45. N.-Y. Journal, Mar. 22, 1794; Richard Harison to Rufus King, Apr. 18, 1794, King Papers, N.-Y. Hist. Soc.

46. Lincoln, ed., Messages from the Governors, II, 346-47; Carroll and Ashworth, George Washington, VII, n.162; Bemis, Jay's Treaty, 239-40.

47. Henry Van Schaack to Theodore Sedgwick, Mar. 20, 23, 1794, cited in Joseph Charles, Origins of the American Party System; Three Essays (Williamsburg, 1956), 100, n.16. See also Henry Van Ingen to Henry Glen, Mar. 26, 1794, Glen Papers, N.Y. State Hist. Assoc.

48. Albany Register, reprinted in Kingston Rising Sun, Apr. 12, and N.-Y. Journal, Apr. 16, 1794; see Elkanah Watson, Commonplacebook, Watson Papers, N.Y. State Lib.

49. N.-Y. Journal, "The Ghost of Warner," Apr. 30, "Yankee Doodle," May 7, 1794; N.Y. Columbian Gazetteer, Mar. 27, 1794.

50. John Laurance to King, Mar. 23, 1794, King Papers, N.-Y. Hist. Soc.

51. Schuyler to King, Mar. 23, Steuben to King, Mar. 25, 1794, ibid.

tion for forts for New York City and the frontier from £40,000 to
£30,000, but the final appropriation was passed with all but five members of the assembly voting for it.[52] In Philadelphia the pattern was
similar. A thirty-day embargo at first was defeated by a narrow margin
in the House, then passed easily. It also got through the Senate, where
Aaron Burr was active on its behalf.[53] At the same time Federalist
leaders redoubled their efforts to get an envoy to Britain named,[54]
with Hamilton pumping for John Jay, who alone among the New York
Federalists commanded a reputation which could placate the opposition.

These policies rallied the Federalists' nervous mercantile supporters in New York. The Federalist problem in the city was never as
sharp as elsewhere, most likely because the losses to New York shippers
were relatively small. The actions of the Chamber of Commerce suggest only a minor schism among the merchants. The Chamber included a large number of merchants who had been Tory or neutral in
the Revolution, enough to elect a Tory president in 1784, the first year
of peace. But it also included a sizable number of Whigs and a
minority of Clintonians who elected John Broome president in 1785
and kept him there until 1794. The Chamber was slow to react to the
crisis with Britain. In September 1793, in response to a circular letter
from Secretary of State Jefferson, the Chamber appointed a committee
"to receive complaints of vexation and spoliation" with William Neilson, a former Loyalist, as chairman. Six months later the committee
reported that after meeting repeatedly "no 'evidence of spoliation'
hath yet appeared to warrant an application to the government and
but one instance of 'vexation.'" At a meeting in March the Chamber
ordered the report printed.

Apparently, however, there was some dissatisfaction with the report.
The meeting, one merchant informed Senator King, "was not composed of the great sufferers," i.e., shippers with serious losses. Neilson
then announced that his committee would continue to meet regularly
every Tuesday evening at Tontine's to hear complaints from "all persons who have sustained any injuries from any of the beligerent
powers." At the same time the Chamber appointed another committee
headed by Comfort Sands, a Federalist but a Whig of '76, to prepare

52. *Journal of the Assembly of N.Y.*, 17th Sess., 153; *N.-Y. Journal*, Mar. 29, 1794.
53. *Annals*, 3d Cong., 1st Sess., 329-31; Schachner, *Founding Fathers*, 301.
54. Mitchell, *Alexander Hamilton*, II, 331-37.

a resolution expressing their opinion. At its meeting in early April after the crisis had escalated, the Chamber approved Sands' report which recognized that "a general interruption is now experienced" in trade but blunted condemnation of Britain by lumping her seizures with those by Algerian corsairs and the French. The Chamber expressed confidence that Congress would take action "against any and every power whatsoever" that violated American rights.[55]

When Congress adopted the embargo New York City merchants went along with the measure, all, one of them said, "except a few who may be agents of Britain and have other foreign ships at hand." William Neilson protested to Senator King; he had two ships loaded ready to sail; he saw the value of an embargo on trade to the West Indies, but why to Europe?[56] The embargo, distasteful as it may have been, took the wind out of the sails of Madison's scheme for commercial discrimination and all proposals for debt sequestration, not to mention the Chancellor's proposals for war.

For a few weeks merchants hung in suspense. On the confirmation of John Jay as envoy they breathed easier. The news that England had issued new instructions on seizures and that Pitt was friendly to America helped to "soften" their resentment.[57] In May the Chamber of Commerce with apparent unanimity praised Washington enthusiastically for appointing Jay, glorifying peace and negotiations. At the annual election of officers, Federalists tried to remove John Broome as president, running Gulian Verplanck, a Jay-ite, against him. Broome had sinned by joining the Livingstons' committee to protest administration policy. There was a tie vote, 17–17, and at a second election Comfort Sands was chosen, apparently with the support of both factions.[58] Obviously the crisis with Britain had produced dissidence among city merchants. But the losses of New York's merchants were

55. For a very sparse record, Sept. 10, 1793, Mar. 4, 1794, Minutes of the Chamber of Commerce of New York City, Vol. I (photostat), N.Y. Pub. Lib.; N.Y. *Diary*, Mar. 3, Apr. 8, 1794; N.Y. *American Minerva*, Mar. 5, 7, 1794. Phila. *Dunlap and Claypoole's American Daily Advertiser*, Mar. 8, 1794; Herman LeRoy to Rufus King, Mar. 5, 1794, King Papers, N.-Y. Hist. Soc.

56. Peter Elting to Peter Van Gaasbeck, Apr. 17, 1794, Van Gaasbeck Papers, Kingston Senate House; William Neilson to King, Apr. 2, 1794, King Papers, N.-Y. Hist. Soc.

57. See letters to King, Mar. 28-Apr. 30, 1794, from Herman LeRoy, John Alsop, and John Laurance, King Papers, N.-Y. Hist. Soc.

58. Minutes of the Chamber of Commerce, May 6, 1794, N.Y. Pub. Lib. For Jay's appraisal of Verplanck, see Jay to King, May 3, 1794, King Papers, N.-Y. Hist. Soc. For Broome, see Scoville, *The Old Merchants of New York*, 213-15, 232-36.

not great enough to lead to open protest; and even merchants whose ships had been seized recognized that negotiations alone offered hope of restoring their property or indemnifying them for their losses.

IV

If Federalists retained support among merchants, they lost it among mechanics, a fact that was clear in the spring elections for assembly and senate. The elections were held in the last few days of April before the month-old embargo, Jay's mission, or the news of the softening of British policies could counteract the months of feverish Republican agitation. In the city the elections coincided with a patriotic turnout of artisans organized by Republicans to help construct the new fort on Governor's Island authorized by the state. The Commissioners of Fortifications issued a call for "voluntary contributions of labor" by "a fatigue party of citizens." Governor Clinton was chairman, and Ebenezer Stevens, the Genêt-ite merchant, was an active commissioner along with three Federalists. The Democratic Society was the first to issue a call to its members to donate their services; Tammany and most of the craft groups followed suit. Beginning at the end of April, for several weeks "hardly a day passed," Greenleaf reported, without a volunteer party of fifty to one hundred men rowing out to Governor's Island to put in a day's work. On the site a Federalist noted that Governor Clinton was "conspicuous" several days before the polls opened.[59]

In the election campaign the new Democratic societies were active in the city and Ulster County. The Livingstons also campaigned both in the city and the Hudson Valley. The Republican assembly ticket in the city showed an effort to capitalize on events. Two candidates had run before, William Denning, chairman of the resolutions committee delegated by the "Town Meeting" to protest British policy, and John Campbell, vice-president of the Mechanics Society. Four were new: Isaac Stoutenbergh, Peter Livingston, Ebenezer Stevens, and Peter Elting, the last three of whom had also served on the resolutions committee. David Gelston, president of the Democratic Society, again ran for the senate.[60]

Republicans for the first time in a decade were able to pitch their

59. Proceedings of the Commissioners of Fortifications for the City of New York and its Vicinity, N.-Y. Hist. Soc.; N.Y. *Diary*, Apr. 29, 1794; *N.-Y. Journal*, May 3, 10, 1794; Herman LeRoy to King, Apr. 25, 1794, King Papers, N.-Y. Hist. Soc.
60. N.Y. *Daily Advertiser*, Apr. 11, 1794; *N.-Y. Journal*, June 7, 1794.

appeal to patriotism. "Lucius," a well-informed Republican, possibly Melancton Smith, after listing ten prominent city Federalists, claimed that with two exceptions there was "not a single name" among them entitled to be called a Whig. Few in fact were even native Americans. Most Federalists were loyal to the United States, he claimed, only as long as the government was able to pay the interest on their funded certificates. They were composed of "a group of Scotch, English and Irish factors and merchants." Republicans, by contrast, said "Lucius," listing a dozen leaders, were "natives and Whigs" and were supported by "a group of industrious mechanics, continental officers, etc." "Let us have done with these new fangled distinctions of Federalist, Anti-federalist and Republican," he concluded, "and go back to the old and true test of 1776. Was he Whig or Tory then? And what is he now?" In counties like Dutchess, where the anti-Federalist tradition still glowed, Republicans modified this claim, contending that the current struggle between "Republicans" and "Aristocrats" continued the old battles between "anti-Federalist" and "Federalist," as well as "Whig" and "Tory."[61] In strong Federalist counties, they bypassed the battle of 1788.

Republicans also revived the issue of Hamiltonian finance. "The Ghost of Warner" lambasted one foe as "some person who has purchased the certificates of soldiers, or the widows or children of soldiers for perhaps eighteen pence on the pound and have now funded them at twenty shillings on the pound." "Legion" attacked Federalist candidates as "high speculators, great stockholders, devotees to great or little men in office, immoral characters and warm advocates of the funding system—a child of monarchy."[62]

Wherever they could, Republicans played on local grievances, blending them in with the larger issues. In Ulster County they blasted an incumbent Federalist assemblyman for voting against the forts but in favor of "supply bills for the rich" and "granting relief against forfeited estates" to former Tories, and also linked Federalists at Kingston to town trustees who had sold the common lands.[63] At Albany,

61. "Lucius," N.Y. *Diary*, Mar. 8, 1794. "Lucius," I am convinced, was Smith's pseudonym in 1792. For Dutchess themes, see *Poughkeepsie Journal*, Feb. 19, Mar. 5, Mar. 19, and Apr., 1794, *passim*.

62. "Ghost of Warner," *N.-Y. Journal*, Apr. 2, 1794, "Legion," *ibid.*, Apr. 23, 1794.

63. "An Admirer of Truth," and "An Old Whig," Kingston *Rising Sun*, Apr. 26, 1794; "A Commoner" and "A Citizen," *ibid.*, Mar. 1, 1794; James Oliver to Peter Van Gaasbeck, Apr. 10, 1794, Van Gaasbeck Papers, Kingston Senate House; Marius Schoonmaker, *The History of Kingston, New York . . .* (Kingston, 1888), 368-69, 381.

Elkanah Watson made an issue of the failure of the city fathers to keep the streets clean and in good repair. "Wealth and connections," it was said, had forced a plan of private streetcleaning expensive to "the gentle and the poor, the widow and the orphan," indicating that men worth £1500 a year were too influential in city affairs.[64]

Everywhere Republicans believed they were standing at Armageddon. "Never was a more important crisis than the present," wrote Beriah Palmer of Saratoga County. "In all ages and countries," there were men who wanted to "deprive the community of that Natural Berth Right which God and Nature has given us and now is the time if ever there was a time for us to step forward." But they toned down the war theme they had struck earlier. On the eve of the election the Democratic Society of New York filled up two pages of the city newspapers with a reprint of a resolution of the Democratic Society of Chittenden, Vermont, expressing a wish for peace "if it can be maintained on honorable terms."[65]

Republican gains were uneven. Federalists retained control of both assembly and senate but in the two new centers of the Democratic societies, Ulster and New York City, the Republican vote soared.[66] In Ulster, where exertions were "immense on both sides," Republicans picked up an average of 500 more votes than in 1793 and ousted all the Federalist incumbents.[67] In New York, Republican gains exceeded their expectations. Three weeks before, Chancellor Livingston had persuaded Edward not to run again—he had gotten only 200 or so votes the year before. "The mechanics and cartmen," he wrote, were Federalist; "I find no class of people on which you can depend." The Chancellor was wrong. Although the Federalists won, the Republican ticket averaged about 1250 votes, three times the average of 1793, and Peter R. Livingston, their front runner, came within 130 votes of the low man on the Federalist ticket. Republicans ran strongest in the

64. In the *Albany Register*: "City," Feb. 3, "Querest Junior," Apr. 28, "A Freeholder," July 22, "Equality," Jan. 27, 1794. For Elkanah Watson's articles on these issues, see his Commonplacebook, Watson Papers, N.Y. State Lib.

65. Beriah Palmer to Henry Wilson, Mar. 26, 1794, Van Cortlandt Papers, N.Y. Pub. Lib.; N.Y. *Diary*, Supplement, Apr. 26, 1794; *N.-Y. Journal*, Supplement, Apr. 30, 1794.

66. Philip Ten Eyck to John B. Schuyler, June 5, 16, 1794, Schuyler Papers, N.Y. Pub. Lib. Rufus King was re-elected senator by the state legislature, Jan. 27, 1795, by a vote of 35 to 30.

67. John Addison to Peter Van Gaasbeck, May 3, 1794, Van Gaasbeck Papers, Kingston Senate House; Kingston *Farmer's Register*, June 1, 1793; Kingston *Rising Sun*, May 31, 1794.

poor sixth ward. The narrow gap between the two tickets, only three to four hundred votes, presaged an end to an era of easy Federalist victories.[68]

The election results, uneven as they were, stiffened the Republican spine. In May, Chancellor Livingston took delicious pleasure in rejecting Washington's offer to appoint him minister to France. The Federalists, as soon as they had been guaranteed Jay's mission to England, had moved to placate both France and the Republicans by replacing Gouverneur Morris with a Republican as minister to France. Republicans in Congress urged Burr, who was unacceptable to Washington, then Madison, who was uninterested, and finally Chancellor Livingston, who, Washington may have reasoned,[69] might still be won over. Republicans were enthusiastic. Monroe, writing from the capital, told Livingston his acceptance was "wished by the republican interest here"; Edward pointed out that "the groundwork of the future connections between the two republics is to be laid."[70]

The Chancellor could not refrain from writing a stinging letter of rejection. He was gratified, he told Washington, that "my enemies have been less successful than I imagined in depriving me of your favorable opinion. Yet having long since had reason to suppose that I should not soon be called to any public employment out of this state" he could not "make immediate arrangements for a permanent residence abroad." Undeterred, Washington asked again; "what will be the shortest time necessary for your preparation?" Again Livingston refused, this time with an evasion about the "important personal sacrifice" he could not risk.[71] To Monroe he gave his real reasons: if he resigned as chancellor, the Council of Appointment which would be Federalist would give it to someone "of very different political sentiments"; secondly, his absence "would also have some effect on the politics of this state which it is very important to set right"; third,

---

68. R. R. to Edward Livingston, Apr. 10, 1794, R. R. Livingston Papers, N.-Y. Hist. Soc.; *N.-Y. Journal*, June 7, 11, 1794.

69. Carroll and Ashworth, *George Washington*, VII, 169-71; Schachner, *Aaron Burr*, 136-37; Brant, *James Madison*, III, 400, John Jay to King, May 3, 1794, King Papers, N.-Y. Hist. Soc. George Clinton's name appears on a "List of Names from Whom to take a Minister to France, May 19, 1794," George Washington Papers, Lib. Cong., but if his name was brought up, it figured in none of the discussion.

70. Monroe to R. R. Livingston, May 9, 1794, cited in Livingston, *The Livingstons*, 338; Edward to R. R. Livingston, May 1, 1794, R. R. Livingston Papers, N.-Y. Hist. Soc.

71. Washington to Livingston, Apr. 29, May 14, Livingston to Washington, May 10, May 15, 1794, R. R. Livingston Papers, N.-Y. Hist. Soc.

if he took the post, his views were so different from the administration's that "I should either be compelled to violate my own principles by yielding to theirs, or risk my reputation by incurring their resentment."[72] On Livingston's refusal Washington appointed Monroe, the Chancellor's political alter ego as it were, with whom the New York leaders would maintain a cordial liaison in the next few years.[73]

When Jay was ready to depart for England, Chancellor Livingston sent his card to his old college classmate and co-worker, wishing him "a safe passage" and a successful mission; Jay was arch in his reply. As Jay was boarding his ship, Livingston boarded a French vessel in the harbor, joining Governor Clinton and the French consul in a celebration at which "a brilliant circle of female republicans" sang the Marseillaise and "Americans and French appeared like a band of brothers."[74]

Not only aristocrats but ordinary citizens as well made a display of their displeasure with the Federalists. At Jay's leave-taking, the militia refused to parade and the crowd that saw him off was closer to 200 than to the "immense concourse" Noah Webster's paper claimed. The same day, Tammany heard an impassioned plea from John Johnson to maintain "a firmly cemented union of all the civic and military virtues." The peril was still enormous, he maintained. "At the hand of France, despotism had received his mortal wound. This is the cause of the Monster struggling so violently and bellowing so loud." Thus, "he may yet make the effort of despair and wrap the whole world in flames." "Who knows," Johnson asked, "but before the flight of another month, the storm which now lowers in our horizon may rapidly rise and involve us in destruction?"[75]

In the spirit of Johnson's plea, dozens of groups of craftsmen and professionals turned out to work on the fort on Governor's Island

72. Livingston to Monroe, May 16, 1794, Monroe Papers, Lib. Cong., draft in R. R. Livingston Papers, N.-Y. Hist. Soc.

73. Dangerfield, *Chancellor Robert R. Livingston*, 268-69; Monroe to Jefferson, May 26, 27, 1794, in Hamilton, ed., *Writings of Monroe*, I, 297-300; William P. Cresson, *James Monroe* (Chapel Hill, 1946), 128-29. See correspondence from Livingston, Burr, and Melancton Smith to Monroe in France in Monroe Papers, Lib. Cong., cited in Beverly Bond, *The Monroe Mission to France, 1794-1796* (Baltimore, 1907), 75.

74. Livingston to Jay, May 11, Jay to Livingston, May 11, 1794, R. R. Livingston Papers, N.-Y. Hist. Soc.

75. *N.-Y. Journal*, May 14, 1794; Rev. John B. Johnson, *An Oration on Union Delivered in the Dutch Reformed Church of New York, May 12, 1794, the Anniversary of the Tammany Society* (N.Y., 1794), 12, 15, 19.

through May and June. Henry Wansey, a visiting British clothier, took it all in one day:

> As I was getting up in the morning, I heard drums beating and fifes playing. I ran to the window, and saw a large body of people on the other side of the Governor's House, with flags flying, and marching two and two towards the water-side. What, thought I, can the meaning of this be? The peaceful Americans with the ensigns of war? What! have the Americans a standing army too in time of peace? The sound of the drum is what I have not heard since I left England. I hastened down stairs, and the mystery was soon explained: it was a procession of young tradesmen going in boats to Governor's Island, to give the state a day's work. Fortifications are there erecting for strengthening the entrance to New York Harbour; it is a patriotic and general resolution of the inhabitants of this city, to work a day gratis, for the public advantage, on these fortifications. To-day, the whole trade of carpenters and joiners; yesterday, the body of masons; before this, the grocers, school-masters, coopers, and barbers; next Monday, all the attorneys and men concerned in the law, handle the mattock and shovel, the whole day, and carry their provisions with them.[76]

And there were still others: ship carpenters, journeymen hatters, cordwainers, peruke makers, tallow chandlers, tanners and curriers, and sailmakers; Columbia College undergraduates and law students; the St. Andrews Society; the General Society of Mechanics; immigrant groups, styling themselves "English Republicans" and "the patriotic natives of Great Britain and Ireland." Two apprentices even walked thirty miles from upstate to do a patriotic stint.[77] It was, in short, the constitutional parade of 1788 all over again, except this time the parade was under Republican leadership.

Meanwhile, as Congress drew to the end of its session, Republican lines in Philadelphia collapsed. Conflict broke out again over renewing the embargo a second time beyond its May 26 expiration. In New York City two petitions were circulated, one pro, one con,[78] but before the campaign was off the ground, the House defeated a second renewal, 73–13. The three New York State Republicans joined most of their

76. Henry Wansey, *The Journal of an Excursion to the United States of North America in the summer of 1794* . . . (Salisbury, Eng., 1796), May 24, 1794.

77. *N.-Y. Journal*, Apr. 26, 30, May 3, 7, 10, 24, 28, June 18, 21, 1794. See also Stokes, *Iconography of Manhattan*, Apr.-June, 1794, *passim*.

78. *N.-Y. Journal*, May 14, 1794.

party in voting down the measure,[79] the representatives from West-chester and Long Island doubtless influenced by the suffering of farm-ers whose produce for the export trade was returned from a glutted New York City market.[80] The Republican party in the Senate was "completely wrecked," Madison told Jefferson, and in the House was "in a much worse condition than at an earlier period of the session."[81]

With the embargo over and Jay on the high seas the crisis had passed. In the city, merchants were so eager to get back to business as usual that the day after the embargo expired there was "no getting into the customhouse—such was the crowd." But it was still difficult "to appease the restless and irritated part of the community."[82] The parade of artisans to build the fort continued.[83] Upstate in Ulster County, Republicans burned an effigy of their Federalist congressman, Peter Van Gaasbeck, alongside one of the French traitor General Dumourier and another of Benedict Arnold.[84] In some ways Federal-ists would never recover from the stigmas they acquired in the spring of 1794.

V

In only one part of the state, the western frontier, did the New York Federalists come through the crisis of 1794 unscathed politically. In the district-wide election for the state senate in April, the west elected two Federalists by a vote of 5200 with a sprinkling of 250 votes for various opponents. The Federalist vote went up about 2000 from the year before while the anti-Federalist vote dwindled by at least 1000. The elected Federalists were John Frey and Stephen Van Rensselaer, the Albany landlord.[85]

79. *Annals*, 3d Cong., 1st Sess., 683. New York Republicans wavered on earlier votes on the embargo, too. Thus on the vote in *Annals*, 605, Tredwell of Long Island and Van Cortlandt of Westchester were not recorded and Bailey of Dutchess voted no.

80. Gilbert Saltonstall to Rufus and James Backus, Mar. 19, 28, 29, Apr. 2, 1794, in Backus Mercantile Papers, N.Y. Pub. Lib.

81. Madison to Jefferson, May 25, 1794, in Hunt, ed., *Writings of Madison*, VI, 217.

82. Saltonstall to Rufus and James Backus, May 27, 1794, Backus Mercantile Papers, N.Y. Pub. Lib.

83. *N.-Y. Journal*, May 24, 28, June 18, 21, 1794.

84. Justin Foote to Van Gaasbeck, Apr. 15, Cornelius C. Wynkoop to Van Gaas-beck, May 8, John Addison to Van Gaasbeck, May 12, 1794, Van Gaasbeck Papers, Kingston Senate House; *Goshen Repository*, May 6, 1794; Kingston *Rising Sun*, May 7, 10, 1794.

85. *N.-Y. Journal*, June 1, 1794.

Westerners, to be sure, were anti-British. Even before 1794, there was "a strong predisposition against everything that was British," the land agent Charles Williamson wrote. In the westernmost counties Indians were never out of sight or mind and, as one pioneer recalled, the early settlers "saw on more than one occasion the Indians in possession of new broadcloths, blankets and silver ornaments that came from the King's storehouse [at Fort Niagara] the fearful import of which they well understood." Williamson himself was suspect as the agent of a British company and a former captain in the British army. "Every road I talked of," he wrote, "was said to be for the purpose of admitting the Indian and the British; every set of arms I procured— though really to enable the settlers to defend themselves against the Indians—was said to be for supplying the expected enemy."[86]

Understandably tension mounted on the entire frontier in the spring of 1794 with news that Dorchester had provoked the Indians to war, along with rumors that the British were already intriguing with the Cayuga and Oneidas within the state. Instead of deserting the Federalists, however, frontiersmen closed ranks behind them. Like William Cooper, they feared the devastating consequences of war. For protection they had to rely primarily on the federal government. With attack imminent and the settlers "totally destitute of arms and ammunition," western officials sent urgent appeals for help both to Governor Clinton and Secretary of War Knox. Clinton acted promptly and once the legislature appropriated the money, he rushed arms to the frontier, appointing officers to supervise the building of blockhouses. Charles Williamson was more than satisfied with his speed.[87] But the settlers, even in the thickly settled Whitestown area, were still panicky; they feared that the forts were inadequate; there was not enough gunpowder; flight might be necessary.[88]

Weeks after New York City had calmed down, incidents kept pioneers tense. British conduct became "more and more intolerable and insolent."[89] To the north where an Indian raid on a pioneer took

86. Cited in Turner, *History of Phelps and Gorham's Purchase*, 274; Charles Williamson to Sir William Pulteney, ca. 1800, cited in *ibid.*, 288.

87. Nathaniel Taylor and Phineas Peirce to George Clinton, May 5, Israel Chapin to Henry Knox, May 5, Charles Williamson to George Clinton, May 18, 1794, O'Reilly Coll., X, N.-Y. Hist. Soc.; a letter from Albany, N.Y. *Herald*, June 30, 1794; "A Report from a Gentleman in the Genesee," *ibid.*, July 10; also *N.-Y. Journal*, July 16, 1794.

88. Thomas Morris to Stephen Van Rensselaer, July 11, 1794, MS 1955, N.Y. State Lib.

89. A report from Whitestown, *N.-Y. Journal*, July 26, 1794; see other reports from the frontier, *ibid.*, May 28, July 15, 1794.

place, there was talk of taking Canada in the event of war.[90] In the Genesee country a British unit under the orders of Simcoe demanded that Williamson halt the settling of farmers in an area bordering on Lake Ontario, a move which Washington branded "the most open and daring act of the British agents in America."[91] Secretary of State Edmund Randolph protested to George Hammond, the British ambassador. Governor Clinton, not to be outdone, ordered the western militia held "in the most perfect readiness." Williamson, to the chagrin of the British, resisted their pressure.[92]

During the summer the state's forts were completed—six to the west, five to the north. But it was the news of federal action early in September—General Anthony Wayne's spectacular victory over the Indians at the Battle of Fallen Timbers in the Ohio country—that lifted the cloud of war from the New York frontier.[93] In September another symbol of federal power, the Indian commissioner Timothy Pickering, arrived in western New York to negotiate a treaty with the Indian chieftains.[94] Meanwhile, Hammond publicized the fact that he had written Simcoe in Canada warning him against provoking any hostilities.[95]

As a result of all these factors, by late fall the frontier was calm. Talleyrand, after touring the Mohawk Valley, reported that even though the frontiersmen's "resentment is lively enough and their dispositions generally bellicose," there was not "that excess of warlike ardor which has been represented to us as difficult to control and disturbing the pacific views of the government." Nevertheless Westerners still were keenly aware, he observed, that the success of their settlements "will depend a great deal on the action which England takes in the restitution of the forts."[96]

Republicans should have picked up some political chips in the western district from the six months of crisis. Governor Clinton, after

90. A letter from Plattsburgh to Lansingburgh, *N.-Y. Journal*, July 29, 1794; a letter from Plattsburgh, N.Y. *Herald*, Aug. 11, 1794; *N.-Y. Journal*, Aug. 2, 9, 1794.

91. Cited in Burt, *The U.S., G. Britain and Br. North America*, 145.

92. *N.-Y. Journal*, Sept. 3, 1794; Randolph's letter to Hammond is in *N.-Y. Journal*, Sept. 10, 1794; Clinton's letter to the Major General of the Militia of the Western District, *ibid.*, Sept. 17, 1794; N.Y. *Herald*, Sept. 18, 1794; Cowan, *Charles Williamson*, 55-56.

93. *N.-Y. Journal*, Sept. 17, 20, 27, 1794. A report of Sept. 27 indicates this news reached western New York Sept. 3, 1794.

94. Thomas Morris to ?, Sept. 20, 1794, MS 11203, N.Y. State Lib.

95. William Strickland, Journal, Sept. 22, 1794, N.-Y. Hist. Soc.

96. Charles Maurice de Talleyrand, "Notebook," Oct. 30, 1794, in Huth and Pugh, trans. and ed., *Talleyrand in America*, III, 91.

all, had acted decisively—it was not without cause that Simcoe branded him "one of those violent and able anti-Federalists."[97] But if the crisis exposed the pro-British bias of New York City merchants, it showed that the Federalist chieftains of the north, General Schuyler and Stephen Van Rensselaer, were decided patriots. Van Rensselaer, as late as October 1794, shocked a British visitor when he spoke with "great indignation against the retention of the frontier posts . . . and said they *must be given up* or *would be taken,* which the people of the backcountry were eager to do and without doubt could accomplish any time."[98] The commissioners appointed with Van Rensselaer to supervise the building of the frontier forts, Generals Von Steuben and North, were Federalists and, like Schuyler, patriots of '76.

New York's western settlers, contrary to the stereotype of frontiersmen elsewhere, by and large did not become bellicose in 1794; there was too much to lose in the event of war. In January 1795, when Judge Timothy Hosmer of Ontario rejoiced that the war clouds had passed and that "peace extends her olive branch over this western region,"[99] the west shared his sentiments.

By the late summer of 1794, the "spirit of '76," as Jefferson had called it, burned low in the state as a whole. Businessmen had recovered from their shock. "Stocks have mended," one speculator reported, and "real estates have risen in two years nearly 50 per cent."[100] Sarah Jay was probably accurate in writing to her husband that many who had opposed his mission were now for it, that many who had been for war were now for peace, and that the success of his mission was "a universal toast."[101]

Federalists rallied their followers, holding the merchants intact, riveting the frontier to their cause more firmly than ever. Republicans had found a new following among the mechanics of New York City and reinforced their old one in their traditional areas of strength. But their political gains were uneven; they were able to influence events but not to control them. Until Jay's Treaty was received Federalists were able to focus attention on the threat to their political hegemony posed by the new Democratic societies.

97. Cited in Spaulding, *George Clinton,* 155.
98. William Strickland, Journal, Oct. 26, 1794, N.-Y. Hist. Soc.
99. Timothy Hosmer to Oliver Phelps, Jan. 19, 1795, Phelps Papers, N.Y. State Lib.
100. Samuel Ward to William Constable, Aug. 30, 1794, Constable Pierrepont Papers, N.Y. Pub. Lib.
101. Sarah Jay to John Jay, Aug. 2, 1794, Jay Papers, Columbia Univ.

CHAPTER 18

The "Self-Created"

Societies Emerge

1794-1797

During the course of debate at the constitutional ratifying convention at Poughkeepsie in 1788, Melancton Smith remarked that "the great easily form associations, the poor and middling class form them with difficulty." Six years later, in an Independence Day oration, the Reverend Joseph Pilmore could hardly avoid commenting on the number of private associations flourishing in New York City. There were societies "for mutual improvement—to promote patriotic friendship, to diffuse knowledge, to guard and defend the rights of human nature, to give counsel and impart relief to the distressed, to encourage virtue and to promote the happiness of their country." All these, he said, "are truly excellent in their kind and justly deserve the smiles of public approbation."[1]

This striking proliferation of "self created" societies in the mid-1790's, not confined to the city alone, had several important consequences for the Republican movement. A few of the new groups were consciously Republican; others espoused a democratic philosophy; still other non-political groups were vehicles for Republicans who partici-

1. Elliot, ed., *Debates*, II, 246; Reverend Joseph Pilmore, *The Blessings of Peace: A Sermon Preached in Christ's Church, New York, July 4, 1794, at the Joint Request of the Tammany Society and the Society of Mechanics* (N.Y., 1794), 9-10.

pated in their activities. Not all were new—New Yorkers had a tradition of self-organization—but the growth of societies in the 1790's was of greater scope and intensity, reflecting the same awakening of "the poor and middling class" in pursuit of their own interests that was flowing into the Republican movement.

I

There were four Democratic societies in the state with some staying power: one in New York City, two in Ulster County, and one in Columbia County. There were three more of an ephemeral nature: in Kings and Suffolk counties on Long Island and on the distant frontier in Ontario County.[2]

The principal societies came into being about the same time early in 1794 and owed much to the examples set in neighboring Pennsylvania and Massachusetts. They sprang up in counties with traditions of organized political activity. New York City had the Federal Republican Club of 1787-88, the Sons of Liberty and a host of comparable groups in the Revolution; Ulster was a major center of radical whiggery, Columbia a center of organized tenant action.

The New York City Republicans were relatively late in forming their society. In 1793 the Independence Day celebration by Tammany and the Mechanics was already known as an observance of "some of the republican societies,"[3] and Tammany played a leading role in expressing pro-French opinion. An *ad hoc* committee had to be formed to welcome Genêt. No group conducted political discussions, except for the tiny Uranian Society. To fill this gap, two Republican printers organized a debating society late in 1793, "to induce investigation and to promote good speaking." At the first meeting ("Were the French justifiable in beheading their king?"), attendance was poor and the society died aborning.[4] A few weeks later when editor Greenleaf was subjected to a Federalist inquisition Republicans called a special meeting to defend him.[5] Out of such *ad hoc* beginnings the Democratic Society of New York originated.

The leadership of the New York society showed a blend of old and

2. Link, *Democratic Republican Societies*, ch. 1; Link discusses only the three major societies.
3. Entry of July 4, 1793, Anderson Diary, Columbia Univ.
4. *N.Y. Columbian Gazetteer*, Sept. 23, 30, Oct. 7, 1793.
5. *N.-Y. Journal*, Dec. 7, 11, 14, 21, 1793; Tunis Wortman, soon secretary of the Democratic Society, was secretary at this meeting.

new blood. Two of its four presidents were the prominent anti-Federalists and Clintonians, David Gelston and Henry Rutgers; Melancton Smith was also an active member. Yet the group was able to claim that there were "many, very many members" who were "warm advocates for the adoption of the Constitution."[6] Two presidents, Solomon Simpson and James Nicholson, were ex-Federalists, as were Edward and Brockholst Livingston.[7] The routine organizational work was in the hands of young political newcomers not scarred by the battles of the past—articulate men of intellect and strong convictions. The leading secretary was Tunis Wortman, a lawyer of uncommon philosophical bent who probably drafted the society's lengthy public addresses, and in 1800 wrote a full-length treatise on freedom of the press, the only American work of its kind.[8] Donald Fraser was another active member, a prolific writer on moral themes, a teacher who organized the first teachers' association of the city, and a Scot who led the Caledonian Society.[9] A third was William Keteltas, an impecunious lawyer with a flair for dramatizing humanitarian causes.[10]

The society referred to its founders with accuracy as "the old whigs in this city."[11] Commodore Nicholson, the most illustrious, had been the senior officer in the Continental navy.[12] As to the members at large, they were "the heroes and the sons of those heroes" who established independence.[13]

The society probably had from one to two hundred members.[14]

6. For officers, see the *New York City Directory* (1794-98); "Address to the Republican Citizens of the United States by the Democratic Society of New York," supplement to *N.-Y. Journal*, May 28, 1794.

7. William Miller, "First Fruits of Republican Organization: Political Aspects of the Congressional Election of 1794," *Pa. Mag. of Hist. and Biog.*, 63 (1939) 129.

8. Tunis Wortman, *A Treatise Concerning Political Economy and the Liberty of the Press* (N.Y., 1800) and *An Oration on the Influence of Social Institutions Upon Human Happiness . . . before the Tammany Society, May 12, 1796* (N.Y., 1796); cf. Leonard Levy, *Legacy of Suppression: Freedom of Speech and Press in Early American History* (Cambridge, Mass., 1960), 283-89.

9. Fraser wrote: *The Columbian Monitor: The Mental Flower Garden. A Compendium of Useful Information for Gentlemen* (1794); *The Recantation: Being an Anticipatory Valedictory Address of Thomas Paine to the French Directory* (1797); *A Collection of Select Biography . . .* (1798); and *Party Spirit Exposed . . .* (1799).

10. See below, ch. 22.

11. *N.-Y. Journal*, Feb. 22, 1794.

12. Charles O. Paullin, *DAB*, s.v. "Nicholson, James."

13. "Philo Libertas," *N.-Y. Journal*, Mar. 5, 1794.

14. It is difficult to estimate the size of the society. "A.B.," N.Y. *Daily Advertiser*, Mar. 1, 1794, claimed that eighty members of the society met the night before the "Town Meeting," Feb. 1794. The constitution of the society established a quorum of 20 to transact business. In Philadelphia Link found a membership of 300 but

According to Federalists their meetings were attended by "the lowest order of mechanics, laborers and draymen" and were deliberately held at night to accommodate them. The Democrats half admitted the charge—"Workingmen must meet in the evening," they said—but they were accurate in claiming that their members "are composed and mingle with every class of citizens."[15] From what can be learned of its few known members, it appears that its leading officers were merchants of wealth and some status, its lesser officers young lawyers, teachers, and craftsmen, while its rank and file were men of the "middling" and "lower sort."[16]

"To support and perpetuate the EQUAL RIGHTS OF MAN" was the society's "great object"; toward this end they would "constantly express our sentiments."[17] According to their constitution no one could be accepted unless five members could testify that he was a "firm and stedfast friend of the EQUAL RIGHTS OF MAN"; one-fifteenth of the members present might blackball a candidate. "Apotasy from Republican principles" was grounds for expulsion. Characteristically, there were to be no titles; officers were to be addressed as "Citizen President" etc.

Within its first few months, the New York society established the pattern of activities it would follow during its five years of existence: monthly meetings with more frequent meetings at elections or times of political crisis; participation in elections, more or less *sub rosa*; public celebrations and parades, particularly on July Fourth; and the adoption of public addresses to express their opinion. The society was in sporadic contact with the Philadelphia group.[18] More impor-

---

the New York society probably was not as large. At the Independence Day celebration of 1798, the society was assigned "the left of the middle aisle" of a church for its members, the Mechanics the right. The Mechanics had as many as 600 members. Minutes of the General Society of Mechanics and Tradesmen, Soc. Lib., 328.

15. William Woolsey to Oliver Wolcott, Jr., Mar. 6, 1794, cited in Link, *Democratic Republican Societies*, 94; "Address . . . by the Democratic Society," May 28, 1794, broadside; Phila. *Dunlap's American Daily Advertiser*, Jan. 20, 1795, cited in Luetscher, *Early Political Machinery*, 58n.

16. Of 43 men it is possible to identify as members of the society, the occupations ascertained from the *New York City Directory* (various years) were as follows: craftsmen (including petty tradesmen) 9; merchants 14; public officials 2; printers 3; lawyers 4; teachers 2; unidentified, 13. This list is heavily weighted with officers and others prominent in the affairs of the society and therefore is not representative. See Link, *Democratic Republican Societies*, 71-72, for a more definitive analysis of the Philadelphia society.

17. *Constitution of the Democratic Society of the City of New York* (N.Y., 1794).

18. Link, *Democratic Republican Societies*, 132, n.29; Tunis Wortman for the

tant probably were informal contacts with Republican leaders, for example Nicholson with his son-in-law, Albert Gallatin, and DeWitt Clinton with John Beckley. Contact with the upstate societies seemed to work on a similar basis.

There were two Republican societies in the anti-Federalist stronghold of southern Ulster County, one in the town of Montgomery, another in nearby Shawangunk. Both were rural areas inhabited by prosperous yeomen, with a sprinkling of tenants and artisans. In 1794 there also were area meetings of the tanners and curriers, weavers, and carpenters and joiners, all bent on raising their prices. The Governor's nephews, George, Jr., and Charles, had a hand in organizing the Republican Society of Ulster County at Montgomery as did other anti-Federalists. Its two known presidents were military veterans, and several doctors and the principal of the local academy were prominent in its affairs.[19] The Montgomery group was formed, their constitution stated, "for the purpose of political information." Membership was restricted to those approved by a three-fourths vote "for their moral character and republican principles," and members who "shall openly contradict any acknowledged principle of Republican government" were to be admonished first and on the second offense expelled by a majority vote. So exclusive were the leaders that when four hundred or so Ulsterites showed up in 1794 at the society's first Independence Day observance they insisted that they all become members before they could join the celebration; as a result there were two separate dinners.[20] The Republican Society of Shawangunk was formed a few months later. It, too, adopted a constitution, elected known anti-Federalists, and held an Independence Day celebration in July 1794, but seems to have done little else. Possibly it amalgamated with the Montgomery group.[21] The Ulster society at its height had at least 150 members, the Shawangunk group fewer.[22]

Committee of Correspondence of the Democratic Society of New York to the Democratic Society of Philadelphia, [n.d.], Miscellaneous MSS, No. 85, N.-Y. Hist. Soc.

19. Link, *Democratic Republican Societies*, 82, 98, 319; *Goshen Repository*, Dec. 17, 1793, Mar. 4, and 11, and "A Member of the Republican Society of Ulster County," *ibid.*, Oct. 7, 1794; *N.-Y. Journal*, Jan. 18, 1794; *Albany Register*, Feb. 3, 1794; for the labor meetings, *Goshen Repository*, Oct. 14, Nov. 4, Dec. 9, 1794.

20. *Goshen Repository*, Mar. 4, Mar. 11, 1794, "No Deceiver," July 8, an unsigned rebuttal, July 22.

21. *Goshen Repository*, July 1, 29, 1794.

22. For claims and counterclaims, "A Member of Republican Society of Ulster County," *Goshen Repository*, Aug. 5 and Oct. 7, 1794, "An Old Tryed Independent Whig," *ibid.*, Aug. 20.

In Columbia County, the Democratic Society of Canaan was located in the northeastern section of the county on the Massachusetts border, an area of poor farmers and tenants. Hillsdale, scene of the "Indian" tumult that set off a new wave of anti-landlord activity in 1791, was nearby; to the southwest near the Hudson lay the estates of the two Livingston families, neither of which had anything to do with the group. Canaan in the 1792 election had given Clinton a slight edge but the same year had voted two to one for a Federalist congressman.[23] It was a sleepy town—Elihu Phinney set up its first newspaper in 1794 but abandoned it in a few months for more prosperous pastures in Cooperstown on the frontier.[24] The society's chairman was Philip Frisbie, a county judge who sat on the panel of judges in the "Indian" trial of 1791 and a Clintonian assemblyman; one clerk was Dr. Moses Younglove, known as a medical innovator; another clerk was the local tavernkeeper. Younglove and Frisbie were both Revolutionary veterans.[25] The constitution of the Canaanites was short and plain— only seven articles—its orators unpolished, and a major concern was reform of the court system, an issue close to the hearts of tenants.[26]

Country groups, the Ulster and Canaan societies met only a few times a year. The societies per se did not play a role in elections, although their leaders participated in the *ad hoc* committees that were the customary method of electioneering.[27] Instead, they sponsored Independence Day celebrations, adopted resolutions, circulated petitions, and promoted the circulation of a new semi-weekly edition of Greenleaf's paper.[28]

The evidence of other political societies is sparse. From distant Ontario an anonymous writer in the *New-York Journal* mentioned "a little self-created society to which I belong who meet twice a week to

23. In Dec. 1792, the town cast 250 votes for Ezekiel Gilbert, the Federalist candidate for Congress, 134 for Peter Van Ness, an anti-Federalist; *Hudson Gazette,* Feb. 28, 1793. In the 1792 gubernatorial election the town cast 264 votes for Clinton, 224 for Jay; *N.-Y. Journal,* June 6, 1792.

24. For the Canaan *Columbian Mercury* see Brigham, comp., *Bibliography of American Newspapers,* I. Only one issue is extant.

25. Ellis, *Columbia County,* 34, 313, 325; Link, *Democratic Republican Societies,* 57, 82, 98; for Young, see Alexander C. Flick and G. S. Lobrano, *Samuel Jones Tilden; Study in Political Sagacity* (N.Y., 1939), 2-3, 42.

26. *N.-Y. Journal,* Mar. 8, 1794, and *Albany Register,* Mar. 10, 1794. For criticism of the courts, see ch. 24, sec. IV.

27. For Philip Frisbie as chairman of the committee for Republican gubernatorial candidates, *N.-Y. Journal,* Apr. 29, 1795.

28. *Ibid.,* Feb. 11, June 24, 1795.

hear and talk over what news has reached our settlement."[29]   Of the Bushwick Democratic Society of Brooklyn and the Columbian Society of Huntington, Long Island, we know only that they sponsored Independence Day celebrations.[30]   In New York City several other ephemeral organizations blossomed in the shade of the Democratic Society. The Juvenile Republican Society celebrated July 4, 1795, and probably became the Patriotic Junior Association. A Union Society set down its principles in unmistakably Republican language in the city directories and paraded with the Democrats. A Society of Information seems cast in a similar mold.[31]   The Society for Free Debate, stillborn in 1793, came to life under Republican sponsorship in 1797-98 when the Democratic Society began to fade.[32]

The upstate Democratic societies had short lives—perhaps two years —but the New York City group was active as late as 1799,[33] as long as any other in the United States. All were small in numbers; none replaced the loose committee machinery that constituted the Republican party. But they were influential beyond their numbers as catalysts of Republican opinion.

II

The other associations in New York City mentioned by the Reverend Pilmore in 1794 were of several sorts: fraternal, humanitarian, ethnic, religious, military, and cultural. Some were new; some were old. Republicans were involved in all, and each contributed to the Republican tide in one way or another.

Tammany, the most Republican of the fraternal groups, underwent its first transformation in the mid-1790's, identifying itself completely with the Republican cause. Tammany grew to about five hundred members, weighted heavily with artisans and tradesmen.[34] In the mid-1790's it differed from the Democratic Society in that it conducted no debates, took no stand on political issues, and did not participate in elections. Most members of the Democratic Society were members of Tammany, although the reverse of course was not true,

29. *Ibid.*, Feb. 24, 1795.

30. *Ibid.*, July 15, 1795; for the Huntington Society, Sag Harbor, *Frothingham's Long-Island Herald*, July 26, 1797.

31. Link, *Democratic Republican Societies*, 17, and *Argus*, Feb. 7, 1797; *N.Y. City Directory*, 1796, 113, 121; *N.Y. City Directory*, 1797, 82, 84, 85, 97.

32. Duer, *New York During the 18th Century*, 42-44.

33. *N.-Y. Journal*, July 3, 1799; see Link, *Democratic Republican Societies*, 202-3.

34. Paulson, "The Tammany Society," *N.Y. History*, 34 (1953), 72-84.

even of Tammany's officers. The remaining Federalists among its members were increasingly uncomfortable and took the occasion of a dispute early in 1795 to leave. Late in the decade when the Democratic Society faded, Tammany underwent a second transformation, taking over some of the Democrats' functions although even then it did not become an electioneering club.

In the mid-1790's Tammany expressed itself mainly at patriotic celebrations at which the procedure usually was a parade, a public meeting featuring an oration which the society later published, and a dinner or collation ending in a round of ideological toasts, prepared in advance by a committee.[35] Tammany's strength lay in the fact that it remained essentially a fraternal order replete with paraphernalia, ritual, and a rich symbolism featuring the Indian motif. Its meeting place was "the wigwam," its officers "sachems"; on parade its members wore Indian feathered caps or buckskins, and it absorbed an elaborate, fanciful Indian folklore from its orators.[36] Other fraternal groups passed into Republican hands. In the hectic spring of 1794 in the Holland Lodge of the Masons, for example, there was a sharp contest between "anti-Federalists" and "monarchists" in which DeWitt Clinton was elected master.[37] Partisan politics aside, the numerous Masonic lodges mingled men of different classes and nationalities, spread principles of brotherhood and benevolence, and as a result were viewed with "suspicion and prejudice" by some conservatives.[38] The Black Friars, another fraternal order, had a penchant for hearing orations on the theme of the Enlightenment by DeWitt Clinton and Samuel L. Mitchill.[39]

35. Minutes of the Tammany Society (1791-95, 1799-1801), Toasts of the Tammany Society (1792-1808), Columbia Univ. Lib.; Minutes of the Committee of Amusement of the Tammany Society, 1791-95, N.Y. Pub. Lib.
36. Kilroe, *Saint Tammany*, 168-77; Samuel L. Mitchill, *The Life, Exploits and Precepts of Tammany; the Famous Indian Chief . . . Being the Anniversary Oration Pronounced before the Tammany Society . . . May 12, 1795* (N.Y., 1795).
37. John Ludlow to DeWitt Clinton, Mar. 9, 1795, DeWitt Clinton Papers, No. 24, Columbia Univ.; Clinton, *An Address Delivered before the Holland Lodge, Dec. 24, 1794 on His Installation as Master of Said Lodge* (N.Y., 1794) is listed in William Gowans, *A Catalogue of Books on Freemasonry . . .* (N.Y., 1858), No. 15, but is not extant.
38. Rev. Samuel Miller, *A Discourse . . . before the Grand Lodge of the State of New York . . . on the Festival of St. John the Baptist, June 24, 1795* (N.Y., 1795), 25; Bernard Faÿ, *The Revolutionary Spirit in France and America . . .* (N.Y., 1927), 417-19.
39. DeWitt Clinton, *An Oration on Benevolence, Delivered before the Society of Black Friars . . . November 10, 1794* (N.Y., 1795); Samuel L. Mitchill, *An Oration Pronounced before the Society of Black Friars . . . Nov. 11, 1793* (N.Y., 1793).

In the spring of 1794 Republicans also fathered two new humanitarian organizations. Up to this time humanitarianism was by and large the province of conservative Federalist merchants, in particular Quakers who organized the Manumission Society and the debtors' relief society. The new Society for the Information and Assistance of Persons Emigrating from Foreign Countries was led by two Republican printers and booksellers, and by Thomas Greenleaf and Melancton Smith, among others. Its ideology was decidedly Republican; the Reverend Thomas Dunn in his 1794 oration to the group excoriated England, hailed the French Revolution and "the rights of man," and held out America as an "asylum for peace for liberty, and for religion."[40] To the affluent among the immigrants, said the group, they offered congratulations; to those "in the middling rank," information, and to the "unfortunate, the sick, the friendless and to the needy," a helping hand. The society distributed financial aid, made a doctor available, kept a register of immigrants seeking jobs, and protested the inhuman treatment of immigrants by ship captains.[41]

The officers of the new Humane Society were George and DeWitt Clinton, John Lamb, David Gelston, Melancton Smith, and the Reverend William Linn, Republicans all. Its objective was "the general improvement in the medical profession so as to embrace every subject which is connected with the public health and the safety of individuals." Patterned after societies founded in Boston and Charleston in the 1780's, its primary interest was in rescuing victims of "suspended respiration"—persons who appeared to be dead but who might be revived by emergency treatment. For this purpose the society kept special equipment to rush to victims and offered a reward of five dollars for news of sudden deaths. The society functioned for several years.[42]

Republicans also played more of a part in the Manumission Society as it grew to about 250 members. Although it was invariably

40. Thomas Dunn, A.M., *A Discourse . . . October 21, 1794 before the New York Society for the Information and Assistance of Persons Emigrating from Foreign Countries* (N.Y., 1794), 3-4, 23.

41. *New York City Directory* (1794-96); "Society for the Assistance of Persons Emigrating from Foreign Countries . . . June 30, 1794," broadside, N.-Y. Hist. Soc., N.Y. *Columbian Gazetteer*, June 23, 30, 1794; *N.-Y. Journal*, Aug. 30, 1794.

42. *Constitution of the Humane Society of the City of New York* (N.Y., 1794); *New York City Directory*, 1795, 56. Jensen, *The New Nation*, 141. The society, organized in July 1794, should not be confused with the Humane Society organized about 1800, successor to the Society for the Relief of Distressed Debtors.

headed by a Federalist, Melancton Smith was its vice-president and occasionally presiding officer. The society continued to agitate to abolish slavery in New York and to sponsor the African School for Negro Children. Its legal aid committee, which Republican lawyers joined, handled cases of Negroes unlawfully held in bondage, some ninety in 1796 alone.[43] New York Republicans also joined the Pennsylvania anti-slavery society, the mother society of northern abolition.[44]

It is not surprising that new organizations along lines of national origin appeared in the mid-1790's, some of them with a distinct Republican cast. The prewar fraternal societies, St. George's for Americans of British origin, St. Andrews for Scots, and the Friendly Sons of St. Patrick for the Irish, were social groups of successful, assimilated citizens. The newcomers who streamed into the city in the 1790's—the Scots, British, Irish, German, French—were for the most part poor, in dire need, and of course were "greenhorns" to American life. The established nationality groups, save for the German Society, showed little interest in "their own kind."[45]

In the past Federalists had been aware of the need to court nationality groups in election campaigns. They also knew the prestige attached to officeholding in the nationality groups; a Federalist boasted to Hamilton how he had edged Chancellor Livingston out of office in the St. Andrews Society.[46] But to the "new immigrants" of the 1790's Federalists were cool or hostile; such people ran up the cost of charity at the city almshouse, hated Great Britain, and, it was claimed, even brought in yellow fever.[47] By default the Scots, Irish, and French, and to a lesser extent the new English, drifted perceptibly toward the Republicans.

Scottish immigrants formed the Caledonian Society whose president was Donald Fraser, a leader of the Democratic Society. In their native land many Scots had read Thomas Paine and been members of the radical Friends of the People. As an Edinburgh migrant who came to New York in 1794 recalled, "We had some hot characters among us

43. See The Minutes of the New York Society for Promoting the Manumission of Slaves and for Protecting Such of Them as Have Been or May Be Liberated, N.-Y. Hist. Soc.; "Minutes of the Fourth American Convention of Delegates from the Abolition Societies, 1797," *Jour. of Negro Hist.*, 6 (1921), 316-22.
44. Link, *Democratic Republican Societies*, 153-54.
45. Pomerantz, *New York an American City*, 469, 199-209.
46. James Tillary to Alexander Hamilton, Jan. 14, 1793, Hamilton Papers, Lib. Cong.
47. See ch. 22, n. 33.

which all the waters of the Atlantic could not cool." The Caledonian
Society organized late in 1794 met as "Scotch patriots forced from
their native country." Their motto was

> The Rights of man we will defend
> And Objects of distress befriend.

The goals of the society were to provide a fraternal center for mutual
assistance.[48]

Like the Scots, most Irish migrants had a burning hatred of the
British. They became the poorest of the poor, draymen and common
laborers who dwelt in the city's most wretched slums. More than
any other immigrant group they were subject to the slings and barbs
of conservative prejudice.[49] In 1794 the Irish formed *ad hoc* committees to work on the forts and also to welcome the scientist Joseph
Priestley, styling themselves "The Republican Residents of Great Britain and Ireland Residents in New York" and "The Republican Irishmen." Early in 1796 they formed a militia unit, "the New York Hibernian Volunteers," which broke up, according to their minute book,
because they could not make "any further progress in getting any
more uniforms of the color we had chose"—green, naturally, with a
shamrock—and because John Jay refused to commission their officers.
Some time later they formed "the Republican Greens," whose officers
received commissions. In the closing years of the decade the Irish
organized Republican political committees and a mutual aid group,
the Hibernian Provident Society.[50]

The French of the city were divided politically as they were socially. The Republican-minded among them, doubtless with the aid of
French officials, formed *ad hoc* committees for ceremonial occasions
and the Société de Fraternité, probably a benevolent group, and a
French-language paper of a Republican cast. But while they voted
Republican, they do not seem to have been as well organized or as
political as their brethren in Philadelphia who formed a Republican

48. Grant Thorburn, *Forty Years Residence in America* . . . (Boston, 1834), 23,
37-40, 92. *N.-Y. Evening Post*, Dec. 22, 1794; N.Y. *Argus*, Dec. 3, 1795; *N.Y. City
Directory*, 1796, unpaged.

49. See below, ch. 22, sec. I, for conditions of the Irish.

50. N.Y. *Daily Advertiser*, June 3, 11, 1794; *Albany Register*, May 12, 1794; for
the militia, Minutes of the New York Hibernian Volunteers, 1796, N.-Y. Hist. Soc.;
N.Y. *Republican Watch-Tower*, Mar. 18, 28, 1801; for political committees see N.Y.
Time Piece, July 6, Aug. 30, 1798; N.Y. *Argus*, Mar. 24, 1799; *N.Y. Journal*, Mar.
27, 1799; N.Y. *Republican Watch-Tower*, July 9, 1800.

Society.[51] The Germans, who seem to have been taken into the Federalist-oriented German Society, lagged even farther behind their countrymen of Philadelphia who formed the first Republican Society in the United States.[52]

Free Negroes also demonstrated the "spirit of association." "Most of the inferior labor of the town," a traveler noted, was done by blacks; most of the male servants were Negro slaves. Free Negroes who ran "some petty shops" and were in the "inferior trades" were in a "state of want." This poverty notwithstanding, by 1797 abolitionists reported "various associations among the free blacks for mutual support, benefit and improvement." Negroes formed an African Society, an African Methodist Episcopal Church (which by 1800 boasted its own building), and an African Assembly Room.[53] It could not be said of the city's Negroes, however, that they were either political or Republican.

In the established organizations of the city—the militia, the churches and religious groups, and the gentlemen's cultural societies—Republicans were also active, widening the circles of their influence.

The city's militia was "republicanized" in the mid-1790's. The mechanics and tradesmen who made up the rank and file cherished drilling and parading as a badge of their citizenship. Republicans in turn exalted the militia in face of widespread detraction and urged them on to greater proficiency to foil the advocates of a standing army.[54] Many militia officers were members of Tammany, some of the Democratic Society, and the militia parades and toasts each Independence Day left little doubt of their growing Republicanism. In 1795, a year after the militia refused to parade on John Jay's sail-

51. Childs, *French Refugee Life in the United States*, chs. 2, 3, 4, 7 *passim.*; Pomerantz, *New York An American City*, 204-5; George P. Winship, "French Newspapers in the United States from 1790 to 1800," Bibliographical Society of America, *Papers*, 14 (1920), 134-47; N.Y. *Diary*, Mar. 13, 1794.

52. N.Y. *Daily Advertiser*, Apr. 28, 1788; N.Y. *Evening Post*, Jan. 2, 1795; *N.-Y. Journal*, Dec. 30, 1797; see Link, *Democratic Republican Societies*, 5-8; for Germans at work on the fort, N.Y. *Columbian Gazetteer*, May 1, 1794.

53. Strickland, Journal, entry of Sept. 25, 1794, N.-Y. Hist. Soc.; "Minutes of the Convention of the Abolition Society, 1797," *Jour. of Negro Hist.*, 6 (1921), 318-19; Peterson, ed., *Minutes of the Common Council of the City of New York*, II, 137, 151, 159; Olson, Negro Slavery in N.Y., 177-79; Christopher Rush, *A Short Account of the Rise and Progress of the African Methodist Episcopal Church in America* (N.Y., 1843), 9, 11-12, 16-24; N.Y. *Republican Watch-Tower*, Apr. 25, 1801.

54. In the *N.-Y. Journal*: "A Friend to the Country," May 24, 1794; and "Centinel," July 23, 1794; in N.Y. *Argus*: "One of Montagnie's Company," Nov. 24, 1795; Dec. 3, Dec. 7, 1795, Feb. 12, 1796.

ing, Hamilton believed the militia "from the complexion of its officers in general cannot be depended on"—they were "too Jacobinical."[55]

Republicans were leaders in a variety of religious groups embracing all shades of the religious spectrum. Only a handful were active on the religious "left." A Unitarian Society was organized in March 1794, whose minister lectured weekly to large audiences, but there is no evidence that it drew any marked support from Republican quarters.[56] When the Deistical Society was formed in the winter of 1796-1797, DeWitt Clinton, Philip Freneau, and a number of other Republicans were active in it, but so were Federalists. Elihu Palmer, the blind lecturer who led the society, was a member of the Democratic Society but the officers of the Democrats hardly reciprocated.[57] "A Christian Democrat" was probably accurate in rejecting a Federalist charge that "a Deist and a Democrat are principles generally inseparable," and the Patriotic Junior Association was probably typical of rank and file Republicans in offering as a toast to Thomas Paine, "May his Rights of Man be handed down to our latest posterity; but may his Age of Reason never live to see the rising generation."[58]

It was quite typical of Republicans that Henry Rutgers gave land to his own Dutch Reformed church and to the Baptists and Presbyterians,[59] or that Solomon Simpson was president of the Jewish congregation,[60] that Donald Fraser wrote Christian homiletics,[61] and that George Warner was an officer of societies to promote the gospel and Sabbath observance.[62] It was also typical of the Republican societies

55. *N.-Y. Journal*, July 6, 1793; for the officers see *New York City Directory*, 1789-99, *passim*. *N.-Y. Journal*, May 5, July 8, Nov. 28, 1795; N.Y. *Argus*, July 12, Oct. 12, 1796; Hamilton to Oliver Wolcott, July 28, 1795, Lodge, ed., *Works of Hamilton*, X, 112.

56. N.Y. *Daily Advertiser*, Jan. 24, 1794; Pomerantz, *New York An American City*, 388-90; McMaster, *History of the U.S.*, II, 238-41.

57. Adolf Koch, *Republican Religion, The American Revolution and the Cult of Reason* (N.Y., 1933), ch. 3; Herbert Morais, *Deism in the Eighteenth Century* (N.Y., 1934), 130-35; Pomerantz, *New York An American City*, 388-90.

58. "A Christian Democrat," *N.-Y. Journal*, June 3, 1796; N.Y. *Argus*, Feb. 7, 1797.

59. L. Ethan Ellis in *DAB* s.v. "Rutgers, Henry"; Samuel Miller, Jr., *The Life of Samuel Miller*, 2 vols. (Phila., 1869), I, 167.

60. Morris U. Schappes, "Anti-Semitism and Reaction, 1795-1800," American Jewish Historical Society, *Publications*, 38 (1948), 115-16.

61. Donald Fraser, *A Collection of Select Biography: or the Bulwark of Truth, Being a Sketch of the Lives and Testimonies of Many Eminent Laymen who have Professed their Belief and Attachment to the Christian Religion* (N.Y., 1798). Among several hundred subscribers were numerous Republicans.

62. *New York City Directory*, 1794-96; N.Y. *Argus*, July 14, 1796.

that they held their July Fourth observances in a church and frequently invited ministers of the orthodox churches to be their orators.[63] The Presbyterian church, composed of "no aristocrats but good plain republicans," most "of the middling class," as an English traveler observed, very likely had a major share of the Republican political leaders.[64]

Republicans also figured in the gentlemen's literary and debating societies. Three members of the Friendly Club, the most celebrated of such groups, were "a little democratic" while seven were "decided Federalists." Here Republicans-to-be, like Dr. Samuel Mitchill of Columbia or liberals like Dr. Elihu Hubbard Smith, might discuss Godwin, Paine, or Condorcet with Federalists like Charles Brockden Brown, the novelist, or William Dunlap, the playwright.[65] In the Calliopean Society Tunis Wortman and Stanton Latham, both secretaries of the Democratic Society, could try their wings in oratory and disputation.[66] Republicans, gentlemen might well conclude, were everywhere.

III

Collective action by mechanics did not get many of the "smiles of public approbation" the Reverend Pilmore spoke of. Among the mechanics of various strata there were two developments of political significance. Some of the existing mechanic societies embracing for the most part master craftsmen showed a political allegiance to Republicanism. The General Society of Mechanics and Tradesmen, made up of master craftsmen in all trades, went Republican in the mid-1790's. Officially the society, grown from about 250 members in 1792 to about 600 by 1798, remained non-political. Limited as it was

63. Orations were delivered by the following ministers: William Linn (1791); Samuel Miller (1793, 1795); Joseph Pilmore (1794); John Johnson (1794).
64. Strickland, Journal, entry of Sept. 28, 1794, N.-Y. Hist. Soc.
65. Samuel Miller to Jedediah Morse, Apr. 3, 1799, in Miller, The Life of Samuel Miller, 99. Harry R. Warfel, Charles Brockden Brown, American Gothic Novelist (Gainesville, Fla., 1949), 40-44, 81-86; Charles C. Cole, Jr., "Brockden Brown and the Jeffersonian Administration," Pa. Mag. of Hist. and Biog., 72 (1948), 253-63; Dorothy C. Barck, ed., Diary of William Dunlap, 1766-1839 . . . , 3 vols. (N.Y., 1931), I, 1797-98 entries, passim; James E. Cronin, "Elihu Hubbard Smith and the New York Friendly Club, 1795-1798," Modern Language Association, Publications, 69 (1949), 471-79.
66. Minutes of the Calliopean Society (1788-1795), 69-70, 115-16, N.Y. Pub. Lib., see, too, Minutes of the Belles Lettres Society (1799-1806), N.Y. Pub. Lib., and "Regulations of the Belles Lettres Society, 1795," broadside, N.Y. Pub. Lib.

to "charitable purposes" it collected payments for future old age and widows benefits and occasionally made small loans to members. But early in 1794 the society re-elected John Stagg, a Republican who had served as president in 1790. In July 1794 they toasted "the republican societies of New York"; the next year they conducted a joint celebration of the Fourth of July with the Democratic Society and each year thereafter they regularly agreed to a formal request from the Democrats for a joint observance. In December 1794 Stagg presided over a meeting to nominate a Republican congressman, and in 1795 the society officially singled out for toasts Governor Clinton and Thomas Jefferson.[67]

Other craft associations showed a similar bent. The Coopers Society regularly joined the Mechanics, Democrats, and Tammany to celebrate Independence Day; they were led by John Utt, "a strenuous and influential Republican."[68] The Sailmakers Society, who toasted "the societies of America as nurseries of Republicanism," were led by George Warner, "an indefatigable laborer in the democratic vineyard" who later ran on the Republican assembly ticket.[69] The Association of Tallow Chandlers and Soap Boilers chose Republican politicians to plead their case before the state legislature.[70]

Perhaps the most Republican economic group in the city was the Society of the Associated Teachers of New York, the first professional organization of its kind in the United States. Formed in 1794 in the flurry of Republican-oriented organizations, it was led by members of the Democratic Society; members addressed each other in Republican style as "Citizen" and its library was stocked with the works of Thomas Paine, Thomas Erskine, *et al.* The Association took up a variety of problems—payments for teachers, curriculum, professional standards, distribution of state aid to schools—and formally debated such "advanced" educational issues of the late eighteenth century as "whether a republican or monarchial form of government is most

67. Entries of June 4, 1794, June 3, 24, 1795, Apr. 5, May 10, July 1, 1795, Mar. 7, 1798, June 5, 1799, June 18, 1800, Minutes of the General Society of Mechanics and Tradesmen (typescript), at the Society, N.Y.C.; *N.-Y. Journal*, Dec. 3, 1794.

68. George to DeWitt Clinton, Jan. 20, 1801, DeWitt Clinton Papers, No. 63, Columbia Univ.; *N.-Y. Journal*, July 5, 1794.

69. James Nicholson to Albert Gallatin, May 14, 1798, Gallatin Papers, N.-Y. Hist. Soc.; Duer, *Reminiscences*, 59; George Warner, *Means for the Preservation of Liberty* . . . (N.Y., 1797); for the sailmakers' toasts: *N.-Y. Journal*, Nov. 14, 1794; N.Y. *Argus*, Nov. 12, 1795, Nov. 10, 1796.

70. See ch. 22, n.101.

advantageous in a school." When they joined the other Republican societies in public activities the teachers had to defend their rights against the baiting of William Cobbett, the Federalist poison penman of Philadelphia.[71]

Secondly, there was an increase in activity for economic purposes which brought several kinds of mechanics into collision with Federalists. As many as a dozen organized groups of master craftsmen took action either to control the labor market or petition Congress for tariff protection.[72] Journeymen were restive under a decaying apprenticeship system, the flood of unskilled immigrants, and rising living costs. Journeymen printers, house carpenters, and masons conducted strikes for higher wages. Workers dependent on fees and prices set by the state or city government petitioned for increases because, as the repackers of beef pointed out, "for some considerable time past House Rent, Fuel, provisions and the prices of everything necessary for the support of a family have been rising."[73] The Common Council of the city heard from bakers, fish venders, and especially the numerous cartmen who objected to the city's regulations.[74] Not all with whom workers came into conflict were Federalists, but this was true of the "city fathers," and the city's delegation in the state legislature and Congress, and most merchants. Moreover, "combinations" created resistance among those fearful lest their success "excite similar attempts among all other descriptions of persons who live by manual labor."[75] There was thus a ferment of economic discontent among the very groups Republicans were attempting to arouse politically.

IV

Outside New York City the "spirit of association" bloomed less

71. Minutes of the Associated Teachers of New York (1794-1797), N.Y. State Lib.; William Cobbett, *Observations on the Emigration of Joseph Priestley* . . . (Phila., 1795), and for the reply, [Anon], *A Twig of Birch for a Butting Calf, or Strictures Upon Remarks on the Emigration of Dr. Joseph Priestley etc.* . . . (N.Y., 1795), 36-37.

72. For the carpenters and masons, N.Y. *Daily Advertiser*, Mar. 30, 1795; for activities of the Typographical Society, organized in 1794, which in 1798 was the Franklin Typographical Society, clearly identified as composed of journeymen, see Stokes, comp., *Iconography of Manhattan*, VI, 49-50.

73. "A Petition, Jan. 24, 1795," Misc. MSS, No. 86, N.-Y. Hist. Soc.; for petitions from clerks of the loan office and gaugers, *Annals*, 3d Cong., 1st Sess., 525-29.

74. Peterson, ed., *Minutes of the Common Council of New York*, II, for the bakers, Apr. 20, 1795, for the fish venders, Feb. 27, 1797; for the cartmen, see "Regulations of the Common Council . . . 1794," broadside, Lib. Cong., and N.Y. *Argus*, May 15, 1795.

75. N.-Y. *Journal*, Apr. 5, 1794; N.Y. *Daily Advertiser*, Mar. 30, 1795.

luxuriantly. In Dutchess County a Constitutional Society which was active in politics in 1788 and then applied to the legislature for a charter as a combination Tammany and society to promote manufactures, agriculture, and the useful arts does not seem to have lasted beyond 1792.[76] Here and there a new society appeared in the mid-1790's: in Dutchess the Fredericksburgh Union Society; in Schenectady, the Social Society; in Otsego County, a teachers' association;[77] in Rensselaer County, the Scientific Society for the General Diffusion and Promotion of Useful Knowledge (later changed to the hardly less euphonious Schaghticoke Polemic Society). Perhaps the last, whose minutes have survived, is typical of the "spirit of association" in the countryside. A debating society, it met in the town schoolhouse every Saturday afternoon outside the farming season, stirring up farm youths on the pros and cons of "the party spirit," slavery, and universal suffrage. Indirectly, it also helped to promote the fortunes of young Republican political aspirants and inevitably met the "ill-founded and unfavorable apprehensions" of "neighbors and friends."[78]

The yeomanry showed more of an interest in organizing to protect their property. Up and down the Hudson Valley they formed societies to catch horse thieves—private posses in effect.[79] And in at least one town in Ulster, Shawangunk, home of a Republican society, they formed a society to "detect and apprehend" runaway slaves.[80] They were totally uninterested in the Society for the Promotion of Agri-

76. For nominations by such a society at Amenia, possibly anti-Federalist, see Poughkeepsie *County Journal*, Apr. 15, 1788; for notices of meetings, *ibid.*, Dec. 25, 1790, Aug. 25, Oct. 25, 1791, Jan. 5, 1792. For the unsuccessful petition for a charter see *Journal of the Assembly of N.Y.*, 13th Sess., 71.

77. *N.-Y. Journal*, Apr. 29, 1795; *The Constitution of the Social Society of Schenectady, June 28, 1798* (Schenectady, 1798); Cooperstown *Otsego Herald*, Mar. 9, 1797.

78. Minutes of the Schaghticoke Polemic Society, N.-Y. Hist. Soc. The society was organized Jan. 18, 1797; the last entry is Apr. 13, 1799. See the address of the presidents, Jan. 25, Nov. 4, Dec. 23, 1797; Silas Wickes, president and very likely a Republican, was a candidate for the assembly in 1798. Sybrant Velie, another member, was host to the meeting that nominated Wickes; see Troy *Farmers' Oracle*, Apr. 3, 1798; Troy *Northern Budget*, June 5, 1798.

79. Newspaper notices reveal that groups were formed in the following places: Pawlingstown, Dutchess Co. (*Poughkeepsie Journal*, Aug. 11, 1789); Catskill (*Catskill Packet*, Sept. 17, 1792); New Paltz, Ulster Co. (*Poughkeepsie Journal*, Sept. 11, 1793); Beekman, Dutchess Co. (*ibid.*, Apr. 1, 1795); Pittstown and West Hoosick, Rensselaer Co. (*Lansingburgh Recorder*, Feb. 1795); and Montgomery, Orange Co. (Newburgh *Rights of Man*, Aug. 10, 1800). For activities, see Minutes of the Red Hook Society for the Detection of Horse Thieves (1796-1852), N.Y. State Lib.

80. Constitution and Minutes of the Slave Apprehending Society of Shawangunk, Ulster County [founded] May 21, 1796, N.Y. State Lib.

culture, Arts and Manufactures, whose gentlemen directors were equally uninterested in them.[81] As for the tenants, while they again took collective action against their landlords in the mid-1790's, they formed no organizations, or at least none whose traces can be found.

In the small towns it was mostly the traditional organizations which flourished. Republicans often led the militia, glorying in the "citizen soldiers," who were often "ill drilled," not arranged by size, and armed with "muskets and rifles, duck guns, pop guns and bludgeons."[82] Republicans were busy in Masonic lodges which sprang up all over the state and were also used occasionally to further the ambitions of would-be office seekers.[83] Republicans were also active church members, who lingered to talk of politics after Sunday meeting. The Baptists in particular, New England migrants most of them, fathered a cantankerous breed of men, some of whom became Republican leaders.[84] At Newburgh, a few Republicans organized a deist group—the Society of Ancient Druids—which stirred such a hornet's nest in Republican Orange County that its leading light, editor David Denniston of the Newburgh *Rights of Man*, was forced to depart for the more liberal climate of New York City.[85]

In the Hudson Valley cities general mechanics societies made their appearance at Poughkeepsie, Hudson, Catskill, Albany, and Lansingburgh,[86] and a variety of craft and journeymen groups took action to

81. Hedrick, *History of Agriculture in New York*, 112-17; for the indifference to a frontier agricultural society, see Francis Adrian Vanderkemp, *Speech . . . June 1, 1795 . . . at Whitestown for the Institution of a Society of Agriculture* (Whitestown, 1795).

82. *Albany Register*, Sept. 22, 1794. See entry for 1800 of John Maude, "Diary" in Munsell, ed., *Annals of Albany*, III, 62.

83. See the charge in "Cato," Cooperstown *Otsego Herald*, Apr. 26, 1797, regarding Jedediah Peck; a notice in the *Poughkeepsie Journal*, June 6, 1791, refers to lodges in Poughkeepsie, Newburgh, Fishkill, Kingston, and Cooperstown. By the mid-1790's there were many more. Masonic literature, rule books, song books, orations, etc., were published in the following towns in the 1790's: Albany, Ballston, Cooperstown, Duanesburgh, Kingston, Lavanna, Newburgh, and Waterford. See Evans, comp., *American Bibliography*, XI, XII, Appendix.

84. Minutes of Baptist associations were published at Goshen (1792), Lansingburgh (1793), Cooperstown (1796), Waterford (1797), and Albany (1800 for Rensselaerville); see Evans, comp., *American Bibliography*, XI, XII; for an example of a piece of militant democratic Baptist literature, see *A Plea for the Non-Conformists . . .* (Ballston, 1800).

85. Koch, *Republican Religion*, 116-19, 208-20.

86. "An Address to the Society of Mechanics of Hudson and Claverack," *Hudson Gazette*, Mar. 15, 1792; "Constitution of the Mechanics Society of Albany," Munsell, ed., *Annals of Albany*, VII, 240-44; for Lansingburgh, *ibid.*, III, 97 and *Albany Gazette*, Jan. 23, 1795.

regulate prices or wages.[87] The smalltown craftsmen could be militant: the Lansingburgh carpenters pledged to "do everything in their power not only to discourage but also to obstruct" nonunion craftsmen from plying their trade. Even the unskilled workers on Philip Schuyler's western canal project threatened to strike.[88] Mechanics supported upstate printers who brought out their own reprints of books written "by one born of a son of a mechanic" and by mechanics who made good.[89] And mechanics developed a sense of class against "those who disliked the mechanics for joining together" as a speaker at Hudson put it, who doubtless had in mind the legislators who refused to charter upstate mechanics societies.[90]

Mechanics aside, in the other cities of the state there was no organizational growth comparable to New York City. At Albany, the second city, the only new groups to appear in the 1790's were a Humane Society and a debtor's relief society, both in Federalist hands.[91] It is perhaps typical that Elkanah Watson, Albany's Yankee crusader, acted on his own, without forming associations in the style of Philadelphia's Benjamin Franklin, and that late in the 1790's, he left Albany's phlegmatic burgers to return to his native New England.[92]

V

By the late spring and early summer of 1794 the "republican societies" had the initiative in New York City. The continued outpouring of group after group to work on the unfinished fortifications on Governor's Island was one measure of this. Another was the reception given the celebrated scientist, Joseph Priestley, when he dis-

---

87. *Albany Register*, Mar. 11, 1793; *Albany Gazette*, Feb. 27, 1795; Lansingburgh *Tiffany Recorder*, Sept. 23, 1794; *Poughkeepsie Journal*, July 16, 1794; Cooperstown *Otsego Herald*, Feb. 29, Mar. 22, 31, 1796; *Albany Centinel*, July 4, 1795.

88. "Rules and Regulations of the United House Carpenters and Joiners of Lansingburgh and Troy . . . June 17, 1790," broadside, N.Y. State Lib.; Nathan Miller, "Private Enterprise in Inland Navigation: The Mohawk Route Prior to the Erie Canal," *N.Y. History*, 31 (1950), 400-401.

89. See Benjamin Franklin, *The Way to Wealth* (Lansingburgh, 1789; Albany, 1793), *The Life of Dr. Benjamin Franklin Written by Himself* . . . (Albany, 1797); John Bernard, *A Present for an Apprentice or a Sure Guide to Gain Both Esteem and Estate . . . By a Late Lord Mayor of London* (Albany, 1798). Andrew Adgate [Absalom Aimwell, pseud.], *A Lecture; Containing a Short History of Mechanics . . . Reverently Dedicated to the Respectable Supporters of Liberty and Property, the Mechanics of the United States* (Catskill, 1795), a reprint.

90. *Hudson Gazette*, Mar. 15, 1792; *Albany Gazette*, Feb. 27, 1795.

91. *Albany Register*, Jan. 21, 28, May 13, 1793, Dec. 1, 1797; *Catskill Packet*, June 20, 1795.

92. Flick, Elkanah Watson, 102-3, 109-11.

embarked in the city, a political refugee from a "Church and King" mob that had driven him from his native Birmingham. Priestley was greeted by Governor Clinton, Bishop Samuel Provoost of the Episcopal Church, and deputations from the Democratic Society, Tammany, the Associated Teachers, the Medical Society of the State of New York and "the Republican Natives of Great Britain and Ireland." Through all their messages ran the same theme: America was a haven for a distinguished victim of old-world persecution and hated British tyranny. In his replies Priestley was appreciative, but nonpolitical, disappointing the Democratic Society. The Democrats and Tammany invited Priestley to join; he made clear that he was "not to be a public or political character." Nonetheless, Republicans remained his admirers after he left for Pennsylvania to start a new life.[93] Republican printers published his works, a Republican artist put out an engraving of him, and on a return visit, the Democratic Society arranged a lecture series for him.[94]

On July Fourth the societies turned Independence Day into a Republican festival as they would do for years. The day was "more universally celebrated," Greenleaf reported, than it had been for "many years." For the first time Tammany, the Mechanics, several militia companies, and the Democratic Society held a joint parade. They were joined by Governor Clinton, Genêt, and a "long procession of French Jacobins."[95] When the paraders reached Christ Church they entered, each society by prearrangement sitting in its assigned section: the militia officers in front of the pulpit, the Mechanics to the right of the center aisle, Tammany over to one side; in later years the Democrats would be to the left of the center aisle, the Coopers off to another side.[96] The program consisted of the reading of the Declar-

93. For comment on the reactions, Wansey, *Journal of an Excursion*, 87-89; for the messages and Priestley's replies, Edgar Smith, *Priestley in America, 1794-1804* (Phila., 1920), 21-40, and *N.-Y. Journal*, June 7, 18, 1794; N.Y. *Columbian Gazetteer*, June 9, 1794; N.Y. *Herald*, June 11, 19, 1794; entries of June 5, 12, 1794, Minutes of the Associated Teachers, N.Y. State Lib.

94. Horace Johnson to Andrew Craigie, June 4, 1794, Craigie Papers, III, No. 90, Amer. Antiq. Soc.; N.Y. *Herald*, Sept. 10, 1794, and *N.Y. Magazine*, 9 (1794), 558-61; the engraving is advertised *N.-Y. Journal*, July 2, 1794; entry of Oct. 15, 1796, Minutes of the Associated Teachers, N.Y. State Lib.; entries of Aug. 25, Nov. 6, 1794, Anderson Diary, Columbia Univ.

95. *N.-Y. Journal*, July 2, 5, 1794; Kenneth and Anna M. Roberts, trans. and eds., *Moreau de St. Méry's American Journey (1793-1798)* (Garden City, N.Y., 1947), 125.

96. Entry of June 7, 1798, Minutes of the General Society of Mechanics, Soc. Lib., lists the seating arrangements for the first time. The Democratic and Cooper societies met with the other groups for the first time in 1795.

ation of Independence, an ode, and a sermon. In the evening the groups dined separately, toasted each other, and exchanged deputations. The Democrats, with Citizen Genêt as their guest, toasted "Citizen Thomas Jefferson" and "Citizen James Madison," while the Mechanics toasted "the republican societies."[97]

Thus in less than half a year's time, the outlook for the Republican movement was bright, especially in the city. The Democratic societies had pushed themselves to the center of the political stage. The other private associations in various ways contributed to the Republican cause. Tammany and the Masonic lodges spread democratic ideas. Through the humanitarian associations Republicans reached out to the poor and unfortunate. The more active mechanics became, the more they discovered their foes were Federalists. New immigrants who organized would also vote; symbolically Republicans opened the doors of the Humane Society "to any person either an American citizen or a foreigner."[98] Republican leaders active in a variety of organizations—for example, DeWitt Clinton, Melancton Smith, Donald Fraser, and Samuel L. Mitchill—were making friends who might join them at the polls.[99]

New Yorkers were invigorating the tradition of doing things in associations which visitors like Alexis de Tocqueville later found so characteristically American;[100] they were becoming "joiners." If Federalists attacked "self created societies" it was certainly true of New York that "there was not an individual who might not come under the charge of being a member of some one or other self created society," as Congressman Giles of Virginia put it.[101] If Federalists attacked the right of the Democratic societies to exist, others might see a threat to their own rights. Beginning in the summer of 1794 this is precisely what happened—with favorable political consequences for the Republicans.

97. Pilmore, *Blessings of Peace*, 9-10; *N.-Y. Journal*, July 5, 1794; Udney Hay to Edmund Genêt, June 28, Genêt to Hay, July 2, 1794, Genêt Papers, Lib. Cong.

98. *Constitution of the Humane Society of New York.*

99. Clinton was a member of Tammany, the Masons, the Black Friars, and probably the Democratic Society; Smith was a member of Tammany, the Manumission, Debtors Relief, Humane, Emigrant Aid, and probably the Democratic Society; Fraser was a member of the Tammany, the Caledonian, and the Democratic Society, and the Associated Teachers; Samuel L. Mitchill was a member of Tammany, the Emigrant Aid, the American Mineralogical societies, the Friendly Club, the Agricultural Society, and the Associated Teachers.

100. Alexis de Tocqueville, *Democracy in America*, trans. Henry Reeve, ed. P. Bradley, 2 vols. (N.Y., 1945), I, ch. 12, II, Bk. II, ch. 5.

101. Quoted in DeConde, *Entangling Alliance*, 265.

CHAPTER 19

Federalist Counterattack and

Republican Victory, June-December

1794

As the Republican movement gathered momentum in 1794 it was confronted with two tasks: to defend itself against a bitter Federalist onslaught and to bring its patriot supporters to the polls as Republican voters. With John Jay in England, discussion of foreign policy for the time being was put aside. When the Whiskey Rebellion erupted in western Pennsylvania, Federalists made the Democratic societies a major political issue. In defending themselves Republicans presented their philosophy. Then in the congressional elections of December 1794, they scored their first breakthrough in a national election, bringing the first year of their movement to a rewarding climax.

I

Federalists continued to attack the growing Republican opposition with old charges. Republicans, they claimed, were a "faction" stirring up "the spirit of the party"; party was "a monster that devours the public good."[1] But new ammunition had to be cast to confront the rising caliber of the leaders in the Republican camp. Derision was the

1. William Wyche, *Party Spirit, An Oration Delivered to the Horanian Literary Society . . . May 10, 1794 at Tammany Hall* (N.Y., 1794), 12, 16, 17-18.

answer. A mock epic poem "Democracy" by "Acquiline Nimble Chops, Democrat," mercilessly poked fun at the organizers of the New York City public meeting of February 1794.[2] The speakers were mocked as "Squire Pomposo," "mighty Matlack," and "a young man of aristocratic lineage," presumably Edward Livingston. The burden of the satire was that these men were demagogues pretending to be democrats or merchants trying to escape legitimate debts to Britain. The apprentices and journeymen who quit the cobbler's last to attend the meeting were labeled "greasy caps," thoughtless and emotional. At each good point made by a speaker

> Hats, caps, and wigs, and leathern aprons flew
> And puffs of wondrous size and jerkins blue.

To Federalists, discussion by such men was "the pitiful ebullitions of an incoherent mass of people."[3]

Commodore James Nicholson, perhaps the most distinguished and wealthy Republican leader, especially galled the Federalists. To "Nimble Chops" he was "the noted TAR" who scorned a title in others but kept one for himself. Federalists pounced on him for his comment that he "would not be surprised if the British were attempting to bribe the President," twisting this into an accusation that Washington had actually received "British gold." The falsehood, Republicans claimed, "was spread abroad for some electioneering purpose and to expose the reputation of the [Democratic] Society."[4]

Federalists launched their attack on the Democratic societies along several fronts: they were "Jacobins" or "Genetites" ("Genêt's scouting party"), they were exclusive and secretive, and they were "anti-Federalist." Underlying these charges was the assumption, often stated, that the societies did not have a legitimate function because the people had no right to instruct their representatives once elected. The very name Democratic thus was objectionable.

In a formal "Address to the Republican Citizens of the United States," the New York Society took two full pages of Greenleaf's paper

2. "Acquiline Nimble Chops," [pseud.], *Democracy, An Epic Poem* . . . (N.Y., 1794), attributed, falsely I believe, to Henry Brockholst Livingston. James Tillary denied a rumor that Tillary was the author, to R. R. Livingston, Mar. 22, 1794, R. R. Livingston Papers, N.-Y. Hist. Soc.

3. N.Y. *American Minerva*, Mar. 1, 3, 1794.

4. Samuel B. Webb to James Nicholson, May 18, 1794, in Ford, ed., *Correspondence of S. B. Webb*, III, 192-94, exonerating Nicholson; "Candour," *N.-Y. Journal*, May 14, 1794.

to refute such "objections" and present their philosophy.[5] The first charge was that "we have not stiled ourselves Republican, but Democratic, which signifies, as it is alleged a government composed of the whole mass of the people, and not a representative government." The two words, they answered, are "synonymous"; besides, in *The Federalist* Hamilton himself said the term republican had been so variously applied "that it is left without any definite meaning at all." The second objection was that "we are *anti-Federalists.*" "To this we reply—In the first place, we positively deny the charge"—many members were Federalists of '88. But in the second place, suppose the charge were true—the "only essential difference" between Federalist and anti-Federalist then was that the latter wanted to amend the Constitution before, the Federalists after adoption. The amendments "in sundry important instances" have since been adopted—"What then is the charge against the anti-Federalists?" Why revive "a once warm, but long since dead and buried political dispute?" As for "the third objection," "that we are the leaders of faction, possess a turbulence of disposition and intend to overset the government," the society replied, "Not Guilty." "No one may remain a member who is not a lover of genuine republicanism, a man of good moral principles, and strict honor, a friend to his country." They also defied the related charge that they were pro-French: "Yes, fellow citizens, we take pleasure in avowing thus, publicly to you that we are lovers of the French nation, that we esteem their cause as our own." If this was "the language of treason, if this is the language of faction and sedition," then come forward, and try us legally, "punish us for these, our open, our avowed principles, from which no earthly consideration shall ever tempt us to recede." Such a prosecution would only expose the accusers to the wrath of the people, for "he who is an enemy to the French revolution, cannot be a firm republican."[6]

In listing "a few of the advantages of popular associations," the society put first "the promotion of useful knowledge and the dissemination of political information." In republican governments it was the duty of individuals to "acquire a perfect knowledge of government" because "the offices of state are equally open to every class and description of citizens, without any other distinction than that which arises

5. "Address," May 28, is bound between the June 13 and June 14, 1794, issues of *N.-Y. Journal*, N.-Y. Hist. Soc.

6. For another denial of the charge, "A Member of the Democratic Society," *N.-Y. Journal*, Mar. 22, 1794; a paragraph, *ibid.*, June 18, 1794.

from superiority of virtue and talents"; therefore, all individuals "may one day be called upon to take an active share in the administration" of government. Secondly, the societies were essential for the formation of "public opinion," which required that citizens "hear and impartially weigh the arguments on both sides of all questions" and decide as reason dictates. Thirdly, they were necessary to protect popular rights. The people have to "meet for the purpose of examining and discussing whether there is, or is not, any infringement on those rights and in a manly but decent tone express their opinions, and when necessary, *demand redress*."

The Democrats believed that theirs were "the real principles of the constitution and original intention of the revolution." They challenged their opponents to form a society of equal size and compare the records of their members "from the memorable 19th of April, 1775 to the present moment." "You have all the agents from Great Britain, and lovers of the government of that country on your side," they said, "by which means you in a great degree direct our commerce and command our purses." In concluding their defense, the society expressed complete confidence in their "countrymen." "Our calumniators," they told the public in general, were "your enemies, as well as our own."

In the Hudson Valley the country Republicans defended themselves with more wit and brevity. An Ulsterite threw the Federalist derision back in their faces by satirizing "all the respectable Tories" of Orange and Ulster in a mock resolution adopted "in the thirty third year of the reign of their leige Lord King George the third" proclaiming that "the people have no right to assemble to deliberate on political affairs."[7] "A Canaan Democrat" justified the societies in class terms: "mediocrity or poverty joined with modest worth" was no match for "family, estate and the officious promptitude of brilliant parts"; representatives had to be instructed by the people because of "the more alluring and courtly influence of a banking and funding system."[8] A farmer who called himself "An Old Yankee," wrote, "I pronounce them all Democrats where I come from."[9]

7. Kingston *Rising Sun*, Feb. 22, 1794, reprinted from *Goshen Repository*; for defense of the right of exclusion, in *Goshen Repository*: "A Member of the Ulster Republican Society," Aug. 5, "A Member," Aug. 19, Oct. 7, 1794.

8. "A Canaan Democrat," Canaan *Columbian Mercury*, Oct. 1, 1794; for another Canaan defense, *N.-Y. Journal*, July 23, 1794.

9. *N.-Y. Journal*, June 21, 1794; see also "J.M." of Westchester, *ibid.*, Aug. 9, 1794.

In the late summer and fall of 1794 the societies faced a more severe challenge as Federalists stigmatized them as fomenters of Pennsylvania's Whiskey Rebellion, quelled by a federal expedition of 15,000 troops, Alexander Hamilton at their head. The question for New York Republicans was whether they would condone armed resistance to a hateful law and the seeming support of the rebellion by their sister society on the scene.[10]

The New York Republicans left no doubt where they stood. In the western part of the state near Pennsylvania, where a few New York pioneers operated distilleries, a "liberty pole" was raised against the whiskey tax, but this was as far as sympathy with the rebels went.[11] Even the Democratic Society of Canaan in the heart of the landlord country, whose farmers knew what it was to take up arms against oppression, resolved concisely "that whatever may be our sentiments relative to the excise law of the United States, we highly disapprove of that riotous opposition to the laws enacted by the constitutional powers of government . . . as an improper and daring means to seek redress of grievances."[12]

The Ulster Society rejected the accusation that the societies were instigators of the riots and argued that "whenever a law is so odious and unpopular that it cannot be executed by the ordinary authority of government, it is wise and politic to repeal" it. But they condemned "resistance by force to the execution of laws legally enacted by a majority of the representatives of the people" as "highly criminal, subversive of the sovereignty of the people and dangerous to the existence of a free government" and hoped that the insurgents would "resign their arms to the legal and constitutional mode of redress." The sentiments of their New York City brethren were similar.[13] Even Chancellor Livingston vented his spleen on the excise tax as the cause of the rebellion, "the first chapter of the evils I predicted from assump-

10. For differing interpretations of the role of the societies in the rebellion: William Miller, "The Democratic Societies and the Whiskey Insurrection," *Pa. Mag. of Hist. and Biog.*, 63 (1938), 324-49, and Link, *Democratic Republican Societies*, 45-49.

11. For western New York, Cowan, *Charles Williamson*, 106; James Kent, Travel Journal, Lib. Cong., reported 40 distilleries in the Genesee country in 1798.

12. *N.-Y. Journal*, Sept. 10, 1794, and "A Republican," Canaan *Columbian Mercury*, Oct. 1, 1794.

13. *Goshen Repository*, Oct. 28, 1794; for the New York City Society's resolution, *N.-Y. Journal*, Aug. 27, 1794.

tion" of the state debts, and hoped that "the business will blow over without bloodshed."[14]

Late in the year the threat moved closer to home after Washington condemned "certain self created societies," and Federalists in Congress attempted a motion of censure, singling out the New York City group for criticism in the course of debate. Madison led a spirited resistance in the House—"opinions are not the object of legislation"—as did Burr in the Senate. Greenleaf, in publishing the debate, warned that the "liberty of *meeting* to converse on political topics, of *speaking, writing,* and *publishing* the political sentiment of its hitherto supposed independent citizens," was at stake. Censure failed; the state's three Republicans voting with Madison, the six Federalists, including the three from the districts with the societies, voting for censure.[15] New York Federalists were unrealistic in predicting that the societies "have spit their venom and will be heard no more."[16]

This first Federalist attempt at repression only confirmed Republicans in their convictions. They were similarly unshaken by the news from France of the intensified Jacobin "Reign of Terror." The reaction of Reverend William Linn, junior minister at the Presbyterian church, was typical. An idealistic young man given to poetry who had deserted the study of law in Hamilton's office to join the ministry, Linn wrote a discourse early in 1794 in which he envisioned the French Revolution as "preparing the way for the pure and peaceful religion of Christ." In the fall the latest news from France made him pause as he prepared his essays for the printer. He added a preface: "The events which have taken place during the summer," he wrote, "confirm . . . [me] in the opinion that civil liberty will unanimously prevail and that God is preparing the way for the introduction of a glorious scene upon earth."[17]

When the news arrived of the execution of Robespierre, New York's Republicans were, a Frenchman observed, "profoundly grieved as at the loss of their father, their leader, their friend." Nevertheless,

14. R. R. Livingston to James Monroe, Sept. 18, 1794, Monroe Papers, II, Lib. Cong.

15. *Annals*, 3d Cong., 2d Sess., 899-946, vote at 914; Miller, "The Democratic Societies," *Pa. Mag. of Hist. and Biog.*, 63 (1938), 335-39; Brant, *James Madison*, III, 416-18; *N.-Y. Journal*, Dec. 12, 1794.

16. Peter Van Schaack to Theodore Sedgwick, Dec. 23, 1794, Sedgwick Papers, Mass. Hist. Soc.

17. Rev. William Linn, *Discourses on the Signs of the Times* . . . (N.Y., 1794) 12-13.

the Democrats and Tammany celebrated the third anniversary of the French Republic with a feast at which Fauchet, the new French minister, shared the honors with Governor Clinton. Seven troops of militia paraded, adorned with the French national cockades. The Democratic Society expressed its "warmest approbation" of James Monroe's Francophile speech to the French National Convention, and the republican sailmakers toasted a "perpetual union" of France and America.[18] Democrats welcomed Genêt's marriage into "one of the most distinguished families in this country,"[19] and continued to treat Genêt as a welcome ally.[20]

Continuing British seizures of American ships hardened New York Republicans in their Anglophobia. In September the Britsh took three merchant vessels off Sandy Hook, owned by of all people John Livingston, the Chancellor's brother, and David Gelston, president of the Democratic Society. Gelston fumed: "It looks as though the British were determined to plunder and robb us on our own coasts until they have taken everything we have and then laugh at us. It is said by them we have not spirit to resist any insult or offense."[21] Even merchants in conservative pro-British circles were "greatly disgusted."[22]

Thus confirmed in their faith, defiant of their detractors, and working in a political atmosphere that continued to favor them, Republicans warmed to the congressional elections of 1794.

II

Republicans who had elected only three out of ten congressional seats in 1792 won six out of ten races in December 1794. They returned their three incumbents in the Long Island, Westchester, and Dutchess districts, recaptured one old one, Ulster-Orange, and took two new ones: Washington-Saratoga and New York City. Republicans thus took the entire southern part of the state, the middle Hudson Valley, and the northern frontier.

18. Roberts, trans. and ed., *Moreau de St. Méry's Journey*, 143-44; Strickland, Journal, Sept. 22, 1794, N.-Y. Hist. Soc.; *N.-Y. Journal*, Sept. 24, Nov. 15, 1794.

19. Donald Fraser to Edmund Genêt, Nov. 11, 1794, Genêt Papers, Lib. Cong.

20. For continuing recognition see the account of the observance at Jamaica, *N.-Y. Journal*, July 4, 1794; G. N. Bleecker to Genêt, Feb. 4, 1797, Genêt Papers, Lib. Cong.; James Nicholson to Albert Gallatin, July 2, 1796, Gallatin Papers, N.-Y. Hist. Soc.; Minnegerode, *Jefferson, Friend of France*, 388.

21. David Gelston to Governor Clinton, Sept. 8, 1794, Jay Papers, Columbia Univ.; R. R. Livingston to James Monroe, Sept. 18, 1794, R. R. Livingston Papers, N.-Y. Hist. Soc.

22. Strickland, Journal, Sept. 1794, in particular Sept. 24, N.-Y. Hist. Soc.

In their three old districts the Republican victories were nothing to boast about. On Long Island, which they had taken with ease two years earlier, "all interests split." Jonathan Havens, the Republican, defeated Samuel Jones, who had gone over to the Federalists, and two other candidates, with less than a plurality. In the Westchester-Richmond district Philip Van Cortlandt, the Republican incumbent who defeated Richard Hatfield by 200 votes in 1792, squeaked through by only twenty votes. In Dutchess the Republican incumbent Theodorus Bailey won by a safe margin over strong Federalist opposition.[23]

In New York City the victory of Edward Livingston over the Federalist John Watts by a vote of 1843 to 1638 represented a spectacular Republican climb from 1792 when Watts had defeated William S. Livingston. In accordance with the non-party tradition, Edward Livingston was nominated at several public meetings to which all "friends of this nomination" were invited. Privately Republican leaders acknowledged what Federalists charged—that Livingston was the choice of the Democratic Society. His support showed the new elements attracted to the Republicans. The chairmen of various nominating meetings were Ebenezer Stevens, the Genêt-ite merchant; John Stagg, president of the General Society of Mechanics and Tradesmen; and Thomas Ivers, ropemaker and popular Whig of the 1770's.[24]

The choice of the Chancellor's 34-year-old brother as a candidate was a shrewd move. A lawyer, the owner of a country estate, the son-in-law of a prominent merchant, he was hardly a Jacobin "sans culotte"; in fact he made no effort to disguise his class status. He was known by the sobriquet of "Beau Ned," the young dandy. He could command support from his numerous tribe of relatives and among merchants who remembered his role in the abortive "State Bank" of 1792. At the same time he was a member of the Democratic Society and Tammany. An eloquent orator and man of charm he nevertheless had been completely unsuccessful in running for the assembly since 1791.[25]

In the two weeks of electioneering Republicans were "all active . . .

23. For brief identifications of candidates in all districts by Greenleaf, see *N.-Y. Journal*, Dec. 17, 1794, also *Albany Register*, Dec. 15, 1794, and *Albany Gazette*, Dec. 8, 22, 1794; for the returns see Appendix, Table 6.

24. *N.-Y. Journal*, Nov. 26, 29, Dec. 3, 1794; Miller, "First Fruits of Republican Organization," *Pa. Mag. of Hist. and Biog.*, 63 (1939), 119-20.

25. Charles H. Hunt, *The Life of Edward Livingston* (N.Y., 1864), chs. 1-3; William Hatcher, *Edward Livingston: Jeffersonian Republican and Jacksonian Democrat* (Baton Rouge, La., 1940), 1-36.

every nerve is in motion by them," appealing to patriotism, republicanism, and class. The contest, one writer put it, was between "Whigs and Tories or [between] friends and enemies to the French or [between] the swinish multitude and the better sort." The issue was: "shall British influence . . . prevail?" "Whigs," intoned this writer, "muster all your force and let EDWARD LIVINGSTON, the poor man's friend and the uniform assertor of the Rights of Man go to Congress." Livingston and all but a few of his family were "tried whigs of '76." Watts had remained in occupied New York City during the Revolution; "no republican saw him [then], except those unfortunate brave men who looked at him through their prison windows." As a congressman, he was inactive, a "paper man" and, by implication, a "friend to British measures."[26]

Federalists attacked Livingston as the candidate of the Democratic Society, as a disappointed office seeker, and an untried young man who grew rich on bankruptcies. Speaking to the rich, they claimed that Republicans would "level all distinctions, property and rights"; to the poor, they stressed Livingston's aristocratic lineage. Over and above this, national policy was at stake. The treaty which Jay was negotiating would restore the frontier posts, satisfy merchants, and maintain peace.[27]

A year and a half before, when Livingston ran for the assembly, he had drawn about 200 votes. In his race for Congress he converted a Federalist majority of 1200 votes in 1792 to a Republican majority of 200 in 1794. The "federal interest," Noah Webster claimed, was "ill managed" and rent by "some improper jealousies." Watts ran strongest in the old wealthy downtown wards; Livingston drew some support there but his percentage increased in the uptown wards on the east and west sides of town, the home of the mechanics and immigrants who had worked on the fort the spring gone by.[28] Essentially Livingston owed his victory to the events of 1794.

In the Ulster-Orange County district, home of the second Democratic Society, the Republican triumph was even more striking. Two

26. N.Y. *Daily Gazette*, Dec. 2, 1794; in *N.-Y. Journal*: "An Old Whig," Dec. 3, "A Plebeian," Dec. 6, unsigned, Dec. 10, 1794.

27. In N.Y. *Daily Advertiser*: "Sene," Dec. 1, "Montgomery," Dec. 3, Edward Livingston's reply, Dec. 6, 1794; in N.Y. *American Minerva*, articles Nov. 27, Dec. 5, Dec. 9, cited in Miller, "First Fruits of Republican Organization," *Pa. Mag. of Hist. and Biog.*, 63 (1939), 140-41; "P," N.Y. *Herald*, Dec. 1, 1794.

28. *N.-Y. Journal*, Feb. 7, 1795. Noah Webster to Theodore Sedgwick, Dec. 15, 1794, Sedgwick Papers, Mass. Hist. Soc.

years earlier the Republican incumbent, John Hathorn, had lost to the Federalist merchant of Kingston, Peter Van Gaasbeck, by a hair's breadth, 1448-1464. When Van Gaasbeck, fearing defeat, refused to run again Federalists divided over backing another Kingstonian, Conrad Elmendorph, who was probably a former anti-Federalist. Republicans united behind Hathorn, who was nominated by leaders of the Democratic Society in the southern part of the county. Raising the old anti-Federalist battle cries about "a consolidated system" and the "funding junto," Hathorn swept the district, 1519-583.[29]

The triumph of John Williams, the *nouveau-riche* landholder of Washington County, gave Republicans their third new seat.[30] In 1792 Williams, the veteran anti-Federalist and Clintonian, had been nosed out for Congress because anti-Federalist votes were diverted to a third candidate. Williams had recently been elected to the state senate again as a foe of "the patroon influence" and an "overgrown landlord," namely Stephen Van Rensselaer.[31] Philip Schuyler sneered at the "virtuous character Williams" a reference to his expulsion from the senate in 1777, expecting him to lose.[32] In the campaign Federalists called Williams "the nabob" of Salem, accusing him of pressuring his tenants and of donating land to a church only in penance for his sins.[33] Williams offered himself as a spokesman for the pioneer farmers of his county. This time he won, 1297–1079, even though 309 votes were again drawn off to a third candidate.[34]

In the four districts which Federalists retained, their strength rested heavily on votes dependent on landlords and land proprietors. In Albany, center of the Schuyler influence, the incumbent Federalist

29. *Albany Gazette*, Dec. 8, 22; *Albany Register*, Dec. 15, 1794; *Goshen Repository*, "Candidus," *ibid.*, Nov. 18, 25, Dec. 2, 1794; for returns *N.-Y. Journal*, Feb. 21, 1795; Peter Van Gaasbeck to Rufus King, July 19, 1794, King Papers, N.-Y. Hist. Soc.

30. For background see ch. 2, sec. III; for his economic activities at this time, John Williams Papers, vols. I, II, IV, and Assessment Roll for the Town of Salem for 1795, III, N.Y. State Lib. For a description of the area, see Kent Travel Journal, May 17-June 22, 1795, Kent Papers, Lib. Cong., and Salem *Washington Patrol*, May-Nov., *passim*.

31. "A Conversation Between an Old Whig and Robert the Schoolmaster," Apr. 23, 1794; "Mr. Printer," by Thomas Sickels, Apr. 24, 1794, and "A Farmer," 1794, all broadsides in Williams Papers, III, N.Y. State Lib.

32. Philip Schuyler to Rufus King, Nov. 24, Dec. 30, 1794, King Papers, N.-Y. Hist. Soc.

33. *Albany Gazette*, Dec. 8, 1794.

34. *N.-Y. Journal*, Feb. 11, 1795. Judge Webster, an anti-Federalist, had 305 votes. John Woodworth to Williams, Apr. 20, 1795, Williams Papers, III, N.Y. State Lib.

Henry Glen was returned with only a token challenge.[35] In the Rens-selaer-Clinton district the Republicans gave Stephen Van Rensselaer's choice, Congressman John Van Allen, a fright by nominating Thomas Tredwell, the incumbent Republican congressman from Long Island who had moved to Plattsburgh in Clinton County where he owned land. After his agent, Thomas Witbeck, made his rounds, however, the patroon was able to assure Van Allen that "our old friends are all true." The vote was a lopsided 1109–298. Van Rensselaer delivered his tenants in his own county and Tredwell's small vote came entirely from Clinton County.[36]

In Columbia County the Livingstons made clear that whatever their posture on national policy, they would sooner back a Federalist than elevate a traditional foe of the landlords. To oppose the incumbent Federalist, Ezekiel Gilbert, Republicans were unable to produce a man satisfactory to the Livingstons, or even to agree among themselves. Matthew Adgate, the senior assemblyman, insisted that he alone could carry his home town, Canaan, center of the Democratic Society, and the northern part of the county. John Bay, the junior assemblyman from the southern part of the county, refused to withdraw. Since 1785 the Livingstons had opposed Adgate, whom Hamilton had characterized as "a New England adventurer" with "levelling" principles.[37] Adgate asked for support from William Wilson, Chancellor Livingston's steward on the lower manor, but Wilson, who saw no prospect of a Republican victory, backed Gilbert.[38] The tenants of the small lower manor and the large upper manor turned out for Gilbert, their votes added to those of normally Federalist Hudson and Kinderhook giving Gilbert the victory, 768 to 441 for Bay and 419 for Adgate. Sixty per cent of Adgate's vote came from Canaan.[39] Had

35. *Albany Gazette*, Feb. 20, 1795; Schuyler to King, Nov. 24, Dec. 2, 1794, King Papers, N.-Y. Hist. Soc. The results: Henry Glen, 703, James Fairlie, 82.

36. *Albany Gazette*, Feb. 10, 1795. Thomas Witbeck to John Van Allen, Nov. 17; an undated letter written after Nov. 17; Dec. 7, and another undated letter written after Dec. 7; Stephen Van Rensselaer to John Van Allen, Dec. 4, 1794; Van Rensselaer MSS, N.Y. State Lib.; Schuyler to King, Dec. 2, 1794, King Papers, N.-Y. Hist. Soc.

37. Hamilton to Robert Livingston, Apr. 25, 1785, Livingston to Hamilton, June 13, 1785, Syrett, ed., *Hamilton Papers*, III, 608-9, 614-16.

38. Michael Adgate to William Wilson, Dec. 3, 1794, Wilson to Ezekiel Gilbert, Dec. 23, 1794, Wilson Papers, Clements Lib.

39. *Albany Gazette*, Feb. 16, 1795; Peter Van Schaack to Theodore Sedgwick, Dec. 23, 1794, Sedgwick Papers, Mass. Hist. Soc. Van Schaack, a resident of the district, makes no mention of Democratic society activities.

Republicans been united, even without Livingston support, they might have taken the district.

In the western district, the fourth the Federalists kept, a victory was all but inevitable with the future of the region riding on John Jay's success in London at restoring the forts. Adding to the grievances stemming from the election of 1792 which westerners held against the Governor was his recent refusal to call a special election in their district when the Federalist congressman, Silas Talbot, resigned.[40] In 1792 Talbot had won in a three-way race in which the anti-Federalist John Winn was second and the Federalist William Cooper, third. Now it was Cooper against Winn, sheriff of Montgomery County, with a young Federalist lawyer, James Cochran, entering the race at the last minute. Cooper's friends campaigned for him as "the father of his country," attacking Winn's supporters as "Jacobins." Winn made an issue of Cooper's "oppressions" in Otsego, while Cochran's appeal was personal and local. Cooper won with 2535 votes to 1426 for Winn and 535 for Cochran. Otsego gave Cooper half of his vote. Winn's vote, while twice what he received in 1792, was almost all from his home county, as was Cochran's.[41] It was the last congressional race in the western district for years in which Republicans would sponsor their own candidate. Shortly after the election, Philip Schuyler asked Rufus King to get a federal appointment for James Cochran to quench his political ambitions.[42]

The Republican victory—six out of ten seats—was as unexpected to the Republicans as to the Federalists.[43] The Democratic societies in two districts, Ulster and New York City, had proven their vote-gathering capacity; less so the Canaan society. But Republican margins of victory, save for Ulster-Orange, were narrow. They were plagued

40. N.Y. *Herald*, Nov. 8, 1794; DeWitt Clinton on behalf of the governor to the Members of Congress from New York, Dec. 19, 1794, published in N.Y. *Herald*, Jan. 31, 1795; the answer of six Federalist congressmen and DeWitt Clinton's response, N.Y. *Herald*, Mar. 18, 1795; see also *Albany Gazette*, Nov. 3, 1794.

41. William Cooper to Ebenezer Foote, Nov. 29, 1794, Cooper MSS, N.Y. State Hist. Assoc.; James Cochran to Stephen Van Rensselaer, Dec. 15, 1794, MS 1833, N.Y. State Lib.; *Albany Register*, Nov. 10, 24, 1794; *Albany Gazette*, Oct. 27, Nov. 20, 27, Dec. 1, 4, 1794; *N.-Y. Journal*, Nov. 19, 1794; for returns Cooperstown *Otsego Herald*, Apr. 17, 1795, very likely more accurate than those in *Albany Gazette*, Feb. 10, 1795 and *N.-Y. Journal*, Feb. 14, 1795.

42. Schuyler to King, Jan. 20, 1795, King Papers, N.-Y. Hist. Soc.

43. R. R. Livingston to James Monroe, Feb. 18, 1795, Monroe Papers, III, Lib. Cong.; William Van Ingen to Henry Glen, Jan. 2, 1795, Glen Papers, N.Y. State Hist. Assoc.

by third candidates on Long Island and the northern frontier and by disunity in Columbia which seemed beyond repair. There were grounds for only a cautious optimism.

In the senatorial election of January 1795 Republicans suffered an expected blow when the state legislature elected the previous spring returned Rufus King for a second term. At first there was talk among northern Federalists of returning Philip Schuyler instead; otherwise, Egbert Benson explained to King, both senators, he and Burr, would be from the southern district. Republicans seem to have sounded out Samuel Jones, the former Clintonian, about accepting their support. But at the Federalist caucus Schuyler branded talk of his running a Republican plot, Jones endorsed King, and the caucus voted unanimously for the incumbent Yankee. In the legislature Republicans went through the motions of supporting Dr. Thomas Tillotson, the Chancellor's brother-in-law, but King was re-elected by five votes in the assembly and two in the senate.[44] Thus in the fourth Congress New York would continue to be represented in the Senate by King and Burr, but with the three new Republican congressmen, John Williams, Jonathan Havens, and above all in Edward Livingston, the Republican interest would for the first time acquire able and articulate spokesmen.

III

Early in 1795, after roughly a year of the Republican movement, the New York Republicans had a good deal to crow about. The increase in their strength could be measured not only at the polls but in the flourishing state of their newspapers. Greenleaf, the dean of Republican printers in the state, claimed that the circulation of his *New-York Journal* went up one-third in 1794 to two thousand—which, if true, was three times that of the average New York City paper. In the spring of 1795 he launched a daily, the *Argus*, and converted the *Journal* into a country semi-weekly. In New York City merchants boycotted Greenleaf, sending their advertisements elsewhere, but the *Journal* became a statewide organ of Republicanism.[45] Meanwhile, Barber and Southwick claimed the circulation of the *Albany Register*, now

44. Schuyler to King, Jan. 6, 20, 1795. Benson to King, Jan. 15, 1795, Schuyler to Alexander Hamilton, Jan. 25, 1795, Robert Troup to King, Jan. 27, 1795, King Papers, N.-Y. Hist. Soc.; *Journal of the Assembly of N.Y.*, 18th Sess., 32.
45. *N.-Y. Journal*, Jan. 3, Feb. 11, June 24, 1795; N.Y. *Argus*, July 22, 1795; Philip Freneau to DeWitt Clinton, Nov. 8, 1795; DeWitt Clinton Papers, No. 35, Columbia Univ.

bi-weekly, was up one thousand by 1794 and another five hundred by June 1795. It even survived the resolution of Otsego County Federalists to discourage subscriptions "from its being too deeply tinged with DEMOCRATIC and anti-Federalist principles."[46]

In the Republican sunshine some new papers bloomed, although most withered on the vine. In New York City the *Columbian Gazetteer* was enlarged and appeared as the *New-York Evening Post* for six months. In the Hudson Valley there were the *Poughkeepsie Republican Journal* and the *Newburgh Packet* and to the north, the *Salem Times*. Federalists matched these by papers at Schenectady and Salem and by no fewer than five papers on the western frontier, but even Federalist papers gave wider currency to Republican contributors and stimulated political debate.[47]

As the state's Democratic societies surveyed the political scene on the occasion of their first anniversary, they were in a fighting mood. The Canaan Democrats saw tyranny everywhere on the defensive: in Europe democracy was regenerating the continent, in America the advocates of a standing army and "titular pomp" were "baffled and mortified" and the abuses of aristocracy were exposed by a vigilant press. The fundamental issue, of course, remained: "whether the real object of government shall be the general benefit of the community or the emolument and aggrandizement of the few"; the Democratic societies therefore were more necessary than ever.[48]

The New York City Democrats were also defiant. "Our principles may be gibbetted," the secretary, Tunis Wortman, wrote to their sister association in Philadelphia, but "rather than consent to abandon them we would be gibbetted ourselves." The society's second public "address" was a pithy performance, breathing a new sense of confidence.[49] Was the charge against them "fomenting insurrection?" They were "condemned without proof." Was the charge that they were "self created?" "By whom then ought we to have been consti-

46. *Albany Register*, Jan. 4, June 2, Dec. 8, 1794.

47. Political identification is based on my own judgment and Stewart, *Jeffersonian Journalism*, Appendix; for dates and publishers see Brigham, comp., *Bibliography of American Newspapers*, II, "New York."

48. *N.-Y. Journal*, Mar. 18, 1795, and *Catskill Packet*, Apr. 11, 1795. The address of the Ulster Society is in *Goshen Repository*, Feb. 24, 1795.

49. Tunis Wortman for the Committee of Correspondence of the Democratic Society of New York to the Democratic Society of Philadelphia, [n.d.], Misc. MSS, No. 85, N.-Y. Hist. Soc.; *N.-Y. Journal*, Jan. 17, 1795. See also the articles developing democratic political theory, *ibid.*, by "Agis," Nov. 28, 1794, Jan. 31, 1795, and "Democritus," Feb. 7, Mar. 25, May 20, 1795.

tuted?" "Are not all private associations established in the foundation of their own authority?" "Is it for assembly we are accused?" "What statute has deprived us of the right?" "Is it for presuming to disapprove of any of the measures of the administration that we are censured?" "The government is responsible to its sovereign the people . . . and any part of the people have the right to express their opinions on the government." Did they disagree with the government? Most certainly it was a right of the people, for even if they were in error, argument would correct them; suppression would not. Where would the country have been without popular societies? It was free inquiry that secured liberty from Great Britain and produced the Constitution.

In a concluding section, the address restated their fundamental principles. Under a republican form of government sovereignty rested in the people who delegated it to a representative government. "THE RESPONSIBILITY OF PUBLIC FUNCTIONARIES *presupposes* A RIGHT OF INVESTIGATION INTO THEIR PROCEEDINGS." Democracy declined "and the EMPIRE OF DESPOTISM was established only where there was ABJECT IGNORANCE." History thus proved that the societies were essential for the survival of a democracy.

Reverend John McKnight, senior minister of the Presbyterian church at New York City, delivered a "Thanksgiving Sermon" that was also a summation of Republican principles of 1794-95. McKnight gave thanks to "the goodness of God" for five blessings America enjoyed. The first was the blessing of prosperity. The second was the blessing of peace: we had "kept ourselves clear of the vortex of European politics and from being involved in the miseries of war"; and further peace was presaged by the rumor of successful negotiations with Britain. The blessing of peace was internal as well. The Whiskey Rebellion was "unjustifiable and highly criminal" even "when all due allowances are made for the supposed noxious and unexceptionable nature of the excise law." In a republic the minority had to acquiesce to majority rule. The third blessing was the federal and state constitutions which "established liberty and order." The fourth was "religious liberty." The fifth was American freedom compared to "the tyranny and oppression" and "heathenish darkness" under which most of the world labored. If citizens would praise God, adopt republican manners, and banish the "influence of faction and party," the country's blessings would be complete.[50]

50. John McKnight, *The Divine Goodness of the United States of America . . . A*

After the first year of the Republican movement, the conservative patriotic theme of McKnight's sermon, combined with the defiant libertarian theme of the address of the Democratic Society, expressed the Republican mood.

Thanksgiving Sermon . . . Feb. 19, 1795 (N.Y., 1795), 14. The subscribers, listed in the appendix, include the city's leading Republicans.

CHAPTER 20

Federalist Resurgence:

John Jay Becomes Governor

1795

———•———

In the gubernatorial election of 1795, Republicans faced an uphill struggle. George Clinton, it was rumored, might not run. For the Federalists John Jay, who had actually gotten a majority of the ballots cast in 1792 and was now on the vastly popular mission to England, was likely to be the candidate again. Moreover Hamilton, just retired from the Treasury, was back in New York, ready to give his full attention to a political campaign in his adopted state for the first time since Republicans had made their first political breakthrough in the congressional elections. Would the Republicans be able to transfer some of their new-found patriotic following on national questions to their candidates for state office?

I

As early as December 1793, Federalist political managers had conversations with Jay about running for governor again. He preferred to remain on the Supreme Court, Egbert Benson reported to King, but "he would not desert them."[1] When King and Hamilton promoted his mission to England in May 1794, they were counting on him

1. Egbert Benson to Rufus King, Dec. 18, 1793, King Papers, N.-Y. Hist. Soc.

to return before the elections in April 1795, doubtless with a treaty that would be a political asset. In November 1794, when it was not clear when Jay would be back, Schuyler was frankly worried, especially because Aaron Burr once again was after the gubernatorial nomination. If Jay was not going to arrive by the spring, the Federalists would need a substitute or else they might "reelect Clinton as the least of two evils." By December Schuyler was relieved to learn that Jay would get home in time for the campaign and expected that Burr would be his opponent, that Clinton would back Burr and have himself elected to the Senate from which vantage point he would be a candidate for the vice-presidency.[2]

Canny politician that he was, George Clinton delayed his decision on running—or at least the announcement of it—until as late as possible. He was, Republicans were told, "ready to do what is thought best by his party."[3] His political liabilities were heavy: added to the land scandal and the disputed election of 1792, he was now Citizen Genêt's father-in-law. On the other hand he had enhanced his reputation as a staunch Whig in the war crisis of 1794. He had a genuine excuse not to run if he so chose. He had been "in bad health for some months"; all knew that rheumatism had kept him from attending the opening of the legislature in 1795, forcing it to move to Poughkeepsie to accommodate him.[4] In the shadow of this uncertainty about Clinton's plans, Senator Burr, Chancellor Livingston, and Chief Justice Yates joined in the competition for the gubernatorial nomination.

Burr, as was usually the case, was active in his own behalf. He "has hired Mrs. Metcalf's house" at Albany, Chancellor Livingston heard, "in order I suppose to obtain a northern interest." In November 1794, he traveled through the state, his absence from the Senate preventing a quorum and prompting "a snarling bark" from the Federalist Noah Webster at "the little Senator."[5]

Burr's candidacy once again brought strange fellows into one political bed as it had in 1792. His major supporter was the lame-duck Congressman Peter Van Gaasbeck, the Federalist political boss of Ulster, more convinced than ever of the need for a Republican

2. Schuyler to King, Nov. 24, Dec. 16, 1794, King Papers, N.-Y. Hist. Soc.
3. R. R. Livingston to William Wilson, Jan. 5, 1795, Wilson Papers, Clements Lib.
4. John S. Hobart to John Jay, Jan. 7, 1795, Jay Papers, Columbia Univ.; George to Cornelia Clinton, Oct. 25, 1794, Clinton MSS, N.-Y. Hist. Soc.; Lincoln, ed., *Messages from the Governors*, II, 348.
5. R. R. Livingston to Edward Livingston, Feb. 12, 1794 [possibly misdated—1795?], R. R. Livingston Papers, N.-Y. Hist. Soc.; *N.-Y. Journal*, Nov. 19, 1794.

candidate to carry his county. Van Gaasbeck, who now kept Burr's portrait by Vanderlyn, the local artist, over his mantel, continued to be his moneylender and legal client.[6] To the north Burr this time had the support not only of Thomas Witbeck, Stephen Van Rensselaer's steward, but also of Congressmen Van Allen of Rensselaer and Gilbert of Columbia.[7] In New York City his Republican backers of 1792, Marinus Willett and Melancton Smith, were probably augmented to include Matthew Davis, John Swartwout, and a number of others—precisely when each can be reckoned a Burr-ite is difficult to establish. These men aimed to discourage their party from nominating Clinton, whom they considered a weak candidate, and forge a bipartisan coalition for Burr as an independent man above both parties.[8]

Burr's backers traded on his popular reputation for liberalism and nonpartisanship. One man wrote that he was supporting Burr "but not because I know him to belong to either one faction or another but because I believe him to belong to none."[9] An Ulster Federalist conceded that his "abilities as a statesman, Philosopher and soldier are well known by every enlightened man and every soldier"; there was some doubt only as "to honesty."[10] At the same time Congressman Van Gaasbeck privately reassured Hamiltonians like Stephen Van Rensselaer that "as to his politics he and I often differ in our votes on particular measures, but I consider him to be an upright man and as good a friend to the Constitution and good government as you or I." Young Van Rensselaer, however, was not impressed. Nor were other

6. For Burr's law practice in Ulster see [Anon], "Aaron Burr and Ulster County," *Olde Ulster*, 8 (1912), 137-41; for Burr's relation to Van Gaasbeck, see Burr to Van Gaasbeck, Feb. 2, July 16, 1793, Apr. 14, May 8, 1795 ("I am in real distress"), and May 27, 1795; Apr. 9, 13, 23, 25, May 14, 1796, Aug. 23, 1797; for the portrait, La Rochefoucauld-Liancourt, *Travels*, II, 231.

7. See Stephen Van Rensselaer to Van Gaasbeck, Oct. 22, 1794, Van Gaasbeck to Van Rensselaer, Dec. 22, Dec. 30, 1794, Van Gaasbeck Papers, Kingston Senate House; Schachner, *Aaron Burr*, 140, completely neglects the effort to secure a gubernatorial nomination for Burr.

8. See Willett to Peter Van Gaasbeck, Feb. 14, 1795, Van Gaasbeck Papers, Kingston Senate House; for Swartwout and Davis, see Schachner, *Aaron Burr*, 139; the support of some Democratic Society leaders may be inferred from the vote in the Republican caucus; see footnote 19, below. Cheetham, *A View of Aaron Burr*, 19.

9. "A Correspondent," *Albany Gazette*, Dec. 4, 1794, "Fair Play," Dec. 8, "A Citizen," Dec. 11, 1794.

10. Philip Ten Broeck to Peter Van Gaasbeck, Feb. 3, 1795, Van Gaasbeck Papers, Kingston Senate House; John Addison to Van Gaasbeck, Aug. 3, 1793, wrote "Whether Mr. B—— can make every crooked thing of his straight I have my doubts."

conservative Federalists like William Cooper of Otsego, Peter Van Schaack of Columbia, or James Kent of Dutchess, all of whom rejected overtures from Burr's supporters.[11]

Chancellor Livingston conducted his operation for the gubernatorial nomination under his customary mask of diffidence which shielded him from rebuff. Early in 1795 Schuyler heard that Livingston "has proposed to our friends at New York to form a coalition, I do not know on what principles"; Schuyler was utterly opposed. The Chancellor reported to William Wilson, his bailiff, "I have done nothing nor do I care sufficiently about the matter to give myself much trouble, while my friends remain inactive."[12] Actually the Chancellor's problem was that Robert Yates, the anti-Federalist who had been put up by the Federalists in 1789, had far more support than he as a bipartisan candidate, especially in "the northern interest," as upstaters north and west were called.

Late in January 1795, Governor Clinton issued an announcement that he would not be a candidate. In a brief farewell addressed "to the Freeholders of the State of New York," he said that the "declining condition of my health" had forced him to withdraw; indeed, it had been his intention to do so "for a considerable time."[13] After thirty years of public office he concluded with a simple affirmation of his principles: "It has been my invariable object to promote and cherish the republican system of government as well as from a sense of duty, as from a full conviction that it is the only one calculated for the happiness and dignity of men."

The scramble now was on. The Burr-ites "have redoubled their exertions," Schuyler told King, imploring him to come up from Philadelphia to confer. Livingston dropped his mask, at least to Dr. Wilson, whom he beseeched to arrange a meeting on his behalf at Hudson or Kingston so that the pressure there "would compel them to take me up here" in New York City. But the cautious Livingston warned

11. Van Gaasbeck to Van Rensselaer, Dec. 30, 1794 (copy), Van Gaasbeck Papers, Kingston Senate House; William Cooper to Ebenezer Foote, Nov. 28, 1794, Cooper MSS, N.Y. State Hist. Assoc.; Aaron Burr to Foote, Dec. 10, 1794, Foote, ed., *Ebenezer Foote*, 50; Josiah Hoffman to Rufus King, Nov. 11, Dec. 26, 1794, King ed., *Correspondence of Rufus King*, I, 581, 583; Peter Van Schaack to Theodore Sedgwick, Dec. 23, 1794, Sedgwick Papers, Mass. Hist. Soc.; James to Moss Kent, Jan. 12, 1795, Kent Papers, II, Lib. Cong.

12. Schuyler to Hamilton, Jan. 5, 1795, Hamilton Papers, Lib. Cong.; R. R. Livingston to William Wilson, Jan. 5, 1795, Wilson Papers, Clements Lib.

13. Dated Jan. 22, 1795, published in *Albany Gazette*, Jan. 30, 1795.

that he personally "must not appear to have any agency in the business." Actually, as far as the Republican nomination was concerned, the Chancellor was too late. He was already aware that "many of the Republicans" favored Yates as the man "most agreeable to the common people" and most popular in the north. A few days later Livingston reported that the Republicans "have fluctuated for some time between me and Yates and as far as I have learnt will ultimately fix on Yates." He put on his mask once again: "I am perfectly indifferent to the thing myself."[14]

Federalists decided on their ticket first. Hamilton whipped the wavering into line, rejecting a proposal that he become the candidate for governor, with the merchant Nicholas Cruger, his onetime patron, as lieutenant-governor,[15] squelching talk of Van Rensselaer as a gubernatorial candidate by saving the second place on the ticket for him. For some Federalists, Yates was still a temptation. "Should Jay not come," one Albany Federalist wrote, "Yates be left out and a middle man be taken up by us, the opposition by taking Yates with those they would detach from our side would be in my opinion a very decided majority and defeat our election."[16] But Yates, confident of the Republican nomination, ended such speculation by rejecting a Federalist overture. The Federalist supporters of Burr, however, kept up the pressure. In Kingston a Federalist reported that "the largest meeting I ever recollect seeing here" voted for Burr by a two-thirds majority, with the rest split between Jay and Livingston, plus a few for Yates.[17] Despite these upstate rumbles, Hamilton and Schuyler retained control of the Federalist party. In New York City early in February, a caucus of Federalist members of the state legislature attended by the county leaders as well nominated Jay and Van Rens-

14. Schuyler to King, Jan. 28, 1795, King Papers, N.-Y. Hist. Soc.; Livingston to Wilson, Jan. 25, Feb. 1, 1795 [the latter misdated 1796], Wilson Papers, Clements Lib.

15. David Campbell to Hamilton, Jan. 27, 1795, Hamilton Papers, Lib. Cong.; *Albany Gazette*, Feb. 2, 1795; Schachner, *Alexander Hamilton*, 339-40, 346-47; Mitchell, *Alexander Hamilton*, II, 367-68.

16. William Van Ingen to Henry Glen, Feb. 1, 1795, Glen MSS, New York State Hist. Assoc.; for Yates's support in the middle Hudson Valley, see Henry Livingston to Samuel B. Webb, Feb. 14, 1795, Ford, ed., *Correspondence of S. B. Webb*, III, 196; for New York City Federalist support, see Josiah Hoffman to Ebenezer Foote, Foote, ed., *Ebenezer Foote*, 51.

17. John Addison to Van Gaasbeck, Feb. 2, 1795, P. Ten Broeck to Van Gaasbeck, Feb. 3, 1795, Van Gaasbeck Papers, Kingston Senate House.

selaer, the 1792 ticket. At Albany Federalists followed suit, by "unanimous vote," Schuyler exulted.[18]

A few days later, about forty Republican members of the state legislature and New York City leaders met in the city. The Democratic Society had met a few nights before. Livingston, whose upstate support had not materialized, withdrew and Yates won handily, the caucus giving Burr no more than six votes, all from New York City.[19] To run with Yates, Republicans chose William Floyd, an old Whig and Clintonian.

Unabashed, the Burr-ites, hoping to win in a three-way race, agitated for their favorite for about a month more, sustained by the half-promised support from a few leaders in Albany and Ulster. Van Gaasbeck continued his effort to convert Stephen Van Rensselaer: Yates was not strong enough; Burr had the greatest chance of success; it was crucial to "break the aristocratic chains we have so long bore the shackles of"—this to the largest landlord of the state. From New York Marinus Willett extended encouragement to Van Gaasbeck— "you have the people's interest at heart."[20]

Party lines were too tightly drawn, however, to allow much hope for a third candidate. The New York City Burr-ites withdrew in favor of Yates and when the Federalist, Thomas Witbeck, reached the city and found his favorite, Burr, "deserted by both parties," Burr was "out of the question" for him too. The Kingston Federalists split— Ebenezer Foote called it "altogether a farce to talk any further of Burr," but Van Gaasbeck was willing to put up Burr even if it meant getting only Ulster's support. Senator King now stepped in to dissuade Van Gaasbeck from so dangerous a tactic. Finally, at the end of March when Burr wrote to say he would not run, Van Gaasbeck grudgingly switched to Jay.[21]

18. Hoffman to Foote, Feb. 12, 1795 in Foote, ed., *Ebenezer Foote*, 51; *Albany Gazette*, Feb. 20, 1795; Schuyler to Nicholas Low, Feb. 23, 1795, Schuyler Papers, Box 2, N.Y. State Lib.

19. *N.-Y. Journal*, Feb. 6, 11, 1795; Cheetham, *A View of Aaron Burr*, 19-22.

20. Van Gaasbeck to Van Rensselaer, Feb. 12, 1795, *ibid.*, and copy of a letter, Van Gaasbeck to ?, Feb. 13, 1795, Willett to Van Gaasbeck, Feb. 14, 1795, Van Gaasbeck Papers, Kingston Senate House.

21. For the last phase of the Burr candidacy, see Foote to Van Gaasbeck, Feb. 24, Cornelius Wynkoop to Van Gaasbeck, Feb. 19, Moses Yeomans to Van Gaasbeck, Feb. 29, Burr to Van Gaasbeck, Mar. 25, Apr. 14, May 8, Van Gaasbeck to Burr, Apr. 13, 1795, Van Gaasbeck Papers, Kingston Senate House; Foote to Van Gaasbeck, Mar. 18, Rufus King to Van Gaasbeck, Mar. 25, S. Miller to Van Gaasbeck, Mar. 29, Thomas Witbeck to Van Gaasbeck, Mar. 28, Van Gaasbeck Papers, F.D.R. Lib.,

On the surface the Republican factions closed ranks behind Yates. Burr's Republican followers joined Yates's election committee although the great man himself took off for Philadelphia where he sat out the campaign as he had in 1792. Chancellor Livingston never exerted himself for Yates, although it seems he could not resist getting a few licks in the papers about Jay's rumored treaty.[22] But his family was active in New York City as were his land agent and surveyor upstate. The leaders of the Democratic societies in New York, Ulster, and Columbia campaigned for Yates as did the old Clintonian leaders elsewhere.[23]

In New York City Republicans were able to enlist some of their new-found national following on behalf of Yates. The city election committee with ninety-nine members, five times the size of Clinton's 1792 committee, was a cross section of the middling and well-to-do classes of the city, heavily weighted for the first time with artisans and small tradesmen. Leaders of the Democratic Society, Tammany, and the Associated Teachers graced the committee. For the first time, too, city Republicans offered a strong assembly ticket.[24]

Despite these Republican resources all agreed that Federalists had the better prospect of winning. Schuyler counseled his cohorts to make the most of the bandwagon psychology "as it tends to encourage the timid and prevents the exertions of the enemies." Federalists counted on offsetting any losses among their "apostate friends" in Ulster by a heavy majority on the western frontier and among the patroon's tenants.[25] That Republicans could overcome these advantages was doubtful.

Stephen Van Rensselaer to Foote, Mar. 4, Burr to Foote, Mar. 30, 1795, Foote, ed., *Ebenezer Foote*, 51-53.

22. For the New York City committee, *N.-Y. Journal*, Mar. 11, 1795; Van Gaasbeck to Foote, Apr. 16, 1795, Foote MSS, N.Y. State Lib.; for Livingston's indifference see letters to William Wilson, before Apr. 23 and Apr. 24, 1795, Wilson Papers, Clements Lib.; for the anti-Jay articles see footnote 35.

23. *N.-Y. Journal*, for Ulster, Feb. 28, for Columbia County, Apr. 29, and a summary listing, Apr. 29, 1795; for New York City, see also a broadside on the nomination of Yates and Floyd, n.d., N.-Y. Hist. Soc.; for a summary listing of local meetings, see *N.-Y. Journal*, Apr. 29, 1795.

24. *N.-Y. Journal*, Mar. 11, 1795; for occupations *New York City Directory*, 1795. Of about 80 who could be identified, there were 27 merchants, 6 lawyers, 13 grocers, 27 artisans, 1 gauger, and 2 cartmen. A meeting of cartmen also supported the Republicans for the assembly ticket, *N.-Y. Journal*, Apr. 22, 29, 1795.

25. Schuyler to Nicholas Low, Feb. 23, 1795, Schuyler Papers, Box 2, N.Y. State Lib. Abraham Van Vechten to Foote, Mar. 20, Van Rensselaer to Foote, Mar. 4, William North to Foote, Mar. 21, 1795, Foote, ed., *Ebenezer Foote*, 51-52, 57-58; Jacob Radcliff to Van Gaasbeck, May 10, 1795, Van Gaasbeck Papers, F.D.R. Lib.

II

The election campaign was not as "dull" and "listless" as some historians have contended.[26] There was more participation in politics than ever before, judging by the unprecedented number of town and county electioneering committees. The forums arranged by these groups, "designed to collect the opinions of the whole town," were on occasion wild. At a Lansingburgh meeting, for example, four or five people tried to speak at once, according to one reporter, and there were loud harangues and accusations of "falsehoods and bugbear stories." In the campaign "a beaver hat, an oyster supper or a glass of grog" brought out the voters.[27] And at the polls there was the largest turnout for a gubernatorial election in New York history, 25,000 voters, 8600 more than three years before.

What gave the campaign a deceptive surface calm was an effort by each party to give the appearance of nonpartisanship. Both parties still avoided a label and clung to the customary usage in state politics of "the supporters of Mr. Jay" or "the friends of Mr. Yates." The official Republican campaign address represented Yates and Floyd as "the candidates most likely . . . to compose the divisions among us," making the most of the fact that Yates, the Federalist candidate in 1789, had already received "the approbation of our political antagonists," while Federalists appealed for Jay as a man capable of putting an end "to the intestine broils and party divisions of the state."[28]

There was also an ambiguity to the reputation of the candidates which made them difficult to attack. Both Jay and Yates were chief justices, Jay of the federal, Yates of the state supreme court. Jay had tarnished his image as a Federalist above the battle by his sallies against Genêt, but as the man chosen to negotiate with England he symbolized the prospect of peace to which even Republicans had to give obeisance. Yates, a moderate anti-Federalist of 1788 who had run on the Federalist ticket in 1789 and supported Jay in 1792, had in no way identified himself with the new ideological Republicanism. Yates, in short, was not Clinton and Jay was not Hamilton.

William Floyd, Yates's running mate, was similarly above controversy. The signer of the Declaration of Independence had been a

26. Spaulding, *George Clinton*, 217; Monaghan, *John Jay*, 405.

27. Lansingburgh *American Spy*, Mar. 17, 1795; "Inspector," Lansingburgh *Recorder*, Apr. 26, 1795; *N.-Y. Evening Post*, Apr. 17, 1795.

28. "To the Free Electors of the State of New York" [Republican], *N.-Y. Journal*, Apr. 1795, *passim.*; *Albany Gazette*, Mar. 23, 1795.

supporter of the Constitution in '88 and an anti-Federalist in the first Congress. His supporters based their appeal for him on the many "important stations" he had "ably and faithfully discharged" as state senator, member of Congress, general of the militia, presidential elector, and Indian Commissioner. It was true that "his situation in life, his probity, his respectability, are such that no reasonable objections can be made to him."[29] As a Long Islander who had moved to Oneida County the year before, he could appeal to both "southern" and "northern" interests.

By contrast, the choice of Stephen Van Rensselaer as Jay's running mate was a brazen identification of the Federalists with national Federalist policies and aristocratic wealth. Late in 1794, the English traveler, William Strickland, was struck by the fact that "the Van Rensselaers, the Schuylers, and some other great families of this state are the objects of universal jealousy." It was "not on account of their wealth but on account of the undue political influence their wealth gives them. When Van Rensselaer joins with his father-in-law, Schuyler, all opposition to him is in vain; so great is their influence from the multiplicity of their tenants all of whom are voters." Thus, the astute Englishman concluded, "had property an equal influence under every form of government."[30]

Both parties campaigned on two levels. The official Republican committee, "desirous of conducting the ensuing election with moderation, temper and urbanity," extolled Yates's democratic virtues, not Republican policies. "His sentiments are republican, his manners plain; his integrity unquestionable, and his ability adequate." Yates knew the people of the state, having visited every county as a judge. Their major mark against Jay was that he "has been entirely unconnected with the affairs of this state for a number of years" and "has been for a great part of the time out of it, and is now in Europe."[31]

On the unofficial level, however, local leaders again inflamed class feeling. Abraham Yates writing again as "Rough Hewer," argued that Jay's opinions at the Poughkeepsie convention showed he had "high notions of government . . . nothing short of a limited monarchy will

29. *N.-Y. Journal*, Mar. 11, 21, 1795; see Richard Morris in *DAB* s.v. "Floyd, William."

30. Strickland, *Journal*, Oct. 26, 1794, XIV, 321-26, 342, N.-Y. Hist. Soc.

31. "To the Free Electors of the State of New York," *N.-Y. Journal*, Apr. 1795, *passim*.

suit him."[32] He had a "mean opinion of the people and popular government" because he refused to seek elective office, and had a "courtly education" and was "by nature haughty, vindictive and unsocial." As to his running mate, "who is Stephen Van Rensselaer?" "Rough Hewer" asked. He had no abilities—"but he has grand connections; he is Hamilton's brother-in-law, Schuyler's son-in-law and Schuyler's humble servant. But above all he is immensely rich—he has 21 square miles of land, a vast number of tenants, and of course can command a vast number of voters." Was it right for such a man to be lieutenant-governor? "Talent and virtue, not birth and riches should entitle a man to the suffrages of freemen."

Elkanah Watson of Albany pitched his appeal for Yates to "the Northern and Western interest of this state."[33] Men in these sections, he wrote, have "been obliged to trudge away to New York whenever we have any business to transact with the Executive Department. The next census will infallibly fix the legislature North after it appears— and I therefore think our Governor should be a Northern Man." Watson asked whether "we New England men (who already compose one-half of the population of this State and will in five years more grow to at least two-thirds) are to be forever the dupes of the presumptuous assumptions of self created societies who call themselves committees of correspondence," a reference not to Republican but to Federalist nominating methods.

Republicans also tried to inject foreign policy as an issue, doing the best they could with what little they knew of Jay's Treaty. Completed in London in November 1794, the treaty had arrived in Philadelphia in March, but its provisions were kept secret while the Senate debated ratification. In January Chancellor Livingston got wind of its contents from a London correspondent who sent him a cursory summary from the British papers. He spread the worst rumors he could, prompting Schuyler to curse him as an "apostate to the General Government."[34] In the campaign Livingston probably was responsible for a series of articles by "Montgomery," revealing the news about the

32. "Rough Hewer," *N.-Y. Journal*, Apr. 4, 1795, reprinted from *Newburgh Packet* and probably the *Albany Register*; see too "Address of the Ulster Committee," *N.-Y. Journal*, Apr. 22, 1795.

33. MS fragment, Elkanah Watson Papers, Box 2, Folder 7, N.Y. State Lib.

34. Robert R. Livingston to James Madison, Jan. 30, 1795, Madison Papers, Lib. Cong.; Madison to Livingston, Feb. 8, 1795, Bancroft Transcripts, N.Y. Pub. Lib.; Schuyler to King, Jan. 20, 1795, King Papers, N.-Y. Hist. Soc.

treaty Livingston had received. He questioned the value of "a treaty of any kind with Britain" because "we should avoid any connection whatever with her."[35] "Rough Hewer," for want of more information, was reduced to sniping at the absence of "a republican style" in Jay's diplomacy, denouncing "the flattery, kisses and caresses" the minister had lavished on the British.[36] Thus really bereft of a solid issue, the Republicans in their eleventh-hour appeals ended up by emphasizing Jay's absence from the state, raising a doubt as to whether he would return in time to assume his duties if elected.[37]

The Federalists, on their high level of the campaign, appealed to Yates's former supporters, stressing the fact that Yates himself had backed Jay in 1792. They also took pains to establish that Jay did not have a large fortune, was not an aristocrat but a "determined republican," and in framing the state constitution, had advocated a £100 freehold suffrage and not a £1000 freehold as charged. A true republican, they added, "regards with equal eye the *rich* and the *poor*."[38] On the "lower level," Federalists attacked the "pestilent Democratic Societies" as instigators of "the whiskey insurrection" and war with Britain, and they fanned the embers of the land sale to Macomb and the 1792 canvassers' decision.[39] Perturbed over Jay's absence, in the last weeks of the campaign they could do no more than reassure the voters that he would arrive shortly.[40]

35. "Montgomery," Apr. 8, 11, 15, 22, 25, 1795, *N.-Y. Journal.* There are no drafts in the Livingston Papers but the contents of the articles and use of the name of the Chancellor's brother-in-law who had fallen in the Revolution as pseudonym suggest Livingston as the author.

36. "Rough Hewer," *N.-Y. Journal,* Apr. 4, 1795; see also in *N.-Y. Journal:* "A Letter from Ontario," Feb. 24, an article, Mar. 7, and "Franklin," Apr. 1, 1795; see John Speyer to DeWitt Clinton, Feb. 20, 1795, DeWitt Clinton Papers, No. 26, Columbia Univ.

37. "To the Electors of the State of New York . . . ," New York, Apr. 23, 1795, by William Gilbert *et al.,* broadside, N.Y. Pub. Lib.; "A Federalist" [pro Yates], *Poughkeepsie Journal,* Apr. 22, 1795; a letter from New York, *Albany Gazette,* Apr. 27, 1795; "Caution," *N.-Y. Journal,* Apr. 25, 1795; an editorial paragraph, *ibid.,* Apr. 29, 1795.

38. "A Friend to Candour," *Albany Gazette,* Mar. 23, 1795; "Fellow Citizens . . . Albany by the Albany Federal Committee" [n.d.], broadside, N.Y. Pub. Lib.; and in *Albany Gazette:* "A Friend to Truth," Mar. 13, "A Free Elector," Mar. 23 and 27, "Jeremy Twitcher," Mar. 27, 1795.

39. "A Friend to Truth" and "An Independent Elector of Rensselaer-wyck," *Albany Gazette,* Mar. 13, 1795; "A Friend to the Right of Suffrage," Cooperstown *Otsego Herald,* June 19, 1795.

40. Ezekiel Gilbert to Van Gaasbeck, Apr. 26, 1795, Van Gaasbeck Papers, Kingston Senate House; broadside issued by the Federalist Committee at New York, Apr. 17, 1795, and at Albany, Apr. 25, 1795, N.Y. Pub. Lib.

Anticipating victory, the Federalists ended their campaign with a burst of energy to get out the vote. The Ulster brethren were urged to spare no pains to cut down the size of the Republican majority. From Kingston, Van Gaasbeck marshaled his host: every part of the county was assigned to a different man, circulars were distributed, and instructions issued to have "horses and carriages ready to conduct the infirm to the Pole."[41] In Van Rensselaer's domain, according to Republicans, Federalists coerced tenants, "imposing the will of the few over the many."[42] In the western district pressure probably was not necessary. In Oneida County, wrote one Federalist, "I do not know an influentual man who advocates Yates and Floyd."[43]

The results ran more or less true to Federalist predictions. Jay won by a vote of 13,481 to 11,892.[44] With 8601 more votes cast than in 1792, Jay's margin was 1589 votes or a margin of 6 per cent, compared to Clinton's disputed margin of a fraction of 1 per cent in 1792. Van Rensselaer, however, barely nosed out Floyd by 627 votes. Federalists took the southern district by a wide margin on the basis of the strong support for Jay in Westchester, his home county. They also carried New York City by a better than 2-to-1 majority. Republicans retained the middle district, but by a smaller margin than usual, Ulster, their customary stronghold, giving about a third of its votes to Jay. They took the eastern district by a narrow margin, aided by a heavy turnout for Yates in Canaan (center of the Democratic Society) and on the upper manor Livingston estate. The lower manor, however, went for Jay, 51 to 22; perhaps the diffident Chancellor just did not care enough to press the issue among his dependents. In the upper Hudson, Federalists triumphed easily on the basis of the expected Schuyler-Van Rensselaer influence, although Yates ran better in this, his home area, than had Clinton. Similarly in the western

41. For the closing campaign in Ulster, see Foote to Van Gaasbeck, Mar. 18, Josiah Hoffman to Foote, Apr. 25, Apr. 27, 1795, Foote, ed., *Ebenezer Foote*, 54, 64; Foote to Van Gaasbeck, Apr. 10, 1795, Van Gaasbeck Papers, Kingston Senate House; Foote to Van Gaasbeck, Apr. 25, 1795, Van Gaasbeck Papers, F.D.R. Lib.; Samuel Barker to Foote, Mar. 24, 1795, Van Gaasbeck to Foote, Apr. 16, 22, Johannes Miller to Foote, Apr. 19, 1795, Foote MSS, N.Y. State Lib.

42. "Suilbup," *N.-Y. Journal*, Apr. 25, 1795, and "Rusticus," *ibid.*, Mar. 21. See also "An Independent Elector," *Albany Gazette*, Apr. 6, 1796. According to the charges, tenants were threatened with "fines for alienation" and those with perpetual leases were charged with quarter sales, "creating the most humiliating dependency."

43. *Albany Gazette*, Apr. 27, 1795.

44. Complete returns are *ibid.*, June 12, 1795. See Appendix, Table 4.

district, Yates who was identified with "the northern interest" kept down the Federalist margin in the older settlements, but could do little to overcome the Federalist lead in Otsego and Ontario, the land magnates' preserves. Van Rensselaer was saved only by his heavy support in his tenanted domains and on the western frontier.

The picture was not all bleak for Republicans. They received 3500 more votes than in 1792. Federalists were not taking away Republican votes; they simply got about 5000 new voters, on the frontier in particular. Republicans also made gains in Federalist counties, doubling their vote, for example, in Albany and emerging at last with a respectable minority in Otsego. But they fared poorly in the assembly voting. Federalists regained Ulster and retained New York City, where Republicans drew about 700 votes fewer than Edward Livingston had attracted in his race for Congress in December 1794.

Why, in the midst of a tide of Republicanism which enabled Republicans to capture six of the ten congressional districts in December 1794, were Federalists able to take the governorship and retain control of the state assembly and senate only four months later? One reason was that the gubernatorial electorate was composed of freeholders worth £100 and more and excluded the 40-shilling renters who could vote in congressional contests. Thus, several hundred men in New York City who voted for Edward Livingston were not qualified to vote for Yates. They could vote for the assembly, however, yet did not. In the congressional victories of December 1794, Republicans rode the crest of a patriotic anti-British wave. By the spring of 1795 the crest had passed. Moreover, the conciliatory Federalist foreign policy which had alienated some voters in 1794 now seemed attractive, especially in the war-timid west. John Jay could not be successfully tarred as either pro-British or as a high-flying aristocrat. Whatever his private views about "the many" and "the few," Jay could be presented to the public in moderate republican hues. Hamilton, back at the helm in New York, had steered the Federalist ship well.

A month after the election, the victorious candidate arrived in New York from London. A crowd greeted him at the wharf and escorted him to his home amidst the ringing of bells and the firing of cannon (powder courtesy of the Chamber of Commerce). Jay's conservative Whig colleagues of the Revolution—Schuyler, Benson, Hobart—all sent letters of congratulations.[45] On July 1, Jay was inaugurated.

45. Minutes of the Proceedings of the Chamber of Commerce of the City of

In his first address to the legislature as governor, Jay confirmed the republican coloring Federalists had assumed. As if speaking to the thousands of New Yorkers suspicious of him as an "aristocrat," Jay said he assumed the following "obligations" as governor: "To regard my fellow citizens with an equal eye; to cherish and advance merit wherever found; to consider the national and state constitutions and governments as being equally established by the will of the people; to respect and support constituted authorities under each of them; and in general to exercise the powers vested in me with energy, impartiality and prudence."[46] In rejecting class and aristocratic distinctions, consolidated government, and an unlimited executive, George Clinton could not have done better.

New York, I, June 2, 1795, N.Y. Pub. Lib. Jay resigned as Chief Justice of the U.S. Supreme Court.

46. Lincoln, ed., *Messages from the Governors*, II, 358-66.

PART V

The Republican Movement Deepens

1795-1797

CHAPTER 21

Republican Wrath:

The Storm over Jay's Treaty

1795-1796

On July 1, 1795, the day John Jay was inaugurated governor, the newspapers carried the first summaries of the treaty he had wrought in London. "The crisis is at hand," wrote Greenleaf, the Republican editor. Federalists had brought their ship into the harbor just in time. Within days the storm was upon them. On July 4 Greenleaf threw out his advertisements and ran the entire document, "Treaty Authentic," on the first and second pages. Soon there was news of the two and a half weeks of secret debate in the special session of the Senate which had ratified the treaty by a vote of 20-10, the exact two-thirds required, and of how Rufus King had supported the treaty warmly and Aaron Burr had lost his moves to renegotiate the objectionable articles and postpone ratification.[1]

Hamilton himself hesitated before supporting the treaty; Jay had obtained even less than his New York advisors had agreed upon in drafting his instructions.[2] The commercial interests of New York were adversely affected, as they were everywhere. The treaty did not recog-

1. *N.-Y Journal*, June 27, July 1, 4, 1795.
2. Bemis, *Jay's Treaty*, ch. 13; Burt, *The U.S., Gr. Britain, and Br. North America*, ch. 8; DeConde, *Entangling Alliance*, ch. 4; Beard, *Economic Origins of Jeffersonian Democracy*, ch. 10.

nize the traditional American principle that free ships make free goods. Britain agreed on compensation for illegal ship seizures, providing a mixed commission to settle claims, but insisted that claimants first exhaust the ordinary judicial channels—a tedious process. Worse still, the contraband list was extended to cover naval stores. The United States agreed to indemnify Britain for losses suffered at French hands in American waters and to prevent the French from outfitting ships in American ports or Americans from serving under the French flag. But on British impressment of American seamen, the treaty was silent.

In dealing with long-standing British commercial restrictions, the agreement took away with one hand what it gave with the other. The British East Indies were opened to American trade, but trade to India was barred and what was really crucial, under XII, trade to the British West Indies was limited to small seventy-ton vessels, a provision so objectionable that it was stricken from the treaty by the Senate. To cap the restrictions which Jay accepted, the United States agreed not to pass discriminatory duties on British trade or to resort to sequestering British debts or assets.

Jay's treaty also dealt unevenly with the issues hanging fire from the peace treaty of 1783. Great Britain agreed to evacuate the forts by mid-1796, but British fur traders were to retain rights equal to Americans. The United States agreed to assume the debts private citizens had contracted to the British prior to the Revolution, but nothing was said about compensation for slaves carried off by the British during the war.

One-sided as the treaty was, it secured several gains especially important to New Yorkers. It restored the forts, even if belatedly. It provided machinery for compensation for ship seizures, cumbersome though it was. And implicitly, by ending the threat of war, it spelled security for the import trade from Britain, the foundation stone of the Hamiltonian financial edifice. These gains ultimately enabled Federalists to weather the most furious political storm of the era in New York.

I

The treaty was not a complete surprise to either party. Chancellor Livingston had already publicized the information he had received from London. Hamilton on an upstate tour with Congressman Glen seems to have prepared leading Federalists of the western district for the worst.[3] Even so, the impact of the treaty was electric. In New York City it was greeted with "universal execration" and "almost universal abhorrence," Chancellor Livingston was told. "Had a petition immediately been prepared to be presented to the President against its ratification," Brockholst Livingston claimed, "nine merchants in ten would have signed it; and not a mechanic would have refused." Within a few days, petitions were circulated and were "very generally signed."[4]

From the Federalist point of view, the treaty could not have been more ill-timed. On July Fourth, the Democratic Society, Tammany, the Mechanics, and the militia companies turned their joint observance of Independence Day into a political protest against the Federalist treaty. At nine in the morning the societies assembled in full force, each carrying its insignia, and marched into the Presbyterian church, crowding it to capacity. The program began with Congressman Livingston reading the Declaration of Independence. The Reverend Samuel Miller followed with a sermon which was greeted with "universal applause," rehearsing the glories of the struggle for emancipation from Britain and warning Americans not to give up the right "to keep a watchful eye on the servants of the public." An "Ode to Freedom" concluded the ceremony. The societies then paraded down Broadway, the line of march stretching "farther than the eye could see." At the customary dinners in the evening, the Democrats and Tammany asked Washington to withhold his signature from the treaty. When the militia toasted, "May the cage constructed to coop up the American eagle prove a trap for none but Jays and Kingbirds," there were nine cheers. The merchants (who had invited Governor Jay to be their guest before they knew about the treaty) wished "firmness" to the President and an honorable peace, but not even they, said Brockholst Livingston, dared "to lisp a syllable" in favor of the treaty.[5]

3. Journal of Henry Glen, N.Y. State Hist. Assoc., May 13 to June 7, 1795; see also Henry Van Allen to Peter Van Schaack, Feb. 4, 1795, Van Schaack Papers, Lib. Cong.

4. Edward to R. R. Livingston, July 6, Maturin to R. R. Livingston, July 15, 1795, Livingston to Monroe, July 10, 1795, R. R. Livingston Papers, N.-Y. Hist. Soc.; "Decius," No. 1 [Brockholst Livingston], N.-Y. Journal, July 11, 1795.

5. N.Y. Journal, July 8, "Decius," ibid., July 11, 1795. Samuel Miller, A Sermon, Delivered at the New Presbyterian Church, New York, July 4, 1795 . . . at the Request of, and Before, the Mechanic, Tammany and Democratic Societies and the Militia Officers (N.Y., 1795), 25-28.

The Livingstons threw themselves into the battle as never before. The Chancellor began with a torrent of letters. Informing Madison of the state of New York opinion, he pleaded with him to write to Washington and "write to the public, show the danger, the unconstitutionality of many parts of the treaty." He wrote to Sam Adams, whom he had not seen in twenty years, to write to the President; "perhaps Washington will pay some respect to the voice of the old whigs of '75." And he brought James Monroe in France up to date. In his own letter to the President, Livingston appealed to Washington to be "the saviour of your country" once again, to rise "above the violence of parties." In his judgment, the treaty did not provide "the slightest satisfaction of our injuries," took commercial retaliation "out of our hands," and, "above all," threatened a "rupture with France." "England, notwithstanding her professions I consider a secret enemy," he concluded, "France as our most constant ally—a war with her would be the signal for a civil war among ourselves."[6]

The Livingstons also took to the papers. Brockholst Livingston, writing as "Decius" (the heroic military tribune), offered a short series dissecting the treaty clause by clause; following this with another as "Cinna" (the patrician leader of the democratic party).[7] At Clermont the Chancellor, as "Cato" (the rustic, traditional conservative), mobilized his clan to turn out a series of sixteen articles that ran well into September. In New York City, Maturin Livingston gave him his deadlines and read proof. Maturin and Edward sent source materials to Dr. Tillotson in Dutchess who forwarded them to Clermont. Edward tried, unsuccessfully, to place the articles in the Federalist *Daily Advertiser* or *The Herald*, "the only paper that has a country circulation."[8]

Republican papers teemed with articles, short and long, condemn-

6. R.R. Livinugston to Madison, July 6, to Washington, July 8, to Monroe, July 10, to Samuel Adams, July 10, 1795, R. R. Livingston Papers, N.-Y. Hist. Soc.

7. "Decius," N.Y. *Argus,* July 10, 11, 13, 14, 1795; "Cinna," *N.-Y. Journal,* Aug. 1, 12, 15, 19, 1795; the authors are identified in Robert R. Livingston to James Monroe, Aug. 25, 1795, Monroe Papers, III, Lib. Cong.

8. "Cato," *N.-Y. Journal,* July 15 to Sept. 30, 1795, *passim,* later in pamphlet form as "Cato," *Examination of the Treaty with Great Britain . . .* (N.Y., 1795) and reprinted in *The American Rememberancer, or an Impartial Collection of Essays, Resolves, Speeches, etc., Relative,* or *Having Affinity to the Treaty with Great Britain,* 2 vols. (Phila., 1795), II. Drafts of several articles in the series in Livingston's hand are in R. R. Livingston Papers, N.-Y. Hist. Soc. For arrangements see: Maturin to R. R. Livingston, July 15, Aug. 17, Thomas Tillotson to Livingston, July 18, R. R. to Edward Livingston, July 19, 1795.

ing the treaty. There was sentiment in the city to burn Jay in effigy—"Sir John Jay" they called him—as Republicans prepared a "Town Meeting" to express the popular will.[9]

II

Boston's "Town Meeting" once again was the inspiration for the New Yorkers. When news of it reached the city, according to Hamilton, "the leaders of the [Democratic] clubs were seen haranging in every corner of the city, to stir up citizens into an imitation of the example of the meeting in Boston." Notices were placed in the papers calling all citizens to assemble on Saturday, July 19, at noon.[10] "Our demagogues always fix their meetings at the hour of twelve," one Federalist complained, "in order to take in all mechanics and labourers —over whom they alone have influence." Peter R. and Brockholst Livingston "appeared the leaders," assisted by Edward Livingston, James Nicholson, and other members from the Democratic Society.[11]

On Friday Hamilton, King, Mayor Varick, and a handful of Federalist merchants met until late in the night to map a counterstrategy. Early Saturday morning they put out a handbill recommending "a general attendance" at the Republican meeting in order that "the true sense of the city" may appear and pleading for a "fair and rational discussion" of the treaty. They intended to challenge the Republicans.[12]

New York City had not seen the likes of the "Town Meeting" since 1775. At noon, a crowd estimated by all parties at nearly 5000 assembled in front of the city hall. The working population turned out en masse: "respectable mechanics," laborers, cartmen with their horses, "the hod men and the ash men and the clam men," as one scoffer remarked,[13] especially recent immigrants—Scottish, Irish, English, and French.

Judging by the account in Greenleaf's Republican paper—the ful-

9. In N.-Y. Journal, July 8, 15, 18, 22, 1795.
10. "Camillus," No. 1 [Alexander Hamilton], N.-Y. Journal, July 22, 1795. "Cinna" [Brockholst Livingston], ibid., Aug. 12, 1795, claimed "some of the most active members enemies of the treaty belong to no club at all." N.-Y. Journal, July 16, 17, 1795.
11. Benjamin Walker to Joseph Webb, July 25, 1795, Ford, ed., Correspondence of S. B. Webb, III; Seth Johnson to Andrew Craigie, July 23, 1795, Craigie Papers, III, No. 97, Amer. Antiq. Soc.
12. In The American Rememberancer, II, 176-77; see also "Cinna," No. 3 [Brockholst Livingston], N.-Y. Journal, Aug. 12, 1795.
13. Grant Thornburn, Forty Years Residence (Boston, 1834), 37-40.

lest one available and one which Edward Livingston told his mother was "true and accurate"[14]—Federalists tried to take over or disrupt the meeting. At the stroke of twelve Hamilton, surrounded by a knot of supporters, mounted the steps of a nearby building and began to speak. There were cries of "Let us have a chairman," and Colonel William S. Smith, whom Republicans had agreed on in advance, went to the balcony of the city hall to preside. Peter R. Livingston asked for the floor; Hamilton claimed it. "In an instant nothing was to be heard but hissing and 'hear him, hear him.'" Smith, putting the question as to which man was first, declared the vote in favor of Livingston.

Livingston proposed that all those who opposed the treaty should file off to the right, those who were in favor to the left. Hamilton continued his harangue; there should be no vote before a full discussion, but the crowd drowned him out with "hissings, coughings and humphing." Brockholst Livingston shouted him down: the treaty had been published two weeks earlier; everyone had formed his opinion; discussion meant procrastination and besides it was impossible under the circumstances. If there were people who had not yet made up their minds, he suggested they meet in a nearby church where he would be glad to debate the treaty. In response to Peter Livingston's plea "a large body" moved to the right in opposition to the treaty, another large number stood where they were, and according to Greenleaf's account, none went to the left. After this victory a group of several hundred marched off to the Battery where they burned the treaty.

Hamilton would not give up. He handed in a written resolution, declaring it "unnecessary to give an opinion on the treaty" and expressing confidence in "the wisdom and virtue of the President to whom with the Senate the discussion of the question constitutionally belonged." At this there were roars from the crowd: "We'll hear no more of it" and "tear it up." A Republican shouted out a motion for the election of a committee of fifteen to draw up a resolution condemning the treaty. Fifteen names were read and greeted with hurrahs although they were "indistinctly heard if at all by many." Hamilton now put his own resolution to the clique around him and a few "ayes" were heard. Calling on "the friends of order" to leave, he went off with a small number of his followers. At 1:30 Colonel Smith

14. "The Meeting," N.Y. *Argus,* July 20, 1795; *N.-Y. Journal,* July 22; Edward to Margaret Beekman Livingston, July 20, 1795, R. R. Livingston Papers, N.-Y. Hist. Soc.

adjourned the meeting, announcing it would reconvene on Monday noon to hear the committee's resolutions.

Accounts left by other observers round out Greenleaf's version with a few touches less flattering to Republicans. The sense of the meeting was not quite as clear as Republicans contended. Colonel Smith clearly got more than he bargained for. In a statement defending his rulings as chairman, he explained that on Hamilton's resolution there was "so much disorder that it was difficult to pronounce with certainty where the majority lay." And on the resolution for a committee of fifteen "the noise was so considerable" he was uncertain "whether this proclamation was understood by the meeting at large."[15]

There was also violence directed at Hamilton, although it is not likely that he was stoned, as many contemporaries were told. Seth Johnson, a Federalist who was at the meeting, reported "it is said in the heat of the business that Edward Livingston pointed to Mr. Hamilton and said 'Take care, or that man will ruin you' which in the temper of those around him, might have led to assassination . . . Stones were thrown at Hamilton one of which grazed his head." However, an eyewitness account by Grant Thorburn, then a young Scottish lad, who watched the proceedings from the vantage point of a buttonwood tree near the building where Hamilton stood, may be more accurate than Johnson's, even though penned years later. Hamilton's eloquence, wrote Thorburn, "inflamed their [the crowd's] plebeian souls; they cut short his speech, forced him from the stoop and dragged him through the gutter." Whichever version is correct, there is no contemporary evidence at all for the heroic story Hamilton's son told years later that his father, with blood streaming down his face, said "If you use such knockdown arguments, I must retire."[16]

It also seems that there was a question as to the strength of anti-treaty sentiment in "the lower class." At the decisive voting, according to Seth Johnson, the Livingstons were "supported by a few of the principal citizens, the rest being made up of men of the lower class." A Republican concurred; turning the Federalist taunt into a badge of

15. N.Y. *Herald*, July 22, 1795.
16. Seth Johnson to Andrew Craigie, July 23, 1795, Craigie Papers, III, No. 97, Amer. Antiq. Soc. Thorburn, *Forty Years Residence*, 37-40, and Thorburn, *Fifty Years Reminiscences of New York* . . . (N.Y., 1845), 149-50; John C. Hamilton, *History of the Republic . . . as Traced in the Writings of Alexander Hamilton and his Contemporaries*, 7 vols. (N.Y., 1857-64), VI, 225; Mitchell, *Alexander Hamilton*, II, 342-43, rejects John Hamilton and questions the violence but does not make use of the Johnson letter cited above.

honor: "There was not a whole coat"—the outer garment of the well-to-do—"amongst all those who voted against the treaty." On the other hand Federalists were probably right in insisting that not *all* mechanics present voted against the treaty, but probably wrong in claiming that the anti-treaty vote "was not a majority of the lower class."[17]

All afternoon the tension continued. A group of Revolutionary War veterans paraded, displaying French and American flags with a British flag beneath them upside down. They burned a picture of John Jay "holding a balance containing American independence and British gold, the latter predominating."[18]

The tempers of political leaders frayed, Hamilton's to the breaking point.[19] By chance a few of the leading Federalists, while strolling down the street, encountered their opposite numbers among the Republicans. James Nicholson, officer of the Democratic Society, and Josiah Hoffman, Federalist assemblyman, fell into an argument at once, and soon exchanged personal recriminations. When Hamilton intervened, Nicholson told him to stay out, muttering that he was "an abetter of Tories" and "other harsh expressions." Hamilton had been furious with Nicholson for weeks for spreading the rumor that he "had invested £100,000 sterling in the British funds whilst he was Secretary of the Treasury, which sum was still held by a Banking house in London, to his use and interest."[20] Hamilton insisted that the street was no place for a quarrel; he would be happy to discuss Nicholson's accusations with him on a more suitable occasion. Nicholson scoffed; Hamilton, he said, had refused an earlier offer to meet so that Nicholson could present proof of his British funds charge. Hamilton denied he had ever declined an interview with Nicholson, and with his honor at stake, challenged Nicholson to a duel, which the 59-year-old Commodore accepted.

A few minutes after this fracas, the Federalist strollers stopped in

17. Johnson to Craigie, July 23, 1795; "Slash," *N.-Y. Journal*, July 25, 1795; Benjamin Walker to Joseph Webb, July 24, 1795, Ford, ed., *Correspondence of S. B. Webb*, III, 197-98.

18. "Seventy-six," N.Y. *Argus*, July 22, 1795.

19. The incident can be reconstructed from the exchange of notes between Nicholson and Hamilton, and between their seconds, July 20-26, 1795, Nicholas Fish Papers, Columbia Univ., reprinted in Milton H. Thomas, "Alexander Hamilton's Unfought Duel of 1795," *Pa. Mag. of Hist. and Biog.*, 78 (1954), 342-52; for a secondary account, Mitchell, *Alexander Hamilton*, II, 382-88.

20. John Beckley to James Madison, May 25, 1795, Madison Papers, N.Y. Pub. Lib., quoted at length in Mitchell, *Alexander Hamilton*, II, 699. Schachner, *Alexander Hamilton*, 341.

front of Edward Livingston's house where they encountered a number of the clan who had organized the morning's affair. Hoffman got into another warm exchange, this time with Peter R. Livingston. Rufus King and Edward Livingston intervened, but Hamilton again "stepped forward declaring that if the parties were to continue in a personal way, he was ready that he would fight the whole [Republican] party one by one . . . the whole detestable faction." Maturin Livingston called this a challenge; Hamilton said he already had one duel but that he was willing to take on another. But by the code of the day the exchange was neither a formal challenge nor acceptance and the duel was squelched.[21]

The duel between Hamilton and Nicholson was narrowly averted. For a week their seconds—DeWitt Clinton, Brockholst Livingston, and Udney Hay for the Republican, Rufus King and Nicholas Fish for the Federalist—feverishly negotiated an apology by Nicholson acceptable to Hamilton. On Saturday, July 25, with the duel scheduled to take place Monday morning, Hamilton made out his will. Finally on Sunday night, there was agreement on a fourth draft of a statement in which Nicholson wrote that "he does not recollect and is not conscious of having made" the accusation that Hamilton had previously declined an interview to answer his charge. He did not intend any "imputation" and "regrets the pain caused Hamilton." Two days later Hamilton, convinced that "our Jacobins mediate serious mischief to certain individuals" and the militia "cannot be depended on,"[22] suggested to the Secretary of Treasury that federal troops be kept at Fort Jay. He and his friends must have thought they were facing Marat, Danton, Robespierre, and the mobs of Paris.

Meanwhile, over the previous weekend the resolutions committee of fifteen—most of them merchants and three or four of them entirely new to Republican politics—drafted a list of twenty-eight objections to the treaty. On Monday a crowd estimated at from five to seven thousand reassembled; this time Federalists stayed away. At noon Colonel Smith called the meeting to order. Saturday's appointment of the committee was confirmed and Brockholst Livingston read the committee's objections to the treaty, one by one, so that no one could

21. Edward to Margaret Beekman Livingston, July 20, 1795, R. R. Livingston Papers, N.-Y. Hist. Soc. For Nicholson's earlier attack against Washington, see ch. 19, n.4.

22. Hamilton to Robert Troup, July 25, to Oliver Wolcott, July 28, 1795, Lodge, ed., *Works of Hamilton*, VIII, 351-55.

say New Yorkers did not know what they were voting for. Livingston moved the question, and a resounding and unanimous "yes" swept the crowd. At 1:15 Smith adjourned the meeting.

The resolutions followed closely the line of criticism in Chancellor Livingston's articles, attacking most sharply the commercial aspects of the treaty: the rejection of the principle of "free vessels . . . making free goods," the additions to the list of contraband, the silence on the impressment of seamen, the abandonment of the "invaluable prerogative" of passing "discriminating acts" in regulating trade and confiscating or sequestering British properties. On the two most favorable features of the treaty the Republicans cast doubt. If the return of the forts was promised, why delay another eighteen months? Britain might wiggle out again, and even if the forts were returned, the fur trade might remain in British hands. As to the process for indemnifying Americans for illegal captures, it was "on a footing too precarious to expect any compensation." They also condemned the provision which permitted British subjects to hold lands previously purchased in the United States, which would override New York State's laws confiscating Tory land and prohibiting alien landholding. And they enumerated the ways in which the treaty usurped the powers of Congress, anticipating a theme Republicans would take up later in the year. Underlying this attack were two general principles: that the disadvantages were "the more striking" because they could have been avoided, and that the treaty, by aiding Britain in her war, was "peculiarly hostile to" France and might lead to war with her.[23]

III

Stunned by the two town meetings, Federalist leaders tried to rally their supporters. At a thinly attended meeting Hamilton delivered a harangue about "the rabble" and the "self created society" responsible for the opposition. For "the true sense of the people" he proposed a petition "to go around in the several wards of the city to the people individually." At a second meeting this plan was abandoned.[24]

Even the Chamber of Commerce was no longer "safe." A day after the second town meeting, more than seventy members of the Chamber met at "the most respectable meeting ever held," as the secretary noted.

23. *N.-Y. Journal*, July 22, 25, 1795.
24. "J.H.," N.Y. *Argus*, July 30, 1795; "Cinna" [Brockholst Livingston], *N.-Y. Journal*, Aug. 12, 1795.

The treaty was read, a resolution of approval was put and after a brief discussion was passed, the secretary noting "ten dissentments."[25] The vote, however, masked more than it revealed. "Of the about seventy who were present," a writer in the *Journal* claimed, "the minority which was ten, owns more tonnage than the other sixty put together." Another writer, "A Republican," who named names, claimed that actually eleven members dissented, five others withdrew from voting, two more were "pointedly absent," and still another, although he voted for the resolution, favored only part of it. Thus he said nineteen members were critical of Jay's handiwork. And to detract from the patriotism of the fifty-nine pro-treaty merchants he reviewed their whereabouts during the American Revolution: only eighteen had been outside British lines; eight were refugees who joined the British; seventeen had remained behind British lines for the entire war; six were migrants from Britain during the war and ten were migrants since.[26]

Even the resolution the Chamber passed was apologetic: the treaty contained "as many features of reciprocity, as . . . could reasonably be expected"; its merits were "the precarious privileges" of trade to Britain and her colonies "changed into permanent rights," "a quiet surrender of the western posts, and an amicable adjustment of the British debts, a fair compensation for the spoilations upon our commerce and for the prevention of future depredations." Above all, the consequence of rejecting the treaty would be war.[27]

As the Federalist defense gained momentum it was this theme—the danger of war—that they played to the hilt. Hamilton, assisted by Rufus King and John Jay, as "Camillus" (the savior of Rome after the Gallic invasion), and James Kent and Noah Webster collaborating as "Curtius" (the legendary patriotic knight) painted lurid pictures of the consequences of war: Indian attacks on the frontier, the death of commerce of the seas, internal civil war. And as might be expected,

25. Minutes of the Chamber of Commerce of the City of New York, July 21, 1795, N.Y. Pub. Lib.; Christopher Gore to Rufus King, July 24, 1795, King Papers, N.-Y. Hist. Soc.

26. "A Republican," *N.-Y. Journal*, Aug. 8, 1795; see also the report of the Chamber minority in Philadelphia *Aurora*, July 28, 1795, not located in New York City papers. The claim that the minority against the treaty "owns more tonnage than the other sixty put together" might well be true. For example, John Mumford and Robert Murray who voted in the minority filed claims under the Jay Treaty for eight captured vessels (owned either by Murray and Mumford, Robert Murray and Co., or D. and G. Mumford). See the Report of the Claims Commission cited in n.38 below.

27. *N.-Y. Journal*, July 29, 1795.

they made an *ad hominem* attack on Republicans, the Livingstons in particular. Congressman Gilbert of Columbia County vilified the national movement as a "heterogeneous mass" consisting "greatly of negro representation, of British debtors, fraudulent bankrupts, of mere nabob pride and democratic fury; anti federal tribes, factious demi-goges french partizans; imported Scots Irish [and] English malcontents."[28]

As news of the treaty spread through the state, new waves of anti-British feeling rolled in. On Long Island six Suffolk towns sent delegates to a county-wide anti-treaty meeting, the first of its kind. In Ulster, the Republican Society called a meeting attended by "a large proportion of old respectable farmers and early and decided patriots of the revolution." Only a "very few" Jay-ites, it was claimed (those "who are eat up with party"), favored the treaty. In Columbia County, the Canaan Democratic Society organized a protest.[29]

To the north, anti-treaty sentiment thinned out. At Albany, Republicans did not risk a meeting, few joining the editor of the *Albany Register* in his jibes. At nearby Troy, Federalists sneered at the men who burned Jay in effigy as "not more than ten sans culottes full of RUM and patriotism."[30] At Salem, Washington County, the Federalist editor of the *Washington Patrol* at the first news of the treaty cautioned against a hasty judgment. On receiving the full document and news of the protest, he inveighed against the "Town Meetings." A week later he featured an article of endorsement side by side with the favorable resolution of the New York City Chamber of Commerce.[31]

To the west anti-treaty sentiment evaporated. Independence Day celebrants at Cooperstown condemned opponents of the treaty as "Frenchified" or "factious anarchists and disorganizers." Jedediah Peck of Otsego disparaged Republicans as either "knaves unwilling to pay their honest debts" to Britain or "those who seek a war to re-

28. Mitchell, *Alexander Hamilton*, II, 344-45; Monaghan, *John Jay*, 396-97, 402; Horton, *James Kent*, 106-7; James to Moss Kent, July 27, 1795, Kent Papers, Lib. Cong.; Ezekiel Gilbert to Peter Van Gaasbeck, Apr. 17, 1796, Van Gaasbeck Papers, Kingston Senate House.

29. *N.-Y. Journal*, July 8, 11, 18, 28, Aug. 12, 15; Sag Harbor *Frothingham's Long Island Herald*, July 6, 1795; *Goshen Repository*, Aug. 18, 25, 1795; *Albany Register*, July 20, Sept. 7, 1795; John Wynkoop to Peter Van Schaack, Sept. 7, 1795, Van Schaack Papers, Lib. Cong.

30. *Albany Register*, July-Aug., 1795 *passim*; Aug. 3 for editorial; *Albany Gazette*, Aug. 3, 1795.

31. Salem *Washington Patrol*, June 15, July 29, Aug. 5, 12, 1795.

plenish their fortunes by privateering and plundering honest traders on the sea." From Lake Oneida Francis Adrian Vanderkemp wrote of the treaty that "everyone considers it as an eminent blessing."[32]

New York's frontiersmen were of course not pro-British. After touring the area north of Albany in mid-August, La Rochefoucauld-Liancourt, the French traveler, found the number of "noncontents" with the treaty to be great although probably not a majority; the "universal sentiments," he said, were "good wishes for the success of the French, a detestation of their crimes and decided hatred against the English." To the west celebrants in Steuben County hoped that France "may . . . teach John Bull to bend his stubborn will to republicanism and virtue or his neck to the Guillotine." But whatever the treaty did not do, it accomplished the objective uppermost in the minds of westerners: it restored the forts. Accordingly, enthusiasm in favor of the treaty mounted on the frontier as opposition rose elsewhere.[33]

In mid-August Washington signed the treaty. In his replies to the New York Chamber of Commerce the President was appreciative, to the New York "Town Meeting" committee he was curt, to Chancellor Livingston he was apologetic.[34] At summer's end John Jay was convinced that things had quieted down "except in places where Jacobin societies have been set up or in neighborhoods where some leading malcontents have influence."[35] In New York a yellow fever epidemic which drove 10,000 residents into the countryside and took the lives of hundreds put politics out of everybody's mind. The first and stormiest phase of the treaty fight was over.

IV

In September Republicans launched the second round of their attack with the goal of getting the House of Representatives to withhold the appropriations necessary to execute the treaty. They began

32. Cooperstown *Otsego Herald*, July 10, 21, 24, 31, Aug. 14, 21, Dec. 13, 1795; Jedediah Peck, "An Address to the Free Citizens of the United States of North America," in *The Political Wars of Otsego or the Downfall of Jacobinism and Despotism. Being a Collection of Pieces Lately Published in the Otsego Herald* (Cooperstown, 1796), 97. Vanderkemp cited in Harry Jackson, *Scholar in the Wilderness: Francis Adrian Van der Kemp* (Syracuse, N.Y., 1963), 118.

33. La Rochefoucauld-Liancourt, *Travels*, I, 379, 381-82.

34. *American Remembrancer*, II, 179; Washington to Livingston, Aug. 20, 1795, Bancroft Transcripts, N.Y. Pub. Lib.; *N.-Y. Journal*, Aug. 19, 1795.

35. Jay to Thomas Pinckney, Aug. 17, Jay to James Duane, Sept. 19, 1795, Johnston, ed., *Correspondence of John Jay*, IV, 85; Peter Van Schaack to Theodore Sedgwick, Aug. 15, 1795, Sedgwick Papers, Mass. Hist. Soc.

with a national petition campaign managed by John Beckley from Philadelphia, the most ambitious project they had undertaken. In New York State, DeWitt Clinton was the coordinator.

From New York City he sent petitions to local leaders through the state. Republican papers printed the petition; the city paper listed the place in each ward where citizens could sign. From Saratoga County a few Republican stalwarts set out for Federalist Otsego, their saddle bags stuffed with petitions. Shrewdly the solicitors took pains, as Thomas Tillotson put it, to avoid "mixing the enmity to Mr. Jay on state politics with the opposition to the treaty on national grounds." George Clinton, Jr., and Chancellor Livingston explained the new issue in the newspapers and Livingston brought out his "Cato" series in pamphlet form.[36]

To the basic issue of the merits of the treaty, Republicans added two new questions. The first was constitutional: would the country be ruled by "the mere will and absolute discretion of the President and Senate, in conjunction with a foreign power," or would the House, "as that great and dernier constituted authority," restore constitutional government? The second was emotional: the treaty might produce the sad spectacle of war with France, "that magnanimous republic." Congress thus had to preserve "the blessings of peace."[37]

With such appeals the petition campaign should have gone well. The British, moreover, helped by a new wave of ship captures which Greenleaf sarcastically reported under the heading "First Fruits of the Treaty of Amity, Commerce and Navigation." Under an Order in Council of May 1795, British ships seized all vessels carrying provisions to France. Over the summer they took some 27 ships owned by New Yorkers, a larger number than in the 1793-94 crisis, and a larger share of the total number of American vessels seized in 1795 which came to 120. Robert Murray and the firm of Murray and Mumford alone accounted for a half dozen of the losses. Such old anti-Federalists as Melancton Smith (of Smith and Wyckoff) and Zephaniah

36. John Beckley to DeWitt Clinton, Sept. 13, 1795, George Clinton, Jr., to Clinton, Oct. 19, 1795, Thomas Tillotson to Clinton, Oct. 24, 1795, DeWitt Clinton Papers, Columbia Univ.; R. R. to Edward Livingston, Aug. 30, 1795, Maturin to R. R. Livingston, Sept. 21, 1795, R. R. Livingston Papers, N.-Y. Hist. Soc.; N.Y. *Argus*, Nov. 16, Dec. 5, 8, 9, 12, 1795; *Albany Register*, Oct. 26, 1795, "Cato" [R. R. Livingston], No. 15 and 16, *N.-Y. Journal*, Sept. 23, 30, 1795; "Polybius" [George Clinton, Jr.], *Newburgh Packet*, reprinted in *N.-Y. Journal*, Nov. 18, 1795; *Albany Gazette*, Oct. 23, 1795.

37. *Albany Register*, Oct. 26, 1795; N.Y. *Argus*, Nov. 8, 1795.

Platt were among the victims, suggesting that a number of men had responded to the lure of combining profit with Republicanism by supplying France.[38]

Among common folk there was a growing resentment over Federalist efforts to discredit critics of the treaty as "the swinish multitude" and "the rabble" and to fob off the town meetings as "the mobs of Paris called by nobody." A Democratic Society orator at Canaan pointed out that "the aristocratic conspiracy" first had attacked the Democratic societies as secret; yet when "open assemblages" were held they were even more horrified. This proved they were opposed to the right of petition and to the people governing themselves.[39]

There was a general mood of defiance against the Federalists. Republicans rejoiced that Hamilton "and his chickens however abundantly rich from the funding system appear . . . to have really got the pip" for the treaty. "The floodtide of abuse is still rolling in," a Federalist leader reported.[40] For the first time Republicans felt safe in criticizing President Washington, not only for signing Jay's Treaty, but for allegedly overdrawing appropriations and even for his military record.[41] They mocked Governor Jay when he suggested in his Thanksgiving Proclamation that they pray for Washington as one of their blessings (perhaps they should also pray for Hamilton as "defender of the faith") and scorned the celebration of Washington's birthday as America's "political Christmas."[42]

Slowly, however, the "floodtide" receded. By December, after Congress convened, the state was "more and more composed," Jay reported.

38. N.-Y. Journal, Oct. 14, 24, 1795; Report of the Claims Commission Under Article VII, Jay Treaty, Record Group 76, National Archives, Washington, D.C. See after the alphabetical list of claims, Class 14, "Vessels Going to France or Other Markets and taken by British Cruizers . . . under the Provision Order in May, 1795." The seizures which bear dates were in June, July, and August; hence the news arrived in September.

39. N.-Y. Journal, Oct. 14, 1795; for other resentment see N.-Y. Journal, July 29, Aug. 1, 8, Sept. 26, Oct. 3, 14, 21, 28, Nov. 18, 1795; N.Y. Argus, Nov. 10, 23, 1795; Minutes of the Calliopean Society of New York City, 116-17, N.-Y. Hist. Soc.

40. James Watson to James Wadsworth, Nov. 8, 1795, Wadsworth Papers, Conn. Hist. Soc.; N.-Y. Journal, Oct. 24, 31; N.Y. Argus, Nov. 7, 11, 13, 1795.

41. See "Hancock," "Valerious," and "Belisarius," reprinted from Philadelphia Aurora in N.-Y. Journal, Aug.-Nov., 1795, passim; for a debate over financial questions which discussed Washington, see ibid.: "A Calm Observer" and "An Observer" [Oliver Wolcott and Alexander Hamilton], Oct. 20, 21, 26, 31, Nov. 4, 7, 21, 25, 1795. See Carroll and Ashworth, George Washington, VII, 318-22.

42. "Communication," N.-Y. Journal, Nov. 14, 1795; John Sloss Hobart to Jay, Nov. 18, 1795, Johnston, ed., Correspondence of John Jay, IV, 195-96; N.Y. Argus, Mar. 6, 1796.

"The farmers are so intent on improving the means of getting rich," another Federalist claimed, "that they can hardly be got to lend an ear to any political subject, however interesting." Moreover, fear stayed the hands of some farmers from signing the Republican petition: in Columbia, a landlord county, it had to be circulated secretly; even so a Federalist leader wrote his friends at the capital to have the local names sent back. On the frontier the treaty was "universally considered," Vanderkemp reported, "a heavenly blessing for our western world."[43]

Early in January 1796, Robert R. Livingston warned Edward at Philadelphia that the petitions "will not be so respectable as to give much weight to your measures." By mid-February Federalists reported from the upper Hudson that "the treaty is hardly spoken of and the general language is that the Father of his Country, our beloved President will watch over us, and that what he has done cannot fail of being right."[44] In the state legislature when Virginia's resolutions for a constitutional amendment to require the approval of the House for any treaty impinging on its legislative powers came up, the ranks of the Federalist majority held firm in voting down the proposal.[45]

Thus as Republicans opened their battle in Congress their political support was waning. Correctly reading the signs, Chancellor Livingston counseled Edward to be careful not to "wound" Washington in whom the people had confidence and to work closely with his Republican colleagues. Edward should also raise such questions as an appropriation to complete New York City's fort and the return of impressed seamen on which he would have broad patriotic support. In March, however, despite this warning, young "Ned" precipitated a debate prematurely with a motion requesting Washington to give the House the diplomatic papers of Jay's mission. The "older members," he reported, were against him.[46] Madison, alarmed at the temper of

43. Jay to Washington, Dec. 14, 1795, Johnston, ed., *Correspondence of John Jay*, IV, 197; Van Schaack to Sedgwick, Dec. 14, 30, 1795, Sedgwick Papers, Mass. Hist. Soc. Francis Adrian Vanderkemp to Peter Van Gaasbeck, Dec. 20, 1795, Vanderkemp Papers, N.-Y. Hist. Soc.

44. R. R. to Edward Livingston, Jan. 5, 1796, R. R. Livingston Papers, N.-Y. Hist. Soc.; Peter Van Schaack to John Van Allen, Feb. 15, 1796, Van Allen Papers, Albany Institute.

45. Lincoln, ed., *Messages from the Governors*, II, 366-67.

46. Robert R. to Edward Livingston, Oct. 30, Dec. 20, 1795, Jan. 5, Jan. 21, Feb. 5, 1796; to Madison, Nov. 6, 1795; to Monroe, Dec. 13, 1795; Edward to Robert R. Livingston, Dec. [n.d.] 1795, Jan. 20, Feb. 8, 1796, R. R. Livingston Papers, N.-Y. Hist. Soc.

the House, thought Livingston would "probably let it sleep or withdraw it." But when Livingston pushed his point and debate began "rather abruptly," he entered the fray to soften Livingston's request in the hope of saving it.[47]

New York's congressmen were in the center of the debate. The Federalists were choleric. Ezekiel Gilbert of Columbia sputtered that Livingston's motion was "unconstitutional, unprecedented, inexpedient, improper and dangerous to the peace and prosperity of the government." William Cooper, speaking as if he were on the stump in frontier Otsego, said it was "rebellion" and "a usurpation of power." When someone asked Livingston sarcastically whether the information about the treaty diplomacy was wanted for purposes of impeaching Washington, Jay, or both, Livingston replied coolly that the papers themselves might settle that point.[48] In defense of his colleague Jonathan Havens of Long Island offered a tightly reasoned brief on the distribution of powers in the federal government which led to the conclusion that the House could not abdicate its power of appropriations to the Senate or executive. John Hathorn of Ulster was sympathetic.[49]

In defense of his own resolution, Livingston offered an eloquent speech on what he called "the most important question that has ever been agitated within these walls": whether a treaty was paramount to statutory law. If this were true, it would lead to "the substitution of a foreign power in lieu of the popular branch." The proper republican position was that "every treaty operating on objects submitted to the Legislative power should receive its sanction before it took effect"; the House, therefore, had authority to act. For precedent, Livingston turned to Britain and recited at length the relations of Crown and Parliament. In examining the American Constitution, he justified his interpretation by three authorities: the construction of the framers, the practice of the government since 1788, and the present ideas of the people.[50]

When John Williams rose to answer Livingston he gave the first sign of his desertion to the Federalists. Identifying himself as an anti-Federalist in 1788 who had opposed the treaty-making clause of the

47. Cunningham, *The Jeffersonian Republicans*, 80-83; Brant, *James Madison*, III, 433-39.
48. *Annals*, 4th Cong., 2d Sess., 437, 541-42, 426.
49. *Ibid.*, 482-89.
50. *Ibid.*, 627-42.

Constitution and as a man who agreed with Livingston on most measures, the congressman from New York's northern frontier said his sole concern was to execute the treaty by June 1, the date by which the British had agreed to give up the frontier posts. There was no need to call for the official papers—it was a bad precedent, he said. Treaties were the will of the people as much as acts of Congress; in fact, it would be well to guard against excessive power in the legislative as well as the executive branch in light of the tendency for excessive spending. If the treaty was constitutional, the House was bound to put it into effect; otherwise, only a constitutional amendment could give the House a coordinate power to pass on it. The heart of the matter was the treaty proper, which he believed should pass without a day's delay.[51]

On March 24 the vote was taken and Livingston's resolution passed sixty-two to thirty-seven. When Washington refused to turn over the papers, the House then affirmed its right to make the request. On these and the related votes, the New Yorkers divided five to five, the frontier Republican Williams joining the four Federalists.[52]

In April when the House took up the substantive question of their right to sanction or refuse treaties, New York's two frontier congressmen, Williams and Cooper, were desperate to guarantee that the forts would be turned over in June. As Cooper rose to speak, Livingston archly reminded him that if he "delivered his sentiment with that ability, politeness and delicacy of manner with which he generally expresses himself he would be duly attended to" but that "if he did it in the way in which he sometimes delivered himself, he might as well be silent." Cooper was furious: "let him deliver his sentiment on which way he would, he had no doubt that it would be as satisfactory to his constituents as the conduct of that gentlemen to his."[53] Obviously no aristocrat to the manor born was going to tutor a self-made frontier land magnate.

A few minutes later Williams flared up. As he argued the interest of New York City in the treaty, one of the urban Republicans smiled—possibly Livingston but more likely Congressman John Swanwick, the Philadelphia merchant Republican—it was amusing, after all, to receive instructions from a frontiersman. Williams, the House annalist

51. *Ibid.*, 642-50. Cooper and Gilbert spoke briefly, *ibid.*, 676-83.
52. *Ibid.*, 759-768, 782.
53. *Ibid.*, 946.

noted, "here took notice of a smile which he observed upon the countenance of a gentleman near him which he said he despised."[54]

Williams in democratic fashion offered his opinion as the voice of his constituents. When he left northern New York in December, he said, three-fourths of the people there were against the treaty. His letters now informed him that "a very large majority" were for it. "The people are the sovereign; their will shall be my guide from which I shall not knowingly depart." The frontier posts were "an object of the first magnitude" commercially because they dominated the channels of trade to Canada via the St. Lawrence and Lake Champlain. More important, if the treaty was not executed, war, by destroying American commerce would reduce the revenue on imports and necessitate a land tax that would add to the burden on farmers. Williams, himself, "could not boast of having vessels"—another barb at Swanwick—"but he had a few acres of land on the frontier which he wished to have settled" (a modest claim); and "in the district which he represented, hundreds of industrious families, some with six or eight children apiece, lived in log huts, and who, at the sound of war with the Indians would fly from their habitations. Gentlemen who lived surrounded by luxuries in a city do not think of the situation of this class of their citizens who were nevertheless worthy of their consideration."[55]

Cooper dwelt on another frontier economic interest: once the garrison at Fort Oswego was removed, trade with Canada would fall to Americans. He too feared taxes; should the treaty be destroyed and war result, "Why our commerce will be cut up, of course, our revenue destroyed, our farmers impoverished, and on them we must cause to be assessed direct taxes to create supplies or the government will fall to pieces." Columbia's Ezekiel Gilbert focused on two other interests well understood upstate: the fur trade—once the posts were restored, it might be possible for American traders to enter British territory on a reciprocal basis; and western land—its value would go up once the interior was secure.[56]

In face of such powerful economic and emotional appeals and changing sentiment in their own districts, Republican congressmen from the lower Hudson Valley vacillated. At a caucus of House Re-

54. *Ibid.*, 949.
55. *Ibid.*, 1065-77.
56. *Ibid.*, 1095-97, 1203-13.

publicans, the first of its kind, the party split; a majority favored an anti-treaty vote but the minority, as Albert Gallatin recalled it, "were left at full liberty to vote as they pleased."[57] Williams was lost; Livingston and Hathorn of Ulster stood with the majority but Bailey of Dutchess, Havens of Long Island, and Van Cortlandt of Westchester, John Beckley reported to DeWitt Clinton, "may want the necessary stamina to carry them thro'," not because they favored the treaty but "more from their respective situations in their districts than from any other cause." Elected by "small majorities," "they perhaps wish to steer their course which will best insure their re-elections." Only if the three stood firm, could the treaty be rejected—the parties were that evenly divided. Beckley knew New York politics well. Van Cortlandt had received a laconic note from his son in Westchester to "Be prudent in your vote in Congress"—the meaning of which could not have escaped a man elected by a margin of twenty votes. To guarantee his prudence Federalists laid plans to "prepare a reception" for him on his return trip to New York. Ten days later Beckley reported no change: "our three friends are certainly wavering." A Republican victory in the forthcoming New York City election therefore was vital "in confirming the timid and the wavering."[58]

Actually it was too late for Republicans at home to stem the tide. Even though British seizures were continuing, the fear of rejecting the treaty was overpowering. For three days in New York City Federalists took a petition from door to door with one simple thought, the treaty or war. Under the banner, "Washington and Peace," they collected 3200 signatures, a number, Hamilton boasted, "within about 300 of the highest poll we ever had in this city on *both sides* at the most controverted election." To keep the merchants in line, the leading insurance brokers, at Hamilton's instigation, agreed to stop writing policies on shipping until the House executed the treaty.[59]

57. Cunningham, The Jeffersonian Republicans, 81-83.
58. Beckley to Clinton, Apr. 11, 21, 1796, indicating a letter from Clinton, Apr. 16, DeWitt Clinton Papers, Columbia Univ.; John Hathorn to ?, Apr. 20, 1796, Emmet Coll., No. 683, N.Y. Pub. Lib.; for Williams, see Beckley to James Madison, Apr. 20, 1795, Madison Papers, XVIII, Lib. Cong.; Rufus King to Alexander Hamilton, Apr. 17, 1796, Hamilton Papers, Lib. Cong.
59. Hamilton to Rufus King, Apr. 15, 18, 20, 23, 24, 1796 (the latter erroneously dated 1795), Lodge, ed., Works of Hamilton, X, 157-63 98; for insurance pressure, see "Circular letter . . . by Nicholas Low, Archibald Gracie and Julian Verplanck . . . New York, May 3, 1796," broadside, N.Y. Pub. Lib.; for the petition, N.Y. Argus, Apr. 21, 1796.

At Albany Federalists launched a petition at a meeting composed "principally [of] merchants" and, according to Schuyler in three hours had four hundred signatures including "many decided anti-Federalists." Other petitions were sent to surrounding towns where few refused to sign.⁶⁰ On the western frontier it was the same story. In Otsego, Cooper's district, it was said that 5365 signed with no more than ten freeholders opposed.⁶¹

Republican last-ditch efforts were confined to New York City and even there were ineffective. Greenleaf insisted that three or four thousand attended an open air anti-treaty meeting in "The Fields," but Federalists were probably closer to the truth in claiming a crowd of no more than fifteen hundred, made up "almost totally of those who at twelve o'clock could be spared from their manual labors." Fully one-third, a Federalist wrote, "as is usually the case," were "negroes, sweeps, boys, apprentices, Frenchmen and curious people opposed to the meeting." "Few, very few indeed of the heads of the party were to be seen." The "merchants and traders" as well as the "substantial mechanicks" were almost universally pro-treaty.⁶² Republicans did not risk circulating a counter-petition and instead sent a committee to deliver their resolutions to Livingston. When the congressman presented the House with petitions giving both views among his constituents, it was clear that Republicans had lost the race to rally opinion.⁶³

The elections of April 1796 told the same story. "The British treaty defeated and a Republican president to succeed Mr. Washington"—these were the goals, John Beckley trumpeted from Philadelphia.⁶⁴ The new assembly and senate would choose the next presidential electors. As a result of reapportionment there were twenty new senate seats and thirty-four new assembly seats, the major part in the western district. Republicans knew the stakes. In the southern district at a meeting in New York which Melancton Smith called "the

60. Philip Schuyler to Hamilton, Apr. 25, 1796, Schuyler Papers, Morristown National Historical Park; Stephen Van Rensselaer to William Cooper, Apr. 25, 30, May 6, 1796, Cooper MSS, N.Y. State Lib.; N.Y. *Argus*, Apr. 29, May 2, 1796; *Albany Gazette*, May 2, 1796.
61. Cooperstown *Otsego Herald*, May 12, June 16, 1796; "An Address to the Free Citizens of the United States of North America," in Peck, *Political Wars*, 95-103; see also *Whitestown Gazette*, "Agricola" and a letter from Oswego, Aug. 9, "The Democrat's Soliloquy," Aug. 16, 1796.
62. N.Y. *Argus*, Apr. 29, 1796; William Willcocks, *Albany Gazette*, May 2, 1796.
63. *Annals*, 4th Cong., 2d Sess., 1228; *Albany Gazette*, May 2, 1796.
64. John Beckley to DeWitt Clinton, Apr. 11, 1796, DeWitt Clinton Papers, Columbia Univ.

largest and most respectable ever attended," they nominated Aaron Burr for the state senate.[65] Burr would resign his seat in the United States Senate if elected; he was near the end of it anyway. In the city Republicans put together their strongest assembly ticket thus far: General James Alner, a hero of the Revolution, Peter R. Livingston and DeWitt Clinton, leaders of the anti-treaty campaign, Henry Rutgers and Tunis Wortman of the Democratic Society, and William Keteltas, a young lawyer who had just emerged from prison, a hero in the *cause célèbre* of two Irish ferrymen—a case to be described presently. Calling themselves the "Republican Whig" ticket, they campaigned as the party of "Public Liberty, the Constitution and Peace."[66] Elsewhere in the state, however, Republican efforts were not comparable.

In the midst of the state balloting, the House ended the treaty issue by voting 51-48 for an appropriation to execute Jay's Treaty. Among the New York Republicans, Livingston of New York City and Hathorn of Ulster voted nay, as expected; Havens of Long Island joined them but, true to Beckley's fears, Van Cortlandt of Westchester and Bailey of Dutchess defected. A little later Van Cortlandt addressed an apologetic letter to his constituents defending his vote.[67]

In June with the election returns before them Republicans stared political disaster in the face. The centers of Republican anti-treaty sentiment in 1795, New York City, Ulster, Dutchess, all elected Federalists. In New York City the Federalists won all twelve seats; the Republican vote climbed by five hundred over the year before, but the Federalist vote climbed more. In the southern senatorial district, Burr lost by a two-to-one vote even though he ran better than any Republican before him.[68] Of the twenty-three senate seats contested in the state as a whole, Federalists took all but one; they made gains in the assembly as well. The western and northern centers of pro-treaty sentiment went resoundingly Federalist. The line-up in the next legislature would guarantee Federalist presidential electors and Federalist senators to replace Rufus King, just confirmed as Minister to Great

65. Melancton Smith to John Smith, Mar. 12, 1796, John Smith Papers, N.-Y. Hist. Soc.

66. "Let every True Whig . . . Apr. 19, 1796," broadside, N.Y. State Lib., and another, undated, in N.-Y. Hist. Soc., misfiled under 1791; *N.-Y. Journal*, Apr. 19, 22, 29, 1796.

67. *Annals*, 4th Cong., 2d Sess., 1291; Brant, *James Madison*, III, 438-39. Philip Van Cortlandt, "Circular Letter," May 20, 1796, in Van Cortlandt-Van Wyck Papers, N.Y. Pub. Lib.

68. Hammond, *Political Parties*, I, 100; *N.-Y. Journal*, June 3, 4, 7, 1796.

Britain, and Aaron Burr, whose six-year term was drawing to a close.

Surveying the election in the country as a whole, Madison commented to Jefferson that "the crisis which ought to have been so managed as to fortify the Republican cause, has left it in a very crippled condition."[69] In New York, Republicans who were at the dizzy pinnacle of political influence in July 1795 a year later were in a slough of despair. The reasons for Federalist success were not hard to fathom. Everywhere there was a fear of war if Jay's Treaty was rejected. For New Yorkers the positive features of the treaty were in the end decisive. The recovery of the forts, with its prospects for safety, land values, frontier commerce, and the fur trade, was crucial to the northern and western frontier. In July 1796, about twenty wagons from the north arrived at Albany laden with furs—"the old fur traders in this city look very pleasant this day," a visitor observed. "A renewal of this gainful business is anticipated."[70]

For the merchants of New York City the import trade, the revenue, and in turn Hamiltonian finance had been saved. And those who had suffered ship losses would make full use of the claims machinery set up by the treaty.[71]

Republicans had collapsed for a number of reasons. In the southernmost counties, Long Island, Westchester, and Dutchess, the wavering Republican congressmen very likely were affected by the commercial orientation of their farm constituents to the New York City market. The anti-Tory implications of the Republican campaign doubtless revived latent fears among the numerous former Loyalists of the area. In New York City the defectors in the mercantile community were probably tugged back into line by the prospects of indemnification or the pressures of insurance underwriters. In the state as a whole Republicans were no match for the two strongest political figures the Federalists could muster: Governor Jay whose reservoir of popular support was at its fullest, and President Washington whose popularity was hardly diminished. It is therefore not surprising that the Republican storm of 1795 was no more than a squall in 1796 and that Federalists kept control of the ship of state.

69. Madison to Jefferson, May 22, 1796, cited in Malone, *Jefferson and His Time*, III, 259.
70. Jeremy Belknap, *Journal*, July 1, 1796, p. 30.
71. New Yorkers filed 71 claims before the Jay Treaty Claims Commission whose records are cited in n.38 above.

CHAPTER 22

"A Question Between the Rich and the Poor":

New York City Politics

1796-1797

―――•―•―――

"In the view of the common people," Alexander Hamilton wrote, "the elections for assemblymen and senators in New York City in the spring of 1796 was a question between the rich and the poor." The city's first class conflict of the Federalist era, it was correctly attributed by Hamilton to "the vile affair of whipping Burke and McCredy," two Irish-born ferrymen who had been severely punished by the Federalist magistrates for the crime of talking insolently to one of their number.[1] Coming to public attention precisely when the battle to defeat Jay's Treaty reached a crescendo in Congress, Republican leaders seized on the issue and made it a *cause célèbre*. From the tumult a new urban democratic leader emerged, William Keteltas, the likes of whom New York had not seen since the "liberty boy," Alexander McDougall, won a reputation as the "John Wilkes of America" in 1769-1771.

I

The ferrymen incident was an explosive spark that set off a number of combustible elements building up in the life of the city for several

1. Hamilton to Rufus King, May 4, 1796, Lodge, ed., *Works of Hamilton*, VIII, 395-96. The correct name of the second ferryman was Crady, not "McCredy," while "Burke" usually was spelled "Burk."

[468]

years. The city's growth in the middle 1790's was phenomenal. A population of 33,000 in 1790 had grown to a probable 45,000 by 1795 and to 60,000 by 1800. From September 1794 to September 1795 alone, one merchant calculated that from 1000 to 1200 new houses were built.[2] The boom resulted from natural growth, migration from New England, and beginning about 1793 immigration from France, the French West Indies, Ireland, Scotland, and England.

With growth came prosperity, the consequence of the burgeoning export trade and the demands of a growing population.[3] And with prosperity came pockets of poverty new to the city in intensity and scope. New York, like "all great towns," the worldly Frenchman La Rochefoucauld-Liancourt observed, "contains at once more riches and more wretchedness than towns less populous and commercial."[4] "On all sides," the Englishman John Payne recorded, "new houses are rising and streets extending."[5] Some two hundred and fifty mansions assessed at over £2000,[6] a handsome Broadway, fashionable restaurants and gardens, the new Tontine's Coffee House—all betokened a wealth that prompted one visiting Englishman to think of New York as "a London in miniature" with "its populous streets, hum of business, busy faces, shops in style etc."[7] On the other hand there was a New York that reminded another Englishman of Liverpool with its narrow, dirty and crowded streets, and its poverty.[8]

As shipping, shipbuilding, and manufacturing expanded, the number of wage workers with little or no property leaped ahead. By the mid-nineties there were hundreds of common laborers on the docks stowing barrels and crates in the hot sun from dawn to dusk. There were more cartmen or draymen to lug freight around the city, some 500 of them licensed by the city, men known for their "quick tempers"

2. Seth Johnson to Andrew Craigie, Sept. 21, 1795, Craigie Papers, III, No. 98, Amer. Antiq. Soc. Matthew Davis estimated that the number of families went up from 4700 in 1791 to 9000 in 1795, an exaggerated estimate; see Davis, *A Brief Account of the Epidemical Fever* . . . (N.Y., 1795), 6.

3. Timothy Pitkin, *A Statistical View of the Commerce of the United States* . . . (New Haven, 2nd ed., 1835), 50-51, 96, 105.

4. La Rochefoucauld-Liancourt, *Travels*, II, 205.

5. John Payne, *New and Complete System of Universal Geography*, 4 vols. (N.Y., 1799), IV, 302.

6. Wilson, ed., *Memorial History of New York*, III, 150-52.

7. William Priest, a traveler cited in Stokes, *Iconography of Manhattan*, V, Sept. 21, 1797.

8. Isaac Weld, Jr., *Travels Through the States of North America and the Provinces of Upper and Lower Canada During the Years 1795-1796, and 1797* (London, 1799), 264-66.

and "mistreating their horses."[9] There was also a good sprinkling of factory workers—in tanyards, in fur, glue, and soap-making establishments, in a few textile mills. While craftsmen worked in pleasant shops often located in their own homes, fur workers toiled in "damp cellers which exude fumes so noxious especially during the great heat of summer, as to suffocate passersby on the sidewalks,"[10] and the tanyards were located in a part of town known as "The Swamp."[11] There were also hundreds of workers eking out a marginal living as tea-water men, food hawkers, chimney sweeps, and the like.

Skilled craftsmen seem to have prospered. Compared to their European counterparts, La Rochefoucauld-Liancourt observed, they were "much better paid" and "live Well"—"the proverbial wish of having a chicken in the pot is more than accomplished in America."[12] Or if they were dissatisfied, they could migrate to "the new settlements," where they would be well paid, or so it seemed to an English observer, Henry Wansey. Even craftsmen in the new cotton mill at Hell's Gate were "ready to leave the factory as soon as they have saved a few pounds, in order to become landholders up the country, and arrive at Independence."[13]

The unskilled common laborers, on the other hand, could not make good such aspirations. The price inflation that brought prosperity to the merchant brought privation to mechanics. "For some considerable time past," one group reported early in 1795, "house rent, fuel, provisions, and the prices of everything necessary for the support of a family have been rising," many to twice their previous level.[14] Rising prices put flour, beef, pork, and butter out of the reach of many who had to "pay through the nose"—and this in a land "said to flow with milk and honey."[15]

There were unmistakable signs of a grinding poverty in the city. The almshouse was constantly filled. From 1794 through 1797 there usually were from 600 to 800 paupers getting assistance.[16] In January

9. Roberts, trans. and ed., *Moreau de St. Méry's American Journey*, 124-25, 127, 158-59, 162.

10. *Ibid.*, 164.

11. Frank Norcross, *History of the New York Swamp* (N.Y., 1901), 8-11.

12. La Rochefoucauld-Liancourt, *Travels*, II, 671.

13. Wansey, *Journal of an Excursion*, 83-84.

14. "Petition of the Repackers of Beef and Pork to the State Legislature, Jan. 24, 1795," Misc. MSS, N.Y.C., No. 86, N.-Y. Hist. Soc.

15. "Jehoshaphat," *N.-Y. Evening Post*, Jan. 14, 1795.

16. Peterson, ed., *Minutes of the Common Council*, II, Feb. 5, 1795, Feb. 1,

1797, some six hundred journeymen mechanics and tradesmen "now out of employment" signed a public petition requesting assistance because "in consequence of the season, without work" many "by reason of large families" were "in want of sufficient FIRE and WOOD."[17]

There were also signs of a *lumpen proletariat*. A doctor described one of his patients as "a most wretched looking drunken being who gets his living by chimney sweeping and picking up rags."[18] There were 709 licensed taverns and grog shops in the city in 1795, almost twice as many as in 1790, one for every 60 inhabitants.[19] "Whole sections" of the city were "given over to streetwalkers for the plying of their profession."[20] In 1793 authorities could not quell a mob of "boys apprentices, and Negroes, as well as sailors" who demolished two bawdy houses.[21]

The housing shortage was probably the most acute problem for the poor. When newcomers began streaming in during the mid-90's, the city had not made up the deficit of housing created by fires during the British occupation. In the old parts of town, on the lower east side where the streets were "small and crooked" and the footpaths narrow, La Rochefoucauld-Liancourt found the houses "mean, small and low, built of wood." On the new west side near the Hudson they were "much better built" and on Broadway the homes of the "opulent inhabitants" were unmatched for "elegance."[22] But the upper east side near the East River, where most of the poor flocked, was a true slum. As a doctor described it, it had "narrow, crooked, flat unpaved, muddy alleys," was filled with swamps, stagnant waters, and "little decayed huts," some inhabited by several families, and was scented by an intolerable stench from garbage piled in the streets, the tanyards, and putrefying excrement at the docks.[23] Inevitably there were complaints of high rents and "unfeeling" and "insolent" landlords.[24] If middle-

1796; Pomerantz, *New York An American City*, 331-34; La Rochefoucauld-Liancourt, *Travels*, II, 460-61.

17. N.Y. *Argus*, Jan. 14, 1797.

18. Entry of Aug. 2, 1794, Anderson, Diary, Columbia Univ.

19. Peterson, ed., *Minutes of the Common Council*, II, 606.

20. Roberts, trans. and ed., *Moreau de St. Méry's American Journey*, 156.

21. N.-Y. *Journal*, Oct. 19, 1793; entries of Oct. 14, 16, 1793, Anderson Diary, Columbia Univ.

22. La Rochefoucauld-Liancourt, *Travels*, II, 457-58.

23. Dr. Elihu Hubbard Smith, "Letters to William Bull . . . on the Fever," Noah Webster, Jr., comp., *A Collection of Papers on the Subject of Billious Fevers* (N.Y., 1796), 66-74.

24. N.-Y. *Journal*, Feb. 12, 1794; N.Y. *Columbian Gazetteer*, Feb. 14, 1794.

class lawyers like James Kent complained that New York in the summer was a "hot, noisy, hateful city," the feelings of the slum dwellers can be imagined.[25]

Foremost among the sufferers were the most recent migrants from Ireland who crowded down the gangplanks from the fall of 1794 through the summer of 1795. They were, as one New Yorker put it, "the wretched and depressed poor" who were eager to migrate to a new land.[26] Once here they occupied the lowest rung on the occupational ladder, toiling in the out-of-doors as common laborers, dockworkers, and draymen. Their housing was abominable; "in consequence of the enormous price of rents," wrote Matthew Davis, the Republican printer, they "were reduced to the necessity of living, or rather existing in damp cellers" in the swampy part of town.[27]

The increase in the number of the poor, their location in distinct parts of the city, and the identification of the poor with new immigrants heightened the sense of class distinctions in the city. The "first class" in America, La Rochefoucauld-Liancourt observed after his sojourn in New York, was composed of merchants, lawyers, "landowners who do not cultivate their land," doctors, and clergymen; the second of "inferior merchants, the farmers and the artisans"; the third, of "workmen who let themselves by the day by the month etc." "In Balls, concerts, and public amusements, these classes do not mix." The third class, moreover, was below respectability. "Everyone calls himself, and is called by others, a *gentleman*," he pointed out, "except the laborer in ports, and the common sailor."[28] Federalists recognized this same distinction when they claimed that the "substantial mechanicks," the property-owning craftsmen, supported them while "the lowest order of mechanics, laborers and draymen" attended Democratic Society meetings.[29] So did Republicans when they accused the "opulent politicians and the lordlike landholder" of looking upon "the honest laborer" as "a distinct animal of inferior species."[30]

25. James to Moss Kent, June 22, 1796, Kent Papers, II, Lib. Cong.
26. Smith, "Letters to William Bull," Webster, comp., *Collection on Fevers*, 66-74, 79-89.
27. Davis, *A Brief Account of the Epidemical Fevers*, 6, 16-17. Davis lists the dead, 58-67. The occupations, where given, are predominantly those of craftsmen or laborers. There were 37 names beginning with "Mc."
28. La Rochefoucauld-Liancourt, *Travels*, II, 671-72.
29. William Willcocks, *Albany Gazette*, May 2, 1796; William Woolsey to Oliver Wolcott, Mar. 6, 1794, cited in Link, *Democratic Republican Societies*, 94.
30. "J.L.," N.Y. *Argus*, Apr. 27, 1796; N.Y. *Diary*, Jan. 18, 1795, cited in Luetscher, *Early Political Machinery*, 58.

The yellow fever epidemic that struck the city in August 1795 helped to bring social tensions to a head. The fever took its heaviest toll among the "new residents," especially the Irish.[31] Already fatigued by the overseas voyage, forced to live in unsanitary conditions and to do the hardest work, the Irish succumbed by the hundreds. While the well-to-do were able to evacuate the city, slum dwellers were unable either to leave or to obtain medical help. In ignorance, many avoided the Lazeretto set up for their assistance at Bellevue Hospital. The near-dead were rejected at the hospital, put in carts "like calves and other livestock," and "drawn thence in succession to the doors of several members of the Health Committee over the stony roughness of the pavement and under the scorching rays of a noon-tide sun." Some seven hundred New Yorkers perished in this living Dante's Inferno, the city counting the last deaths November 1, a week or so before the ferrymen incident.[32]

Native-born New Yorkers of conservative bent were already brimming over with hostility toward the new immigrants. If Noah Webster, the Yankee editor, is a reliable guide, they already looked upon immigrants as harboring many "warm democrats." The formation of associations along ethnic lines by the Scots, Irish, and French confirmed their suspicions, as did the turnout at the "Town Meetings" in 1795. Conservatives doubtless blamed immigrants for the high cost of maintaining the poorhouse and for the fever as well, rationalizing the high mortality rate among the Irish as the result of heavy drink.[33] Humanitarians on the other hand, including a number of Republicans, had their consciences pricked by the suffering in their midst which the fever revealed.[34] As for the poor Irish and slum residents, their resentment seemed to simmer, waiting to burst forth.

Before the fever struck, there was a smoldering discontent with the governing body of the city, the Common Council. In the mercantilist

31. N.Y. *Argus*, Oct. 17, 1795; see also "A Passenger," *ibid.*, Sept. 29, 1795.

32. Smith, "Letters to William Bull," Webster, comp., *Collection on Fevers*. For verification see Valentine Seaman, "Account of the Yellow Fever in New York in 1795," *ibid.*, 5-7; Richard Bayley, *An Account of the Epidemic Fever* (N.Y., 1796), 59-66, 122. Bayley was a health officer of the city.

33. Noah Webster to Theodore Sedgwick, Jan. 2, 1795, cited in Richard E. Welch, Jr., *Theodore Sedgwick, Federalist; A Political Portrait* (Middletown, Conn., 1965), 133; Seth Johnson to Andrew Craigie, Sept. 21, 1795, Craigie Papers, III, No. 98, Amer. Antiq. Soc.

34. See the pamphlets of Smith, Seaman, Bayley, and especially Davis cited above; see N.Y. *Argus*, Sept.-Nov. 1795, *passim*, for appeals for charity.

tradition, the city government supervised the local retail market, licensed tradesmen, set prices on such commodities as bread, and regulated the activities of the cartmen. Consumers complained that the council did nothing to prevent the sharp practices of tradesmen which boosted the prices of necessities. Petty tradesmen like bakers and cartmen protested that prices or rates set by the Council were inadequate in the face of spiraling costs.[35] Citizens in all walks were irritated by inadequate police protection, "dirty streets," and the filth and stench around the piers.[36] Justice as meted out by the city magistrates in the Court of General Sessions was still another cause for grumbling. Of Mayor Richard Varick who sat as chief judge it was claimed, "The lawyers say you are passionate" and "criminals say you are cruel."[37] For poor and defenseless petty offenders justice was summary and punishment at the pillory or in the stocks harsh. At the jail, conditions were noisome.[38]

After 1790-91 Federalist control of the city government went unchallenged in the city elections each September. It was the chronic lament of the Republican editor, Greenleaf, in fact, that few even bothered to vote for alderman. Mayor Varick, although appointed by Governor Clinton, was staunchly Federalist as were most of the aldermen.[39] Early in the decade there was so little interest in city affairs that a motion in the legislature to have the mayor elected rather than appointed stirred hardly a ripple.[40] In the fall of 1795, in spite of the many complaints, the Common Council once again was returned without a contest.[41]

Potentially, however, the political situation was hazardous for the Federalists. The electoral census, published in January 1796, revealed that there were about 900 more voters in the £100 electorate than in 1790, for a total of 2100; but there were 2300 more 40-shilling renters, for a total of almost 5000. There were thus more than twice as many propertyless as propertied voters. Moreover, the poorer voters were concentrated in the newly built part of town, the fifth and especially the seventh wards along the East River, and the fourth and especially

35. See above, ch. 18, n.74.
36. See footnote 94 below.
37. John Clark, a letter, *N.-Y. Journal*, Dec. 26, 1795; Duer, *Reminiscences*, 29.
38. Pomerantz, *New York An American City*, 308-16.
39. *Ibid.*, 42-44.
40. "Atticus," *N.-Y. Journal*, Apr. 7, 1792.
41. *Ibid.*, Oct. 3, 1795.

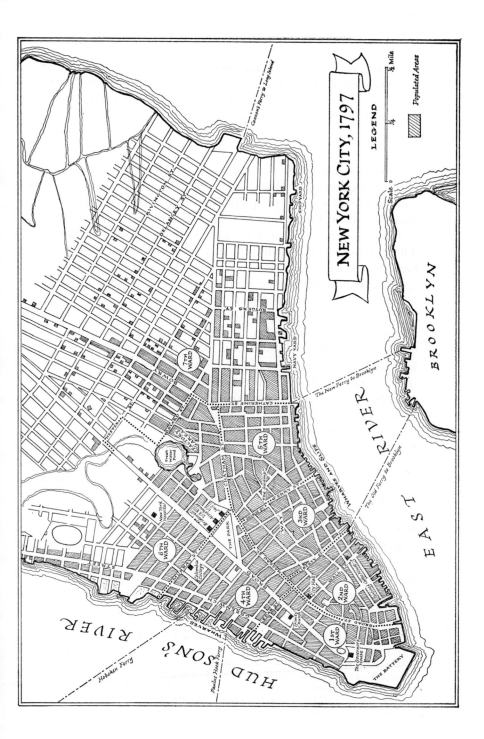

NEW YORK CITY, 1797

LEGEND

Scale 0   ¼   ½ Mile

▨ Populated Areas

BROOKLYN

EAST RIVER

The New Ferry to Brooklyn

The Old Ferry to Brooklyn

HUDSON'S RIVER

Hoboken Ferry

Paulus Hook Ferry

WHARVES

THE BATTERY

1ST WARD

2ND WARD

3RD WARD

4TH WARD

5TH WARD

6TH WARD

7TH WARD

THE PARK

Fresh Water Pond

SHIP YARD

NAVY YARD

Corlears Ferry to Long Island

CATHERINE ST.

RIVINGTON ST.

DELANCEY ST.

BROADWAY

WALL AND SOUTH STS.

the sixth to the west along the Hudson River. In the seventh, known as the "cartmen's ward," 40-shilling voters outnumbered the £100 voters by 870 to 311; in the sixth the proportion was 1298 to 223.[42] Here was the Republican potential.

II

The ferrymen affair was the spark which ignited the fuse to the political explosion in New York City. The incident itself was commonplace.[43] A small barge poled by two men took travelers and produce across the East River between lower Manhattan and Brooklyn. A business venture, it was owned by John Hicks and manned by Thomas Burk and Timothy Crady, two Irish immigrants who had been in the city a scant year and a half. The reputation of the service appears to have been poor even though the ferrymen, according to Hicks, were "industrious, sober, honest."

One day early in November 1795, Gabriel Furman, a merchant who was the Federalist alderman representing the well-to-do first ward, was returning to Manhattan from Brooklyn. Arriving at the ferry a few minutes before the scheduled time of departure, Furman asked the ferrymen to leave earlier. They refused; Furman insisted, and some hot words were exchanged. The alderman complained to Hicks, who ordered the boat off. Before reaching the Manhattan wharf, the alderman, according to one witness, renewed the dispute upbraiding "the rascals" and threatening to commit them to jail. Crady was enraged—"They were as good as any buggers"—and threatened to use his boathook against anyone who tried to arrest him. Furman called the high constable and second alderman and ordered the men arrested for insulting a magistrate. When Crady resisted, he and Burk were seized and Furman marched them through the streets, inveighing against them as "impudent rascals." He also either punched them in the back several times with his cane or brandished his cane menacingly. The two were committed to jail on Furman's order, without the necessary oath and without legal process, it seems. Then they were

42. N.Y. *Daily Advertiser*, Jan. 15, 1791, "Supplement," Jan. 27, 1796; see N.Y.C. map.

43. See Pomerantz, *New York An American City*, 263-68 for a brief account. The account herein is based on contempory newspaper accounts by Keteltas, "One of the People," *N.-Y. Journal*, Dec. 26, 30, 1795, a signed article, *ibid.*, Feb. 23, 1796, and an excellent detailed unsigned series of articles reviewing the case, under the title "Richard Varick," N.Y. *American Citizen*, Sept. 1, 2, 3, 1801. The Sept. 2, 1801, article attributed "One of the People" to Keteltas. The "Varick" articles very likely were also by Keteltas.

accused as vagrants. The next day Hicks' son appeared at Furman's house to ask for the release of the men; they had saved their money and clearly were not vagrants. Hicks offered bail. Furman refused. They remained in the Bridewell jail for twelve days, awaiting trial.

In jail Burk and Crady attracted the attention of a young Republican lawyer, William Keteltas, who attended their trial. The trial was before the Court of General Sessions—Mayor Varick and three Federalist aldermen. There was no jury. Burk and Crady, without counsel, faced a chief judge so prejudiced against the Irish that two months after the trial he still could not get Crady's name straight. "O'Grady" Varick called him, "McCredy," Hamilton called him—after all what difference did the name of a poor Irish ferryman make?[44]

At the trial it was obvious that the judges were out to make an example of two insolent Irishmen. "You rascals, we'll trim you," Varick allegedly said, "we'll learn you to insult men in office!" There were two formal charges: insulting an alderman engaged in the execution of the duties of his office, and threatening the high constable. To both charges Crady and Burk pleaded not guilty. Furman was the only witness called and naturally gave a highly colored version of the incident, making Crady the principal villain.

The ferrymen were not allowed to speak in their own behalf. John Hicks, who sought to testify as a character witness for Burk, could do no more than force an unwanted sentence or two on the judges. The magistrates, acting with customary dispatch, found the two guilty on both counts, sentencing both to two months at hard labor and Crady to twenty-five lashes as well. Burk narrowly escaped a similar fate.

For more than a month scarcely a ripple was heard of the case. Then the two ferrymen and several other prisoners broke out of jail—a not uncommon event—and fled to Pennsylvania. A few days later, the first article about the affair appeared in Greenleaf's papers, a two-column account signed "One of the People," written by Keteltas.[45]

Keteltas described the incident and the trial which on the surface alone condemned the magistrates. He castigated "the tyranny and partiality of the court" and concluded that Burk and Crady were punished to "gratify the pride, the ambition and insolence of men in office." Varick and the magistrates issued a prompt denial in the papers. Within a few days the other principals were in print, their

44. Richard Varick to Ebenezer Foote, Jan. 28, 1796, Foote, ed., *Ebenezer Foote*, 69.
45. "One of the People," *N.-Y. Journal*, Dec. 26, 30, 1795.

testimony marshaled by the young lawyer. Hicks offered an affidavit as to what happened at the dock, another man described the treatment the ferrymen received from Furman in the Manhattan streets, and Hicks's son recounted how Furman highhandedly refused to allow bail.[46]

At this juncture Varick was vulnerable to criticism because of another incident reported only the week before. In response to the demands of the captain of the *Thetis*, a British man-of-war in the New York harbor, Varick and the aldermen, including Furman, delivered up nine prisoners from the Bridewell, accepting the British claim that they were deserters. Others presented affidavits to the contrary. Immediately the cry went up that Varick had helped to "crimp" the men on board, collaborating with the British "tyrants." Coming just when Republicans were renewing agitation against Jay's Treaty, it was an explosive issue. John Clark, a former sergeant of the New York line who had visited Washington early in 1794 on behalf of the New York war veterans, took the lead in pressing the "crimping" issue.[47]

Writers immediately picked up the ferrymen case. There was absolutely no law, wrote "Cleon," by which a person could be punished for "insulting language." "Do we live in a city where the Mayor or an Alderman or two have a right to strip us naked and give us as many lashes as they please at a whipping post for what they may deem an insult to a magistrate?" "Sidney" pointed out the violations of legal rights involved: no indictment by a grand jury, no jury trial, a summary and arbitrary trial under a law that gave no authority to punish an insult to a magistrate in his capacity as a private citizen. "A Friend to the Mighty" sarcastically suggested that to distinguish the "worthy magistrates" from "the swinish multitude" the magistrates might hang gold chains around their necks inscribed "I am born to govern, therefore approach me with reverence."[48]

Cleverly, Republicans linked the ferrymen case to their other scores against the Federalists. "What a falling off is there!" wrote "Brutus." "People in office who are guided by a British influence and aping the customs and manners of petty tyrants who exist under monarchy—men taking up them to ratify a treaty, without consulting the will of the people—Aldermen punishing citizens for daring to

46. See also Keteltas' review of the case, *ibid.*, Feb. 23, 1796.
47. *Ibid.*, Dec. 10, 1795; N.Y. *Argus*, Dec. 19, 22, 1795.
48. *N.-Y. Journal*, Dec. 30, 1795, Jan. 2, 5, 1796.

speak to them, refusing them a fair trial and whipping them like slaves —sending men on board a British vessel to serve a tyrant and in irons without their consent and in contradiction to the laws of the United States."[49]   In a satiric doggerel poem, "The Strange and Wonderful Account of a Dutch Hog," the cartmen were reminded that Mayor Varick—"varick" meant "hog" in Dutch—was also their special enemy:

> He often sits upon a bench,
> Much like unto a judge, sir,
> And makes the wretches' bosom wrench
> To whom he owes a grudge, sir.
>
> But now he does a great offence
> It is no thing to mock at
> He takes away the cartmen's pence
> And puts them in his pocket.
>
> He acts as tho' he favors POWER
> Were made but for his use, sir.
> And when it is—in luckless hour,
> He'd turn it to abuse, sir.
>
> For once two Ferrymen
> Some thought let freely slip, sir,
> But ah! he sent them to a Den
> And made them feel the whip, sir.
>
> Oh, send him to his Pen to close
> 'Twould be a funny joke, sir.
> An iron ring upon his nose
> And on his neck a yoke, sir.[50]

Keteltas pressed the case aggressively on several fronts. He appealed first to the grand jury for an indictment against Alderman Furman for assault and battery and false imprisonment. He also petitioned the state assembly, then meeting in the city, to impeach the magistrates for their "illegal and unconstitutional" acts, asking permission to come before the house to substantiate his charges. John Hicks, the ferry owner, backed him up with a separate petition.[51] Simultaneously, Keteltas issued a dramatic public appeal to Burk and Crady to return to New York City. "The people," he said, "will support the law, vindicate your innocence and punish the guilty. . . .

49. *Ibid.*, Jan. 5, 1796.
50. "The Strange and Wonderful Account of a Dutch Hog," [1796], broadside, Acc. 7765, N.Y. State Lib.
51. *Journal of the Assembly of N.Y.*, 19th Sess., 11, 24.

Sounds like Brockholst

Heaven forbid that it should be said that the State of New York is no longer an asylum for the persecuted sons of men of any clime."[52]

III

The ingenious steps taken to publicize the ferrymen's case showed that the man who made it his own had an uncommon flair for dramatizing an issue. Identified in the papers solely as "a young lawyer of veracity and reputation," William Keteltas was born in 1765, the sixth of ten children of Abraham Keteltas, a prosperous Presbyterian minister of Queens County active in the Revolution as chairman of the Jamaica Committee of Safety and as a member of the state convention. "The young man," it was claimed in an article William himself probably wrote, "seems to possess the independent spirit of the father."[53] As a child, William shared his family's "easy and affluent" life; in the Revolution when the family took refuge in Connecticut he suffered in "wretched indigence" and saw his mother "sickly and sometime insane."[54] During or after the war, like a good many other Long Island patriots, he settled in Poughkeepsie, where he read law and was admitted to the bar.

He may have been active in politics as early as the ratification controversy but characteristic of the new Republicans of the mid-90's he called himself "neither anti-Federal nor Federal and yet both" —he was in favor of the Constitution, he said, and also the first ten amendments.[55] He first seems to have caught public attention in 1789 in a long-winded newspaper attack against the chief magistrate of Dutchess County, a controversy in which he championed "the rights of mankind."[56] He won a reputation in Poughkeepsie as someone who was "always in hot water."[57] To the conservative James Kent he was "a certain fanatical demagogue,"[58] while even to Smith Thompson, a Republican lawyer, he had a "proud and haughty spirit" that was a "species of insanity." "He seems not in his proper element unless in some quarrel," according to Smith, who almost fought a duel with him. Keteltas was forced to profess his faith at a public meeting,

52. *N.-Y. Journal*, Jan. 29, 1796.
53. "A Dialogue Between 1776 and 1796," *ibid.*, Feb. 5, 1796.
54. Abraham Keteltas to Gov. George Clinton, Dec. 8, 1778, Emmet Collection, No. 10686, N.Y. Pub. Lib.; Franklin B. Dexter, *Biographical Sketches of the Graduates of Yale College* . . . , 6 vols. (N.Y., 1885-1919), II, 289-91.
55. "A Dialogue," *N.-Y. Journal*, Feb. 5, 1796.
56. Poughkeepsie *Country Journal*, Feb. 10, 1789.
57. "A Citizen," N.Y. *Herald*, Mar. 19, 1796.
58. James Kent to Moss Kent, Mar. 12, 1796, Kent Papers, II, Lib. Cong.

said Smith, but wore "the Christian garb" only a short while before he discarded it to become a deist.[59] He probably came to New York City in 1794.

When the ferryman case occurred, Keteltas, with a wife and several children, was no more than a struggling young lawyer uncommonly devoted to libertarian principles, a member of both Tammany and the Democratic Society.[60] It was claimed, however, that he was "merely the catspaw of a certain family"—the Livingstons. Brockholst Livingston, to whom Keteltas may have been related by marriage, seems to have taken a part in defending him.[61]

The grand jury to which Keteltas first turned rejected his plea.[62] The assembly, however, referred his petition to impeach the magistrates to a special committee. Headed by the Ulster Federalist Ebenezer Foote, the committee summoned records and examined witnesses in a two-week inquiry. In its lengthy report it supported the conservative version of the affair, placing the onus for the incident on the ferrymen who "for some time past have been generally strangers [to the country] ignorant of their duty, given to intoxication and uncivil and abusive to passengers." Although the committee conceded that at the trial Mayor Varick had not given Burk and Crady an opportunity to present character witnesses, they pronounced the trial itself fair. On the grounds of insufficient evidence to warrant impeachment proceedings, they recommended that Keteltas' petition be dismissed.[63]

When the report was turned over to the assembly for debate, Keteltas tried to mobilize public pressure, obtaining a hundred or so signatures to a petition which, by demanding a full investigation of the charges, implied that the committee's inquiry was deficient. Citizens were urged to attend the legislature's debate. In the *New York Journal* Republicans clarified the violations of constitutional rights in the case.[64]

In the legislative debate, a vociferous minority led by John Bird

59. William Keteltas, *Poughkeepsie Journal*, July 31, 1793; Smith Thompson, *ibid.*, Aug. 7, 1793.

60. Link, *Democratic Republican Societies*, 58n., 86, 153, 187.

61. "A Citizen," N.Y. *Herald*, Mar. 19, 1796, for the "catspaw" charge. Brockholst Livingston married Catherine Keteltas, daughter of Peter Keteltas, a merchant. The relation to William's family, while not clear, is possible in view of the small number of Keteltases in the area. A genealogical search was inconclusive.

62. "A Citizen," *N.-Y. Journal*, Feb. 2; "Enquiry," *ibid.*, Feb. 5, 1796.

63. *Journal of the Assembly of N.Y.*, 19th Sess., 24, 48, 67-68.

64. See especially "A Citizen," N.Y. *Argus*, Feb. 2, 1796; "One of the People," *ibid.*, Feb. 9, 1796, "Sidney," *ibid.*, Jan. 5, 1796.

and Adam Comstock, two Saratoga County Republicans who had served on the committee of inquiry, challenged the report. Taking the position that what Burk and Crady did was not a criminal offense and consequently not punishable, they argued that the trial was improper and illegal. They also charged that the committee had suppressed testimony and refused to hear testimony on behalf of the ferrymen. A host of leading upstate Federalists rallied to the conservative defense—William North, the landlord, Thomas Morris, the western land proprietor, and Abraham Ten Broeck, the Albany merchant. Their chief defense was a legalistic argument that because the assembly lacked jurisdiction to judge the case, the petitioner's proper recourse was to a court of law. A Federalist motion to dismiss Keteltas' petition passed, fifty-two to ten,[65] Bird and Comstock rallying only part of the Republican minority.

In a few days Keteltas published a factual summary of the debate in Greenleaf's paper attacking the assembly for "the most flagrant abuse of [the people's] rights" since Independence.[66] The assembly, he charged, was sympathetic to Varick and was protecting him against impeachment to save his reputation. But what of the reputation of Burk and Crady ruined by Varick? Justice should not incline one way or the other, but if a choice were necessary, it should be stern with the "guilty rich" and not lead to "oppression of innocent poor . . . the rich having a consolation in wealth to soften the anguish of distress, while the poor are left without hope to perish." In his article Keteltas repeated Assemblyman Bird's comment that the committee had not reported all the evidence to the assembly.

This accusation infuriated Federalist legislators. Two days later they introduced a resolution which called Keteltas' accusation "unfounded and slanderous" and praised the committee for performing with "ability, fidelity and impartiality." David Brooks, a committee member from Dutchess, was enraged, crying out to the house, "Do me justice." In vain Bird and Comstock tried to point out that some parts of the story had indeed been kept back but debate grew so hot that the speaker adjourned the meeting. A few days later when the resolution to censure Keteltas was taken up, it passed by unanimous vote.[67]

65. *Journal of the Assembly of N.Y.*, 19th Sess., 67-71; *N.-Y. Journal*, Feb 16, 19, 1796.

66. N.Y. *Argus*, Feb. 22, 1796, and *N.-Y. Journal*, Feb. 23, 1796.

67. *Journal of the Assembly of N.Y.*, 19th Sess., 102; see also "A Communication," *N.-Y. Journal*, Mar. 1, 1796, describing the debate.

On the day of this vote, news reached the city from Pennsylvania that Timothy Crady was probably dead. He had not been well when he was flogged and sympathizers drew the obvious conclusion. "Being an innocent man," one wrote, "and in ill health, when loaded with infamy, disgrace, and wounds, stript of his good name in a strange land . . . the burden became insupportable and he sunk into his grave."[68] By this time, however, Keteltas, rather than Burk or Crady, was the principal figure in the case. The question had shifted from justice for two humble ferrymen to the constitutional right of a citizen to criticize the legislature.

Keteltas responded to the assembly's censure with another stinging article.[69] He had done nothing wrong; his allies were "the Constitution, the law, truth and conscious rectitude." Assemblyman Bird himself had said that testimony was suppressed; he was only repeating what Bird had said on the floor of the assembly; indeed, he was censured solely for "speaking the truth." The assembly resolution, not his article, was "unfounded and slanderous." He had taken the proper legal avenues to redress an injustice, appealing to the grand jury, the assembly, and most recently the Council of Appointment which had appointed Varick. Yet the mayor and the alderman remained unpunished.

To Federalists this was the last straw. Thomas Morris moved to summon Keteltas before the bar of the house for "a breach of the privileges" of the assembly. Both of the lawyer's articles, Morris' resolution declared, were "highly injurious to the honor and dignity" of the assembly and were "calculated to create distrust and destroy that confidence" which the people have in their representatives. Some Federalists also wanted to bring in editor Greenleaf. Supporting Morris were Brooks of Dutchess and James Watson of New York City, a wealthy merchant, who considered Keteltas "crackbrained or crazy."[70]

With the constitutional question clearer, the opposition in the assembly rallied. "Shall we attempt to prevent citizens from thinking?" Bird asked, "from giving their opinion on acts of the legislature? Shall we stop freedom of the press?" All Keteltas had done, said Comstock, was to recite events. The legislature "could not prevent the citizens from hearing, thinking [or] expressing their opinions." This time the Federalist victory was by a narrow vote, thirty-three to

68. "A Citizen of New York," *N.-Y. Journal*, Jan. 4, 1797.
69. N.Y. *Argus*, Mar. 5; *N.-Y. Journal*, Mar. 8, 1796.
70. *Journal of the Assembly of N.Y.*, 19th Sess., 120; *N.-Y. Journal*, Mar. 11, 1796.

twenty-seven; Keteltas was called to appear before the assembly the next day.[71]

Immediately Republican leaders went to work. The next morning when Keteltas appeared, he brought with him the largest crowd of New Yorkers ever to attend a meeting of the assembly—perhaps two thousand people. "The house was so crowded with citizens," according to Greenleaf's account, that it was impossible to get in. The stairways, the aisles, the back of the chamber, all were jammed. Among the crowd were several leaders of the Democratic Society and at least one of the Livingstons, probably Brockholst, who was very busy arguing with several assemblymen before the proceedings started.[72]

Keteltas was sworn in at once. He was then asked if he had written the two articles that appeared in the *Argus* and *Journal* and caused them to be published. He replied, "Yes." Without debate the assembly then found him guilty of "a misdemeanor and contempt of the authority of this House" but offered to discharge him if he would ask the pardon of the House. To this the young lawyer's reply was simple: "I am not conscious of having committed any offense and therefore I *will not* ask the pardon of this House."[73]

"At this moment," according to Greenleaf's correspondent, "three cheers and clapping of hands *comme un éclair* [in a flash] burst forth from the spectators at the bar which was [so] crowded that the jolting of the one moved the whole body like the wave of the sea . . . the huzza ran through the ranks like wildfire." The cheering "created the greatest confusion," Stephen Van Rensselaer wrote.[74]

Frantically William North, the speaker, banged the gavel while the sergeant-at-arms scurried to and fro to quiet the crowd. When order was finally restored, Abraham Ten Broeck moved that Keteltas be jailed "until the further order of the House." There was no debate, the resolution passed, and North handed the clerk a warrant for Keteltas' arrest.[75] Before Keteltas could be served, however, the crowd

71. *N.-Y. Journal*, Mar. 11, 1796.

72. *Ibid.*, Mar. 8, 1796. A Federalist assemblyman said the crowd was 2000; see John Addison to Peter Van Gaasbeck, Mar. 10, 1796, Van Gaasbeck Papers, Kingston Senate House; "A Citizen," N.Y. *Herald*, Mar. 19, 1796.

73. *Journal of the Assembly of N.Y.*, 19th Sess., 122-23. According to the newspaper report, Keteltas emphasized "will not."

74. Stephen Van Rensselaer to ?, Mar. 11, 1796, Van Rensselaer MSS, N.Y. State Lib. See also John Addison to Peter Van Gaasbeck, Mar. 10, 1796, Van Gaasbeck Papers, Kingston Senate House.

75. *Journal of the Assembly of N.Y.*, 19th Sess., 123.

lifted him into a "handsome arm chair" which eight men carried out of the chamber into the streets and off to the jail. The crowd streamed after them with loud cries of "The Spirit of 1776." At the jail Keteltas stood on a chair and addressed the throng: "Fellow citizens, the legislature have resolved that I shall be carried to gaol—It is my desire to comply because I wish ever to comply with the laws of my country. The Constitution has provided me with redress; and I wish to wait the time when that redress will be afforded me."[76]

With that he entered the jail and the crowd returned to the assembly in the hope of escorting Keteltas' defenders Bird and Comstock to their homes. When they declined, the crowd dispersed. About this time Governor Jay appeared on the scene, ready to do battle with the mob, his sword at his side. He was somewhat tardy, Greenleaf jibed, because he had to change into "regimentals" appropriate for the occasion.[77] Meanwhile, the assembly, before it adjourned, appointed a committee to investigate the instigators of the "indecent huzzahing," ordering a hearing for the following day.[78]

The next morning the committee brought two men before the assembly, Azarias Williams, Secretary of the Democratic Society, and Thomas Gilbert, a member. Gilbert, who was called first, showed he was not of the same mettle as Keteltas. Pleading guilty to the charge of insulting the house, he offered an apology "with tears in his eyes." He did not consider his action an insult, he explained; he had acted on an impulse.

Williams came next, advised by two attorneys: Brockholst Livingston and Robert Troup, Alexander Hamilton's political co-worker. Williams was accused of instigating the demonstration as well as joining it. The second charge he admitted, the first he denied. To back its accusation, the prosecutors then introduced two informers present in the crowd the day before who testified that Williams was a leader of the affair. The house voted Williams guilty on both counts and called him up again. Again the Democrat stood his ground.

"I can only say as I have before declared that I did not intend to insult the dignity of this house and that I am sorry for what I did."

Federalists were still not satisfied.

"I have nothing further to say," said Williams.

The warrant for his arrest was then handed him, and Williams

76. *N.-Y. Journal*, Mar. 8, 1796.
77. *Ibid.*
78. *Journal of the Assembly of N.Y.*, 10th Sess., 124.

brought before the bar of the house again. This time he broke, asked the pardon of the House, and was discharged.

Somewhat sheepishly a few days later Williams explained his actions to his Republican public; he had important business out of town; his friends persuaded him to make the final plea; he hoped that everyone understood he had not deserted Keteltas. While some Republicans doubtless were disappointed, others anointed both Gilbert and Williams as "true republicans" for "confessing their error and yielding obedience" to the elected representatives of their country.[79]

IV

Keteltas was jailed for "a breach of the privileges" of the house. In keeping with the precedent established by the British Parliament and zealously followed by the assembly of the Colony of New York, the legislature could summon a citizen, act as accuser, prosecutor and judge, and imprison him for the life of its session. Indeed, in the late colonial era in New York, the failure of common law prosecutions against political critics, as in the Zenger case, "made the courts a mere formal threat against unfettered discussion," as the most recent authority has made clear. "The actively suppressive power was exercised by an unlimited discretion in the legislature to move against supposed breaches of parliamentary privileges."[80] The handling of Keteltas showed that the assembly had not abandoned any of the prerogatives it had asserted as late as 1769-71 in the famous case of Alexander McDougall. The leader of the city's Sons of Liberty, who had criticized the assembly for betraying the province by voting to supply provisions for the King's troops, was first charged by the assembly with seditious libel, then indicted by a grand jury, and after his trial was indefinitely postponed he was recommitted by the assembly for a breach of privilege. Then the Livingstons, George Clinton, a fledgling Ulster assemblyman, and John Lamb, a fellow Liberty Boy—Republicans of the nineties—were his defenders.[81]

Keteltas, Federalists should have known, was not the kind of man whose ardor could be cooled by dank prison walls. He continued his defense from prison, although with a spirit of legalism that set him

79. *N.-Y. Journal*, Mar. 15, 1796, including a letter by Williams; Van Rensselaer to ?, Mar. 11, 1796, Van Rensselaer MSS, N.Y. State Lib.; James Oliver to Van Gaasbeck, Mar. 10 [?], 1796, Van Gaasbeck Papers, Kingston Senate House.

80. Levy, *Legacy of Suppression*, 48 and 15-17, 20-21, 23-24; Mary P. Clarke, *Parliamentary Privilege in the American Colonies* (New Haven, 1943), 125-31.

81. Levy, *Legacy of Suppression*, 78-85; Dillon, *The New York Triumvirate*, ch. 6.

apart from McDougall. He released news confirming the rumor of Crady's death which he had received from Burk who had recently returned to Brooklyn. In keeping with his respect for the law, Keteltas informed the jailer of Burk's whereabouts, only to be told that "he should not trouble himself about the said Burk except he came in his way." Dutifully Keteltas called the attention of the court to the jailer's violation of the law.[82] In a few weeks he was ready with his own defense, a series of five articles that ran for a week in Greenleaf's papers.

Keteltas' defense followed along the lines of a cautious libertarianism laid down a few weeks earlier by "Camillus Junius," a lawyer, who likely as not was Brockholst Livingston.[83] In a cogent, learned article "Camillus Junius" developed the thesis that "the house of assembly have not any privileges which can be infringed by those, or similar publications" of Keteltas. Examining the Constitution and statutes of the state, he insisted that the assembly had the privilege of "freedom of speech in debate" and "from arrest during the session"—but "that there is none other than the two I have mentioned." "Will it be said," he asked, "that Mr. Keteltas' publications interrupted the proceedings of the house or disturbed its deliberations? Can it be said that the suppression of them was 'indispensably necessary for the performance of their constitutional duties?' " His answer was no; therefore, Keteltas' imprisonment was illegal.

For a moment "Camillus Junius" pushed into new philosophic territory. What, he asked, if an individual publishes "falsehoods which have an evident tendency to destroy that confidence which is reposed by the constituent in his representative?" Ought not the house possess a "right to punish the offence?" "I answer *no*." His reasoning was partly pragmatic: such action would "itself excite suspicion, and incite distrust." He emphasized the "consequences that must result, the danger to freedom" from "such extraordinary prerogatives" as the assembly claimed. If "we relate any circumstances which passed in the house" or call a law "a bad one," there was the risk of a breach of privilege. Granting that punishment was unlikely when there were annual elections, the writer pointed to what the United States Senate might do if such a principle were recognized. Suppose "I was to declare" that some of the senators who voted for Jay's Treaty were "incompetent to decide thereon." "Admit this to be false," still it

82. *N.-Y. Journal*, Apr. 1, 1796.
83. "Camillus Junius," N.Y. *Argus*, Mar. 15, 1796.

would "create distrust" and would be "a contempt" and a "breach of the privileges of the Senate."

> I should be brought to their bar (perhaps in the city of Washington, where exclusive jurisdiction prevails)—It would be demanded of me, "Were you the author of such language?"—If I denied it, it would be proved against me, and increase my guilt—If I confessed, I would (as if by magic) be *already convicted*, and even the solitary comfort of explaining my motives, would be refused.—Sure a doctrine so monstrous so pregnant with oppression, can never be received in a new country.

Such were "the dangerous extravagencies" to which the principle adopted by the New York assembly pointed.

After this bold sally, however, "Camillus Junius" retreated, unwilling to discard the concept that "contempt and insult" to the house should "pass unpunished." "A libel tending to asperse or vilify the house of Assembly or any of its members may be as severely punished in the Supreme Court as a libel against government." The remedy thus was the *court*, not the legislature. Otherwise, one of the "first principles of natural justice" would be violated—"which forbids us to be judges when we are party to the cause." For his final argument the lawyer fell back still further. Assuming that the assembly had the power to punish Keteltas, the "manner" in which they acted was "unreasonable" because they did not inquire into the "motive or intention of the publications." If the articles were "written with a pure intention," as "Camillus Junius" claimed, no crime had been committed.

In a second piece addressed to the assembly after it had jailed Keteltas, "Camillus Junius" combined his several themes. "Liberty of the press" was at stake. "I am no friend to the doctrine of libels, but it is a perfect guardian of the press compared with our late decision." Trial by jury and separation of powers were also at stake—"the manifest injustice of first making yourselves party to a cause, and then constituting yourselves judges." And thirdly, by keeping Keteltas in jail, "you have falsified one maxim of law, 'that there is no wrong without a remedy.'" There was "no relief by ordinary means" inasmuch as a judge could not grant habeas corpus for the length of the session. Appealing to the assembly to display "humanity" and not a "vindictive temper," he asked for Keteltas' "immediate discharge."[84]

84. *Ibid.*, Apr. 6, 1796.

Keteltas' own defense clung to "Camillus Junius's" narrowest theme. He began on a lofty note of defiance: he was "within the iron grate for an honest, but successful attempt to support inviolate the law in defence of injured innocence"; he could not ask the pardon of the house, "without being guilty of treason to my God, my Country, and my conscience." In his argument, however, he did no more than review in a pedestrian fashion the history of legislative privileges in the British House of Commons, the colonial assemblies, and under the constitution of New York, all for the purpose of showing that the privileges of the assembly were limited to freedom of debate and from arrest and that he had violated neither. Coke and Blackstone were his authorities. His publications had done no more, Keteltas insisted, than to "echo Mr. Bird's express words"; if they were false, the house might well call the assemblyman to the bar. If he had breached the privileges of the house, he asked, "should I not have been prosecuted in the courts?" "Should I not have been permitted to have made a defence." He ended with the legalistic hope that "at some future day" a court would find the action against him unconstitutional, tyrannical and illegal."[85]

Before adjourning, a little over a month after they had jailed Keteltas, the assembly passed a bill drastically amending the criminal code to abolish capital punishment for all but two crimes and to eliminate whipping altogether. Advocated for several years by Republican, Quaker, and conservative humanitarian reformers and pushed by Governor Clinton, the measure may well have received the impetus necessary for its final passage from the reaction to the ferrymen affair. Whatever the assemblymen may have thought of Keteltas, the affair of Burk and Crady and the cheering mob seem to have had an effect on them.[86]

After the legislature adjourned, Keteltas' friends obtained the release of the unrepentant heretic on a writ of habeas corpus. When he stepped out of the jail, a crowd placed the Republican martyr in a phaeton which they drew through the streets to the accompaniment of beating drums. The carriage was decked with an American and French flag, a cap of liberty, and a picture of a man being whipped, bearing the inscription, "What you rascal, insult your superiors." When they reached his home, Keteltas made a short speech of appreciation and

85. "The Defence" by William Keteltas, Nos. 1-5, N.Y. *Argus*, Apr. 4, 5, 7, 8, 12, 1796.
86. See below, ch. 24, sec. II.

struck the same note of legalism he had used a month before on entering prison: "Your decorum, combined with all your insignias evidence to us your attachment to the constitution and laws of your country—they are the best supporters of liberty, and I am sure you revere them." After three cheers, the crowd dispersed.[87]

When Keteltas got out of prison, the Republicans were in the midst of their last-ditch battle against Jay's Treaty which had melted into the spring election campaign. The New York City Federalists had already nominated a ticket which included four assemblymen who had voted to jail Keteltas and for senator, James Watson, who had taken a leading part in the episode. Three days after Keteltas was released, the Republican leaders nominated him for the assembly. He was chosen along with eleven others at a meeting presided over by Henry Rutgers, president of the Democratic Society.[88]

In the hectic campaign, Keteltas shared the limelight with Jay's Treaty. A readable article couched as "A Dialogue between an Old Tory and a Young Republican" typified the Republican appeal to class and patriotism. The "Old Tory," rich and well dressed, observed that Keteltas' supporters were "ragamuffins." The irate "Young Republican" slapped back, arguing that these were "the men whose mechanical labours, the necessaries and conveniences of life are produced in abundance." It was "such men as these [who] were the triumphant victors at Breed's Hill, at Saratoga, at Yorktown"; they were entitled to "respect" and not ridicule. Men had to be judged by "merit" and not "money."[89]

Although Federalists carried the city for their entire assembly slate of twelve candidates, they won by only 2250 votes to 1775 for the Republicans. More voters turned out than ever before and the total Republican vote was about 500 more than the year before, an increase of nearly one-third. Keteltas who had never run for any office before, came in ninth on the ticket, a hundred or so votes behind the leading Republican vote getter.[90]

Federalists were shocked. "You will easily perceive," Hamilton wrote King, "how much the ferrymen case embarassed and jeopard[iz]ed" the Federalist cause.[91] Another Federalist analyzed the class antagonism which the returns revealed. Of the 2250 votes his party

87. N.-Y. Journal, Apr. 15, Apr. 19, 22, 1796.
88. Ibid., Apr. 19, 1796.
89. Ibid., Apr. 22, 1796.
90. Ibid., June 3, 4, 7, 1796.
91. Hamilton to King, May 4, 1796, Lodge, ed., Works of Hamilton, VIII, 395-96.

received, 1140 were from voters in the £100 freeholder group; thus half the Federalist voters were men of property. Of the 1750 Republican votes, on the other hand, only 575 were from the £100 group while 1200 were 40-shilling renters. Thus, less than one-third of the Republican voters were men of substantial property and two-thirds had "no real property."[92] Republicans ran very strong in the poor wards. In fact in view of the tide which had set against them because of their intransigence over Jay's Treaty, Republicans owed their large vote to the raw social issues raised by the ferrymen-Keteltas affair.

Four months later Federalists again felt the impact of the affair in the September elections for the Common Council, even though the suffrage requirement of £20 or more excluded the poorest assembly voters, the 40-shilling renters.[93] In the election the year before voters had been indifferent; in 1796 they were aroused. "A Change of Men is Recommended," Greenleaf captioned his appeal. Wealth should not be the standard because "riches are not always accompanied by that wisdom and integrity which are requisite in good magistrates." Republicans raised the issues of reforming the Bridewell court, cleaning the streets and piers, decreasing taxes, and curbing the practice of forestalling in the market, for which the blame belonged on the rich and not the "small grocer."[94] The result was the election of two Republicans, Ezekiel Robins, a well-to-do hatter despised by Mayor Varick, and Jacob de la Montagnie, a leader of the Democratic Society. The Federalists challenged the latter's election, but when a second was held, he was returned by a larger majority. Times indeed had changed in city politics.[95]

Keteltas doggedly kept with his case. Late in 1796 a damage suit he had filed against Varick and the magistrates on behalf of Burk was scheduled to come up before the state supreme court. Keteltas employed as his co-counsel Alexander Hamilton, who it may be surmised either had drawn a political lesson from the elections gone by or was interested in promoting an out-of-court settlement to wind up the case. Keteltas was asked by a person he would not name to withdraw the suit; he refused, unwilling to be party to a "compromise" when justice was involved. But Burk was interested in financial compensa-

92. An anonymous article, N.Y. *Herald*, June 15, 1796.
93. Pomerantz, *New York an American City*, 65-69.
94. See in N.Y. *Argus*: "C.D.," July 7, "An Inhabitant of Broad Street," July 21, "An Elector," Sept. 20, "A Citizen," Sept. 22, "A Freeholder," Sept. 22, and an editorial paragraph, Sept. 29, 1796.
95. Pomerantz, *New York An American City*, 120-21.

tion and a day before the trial was to take place Varick and others
agreed to pay him $500 to withdraw the suit, a handsome sum for a
ferryman. Hamilton and Samuel Jones apparently arranged the settlement. Burk left the state, and Keteltas heralded the outcome as a
vindication of his cause.[96]

Keteltas' next step, early in 1797, was a suit against the speaker
of the assembly, William North, for having arrested him by improper
procedures. North informed the assembly of the action, confident
that the courts would not "abet an attempt to intrench on the privileges of the representatives of the people." The assembly concurred by
a vote of eighty-eight to one, directing the state's attorney-general to
defend the speaker. Adam Comstock, the Saratoga Republican, was
the sole dissenter.[97]

Keteltas' case did not come before the circuit court until December
1797, when it was tried without a jury before John Sloss Hobart, a
firm Federalist. North's chief counsel was Hamilton, now in a more
natural political posture, while Keteltas was his own advocate. For
some reason, however, he did not advance the constitutional argument about the limits of the privileges of the assembly which he had
argued while in prison, and instead based his case on the claim that
he was arrested on a "spurious warrant." Keteltas contended that the
warrant used for arrest at his hearing on March 8, 1796, had been
issued March 6 on the basis of the resolution calling him before the bar
of the assembly. The warrant was improper, according to Keteltas,
because it was issued only by the speaker on his own authority. In
North's defense Hamilton called the sergeant-at-arms who testified
that North had handed a warrant to the clerk who had handed it to
him; he then called the jailer who testified he in turn had received the
warrant along with Keteltas. Keteltas in his defense offered to read
the house journal for the day of his arrest and to introduce witnesses
to prove there was nothing in the assembly's proceedings authorizing
the issuance of a warrant. Hamilton objected; Hobart sustained him,
the journal was not introduced, and Hobart dismissed Keteltas' suit. If
the opinion was confirmed, "A Spectator" observed, in concluding the
only account of the case available, "the freedom of the press is taken

96. "A Citizen of New York," *N.-Y. Journal*, Jan. 4, 1797, and William Keteltas,
ibid., Feb. 8, 1797. This example of Hamilton's political astuteness has escaped
his biographers.

97. *Journal of the Assembly of N.Y.*, 20th Sess., 59, 63, 69.

away and personal liberty is no longer secure in the state of New York." Keteltas talked of an appeal but did not follow it up.[98]

After initiating the suit against North, Keteltas renewed his plea to the Council of Appointment to remove Mayor Varick from office. There were more grounds than ever, he wrote, to oust this "tyrant." Emboldened by his victory in the ferrymen case, Varick, according to Keteltas, had revoked the licenses of men who signed the petition to the legislature asking that he be impeached and refused licenses to others. He had also threatened a lawyer in his court, had refused arbitrarily to allow men to become freemen, and had gone so far as to imprison a poor German woman in the dead of winter without fuel.[99] With John Jay governor and the council in safe Federalist hands, however, Keteltas' appeal again fell on deaf ears. Even so Varick was alarmed. He suggested to John Jay that the city magistrates be released from holding police court—the court over which he presided in the ferrymen case. "I think our city government is enervating fast," he lamented to James Kent, "and I fear it will be ruined in time and abandoned to unprincipled men and to mobs."[100]

After 1796 interest in the ferrymen case naturally subsided; Republicans did not renominate Keteltas for the assembly in 1797. However, they were quick to learn the lesson of 1796: the tactic of seizing upon a popular, explosive issue close to the hearts of the laboring population. Early in 1797 Federalists presented the Republicans with another such golden opportunity. In February the Federalist-controlled assembly passed a law requiring the manufacturers of soap and candles to move their factories to the outskirts of the city. The ostensible reason was that the "noxious vapors" from their boiling vats were the cause of yellow fever. The assembly acted quickly, without giving the chandlers an opportunity to present their views. Immediately, as less astute politicians might have anticipated, there was a "great outcry" from the Association of Tallow Chandlers and Soap Manufacturers, which dispatched a petition signed by seventy-five mem-

98. "A Spectator," *Time Piece*, Dec. 22, 1797, reprinted in *N.-Y. Journal*, Jan. 14, 1798. See also "Richard Varick," N.Y. *American Citizen*, Sept. 3, 1801. *Journal of the Assembly of N.Y.*, 19th Sess., 123, reports a resolution prior to North's handing the clerk the warrant.

99. "A Citizen of New York," *N.-Y. Journal*, Jan. 4, 1797; William Keteltas, *ibid.*, Feb. 8, 1797.

100. Richard Varick to John Jay, Jan. 10, 1797, John Jay Papers, abstracts, Columbia Univ.; Varick to James Kent, Feb. 24, 1797, cited in Pomerantz, *New York An American City*, 122.

bers. The law, they wrote, was "peculiarly hard, their expulsion [from the] city rigorous in the extreme, utterly ruinous to the [greater] part of them and needlessly severe." The chandlers warned others of the dangers: the action was discriminatory; it violated the rights of property; it would also mean a loss of work to ashmen who could not afford to cart the ashes needed in making soap so far from the city. The starch makers, fearful that they would be next, sent off their own petition to the assembly.[101]

Republican leaders at once entered this new battle on the side of the chandlers. Brockholst Livingston was counsel for their association and at their request Samuel L. Mitchill, the Columbia scientist, prepared a lengthy treatise which the Association brought out as a pamphlet exonerating the chandlers' "pestilential vapors" and placing the blame for the fever exclusively on "septic acid vapor."[102] Mitchill sent a copy to Robert R. Livingston, proud that he had written it "in as familiar and popular stile as I could." The patrician Chancellor, who had fearfully vetoed a charter for the General Society of Mechanics in 1785, praised Mitchill and the aggressive chandlers—"those respectable and useful citizens."[103]

The chandler issue boiled through March. In April 1797 Republicans placed Mitchill on their assembly ticket, together with the two aldermen elected in the wake of the ferrymen affair, Aaron Burr, a tanner, a hatter, and a sailmaker. In further pursuit of the mechanic vote, Republicans made much of the low state of American manufactures in the face of British imports, a situation they related to Jay's Treaty. Republican prospects were so bright that Federalists ran only half a ticket, endorsing six Republicans, an unheard-of event.[104] For the first time in the decade Republicans swept the field, deluging the Federalists. The vote for Republican candidates ranged from 1600 to 2100 votes while the Federalists received a scant 600 to 700, a catastrophic drop from the year before. Republicans ran exceptionally well in the poorer wards.[105]

The ferrymen-Keteltas campaign did not, as "Brother Jonathan"

101. The original petition is in Assembly Papers, Box 5, No. 113, N.Y. State Lib., in charred condition; N.-Y. Journal, Feb. 18, Feb. 23, Mar. 8, Mar. 11, 1797.
102. Samuel L. Mitchill, The Case of the Manufacturers of Soap and Candles in the City of New York Stated and Examined (N.Y., 1797).
103. Samuel L. Mitchill to Robert R. Livingston, June 9, 1797, Misc. MSS, N.Y. Hist. Soc.; Livingston to Mitchill, July 18, 1797, Livingston MSS, N.Y. State Lib.
104. An editorial, N.-Y. Journal, Mar. 8, 1797, and "Scrutator," ibid., Apr. 15, 1797; for other election articles, ibid., Apr. 26, 1797; Time Piece, Apr. 24, 28, 1797.
105. N.-Y. Journal, June 4, 1797.

claimed in 1800, settle the question of "whether the rich and the poor were to be regarded alike . . . at the bar of Justice." But he hardly exaggerated in claiming that the episode led "mechanics and yeomen" to desert the Federalists and "has not a little contributed to their downfall in this state."[106]

106. "Brother Jonathan," N.Y. *American Citizen*, Apr. 21, 1800.

CHAPTER 23

Pioneer vs. Proprietor:

Frontier Federalism Divides

1796-1797

As the Democratic-Republican movement crystallized in the east, sinking roots among the poor and "middling classes" of New York City, Federalists reached the apogee of their strength on New York's western frontier. In 1794 the west elected the aristocratic-landlord Federalist, Stephen Van Rensselaer, to the state senate and sent the "Bashaw of Otsego," William Cooper, to Congress. In 1795 it provided John Jay with his margin of victory as governor. In 1796 it was all but unanimous behind Cooper, as an energetic advocate of Jay's Treaty.

Yet even as Federalism climbed to a peak, it began to corrode, with Republicanism emerging as a current within the Federalist party. Beginning in the spring elections for the state legislature in 1796, the wealthy western land proprietors and Albany landlords who dominated the party were challenged. In the winter of 1796 Judge Cooper was defeated in his bid to return to Congress. By the spring of 1797 there were two rival Federalist senate slates for the district. In this process there appeared from within the Federalist fold a leader who has been characterized as the personification of frontier Jeffersonianism, Jedediah Peck of Otsego County.

The Federalists of western New York were victims of their own success. Federalism developed in the district on three pillars: dependence on land proprietors who enjoyed a social cohesion natural to the first phase of frontier development; dependence of the area on the national government for protection; and the fortuitous factor that an anti-Federalist, George Clinton, was in power in the state government. The first factor united pioneers behind proprietors like William Cooper; the second united them behind President Washington, Secretary of War Knox, and diplomat John Jay, while the third threw them into the arms of Philip Schuyler and Stephen Van Rensselaer, eastern-landlord Federalists who exploited the district's grievances against Clinton.[1]

Beginning about 1796, the props were loosened around the base of each of these three pillars. Internally, rapid social-economic change brought the latent conflict between pioneer and proprietor to the surface. Nationally, the success of Federalists in restoring the British-held forts removed the external threat, lessening the ties of dependence to the federal government. In state affairs, the election of John Jay as governor eliminated Clinton as a whipping boy. The result was a two-way split within the party: of western Federalists against the eastern Federalists of the "Albany junto," and of pioneer farmer Federalists against land proprietor Federalists within the district.

I

Changes within the west in the middle 1790's set the stage for this new political conflict.[2] Migration increased. The magnet again was land on generous terms, especially from the European land companies now commencing operations. New roads and improved waterways eased the way into the interior while American military victories in the Northwest lessened the fear of Indians. General Anthony Wayne's famous victory at Fallen Timbers occurred in August 1794. The following winter, 20,000 migrants poured through Albany on their way west. The electoral census of 1795 found some 14,500 men in the district eligible to vote, which meant a total population of close to 80,000.[3]

Like the earlier migrants, the new settlers came mostly from New

1. See above, ch. 12.

2. Hockett, *Western Influences on Political Parties*, 62-65, attributes Federalism on the New York frontier solely to the New England background of the migrants and assigns their transformation to Republicanism to the "solvents of the frontier."

3. *Albany Gazette*, Mar. 6, 9, 1795; for the electoral census, N.Y. *Daily Advertiser*, Jan. 27, 1796; see Appendix, Table 3.

England. There were more than before, however, from New Jersey, Pennsylvania, and Delaware, and a bigger sprinkling of foreign born: Hamburg Germans and poor Scots in the Genesee country, refugees from the French Revolution in the Black River country, Irishmen in Tioga County, Dutch in Oneida—almost all brought by the European land companies.[4]

In the middle 1790's the agents representing these companies were the most significant new factor on the New York frontier. In 1793 Charles Williamson began in earnest his "hot house" development of the Genesee area for the Pulteney Associates of England. A little later, Joseph Ellicott, Theophile Cazenove, and John Lincklaen took the first steps to promote the Holland Company's vast holdings east and west of the Pulteney land. Shortly, they were joined by the agents of the Chassanis Company of Paris on land north of the Mohawk River and east of Lake Ontario.[5] Town names bear testimony to the work of the land agents: Pulteney and Bath, named after the owners Williamson represented and their English country seat; Williamsburgh, named for himself; Cazenovia, named after the Holland Company's agent.

The new settlers made their way into all parts of the west. They filled in the accessible Mohawk Valley and thickened settlement immediately south in Otsego County. For the first time, they coursed over the military bounty land in the southern tier and settled in great numbers in the rich Genesee country to the west. Sections within the vast interior were now at markedly different levels of development, with pioneers opening new areas engaged in subsistence agriculture, in contrast to settlers on the land five to ten years who were ready to enter the commercial phase of farming, eager to market crops for a profit.[6]

The Mohawk Valley, the oldest section of the frontier, with the best water and land transportation to eastern markets, now took on an

4. Cowan, *Charles Williamson*, 77-78; T. Wood Clarke, *Émigrés in the Wilderness* (N.Y., 1941), 29-50.

5. See Royal L. Garff, Social-Economic Conditions in the Genesee Country, 1787-1812 (unpubl. Ph.D. diss., Northwestern Univ., 1939); Paul D. Evans, *The Holland Land Company* (Buffalo, 1924); Alta M. Ralph, "The Chassanis or Castorland Settlement," N.Y. State Hist. Assoc., *Quarterly Journal*, 10 (1929), 333-45; Neil A. McNall, *An Agricultural History of the Genesee Valley, 1790-1860* (Phila., 1952), ch. 2. See 1796 state map.

6. For travelers' descriptions of the New York frontier at this time, see Huth and Pugh, trans. and ed., *Talleyrand in America*, III, 86-90, and especially La Rochefoucauld-Liancourt, *Travels*, I, 99-174, 343-88, on whom I rely for many of the points below.

air of prosperity. Oneida, the westernmost county in the valley, was becoming "the third county in the state for population and wealth," an area of "rich and flourishing farmers," with booming towns at Whitestown, Utica, Paris, and Rome.[7] Otsego County was similar, although its prosperity was inhibited by the absence of good roads to Albany. The county now had a population upwards of 20,000, thanks to Judge Cooper's promotional efforts. Cooperstown, the county seat, could boast of a church, a library of twelve hundred volumes, a newspaper, a Masonic lodge, and even water pipes in the village houses. As far as the new editor was concerned, however, it was still "about 75 per cent below proof—no life—no society—no telegraph."[8]

By contrast, south-central New York, embracing Tioga and Onondaga counties, was relatively backward, unfavored by land promoters or natural transportation. Onondaga, the site of the military tract, was further retarded by a welter of conflicting land claims.[9] Tioga, even at the end of the decade, was "on the whole a poor county and very thinly settled." Newton, its principal town, was "inelegant and lifeless." In both counties, by Federalist standards, the "lower class of people" were "more rude and immoral," their court sessions more disorderly than those held by "substantial farmers" elsewhere.[10] Western Ulster and southern Otsego, later united into Delaware County, was a similar area, "hard featured and forbidding," "the roughest and most mountainous" in the state, populated mostly by "raftsmen, squatters, insolvent emigrants and demagogues," who, conservatives believed, were "so easily wrought upon by every designing fellow."[11]

The Genesee country, the westernmost area then being settled, enjoyed the most spectacular growth because of the Pulteney Company's lavish investments. In order to leap over the initial frontier phase Charles Williamson sowed a fistful of wilderness towns, erected sawmills and gristmills, cut roads and cleared waterways, built docks, taverns, stores and several schools, set up two printers, and built a

7. Kent, Travel Journal, 1798, Kent Papers, Lib. Cong., an excellent contemporary account.
8. "Extract from a Letter from Cooperstown," N.Y. *American Minerva*, May 17, 1794; Cooper, *Chronicles of Cooperstown*, 32-58; Elihu Phinney to William Cooper, Nov. 4, 1796, in Cooper, *Legends and Traditions*, 162.
9. Jeanette B. Sherwood, "The Military Tract," N.Y. State Hist. Assoc., *Qtly. Jour.*, 7 (1926), 169-80.
10. Kent, Travel Journal, 1798, Kent Papers, Lib. Cong.
11. *Ibid.*, July 4, 1799 and Journal for 1801, 74; Ebenezer Foote to Peter Van Gaasbeck, Oct. 12, 1796, Van Gaasbeck Papers, F.D.R. Lib.; John Addison to Van Gaasbeck, Feb. 4, 1796, Van Gaasbeck Papers, Kingston Senate House.

hotel that was luxurious even by eastern standards, and a track whose annual races advertised the area's attractions.[12] He also granted generous mortgages. By 1796, Williamson could boast of 15,000 settlers and "an appearance of respectability" unprecedented for so early a stage of the frontier. While Cooper to the east started with only poor pioneers, Williamson had "a most respectable yeomanry," as well as a sprinkling of "gentlemen."[13]

Compared to 1792, the signs of progress on the New York frontier were many. Half a dozen newspapers appeared, several supported by Williamson and Cooper, one by a New York City printer, and others by village businessmen.[14] Here and there churches were built, and missionaries appeared, a sure sign that the area was safe for civilized easterners. A few schools were also organized.

This impressive growth had important social consequences. Class differences, obscured when there was little wealth to display, became more apparent. A country gentry emerged.[15] As land proprietors, land agents, and village merchants prospered, they abandoned their log cabins to build "genteel frame houses," importing fancy furniture from the east over newly hewn roads. A few built mansions and acquired slaves. The boom towns were complete with thriving merchants and artisans and within a few years were "overstocked with lawyers . . . young men of promising talents and great activity."[16] In the countryside the middle class of yeomen prospered.

Some of the new gentry adapted to pioneer ways, as had William Cooper. Charles Williamson, the most important new figure in the "western theatre," was transformed from an English squire into a frontier democrat. Pioneers recalled that Williamson "was at home in every log cabin, a welcome cheerful and contented guest." La Rochefoucauld-Liancourt, who had an eye for such things, was impressed that "his way of living is simple neat and good. . . . We met with no circumstances of pomp or luxury, but found good ease, humor and

12. Cowan, *Charles Williamson*, *passim*.

13. Williamson, *Description of the Genesee Country*, especially 6-12.

14. See Frederick Follett, *History of the Press in Western New-York from the Beginning to the Middle of the Nineteenth Century* (Rochester, 1847, N.Y., 1920), 1-3 and *passim*. The papers were Cooperstown *Otsego Herald*, founded by William Cooper, 1795; *Bath Gazette* and Geneva *Ontario Gazette*, founded by Charles Williamson late in 1796; *Johnstown Gazette* founded in 1795; Whitestown *Western Centinel*, founded 1794.

15. See Williamson, *Description of the Genesee Country*, 10, 11, 19, 21; Frost, *Life in the Upper Susquehanna*, ch. 1; Neil A. McNall, "The Landed Gentry of the Genesee," *N.Y. History*, 26 (1945), 162-76.

16. Jonas to Zephaniah Platt, June 10, 1800, Platt Papers, N.Y. State Lib.

plenty." Williamson received all visitors, no matter how humble, "with the same attention, civility and good nature."[17]

Some of the new "gentry" did not adapt. One of Williamson's agents, for example, had "a certain loftiness . . . that is better adapted to a city merchant than the country land agent."[18] The Dutch and French agents, in particular, introduced an aristocratic tone to their neighborhoods. "Although we are in the woods," Adam Mappa's wife wrote, "we are yet constantly with the fashionable people of the country, and without being proud, it is well to maintain one's position." Francis Adrian Vanderkemp sent east for slaves for his wife.[19] Even Whitestown, settled by Yankees, had "an excellent genteel society," in Judge James Kent's eyes "the best in the state outside the cities."[20]

Such pretensions, mild as they were, were a contrast to the democratic ways of the yeomanry. Vanderkemp, a Dutch immigrant, painted a romantic picture of this type in an oration delivered at the founding of the Western Agricultural Society in 1795: a cheerful, courageous farmer, an energetic improver by day, a self-educated man who read Sidney, Locke, Montesquieu, or John Adams in the evening, instructed his children in religion and the laws of government and "cries out in ecstasy, I too am a Free American."[21] Other observers saw the seamier side. The frontier yeoman usually was a careless farmer indifferent to scientific farming—a fact Vanderkemp discovered when his Agricultural Society failed dismally. He often "begins by prodigous efforts," then with "his subsistence assured, he stops and falls into indolence." There was a "filthiness of his house and person" which Talleyrand found "beyond all description."[22] And so indifferent was he to learning that he was slow to seize even the meager opportunities offered by the state's new common school law.[23]

Such social and economic changes strengthened the dominance of Federalist landholders. The new land agents and proprietors almost

17. Turner, *History of Phelps and Gorham's Purchase*, 275; La Rochefoucauld-Liancourt, *Travels*, I, 138, 140; Cowan, *Charles Williamson*, 168-69.

18. An observation of Robert Troup about John Johnstone, cited in Cowan, *Charles Williamson*, 248.

19. Mrs. Adam Mappa to Adam Mappa's sister, July 1, 1795, in Helen L. Fairchild, ed., *Francis Adrian Van der Kemp, 1752-1829, An Autobiography* (N.Y., 1903), 151-52; Vanderkemp to Peter Van Gaasbeck, Aug. 1, 1796, Vanderkemp MSS, N.-Y. Hist. Soc.

20. Kent, Travel Journal, 1798, Kent Papers, Lib. Cong.

21. Vanderkemp, *Speech . . . June 1, 1795 . . . at Whitestown*, 7.

22. Huth and Pugh, trans. and ed., *Talleyrand in America*, a letter of Oct. 30, 1794, 90.

23. La Rochefoucauld-Liancourt, *Travels*, II, 447-49.

all gravitated to Federalism. The thriving towns were centers of Federalism whose influence radiated to the countryside, their newspapers dispensing doctrine reprinted from Federalist papers of New York and Philadelphia. Charles Williamson, in particular, added reserves to the Federalist armies. Williamson rapidly made common cause with New York and Albany merchants and lawyers; they sought him out for land or political support while he approached them for the aid they could render as lawyers and in the state legislature.[24] Locally the Britisher repeated Cooper's formula for political success. What support he did not win as a result of lavish investments and generous credit, he took by virtue of his tremendous power. He was "the lord of clan," James Kent reported. A committee which nominated him for public office was composed of the printer of the newspaper he established, the lawyer he retained, the keeper of the inn he built, and the local sheriff.[25] Like Cooper, Williamson was toasted with a combination of sycophancy and respect as the man who "has turned the howling wilderness into a fertile plain."[26]

Developments precisely such as this also helped to mature the seeds of conflict latent in the region. The foreign land companies excited apprehension for a number of reasons. Williamson by withholding choice tracts from sale "leaves the other settlers in want of good hay and pasturage and in too great humility and dependence."[27] The companies also exerted pressure on the state legislature for the unrestricted right of aliens to hold land in New York, a privilege hitherto granted to individuals only by special act.[28]

Popular suspicion of the companies was reflected in Vanderkemp's oration at Whitestown in 1795. Three years earlier he had heaped praise on "prudent" and "benevolent" land proprietors. He now spoke of a common fear that "we seem . . . to be injured by the rapacious avidity of European and American speculating land jobbers who consider our rich soil as an inexhaustible gold mine." He hoped that "they too *must, will and actually do* contribute considerably to our advancement and convenience. They too *shall be obliged* to advance

24. Cowan, *Charles Williamson*, 42-43.

25. Kent, Travel Journal, July 2, 1798, Kent Papers, Lib. Cong.; for nominating meetings see *Bath Gazette*, Mar. 9, 1797, Apr. 12, 1798; for Williamson's founding of papers, Turner, *History of Phelps and Gorham's Purchase*, 457-58.

26. *Bath Gazette*, Feb. 23, 1797; see also *ibid.*, July 7, 1797, July 1, 1798, for toasts on other occasions.

27. Kent, Travel Journal, July 2, 1798, Kent Papers, Lib. Cong.

28. See below, ch. 24, sec. V.

our gigantic progresses in order to reap the proposed advantages of their acquisitions,"[29] but obviously fear mingled with this hope.

The proprietors, both individuals and companies, also were the objects of discontent as the debtor-creditor relationship came to the fore. Most proprietors granted mortgages on generous terms. In the course of time while some farmers prospered and met their obligations, others failed to emerge from poverty, the result of the normal difficulties of pioneering and especially the lag in transportation. In 1793-94 there was enough mortgage indebtedness in Ontario County to lead the land jobbers attempting to form a separate state in western New York to promise debtors relief, but not enough to enlist much of a following.[30] In Otsego debts to William Cooper ripened about 1797, producing a severe crisis late in the year. On Pulteney land when the first interest payments fell due in 1797 Williamson would collect less than half the money owed the company.[31] As the initial capital-poor phase of the frontier faded, the promoter was less an investor and more a *rentier*. The debtor might now begin to see him less as a benefactor and more as a wealthy man enriched by the sweat of the debtor's brow.

Absentee owners also provoked antagonism for their policies toward squatters. In spite of the availability of land on easy credit, hundreds, and perhaps thousands, of migrants persisted in "making a pitch" either on privately owned land or the public domain, some in hope of securing title, others as "birds of passage," who expected to move on. Among landholders there was a discernible zeal in evicting "turbulent squatters" to induce settlement by "industrious" farmers. Squatters often resisted.[32] They also petitioned the legislature to confirm their titles. Speaking as men "scattered abroad in a howling wilderness" who had enriched the country by their labor, they often knew enough to contrast their lot with that of the Macombs who had been treated with such indulgence by the state.[33]

Such antipathies to companies, proprietors, and absentee owners

29. Vanderkemp, *Speech at Whitestown*, 8.

30. See above, ch. 17, sec. I.

31. Robert W. Silsby, "Mortgage Credit in the Phelps-Gorham Purchase," *N.Y. History*, 41 (1960), 8-9; for the general problem, McNall, *Agricultural History of the Genesee Valley*, ch. 3, especially 39-41.

32. Seth Johnson to Andrew Craigie, Aug. 27, 1797, Craigie Papers, III, No. 104, Amer. Antiq. Soc.; Brockholst Livingston to John Jacob Astor, Nov. 21, 1795 (copy), Astor MSS, N.Y. Pub. Lib.; Elkanah Watson to James Caldwell, May 24, 1798, Caldwell MSS, N.Y. State Lib. All these landholders wrote of trouble with squatters.

33. "Observer," *Albany Register*, Dec. 5, 1796; a random check turned up some dozen petitions each for 1796 and 1797 in Assembly Papers, Box 5, N.Y. State Lib.

were neither universal nor virulent in the mid-1790's, but they bubbled below the surface ready to flow into the political stream. Westerners were political; politics was "the universal topic in this country," La Rochefoucauld-Liancourt found after a trip through the New York frontier.[34] Westerners were avid for news; in distant Ontario when an eastern newspaper arrived it was "borrowed from one to the other to the distance perhaps of twenty miles."[35] And the democratic impulses of Yankee pioneers were kept alive as they came together to elect their own militia officers, direct their own churches, form Masonic lodges, deliberate in juries, and make the town nominations for political office.[36]

Among New York's pioneers, moreover, there was the same cluster of prejudices common to the breed on other frontiers. They were suspicious of lawyers. A man defending a lawyer as a candidate had to remind westerners that lawyers had been "defenders of their constitutional rights in the American Revolution."[37] They were hostile to "avaricious" innkeepers, who allegedly conspired to "extort from the poor and indigent" by their "extraordinary prices" and bad liquor, and to storekeepers who often made 100 per cent profit in their sales.[38] Above all they had an understandable sectional pride as men who had "tamed the howling wilderness," a phrase often on western lips. They were quick to react to any violation of their "rights," as was indicated by the violent response to the canvassers' decision of 1792 counting out the ballots of western counties.

The New England heritage common to most migrants heightened their cohesiveness. There was no love lost on the old Dutch or German settlers. The Dutch boys in Otsego, sons of the first settlers, one New Englander recalled, were "much inclined to flog the 'Yankee' as they called us," while Yankees spoke of their neighbors as "the churlish, ignorant, unenterprising Dutch."[39] In local elections New Englanders often stuck together behind one of their own kind. "Yankees love molasses," Philip Schuyler lamented to an associate after a nomination did not go his way, "that is they retain their national predelec-

34. La Rochefoucauld-Liancourt, *Travels*, I, 366.

35. "A Letter from Ontario" in *N.-Y. Journal*, Feb. 24, 1795.

36. See above, ch. 18, sec. IV.

37. "Dialogue between Farmer Overturn and Farmer Touchstone," Whitestown *Western Centinel*, Mar. 26, 1794.

38. "A Friend to the Public," *Catskill Packet*, Feb. 21, 1795; La Rochefoucauld-Liancourt, *Travels*, I, 162.

39. Beardsley, *Reminiscences*, 69; Kent, Journal, 1798, Kent Papers, Lib. Cong., 130; for background, Fox, *Yankees and Yorkers*, ch. 8.

tions notwithstanding immigration, change of circumstances and society."[40] The Yankee heritage fortified sectional antipathy to the
east.[41] Here then was an explosive potential in western politics.

II

Western sectionalism was apparent in the mid-1790's in the mounting pressure on the state government. Westerners wanted the same
things they had demanded before: more roads, new county divisions,
and more political power.

The demand for roads remained paramount. While frontiersmen
watched the progress of the western canal with mingled enthusiasm
and skepticism, they did not let up in their demand for traditional
overland transport. In 1793 and 1794 the legislature again obliged
with a road into the military bounty lands in the southern tier and
another to Old Fort Schuyler on the Mohawk, halfway to the Genesee
country.[42] Yet Otsego was still "one of these settlements buried in
the land," Talleyrand's phrase, and the Genesee country was still un-
satisfied. Cooper and Williamson continued to lobby for roads.[43]

The demand for political changes became more insistent with
growth. Not a session of the legislature passed without several petitions
requesting that new counties and towns be carved out of older political
jurisdictions.[44] Behind the demand lay the proprietor's desire for more
controllable government. Williamson in 1793 was barely able to quell
a near rebellion among his colony of Hamburg Germans;[45] Cooper
wanted to rid himself of the potentially dangerous Delaware section of
Otsego. By 1795 two more new counties were created, Onondaga and
Schoharie, followed by Steuben to accommodate Williamson in 1796
and Delaware to take care of Cooper in 1798.[46]

Western pressure for another reapportionment of the legislature
also increased. Westerners rightly considered themselves under-repre-

40. Philip Schuyler to Ebenezer Foote, Feb. 15, 1801, Foote MSS, N.Y. State Lib.
41. See for the election of 1795 the appeal to "We New England Men" in
Elkanah Watson, draft of an article, [1795], Watson MSS, Box 2, Folder 7, N.Y.
State Lib.
42. Laws of the State of N.Y., 16th Sess., chs. 37, 53; 17th Sess., ch. 29.
43. Huth and Pugh, trans. and ed., Talleyrand in America, 85; Cooperstown
Otsego Herald, Dec. 31, 1795, Jan. 28, Mar. 3, 1796; Charles Williamson, Observations on the Proposed State Road, 6-7.
44. Journal of the Assembly of N.Y., 16th Sess., 147, 149, 18th Sess., 10, 132-33,
136.
45. Turner, History of Phelps and Gorham's Purchase, 256-60; Cowan, Charles
Williamson, 77-80.
46. Laws of the State of N.Y., 17th Sess., ch. 18, 18th Sess., ch. 42.

sented both in the state legislature and Congress and were extremely sensitive on the subject. A bone of contention with Governor Clinton was his failure to call a special election in 1794 when Congressman Silas Talbot resigned. Westerners who claimed that they were entitled to two congressmen were for a year or so without even one.[47] The western campaign for more state representation reached a peak in 1795 when the electoral census, mandatory under the state constitution, fell due. In the assembly westerners organized for the first time as a bloc to put in a "Northern" man as speaker, electing William North, a Federalist landlord from Duanesburgh, against James Watson, the Federalist merchant of New York City, by a vote of thirty-three to twenty-eight. Four years earlier, eastern Federalists had acquiesced in reapportionment; now they expressed alarm at the prospects of a census which, a Hudson Valley leader feared, "may introduce a new order of things" in the state. As a result, in the debate over a new census, "eastern and southern interests . . . clashed considerably" but the census carried.[48] When the census returns were in, "the new order of things" was apparent. Six western counties which in 1790 had fewer than 2,500 voters in 1795 had 14,525—or nearly one-fourth of the state's 64,017 voters. Moreover, most western voters met the qualified £100 requirement to vote for governor.[49]

Such fears as eastern Federalists had were dissipated by their gubernatorial victory in 1795, which they owed to western support.[50] If "we only use our victory with moderation," Ontario's Thomas Morris counseled Stephen Van Rensselaer, "it will be the means of destroying all kind of opposition to federal measures."[51] When state apportionment came to a vote early in 1796 it passed the Federalist-dominated legislature with little acrimony, except for the expected bargaining for seats. Of the eighteen seats added to the senate twelve went to the west; of the thirty-four added to the assembly twelve went to the west. In all there would be seventeen senators and twenty-four assemblymen from the interior—about a fourth of the legislature.[52]

47. *Journal of the Assembly of N.Y.*, 18th Sess., 33; see ch. 19, n.40.

48. Hammond, *Political Parties*, I, 87; *Albany Gazette*, Feb. 27, 1795; Peter Van Schaack to John Van Allen, Feb. 15, 1796, Van Allen Papers, Albany Institute.

49. N.Y. *Daily Advertiser*, Jan. 27, 1796.

50. Stephen Van Rensselaer to Peter Van Schaack, June 18, 1795, cited in Fink, Stephen Van Rensselaer, 67.

51. Thomas Morris to Stephen Van Rensselaer, June 19, 1795, MS 1952, N.Y. State Lib.

52. Hammond, *Political Parties*, 95, 101; *Laws of the State of N.Y.*, 19th Sess., ch. 19.

At the same time Federalists shuffled the counties to their advantage. Republicans, aware that they were swamped by the huge Federalist majority in the district, tried to divide it into two senate districts, grouping together the four counties of their maximum strength. Instead, Federalists kept the district intact and attached Saratoga County to the eastern senatorial district in which Albany could neutralize its Republicanism.[53]

The next western goal was to locate the permanent state capital in a town close to the district. Invariably at the end of each session, the solons argued as to whether they should meet next at New York, Poughkeepsie, or Albany. By the mid-1790's it was taken for granted that the capital would have to settle down. Westerners thought it should be near them because of "the vast field of legislation in the Western District," and some even talked of holding out for Rome, Paris, or Whitestown.[53] Eastern Federalist leaders were apprehensive, some out of fear for the loss of law business, others, even Philip Schuyler, out of fear that it would make their task of political management more difficult.[54] But reassured by the favorable Federalist trend in the district, they acquiesced. In March 1797, the legislature voted Albany as New York's permanent capital.[55]

Thus in the demands it sought from the state government—more roads, more representation, more of a voice—the west fared well in the middle 1790's just as it had before. Indeed, the apportionment of 1796 was a quiet political revolution, which shifted the geographic locus of power. In meeting these needs eastern Federalists once again served the area well. At the same time every gain fed western sectionalism further. Against this background, in the spring of 1796 the first serious fissure appeared within the Federalist fold—just as the battle over Jay's Treaty drew to a close, as Federalists enjoyed their first year in control of the executive branch of the state government, and as the large number of newly created seats in the legislature beckoned ambitious western politicians to seek office.

53. *Journal of the Assembly of N.Y.*, 19th Sess., for Republican maneuvers, 106-7, 112; for Williamson's petition, 49; for Otsego pressure, 39, 144; for the new counties, *Laws of the State of N.Y.*, 19th Sess., ch. 29.

54. See "Communication," Whitestown *Western Centinel*, "Extraordinary," Nov. 21, 1796; Richard Harison to Peter Van Schaack, Feb. 7, 1797, Van Schaack Papers, Lib. Cong.; Hammond, *Political Parties*, I, 105; Philip Schuyler to Phillip J. Schuyler, Jan. 23, 1795, a calendar note, N.Y. Pub. Lib., letter not located.

55. See the heated exchange in Whitestown *Western Centinel*, Dec. 7, 14, 21, 1796, by Arthur Breese and his opponents.

III

The split among Federalists began as a rebellion against William Cooper, first in his home county, Otsego, then in the district as a whole. The "stolen" gubernatorial election of 1792 had solidified the county behind Cooper. At the end of 1792, when he ran for Congress and lost, Cooper carried Otsego 791–212. Late in 1794 when he was elected, he carried Otsego 1241–229. The legislative inquiry into Cooper's highhanded electioneering tactics did not shake his power nor did the two successful slander suits against him, one by Governor Clinton, the other by John Harper, a county judge. Cooper even brought a successful countersuit against Harper and another judge for "defaming his character," recovering his own payment.[56]

Within Otsego Republican strength was confined to one or two towns. In Harpersfield, for example, it seems to have rested on the influence of a Republican land proprietor, Alexander Harper, formerly a state official under Clinton.[57] In Unadilla vigorous electioneering had some effect. The Republicans, as Jacob Morris described it, "had held several meetings, had written enumerable circular letters, had dispatched many expresses, and had rode day and night to the no small injury of the neighing quadrupeds." On election day "every man in the town on that side who was able to travel was brought up both white and *black*—they had indeed laid their plans so well as to keep at home many of our friends on the Otsego patent and to draw over to their interest many wavering persons." Even so Federalists kept the town, 73 to 68![58]

With Otsego almost a one-party county, it was inevitable that the Federalist party embraced a welter of diverse elements. Ambitious politicians had only two practical choices, either to play along as part of Judge Cooper's "interest" or to fight him from within the party. The first dissident was one Joseph White, a circuit-riding doctor, who dispensed the ideas of the Enlightenment as well as pills. In 1795 while supporting John Jay, White ran for the assembly against Jacob Morris, Cooper's associate, another wealthy landlord Federalist. He

56. For returns, *N.-Y. Journal*, Mar. 2, 1793; Cooperstown *Otsego Herald*, Apr. 17, 1795; William Cooper to Benjamin Gilbert, Mar. 8, 1794, in Cooper, *Legends and Traditions*, 143-44; *Catskill Packet*, Apr. 22, 1794; *Albany Register*, Nov. 10, 1794; Cooperstown *Otsego Herald*, Oct. 16, 1795, *Albany Gazette*, Oct. 26, 1795.

57. Alexander Harper to John McKesson, July 5, 1794. McKesson MSS, N.-Y. Hist. Soc.

58. Jacob Morris to William Cooper, Apr. 2, 1794, in Cooper, *Legends and Traditions*, 147-49.

lost but with support from the northern towns in the county, and from Republicans, he took 40 per cent of the vote.[59] White was soon back in Cooper's fold but his opposition paved the way for two dissidents of a stronger mettle: Jedediah Peck and Moss Kent, each of whom represented a different strand of dissatisfaction with the wealthy landholder's brand of Federalism.

Moss Kent's dissatisfaction was mostly personal. A brother of James Kent, later famous as chancellor and chief justice of the New York Supreme Court, Moss was a young lawyer who came to Cooperstown early in the decade and became Cooper's legal agent and protégé. He lived in the proprietor's home and was a favorite of Madame Cooper and their daughter. Co-owner of a store and a pearl ashery, he also engaged in land speculation with Cooper's aid. Politically, Kent was a Federalist of strong convictions; locally he was an active supporter of his patron. In 1794 he campaigned for Cooper for Congress and testified on his behalf in the slander suit against him.[60] Like his brother, however, Moss Kent was a studious and genteel person repelled by the coarse ways of Cooper, a "self made man," and was anxious lest he be regarded as "a tool" of the proprietor. Like many another frontier lawyer he had his eye on election to the state legislature in order to build his reputation.[61]

Jedediah Peck's dissatisfaction grew out of his roots among the common folk. In his middle-forties, Peck was a sometime surveyor, millwright, and farmer. "Insignificant in aspect," he was "small in stature with peculiar features, wearing shabby clothing and with a gait ungainly."[62] From a Connecticut family of thirteen, he began life as a bookkeeper, then served three years with a Connecticut regiment in the Revolution. He moved to Cooperstown in 1790, following his brother-in-law, a doctor. Self-educated, he was well read in the Bible, an ardent Baptist, and a part-time preacher. An Otsego pioneer recalled him as "illiterate but a shrewd cunning man. . . . He

59. "An Address to the Medical Society of Otsego County," Cooperstown *Otsego Herald*, Oct. 23, 1795; Frost, *Life in the Upper Susquehanna*, 47; for the returns, Cooperstown *Otsego Herald*, May 29, 1795, and "A Friend to Truth," *ibid.*, May 8, 1795; for White's background, see Duane H. Hurd, *History of Otsego County, New York* . . . (Phila., 1878), 124.

60. For Kent's Federalism, Kent to Peter Van Schaack, Mar. 14, Oct. 12, 1792, Van Schaack Papers, Lib. Cong.; for background, Alexander, ed., "Judge James Kent's 'Jaunt' to Cooperstown, 1792," *N.Y. History*, 22 (1941), 543, n. 11.

61. See Moss to James Kent, Dec. 25, 1794, Jan. 4, 1795, Feb. 27, 1796, Kent Papers, II, Lib. Cong.

62. Throop Wilder, "Jedediah Peck, Statesman, Soldier, Preacher," *N.Y. History*, 22 (1941), 291, 290-300.

had not talent as a preacher or speaker; his language was low and he spoke with a drawling, nasal Yankee twang, so that on public speaking he was almost unintelligible."[63]

Although it is invariably overlooked by historians, Peck, like Kent, was a Federalist and a cog in Judge Cooper's "machine." He was appointed a justice of the peace and county judge with Cooper's influence, he testified on behalf of the proprietor before the assembly in 1793, probably campaigned for him for Congress in 1794, and fought for Jay's Treaty in the spring of 1796. He was also on cordial terms with Stephen Van Rensselaer.[64]

In 1796 both Kent and Peck wanted Federalist nominations to the state senate. With twelve additional senate seats allotted to the district and the Jay Treaty agitation at its height, Federalist nomination would be tantamount to election. Nominations for the entire district were worked out by Albany Federalists in consultation with the leaders dominant in each county. The Albany leaders did not dictate the nominations—"I wish you immediately to inform me who you wish for your county," Stephen Van Rensselaer wrote William Cooper as soon as the legislature had set the new apportionment. But with twelve candidates to be chosen from nine counties, including Albany, it was inevitable that the Federalist circle at Albany, led by Philip Schuyler, would show a strong hand. Except for Otsego, there was apparently little problem in working out the nominations for the western counties; "the gentlemen from Herkimer," Van Rensselaer wrote, have made their nomination "the Montgomery folks," theirs, etc.[65] The Federalist ticket was unabashedly weighted with large landholders, among them Thomas Morris, Charles Williamson, Peter Smith, and Vincent Matthews, shortly a lawyer for the Holland Land Company.

Two places on the ticket were reserved for Otsego, Van Rensselaer informed Cooper, "I wish to hear your sentiments on the subject." One spot, it was taken for granted, would go to Jacob Morris, the ranking incumbent assemblyman. The question was whether the second place would go to Moss Kent or Joseph White. Peck never seems to have been considered seriously; with some in Otsego he had

63. Beardsley, *Reminiscences*, 72.
64. Peck to Van Rensselaer, Sept. 3, 1793, Peck MSS, N.Y. State Lib.; for Peck's testimony, *Journal of the Assembly of N.Y.*, 16th Sess., 204; for Cooper's support, "Minutes of a Meeting, Dec. 21, 1793," Cooper MSS, N.Y. State Hist. Assoc.
65. Stephen Van Rensselaer to William Cooper, Mar. 7, Mar. 15, 1796, Cooper Transcripts, N.-Y. Hist. Soc.

the reputation of being "either an insane man or a vulgar black-guard."[66] The candidates proposed at Albany, Van Rensselaer told Cooper, were Morris and White. Cooper probably toyed with backing Kent but ended by backing White, much to the annoyance of many Otsego County Federalist leaders and of Kent himself, whose pique suggests he considered himself betrayed.[67] Thus bypassed, Kent and Peck each began a separate campaign for the senate. Kent, with the endorsement of a number of Otsego County Federalists and of Republicans in the entire district, was the only Federalist to receive official Republican support;[68] Peck had little more than a personal following.

In his campaign Kent exploited opposition to both Cooper and the Albany junto, displaying a letter Cooper had written to him imploring him to withdraw lest White's chances be jeopardized. An article in the Whitestown *Western Centinel* charged that the official ticket had been concocted by "those few great men" in New York City, passed on to Albany, and then sent into the western district. The perpetrators were "this self created society in imitation of the Democrats of this country and the Jacobins of France whose principles and conduct they appear to condemn."[69] In the same vein "A Hawk" railed at the Albany-dictated ticket as an "attempt to introduce a cabinet nomination and influence characteristic of a court party in a kingly government."[70]

Unlike Kent, Peck based his campaign on a broad democratic appeal. Writing under the pseudonym, "A Ploughjogger," he sided up with "my brother farmers, mechanicks and traders," by apologizing for his simple style; if he happened to spell a word wrong, he knew they would excuse him. Thus established, he warmed to his theme: the number of lawyers on the Federalist ticket. In all of Otsego County there were 3119 electors and only six lawyers, yet three of the six were candidates for the assembly, and there was only "one honest one among them." "These lawyers are an intriguing set, it is they that have wooled up the practise of the law in such a heap of

66. Benjamin Gilbert, in Cooperstown *Otsego Herald*, Nov. 22, 1795.

67. Van Rensselaer to Cooper, Apr. 25, 1796, a letter indicating that Cooper had written him but not clear as to Cooper's desires, Cooper Transcripts, N.Y. Hist. Soc.

68. *Albany Register*, June 17, 1796; "A Western Man," Cooperstown *Otsego Herald*, July 7, 1796.

69. Summarized in Van Rensselaer to Cooper, Apr. 30, 1796, Cooper Transcripts, N.-Y. Hist. Soc.

70. "A Hawk," Whitestown *Western Centinel*, Apr. 6, 1796.

formality on purpose so that we cannot see through their entanglement to oblige us to employ them to untangle them, and if we go to them for advice they will not say a word without five dollars."[71] Moreover, warned Peck, the lawyers were so skilled in sophistry that they would prove it by their clever answers to this article.

Peck's special target was Jacob Morris, whom he drew into an acrimonious exchange in the *Otsego Herald*. Peck branded Morris' assembly proposal to transfer the nominating power from the Council of Appointment to the governor alone as "a wide stride toward monarchy." Morris had also voted against the abolition bill; "Sin lieth at your door," the Baptist Peck thundered. "You acknowledge you voted to hold your fellow creatures in slavery who are as good as you by nature and some of them I believe much better by practise, yea you hold some of them in slavery yourself."[72]

Peck's campaign threw the county's Federalist leaders into a panic, the Cooperites for obvious reasons, Moss Kent's supporters for fear he would jeopardize their man's chances. Federalists appealed to him not to split the county's votes. This failing, they challenged his Federalism, accusing him of seeking support from Republicans in Saratoga County. Peck was furious; if an anti-Federalist voted for him, he asked, does that make him one? His accuser was but "a monarchite under the garb of Federalism." Peck equated his enemy with the Republicans; "you are as bad as they are," he told Jacob Morris.[73]

In the district as a whole, the entire "Albany ticket" of Federalists swamped both the Republicans and the dissident Federalists, averaging about forty-five hundred votes with only a few Republicans receiving as many as a thousand. Moss Kent with two thousand votes had the highest number of any man not on the regular ticket.[74] The voters of Otsego, however, rejected the "Albany influence." Here Kent ran about seven hundred votes ahead of Morris and White and would have done better, he thought, had his name not been misprinted on the ballot as "Moses Kent." Running for the senate, Peck got only half as many votes in the county as Kent, but a Federalist candidate for the assembly whom he had singled out for criticism

71. "A Ploughjogger," reprinted from *Otsego Herald* in Peck, *Political Wars of Otsego*, 38-42.

72. *Ibid.*, 13-37, for five articles by Peck and two by Morris; for the issue, Hammond, *Political Parties*, I, 97-98.

73. Peck, *Political Wars of Otsego*, 42-43, 53-57; for anti-Peck articles, "Hocus Pocus," and "An Elector," Cooperstown *Otsego Herald*, Apr. 21, 1796.

74. *Albany Register*, July 1, 1796; Cooperstown *Otsego Herald*, July 7, 1796.

ran a poor fifth and almost lost. If Peck was nothing more than a nuisance, Kent clearly was a force to be reckoned with. Kent continued to live with Cooper a little longer, skirting all discussion of politics; inwardly he seethed at the man whose "heart is as base as his courage is trifling."[75]

IV

Nine months later the revolt within the Federalist party spread to the entire district, leading to William Cooper's defeat in the congressional election. With the western forts finally restored, the west could relax and enjoy an internal fight which otherwise would have been a luxury. Rivalry among land proprietors was now added to sectional feeling against "the Albany influence" and democratic feeling against Cooper's arrogance.

When Cooper had run for Congress in 1794, his principal opponent had been John Winn, a Republican. James Cochran, a young Federalist lawyer who had entered the race late and who had to contend with the rumor that he was a candidate against his own wishes, came in a poor third.[76] In 1796 Cochran ran again and Winn bowed out. Desperately Philip Schuyler tried to head Cochran off. "The general in Mr. Cochran's presence," Cooper was informed, "said he was sure James had more sense than to be a candidate," but to no avail.[77] Cochran picked up backing from Winn's supporters and most of the leading Federalists outside Otsego, including Thomas Morris of Ontario, John Lincklaen, agent of the Holland Land Company, and Hugh White and Jonas Platt of Oneida.[78] Cooper claimed that Morris and Charles Williamson were backing him, but Moss Kent, who was active on behalf of Cochran,[79] said he was a "notorious lyer." Jedediah Peck, on

75. Cooperstown *Otsego Herald*, June 9, 1796; Moss Kent to James Kent, July 8, 1796, Kent Papers, II, Lib. Cong.

76. William Cooper to Ebenezer Foote, Nov. 29, 1794, Cooper MSS, N.Y. State Hist. Assoc.; James Cochran to Stephen Van Rensselaer, Dec. 15, 1794, MS 1833, N.Y. State Lib.; for nominations, *Albany Register*, Nov. 24, *Albany Gazette*, Oct. 27, Nov. 20, Dec. 4, Dec. 1, 1794; for returns, *Albany Gazette*, Feb. 10, 1795. For their political partnership letters from Van Rensselaer to Cooper, Jan. 13, Apr. 2, 1794, Cooper Transcripts, N.-Y. Hist. Soc.; Schuyler to Rufus King, Jan. 20, 1795, King Papers, N.-Y. Hist. Soc.

77. Philip Schuyler and Van Rensselaer to William Cooper, Sept. 9, 1796, Cooper Transcripts, N.-Y. Hist. Soc.

78. For Cochran nominating meetings in which supporters are indicated, see Cooperstown *Otsego Herald*, Oct. 27, Nov. 3, 17, 1796; *Whitestown Gazette*, Oct. 25, Nov. 1, 15, 29, 1796.

79. Moss Kent to James Kent, Dec. 19, 1796, Kent Papers, Lib. Cong. For his personal status see letters of Nov. 17, 27, 1796.

the other hand, returned to Cooper's camp to preside over a meeting that nominated him.[80] With three newspapers churning out propaganda, the campaign turned into a knock-down, drag-out scrap, by far the liveliest election campaign the region had ever witnessed.

Cooper's wealth and arrogance were the major issue. One of Cooper's supporters appealed for him as "a man of large property"; this was the spark that was needed. "Have we resisted monarchy and aristocracy and shall we fall down and worship the golden calf?" asked an irate westerner. What talents did Cooper have for Congress, asked another, "but what his situation as a man of great property gave him?" "His humor is too lofty," said "Diogenes," "his discourse too peremptory, his tongue too filled, his eye too ambitious, his gait too majestical, his general behaviour too vain, too ridiculous and thrasonical." "Too much riches is dangerous in a republican governor," said "A New England Man."[81]

Sectional feeling was triggered when a leading Albany Federalist, Leonard Gansevoort, sent a letter into the district endorsing Cooper. There was a precedent for Albany Federalists' playing a role in the state senate elections, but the frontier had been a separate congressional district for almost four years. "Timothy Thistle" laced into Gansevoort mercilessly. It was "a radical defect and absurdity in our government that any person should be elected by the suffrages of the people where he resides." A meeting in Herkimer County, he jibed, had agreed to nominate a candidate for Congress from Albany; he hoped Gansevoort would not consider this interference "officious or indelicate."[82] Westerners got the point.

James Cochran in contrast to Cooper was presented as "one of those independent lawyers not only in disposition but property," and as a "modest man of merit." He was not a legislator, it was true, but he was well informed, capable, impartial, a person of integrity, and although a young man, a member of the Board of Regents. If elected, it would not be by "that dangerous and domineering influence which property gives."[83]

80. Cooperstown *Otsego Herald*, Sept. 8, 1796.

81. "Communicated," Whitestown *Western Centinel*, "Extraordinary," Nov. 21, 1796; "Argus," Cooperstown *Otsego Herald*, Nov. 24, 1796; "Diogenes," *Whitestown Gazette*, Dec. 6, 1796; "A New England Man," *ibid.*, Dec. 13, 1796.

82. "Timothy Thistle," Whitestown *Western Centinel*, Oct. 5, 1796, *Albany Gazette*, Oct. 16, 1796, *Whitestown Gazette*, Oct. 18, 1796; see in same vein, "A Friend to Merit," and "Argus," Whitestown *Western Centinel Extra*, Dec. 5, 1796.

83. "Hampden," Cooperstown *Otsego Herald*, Sept. 29, 1796; "T.," *Whitestown Gazette*, Dec. 6, 1796.

When Cooper lashed out, Kent feared that he "would not stick at bribery and corruption to ensure his success"; "he is a person that pays no regard to truth and cares not whom he slanders to answer his own purposes."[84] Cooper's defenders appealed to individualist rather than democratic values. The proprietor's wealth was not a mark against him, one man claimed, because Cooper was a self-made man. He had converted the wilderness into "smiling gardens and luxurious fields," said another. "Ploughjogger" Peck exalted Cooper as the "poor man's benefactor and the widow's support, the Father of his County." On national issues, much was made of Cooper's plaintive pleas in Congress for Jay's Treaty. In their offensive against Cochran, the Cooper Federalists added to their old accusation that he was a "stripling upstart," a new one that he was being backed by Republicans. Had not Greenleaf, "a true blooded anti-Federalist," honored him with the "gracious christening of the republican party?"[85]

Cochran won the election by a margin of seventeen votes, 2992 to 2975; forty votes in Steuben County were diverted to Charles Williamson. Cochran's vote doubled that of the Republican, John Winn, in 1794. He drew his support from all counties and social strata: well-to-do farmers along the Mohawk, poor newcomers in Tioga and Onondaga, and pioneers in the domain of the land proprietors in Ontario and Steuben. Although Cooper fared better in his home county than in 1794, his support outside Otsego evaporated except for one county.[86]

Cooper blamed Moss Kent for his narrow defeat; he would not even speak to him at the local tavern. Anti-Cooperites, Republican and Federalist, toasted the defeat of "the corrupt influence."[87] In the east Robert R. Livingston heard the happy news that interference by "the old Sachem and his son-in-law"—Philip Schuyler and Stephen Van Rensselaer—had become a kiss of death in the west. Cochran's success was "likely to break the bond of connection that has so long subsisted with the Albany chiefs."[88] To bail Cooper out, Federalists at the next session of the legislature divided the huge western district

84. Moss to James Kent, Sept. 28, Dec. 15, 1796, Kent Papers, II, Lib. Cong.
85. "Scander," *Whitestown Gazette*, Nov. 1, 1796; "Herkimer Farmer" and "A Ploughjogger," *ibid.*, Dec. 13, 1796; "Federal Elector," *Albany Gazette*, Dec. 2, 1796; "Manlius," *Otsego Herald*, Dec. 8, 1796; "Plain Truth," No. 1, *ibid.*, Jan. 12, 1797.
86. *N.-Y. Journal*, Jan. 14, 17, 1797. See Appendix, Table 6.
87. James to Moss Kent, Jan. 8, Moss to James Kent, Mar. 21, 1797, Kent Papers, II, Lib. Cong.; Whitestown *Western Centinel*, Mar. 1, 1797.
88. Thomas Tillotson to Robert R. Livingston, Jan. 20, Feb. 5, 1797, R. R. Livingston Papers, N.-Y. Hist. Soc.

in two, making Otsego predominant in its district, and lopped off the politically unreliable southern towns of the county, placing them with western Ulster in a new county, Delaware.[89]

In 1797 the inner-party turmoil among Federalists continued. There was a "violent party animosity" between partisans of Thomas Morris, the Ontario landholder who had backed Cochran, and Dr. White, Cooper's senator from Otsego, for the western place on the Council of Appointment, which Morris won.[90] In the spring election to fill three senate seats for the entire district two rival Federalist slates competed. All the candidates, one writer explained, "were good federal men"; the difference was between "present rich landholders and the free and independent Farmers and Yeomen of the district." Cooper again was a target.[91] The candidates backed by him lost in the district as a whole and carried Otsego by six hundred votes less than he had anticipated. To Moss Kent it was another "glorious victory over corruption and intrigue."[92]

Jedediah Peck, however, still had not come into his own; in a race for the assembly in the spring of 1797 he again fared poorly. In the year gone by he had filled up the columns of the *Otsego Herald* with his long-winded, often pettifogging diatribes and the editor complained that as a result circulation had dropped from 800 to 300.[93] Peck published his essays in book form late in 1796 as *The Political Wars of Otsego or the Downfall of Jacobinism and Despotism* (with the support of 200 subscribers). The book summed up the peculiar brand of Republican Federalism his dissidence had assumed. Included were fulsome espousals of pure Federalism in support of Jay's Treaty and in tribute to George Washington, liberal polemics against Jacob Morris's conservative legislative record, a weary post-mortem on his own defeat, plus some remarkable political essays. In "Jack Tar's Journal," a satirical review of recent American history, Peck compared the young nation to a ship that had to steer between "running aground on Cape Monarchy" and "the quick sands of anarchy." The Republican

89. *Laws of the State of N.Y.*, 20th Sess., ch. 33; for the mixed feelings of the Ulster Federalists about Delaware, see John Addison to Van Gaasbeck, Feb. 14, 1796, Van Gaasbeck Papers, Kingston Senate House; and Ebenezer Foote to Van Gaasbeck, Oct. 12, 1796, Jan. 20, 1797, Van Gaasbeck Papers, F.D.R. Lib.

90. Moss to James Kent, Jan. 8, 1797, Kent Papers, II, Lib. Cong.

91. "Argus," Cooperstown *Otsego Herald*, Apr. 13, 1797; "Citizen," Whitestown *Western Centinel*, Apr. 19, 1797; "Cincinnatus" and "An Elector of the Western District," *Albany Gazette*, Mar. 13, 1797.

92. Moss to James Kent, Apr. 27, May 1, 1797, Kent Papers, II, Lib. Cong.; for returns, *N.-Y. Journal*, June 14, 1797; Cooperstown *Otsego Herald*, June 29, 1797.

93. Elihu Phinney, Cooperstown *Otsego Herald*, Nov. 15, 1796; *ibid.*, June 1, 1797.

party to Peck was "a beast with seven heads and ten horns" which originated as a coalition of "libertine whigs and revengeful or avaricious tories."[94] Republican government, however, was "the literal and peaceable kingdom of the messiah," while monarchy was "the literal kingdom of Satan and the anti-christ or the image of the beast." Representative forms, as an adaptation of "democratical government" to the needs of a large territory, required constant vigilance on the part of the people. Clearly, Peck had blended some Tom Paine with the Bible. He thought of himself as a third force, battling "anarchists" and "jacobites" on the one hand and "monarchites" on the other.[95]

In 1798 Federalist dissidence matured. In December 1797 Judge Cooper called in the arrears on his mortgage payments for the first time in eleven years.[96] In April 1798 Jedediah Peck was elected to the assembly, with the highest vote in the county, doubling his vote of the previous year. One of his first interests in the assembly was the abolition of imprisonment of debtors.[97] Within the year he was acting in concert with Aaron Burr as a Republican and at Judge Cooper's behest was imprisoned under the Sedition Law for circulating a petition to repeal that law.[98]

In the congressional elections late in 1798 with the western district divided in two, Moss Kent, still a Federalist, ran against Cooper and doubled the previous anti-Cooper vote in Otsego but lost the district by a narrow margin. In the second western district two Federalists were also pitted against each other.[99]

In state politics eastern Federalists were almost as worried about the powerful western wing of their own party as they were about Republicans. "It will not be long before the seat of government is removed to that quarter," Robert Troup informed Rufus King; "the northern and western interests are much too powerful for us."[100] Thus shortly after the end of Washington's reign, a political eruption on the western frontier had challenged the great landholders within the district and the eastern "aristocrats" without who dominated the party.

94. "An Address to the Free Citizens of the United States of North America" in Peck, *The Political Wars of Otsego*, 93-103.
95. "Monarchical and Representative Government Contrasted," *ibid.*, 9-10.
96. Cooperstown *Otsego Herald*, Jan. 4, 1798.
97. *Ibid.*, May 31, 1798; Frost, *Life in the Upper Susquehanna*, 54-55.
98. James Morton Smith, *Freedom's Fetters; The Alien and Sedition Laws and American Civil Liberties* (Ithaca, N.Y., 1956), 390-98.
99. *N.-Y. Journal*, June 16, 20, 1798.
100. Troup to King, Nov. 16, 1797, King, ed., *Correspondence of Rufus King*, II, 110. See also, James Kent to Moss Kent, Feb. 4, 1797, Kent Papers, II, Lib. Cong.

CHAPTER 24

"The Spirit of Reformation":

The State Government

1793-1796

At its onset, the Republican movement in New York was a response to national issues, in essence a patriotic reawakening. It was not long before Republicanism contributed to what Dr. Phineas Hedges, an Ulster County Republican, called "the spirit of reformation."[1] From 1789 to 1792, during George Clinton's fifth term as governor, reform made little headway.[2] From 1793 to 1797, during Clinton's sixth term and the beginning of John Jay's first, the state government felt the impact of the reform movement. There were two major victories: the inauguration of state aid to "common schools" and the revision of the draconic criminal code. Abolition came close to success, again failing by one vote. There was a successful effort led by Federalists to curb the flagrantly pro-speculator land policy, and a less successful effort led by Republicans to curb the excessive demands of the new canal companies. The movements for reform were bipartisan; Federalists controlled the legislative branch, Republicans the executive, until Jay took over in 1796. Republicans, however, played a larger role in reform than historians have allowed. On

1. Phineas Hedges, M.D., *An Oration Delivered Before the Republican Society of Ulster County . . . At Montgomery, July 4, 1795* (Goshen, 1795), 3-4.
2. See above, ch. 11, secs. V, VI.

the other hand neither they nor the Federalists took up the pleas of tenants or imprisoned debtors or showed interest in revising the undemocratic features of the state constitution.

I

The reform current in New York was fed by several streams of different origins. The oldest was the genteel humanitarianism found among merchants, lawyers, and ministers in New York City. Essentially Christian, philanthropic, and benevolent, it had a long tradition, especially among the Quakers and Anglicans. Thomas Eddy, a Quaker merchant, was outstanding. The son of an ironmonger, he was a successful insurance broker who struck it rich as a securities speculator early in the 1790's. He became known as "the John Howard of America" for his prison reform and was active in reform of Indian policy and a number of other Quaker-sponsored philanthropies. Matthew Clarkson, another wealthy Quaker, was the president of the Manumission Society.[3] Clarkson was a Federalist assemblyman; Eddy worked with Philip Schuyler.

Another current for reform came from the victims of "oppression." Issues of social justice, as the furor over the ferrymen-Keteltas case indicated, aroused the urban poor. Their counterparts in the countryside were the tenants of the upper Hudson Valley who resumed their challenge to landlordism in the mid-1790's. Debtors and their wives pleaded their own cases. Slaves and freed Negroes were also heard from: "Has God appointed us their slaves," a Negro wrote Governor Jay; "I answer NO!"[4]

A third current stemmed from New England migrants. Products of a less stratified society than New York's, they brought with them a hardheaded Yankee equalitarianism and an improving spirit. Elkanah Watson crusaded for everything from banks and canals to free schools and penal reform to water spouts on houses that would not drench passersby on Albany streets. Projects "popped into my busy and restless brain on my pillow while sleeping profoundly," Watson explained.[5] Ambrose Spencer, a lawyer from Hudson, was active in the state senate on behalf of a more humane criminal code, relief for debtors, and the abolition of slavery. Jedediah Peck, the Connecticut

3. Pomerantz, *New York An American City*, 316-38, Michael Kraus, *The Atlantic Civilization: Eighteenth-Century Origins* (Ithaca, N.Y., 1949), ch. 6.
4. William Hamilton to John Jay, Mar. 8, 1796, Jay Papers, Columbia Univ.
5. Flick, *Elkanah Watson*, 105, 102-114.

Yankee, became an advocate in the 1798 assembly of relief for debtors and electoral reform; in later years he won fame as the "father" of the common school system of New York.[6] Watson, Spencer, and Peck all began the decade as Federalists and ended it as Republicans.

Finally, there was a commitment to reform among Republicans, especially in New York City. William Keteltas, the ferryman's champion, made his next appearance on the New York City scene in 1800 as the editor of *Forlorn Hope*, a paper which he edited while in the debtor's prison.[7] Tunis Wortman, the brilliant young secretary of the Democratic Society, developed a sociology of reform in an *Oration on the Influence of Social Institutions Upon Human Nature and Happiness.*[8] DeWitt Clinton presented in several orations a philosophy of reform that he would later apply in office on behalf of abolition, debtors' relief, free schools, and eleemosynary institutions.[9] In Congress Edward Livingston showed a similar concern with federal laws on debtors and the criminal code.[10]

Republican reform sentiment was expressed by the toasts of the popular societies, by editors who opened their pages to articles by reformers,[11] and in the circulation of the works of the European Enlightenment.[12] It was especially apparent among young men, particularly in Columbia College commencement addresses, and in essays of fledgling undergraduates like Daniel Tompkins.[13] It was typical of Republicans that having given little heed to social questions, they embraced them all at once. Thus when the Tammany Society first showed any interest in reform, it offered three consecutive toasts:[14] "A speedy abolition of every species of slavery throughout America,"

6. George Lankevich, The Early Political Career of Ambrose Spencer (unpubl. M.A. thesis, Columbia Univ., 1960), 30-36. Sherman Williams, "Jedediah Peck, The Father of the Public School System of the State of New York," N.Y. State Hist. Assoc., *Qtly. Jour.*, 1 (1920), 219-40.

7. Pomerantz, *New York An American City*, 324-27.

8. Delivered before Tammany, May 12, 1796 (N.Y., 1796).

9. Dixon Ryan Fox in *DAB* s.v. "Clinton, DeWitt."

10. See below, ch. 25.

11. See *New York Magazine*, 4-7 (1793-97), *passim*, which reprinted excerpts from Godwin, Rousseau, Priestley, Wollstencraft and other articles dealing with crime, education, and women's rights.

12. For evidence of circulation of such books, see the discussion of the "Friendly Club," ch. 18, sec. II; for Wortman, *An Oration*, 8-9, 11, 13-14, 20-21; also New York Society Library, *Charter, By-Laws and Names of Members—with a Catalogue of the Books* (N.Y., 1789), re-issued 1791, 1792, 1793, 1800.

13. See *N.-Y. Journal*, May 4, 1793; N.Y. *Daily Advertiser*, May 9, 1794; Irwin and Jacobsen, eds., *A Columbia College Student in the Eighteenth Century, passim*.

14. *N.-Y. Journal*, "Extraordinary," Dec. 6, 1794.

"A happy melioration of our Penal Laws, respecting criminal punishment and imprisonment for debt," and "The establishment of public schools." To its Republican slogans Tammany added three others: "The Empire of Philanthropy," "The Genius of Universal Emancipation," and "Humanity."[15]

Among Republicans in the countryside and small towns the commitment to reform was only a shade less apparent. Dr. Hedges made "reformation" the theme of an Independence Day oration before the Democratic Society of Ulster. The Democratic Society at Canaan dispatched a lengthy petition to the legislature requesting reform of the court system.[16] *The Newburgh Packet*, a warm Republican paper, ran a series of articles expounding a philosophy of reform.[17] At Albany, Barber and Southwick, the Republican printers, brought out Thomas Paine's *Agrarian Justice* with its program for sweeping social reform, expanding the thesis of the second book of *The Rights of Man*.[18]

George Clinton's addresses to the legislature measure the impact of reform sentiment. Up to 1792, he mentioned no question of reform except education, which he pressed primarily on behalf of the existing secondary academies and Columbia College. In 1794 Clinton asked for aid to common schools and for reform of the criminal code; in 1795 he devoted half of his message to these two subjects and to "correcting our system of jurisprudence."[19]

The growth of a Republican philosophy of reform can be traced in Republican orations before the various societies. In 1793 Dr. Samuel L. Mitchill, the Columbia scientist—still a Federalist but a Republican-to-be—raised reform gingerly in the context of a paean of praise to those American institutions which induced "a love of country." In his concluding section he paused briefly "to merely enumerate the glaring deformities" of the country "to show you that I see them and earnestly hope that they will soon be removed." In summary fashion he listed eight "deformities": "imprisonment for debt, capital punishment, domestic slavery, the Indian War, neglect of the old soldiers, duelling, retention of insignificant titles and carelessness

15. In Mitchill, *Life of Tammany*, 35-36.
16. *N.-Y. Journal*, Oct. 4, 1794, reprinting a resolution passed July 11, 1794.
17. "Hortensius," Nos. 1-4, *Newburgh Packet*, June 28, July 12, 19, 26, 1796. The author possibly was David Denniston, a warm deist.
18. Paine, *Agrarian Justice* (Albany, 1797). Barber and Southwick also reprinted Jean Jacques Rousseau, *Treatise on the Social Compact* (Albany, 1797).
19. Lincoln, ed., *Messages from the Governors*, II, 332-37, 348-50.

about education."[In a conservative vein, he warned against haste in correcting such abuses, citing Condorcet's maxim, "If we attack oppression before we have taught the oppressed, we shall risk the loss of liberty."[20]

A year later, young DeWitt Clinton, addressing the same fraternal society, the Black Friars, devoted his entire oration to the theme, "the progressive amelioration of the world." He vividly described the "miseries of life" around us: "disease and poverty . . . oppression and calumny. . . the loss of friends and reputation . . . the prison, the house of madness, the retreat of poverty, the horrid gibbet and the blood streaming scaffold."[21] Clinton then made his specific reforms clear by painting a picture of the society he envisioned after the spread of "the spirit of benevolence." "Schools of virtue and seminaries of learning will be founded, agriculture, commerce and manufactures encouraged, the polite arts and the useful sciences patronized and the rights of nature and the rights of religion respected." At that time, "it will also be the object of the Nation to assuage physical evils by the establishment of hospitals, almshouses and public granaries and to alleviate by proper corrective the moral ills which prevail." In the future, "the shackles of slavery will then fall to the ground and the horrid institution of capital punishment be only seen on the descriptive canvass." In addition the "chicanry of law" will be banished and "the long catalog of crimes which disgraces our statute books [will be] considered as the forgery of misanthropists or as the invention of diabolical spirits." "A university for the illumination of the world" would also be founded. Clinton offered a Baconian vision of worldwide progress. "Great improvements must also take place. . . . The hand of art will change the face of the Universe; mountains, deserts and oceans will feel its mighty force."[22]

In the countryside the spirit of Dr. Hedges' oration to the Ulster Republican Society was affirmative, reflecting the prosperity of an area of yeomen. "We are a comparatively happy land. We are in the lap of plenty," he said, yet "we are far from a state of moral political perfection." First, representation in government was based on property—it should be based on people. Second, there was "the homage paid to the wealthy in American life . . . while the poor and virtuous are treated with neglect and with scorn." Third, the decisions of

20. Mitchill, *Oration Before the Black Friars*, 32.
21. DeWitt Clinton, *Oration on Benevolence*, 16-17.
22. *Ibid.*

the courts were too often outrages against justice; there "the great work of reformation is but just begun." Last and to him most important, "the severity of the criminal code is a reproach to freedom and to justice."[23]

As Republicans analyzed the task of reform that confronted them they varied in their analysis. "Hortensius" was convinced that vested interests would resist change. "Men of property," he wrote, "have always been the devotees of those systems under which they lived; they have always regarded every attempt at reformation as levelled against their elevation and their power; they have looked upon the most trifling change as the certain precursor of political destruction." "To effect a revolution under such circumstances by the operation of reason," he concluded, "is utterly impossible."[24] Tunis Wortman was more typical of Republican thinking in his implicit faith in reason. He devoted his 1796 address to Tammany—Greenleaf called it a "chef d'oeuvre of the kind"—to refuting "that monkish and dishonorable doctrine which teaches the original depravity of mankind" with an environmentalist view of human nature. Man was "the creature of education and the child of habitude," Wortman argued; his manners, virtues, and vices were not innate but socially formed. The "melancholy opinion" of the origins of human nature was "the constant and uniform theme of tyrants," a rationalization of "excessive energy" in government and an excuse for "rigid and penal codes of law." On the other hand, "by tracing the existing evils in society to human and secondary causes, we become enabled to discover and apply judicious means of remedy." After rejecting the "monkish view," Wortman concluded that by a "well organized society" the best in human nature could be developed and "virtue and talents" advanced. Presumably no vested interests stood in the way. Society constantly had to "remedy existing evils." Its true heroes, therefore, were scientists and reformers.[25] Some New York Republicans clearly aspired to be such heroes.

II

In many ways the setting was ripe in New York by 1795 for a flowering of reform. The war scare of 1794 was over, the defense of the state provided for. The state government not only had not been "consolidated," but its annual income from land sales and invest-

23. Hedges, *An Oration*, 14.
24. "Hortensius," *Newburgh Packet*, July 19, 1796.
25. *N.-Y. Journal*, July 7, 1796; Wortman, *An Oration*, 5-6, 8-10, 16.

ments in securities and bank stock was higher than at any time in the state's history. Thus there was money to spend—$484,000 in 1794, $305,000 in 1795—and no excuse for parsimonious country legislators who were fearful of taxing their agrarian constituents, not to spend it.[26]

In 1795 the legislature granted the first state aid to "common schools." Republicans took it for granted that there should be public support for elementary education. Reverend Samuel Miller in his sermon to the societies of New York City said that legislative aid to establish "public schools" was "so plainly and intimately connected with the welfare of all republics that neither proof nor illustration on the subject are necessary."[27] Education had to become "equally accessible to every citizen of America," the Mechanics Society resolved, both to safeguard republican government and make it possible for all positions in government and society to be open to "virtue and talent."[28] In 1793 and 1794 Governor Clinton and the Board of Regents pleaded for aid to "the lower branches of education" which were "greatly neglected," calling special attention to the plight of "the numerous infant settlements annually forming in our state chiefly composed of families in very indigent circumstances."[29] Finally in 1795 Clinton ended his address to the legislature with a plea for "the establishment of common schools" on the grounds that the benefits of the academies "liberally endowed" by the state were "principally confined to the children of the opulent," a remark that prompted the old conservative Egbert Benson to say: "What a detestable rascal he is."[30]

In the assembly a common school bill was brought in by a bipartisan committee over which Jonathan Havens, the Suffolk Republican, presided and on which Adam Comstock, Keteltas' defender, was active. They proposed that the state distribute a fixed sum annually to each county over a five-year period "for encouraging and maintaining schools." Debate turned on the amount of money to be appropriated, the proposals running from $20,000 to $40,000 a year, and whether the

26. For state receipts, 1789-97, see Appendix, Table 7; for expenditures, Table 8.
27. Miller, *Sermon at the New Presbyterian Church, New York, July 4, 1795*, 28-29.
28. Entry, July 1, 1795, Minutes of the General Society of Mechanics and Tradesmen, I, at the Society, N.Y.C.; for Tammany, *N.-Y. Journal*, Dec. 6, 1794; for the Democrats, *ibid.*, July 8, 1795.
29. "Annual Report of the Board of Regents" in *Journal of the Assembly of N.Y.*, 16th Sess., 210-11; *ibid.*, 17th Sess., 32. Clinton was Chancellor of the Regents.
30. Lincoln, ed., *Messages from the Governors*, II, 350; Egbert Benson to Rufus King, Jan. 15, 1795, King Papers, N.-Y. Hist. Soc.

towns should be required to match half of the grant. Republicans and Federalists were both divided over the amount. The assembly voted for $30,000, Republicans defeating the matching requirement; the senate then lowered this to $20,000, a sum the assembly agreed to, and against the wishes of most Republicans, included the matching requirement. Money would be distributed to counties in proportion to the number of qualified assembly voters. Thus New York City, for example, received the largest amount, £1888, compared to frontier Onondaga which received a scant £174.[31] The following year the state loosened its purse strings for higher education, with a generous grant to Union College, recently founded at Schenectady, and a lesser one to Columbia, which it had previously aided. It also encouraged the formation of local libraries, a measure Clinton had urged years before, by making it easy for groups to incorporate library associations, although it appropriated "not one shilling of the state's money" for books, as La Rochefoucauld-Liancourt observed.[32]

To Republicans the common school law was a landmark. It will have "the most beneficial tendency of any law since the Revolution," said Elkanah Watson. It "will dispel ignorance, the bane of republicans" among the poor. Greenleaf took the unusual step of publishing the entire law on the front page of his paper under the heading "PRO BONO PUBLICO."[33]

In New York City there was a spat over the distribution of the state grant. The legislature provided for the Common Council to apportion the city's share among existing schools, which meant the charity schools of the religious societies and the private academies catering to the "middling sort." There was protest: where was money to aid the children of "the hard working part of the community?" The council compromised. Rejecting a petition from the private school teachers, they voted eight to three to distribute the money to the charity schools and at the same time asked the state for authority to found municipal schools. They distributed the state grant to five Protestant schools and the African Free School managed by the Manu-

31. *Journal of the Assembly of N.Y.*, 18th Sess., 66, 71, 79-82, 132, 149, 151. *Laws of the State of N.Y.*, 18th Sess., ch. 75. The law set no other requirement than the teaching of "the English language, or English grammar, arithmetic, mathematics and such other branches of knowledge as are most useful and necessary to complete a good English Education."

32. *Laws of the State of N.Y.*, 19th Sess., chs. 19, 43. La Rochefoucauld-Liancourt, *Travels*, II, 449.

33. *Albany Register*, Nov. 20, 1795; *N.-Y. Journal*, Nov. 25, 1795; Flick, *Elkanah Watson*, 136-38.

mission Society. In 1797 the legislature complied with their request, authorizing the founding of free public schools, and limited the sectarian schools to one-sixth of the total appropriation, a decision that spread educational opportunity.[34]

In the state as a whole the results of the law were disappointing. By mid-1797 La Rochefoucauld-Liancourt found that "little has yet been done." The "establishment of free schools" was not a "necessary consequence" of the law, money spent on existing schools was of little use to the poor, and there was discrimination against the children of Negroes, free and slave. New York, he concluded, lagged far behind its New England neighbors. On the other hand the Board of Regents report for 1798 showed that 1352 schools in 16 of the 23 counties of the state had received aid to educate a total of 59,660 children, no small number.[35] Nevertheless, in 1800 when the law expired, Clinton wrote it off as a failure while Elkanah Watson, who considered the money "literally thrown away," called on the legislature to establish really "free schools."[36] In 1805 under the leadership of Jedediah Peck, by then a leading voice of western Republicanism, the common school act was renewed.[37] In spite of its serious shortcomings, however, the act of 1795 may be regarded as the first fruit of Republicanism harvested in the state government in the middle 1790's.

"The great penal reform year in New York"—1796—was an achievement which also owed much to Republican opinion, although it has usually been credited exclusively to Quakers and, because it was adopted while Jay was governor, to Federalists.[38] New York's criminal laws, a frontier scribe wrote, "like those of Draco, written in blood, stand in this liberal and enlightened age as monuments of ancient barbarity."[39] Death was prescribed for thirteen crimes on the first offense, including burglary, forgery, arson, and housebreaking and for an equal number on the second offense. Hangings were a common

34. "A.B.C.," three articles, N.Y. *Argus*, May 14, 17, 19, 1796; Pomerantz, *New York An American City*, 423-29.

35. Samuel S. Randall, *History of the Common School System of the State of New York* (N.Y., 1871), 7-9; La Rochefoucauld-Liancourt, *Travels*, II, 447-49.

36. A draft of a petition signed "A Layman," Elkanah Watson Papers, Box 2, No. 9, N.Y. State Lib.

37. Lincoln, ed., *Messages from the Governors*, II, 512, 528, 540.

38. Schneider, *History of Public Welfare in New York*, I, 145-46. See W. David Lewis, *From Newgate to Dannemora: The Rise of the Penitentiary in New York, 1796-1848* (Ithaca, N.Y., 1965), 1-5, 29-30, and especially 5, n.9, which is misleading in implying Republican indifference to penal reform.

39. An editorial, Salem *Washington Patrol*, May 27, 1795.

occurrence and lurid gallows confessions a popular literature.[40] For minor offenses whipping was customary—a man could get thirty-nine lashes for stealing a coat or a watch—and the whipping post and pillory were a common sight in every village.[41] Actually few convicted criminals were ever sentenced to jail; the prisons were filled mostly with debtors, vagrants, the accused waiting trial, and slaves receiving punishment.

To Republicans this criminal code was an anomaly in a progressive age—cruel, vindictive, and irrational.[42] DeWitt Clinton prepared a lengthy manuscript on the subject intended, it would appear, for a debate.[43] His uncle gave strong leadership on the subject. Broaching it the first time in 1794 Governor Clinton spoke of "the sanguinary complexion of our criminal code," regretting that "so little attention has hitherto been paid to a due proportion between crimes and punishment." It was "becoming the policy of a modern legislature," he argued, "to prevent crimes rather by the certainty than the severity of the sanction."[44]

The initial response to this plea in the assembly was positive. Although a committee composed of Federalists and Republicans recommended the abolition of the pillory and whipping, the abolition of capital punishment in all cases except willful murder and treason, and the building of jails at Albany and New York to be financed by a lottery, a bill never came out of committee.[45]

The following year, 1795, in opening the assembly, Clinton placed the revision of the criminal code second in importance only to completing the state's fortifications. The forts in fact might serve as prisons, he suggested. At this session, the committee's recommendations came to a vote but ran into a controversy over the location of the new prison. In the assembly Hudson and Albany lost in favor of New York City but the senate killed the entire bill, largely, it was claimed, be-

40. See, for example, *The Narrative of the Life of Francis Uss* . . . (Poughkeepsie, 1789); *The Narrative of Whiting Sweeting* (Lansingburgh, 1791); *The Narrative of the Life and Dying Speech of John Ryer* . . . (Poughkeepsie, 1793).
41. For example, Cooper, *Chronicles of Cooperstown*, 44; Schoonmaker, *History of Kingston*, 373.
42. For opinions, see in *N.-Y. Journal*, "An Extract . . . ," Mar. 18; "An Humane Elector," Apr. 25, 1795; "Reason," *N.-Y. Evening Post*, Mar. 16, 1795; "An Address," Lansingburgh *Tiffany's Recorder*, May 27, 1794. Hedges, *An Oration*, 13-14. "Hortensius," No. 2, *Newburgh Packet*, July 12, 1796.
43. On Capital Punishment, n.d., DeWitt Clinton Papers, Misc., XXIV, Columbia Univ.
44. Lincoln, ed., *Messages from the Governors*, II, 332-37.
45. *Journal of the Assembly of N.Y.*, 17th Sess., 108.

cause of the efforts of the legal scholar, Samuel Jones, a Federalist.[46]

In January 1796 John Jay took up the issue briefly in his opening message.[47] More important, the Quaker reformer, Thomas Eddy, enlisted Philip Schuyler's support. Schuyler journeyed with Eddy to Philadelphia where he was impressed with the pioneering methods of the new Walnut Street prison. On their return Eddy distributed copies of Pennsylvania's penal code to New York legislators, and Schuyler drew up a reform bill which Ambrose Spencer introduced and defended in the senate.[48] All were Federalists. Meanwhile, Keteltas and the Republicans had thrust the case of the whipped ferrymen before the assembly, dramatizing the barbarity of the code. On March 7 the assembly sent Keteltas to jail; on March 26 they and the senate passed the revised criminal code without debate. They did away with capital punishment for all crimes except treason, murder, abetting murder, and stealing from a church—the last, in La Rochefoucauld-Liancourt's opinion, "a remnant of the barbarian prejudices which proves the influence of priests." Life imprisonment was substituted for crime previously punishable by death, and prisons were authorized at Albany and New York. Whipping was also abolished. Within a year or so New York's Newgate Prison was constructed in Greenwich Village on Manhattan Island under the supervison of Eddy, who remained its guiding light for many years.[49]

According to a Federalist poet, St. John Honeywood, credit for the law which marked the end of a barbaric age belonged to John Jay,

> Beneath whose guardian care our laws assume
> A mild form, and lose their gothic gloom.[50]

To Greenleaf, the Republican editor, it was "a glorious work of reformation," and while he made no special claims, he might have be-

46. Lincoln, ed., *Messages from the Governors*, II, 348-50; *Journal of the Assembly of N.Y.*, 18th Sess., 13, 108, 113-14, 118-19, 175, 180; "An Humane Elector," *N.-Y. Journal*, Apr. 25, 1795.

47. Lincoln, ed., *Messages from the Governors*, II, 358-66.

48. Samuel Knapp, *The Life of Thomas Eddy* (N.Y., 1834), 56-57; Arthur Ekirch, "Thomas Eddy and the Beginnings of Prison Reform in New York State," *N.Y. History*, 24 (1943), 376, writes that Eddy was "neither a staunch Federalist nor a Jeffersonian."

49. La Rochefoucauld-Liancourt, *Travels*, II, 446-47; *Journal of the Assembly of N.Y.*, 19th Sess., 109-10, 113; *Laws of the State of N.Y.*, 19th Sess., ch. 30.

50. Saint John Honeywood, "On Crimes and Punishments" in *A Poem on Reading President Washington's Address, Declining Re-election to the Presidency* (Albany, 1796), 108.

stowed some credit on Burk, Crady, Keteltas, Governor Clinton, and the Republican reformers.[51]

III

The move for abolition failed in the mid-1790's as it had in 1790. This time, however, it received unmistakable support from Republicans where before it got very little from anti-Federalists. In New York City, Tammany, the Mechanics, and the Sailmakers societies, even "the Republican Natives of Great Britain and Ireland," among whom were workers who had to compete with the labor of slaves and free Negroes, expressed anti-slavery sentiment.[51] The Democratic Society took no stand but several of its leaders were members of the abolition society at Philadelphia and many Republicans were active in the Manumission Society.[52] Virtually all the Republican printers in the city published anti-slavery articles, books, or pamphlets at one time or another. The result was that the Manumission Society gained support among artisans and the poor where previously it had none.[53]

In contrast to the religious benevolence which guided the gentlemen of the Manumission Society, Republican abolitionism was inspired by the new egalitarianism of the mid-1790's. Typically, a New Yorker, observing that the theme of the Republican Independence Day celebration of 1793 was "all men are born free and equal," asked: "amid this grand display of patriotism, philanthropy and liberality, let me ask you, ARE NEGROES MEN?" Another man, horrified at the sight of a Frenchman beating his female slave, wrote, "Good Lord

51. N.Y. *Argus*, July 2, 1796. Elkanah Watson in his Commonplacebook, 27, cited in Flick, *Elkanah Watson*, 113-14, claims credit for a petition which "inundated" the legislature and led to the passage of the bill but the petition he referred to was submitted at the following session, for what purpose it is not clear. *Journal of the Assembly of N.Y.*, 20th Sess., 100, 1796-97.

52. For Tammany, *N.-Y. Journal*, "Extraordinary," Dec. 6, 1794; for the Mechanics, Minutes of the General Society of Mechanics, Society Lib., July 1, 1795; for the Sailmakers, *N.-Y. Journal*, Nov. 14, 1795; for the immigrants, Edgar A. Smith, *Priestley in America, 1794-1804* (Phila., 1920), 37; for the Democrats, Link, *Democratic Republican Societies*, 154, and see the discussion of the Manumission Society above, ch. 18, n.43.

53. Ellis *et al.*, *History of New York*, 186, repeats the traditional view that "the fight for emancipation was led by the Quakers and some of the old landed families whereas white mechanics feared that freedom would swamp them with cheap labor." For summaries of abolitionism which also neglect the Republicans, see Olson, *Negro Slavery in New York*, ch. 10, and McManus, *Negro Slavery in New York*, chs. 10, 11.

deliver us, if this is the language of freedom . . . in vain did our political fathers struggle seven years for a redress of grievances."[54]

Republicanism also contributed to anti-slavery sentiment in the Hudson Valley centers of slaveholding. In Ulster County, in the election of 1792 John Jay's record as past president of the Manumission Society was a handicap. By 1796 abolitionist talk was so rife that Ulster's slaveowners formed a society to capture runaways who picked up the idea from "some mischievous whites" that they were already freed.[55] In the upper Hudson Valley, Barber and Southwick published an edition of the poems of Phyllis Wheatley, the slave poetess, and sandwiched into their country almanac the exchange of letters between the Negro scientist Benjamin Banneker and Thomas Jefferson in which the Virginian expressed happiness at proof "that nature has given to our black brethren talents equal to those of the other colours of men."[56] On the frontier, abolitionism was warmly supported by the Republican-to-be Jedediah Peck of Otsego.

The change of attitude among Republicans was striking in Greenleaf's paper. In contrast to 1790 when articles against the emancipation bill went unanswered, a pro-slavery article in 1796 launched a groundswell of anti-slavery replies. The debate was touched off when "Justice" defended slavery as the only means of support for the small slaveholding farmer in his old age, attacking abolition as a deprivation of the rights of property and an ex post facto law. The first reply came from "A Consistent Democrat," who identified himself as a deist and a member of the Democratic Society. Attacking slavery on the grounds of humanity, reason, and justice, he challenged his fellow democrats to take a stand. "Africanus" responded with a plan for gradual, compensated emancipation, "Humanitas" with an attack on slavery on the grounds that men should live by their own labor, and "Reflection" with an argument in behalf of the equality of man. When "Another Democrat" muddied the waters by calling "Consistent Democrat" an infidel, the latter rejoined: "Infidel" was "one of those knock me down arguments." His religion, he explained, was

54. "A.B.," *N.-Y. Journal*, July 13, 1796; "A Man," N.Y. *Argus*, June 9, 1795.
55. Constitution and Minutes of the Slave Apprehending Society of Shawangunk, Ulster Co., May 21, 1796, N.Y. State Lib.
56. Phillis Wheatley, *Poems on Various Subjects, Religious and Moral* (Albany, 1793). *Poor Richard Revived . . . or Barber and Southwick's Almanac for 1797* (Albany, 1796), 3-13; for other Hudson Valley sentiment see toasts at Lansingburgh, *Albany Register*, July 18, 1796; "To the Humane," *Poughkeepsie Journal*, Apr. 16, 1794; "Philanthropus," *Goshen Repository*, Mar. 3, 1795.

"do unto others as ye would have that they should do unto you" and "let the oppressed go free."

Finally "W" offered a carefully argued rebuttal of the most prevalent pro-slavery rationalizations. To the argument that slaves did not want to be liberated, he answered that the many risks slaves took to be free showed "an innate love of freedom." To the appeal that they were not educated, his response was: educate them. There was a right to take property, he pointed out, if the owner was compensated, as he was, for example, when the government built roads. "I have seen negroes die in the Revolution," he concluded, citing the Declaration of Independence. "Are negroes men? And did God create them?"[57]

When Jay addressed the legislature in 1796, he, like Governor Clinton, was silent on abolition. According to later testimony by his son, William, himself an abolitionist, his father was afraid that a recommendation by him "would enlist the spirit of party in opposition." A few days after the session began, however, "an intimate friend of the governor obtained leave to introduce a bill."[58] The bill was brought in by James Watson, the New York City merchant Federalist. Federalists nevertheless were not united on the issue, a fact historians have ignored. Although Watson supported it "with a great deal of pathos," his Federalist colleagues from Ulster and Otsego spoke at length against "the abolition business."[59] Republicans, too, were divided, but had Federalist leaders whipped their own party into line, abolition might well have passed.

The fundamental issue of freedom was complicated by the problem of whether emancipation should be gradual or immediate, compensated or uncompensated. The Federalist bill called for the gradual freeing of children of slaves and made no provision for compensation.

The opponents failed to prevent this measure from being taken up, but when the substantive issue was presented, defeated it thirty-three to thirty. The committee was then instructed to draw up a bill for compensated emancipation of slave children—which the politician-his-

57. *N.-Y. Journal*: "Justice" and "A Consistent Democrat," Jan. 26; "Africanus," "Humanitas," "A Consistent Democrat," "Reflection," Jan. 29, "Another Democrat," Feb. 2; "A Consistent Democrat," Feb. 5, "W.," Feb. 5, 1796.

58. William Jay, *The Life of John Jay*, 2 vols. (N.Y., 1833), I, 391.

59. James Oliver to Peter Van Gaasbeck, Mar. 5, 1796, Van Gaasbeck Papers, Kingston Senate House; Hammond, *Political Parties*, I, 99; N.Y. *Argus*, Jan. 22, 1796; Jacob Morris, a letter in Cooperstown *Otsego Herald* reprinted in Peck, *The Political Wars of Otsego*, 17-20.

torian Hammond claims was a device to kill the measure. On this the assembly divided dramatically thirty-one to thirty-one and the Federalist speaker, Ebenezer Foote of Ulster, broke the tie, sending the bill back to commitee. The anti-abolitionists rejoiced at this "mortal wound" which killed the bill. On the tie vote anti-abolitionists who wanted no bill at all voted with abolitionists who probably wanted a better bill.[60]

Undismayed, the supporters of abolition renewed their efforts at the following session in the winter of 1796-97. This time Philip Schuyler, to reduce the opposition within Federalist ranks, drafted a substitute proposal "more agreeable to the owners of slaves."[61] The Manumission Society again "waited on" the assemblyman but to no avail.[62]

The basic opposition to emancipation came, as La Rochefoucauld-Liancourt observed, from the "pecuniary interest" in slavery, not only of "the richest and greatest proprietors," he accused, but of several thousand lesser ones. "A most enlightened lawyer" with otherwise "liberal opinions" declared to him "that it would be an attack upon property to declare even the children of female slaves free."[63] The obduracy of the slaveholders notwithstanding, slavery was doomed by the growing political power of the slave-free frontier and the commitment of Republican opinion in the east not only to abolition but to equal treatment of Negroes in education and before the law. In 1797, William Dunlap, the liberal playwright, wrote that "within twenty years the opinion of the injustice of slaveholding has become almost universal."[64] In 1799 the legislature would pass a bill for gradual, uncompensated emancipation under the combined aegis of Republicans and Federalists.

IV

If Republicans contributed to some reforms they gave no evidence

60. James Addison to Peter Van Gaasbeck, Jan. 20, 27, Feb. 14, 1796, Van Gaasbeck Papers, F.D.R. Lib.; *Journal of the Assembly of N.Y.*, 19th Sess., 51, 64-65; N.Y. *Argus*, Feb. 11, 12, 1796.

61. Philip Schuyler to Samuel Jones, Mar. 4, 1797, Schuyler Papers, N.Y. State Lib.

62. Report of the Committee Appointed to Wait on the Representatives of the City of New York, 1796-97, in New York Society for Promoting the Manumission of Slaves Papers, N.-Y. Hist. Soc.

63. La Rochefoucauld-Liancourt, *Travels*, II, 450.

64. William Dunlap, *Diary*, I, 119; for Republican attitudes to Negro education see N.Y. *Argus*, Nov. 16, 1796, and to equal treatment, "Justice," *ibid.*, Dec. 19, 1796.

of responding to the demand for reform of the debtor laws, the system of tenantry, or the state's political institutions.

Individual debtors continued to press their own pathetic cases on the legislature from the debtors' prisons. At Albany the wives of debtors formed a "club of married women" to campaign for reform; the word "lady," they explained, "we have abolished as a term too aristocratic." The Tenth Commandment, they wrote, ordained "Thou shalt not commit adultery," but "thy husband may be taken from thee, even whilst thou art young for ten pounds, ten shillings." It was better to be a widow in fact than to have a husband in the debtors' prison. But except for Tammany, neither the Republican societies nor leaders responded to such pleas.[65] Republicans were inhibited by a fear that the wealthy bankrupts imprisoned in the panic of 1792 like William Duer and Alexander Macomb, whom they called "wolves" and "swindling sharpers," might escape their just deserts if the law was made more lenient. Republicans also took the side of "honest creditors" seeking restitution for losses. Because friends of such wealthy debtors introduced bills with the ulterior motive of aiding them, Republicans were on their guard against debtor legislation.[66]

In 1797 La Rochefoucauld-Liancourt reported "great complaints" because of the unjustness of the debtors' law. "They talk much of amending the law," said the Frenchman, "but it still exists."[67] In 1799 Aaron Burr with the support of Republicans would take a lead in the assembly to liberalize the law.

The Republicans of the mid-1790's reacted somewhat differently to the new wave of tenant protest than had the popular Whigs in the decades of revolution. In the mid-1790's tenant protest was more orderly, more widespread, and better organized than in the rebellions of 1766 and 1777. Its focus was a challenge to the legality of the land titles of the leading landlords, including Philip Schuyler, John and Stephen Van Rensselaer, the upper manor Livingstons, and James Duane.

Late in 1792, following the trial that acquitted the farmers charged

65. "Uxores Populi," *Albany Register*, Oct. 6, 1794; "Petition of the Albany Debtors," Munsell, ed., *Annals of Albany*, III, 118-19. For Tammany, *N.-Y. Journal*, "Extraordinary," Dec. 6, 1794.
66. "A Correspondent," *N.-Y. Journal*, Mar. 11, 1795; "A Citizen," *ibid.*, Mar. 21, 1795; *Journal of the Assembly of N.Y.*, 18th Sess., 25, 111, 148.
67. La Rochefoucauld-Liancourt, *Travels*, II, 444-45.

with killing the Columbia County sheriff,[68] tenants from a number of townships in the county sent petitions to the legislature challenging the validity of Schuyler's land title, asking for an investigation, but got nowhere.[69] In 1794 tenants of John and Walter Livingston of the upper manor sent off a petition claiming that the Livingston land had been fraudulently obtained, rightfully belonged to the state, and should be granted to them. Amazingly a committee brought in a recommendation that a new survey of the land should be taken, but the legislature shelved the suggestion.[70]

At the next session some 250 Livingston tenants were back with another petition to the same effect. Nearly one hundred of them signed with their mark alone, their illiteracy a sign of their humble status.[71] They recited at length how in 1684-1686 Robert Livingston had converted two grants of 2600 acres from Governor Thomas Dongan into a tract of 175,000 acres by "false and fraudulent" surveys, altering the boundaries. Consequently, Livingston's heirs enjoyed a tract "the right whereof is vested in the people of this state." The tenants were willing to acquire the land from the state on "just and equitable" terms. Most of them, they said, held land "upon Terms and Conditions oppressive and burthensome to the last degree," which tended "to degrade your petitioners from the Rank the God of Nature destined all Mankind to live in, to be SLAVES and VASSALS."

An assembly committee reviewing the records concluded that the state had no claim to the Livingston land. The house then dismissed the petition on the grounds that since the family had been in possession of the land for more than one hundred years it would be improper for the state to resume title "for any real or supposed defects."[72] Thus was theft sanctioned by time.

After the legislature rejected them, the tenants "assumed a more menacing aspect," according to the Livingstons. Tenants and others "from neighboring places" "seated themselves" on land in Livingston Manor and seemed "to expect impunity from their numbers." "This spirit soon broke out into acts of violence in forcibly taking possession of the waste and unimproved lands . . . and in the destruction of wood and timber." The landlords brought ejection suits but the officers

68. See above, ch. 1, sec. II, V, and ch. 9, sec. IV.
69. *Journal of the Assembly of N.Y.*, 16th Sess., 54, 83, 179, 219-20.
70. *Ibid.*, 17th Sess., 135, 157; see Dangerfield, *Chancellor Robert R. Livingston*, 12-14.
71. O'Callaghan, ed., *Documentary History of N.Y.*, III, 499-502.
72. *Journal of the Assembly of N.Y.*, 18th Sess., 125-27, 134-35.

who tried to evict the poachers were "insulted, abused and beaten" and threatened with death. In 1798 in response to a petition from the Livingstons, the legislature with only three dissenting votes authorized the governor to use the militia to establish order.[73]

In Albany County to the north the tenants of James Duane and Stephen Van Rensselaer were bitten by the same bug. In 1794 Duane's tenants secretly circulated petitions protesting Duane's location of a road, a move the overseer seems to have suppressed by calling up back rents. The tenant mood was defiant; would "the whole Township act in Subordination to Mr. Duane?" Tenants next challenged Duane's title. Duane apparently held part of his land on the basis of the law of 1710 which permitted mere occupancy of the land to be made the basis of a legal title even though the governor had made no grant. If the challenge went to a trial, Duane confessed to his lawyer, he feared the worst from a jury because "the levelling principle incident to every republic exposes the landholder to much prejudice." Stephen Van Rensselaer's controversy was over the use of the commons lands of his manor which some of his tenants had occupied, only to be ousted. A series of articles appeared in the *Albany Gazette* reviewing the history of his patent, claiming that it was the patroon, not his tenants, who was encroaching on the commons.[74] But Duane and Van Rensselaer, like Schuyler and the Livingstons, survived these diverse challenges.

Federalists inevitably were hostile to tenant protest. Republicans varied. At least one Republican leader from Columbia County, Peter Van Ness, the unsuccessful Republican candidate for Congress, signed the petition of the Livingston tenants. Abraham Yates may have been behind the anonymous newspaper exposé of the Van Rensselaer land title.[75] In the legislature a few Republicans showed a glimmer of recognition of the justice of tenant claims. But the party leaders backed no measures in the legislature and the Republican societies and newspapers were silent.

73. A Petition from John Livingston for himself and infant sons, Feb. 17, 1798, in Assembly Papers, Executive Messages, Box 33, N.Y. State Lib.; John Jay to the Senate, Feb. 22, 1798, in Lincoln, ed., *Messages from the Governors*, II, 411-12. Tenant activity began in 1795, the ejection suits in July 1796. John to Walter Livingston, Mar. 24, 1795, R. R. Livingston Papers, N.-Y. Hist. Soc.

74. Asa Fitch to James Duane, Dec. 26, 1794 cited in Alexander, *James Duane*, 228; James Duane to Peter Van Schaack, July 9, 1796, Van Schaack Papers, Lib. Cong.; "A Citizen," six articles, *Albany Gazette*, Feb. 2, 9, Mar. 6, 20, 27, Apr. 3, 1795.

75. See Abraham Yates Papers, N.Y. Pub. Lib., for a lengthy History of Rensselaerswyck, which also reviews the history of the land title.

Governor Clinton was responsive only to a peripheral issue, the reform of the courts. Shortly after the Livingston tenants sent their first appeal to the assembly, the Democratic Society at nearby Canaan petitioned the legislature to reform the legal system, claiming that "the timely removal of grievances" was "the best preventative of disturbances." They pointed to the high salaries of judges, "the extraordinary delays of the decisions," "the intricate and antiquated formalities . . . the obsolete phraseology" of the law, and "the vast accumulation of books required, many of them written in dark ages and corrupt government"—all these things perplexed the common man. To reform such abuses the society recommended strict economy in salaries, more "simple and concise modes" of conducting trials, and "a new code of laws and rules in plain English, full concise and unequivocal."[76] Governor Clinton very likely had this in mind when in his next message he laconically asked the legislature to revise "our system of jurisprudence."[77] Nothing, however, came of this reformist effort to eliminate grievances that might lead to further tenant radicalism.

Revision of the undemocratic political institutions of New York was even less of an issue among Republicans. After the canvassers' decision brought to light a variety of unsavory political practices in the 1792 gubernatorial election, a number of electoral reforms were introduced in the 1793 legislature. Of three measures proposed, the most important would have broadened the suffrage to allow mortgage holders to vote. Introduced by Beriah Palmer, a Republican of Saratoga, it lacked united Republican support and was defeated in the Federalist assembly by a two-to-one vote. A second measure, to subdivide the large senatorial districts and the county-wide assembly districts and thereby provide for more direct local representation, also lost. A third to require election inspectors to be freeholders—and thereby less exposed to landlord pressure—fared better but was also defeated.[78] Many Republicans supported one or more of these measures, but no one made them a public issue.

Republican identification with the status quo was even more apparent in their defense of the Council of Appointment.[79] In 1794, in

76. N.-Y. Journal, Oct. 4, 1794. The resolution was passed July 11. The Livingston tenant petition was submitted in March.

77. Lincoln, ed., Messages from the Governors, II, 350.

78. Journal of the Assembly of N.Y., 17th Sess., 95-97, 100, 102-3. No popular discussion of these measures was uncovered.

79. See Hugh M. Flick, "The Council of Appointment in New York State, . . . 1777-1822," New York History, 15 (1934), 253-65.

the first legislature in which they had a safe majority, Federalists moved with lightning speed on the first day of the session to capture control of the council, induced by the prospect of naming one of their stalwarts, Egbert Benson, to the supreme court. "If it had been delayed only for a day, perhaps for an hour," said Schuyler, the Clintonians would have gotten the post. DeWitt Clinton was startled at their "spirit of persecution" which bordered "upon savage barbarity."[80]

A touchy constitutional question arose: who had the power to nominate, the governor alone, or the four senators elected by the assembly?[81] Did the governor offer nominations for the approval of the council, or did the council have a concurrent right to nominate as well as approve candidates? The Federalist majority on the council insisted on the latter and over Governor Clinton's protest appointed Benson, who promptly took office. They also insisted on the right to enlarge the number of local judges and justices of the peace; in fact, they were "properly disposed to grant anything and everything to our friends," one joyous party man reported.[82]

Clinton defended not only the exclusive power of the executive to make appointments but the principle that officeholding should be independent of party allegiance or political pressure. The governor alone, he maintained, was responsible for the execution of the laws; therefore he alone could decide whether additional judicial officers were needed and whether incumbents deserved to be continued. Appointees, it was true, held office at the pleasure of the Council but if displacement by "a capricious arbitrary pleasure" were allowed, the result would be "to deprive men of their offices because they have too much independence of spirit to support measures they suppose injurious to the community."[83] As soon as Jay became governor he asked the legislature for a declaratory law interpreting the ambiguous wording of the state constitution. Jacob Morris, an Otsego Federalist, introduced a bill to give the governor the exclusive right of nomina-

80. *Journal of the Assembly of N.Y.*, 17th Sess., 5; Philip Schuyler to Nicholas Low, Feb. 23, 1794, Schuyler Papers, Box 2, N.Y. State Lib.; DeWitt Clinton to "My dear cousin" [Cornelia Clinton?], Jan. 8, 1794, DeWitt Clinton Papers, N.-Y. Hist. Soc.

81. Hammond, *Political Parties*, I, 79-92.

82. John Addison to Peter Van Gaasbeck, Feb. 15, 1794, C. E. Elmendorph to Van Gaasbeck, Jan. 8, 1794, Van Gaasbeck Papers, Kingston Senate House.

83. For statements by the governor and the three Federalist members of the council, N.Y. *Herald*, Oct. 13, 1794, condensed in Hammond, *Political Parties*, I, 83-85.

tion, which was tabled by a combination of Federalists and Republicans.[84]

The most undemocratic feature of the state's political system—the property qualification for suffrage—drew only a few scattered protests in the mid-1790's and for understandable reasons. The electoral census of 1795 showed that there were 26,000 more voters in 1795 than in 1790, an increase of almost 63 per cent, making a total of 64,000. The increase was in both the more propertied £100 freeholder electorate and the 40-shilling renters. The total electorate in New York City, for example, went up from about 4000 to 7700.[85] Thus even if the proportion of eligible voters to adult white males remained the same, the increase in numbers took the edge off the restrictive nature of the franchise. The legislature, moreover, reapportioned new seats readily.[86] The political experience of Republicans did not suggest to them that they would profit by expanding the electorate. Thus it is not surprising that there was little criticism of the property requirement to vote until 1797 and even then it was confined to a segment of the movement in New York City.[87]

V

The state government gave somewhat less aid to private enterprise in the mid-1790's than earlier, partly because in the midst of the prosperity of the period, as Clinton told the legislature, "the objects of pointed legislative attention are necessarily restricted,"[88] partly because there was a reaction against the largesse of the early 1790's. One group of Republicans became critics of the canal companies and Federalists assumed the uneasy role of critics of favoritism to land speculators.

The legislature, under Federalist control, continued the Clintonian policy of aiding manufacturers with a seeming nonpartisanship. When James Caldwell's tobacco, starch, and cocoa mill at Albany burned down, the legislature responded with a large loan and artisans donated

84. Hammond, *Political Parties*, I, 97-98.
85. See Appendix, Table 3.
86. See account of the assembly in N.Y. *Argus*, Apr. 8, 1796.
87. Hedges, *An Oration*, 12. For the first extensive public discussion of suffrage extension in New York City see in N.Y. *Time Piece*: "On Some of the Principles of American Republicanism," May 5; "Political Greed," Aug. 21; "Communication," Oct. 6 and "Universal Justice," Nov. 10, 1797. See the account of the assembly, N.Y. *Argus*, Apr. 8, 1796.
88. Lincoln, ed., *Messages from the Governors*, II.

their labor to rebuild the factory.[89]   The Hamilton Manufacturing Company at Albany, a glass factory, received a charter of incorporation, a loan which was interest-free the first three years, and tax exemption as well as exemption for its workers from highway, jury, or militia service.[90] James Caldwell was a Federalist, and the glass factory, in spite of its name, was owned and directed by two leading Republicans, Elkanah Watson and Jeremiah Van Rensselaer.

The state also maintained its policy of granting charters of incorporation, but it took pains as before to prevent either a monopoly or excessive powers by its grant. Thus it chartered the Hamilton Manufacturing Company in spite of objections in Albany to "exclusive privileges granted to any one class or description of citizens."[91] But it rejected a request for a charter for a New York City insurance company in response to a cry of "speculation, aristocracy and monopoly" from the existing brokers.[92] Federalists in the legislature were somewhat less hospitable to chartering mechanics' societies than were the Clintonians. In rejecting requests from the Albany and Lansingburgh mechanics, a Federalist committee condemned the groups for "separating citizens into classes" which "may tend to hostility."[93]

The canal companies chartered in 1792 with enthusiastic bipartisan support became objects of criticism when they returned to the legislature to ask for more power and more money. Although influential anti-Federalists were stockholders and members of the board of directors of both the Western and Northern Inland Navigation Companies, the president, Philip Schuyler, controlled both. Because the expected number of stockholders failed to materialize, ownership was vested in a few hundred men, the largest of whom were Federalist landholders who hoped to boost the values of their frontier holdings.[94]

89. La Rochefoucauld-Liancourt, *Travels*, I, 371-73; for loans to manufacturers, see *Laws of the State of N.Y.*, 18th Sess., chs. 40, 45; 19th Sess., ch. 34.

90. Flick, *Elkanah Watson*, 133-36; Hamilton Manufacturing Company, Account Book and Memoranda, and Watson to Nathanial Laurance, Feb. 6, 1796, Watson Papers, N.-Y. Hist. Soc.; Watson to Rufus King, Jan. 22, 1794, King, ed., *Correspondence of Rufus King*, I, 543.

91. "A Communication," *Albany Register*, Apr. 7, 1797.

92. John Delafield to Rufus King, Feb. 17, 1794; Nicholas Low to King, Feb. 19, 1794, King, ed., *Correspondence of Rufus King*, I, 544; Seth Johnson to Andrew Craigie, Feb. 17, 1794, Craigie Papers, Box 9, Amer. Antiq. Soc.

93. *Journal of the Assembly of N.Y.*, 18th Sess. (Feb. 16, 1795), 62; *Albany Gazette*, Feb. 27, 1795, for both the petition and report. The legislature granted a charter, by contrast, to the German Society of New York, whose request had been rejected in 1786. It was liberal in allowing library associations to be incorporated. *Laws of the State of N.Y.*, 18th Sess., ch. 10, 19th Sess., ch. 43.

94. For the business history, Miller, "Private Enterprise in Inland Navigation,"

Before they had dug a spade of earth, the companies precipitated their first controversy in December 1792 by asking the legislature to increase the amount of land they could acquire on either side of their route and to make legal acquisition easier. The legislature obliged, granting them the right to appropriate land up to one hundred feet on either side of any works they might erect and to begin operations without obtaining permission of the owner of the property or a writ of *ad quod damnum*.[95] The Council of Revision, however, vetoed the bill on two grounds. First, it was "subversive of the rights of private property" for it divested "the proprietor of his land in cases not indispensably necessary for the attainment of an object of public utility." The legislature should have imposed restrictions on the company guaranteeing that property taken from individuals would be used only to advance "those interests of the company, in which its private emolument is indispensably connected with the effectual promotion of the public good." Secondly, by allowing the company to begin operations before a writ was granted, the law sanctioned a "destruction of timber and improvements before proper precautions have been taken to ascertain the amount of injury sustained."[96] The assembly overrode the council's veto forty-seven to nine, over the objections of a small group of Republicans led by Assemblymen Comstock and Palmer of Saratoga County and David Gelston of New York City, a stockholder in the Western Company, later a president of the Democratic Society.[97]

The new grant of power set off a clamor in the counties the canals intended to cut through. At the next sitting of the legislature, in 1793, Comstock, fortified with petitions from Saratoga to the west and Rensselaer and Washington to the east, brought in a bill to limit the amount of land the company might take and its right to occupy without consent.[98] Schuyler was incensed, convinced that his trouble came from "political opponents" influenced by "corrupt motives." There was no more danger from the canals, he explained, than from highway companies. Furthermore, the directors were "not so devoid of good sense as wantonly to take any man's property." At the first

New York History, 31 (1950), 401-4, and Davis, *Essays in History of Corporations*, II, 157-67; for Federalist dominance, Fox, *Decline of the Aristocracy*, 150-53.

95. *Laws of the State of N.Y.*, 16th Sess., ch. 8.

96. "Objections by The Council of Revision . . . ," Dec. 19, 1792, Lincoln, ed., *Messages from the Governors*, II, 329-30.

97. *Journal of the Assembly of N.Y.*, 16th Sess., 79.

98. *Ibid.*, 177, 185, 215.

reading Comstock's bill failed. Schuyler armed Assemblyman Josiah Hoffman of New York City with a lengthy defense of the company's need for a 100-foot right of way.[99] The upshot was a compromise: the company was limited to twenty feet on either side of the canal except at the locks where it might take up to 100 feet, and it had to give thirty days' notice to a property owner before entering his land.[100]

Opposition to even this limited grant mounted. Jeremiah Van Rensselaer, the Albany anti-Federalist, resigned from the Western Company, claiming that it was violating its charter. Mayor Abraham Yates of Albany, writing as "Sidney," insisted there was no power "to take the property from one and give it to another for private emolument."[101] There was "so great a clamour" against the Northern Company, said Schuyler, that its operations were obstructed. When landowners demanded damages in the courts, local juries granted them.[102]

The public furor contributed to a blowup on the board of directors of the Western Company which led to the ouster of Elkanah Watson. Watson had been almost as important as Schuyler in promoting the venture. The board appointed him to explore and lay out the route, using the knowledge he had gained from seeing European canals. Schuyler, without technical knowledge, insisted on acting as engineer; there was a dispute over using brick or wood to construct the locks and over hiring a foreign engineer. Watson was "turned out of the directors," he claimed, for "not being a tool of Schuyler" and for opposing his "infamous maneuvers to make the canals subservient to his clandestine and detestable intrigues and party views." At the same time Watson also broke with the Bank of Albany.[103]

When the companies turned to the assembly in 1794 for financial aid, they provoked another flurry of Republican dissent. Both firms were already in desperate straits; in the glow of enthusiasm the promoters had grossly underestimated costs. They needed £12,500 and could not count on their own stockholders to raise it. Governor

99. Philip Schuyler to J.B. Schuyler, Jan. 23, 1793, Schuyler Papers, N.Y. Pub. Lib.; Schuyler to Josiah Hoffman, Feb. 26, 1793, Schuyler Papers, N.Y. State Lib.
100. *Laws of the State of N.Y.*, 16th Sess., ch. 49.
101. *N.-Y. Journal*, Feb. 20, July 24, 1793; "Sidney," July 18, 1793, "Rough Hewer" notebook, Abraham Yates Papers, N.Y. Pub. Lib.; "Sidney," *Albany Register*, Mar. 2, 10, 1794.
102. "To the Stockholders of the Western Inland Navigation Company . . . by Philip Schuyler, June 7, June 17, 1793 [in two parts]," broadside, Schuyler Canal Papers, N.Y. Pub. Lib.
103. Flick, *Elkanah Watson*, 165-67, citing Watson's Commonplacebook, N.Y. State Lib.; Watson, *History*, 62-63.

Clinton recommended aid and Jonathan Havens brought in a sympathetic report. But the Republican critics were unimpressed. The legislative battle was complicated by a difference over the form aid should take. Federalists were divided between a stock subscription and an outright grant. Republicans like Havens favored a loan, while Republicans like Comstock and Palmer opposed aid in any shape. The result was a stalemate and the issue was put over to the next session.[104]

Meanwhile, the Western Company limped along. In 1794 its wooden locks started to decay even before the canal opened. A year later a visitor reported that "progress is slow." Of the scores of newly arrived Irish laborers hired by Schuyler, a good number were former convicts who did not endear themselves to the local populace or to Schuyler. Moreover, his day laborers conducted a strike when he hired other men on a piece-rate basis.[105]

In the assembly in 1795 opponents succeeded in postponing consideration of the company's request for aid until the tag end of the session. After the House defeated Havens' motion for a loan against the companies' real estate as security, it voted to subscribe to 200 shares of stock worth £5000 in each company, but not until Comstock and Palmer had exhausted every parliamentary tactic of obstruction.[106]

In 1796 shortly after the Western Company opened its locks, there were complaints from farmers and merchants about "oppressive" tolls; the toll collectors were subjected to the "grossest abuse." Later on the complaints were expressed in petitions to the legislature.[107] In time, however, the Western Company became moderately successful. But in 1797 the Northern Company had to be abandoned altogether, a complete failure, with a loss of over $100,000 to its investors.[108] The howls of anguish can be imagined. Elkanah Watson, who attributed his break with Schuyler to the "deadly warfare" over the canals, left

104. Lincoln, ed., *Messages from the Governors*, II, 335; *Journal of the Assembly of N.Y.*, 17th Sess., 133-34, 160-61.

105. Strickland, Journal, 296-97, N.-Y. Hist. Soc.; La Rochefoucauld-Liancourt, *Travels*, I, 362.

106. *Journal of the Assembly of N.Y.*, 18th Sess., 137-40; *Laws of the State of N.Y.*, 18th Sess., ch. 38; S. Barker to Ebenezer Foote, Mar. 24, 1795, Foote Papers, N.Y. State Lib.

107. Miller, "Private Enterprise in Inland Navigation," *New York History*, 31 (1950), 404; see also James Kent, Travel Journal, 1798, Kent Papers, Lib. Cong.

108. Davis, *Essays in History of Corporations*, II, 172.

Albany to escape "persecution" by Schuyler and his "satellites."[109] His case was extreme yet there obviously was more "politics" in New York's first venture in promoting canals than historians have allowed.

In land speculation Federalists donned the cloak of reformers. After the Federalist clamor in 1792 over the extravagant disposition of the public domain, the land commissioners, composed of Governor Clinton and his appointees, were more cautious. In 1792-93 they made fifteen grants totaling 245,000 acres, only one of which was relatively large and that at a high price. Nonetheless in 1794, in the first legislature over which they had complete control, Federalists set about "overhawling the land office," as one assemblyman put it. A detailed report revealed that grantees owed some £85,000 to the state and that payments were overdue on sixteen large contracts, including a few held by the largest Federalist speculators. The legislature promptly suspended further sales to those who owed money and gave the delinquents until July 1794 to meet their obligations. The 2,000,000 acres still in the public domain would be sold only in small lots at a minimum of 6 shillings an acre.[110]

Speculators at first were alarmed; Colonel William Smith set off on behalf of several men "to use his influence against the business."[111] But as Alexander Macomb and Daniel McCormick explained to their partner, William Constable, who was still in Europe, the results were not nearly as bad as they might have been. "Attempts were made," wrote Macomb, "to reclaim all the land sold where there was any failure in payment," but these did not pass. And the new policies on unsold land, wrote McCormick, "do not injure us but rather the contrary." The high price being asked would bid up the price on their own land. Moreover, no grants would be made in 1794 because the legislature did not provide funds for a surveyor.[112]

However, Federalists had hardly turned their backs on favors to speculators. A case in point is the plea of the European land companies to lift the legislature's restriction on aliens holding land in New York state except through an intermediary. On behalf of the

109. Elkanah Watson, Journal, Box 2, VIII, inside cover and 438-440, Watson Papers, N.Y. State Lib.

110. William Van Ingen to Henry Glen, Feb. 5, 1794, Glen Papers, N.Y. State Hist. Assoc.; "Report of a Committee," *Journal of the Assembly of N.Y.*, 17th Sess., 54-55, 56, 58-59, 114-17, 149.

111. Seth Johnson to Andrew Craigie, Feb. 13, 1794, Craigie Papers, Amer. Antiq. Soc.

112. Macomb to Constable, Apr. 16, 1794; McCormick to Constable, Apr. 19, 1794, Constable Pierrepont Papers, N.Y. Pub. Lib.

Holland Land Company, Theophile Cazenove retained a galaxy of influential Federalists as lobbyists in the legislature: Herman LeRoy, Samuel Jones, Egbert Benson, and Alexander Hamilton. Their opposition stemmed from several sources: "some of our great landholders and speculators" who wanted to retain the ban in order to keep out competition;[113] demagogic Federalists like Speaker James Watson of New York City who expanded on the dangers of foreigners profiting at the expense of the poor, and of course the democratic prejudices of the average legislator. "The motives and Reasons against permitting wealthy Foreigners to hold large tracts of land," Egbert Benson lamented, "will always and equally continue to operate on Bodies of men composed as our legislatures are."[114]

In 1793 Cazenove got nowhere. In 1794 a bill passed the Senate only to fail in the Assembly. In 1796 a measure got through both houses permitting aliens to hold land for a seven-year period.[115] It passed only because of "my personal influence," said Benson, and there was not "the most remote expectation" of doing better. At this juncture Hamilton and Philip Schuyler came up with a scheme to serve both Hamilton's dissatisfied client and Schuyler's foundering Western Inland Navigation Company. Earlier the Holland Company had indicated that it was willing to invest $300,000 in land development; it also had an obvious stake in the success of a canal to the west. In 1797 the legislature passed a law giving the Holland Company the right to hold land for twenty years provided it either made a loan or purchased stock in Schuyler's company to the tune of $250,000. After the bottom fell out of the land market in 1796, however, Cazenove had cooled to a large investment and found fault with the terms of the bill. The "deal" fell through.[116]

In 1798 the Dutch land agent switched to Aaron Burr who together with Benson wangled a bill through the legislature, after mollifying disgruntled supporters of the canal. Cazenove gave Burr a

113. Samuel Ward to William Constable, Apr. 17, 1794, *ibid.*

114. Theophile Cazenove to Alexander Hamilton and Egbert Benson, May 29, 1797; Benson to Hamilton, Aug. 4, 1797; Hamilton to Cazenove, Oct. 14, 1797, Holland Land Company Papers, Gemeentearchief, Amsterdam, Netherlands, cited with the kind permission of W. J. Van Hoboken, Director of the City Archives, Amsterdam.

115. *Laws of the State of N.Y.*, 16th Sess., ch. 26; 19th Sess., ch. 58; 20th Sess., ch. 36.

116. Paul Evans, *The Holland Land Company* (Buffalo, 1924), 204-14, has the most complete account; for Hamilton's role see Schachner, *Alexander Hamilton*, 373-74, an episode entirely omitted in Mitchell, *Alexander Hamilton*, II.

"loan" of $5500 and later cancelled a $20,000 penalty Burr owed for defaulting on payment for the purchase of 100,000 acres of company land. Burr dispensed at least $5000 more in "legal fees" to such Federalist worthies as Josiah Hoffman, the state attorney-general, and Thomas Morris who managed the bill through the Senate. The Dutch company ended up with perpetual land rights hedged in by a number of restrictions.[117]

Despite these brazen examples of favoritism, Federalists retained their public image as advocates of a pro-settler policy on the unallocated portions of the public domain. When New York acquired a new tract from Indian tribes in 1795, the Federalist legislature provided that 160,000 acres were to be sold in 250-acre lots for a down payment of £10 with ten years to pay the balance, the first meaningful credit extension.[118] In the same spirit, the legislators showed solicitude for squatters who petitioned for the right to purchase state land.[119] And most strikingly, early in 1796 with one and a half million acres remaining in the public domain, Philip Schuyler presented a report to the legislature proposing sales in small tracts on extended credit to settlers alone.[120] He thus had the best of all possible worlds: political champion of the settler, private dealer with alien land companies. In many ways he was a fit symbol of the limitations of the Federalist as land reformer.

The reform movement in New York in the 1790's, this summary suggests, was by no means exclusively Republican; it was bipartisan and nonpartisan. A reform wing clearly existed in the Republican party which had an impact in correcting what Dr. Mitchill called the "glaring deformities" of the day. The reform movement was also limited. Neither Republicans nor Federalists were interested in challenging the economic status quo represented by tenantry or the political status quo represented by the property requirements for suffrage. But the Republican "spirit of reformation" contributed to writing a minor chapter in the history of reform in New York and would lead to still others before long.

117. *Laws of the State of N.Y.*, 21st Sess., ch. 72; Schachner, *Aaron Burr*, 154-59.
118. *Albany Register*, Sept. 18, 1795.
119. For examples, *Laws of the State of N.Y.*, 18th Sess.
120. Philip Schuyler, *Remarks on the Revenue of the State of New York* (Albany, 1796), 16.

CHAPTER 25

State and Nation: Politics,

Congressional and Presidential

1796-1797

———•———

The elections at the end of 1796 measured the strength of the New York Republican movement in the politics of the nation and of their own state as the second Washington administration drew to a close. In the contest for the presidency and vice-presidency, the New Yorkers were a force to be reckoned with. In the congressional elections they had all they could do to defend the six seats they had taken in 1794 against the continuing Federalist counteroffensive.

I

By mid-May 1796 it was "generally understood," as James Madison reported, "that the President will retire" and that there would be a contest for the presidency in which Jefferson would be "the object on one side Adams apparently on the other."[1] Republican leaders in all states seem to have agreed on Jefferson, a choice which met with the approval of rank-and-file Republicans in New York. Even before the presidency loomed, he was referred to by a speaker at the Democratic Society of New York City as "the stable uncorruptible Jefferson" and by a writer in Greenleaf's paper as "undoubtedly the first

1. Madison to Monroe, May 14, 1796, in Hunt, ed., *Writings of Madison*, VI, 301.

[546]

political character in America."[2] On Independence Day 1796, with his candidacy in the offing, Tammany offered a toast to: "Thomas Jefferson—may his integrity and talents again illumine the councils of his country," and Republicans elsewhere singled him out for praise.[3]

The attention of Republican leaders therefore focused, as it had in 1792, on the nomination of a vice-presidential candidate and once again New Yorkers were favored for the same "geographic" reasons. In May Republican senators held an acrimonious caucus at Philadelphia. Aaron Burr and Robert R. Livingston seem to have had more support than Pierce Butler of South Carolina or John Langdon of New Hampshire. Livingston was well known for his record on foreign policy, most recently for the "Cato" articles, and his brother Edward was the toast of Republicans for his fight to hold up the treaty in the House. Burr, although known for his opposition to the treaty, was considered "unsettled in his politics."[4] Although the caucus did not reach a decision, a month later, the knowledgeable Beckley wrote Madison as if a Jefferson-Burr ticket would be widely acceptable: "the whole body" of Pennsylvania Republicans "are decided in favor of Burr." A plan was proposed by some Pennsylvanians "to play off Chancellor Livingston for V.p. upon New York and New Jersey, as the most likely means of a successful diversion there"; Livingston was "however strongly in favor of Burr's election." Beckley thought victory "morally certain" for Jefferson and Burr if "no great schism happens in Virginia."[5]

How the New York leaders felt is difficult to say—the record is meager for all participants. It is certain that George Clinton was not "the favorite candidate of New Yorkers," as Jabez Hammond wrote; ill, in semi-retirement, stigmatized as Genêt's father-in-law, Clinton knew better than to have hopes for high office in 1796.[6] Chancellor Livingston kept himself out of the race; he was not the man to risk a personal political contest unless he was guaranteed success. In

2. N.Y. *Argus*, Oct. 13, 1795, Jan. 26, 1796; see the pseudonym, "Jefferson," *N.-Y. Journal*, Nov. 18, 1795, reprinted from *Newburgh Packet.*

3. *N.-Y. Journal*, July 8, 12, 22, 1796.

4. William Smith to Ralph Izard, May 18, 1796, Ulrich B. Phillips, ed., "South Carolina Federalist Correspondence, 1789-1797," *American Historical Review*, 14 (1909), 780.

5. William Smith to Ralph Izard, *ibid.*; Stephen G. Kurtz, *The Presidency of John Adams: The Collapse of Federalism, 1795-1800* (Phila., 1957), ch. 4; Beckley to Madison, June 20, 1796, Madison Papers, N.Y. Pub. Lib.

6. Hammond, *Political Parties*, I, 103; Spaulding, *George Clinton*, 218, is all surmise.

September, Federalists in New Jersey reported that he "has been talked of" as a candidate—the diversion Beckley spoke of—but this hardly required his permission.[7] The New York Republican leaders, with Clinton and Livingston out of the race, certainly put up no objection to Burr. He had demonstrated his devotion to the cause by his role in the Senate against Jay's Treaty and in defense of the Democratic societies, and had the best prospects of corralling dissident Federalist electors.

In mid-September Washington issued his Farewell Address, confirming his retirement and bringing both the presidential and vice-presidential races into the open. The address with its Hamiltonian tone inspired New York Federalists to poetry, but it stirred New York Republicans not at all.[8] Barber and Southwick, the Republican printers at Albany, brought out an edition of the address[9] but in Republican eyes Washington left the chief office a partisan president.

Burr as always was energetic in promoting his own candidacy. He had not been "promised" the vice-presidency by the Virginia leaders in 1792, as his biographer contends. In fact his abandonment by Virginia Republicans then convinced him that he would have to win their backing in 1796. Burr certainly had this in mind when he visited Jefferson at Monticello in October 1795. Whatever the two talked about, Burr was mending a political fence. Like the Jefferson-Madison jaunt to New York in 1791, Burr's trip set Federalist tongues awagging. In the heat of the presidential campaign in 1796, Virginia Republicans had to issue denials that Burr and Jefferson had mapped "rash and violent measures" for Republicans to pursue in Congress.[10]

Burr was also working his Federalist flank. In February 1796 he dined with Ebenezer Foote, number two man in the Ulster County Federalist machine, who found him as usual "a mighty cunning fellow."[11] In the summer and fall he traveled for six weeks through

7. Jonathan Dayton to Oliver Wolcott, Sept. 15, 1796, in George Gibbs, ed., *Memoirs of the Administrations of Washington and John Adams*, 2 vols. (N.Y. 1846), I, 382-83; Dangerfield, *Chancellor Robert R. Livingston*, Pt. 4, ch. 2, omits this election.

8. Honeywood, *Poem on Reading President Washington's Address*.

9. *The Address of His Excellency, George Washington, President of the United States: On His Declining to be a Candidate for the office of President at the Ensuing Election* (Albany, 1796).

10. Cunningham, *The Jeffersonian Republicans*, 86-87; Malone, *Jefferson and His Time*, III, 276-77; Schachner, *Aaron Burr*, 141-44.

11. Ebenezer Foote to Peter Van Gaasbeck, Feb. 14, 1796, Van Gaasbeck Papers, Kingston Senate House.

New England in search of Federalist electors. By mid-October Beckley, concluding that Burr's efforts "more directed to himself than anybody else," suggested to Madison that Virginia arrange to throw away electoral votes to prevent him from coming in ahead of Jefferson. "Would it not be prudent," he asked, "to vote one-half of Virginia for Clinton?"[12] Beckley thus helped create the "schism" he had warned about.

Meanwhile, New York Federalists were playing the same game with John Adams, their ostensible first choice. Hamilton and King first sought Patrick Henry of Virginia, the popular Whig and former anti-Federalist—a choice that harked back to their experience in New York in 1789 when they ran the safe anti-Federalist, Robert Yates, for governor. Failing to get Henry, they settled on Thomas Pinckney, the former minister to England, resolving to throw away Adams' votes in his favor.[13] New York Federalists were divided over Adams. To commercial-minded, conservative men like Hamilton and Schuyler, he was too republican and too agrarian. To independent-minded Federalists like James and Moss Kent, he was too monarchical, while to others like the Yankee migrant Noah Webster, he was just right.[14]

When the state legislature convened early in November to choose electors, John Jay set the tone with an encomium to Washington, "the father and ornament of his country," and the assembly followed suit, hailing his career as "unequalled in the annals of the world." To no one's surprise the legislature chose twelve electors reported by Greenleaf to be "TRULY FEDERALIST," who would cast their ballots a month later. Some Republicans were hopeful of swaying them by "personal attachments" but George Clinton, labeling them all "tools of faction," predicted a unanimous vote for Adams.[15]

Republicans debated the candidates and the issues in the papers.[16] They began on the same theme stressed elsewhere: the difference in

12. Beckley to Madison, Oct. 15, 1796, Madison Papers, N.Y. Pub. Lib.

13. Schachner, *Alexander Hamilton*, 355-59; Watson, ed., *Memoirs of Elkanah Watson*, 397-400.

14. Kent, ed., *Memoirs of James Kent*, 88-97; *Poughkeepsie Journal*, May 21, 1796; Moss to James Kent, Dec. 10, 1796, Kent Papers, Lib. Cong.; Noah Webster, Jr. [Aristedes, pseud.], *A Letter to General Hamilton . . .* (N.Y., 1800); R. R. Livingston to William Wilson, Dec. 29, 1796, Wilson Papers, Clements Lib.

15. Lincoln, ed., *Messages from the Governors*, II, 300; *Journal of the Assembly of N.Y.*, 20th Sess., 1st meet., 22; *N.-Y. Journal*, Nov. 8, 1796; George Clinton to Michael Lieb, Nov. 19, 1796, Clinton Papers, N.Y. State Lib.

16. For the national campaign, Cunningham, *The Jeffersonian Republicans*, 94-109; Malone, *Jefferson and His Time*, III, 279-84.

the fundamental political philosophies of Jefferson and Adams. In lengthy articles "Polybius" (very likely George Clinton, Jr.) dissected John Adams' *Defence of the Constitution* and "Lucius" (possibly Melancton Smith) actually reprinted a piece from the 1792 campaign which portrayed Adams as an advocate of "kings, lords and commons." Jefferson, in contrast, was offered as "a true Republican" and as someone who, on the basis of his knowledge of commerce and agriculture demonstrated as Secretary of State, would unite both interests.[17]

Republicans also focused on the New York Federalists. To qualify as a Federalist, a satirist explained, one had to "clear [an] estate of 500 pounds a year . . . unless you have money you cannot help us at elections or buy a single vote." Bitterly he catalogued the pressure tactics of the "aristocracy of wealth" in the year gone by: "The Republican debtor was terrified by the menace of a tory or British creditor, the Republican tradesmen were denied the favor of a ministerial and prejudiced bank; and the Republican mechanic and laborer was too often obliged to suppress his private feelings and relinquish his personal independence to retain the employment and patronage of the haughty courtier and supercilious Bashaw." Hamilton was the arch-villain, an "artful and designing man." Had he not said of the Constitution in 1787 that he "did not like it but that he signed it because a good one might be made of it?" In his effort to "improve the constitution" Hamilton had obtained "a national debt, a funding system, stock jobbing and speculation"; but, this Republican warned Hamilton, "you have not triumphed yet!"[18]

Republicans ended the campaign with an impassioned plea on foreign policy. Late in October, Pierre Adet, Fauchet's successor, informed the United States that henceforth France would treat all American ships "in the same manner as they suffer the English to treat them." In mid-November he suspended his functions as minister, appealing to Americans to repudiate Jay's Treaty and fulfill the French alliance of 1778. It was the Genêt issue all over again with even more dangerous stakes. The New York Republicans, true to their pro-French leanings, responded as they had three years before. Appealing directly "to the Merchants and Traders of America,"

17. In *N.-Y. Journal:* "Polybius," No. 1 and 2, Nov. 3, Nov. 7; "Lucius," Nov. 4, 1796, "A Correspondent," *Albany Register,* Oct. 24, 1796.

18. "The Change," a series of four articles, *N.-Y. Journal,* Oct. 28, Nov. 1, 8, 11, 1796; for another summary statement see "No Trimmer," *Newburgh Packet,* Dec. 6, 1796.

"Juno" pointed out that if their commerce was "on the brink of anhiliation" they had Hamilton ("Camillus") to blame. They had allowed him to frighten them into supporting Jay's Treaty by the threat of war; the French Directory and its current policy was the result. They had been "duped" and must now realize that only a "change in both men and manners" in high office would save them. "A Constitutional Federalist" pleaded for an end to "confidence" in Britain, rehearsing a long catalog of her "cruelties and depredations," argued for the "strictest neutrality" consistent with the treaty with France, "that generous nation," and ended with an appeal for the election of "the patriotic Jefferson and the no less patriotic Burr," warning against Federalist "artifice" to divide the ticket.[19]

Early in December New York's electors cast twelve ballots for Adams and Pinckney. Republicans had not swayed them. Neither had Thomas Witbeck, Burr's Federalist supporter, who "was in hopes to have obtained a few votes for my friend Burr so as to have linked him with Adams."[20] And Hamilton apparently was not willing to risk so transparent a tactic as dropping votes for Adams in his own state. By the end of December, the reports from other states trickled in.

When the electoral vote was compiled the score was Adams 71, Jefferson 68, Pinckney 59, Burr 30, and a scattering of 48 votes for nine others, including 7 for George Clinton and 5 for John Jay. Jefferson had lost the main prize by a narrow margin. Burr had been "cut" by the Virginians, Pinckney by the Adams supporters. Virginia cast twenty ballots for Jefferson and only one for Burr, throwing away fifteen on Samuel Adams. Burr picked up half of his votes from four other southern states, half from the successful Republicans of Pennsylvania, and none in New England.[21] As far as the future was concerned, the vote revealed that both parties were divided, the Federalists between Hamiltonians and Adams-ites, the Republicans between Jeffersonians and Burr-ites. In 1801 both the Virginia Republicans and the Hamiltonian Federalists would reap a blighted harvest from the seeds they had sown in 1796.

II

The New York representatives who came up for re-election late

19. In *N.-Y. Journal*: the Adet correspondence to the Secretary of State, Nov. 23; "Juno," Nov. 29, Dec. 6; "A Constitutional Federalist," Nov. 29, 1796.
20. Thomas Witbeck to John Williams, Dec. 10, 1796, Williams Papers, III, N.Y. State Lib.
21. Hammond, *Political Parties*, I, 102-23; Schachner, *Founding Fathers*, 409-10.

in 1796 had had a major impact on the fourth Congress, Republicans foremost among them. Through the first three congresses, the state's anti-Federalists, then Republicans, sat in solemn silence through debate after debate while skilled Federalists like Egbert Benson and John Laurance chaperoned Hamilton's measures through Congress. Men like Thomas Tredwell, John Hathorn, and Theodorus Bailey invariably voted Republican but never led the fight for any cause.[22]

They were "country members" who lacked legislative poise; their constituents, moreover, made few demands upon them. Beginning in the fourth Congress the New York Republicans, elected in 1794, came alive, in particular Edward Livingston, Jonathan Havens, and John Williams.

On two pieces of unfinished business of vital concern to the state—completing the fort in New York harbor and settling the state's Revolutionary War debt to the United States—New York's Republicans led the state's delegation in a vocal effort to sway Congress. The state-owned fort on Governor's Island was incomplete despite a federal grant, despite a supplemental state appropriation, despite the volunteer "fatigue parties" organized by Republicans in the war crisis of 1794. The state had already spent $200,000 and without additional federal aid would have to foot the entire bill to complete the project. Plaintively Edward Livingston pleaded for aid to his district: defense was not a local matter, an appropriation hardly a favor; the city had a right to protection by the federal government. Havens, his Republican colleague from Long Island, discussed the delicate question of jurisdiction, arguing that the state could not cede the fort to the United States, which he granted might be desirable, until the United States agreed to assume its defense. Williams, the agrarian spokesman from the northern frontier, spoke emphatically about the federal government's constitutional obligation to defend the port. Ezekiel Gilbert, ever the practical Federalist, added a word about how small the necessary appropriation actually would be. The New Yorkers argued in vain, however. The vote against them was sixty-four to fourteen, with only four other congressmen joining them.[23]

22. *Annals*, 1st, 2d, 3d Cong. The anti-Federalist and Republican congressmen were: William Floyd (1st), John Hathorn (1st), Jeremiah Van Rensselaer (1st), Cornelius Schoonmaker (2d), Thomas Tredwell (2d, 3d), Theodorus Bailey (3d), Philip Van Cortlandt (3d). A search of the *Annals* and its index shows no occasion on which these men spoke and only a few references to committees on which they served.

23. *Annals*, 4th Cong., 1st Sess., 1361-70.

Underlying this almost unanimous opposition to extending aid to New York was the question of the Revolutionary War debt Congress claimed New York owed the federal government. In 1794, a commission appointed in the first Congress reported that for arms and services provided in the Revolution, New York owed the United States about $2,000,000, plus an additional $800,000 in interest. The debt due from all states together was $3,500,000; thus New York owed more than all the other debtor states combined.[24] If the state had to meet this obligation, the tax burden on its citizens would be staggering. No direct taxes had been levied in New York since 1788. Revenue from land sales and investments in bank stock, federal securities, and private corporations made taxation unnecessary—a factor underlying ex-governor Clinton's long-standing popularity.[25] With John Jay now ensconced as governor and Federalists in control of the legislature, Federalists had an obvious political reason to avoid any action which would force them to introduce new taxes.[26]

To a man, the New York delegation opposed payment of the debt as they held the floor of the House for about a week alternately storming at and imploring Congress to discharge New York from the obligation. Livingston and Williams took the lead. They claimed, to begin with, that the method of apportioning the federal debt was unjust. Because it was done on the basis of state population six years after the war, New York was penalized for the vast migration into the state. If the calculations had been based instead on the immediate postwar population, the state would have been a creditor by two million dollars, not a debtor. Moreover, no account had been taken of the vast destruction on the frontier and in the Hudson Valley or of the costs of war that were never charged to the federal government. Added to this the New Yorkers claimed that an understanding existed at the time the commission was appointed that creditor states would be paid but that the debtor states would be let off. "The settlement was altogether in the dark," said one New Yorker. What's more, the state had never consented to the method of settling the question and therefore was not bound now.[27]

24. See "Report of the Commissioners of Accounts to Congress, Dec. 4, 1793," *Annals*, 3d Cong., 1st Sess., 1311-12, for a statement of New York's debt put at $2,074,846.

25. See "Direct Taxes, A Report to Congress by Oliver Wolcott, Secretary of the Treasury, Dec. 14, 1796," *Annals*, 4th Cong., 2d Sess., Appendix, 2666-68.

26. Lincoln, ed., *Messages from the Governors*, II, 379-85; Philip Schuyler, *Remarks on N.Y. Revenue*.

27. For the debate, see *Annals*, 4th Cong., 2d Sess., 1747-1812 *passim*. Note

With sentiment clearly against them, the New York congressmen tried every possible maneuver to sidetrack a vote. They asked for a rehearing before the commissioners, then moved to postpone a vote three weeks, then one week. On each vote they mustered only twenty-odd votes. Then unable to hold off any longer, they lost the motion to kill the state's debt, fifty-seven to twenty-seven.

Both parties in New York were furious at the outcome. Chancellor Livingston believed that paying the balance would "not only draw from us every farthing in the treasury but bring us considerably in debt which must be made up by direct taxes at a time when Congress will also have to call for a direct tax." The entire settlement had been "brought upon us by Schuyler and our delegates under his direction in the first Congress to favor the schemes of his son-in-law Hamilton and probably his own speculations." The Chancellor's dire predictions of 1791 about the consequences of assumption were being proven. Other Republicans put the blame on Senator King.[28] Schuyler tried to put the blame on Clinton: "the balance against this state would not have been so extensive if the Executive and his incompetent auditor had severally done what was incumbent on them." When this hot potato fell into the state legislature, it was "much debated with us," Troup told King. Federalists divided; Hamilton and Jay were conciliatory; Schuyler and Van Rensselaer adamant. "We shall never pay but at the point of a bayonet," wrote Van Rensselaer. Early in 1797 the issue hung fire.[29] Ultimately New York did not pay.

New York's congressmen lost on the fort and debt issues; they were more influential in shaping the land act that passed the House in 1796, which, had it gotten through the Senate, would have initiated a liberal policy for the public domain. For several years Congress had been spared pressure to reform the essentially pro-speculator ordinance of 1785 because of the availability of land from other sources. But the rapid settlement of state-owned lands in the mid-1790's, the removal of the Indian menace, and the restoration of the British-held forts, all re-

especially Williams' opening address, 1748, and Livingston's closing address, 1802-4. Cooper, Gilbert, Van Allen, and Havens also spoke. For the vote, *ibid.*, 1773-85.

28. R. R. Livingston to William Wilson, Dec. 29, 1796, Wilson Papers, Clements Lib.; Livingston to Thomas Tillotson, Jan. 10, 1797, R. R. Livingston Papers, N.-Y. Hist. Soc.; for political criticism, "An Injured Citizen," *N.-Y. Journal*, Jan. 24, 1795.

29. Schuyler to Hamilton, Jan. 5, 1795, Hamilton Papers, Lib. Cong.; Stephen Van Rensselaer to John Williams, Jan. 16, 1797, and the following letters to Williams: from Schuyler, Jan. 10, Feb. 15; from A. Blanchard, Jan. 31; from Jay, Feb. 24, 1797, Williams Papers, N.Y. State Lib.; Robert Troup to Rufus King, Jan. 20, 1797, King Papers, N.-Y. Hist. Soc.

vived interest in western land among would-be migrants. Moreover, anti-speculator feeling was aroused by an attempt to bribe several congressmen into granting a tract of several million acres. One Philadelphia pamphleteer in warning against sale in large tracts for revenue which would help "sow seeds of aristocracy," pointed to the example of New York where "three men solely from considerations of dependency, can influence as many thousands," presumably a reference to the Schuyler, Van Rensselaer and Livingston families. As a result of such pressure, there was a conflict in Congress in 1796 between what a historian of public land policy calls "the friends of the monied purchaser and the friends of the poor pioneer."[30]

The dispute was over a number of related questions: a fixed price opposed to a sale at auction, the extension of credit, the size of parcels, and whether speculative purchasers should be required to settle persons in a given period of time. Five New Yorkers participated in the debate at length, three Republicans and one Federalist on behalf of a pro-settler policy, and one Federalist in defense of the large promoter. It is impossible not to read into their comments the experience of New Yorkers with land in both the Hudson Valley and on the frontier.

That William Cooper, who claimed to be the state's most successful land promoter, took a consistently pro-speculator position is not surprising.[31] To him New York's experience was proof that selling land in large tracts was the only way to provide the government with revenue. The poor always got their land from the rich, he claimed, pointing out that there were no purchasers of less than one hundred acres from the New York government. The government, moreover, would benefit most, not by establishing a fixed price, but by allowing moneyed men to compete at auction. The minimum price should be set to encourage large purchasers; two shillings was too low because it encouraged settlers, $2.00 too high for merchants; the ideal was ten shillings. Cooper also opposed setting a time limit in which large purchasers had to settle farmers on their land. New York's experience, he claimed, proved it was neither enforceable nor desirable. On

30. Payson J. Treat, *The National Land System, 1785-1820* (N.Y., 1910), 72-77, 89; "Columbus," *Cautionary Hints to Congress Respecting the Sale of Western Lands Belonging to the United States* (Phila., 1795), 12. The 1785 land act provided for rectangular surveys of townships, six miles square, divided into sections one mile square, i.e., 640 acres. Half the towns were to be sold intact, half in the 640 acre sections. All were to be placed on sale at auctions in the East at a minimum price of one dollar an acre, without credit.

31. *Annals*, 4th Cong., 1st Sess., 328-30, 340, 403, 409, 411, 417, 859, 860.

the other hand military warrants, which many moneyed men had bought for a trifle, should be accepted in payment.

Jonathan Havens, the Republican from Long Island, an area pre-eminently of small independent farmers, was at the opposite pole.[32] Not only should all government land be sold in small tracts of 640 acres to actual settlers but special provisions should prevent "monopo-lizing." The receipts from land sales should not be required to pay the public debt, Havens argued. When a proposal was offered to sell land in five-mile tracts, he suggested a price of two cents an acre in order to keep the total price down. At only one point did Havens agree with Cooper. Because a settlement requirement was easily evaded, as an alternative he proposed a tax on non-resident pur-chasers, a restriction hardly more palatable to promoters.

John Williams took a compromise stand consistent for a large pro-prietor elected from a frontier community of pioneers and a man anxious to increase revenue to discharge the public debt.[33] Because "persons of property can generally accommodate themselves," Wil-liams argued, Congress should assist "the lower class of people." Favor-ing a "wholesale-retail" plan, he suggested that land be sold in one-half and one-quarter townships as well as 160-acre lots. To the shock of his fellow frontier promoter, Cooper, Williams made the motion requiring settlement on large purchases. Unless this passed, "the honest industrious settlers shall make roads, bridges and other im-provements, whilst rich holders keep their lands in hand whilst these improvements are made in order to increase the value of their own land." New York had such a requirement but unfortunately "the great landholders" prevented it from being enforced and also thwarted passage of a tax on unsettled land. Crowning his pro-settler approach, Williams spoke against allowing military warrants as payments, sug-gesting instead that settlers be allowed to pay for their land in install-ments.

Even John Van Allen, the Federalist from Rensselaer County stigmatized by Republicans as a "tool" of the great landlords, spoke in behalf of this "wholesale-retail" approach.[34] He was not in favor of "an agrarian law," he explained, but he believed in discrimination on behalf of the "poorer and middle class." No sales should be over 640 acres. If the government sold land to speculators, the price of land

32. *Ibid.*, 335, 339, 341, 408, 412, 403.
33. *Ibid.*, 334-35, 341, 346, 407-8, 410, 417-19, 857, 861.
34. *Ibid.*, 328-30, 344, 422, 856, 859, 865-67.

to settlers would go up; this would be "an indirect tax on the culti-
vator" and "an act of favoritism" to the wealthy.

After this wide-ranging debate, the House passed a "wholesale-
retail" bill, dividing sales between quarter-townships and 640-acre
lots, which pro-settler forces amended by setting aside half of the
640-acre lots in 160-acre sections. The Senate struck out this latter
provision, which lost on a second test in the House by two votes. The
end product was a bill that favored "the monied purchaser" by retaining 640-acre lots, a minimum price of $2.00 an acre, and sales at
auction. There was an innovation of one year's credit for one-half the
purchase price, but this was of scant value when the minimum cost of
a 640-acre lot was $1280 due at the end of one year. Not until 1800
was the lot size reduced to 320 acres and a four-year credit extension
allowed. Thus the net gains of the 1796 act were meager.[35]

Livingston and Williams, quite apart from the debates on land,
the fort, and the state debt, established distinct records for themselves
in the fourth Congress, each in a different Republican mold. Williams, as his vote on Jay's Treaty indicated, by the spring of 1796 was
on his way toward becoming an agrarian Federalist, "an Adams Federalist." Elected as a Republican he spoke of himself as a Republican
in justifying his desertion to the Federalists over foreign policy. His
abiding concern, it seems, was to prevent taxes from falling on the
farmer, a note he had sounded at the 1788 convention in opposing
ratification. He was tireless in fighting increased public expenditures.
He spoke, for example, against an annual salary of $1000 for con-
gressmen to replace the existing $6 a day, against plans for public
buildings in the proposed new capital which were "much too magnificent," against creating a government mint and expanding the army.
His longest speech of the session was against the creation of a navy.
Why, he asked, tax farmers for a navy to protect commerce that would
not even repay the cost of the navy? Any surplus in the treasury
should be distributed to the states to improve marketing facilities for
farmers. As for taxes, they should be levied on luxuries alone. "The
true interests of the country," by Williams' lights, "were the agricultural and everything taken from agriculture to commerce was taken
from the greater and given to the less."[36]

Edward Livingston emerged, as La Rochefoucauld-Liancourt ob-

35. Treat, *The National Land System*, 84-99; Roy M. Robbins, *Our Landed
Heritage: The Public Domain, 1776-1936* (Princeton, 1942), ch. 1.
36. *Annals*, 4th Cong., 1st Sess., 254-57, 305, 313, 365-66, 843-44, 872 ff., 1418-19.

served, as "one of the most enlightened and eloquent members of Congress in the party of the opposition."[37] Livingston led the Republicans nationally against Jay's Treaty, as he led the New York delegation for an appropriation for the harbor fort. Like Williams, he also spoke for economy and against yearly salaries for congressmen, an extensive foreign diplomatic corps, and a mint, the latter "an expensive and extravagant project."[38] His characteristic crusades, however, reflected his urban constituency. After he had been in the House but a few weeks, he moved to establish a committee to investigate the federal criminal code and was appointed its chairman.[39] He was also concerned with the related problem of debtors' imprisonment. Combining humanitarianism with patriotism, Livingston introduced a bill calling for the appointment of agents in foreign ports to arrange for the return of impressed American sailors. In response to the charge that the proposal was unnecessary and overly expensive, he made a heart-rending plea for the suffering seamen and the bill passed by a vote of seventy-seven to thirteen.[40] Livingston also demonstrated another secret of Republican success: an ability to plead the interest of wealthy businessmen, among them a would-be mining company[41] and no less a delinquent land speculator than Alexander Macomb.[42]

Of the New York Republicans, Jonathan Havens of Long Island was active in the Jay Treaty and land debates. An able lawyer and enlightened graduate of Yale, he also spoke forcefully in defense of Jefferson's proposal, which Federalists had ridiculed, for a uniform system of weights and measures.[43] Theodorus Bailey of Dutchess, John Hathorn of Ulster-Orange, and Philip Van Cortlandt of Westchester remained silent as they had been before the Republican upsurge of 1794. Collectively, however, the New York Republicans, up for re-election late in 1796, presented the voters with a clear-cut record that put the two parties in sharper contrast than ever before.

37. La Rochefoucauld-Liancourt, *Travels*, I, 467.
38. *Annals*, 4th Cong., 1st Sess., 254-55, 257, 304-7, 1394.
39. *Ibid.*, 185.
40. *Ibid.*, 381-94, 398, 803.
41. *Ibid.*, 272; see Nicholas J. Roosevelt, J. Hart and associates, *Papers Relative to An Application to Congress for an Exclusive Right of Searching for and Working Mines in the Northwest and Southwest Territory* (N.Y., 1796).
42. *Annals*, 4th Cong., 1st Sess., 1360; 5th Cong., 2d Sess., 1560-61. Livingston introduced a petition asking for a dispensation for Macomb and William Edgar who were unable to meet their payments on an 89,000-acre tract purchased from the federal government in 1787.
43. *Annals*, 4th Cong., 1st Sess., 1375.

III

In the congressional elections of 1796, the Republicans failed to repeat their success of 1794, when they captured six of New York's ten seats in the House of Representatives. In 1796 they retained but four of these six seats, losing one outright and losing John Williams to the Federalists. Everywhere they were confronted by stiffer Federalist opposition.

Once again the most significant Republican victory was in New York City where Republicans were able to capitalize on the discontent stirred up by the ferrymen affair. Edward Livingston's position was so secure that four Federalists refused to risk a race against him. The nomination went by default to James Watson who, Hamilton explained, "had gotten a strong hold on most of the leading mechanics" but who it was admitted was "unpopular and not a character that commanded warmth and zeal."[44] In the midst of the campaign, in fact, there was an attempt to substitute Hamilton for Watson, which the ex-Secretary had to squelch.[45]

Watson was poles apart from Livingston: speaker of the assembly in 1794 who had stalled fortifying the city, chairman of the merchants' committee which attempted to rally support for Jay's Treaty in 1795, chairman of the insurance brokers who threatened merchants in 1796. Republicans pummeled Watson for his wealth and aristocratic leanings. He has "immense property," a "palace on the battery," and "thinks it a degradation to be seen in conversation with a poor man." He was not a regular merchant, but a "speculator," a "stock and land jobber," and a Yankee outsider as well. Furthermore, he had "mediocre abilities" and was "comparatively illiterate"—he could not even spell correctly. It was true that Livingston rode in a carriage, but, said his defenders, he was a modest "truly republican" "native of our state," and a man of talents.[46]

Bereft of issues, Federalists at the eleventh hour undertook to "smear" Livingston. On the evening of the first day of voting, they distributed three thousand handbills charging that he had compromised himself by association with John Swanwick, the Republican merchant congressman who was under attack in Philadelphia for a

44. Hamilton to Rufus King, Dec. 16, 1796, Lodge, ed., *Works of Hamilton*, VIII, 436; James to Moss Kent, Dec. 17, 1796, Kent Papers, Lib. Cong.

45. Robert Troup to Ebenezer Foote, Dec. 10, 1796, Foote, ed., *Ebenezer Foote*, 75.

46. See "If the Cap Fits Put It On," N.Y. *Argus*, Dec. 13, 1796, "Mentor," *ibid.*, Dec. 15, 1796, and several unsigned paragraphs in these issues.

variety of business practices. With typical demagoguery, they scored the Republican candidate as "the Aristocratical, Democratical, Jacobinical Edward Livingston."[47]

City Republicans were far better organized than they had been two years before. Again the Democratic Society played a role, again behind the scenes. This time seven ward committees were formed and "ordered to take a list of all the electors' names in their respective wards and then go to them and remove their objections, if they had any, to Mr. Livingston." The committees met every other evening up to the election. The campaign was conducted with "great spirit," with Republicans "determined to exert every nerve" for Livingston.[48] On the several days of voting Hamilton patrolled the city on horseback, "visiting every polling place." But according to Robert R. Livingston, he was "horribly treated at the different polls."[49] Republicans had done their work well.

Livingston's margin of victory, 550 votes, exceeded Republican expectations. The vote was 2362–1812. He thus doubled the Republican margin of 1784 by bringing out some five hundred new voters to the polls.[50] His greatest majorities, as contemporaries observed, lay in the wards "chiefly inhabited by the middling and poorer classes of the people." At the same time he drew a sizable minority in the well-to-do wards.[51] Clearly Federalist strength was being sapped, a fact which they confirmed two months later when they gerrymandered the Republican seventh ward, the outlying northernmost area known as "the cartman's ward," putting it in the Westchester congressional district.[52]

The Republicans in the other two southern congressional districts

47. "An Impartial History of the Late Election," *N.-Y. Journal*, Dec. 27, 1796; "An American," N.Y. *Argus*, Dec. 15, 1796; *ibid.*, Dec. 14, 1796. For the accusations against Swanwick and the Republican defense see James T. Callendar, *The American Annual Register . . . for the year 1796* (Phila., 1797), 269-75. For the Republican answer to another anti-Livingston handbill see "The Tory Lie Detected. To the Republican Voters of the City of New York" [1796], broadside, Evans 36439.

48. William to Peter Van Ness, Dec. 4, 1796, Van Ness Papers, N.Y. Pub. Lib.; for notice of a Democratic Society meeting, N.Y. *Argus*, Oct. 26, 1796; for vote solicitation by society members, Anderson, Diary, Dec. 14, 1796, Columbia Univ.

49. "An Impartial History," *N.-Y. Journal*, Dec. 27, 1796; R. R. to Edward Livingston, Dec. 20, 1796, R. R. Livingston Papers, N.Y. Hist. Soc.

50. Robert. R. Livingston to Thomas Tillotson, Jan. 10, 1797, R. R. Livingston Papers, N.Y. Pub. Lib.; N.Y. *Argus*, Jan. 20, 1796.

51. See especially "Impartial History," *N.-Y. Journal*, Dec. 27, 1796.

52. *Journal of the Assembly of N.Y.*, 20th Sess., 182.

each fared differently. On Long Island Jonathan Havens, the vocal Republican, won easily, 1259–648; two years before he had faced three opponents and had won without a majority. In Westchester, by contrast, Philip Van Cortlandt, who had wavered on Jay's Treaty because he had been elected in 1794 by a margin of only twenty votes, squeaked in by even less—thirteen votes, 1016 to 1003.[53]

In the two Republican districts of the middle Hudson Valley, Republicans kept Ulster-Orange but lost Dutchess. In Dutchess, Theodorus Bailey, who like Van Cortlandt had also vacillated on the treaty, was defeated, 1220–1048. Two years before he had taken the county by 350 votes. William Keteltas of ferryman fame reminded Dutchess voters that David Brooks, Bailey's opponent, was "a leading character" in imprisoning him and "the greatest enemy to the liberties of the middling class of people," but to no effect. With a little more effort to get out the vote, however, the seat might have been saved, at least so the Chancellor believed.[54] Across the river in Ulster-Orange, the Republican incumbent, John Hathorn, did not run again. Republicans, including the Democratic Society leaders, supported Lucas C. Elmendorph of Kingston to counter the Federalists who put up Conrad E. Elmendorph, his relative. Although the Federalist vote went up by about a thousand votes, Republicans retained their hold on the district, 1936 to 1514.[55]

In the three landlord-dominated districts of the upper Hudson Valley, the Republicans managed to mount only one serious challenge to Federalist control. In 1794 the Republican Thomas Tredwell had made no inroads among the tenants in the Rensselaer-Clinton district against the manor candidate, John Van Allen. In 1796 the Republican candidate John Woodworth launched a vigorous campaign against the "corrupt manor influence" behind Van Allen. During the spring assembly elections a political poet had urged the Rensselaer County tenants to defy the pressure that kept them "under a political cloud of darkness."[56]

> We who have ragged stoneylands,
> With quarter sales and heavy rent,

53. N.Y. *Argus*, Jan. 17, 18, 20, 1797. See Appendix, Table 6.
54. *Ibid.*; William Keteltas in *N.-Y. Journal*, Dec. 9, 1796; Philip Ten Eyck to Philip Schuyler, Dec. 9, 1796, Schuyler Papers, N.Y. Pub. Lib.; R. R. Livingston to Thomas Tillotson, Jan. 10, 1797, R. R. Livingston Papers, N.Y. Pub. Lib.
55. For nominations, *Goshen Repository*, Nov. 15, Dec. 6, 1796; for returns, N.Y. *Argus*, Jan. 17, 18.
56. "An Independent Elector," *Albany Gazette*, Apr. 6, 1796.

Must pay the same to break those bands
And vote for those we afterwards do repent

But come my friends, let's join our hands
Which politically we ought to do yearly
And oppress those aristocratical bands
And give our suffrages freely.

Woodworth picked up this theme, attacking in particular "the unlettered servant of a man of property from the district of Albany"— Thomas Witbeck, Stephen Van Rensselaer's agent—who "dictates to you your representatives." All who were not "tools nor toolmakers," he claimed would vote for him.[57] Van Allen was portrayed as a Tory in the Revolution and mediocre in abilities. Woodworth was thoroughly American, educated since the Revolution, and a man of abilities. In reply, Federalists accused Woodworth of being an anti-Federalist, a charge he denied, and of buying votes by "dispensing grog," a charge that went unanswered.[58] Although Van Allen again won, 1588 to 1152, Woodworth scored heavily among the Van Rensselaer tenants who, "driven by the lash of Widbeck," resembled "a West Indies plantation."[59]

In the other two landlord districts there was no comparable tenant upsurge. In Albany County the Federalist landlords were frightened at first by a secret though abortive campaign to run "a certain Mr. Swart," but Henry Glen, the incumbent, was again elected "without competition," as Greenleaf's paper put it. The influence of Schuyler and Van Rensselaer was "altogether irresistible," La Rochefoucauld-Liancourt observed.[60]

In Columbia, Hezikiah Hosmer, the new Federalist candidate, won easily, even though Republicans ran but one candidate, John P. Van Ness, instead of the two who competed in 1794. Van Ness, a young lawyer recently graduated from Columbia College, had a number of handicaps, not the least being that he was "subject to fits and fallen sickness," a point Federalists made the most of.[61] He also failed to

57. An Oration, July 4, in Lansingburgh *American Spy*, July 19, 1796.
58. In *Albany Register*: "Nestor," Dec. 12, "Argus," Dec. 30, 1796. In Lansingburgh *American Spy*: "Argus," Jan. 10, "Sempronius," Jan. 24, "Plain Truth," Feb. 21, 1797.
59. *N.-Y. Journal*, Dec. 16, 1796; Thomas Tillotson to R. R. Livingston, Feb. 5, 1797, R. R. Livingston Papers, N.-Y. Hist. Soc.
60. Philip Van Rensselaer to William Cooper, Dec. 17, 1796, Cooper Transcripts, N.-Y. Hist. Soc.; *N.-Y. Journal*, Jan. 18, 1797; La Rochefoucauld-Liancourt, *Travels*, I, 372.
61. *Hudson Gazette*, Nov. 28, 1796; Peter Van Schaack to John Van Allen, Jan.

arouse any enthusiasm either in the eastern anti-landlord townships or among the tenants, whose protest against the upper manor's land title had recently come to a head.[62] Chancellor Livingston showed no interest in the campaign[63] although his tenants voted for Van Ness. The upper manor tenants who voted—a third the usual number—were divided, and the Democratic Society voters in Canaan who had poured out for the Republican Matthew Adgate two years before stayed away from the polls. The Republican campaign, in short, was desultory. Hosmer won 1036-758, Van Ness getting fewer votes than the two Republicans together in 1794.[64]

In the two frontier districts to the north and west, a new pattern was emerging which puzzled contemporaries as it has eluded historians. When Greenleaf listed the various nominees, he had no trouble identifying Republicans in the eight districts, but how, after all, was one to classify John Williams, the Republican who voted with the Federalists on Jay's Treaty but was running against the same Federalist he had defeated in 1794, or James Cochran, the Federalist running against William Cooper? In one list Greenleaf made no designation for either; in another he called Cochran a Republican, much to the latter's embarrassment.[65] Cochran was a thoroughgoing Federalist who would prove his loyalty in the fifth Congress by voting with the party on forty-nine out of fifty key votes.[66]

Williams had been elected as a Republican in 1794, winning against the patroon's candidate in a close contest. In 1796 he had the backing of Van Rensselaer, his agent, Witbeck, and Philip Schuyler, who tried unsuccessfully to get James Gordon, the Federalist candidate, to withdraw. Williams won easily, 1325-575, keeping all of his Republican vote while Gordon got only half of his previous Federalist vote. Stephen Van Rensselaer, congratulating Williams on his victory, was hopeful he would soon "take the lead of the Northern interest" and unite with them in the ensuing state election.[67] In the fifth Con-

16, 1797, Van Schaack Papers, N.Y. State Lib.; and a letter with no signature, Cooperstown *Otsego Herald*, Feb. 10, 1797.

62. See ch. 24, sec. IV.

63. R. R. Livingston to William Wilson, Dec. 29, 1796, Wilson Papers, Clements Lib.

64. *Hudson Gazette*, Jan. 30, 1797. In Canaan where in 1794 the vote in favor of the Republican was 266-128, Van Ness got only 68 votes to 131 for Hosmer.

65. *N.-Y. Journal*, Dec. 16, 1796; for the Cochran campaign, see above, ch. 24

66. See Dauer, *The Adams Federalists*, Appendix III, 300, 307, 313.

67. Letters to Williams from Thomas Witbeck, Nov. 3, Dec. 10, 1796, Jan. 28,

gress Williams sided with the Federalists on two-thirds of the votes.[68]

In the state as a whole it was clear that Republicans were not holding their own. They won with safe margins in only three districts, New York, Long Island, and Ulster-Orange. But they barely kept Westchester, and they ran more poorly in Dutchess and Columbia than in 1794. Upstate in the three landlord districts they offered a challenge only in Rensselaer-Clinton. And they lost the frontier districts to a new kind of Federalism represented by Cochran to the west and Williams to the north.

When the state legislature met in January 1797, it added to New York's Federalist delegation in the United States Senate. In November 1796, to replace Rufus King who had been appointed Minister to England, they had already chosen John Laurance, New York City's first congressman. To replace Aaron Burr whose term had expired they now returned Philip Schuyler. Republicans made no campaign against either of these ardent Hamiltonians.[69]

On the surface of things New York's Federalists had reason to rejoice as they celebrated George Washington's birthday in February 1797 with splendid dinners and balls at Albany and New York City. They had helped to elect a Federalist president, reduced Republican strength in the Congress, and sent two of their kind to the Senate. New York State was clearly in the Federalist column; Republicans were on the defensive.

Below the surface the Federalists had cause for anxiety. New York City seemed lost to Federalism; in the spring elections of 1797 it would return its first Republican assembly slate.[70] Even gerrymandering the "cartman's ward" was of scant help. And in the west dissatisfaction with the dominance of William Cooper, Philip Schuyler, and "the Albany junto" was so deep that Federalists believed the only solution was to divide the western district in two, giving one to James Cochran, in order to regain the other for Cooper.[71] In the spring elections of 1797, Cooper's home county would also start to go Re-

---

1797, Stephen Van Rensselaer, Jan. 28, 1797, Williams Papers, N.Y. State Lib.; for returns, N.Y. *Argus*, Jan. 14, 1797.

68. Dauer, *The Adams Federalists*, Appendix III; *Albany Register*, June 22, 25, 1798.

69. *Journal of the Assembly of N.Y.*, 20th Sess., 1st meeting, 18. Seventy votes were cast for Laurance, one for Zephaniah Platt; *ibid.*, 20th Sess., 2d meeting, 68. Eighty-five votes were cast for Schuyler, one for James Kent.

70. *N.-Y. Journal*, Mar. 8, 1797.

71. Thomas Tillotson to R. R. Livingston, Jan. 20, Feb. 5, 1797, R. R. Livingston Papers, N.-Y. Hist. Soc.

publican. Up and down the state Federalists were divided in their opinion of John Adams.[72] Worse still, "many excellent men," as John Jay put it, were retreating rapidly from politics, men who "neglect not to guard their trees and vines from caterpillars . . . yet omit tending to the political grubs."[73]

If at Washington's birthday in 1797 any Federalists paused to recall the public celebrations in New York that had launched the Federalist era when Washington was inaugurated in 1789, they must have been struck by the difference. In 1797 there were no parades and no cheering mobs. On the horizon, only more storms loomed.

72. Elkanah Watson to John Adams, Mar. 5, Apr. 1, Adams to Watson, Mar. 17, 1797, in Watson, ed., *Memoirs of Elkanah Watson*, 397-400.

73. John Jay to Judge Lowell, Feb. 29, 1796, Johnston, ed., *Correspondence of John Jay*, IV, 204-5.

CHAPTER 26

Conclusion

————•————

By 1797 the Democratic Republicans of New York were in full bloom, the contours of the movement clearly shaped. In the political history of New York in the early national period, four broad questions emerge to which this study was directed. Who were the Democratic Republicans? What were the issues that brought the movement into being? What was it like as an organized entity? What was its philosophy?

I

Who were the Republicans in New York? One of the best ways to answer this question is to ask another: who were the Federalists? In the leadership of the Federalists, the continuities in New York politics from the Revolution through the 1790's were striking. The Federalist party of the mid-90's was led by the same men who had led the conservative Whigs in the '70's and the nationalists in the '80's: Philip Schuyler, Alexander Hamilton, and John Jay above all others, James Duane, Egbert Benson, Nicholas Low, John Laurance, Stephen Van Rensselaer among the second-rank figures. These leaders were themselves of the landlord-mercantile aristocracy or were their spokesmen. There were also discontinuities. By the mid-1790's the Federalists had lost the lower manor Livingstons completely, and could not count on the upper manor branch; Gouverneur Morris was in Europe; William Duer was in jail; Duane died in 1794. They also were joined by several new clusters of leaders whose strength lay in rural areas outside the traditional domain of the landlords and merchants: former anti-Federalists like Peter Van Gaasbeck of Ulster County and John Williams of the northern frontier, and William Cooper, Charles Williamson, and Thomas Morris of the west. In New York City and the Hudson Valley they took into their councils such former Tories as Richard Harison, Josiah Hoffman, and Samuel Jones and Yankee newcomers like Rufus King, James Watson, and Ambrose Spencer. These new leaders also tended to be men at the apex of wealth and economic power in their communities, especially on the frontier.

The leadership of the Republicans showed similar continuities and discontinuities. The party was built around the nucleus of George Clinton's anti-Federalists who in the Revolution had been the leaders of the popular Whigs. The anti-Federalist leaders of 1788 in Albany, Ulster, and Dutchess counties, on Long Island and at New York City remained leaders of the Republicans through the 1790's. Yet Clinton had broken "the confederacy" of "all the great and opulent families" which he had mentioned to Rufus King in 1789. Chancellor Livingston's family which had been with him in the Revolution had rejoined him; so had the Van Cortlandts who had deserted in 1787-88. These two landed families contributed Republican congressmen in two districts, New York City and Westchester. The few anti-Federalist leaders of 1788 whom Clinton had lost—Williams, Van Gaasbeck, and Jones—were more than matched by well-known former Federalists who became active Republicans: Brockholst and Edward Livingston, James Nicholson, Samuel Osgood, and Elkanah Watson. Equally important, there were a number of active young newcomers among the Republicans like Tunis Wortman and William Keteltas who counted themselves as neither Federalist nor anti-Federalist in '88. And on the western frontier, Republicans were on the verge of acquiring a new breed of former Federalists among whom Jedediah Peck was a prototype.

The support of both Federalist and Republican leaders changed markedly between the 1780's and the 1790's. The old anti-Federalists were sustained primarily by the yeomanry, both of the substantial and poorer sort. They had created a small following among aspiring entrepreneurs—land speculators, manufacturers, would-be bankers, upstart merchants—but they had lost most of the prewar mechanic following of the popular Whigs to the Federalists. As for the tenants, even though large numbers of them voted anti-Federalist in the convention contest of '88, the leaders feared them as "mechanical creatures" of the aristocracy.

By 1797, Republicans were like the anti-Federalists in one essential: they were still primarily an agrarian party whose strongest vote came from the centers of the yeomanry. Unlike the anti-Federalists, however, Republicans had acquired an urban wing in New York City based primarily upon the mechanics.[1] Their following in this class consisted of entire trades whose interests they espoused, such as the tallow chandlers, trades in need of protection from British manufactures, and the poorer mechanics in general, especially cartmen and laborers, who, if they could not vote, turned out to damn Jay's Treaty at the "town meetings," and packed the assembly chambers to cheer William Keteltas, the ferryman's champion. Republicans also won over a good sprinkling of articulate professionals: lawyers, ministers, doctors, teachers, and young men and women in all classes who gave the movement its tone. Among merchants their degree of success is summed up by an offhand comment by the poet-editor, Philip Freneau. The daily papers, he explained to DeWitt Clinton, "were supported by a mercantile interest which as you know is not republican." He completed the sentence, returned, placed a caret mark between "not" and "republican" to make it read "not generally republican."[2] By 1797 Republicans had won over a small segment of the "mercantile interest," although a growing one.

Republicans also made inroads, though small ones, among the tenantry. In Columbia County, some of their new support was dragooned by the upper manor Livingstons, but the family was so unpredictable that they were more of a handicap than a help; some came from the small, politically inconsequential lower manor. Republicans had only limited success in exploiting the growing anti-landlord sentiment among dependents of Schuyler and Van Rensselaer at the polls. They were willing to climb to office by charging political domination by "the manor lords" but were unwilling to join tenants in challenging the landlords' property rights or the court system that upheld them. Republicans thus broke out of the mold of the popular Whigs who had scorned the tenant rebellions of '66 and '77 and Shays' Rebellion of '86, but in only a limited way.

1. See Young, "The Mechanics and the Jeffersonians," *Labor History*, 5 (1964) 247-76.
2. Philip Freneau to DeWitt Clinton, Nov. 8, 1795, DeWitt Clinton Papers, No. 35, Columbia Univ.

The basis of Federalist support was also broader at the end of the Washington administration than a decade before, as their success in electing Jay in 1795 and six congressmen in 1796 indicated. To a considerable extent Federalist electoral strength continued to be a vote of economic dependents. The safest counties in the state for both gubernatorial and congressional voting were those where the land-lords Philip Schuyler and Stephen Van Rensselaer predominated. In their traditional stronghold, New York City, Federalists owed a good deal of their vote to the influence of merchant over clerk and cartman, of master craftsman over journeyman and of both over laborers. And on the frontier, their newest recruits were often debtors to land pro-prietors and land agents. But the fact remains that most Federalist support was uncoerced, a product of the appeal of their policies. In the 1780's the yeomanry of the southern district was attracted to the Federalists for their leniency to loyalism; in the 1790's a segment of the yeomanry of the Hudson Valley in Whig Clintonian counties like Ulster, Orange and Dutchess also came over, disillusioned with Clintonian policies. On the frontier their support among farmers was based on a variety of policies already analyzed. In New York City Federalists also kept a following among the "leading" and "substan-tial mechanics," who very likely were the more well-to-do master craftsmen and native-born or English-born mechanics. In both parties there was a subtle shift of appeal between 1788 and 1797; Republicans had to attract mercantile and mechanic support and Federalists were tugged by their new and potential yeoman constituents in the Hudson Valley and especially on the frontier.

Ethnic factors seem more important by 1797 than before. The native born and the established immigrant groups, the English, Dutch, Scotch-Irish, and Germans, divided along lines of social economic interests or political tradition. The newcomers from 1793 on, the French, Irish, and Scotch-Irish who were mostly poor, had settled in New York City and had a liberal or radical political heritage, tended to become Republican. Immigrants of English background and those who rose quickly tended to be Federalist. The largest group of new-comers to the state, the New England migrants, went en masse into the Federalist party, especially on the frontier. There, however, they leavened the party in their own Yankee image, contributing to the split of western against eastern Federalist and pioneer farmer against proprietor which paved the way for the emergence of Republicanism on the frontier.

Republicans and Federalists both drew support from almost all religious groups. This much, however, can be said of the Republicans: they obviously had far more adherents among orthodox Protestant denominations than the numerically small deists. Most deists were Republicans, but staunch Baptists like Melancton Smith and Jedediah Peck and the liberal ministers of New York City were more important in shaping the movement than Elihu Palmer, the famous blind deist, or the short-lived Deistical Society of Newburgh. The evidence also suggests that there was significant support for Republicans among Presbyterians, whose church had been synonymous with Whiggery in the Revolution; George Clinton and Aaron Burr were well known as Presbyterians and the Livingstons were heirs to the tradition of the "Presbyterian Party" of provincial days.

II

What were the issues which gave rise to the Democratic-Republican movement, bringing about the alignment just described? Noble Cunningham's generalizations that the Republican party was "a product of national rather than state politics" and that it "was a new growth that sprang from the divisions in Congress and the national government" must be modified for New York, perhaps even more than he concedes.[3] In New York, as we have said, the Republican party was built around the core of the anti-Federalist Clintonian party, the product of Governor Clinton's long tenure in the state government. Men who were attracted to Clinton by his policies and patronage, his principles and reputation, did not need national issues to stimulate them to oppose the Federalists, their traditional political enemies. Indeed the first Washington administration witnessed a duel between two masterful politicians who used the magnet of governmental power to attract substantial interests. Hamilton by his policies on funding, assumption, the tariff, and the bank, hoped to cement an array of interests to the new national government. Clinton used land grants, state investments in canals and roads, and support for manufacturing and banking to attract others and sustain his power. Clintonianism, like Hamiltonianism thus was a positive, dynamic force.

The national policies which did affect New York during Washington's first administration operated differently than most historians have assumed. The "high tone" of the new government, the "aristoc-

3. Cunningham, *The Jeffersonian Republicans*, 256.

racy" that loomed so large in Senator Maclay's diary simply did not strike fire as a public issue. Neither did Hamiltonian finance, at least not at its inception. The anti-Federalists did not vote against funding and the tacit understanding about the settlement of New York's debts of the Revolution to the central government assuaged hostility to assumption. Opposition rose as the orgy of speculation revealed the beneficiaries of Hamilton's program, but even after "the panic of 1792" the political kickback did not last beyond the spring elections. At the end of Washington's first term Federalists won a sweeping vote of approval in the congressional elections.

The Bank of the United States probably had the most serious repercussions within New York of any internal Hamiltonian measure, for it triggered rival business groups into a "battle of the banks." Although the "State Bank" project to counter the potential combination of the Bank of the United States and the Bank of New York failed, the demand for a non-Federalist bank remained, emerging in 1799 to support Aaron Burr's more famous scheme for the Bank of Manhattan. The bank war of New York in 1791-92 also anticipated in more ways than one the business rivalries and "anti-monopoly" spirit of the bank war of the Jacksonian era.

The issue of banking, combined with assumption, was also important for providing the occasion on which the Livingstons first demonstrated their opposition to Hamilton's policies. There is a more complex explanation for Chancellor Livingston's departure from the house of Federalism than his disappointment over not being appointed to high office. An ally of Governor Clinton in the Revolution, he had been slow to join Hamilton and Jay in the battle for a new federal Constitution. He had fought Hamilton on banking policy in 1784; he never favored assumption of the state debts; he also had a latent disagreement with John Jay over the French alliance. Principle thus combined with pique and pride. After 1793 when foreign affairs became crucial, Washington found that he could not bridge the gap between the Chancellor and the Federalists by patronage.

The "republican interest" that came into existence in Washington's first term would not have found a mass following had it not been for Federalist foreign policies in the second. Here the stimulus was unmistakably national and international. The French Revolution helped but it was not as divisive an issue in New York as dramatizers of the period have made it out to be. It operated, moreover, to widen a long-standing schism over the French alliance in which Robert R.

Livingston, the "Gallican," and John Jay, the "anti-Gallican," had long been protagonists. British policy on the high seas and on the frontier, coupled with the Federalist response to them, created the Republican movement in New York, enabling Republicans to catch full sail the strongest winds of nationalism to blow across American political waters since the Revolution.

After men were alienated from the Federalists, Republicans found a receptive audience to renewed attacks against Hamiltonian finance. The evil effects of "the funding system" seemed more visible in the light of the burning effigies of John Jay. Even so, when the inscription for Abraham Yates's tombstone was made public in 1796:

SPECTATOR
Beneath Lies
Abraham Yates, Junior
who uniformly opposed the tyr-
rany of Britain,
and the corrupt, perfidious
funding system;
not for his own good but for the
Public Good.
He has directed this last testi-
monial of the sincerity
of his apprehensions
That it will prove most injurious
to the
Equal Rights of Man
And the essential interests of his country[4]

there probably were not many Republicans who shared the depth of feeling that burned to the last in "Rough Hewer."

After a political following was handed to them by the Federalists, the New York Republicans, it must be said, bungled their chance. They clung to Citizen Genêt after Jefferson advised them to abandon him as a liability; Cornelia Clinton's marriage to the Frenchman was symbolic. They became strident "war hawks" in the spring of 1794, alienating both the commercial interest and the frontier, and by making a last-ditch fight against Jay's Treaty in 1796 they pitted themselves against George Washington whose prestige outmatched theirs.

4. *Albany Register*, July 8, 1796.

In each crisis Federalists were able to outmaneuver the Republicans, making the issue Washington or his traducers, and war or peace with Britain. The result in New York, as elsewhere, was that Republicans were unable to consolidate their gains of 1794, the year of patriotism, thus losing the crucial presidential and congressional elections of 1796.

This extraordinary support for the Federalist party, one of the striking themes of New York politics in the 1790's, was based in large part on the widespread conviction that Federalist policies benefited the state. Hamiltonian financial measures, while they feathered the nests of a good number of wealthy New Yorkers, were also to the advantage of the state treasury as a holder of federal securities and then as an investor in bank stock. The invigoration of commerce lined the pockets of exporting farmers as well as merchants. National military power broke the back of Indian resistance and national diplomacy, however humiliating Jay's Treaty may otherwise have been, restored the forts on New York soil and established a procedure to indemnify shippers for their losses. The results were a boon to pioneer as well as proprietor on the frontier and to all in the east whose prosperity rested on foreign commerce. Federalists, in short, had an outstanding record to point to.

Secondly, Federalists, as the "outs" in the state government, exploited to the hilt Clinton's aberrations from democratic ideals. They campaigned against him for his excessive stay in office and his personal fortune. They hung the albatross of the land office sales of 1791 around his neck for a decade. They championed the "rights of suffrage" after the election "steal" of 1792. Schuyler, western state senator and father of the first canal, espoused the interests of the western district which elected him. In New York City, Federalist humanitarians pioneered as abolitionists, while Ulster Clintonians still defended slavery.

Third, and most important, one face of Federalism was consistently moderate. Under the guidance of Hamilton, Schuyler, Jay, King, and Benson, the New York Federalists established a middle-of-the-road record on issue after issue. They promised amendments to the Constitution in 1788, toned down the "high" Federalists, and ran Robert Yates, a moderate anti-Federalist, against Clinton in 1789; they cooled off the western hotheads who wanted to oust Clinton by extra-legal methods after the election decision of 1792, and did an about-face in 1794, fortifying the state and adopting an embargo in order to avert war. This flexibility continued the tactic cultivated by conservative

Whigs from the 1770's, based on the dictum of Robert R. Livingston to "yield to the torrent if they hoped to direct its course."[5] John Jay's career is the perfect example of this policy. A straight line of moderation runs from his role in getting the state constitution through Abraham Yates's committee in 1777, to the tactics of appeasement to get the federal Constitution through the Poughkeepsie convention in 1788, through his caution as the aggrieved victim of the "stolen" election of 1792, to his conciliatory first message as governor in 1796. This pattern suggests that the process of conservative adaptation to democratic currents began much earlier than Dixon Ryan Fox and many others allowed.

On the other hand these same Federalists had a strain of contempt for the people—a class prejudice—which was a major cause of their undoing. "Aristocracy" was a persistent issue in a state which from 1777 on elected George Clinton because it did not want a Livingston or a Schuyler as governor. It took on new meaning in the 1790's in reaction to the highhandedness of Hudson Valley landlords, western land proprietors, and New York City magistrates. In 1795, Stephen Van Rensselaer, who coerced his tenants at the polls, barely sneaked in as lieutenant-governor. In 1796 just when Federalists were recovering the ground they had lost because of Jay's Treaty, Mayor Varick by his handling of the case of the Irish ferrymen and the assembly by jailing William Keteltas almost gave the city to the Republicans. The same year pioneers on the western frontier exploded against the "Albany junto" which seemingly dictated the nominations of the district and against William Cooper, the "Bashaw of Otsego."

The violent reaction of Federalist leaders to the democratic upsurge of the mid-1790's revealed a growing rigidity. In stigmatizing the Democratic societies as "self created," the "town meetings" as the work of "the rabble," and petitions to Congress as unwarranted, Federalists asserted their elitist notion of representation. Lacking confidence in their ability to win back Republicans as they had once won over followers of the popular Whigs and anti-Federalists, New York's Federalists were on the path to repression which culminated in the Alien and Sedition Laws of 1798. Years later Noah Webster in counseling Rufus King on a way out of the political debacle to which such policies had led them, resorted to the very language Robert R. Livingston had used in 1777: "They have attempted to resist the force of

5. Robert R. Livingston to William Duer, June 12, 1777, R. R. Livingston Papers, N.-Y. Hist. Soc. See above, ch. 1.

current opinion instead of falling into the current with a view to direct it."[6] By then, however, it was too late to repeat the techniques of the conservative holding action of the era of the Revolution.

III

What were the Republicans as an organized movement? Their achievement can be measured against the limitations of the predecessor group which they absorbed. The anti-Federalist party, in itself, was a landmark in New York's history, the first stable political group that did not center on one of the great landed families. It revolved instead around George Clinton's power as governor, not as landholder. More than a personal following, it was a loosely organized collection of the "new men" risen to power in the Revolution who were tied to Clinton by patronage, policy, and family "connections." It functioned cohesively in the state legislature but it was not put to the test as a state-wide electoral party until the gubernatorial campaign in 1789. The anti-Federalists had developed no political societies except for the shortlived Federal Republican Society of New York City and had established only one newspaper for the entire state, Thomas Greenleaf's *New York Journal and Patriotic Register*. Their rural following was unorganized, ill informed, and provincial. To be a rank and file anti-Federalist in 1788 meant only that one voted for Governor Clinton and his followers and supported their policies.

By 1797 there clearly was a Democratic-Republican movement in New York State which embraced not only the Republican party but the Republican societies and the Republican press as well. The societies were distinct from the party, although they took part in elections on a *sub rosa* basis. But there were societies with staying power in only three counties who could not have had more than 500 members, all told. They were more "advanced" than the party and bore the stigma of "Jacobinism" which could not be pinned on local leaders elsewhere. They functioned as the "sentinels" who watched the rulers, as catalysts who produced the "addresses" to rally the citizenry, and as behind-the-scenes organizers. In New York City the Democratic society may be credited with perfecting the techniques of direct democratic expression: the "town meetings," the patriotic parades and celebrations, the circulation of public petitions. None of these tech-

6. Noah Webster to Rufus King, July 6, 1807, King, ed., *Correspondence of Rufus King*, V, 37-38.

niques were new to Whigs who had lived through the 1770's but their scope was far broader.

By 1797 the upstate Republican societies had faded; all would disappear during the Adams administration. In the long run the myriad of other "self-created societies" which blossomed in the mid-1790's may have exerted a more profound political influence. The mechanic, fraternal, humanitarian, ethnic, religious, and militia organizations developed "the spirit of association" fundamental to a democracy. None was new to the 1790's but each in its own way expressed an awakened consciousness on the part of "the middling classes" and to a lesser extent the poor which was the essence of the Republican movement.

The Republican press was indispensable as a vehicle for the movement. With each spurt of Republican sentiment new papers were founded and old ones expanded their circulation. In the mid-1790's Greenleaf's *Journal* was joined by outright Republican papers at Newburgh, Goshen, Poughkeepsie, Kingston, and Albany; elsewhere new "impartial" and Federalist papers stimulated political discussion. The papers ran notices of meetings, nominations, and activities and reported resolutions, toasts, and orations. Most important, they teemed with articles on the issues of the day, long and short, "planted" and unsolicited. The small-town papers were jammed with "intelligence" of national, state, and European affairs, which probably kept their readers better informed on the world beyond their own village than do their counterparts today.

By the end of the era of Washington, Republicans had more of the attributes of a political party than the anti-Federalists. They had a name—usually "Republican"; their candidates often ran on a clearly labeled ticket; committees whose personnel was fairly stable from year to year made their nominations and conducted their campaigns. If Republicans ran as individuals as most still did, it was because it was expedient to avoid the party label. But political leaders knew who "their" men were. There was a process in operation; it went further in some areas, New York City, for example, than others. It also went further in national than state elections. Gubernatorial elections were the least partisan, as is indicated by the efforts of Burr and Chancellor Livingston in 1795 to secure nominations from both "interests" and by the management of the campaign by "the friends of Mr. Yates" and the "friends of Mr. Jay." Yet while the lines were looser in state elections they were essentially the same as in national affairs. In 1796 assemblymen and state senators elected without a label lined up in the state legislature on a predictable partisan basis to choose presidential electors.

Republican campaign methods did not change markedly in this period. Campaign workers made more use of newspapers, pamphlets, and broadsides but they still knew the value of "a beaver hat, an oyster supper, or a glass of grog" to sway a voter.[7] And while the voters heard more and more appeals to lofty principles, one suspects that in more than one township "a large majority gloried" at the election of their favorite because the legislature had located the new county courthouse favorably.[8] On the other hand if campaign methods did not change, it was unquestionably true that more and more people participated in the political process: in making nominations, in campaigning, and in voting.

As a party the Republicans were less unified than the anti-Federalists. Through the election of 1789 George Clinton was the undisputed anti-Federalist leader; he was indispensable for victory in gubernatorial elections and held a tight rein on the patronage. After Chancellor Livingston formed a "coalition" with Clinton to elevate Burr to the Senate in 1791, there were men with their own power base to challenge the Governor. Clinton's prestige also dropped after the land scandal and near defeat of 1792, and once Federalists gained control of the Council of Appointment in 1794 he lost the sinews of his power. As a result factionalism which was under wraps in 1792 when Burr maneuvered to replace Clinton as the Republican vice-presidential candidate was out in the open in 1795 when Clinton retired.

While there was never any love between Clinton, Livingston, and Burr, neither was there the virulent factionalism for which the New York Republicans of the early nineteenth century are so well known. If in Columbia County the Livingstons never got together with the old anti-Federalists on a congressional candidate, they worked unstintingly in harness with the Clintons against Federalist foreign policy. As a congressman Edward Livingston was untarnished in his Republicanism. If Burr sat out the gubernatorial election of 1795, the next year he ran for state senator to bolster the Republican ticket in the contest that would decide the choice of presidential electors. The

7. "Inspector," *N.-Y. Evening Post,* Apr. 17, 1795.
8. Vanderkemp, Journal, 16, N.-Y. Hist. Soc., referring to the 1792 election for governor in Herkimer County.

incentive to oust the Federalists from national power made for cooperation if not cohesion.

If Chancellor Livingston had hopes of "directing" the Republican "torrent" by "yielding" to it, he must have been disillusioned. Control of the party was somewhat diffuse. Clinton, as long as he was governor, ran the party in the legislature together with the leading legislators. Gubernatorial nominations were made by a caucus of legislators attended by other leaders, and then were in effect endorsed at local town and county meetings. Congressional candidates, by contrast, were chosen by the local leaders of the district; when two of the state's six Republican congressmen failed to stand firm on the crucial test of Jay's Treaty in 1796, the statewide leaders were not able to discipline them. Republican factionalism, so scorned by historians, actually was a symptom of a competition for power healthy to a new party.

By virtue of their strength in the state the New York Republicans clearly were a component of a national party; indeed, the national party appears to have been no more than a loose amalgam of the state groups. Neither Jefferson nor Madison had anything to do with organizing the New York Republicans; there would have been a Republican party in New York without them. Nor did the New Yorkers follow Madison's lead either in the fight against Hamiltonian finance in 1789-90 or in the foreign policy crisis of 1794-96 when they took a position to the "left" of the Virginians. They willingly backed Jefferson for the presidency in 1796 because of his opposition to Federalism, not because of his influence among the state party leaders. The New York Democratic Republicans thus cannot accurately be called New York Jeffersonians.

IV

What was the philosophy of the Democratic Republicans of New York? By 1797 they did, indeed, have a political credo distinct from the Federalists and in a number of ways distinct from the anti-Federalists of '88. For many young men who later achieved reputations only as hard-bitten politicians—DeWitt Clinton, Daniel Tompkins, Smith Thompson, Martin Van Buren—the 1790's were a seedbed of their Republican faith, and indeed of a youthful idealism.

First and foremost, Republicans were patriots. "After thy creator, love thy country above all things," read a catechism of the Albany Republicans entitled "The Precepts of Reason." "She alone, ought to fix thy thought and direct thy actions: thy life is hers."⁹ To Republicans the battle against Jay's Treaty, a betrayal of national interest, was a holy crusade; England, a den of iniquity; "Tory," the most odious epithet in their vocabulary; Independence Day, a sacred festival; and Thomas Paine, old "Common Sense" of '76, a near saint. Republican patriots followed the progress of liberty in Europe with bated breath, took Citizen Genêt to their bosoms as a symbol of the French Revolution, and welcomed Joseph Priestley and the victims of European tyranny to America, "an asylum for the oppressed." But they did not cease to think of themselves as the true patriots, loyal to the spirit of '76. "Your drum," ex-Governor Clinton wrote to his new grandson, "Citizen George Clinton Genêt," is "at Granny's braced for you to beat to arms against Tories and aristocrats if necessary."¹⁰

Second, Republicans believed in democracy, as they testified by adopting the name Democratic for their societies, Democratic Republican for their party, and such pseudonyms as "Democratis." They discussed the concept infrequently, yet most probably would have agreed with the simple definition offered at Poughkeepsie: "a government emanating from and being under the influence of the people."¹¹ Unlike Federalists, Republicans believed that elected representatives should express the will of the people and, invigorated by the spirit of direct democracy, instructed officials through the resolutions of societies, public meetings, and petitions. Some Republican congressmen also believed that they had a responsibility to report on their actions to their constituents.¹² As Federalists censured the "self-created societies," denigrated the "town meetings," and jailed protesters like William Keteltas, a libertarian strain never strong in anti-Federalist thinking became more pronounced among Republicans, preparing the ground for the enunciation of a full-blown philosophy of freedom of expression by New Yorkers in the Sedition Law crisis.

Third, Republicans supported the federal Constitution. The Federalist persistence in labeling them "anti-Federalists" missed the mark completely. It was not rhetoric when a New York City orator referred

9. "Precepts of Reason," *Barber and Southwick's Almanack for 1798*, unpaged.
10. George Clinton to Citizen George Clinton Genêt, July 2, 1796, June 1, 1797, Genêt Papers, N.-Y. Hist. Soc.
11. "Gracchus," *Poughkeepsie Journal*, Mar. 17, 1801.
12. A circular letter by Theodorus Bailey of Dutchess County, *Goshen Repository*, Feb. 11, 1794; Egbert Benson to Rufus King, Dec. 16, 1794, King Papers, N.-Y. Hist. Soc., reported that Bailey also sent newspapers to the voters; Philip Van Cortlandt, Circular Letter, May 20, 1796, Van Cortlandt-Van Wyck Papers, N.Y. Pub. Lib.

to Republicans as "sincere friends to Our National Constitution."[13] By 1796, when Abraham Yates died, the old anti-federalism lingered on primarily in such counties as Dutchess and Ulster; the other anti-Federalists had already created a mythology about 1788, maintaining that the sole issue had been whether amendments should be adopted before or after ratification. Republicans had moved toward a "strict interpretation" of the Constitution in the fight over Jay's Treaty, when they defended the legislative powers of the House of Representatives. They already thought of themselves as the "true" upholders of the Constitution against the Hamiltonians. This same strain of Constitutional literalism was also evident in the 1792 controversy over the election canvassers' decision when Clinton's defenders descended to an arid legalism, placing the letter over the spirit of the law.

Fourth, in spite of Federalist efforts to stigmatize them as "revolutionaries," Republicans advocated change by peaceful means. In 1792 when frontier Federalists talked of redressing the canvassers' decision by the sword or a popular convention, Republicans put themselves on the side of "law and order." In 1794 they were quick to disavow the "Whiskey Rebellion." In 1796 they cheered William Keteltas' appeal for confidence in the courts for a legal redress of his unjust imprisonment. And at no time did they sanction extralegal action by tenants against their landlords.

Fifth, Republicans inherited the anti-Federalist attitude toward class. "Wherever the influence of riches are enabled to direct the choice of public offices," said George Warner, a sailmaker, "there the downfall of liberty cannot be very far remote." "Our choice," he continued, "ought only to be direct to men of TALENTS AND VIRTUE whatever their situation in life may be" and "the experience of ages confirms this opinion that a state of mediocrity is more favorable to them both." Melancton Smith had said as much at the Poughkeepsie convention; unlike the anti-Federalists who had faith only in the yeomanry, however, Warner thought of the "tradesmen, mechanics and the industrious classes of society" as the *Means for the Preservation of Public Liberty*, the title of his oration.[14] Other Republicans found a place for merchants in a coalition of "farmers, merchants,

13. George Warner, *Means for the Preservation of Public Liberty . . . An Oration July 4, 1797 . . . before the General Society of Mechanics, Tammany, the Democratic and the New York Cooper Societies* (N.Y., 1797), 15, 9.
14. *Ibid.*, 13-15.

mechanics and common laboring men" necessary to defeat "great land-holders and monied men."[15] None, it seems, found a place for estate holders like the Livingstons. Most Republicans, like most anti-Federalists, still believed that suffrage should be confined to the "middling classes," although Republican success among the propertyless in New York City led to some demands that the suffrage be broadened.

Sixth, Republicans were even less "agrarian" than were the anti-Federalists. Robert R. Livingston and Philip Freneau expressed a distaste for city life and a desire to retreat to a rural haven, but the patrician landlord and the sensitive poet were hardly typical of the Republican movement.[16] In the state legislature Clintonians were dedicated to the pursuit of wealth for the aspiring entrepreneur, be he land speculator or farmer, would-be banker or manufacturer. Republicans thought of themselves as advocates of "the mechanic and useful arts," a phrase that embraced the productive classes of both city and countryside.

Under the imperative of winning support from the commercial community Republicans in New York City constantly wooed "the mercantile interest," from 1789 when they ran John Broome, president of the Chamber of Commerce for Congress, through the campaign for a third bank and the appeals by Genêt and his commercial agents, to the stand of the anti-Jay Treaty minority in the Chamber of Commerce in 1795. "The Colossus of American freedom," Congressman Edward Livingston toasted, "may it bestride the commerce of the world."[17] New York spawned no John Taylor in the 1790's.

Finally, Republicans were mild humanitarian reformers, as the activities of William Keteltas, Tunis Wortman, DeWitt Clinton, Jedediah Peck, and Elkanah Watson attest. "Every mortal is thy brother," read the Albany "Precepts of Reason," "always extend to him the helping hand . . . and always say to thyself, I am a man, nothing which interests humanity is foreign to me."[18] Republican humanitarianism for the most part, expressed middle-class sympathy for the less fortunate: the oppressed slave, the slum-ridden victims of yellow fever, the penniless immigrant, or the cruelly whipped prison-

15. "Scrutator," *N.-Y. Journal*, Apr. 19, 1797.
16. See Robert R. Livingston, "Address to the Agricultural Society of the State of New York," *New York Magazine*, 6 (1795), 95-102; Leary, *That Rascal Freneau*, 108, 260-65, 275.
17. Report of a dinner in New York City in honor of John Adams, *Whitestown Gazette*, Oct. 31, 1797.
18. "Precepts of Reason," *Barber and Southwick's Almanack for 1798*, unpaged.

er. Republican reform sentiment was more urban than rural, more moderate rather than radical, and stopped short of a fundamental challenge to the state's political institutions or landlord system. Nevertheless ideology as well as political necessity pushed Republicans toward ridding society of its "glaring deformities."

In these democratic, libertarian, constitutionalist, humanitarian articles of faith and in their sympathy for "the middling classes," "the mechanic and useful arts," and men of "talents and virtue," Republicans were wedded to a set of convictions that would carry them beyond the immediate battles they were engaged in. In the period that followed, from 1797 to 1801 their ideals and their movement would be put to a test.

Appendix

Bibliographical Essay

Index

Appendix

Table 1
Number of Voters, New York State, 1790[1]

County	1 Free- holders of £100	2 Free- holders of £20	2a[2] Free- holders of £20- £100	3 Tenants of 40 s.	4[3] Free- men	5[4] Total, All Voters	6[5] Assem- bly Voters Only
Southern							
New York	1209	1221	12	2661	93	3975	2673
Richmond	298	274		169		443	169
Suffolk	1511	1827	316	242		2069	558
Westchester	1441	1732	291	1130		2862	1421
Queens	1274	1397	123	438		1835	561
Kings	357	376	19	148		524	167
Middle							
Orange	941	1149	208	584		1733	792
Ulster	1610	1885	275	1096		2981	1371
Dutchess	2413	2780	367	1115		3895	1482
Eastern							
Columbia	2070	2534	464	964		3498	1428
Washington	799	1059	260	514		1573	774
Clinton						176	
Western							
Albany	3967	5122	1255	4030	45	9197	5285
Montgomery	1479	2069	595	1583		3652	2178
Ontario						411	
TOTAL	19,369	23,425	4,185	14,674	138	38,824	18,859

1. "A Census of the Electors and Inhabitants of the State of New York Taken in the Year 1790" signed by Lewis Scott, Secretary's Office of the State of New York, Jan. 11, 1791, published in N.Y. *Daily Advertiser*, Jan. 15, 1791, with

returns for each township and each ward in the city of New York and Albany. It is also reprinted in *Journal of the Assembly of the State of New York*, 14th Sess., 1791 (N.Y., 1791), 13-16. This return is also the basis of the "Summary of the Several State Electoral Censuses" used by most historians, to be found in New York State, Secretary of State, *Census of the State of New York* for 1855 (Albany, 1857), p. x. I have arranged the counties in the senate voting districts of 1790.

2. The original chart in the newspaper, reprinted in the 1855 census, lists only columns 1, 2, 3, and 4. I have added columns 2a, 5, and 6. Most historians, assuming that categories 1 and 2 are mutually exclusive, have added up 1, 2, 3, and 4 to reach a total of 57,606 voters in the state. Column 2, however, *included* the voters in column 1. The correct number of freeholders of £20 to £100 is column 2 minus column 1, as shown in column 2a. With a total of only 4056 freeholders in this category, the total of voters in the state as a whole is 38,834, and not 57,606, the figure commonly used.

My analysis is based on the following evidence. First, the law (*Laws of the State of N.Y.*, 13th Sess., ch. 7, Feb. 18, 1790) instructed the census taker to list all £100 freeholders twice, first separately and then together with freeholders of £20 and more. The law required that the census taker list the name of the head of family in the first column, adult males owning freeholds "of the value of £20; and where such freehold is of the value of £100 or upwards" in the third column, adding explicitly "the same person is to be numbered both in the second and third columns."

Secondly, in 1791 the legislature reapportioned the state on the basis of a total of 38,834 and not 57,606 electors. The total number of voters in all categories for each county, and the state as a whole (column 5) was not printed in the original report of the Secretary, published Jan. 15, 1791. Nor is it to be found in the 1855 census "Summary". But on Jan. 26, 1791, the N.Y. *Daily Advertiser* printed the totals I list in coulmn 5 in a summary of a report on apportionment by a joint committee of the senate and assembly. If one adds the total number of freeholders in both categories (column 1 and 2A) and the 40 s. renters (column 3) with the freemen (column 4), the totals are identical with those used by the legislative committee.

Third, the headings used in the next state electoral census clarify the 1790 census. In 1795 the legislature used more exact language for the catagories (*Laws of the State of N.Y.*, 18th Sess., ch. 11, Mar. 13, 1795). The census taker was instructed to list in the first column the names of heads of families in the second column (Table 3, Column 1) "Electors possessed of the freeholds of the value of £100," and in the third column (Table 3, Column 2) "Electors possessed of freeholds of the value of £20 and under £100." The law now added the injunction "but no person shall be numbered in the third column, who has been numbered in the second column."

Fourth, the number of £20 electors reported in 1795 and subsequent censuses is in line with my reading of the 1790 census. The 4056 £20 freeholders of 1790 went up to 4836 in 1795 and to 5264 in 1800. However, if one accepted column 2 in Table 1 as the correct figure for 1790, for the years 1790-95 one would have to account for a decline from 23,425 to 4836, an impossible loss of 18,587 voters in this category in light of the rise in the number of voters in other categories. The statistics clearly show that there were a relatively small number of freeholds evaluated at from £20 to £100; if a man owned his own farm it seems that it usually was worth more than £100 or it was no problem to have it evaluated at £100 or more.

My corrected reading of column 2 of the 1790 return is not without a few discrepancies. Thus in Richmond County, and in the returns for several wards in New York City (not printed here) there are fewer electors listed in column 2 than in column 1. This can be attributed to confusion in interpreting the 1790 census law, which the legislature obviously tried to correct in 1795. For every other county, and for almost every township in the state, the number of electors in column 2 was greater than in column 1, confirming my analysis.

I am thus "recanting" the analysis I offered in my doctoral dissertation, "Democratic Republican Movement," 37-38, n. 37 (corrected in my article in *Labor History*, 5 [1964], 222), with apologies to those I may have led astray. George D. Luetscher had the matter right in *Early Political Machinery in the United States* (Phila., 1903), 15-16. Scholars of New York history whose interpretation is incorrect include Spaulding, *New York in the Critical Period*, 90-91, Pomerantz, *New York An American City*, 127, and more recently Klein, "Democracy and Politics," *New York History*, 40 (1959), 232-37, Brown, *Charles Beard*, 63-64, and DePauw, *The Eleventh Pillar*, 146.

3. "Freemen" were created by the city government in the two chartered cities of the state. The Common Council of the City of New York did create a few freemen between 1790 and 1795. See Arthur E. Peterson, ed., *Minutes of the Common Council of the City of New York, 1784-1831*, 21 vols. (New York, 1917), I, II, *passim*.

This institution, so important in the colonial period, was obviously on its last legs in the postwar period. See Varga, "Election Procedures," *N.Y. History*, 41 (1960), 272, n. 8; Klein, "Democracy and Politics," *N.Y. History*, 40 (1959), 233-35; Pomerantz, *New York An American City*, 65-67.

4. As indicated in footnote 2 above, column 5 is taken from N.Y. *Daily Advertiser*, Jan. 26, 1791, also in Greenleaf's *N.Y. Journal*, Jan. 27, 1791. It included returns for two frontier counties, Ontario to the west and Clinton to the northeast, which the Secretary of State reported, Jan. 11, 1791, "have sent no returns." It would seem that late returns were filed. Judging by the 1795 returns for these counties which listed a very small proportion of £20-£100 freeholders and 40 s. renters, in 1790 most of the voters in both Ontario and Clinton probably qualified to vote as £100 freeholders.

5. Column 2a plus column 3. Those voters who qualified to vote only for the Assembly, and no other state office. This column is not in any contemporary report and is based on my calculations.

Table 2
Voters in Proportion to Total Adult White Males, New York, 1790[1]

County	1 Total Popu-lation	2 Males over 16	3[2] Males over 21 (AWM)	4 Heads of Fami-lies (HOF)	5[3] Per Cent of AWM who voted only for Senate	6[4] Per Cent of AWM who voted only for Assem-bly	7[5] Per Cent of AWM who voted, all elections	8[6] Per Cent of HOF who voted, all elec-tions
Southern								
New York	33,131	8,500	6,800	6,035	17.7	39.3	58.4	65.8
Richmond	3,835	749	516	566	57.7	32.7	85.8	78.2
Suffolk	16,440	3,756	3,004	2,868	50.2	18.5	67.9	72.1
Westchester	24,003	5,877	4,700	3,797	30.0	30.2	60.8	75.3
Queens	16,014	3,554	2,840	2,548	44.8	19.7	64.6	72.0
Kings	4,495	903	720	546	49.5	23.1	72.7	95.9
Middle								
Orange	18,492	4,600	3,680	2,887	25.5	21.5	47.0	60.0
Ulster	29,397	7,058	5,647	4,354	34.6	24.2	52.7	68.4
Dutchess	45,266	10,968	8,800	6,718	27.4	16.8	44.2	57.9
Eastern								
Columbia	27,732	6,579	5,263	4,279	39.3	27.1	66.4	81.7
Washington	14,042	3,606	2,884	2,483	27.7	26.8	54.5	59.3
Clinton	1,614	546	436	375			40.3	46.9
Western								
Albany	75,736	18,549	14,839	12,319	26.7	35.6	61.9	74.6
Montgomery	28,848	7,857	6,286	4,905	23.5	34.6	58.0	74.4
Ontario	1,075	524	424	204			96.9	
TOTAL	340,120	83,626	66,839	54,884	28.9	28.0	58.0	70.7

1. United States Bureau of the Census, *Heads of Families at the First Census of the United States Taken in the Year 1790—New York* (Washington, 1908), p. 9-10.
2. This first census only recorded free white males over 16. I have calculated free white males over 21 (column 3) as four-fifths of the males over 16 (column 2). This figure comes out somewhat higher than the number of heads of families (column 4), which corresponds with what we know of early American demographic patterns. Most, but not all men over 21, were heads of families.
3. Calculated on the basis of the number of freeholders worth £100 and more (Table I, column 1) who alone could vote for the state Senate and governor. There were no returns by separate categories for Clinton and Ontario.
4. Calculated on the basis of the number of freeholders between £20 and £100 combined with the number of 40 s. renters (Table I, column 6) who could vote only for Assemblymen.
5. Calculated on the basis of both Assembly and Senate electorates (Table I, column 5).
6. Calculated on the basis of the combined Assembly and Senate electorate as a proportion of the number of heads of families (column 4).

Table 3
Number of Voters, New York State, 1795[1]

	1	2	3	4	5	6
County	Freeholds of £100	Freeholds of £20-100	40 s. renters	Freemen	Total no. all voters	Assembly Voters Only[2]
Southern						
New York	2,144	10	4,948	170	7,272	4,958
Richmond	335	21	132		488	153
Suffolk	1,907	302	400		2,609	702
Westchester	1,987	151	1,105		3,243	1,256
Queens	1,372	303	557		2,232	860
Kings	417	22	168		607	190
Middle						
Orange	1,392	172	534		2,098	706
Ulster	2,650	373	1,406		4,429	1,779
Dutchess	3,236	316	2,461		6,013	2,777
Eastern						
Columbia	2,534	283	743		3,560	1,046
Washington	1,886	196	1,288		3,370	1,484
Clinton	336	22	266		624	288
Rensselaer	1,960	413	1,217		3,590	1,630
Western						
Albany	3,264	439	2,311	73	6,087	2,750
Montgomery	1,985	293	1,101		3,379	1,394
Ontario	1,040	108	110		1,258	218
Saratoga	1,978	258	1,034		3,270	1,292
Herkimer	2,478	510	1,173	.	4,161	1,683
Otsego	2,038	382	817		3,237	1,199
Tioga	552	109	504		1,165	613
Onondaga	847	155	323		1,325	478
TOTAL	36,338	4,838	22,598	243	64,017	27,456

1. From "A General account of the number of electors in the State of New York made from the returns delivered into the Secretary's Office of the State of New York, pursuant to an act entitled 'An Act for taking a Census in this State', passed the third of March, 1795," signed by Lewis A. Scott, Secretary, Jan. 20, 1796, published as a supplement to N.Y. *Daily Advertiser*, Jan. 27, 1796.   I have listed the counties by senatorial district as they were rearranged by legislative acts of Mar. 7, 1791 and Mar. 5, 1794.   See S.C. Hutchins, *Civil List* (Albany, 1869), 106-7.   In comparing returns with 1790 it should be borne in mind that new counties have been carved out of two upstate counties: from Albany, Rensselaer and Saratoga; from Montgomery, Herkimer, Otsego, Tioga and Onondaga.   All other counties were geographically intact.

2. The headings have been abbreviated for typographical reasons.   The original headings are as follows: (1) "Electors possessed of freeholds of the value of £100," (2) "Electors possessed of freeholds of the value of £20 and under £100," (3) "Electors, not possessed of freeholds but who rent tenements of the yearly value of 40 s.," (4) "Electors who were freemen on the 14th day of October 1775, and on the 20th day of April, 1777," (5) "Total number of electors."   I have added column 6 by combining the number of voters in columns 2 and 3.

Table 4
Returns for Governor, 1789, 1792, 1795[1]

County	1789 Clinton	1789 Yates	1792 Clinton	1792 Jay	1795 Yates	1795 Jay
Southern						
New York	385	833	603	739	519	1,124
Kings	176	136	244	92	185	171
Queens	482	124	532	288	306	482
Suffolk	353	292	481	228	809	215
Richmond	152	51	106	4	18	214
Westchester	337	442	347	824	397	1,016
Middle						
Dutchess	553	856	751	945	1,031	1,189
Orange	467	113	551	80	765	211
Ulster	1,039	206	947	654	1,185	757
Eastern						
Columbia	823	907	1,303	717	1,232	656
Washington	401	145	758	471	889	599
Clinton[2]	42	3			106	51
Rensselaer			404	717	605	1,075
Western						
Albany	1,000	1,577	414	1,178	850	1,401
Montgomery	181	271	306	424	826	565
Ontario			28	92	69	400
Saratoga			405	461	811	547
Herkimer			247	401	345	1,437
Otsego[2]					455	1,031
Tioga[2]					176	362
Onondaga					127	169
TOTAL	6,391	5,962[3]	8,440[4]	8,332[4]	11,892[5]	13,481[5]

1. The sources are as follows: for 1789, *N.Y. Journal*, June 4, 1789, and for township returns without counties, *N.Y Daily Advertiser*, May 28, 1789 ff.; for 1792, *N.Y. Journal*, May 28 - June 13, 1792; for 1795, *N.Y. Journal*, May 30-June 6, 1795.

2. The returns from Otsego, Tioga and Clinton were disputed in the 1792 election and not counted in the official canvass. For the probable vote in these counties, see ch. 14, sec. I.

3. As reported in the newspapers. This column actually totals 5,956.

4. As reported in the newspapers. These columns actually total 8,427 and 8,315.

5. As reported in the newspapers. These columns actually total 11,706 and 13,672.

Table 5
Returns for Congress, 1789, 1790

District	1789[1]			1790[4]		
	Federalist	Anti-Federalist	Other	Federalist	Anti-Federalist	Other
New York	Jn. Laurance	John Broome		Jn. Laurance		
N.Y.C.	2251	280				
Westch. (lower)	291	92				
total	2542	372		691		
Long Island			Wm. Floyd[2]	J. Townshend	Th. Tredwell	Wm. Floyd[5]
Kings				6	7	83
Queens				581	45	47
Suffolk				5	232	166
Richmond				0	0	23
total			894	592	284	319
Dutchess	Eg. Benson	Theod. Bailey		Eg. Benson	Theod. Bailey	
Dutchess				471	446	
Westch. (upper)				252	21	
total	584	574		723	467	
Ulster-Orange		John Hathorn[3]		P. Van Gaasbeck	C.Schoon-maker	John Hathorn
Ulster				733	376	0
Orange				20	522	61
total				753	898	61
Columbia-East	Ptr. Sylvester	Matthew Adgate	Jn. Williams	Ptr. Sylvester		J. Livingston
Columbia	954	723		914		855
Washington	147	248	14	236		305
Clinton	23	0	36			
Albany (east)	504	530		562		58
total	1628	1501	50	1712		1218
Albany-West	Ab. Ten Broeck	J. Van Rensselaer		Jas. Gordon	J. Van Rensselaer	
Albany (west)				1195	658	
Montgomery				270	359	
total	1215	1456		1465	1017	

1. The sources for the 1789 returns are: *N.Y. Journal*, Apr. 9, 1789 (New York, Long Island and Dutchess), and *Hudson Weekly Gazette*, Apr. 28, 1789 (Columbia-East). I have listed the candidates according to their known political record; they were not designated by party labels at the time.

2. William Floyd ran without opposition and received support from both Federalists and anti-Federalists. He had an Anti-Federalist voting record and became a Republican.

3. John Hathorn, who was well known as an anti-Federalist, ran without oppositon. No returns were reported for his district.

4. The sources for the 1790 returns are: *N.Y. Journal*, May 21, 25, 1790, *N.Y. Daily Advertiser*, May 20, 21, 22, 24, 28, 31, 1790; *Poughkeepsie Journal*, May 29, 1790.

5. There were two other candidates: John Vanderbilt with a total of 327 votes (Kings 209, Queens 64, Richmond 54) and Ezra L'Hommedieu with a total of 147 (Queens 139, Suffolk 7). Tredwell may be regarded as an anti-Federalist.

Table 6
Returns for Congress, 1792, 1794, 1796*

District	1792[1] Federalist	1792[1] Republican	1792 Other[2]	1794[4] Federalist	1794[4] Republican	1794 Other	1796[6] Federalist	1796[6] Republican	1796[6] Other
New York	John Watts 1872	W. Livingston 702		John Watts 1638	Edw. Livingston 1843		J. Watson 1812	Edw. Livingston 2362	
Long Island	H. Peters	T. Tredwell	J. Sands	Sam'l Jones	Jon. Havens	(2 others)[5]	S. Strong	Jon. Havens	
Kings	35	12	425				107	78	
Queens	608	365	300				304	221	
Suffolk	30	1000	44				237	960	
total	673	1377	769	494	815	805	648	1259	
Westchester	R. Hatfield	P. Van Cortlandt		Meyers	P. Van Cortlandt		S. Haight	P. Van Cortlandt	
Westchester	704	880		719	961		859	958	
Richmond	100	123		253	31		144	58	
total	804	1003		972	992		1003	1016	
Dutchess	Jas. Kent 852	Theod. Bailey 979		D. Brooks 1060	Theod. Bailey 1449		D. Brooks 1220	Theod. Bailey 1048	
Ulster-Orange	P. Van Gaasbeck	Jn. Hathorn	(4 others)[3]	C. Elmendorph	Jn. Hathorn	Wm. Thompson	C. Elmendorph	L. Elmendorph	
Ulster	1360	686		543	657		1275	1331	
Orange	104	762		40	862	37	239	606	
total	1464	1448	193	583	1519	37	1514	1937	
Columbia	Ezek. Gilbert 977	P. Van Ness 856	P. Livingston 948	Ezek. Gilbert 768	Jn. Bay 441	M. Adgate 419	H. Hosmer 1036	W. Van Ness 758	

*Footnotes to Table 6 are located on p. 592.

Table 6 (cont.)

District	1792[1]			1794[4]			1796[6]		
	Federalist	Republican	Other[2]	Federalist	Republican	Other	Federalist	Republican	Other
Eastern	J. Van Allen	H. Van Rensselaer		J. Van Allen	T. Tredwell		J. Van Allen	J. Woodworth	
Rensselaer				1071	178		1303	1087	
Clinton				38	120		285	65	
total	1165	870		1109	298		1588	1152	
Washington–Saratoga	Jas. Gordon	J. Williams	J. Thompson	E. Russell	J. Williams	A. Webster	Jas. Gordon	J. Williams	(2 others)[7]
Washington				513	1144	216	96	1084	
Saratoga				566	153	89	479	241	
total	1278	1146	355	1079	1297	305	575	1325	217
Albany	H. Glen 927	J. Van Rensselaer 526		H. Glen 703		J. Fairlie 82	H. Glen[8] 313		Ptr. Swart 167
West	S. Talbot	Jn. Winn	Wm. Cooper	Wm. Cooper	Jn. Winn	James Cochran	Wm. Cooper		James Cochran[9]
Montgomery	694	432	15	304	970	392	289		1046
Herkimer	319	18	54	746	144	106	1069		1086
Tioga	217	12	18	89	88	0	19		169
Ontario	7		83	30	2	37	41		320
Onondaga	0			95	6	0	51		197
Otsego	14	212	790	1271	216	0			152
total	1209[10]	838[10]	961	2535	1426	535	1481		2993

1. The sources are: *N.Y. Journal*, Feb. 20, 23, 1793; *Goshen Repository*, Feb. 28, 1793 (Columbia). Where no returns are listed for a county, none were printed in the papers, or none were located in the papers examined.

2. "Other" does not mean a third party or non-partisan but that there was a third (or sometimes a fourth) candidate in addition to the others. For clarification see the account of the particular congressional election.

3. In Ulster-Orange the other candidates and their votes were: Jesse Woodhull, 31; Cornelius Schoonmaker, 31; William Thompson, 59; John Carpenter, 72.

4. The sources are: *N.Y. Journal*, Feb. 7, 11, 14, 1795; *Poughkeepsie Journal*, Feb. 18, 1795 (Dutchess); *Goshen Repository*, Feb. 17, 1795 (Ulster-Orange); *Albany Gazette*, Feb. 16, 20, 1795 (Columbia, Rensselaer-Clinton, Washington-Saratoga, Albany).

5. On Long Island, John Smith received 251 votes and W. Cornwell 554.

6. The sources are: *N.Y. Argus*, Jan. 13, 14, 17, 18, 20, 1797; *Ulster Rising Sun*, Jan. 27, 1797 (Ulster-Orange); *Poughkeepsie Journal*, Jan. 25, 1797 (Dutchess); *Hudson Gazette*, Jan. 30, 1797 (Columbia).

7. In Washington-Saratoga Russell received 17 votes, Fonda 210.

8. This figure includes returns from Schoharie County, created in 1795. Glen received all of his votes from Albany, Swart received 29 from Albany and 138 from Schoharie.

9. James Cochran was an anti-Cooper Federalist. There is some confusion as to the total vote. *N.Y. Journal*, Jan. 14, 1797, lists returns, in addition to the counties noted, for Durlogh, probably a town of unknown location, which gave Cooper 25 votes and Cochran 23. It also reports 41 votes for Charles Williamson in Ontario. On Jan. 18, 1797 it reports another 99 votes for Cochran from Steuben County created in 1796, increasing Cochran's majority from 18 to 117. The totals listed here include the vote from the town of Durlogh

Table 7
Receipts, New York State Government, *1789-1797*[1]

Source of Receipt	1789	1790	1791	1792	1793	1794	1795	1796	1797
Auction Duties	4,413	6,219	9,192	14,604	20,212	14,798	31,295	25,026	29,100
Fees of Public Officers	17	373			64				1,404
Proceeds of Public Lands		3,164	123,878	325,677	224,172	293,994	142,849	64,546	59,385
Proceeds from State Funds	17,744	24,167	62,653	190,978	136,124	134,298	110,399	105,469	136,340
Dividends from Banks				5,083	9,136	11,538	9,364	7,114	14,764
Miscellaneous	166,193	93,725	60,705	23,158	5,341	29,700	11,711	41,967	24,742
Total General Funds, in Dollars	188,367	127,648	256,428	559,500	395,049	484,328	305,618	244,122	265,735[2]

1. Adapted from Don C. Sowers, *Financial History of the State of New York from 1789 to 1912* (New York, 1914), Appendix II. I have corrected the errors in addition, providing different totals for 1789, 1791, 1795, and 1796.
2. In 1797 the state also received in loan receipts from temporary loans $73,000, making total receipts of $338,735.

Table 8
Expenditures, New York State Government, 1789-1797[1]

General Expenditures	1789	1790	1791	1792	1793	1794	1795	1796	1797
Administrative	37,166	41,089	37,285	45,298	60,426	43,194	49,818	102,389	100,605
Legislative (printing)	3,622	1,957					6,899	832	
Public Health				3,750	1,000	11,007	15,000	23,917	11,875
Common Schools		2,500		19,250	4,000	5,625	9,375	61,125	49,999
Agriculture								1,000	
Defensive	4,660	13,429	2,281	17,097	8,733	160,075	58,328	68,417	10,433
Penal								112,500	87,562
Charitable					500	1,000	7.750		4,500
Public Buildings	6,516	20,000	9,188	1,516	34,248	11,231	15,382	44,626	2,437
Public Lands	9,484	13,458	86	8,038	5,100	4,459	25,235	27,236	14,240
Indian Affairs	8,103	9,100	1,675	1,682	54,625	5,775	5,215	5,780	7,500
Internal Improvements	67,624	2,839	4,707	1,986	58,219	50,775	56,202	28,926	22,125
Supervisory Duties	390	23,891	57,731	72,793	952	883	808		2,050
Bounties	900	565	562	684					
Interest		833	348			4			
Miscellaneous	23,327	5,832	2,085	2,943	5,078		2,555	1,605	
Total Ordinary Expenses	161,792	135,493	115,948	175,037	232,881	294,028	252,567	478,353	313,326
Investments		7,925	8,100	554,600	45,372		56,750	57,500	30,000

1. Adapted from Sowers, *Financial History of N.Y.*, Appendix I. I have corrected discrepancies in the totals for 1789, 1793, 1794, and 1795.

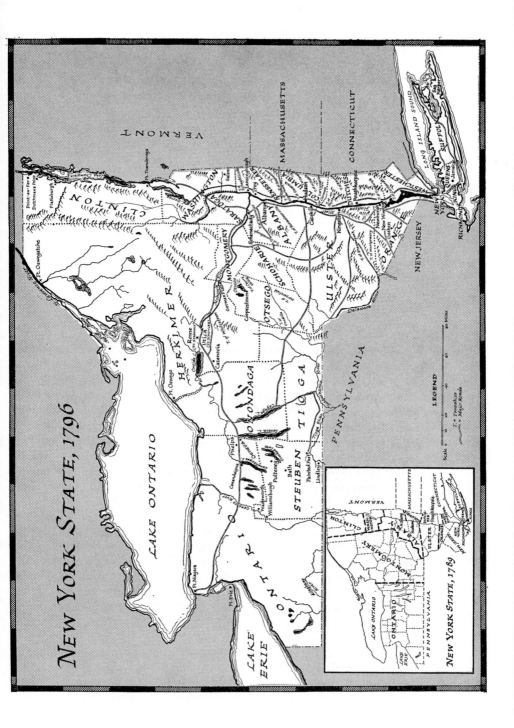

NEW YORK STATE, 1796

NEW YORK STATE, 1789

Bibliographical Essay

———•———

Original Sources

This is a study of the growth of a movement at what is customarily called the "grass-roots" level. I have been interested in politics as it is organized by the leaders, how it appears up front to the voters, how it all turns out in elections, and what the elected do with political power. To catch each of these dimensions it was necessary to make use of a different type of source material. For the organization of politics I have concentrated on the manuscript collections of leaders, high and low, on both sides, and on the records of private associations; for the public campaigns, elections and opinions, on newspapers and contemporary imprints: pamphlet tracts, broadsides, orations and sermons; for the political results, on election returns down to the town and ward level; and for the end product in government, on the legislative record of the state's congressmen in the federal government and the record of the legislative and executive departments in the state government. Throughout I have of course been interested in measuring the results of politics by such quantitative data as election returns, but I have been more interested in getting the feel of politics, and for this purpose I believe there is no substitute for soaking up a wide variety of original sources.

Manuscripts. Manuscript sources are generally rich and include a number of collections relatively unexploited for the study of politics. Of the three conventionally designated factions of the New York Republicans, the Livingstons, the Clintons, and Burr, the sources are fullest by far for the first. The Robert R. Livingston Collection, New

[596]

York Historical Society, N.Y.C., a vast treasure trove which has become available to scholars only in recent years, gives a full picture of the political activities of the lower manor—the Chancellor, his younger brother Edward, and his brothers-in-law—as well as of the upper manor branch of the family. It contains the drafts of numerous hitherto unidentified articles by the Chancellor. I have supplemented it with the Robert R. Livingston Papers, George Bancroft Transcripts, and Stephen Olin Scrap Book at the New York Public Library; Livingston Family Papers, Franklin D. Roosevelt Library, Hyde Park; the collection of Livingston's bailiff, William Wilson, at the William L. Clements Library, Ann Arbor, Mich.; and the Minutes of the Court of Chancery, 1789-1793, Hall of Records, Office of the County Clerk, N.Y. County Court House, N.Y.C.

The surviving papers of George Clinton are sparse. His early papers were destroyed when the British burned Kingston; most of his official papers were destroyed when a fire swept the state library in 1911 leaving ten out of an original fifty MS volumes. There are small collections of Clinton Papers, N.Y. Pub. Lib., and Historical Society of Pennsylvania; there are letters scattered in other collections of the N.-Y. Hist. Soc. and only a handful of unpublished items in the New York State Library Collection, Albany. DeWitt Clinton, the governor's nephew and private secretary in the 1790's, has left a somewhat fuller record in the DeWitt Clinton Papers, Columbia University Library, N.Y.C., but it is still disappointing. Cornelia Clinton's romance with Citizen Genêt comes through in the Edmund Genêt Papers, and the Clinton Family Papers, both at the N.-Y. Hist. Soc.

Aaron Burr's surviving papers create an even more elusive figure; Burr seems to have trusted little to correspondence, and he and his co-workers doubtless deliberately destroyed much of what there was to cover his tracks. I have gone over a good deal of the material, which supplements the selected correspondence published by Matthew Davis in *Memoirs of Aaron Burr . . .* , 2 vols. (N.Y., 1836-37), in Burr Papers at N.-Y. Hist. Soc., N.Y. Pub. Lib., Hist. Soc. of Pa., N.Y. State Lib., and American Antiquarian Society, Worcester, Mass., and in the Eustis and Sedgwick Papers, Massachusetts Historical Society, Boston, but uncovered new material only in the papers of Peter Van Gaasbeck, his client, moneylender, and political supporter, Van Gaasbeck Papers, F.D.R. Lib. and Kingston Senate House Museum.

For the old anti-Federalists who became Republicans there are several small collections well worn by historians: the John Lamb Papers, John Lansing Papers, John Smith Papers, John McKesson Papers, Jonathan Lawrence Papers, all at the N.-Y. Hist. Soc.; the papers of Abraham Lansing and Melancton Smith, N.Y. State Lib.;

Gilbert Livingston Papers, N.Y. Pub. Lib. I have given special attention to three men whose sizable collections reveal different types of
Republicanism: to Abraham Yates, the stormy anti-Federalist intran-
sigent of Albany, whose papers, N.Y. Pub. Lib., are rich for the 1780's
but, like Yates, peter out in the 1790's; to John Williams, the leading
anti-Federalist landholder of the north country who became a Federalist, whose papers, N.Y. State Lib., are helpful for both his politics
and economics; and to Elkanah Watson, the Albany Yankee active in
Republicanism, business, and reform, whose papers, N.Y. State Lib.,
are best for the latter two phases. Unfortunately there does not seem
to be a collection worthy of the name for any New York City Republican. For the 1790's there are only a few items each for James Nicholson, David Gelston, Melancton Smith, N.-Y. Hist. Soc. For the Van
Cortlandts of Westchester it is possible to piece together only the
broad outlines of the family in politics from fragments in the Van
Cortlandt Family and Van Cortlandt Mansion Papers, N.-Y. Hist. Soc.,
the Van Cortlandt-Van Wyck Papers, N.Y. Pub. Lib., and the miscellany assembled in photostats by the research department at Sleepy
Hollow Restorations, Tarrytown, N.Y.

The papers of a number of national Republican leaders were of use
for correspondence with New Yorkers, for John Beckley's reports, and
for observations on the state's politics: the Thomas Jefferson Papers,
examined on the Library of Congress microfilm, and selected items in
transcripts generously provided by Julian P. Boyd; the James Madison
Papers, N.Y. Pub. Lib. and Lib. Cong. microfilm; the James Monroe
Papers, N.Y. Pub. Lib.; the Albert Gallatin Papers, N.-Y. Hist. Soc., of
value for a few reports from Gallatin's father-in-law, James Nicholson,
and other New Yorkers.

The correspondence of the major New York Federalists is more extensive and more revealing than that of their counterparts. Harold C.
Syrett, et al., eds., The Papers of Alexander Hamilton, 11 vols. (New
York, 1961-66), carries Hamilton to June, 1792, after which the older
collections edited by John C. Hamilton and Henry Cabot Lodge must
be supplemented by manuscripts in a number of depositories. The
Syrett edition assembles more writings by Hamilton than we have
hitherto had and is especially valuable for reports to Hamilton from
the New York front by Philip Schuyler, Robert Troup and other political co-workers. The transcripts assembled by the John Jay Papers,
Columbia Univ., supplement the older edition of Jay's writings edited
by Henry P. Johnston in a less spectacular way for this period. Two
volumes of unpublished papers from this collection are being prepared for publication under the editorship of Richard B. Morris. The
Rufus King Papers, N.-Y. Hist. Soc., add to Charles King's edition

here and there, especially with correspondence from New Yorkers in the foreign policy crisis, 1793-94. Philip Schuyler's voluminous papers, N.Y. Pub. Lib., I found indispensable for the politics of the upstate region and the state legislature. I also dipped into Schuyler's Canal Papers and his Land Papers, N.Y. Pub. Lib., and made use of Schuyler Papers, Lib. Cong. and N.Y. State Lib. A project to publish from seven to ten volumes of Schuyler materials is in an early stage at Syracuse University.

The collections of several less well-known Federalists permit one to get at the little understood Federalism of the countryside. The large Peter Van Gaasbeck collection, Senate House Museum, Kingston, part of which is at F.D.R. Lib., Hyde Park, is superb for the functioning of a political machine in Ulster County. For Otsego County, transcripts of William Cooper letters in the Rensselaer-Townshend Papers, N.-Y. Hist. Soc., and a small number of Cooper Papers, New York State Historical Association, Cooperstown, and at N.Y. State Lib., show the modus operandi of the "Bashaw of Otsego." Unfortunately I was not permitted to see the Cooper papers in the hands of the Cooper family, Cooperstown. The letters of Moss Kent to his better known brother in the James Kent Papers, Lib. Cong., clarify the emergence of dissident Federalism in Otsego. For the politics of the proprietors of the "far west," the Genesee country, I have found nothing comparable. There are a few items of political interest in the large Phelps-Gorham Collection, and some scattered Thomas Morris letters, both at the N.Y. State Lib. The O'Reilly Collection, Western Mementos, 1774-1820, vols. 6-10, N.-Y. Hist. Soc., documents the frontier Indian and defense crisis of the early 1790's.

For a number of lesser Federalists there are small collections usually of value for local history: John Van Allen, Rensselaer County congressman, Albany Institute of History and Art; Henry Glen, Albany congressman, N.Y. Pub. Lib. and N.Y. State Hist. Assoc.; Peter Van Schaack of Columbia County, Lib. Cong.; the Sedgwick Papers, Mass. Hist. Soc.; Ebenezer Foote of Ulster County, N.Y. State Lib. and Lib. Cong.; William North, assemblyman from Duanesburg, N.Y. State Lib.; and Richard Varick, mayor of New York City, N.-Y. Hist. Soc.

The manuscript minutes of private societies are indispensable for the "spirit of association." I have used the records of the following groups, the full names of which are in chapter 18; for New York City: Tammany, N.Y. Pub. Lib. and Columbia Univ.; the Federal Republican Club (in John Lamb Papers), the Manumission Society, and the N.Y. Hibernian Volunteers, all N.-Y. Hist. Soc.; the Belles Lettres Society, Uranian Society, and Chamber of Commerce, N.Y. Pub. Lib.;

the Associated Teachers, N.Y. State Lib.; and the General Society of Mechanics and Tradesmen at the society which still bears its name, N.Y.C. For upstate organizations I have examined the records of the Schaghticoke Polemic Society, N.-Y. Hist. Soc.; the Albany Mechanics Society, Red Hook Society for the Detection of Horse Thieves, and the Slave Apprehending Society, Shawangunk, Ulster Co., N.Y. State Lib. Unfortunately only a few pieces of correspondence survive for the Democratic Society of New York City, N.-Y. Hist. Soc., and none for the upstate groups.

Several manuscript collections were used primarily to illuminate specific events, as follows: the Andrew Craigie Papers, Amer. Antiq. Soc., for the bank war of 1792 and the Jay Treaty crisis; the William Constable Land Papers and Constable-Pierrepont Papers, N.Y. Pub. Lib., for the state land sales of 1791; the Proceedings of the Commissioners for the Defense of New York City, N.-Y. Hist. Soc., for the war crisis of 1794; the Edmund Genêt Papers, Lib. Cong. and N.-Y. Hist. Soc., for French dealings with New York businessmen and politicians.

For perhaps one hundred individuals not mentioned above but noted in the footnotes I have examined from one to a score of manuscript items in the following libraries: N.-Y. Hist. Soc., N.Y. State Hist. Assoc., N.Y. Pub. Lib., N.Y. State Lib., and Lib. Cong. Unfortunately the published guides to these five libraries, at which most of the manuscripts for this study are located, are outdated. The most valuable aids to locating historical MSS for early New York history remain Works Projects Administration, Historical Records Survey, comps., *Guide to Depositories of Manuscript Collections in New York State (Exclusive of New York City)* (Albany, 1941), vol. I, and Evarts B. Greene and Richard B. Morris, eds., *A Guide to the Principal Sources for Early American History (1600-1800) in the City of New York* (N.Y., 1929, rev. edn., 1953).

Personal Accounts. Travel journals, memoirs, and diaries provide the best descriptions of conditions. Of the travel accounts by foreigners, the three most perceptive are F. A. F. de La Rochefoucauld-Liancourt, *Travels Through the United States of North America, . . . in the Years 1795, 1796, 1797 . . .*, 2 vols. (London, 1799), thorough and vivid for all parts of the state; William Strickland, *Journal of a Tour . . . 1794-1795*, N.-Y. Hist. Soc., best for the Hudson Valley; and Hans Huth and William Pugh, trans. and ed., *Talleyrand in America as a Financial Promoter, 1794-1796: Unpublished Letters and Memoirs*, American Historical Association, *Annual Report for the Year 1941* (Washington, 1942), III, best for the frontier. I also found useful the published journals of these Englishmen: Francis Bailey, John Bernard, Henry Wansey, and Isaac Weld, Jr., and of the Frenchman, Brissot de Warville.

Of foreigners who came to stay in New York, at least for a while, Kenneth and Anna M. Roberts, trans. and ed., *Moreau de St. Méry's American Journey (1793-1798)* (Garden City, 1947) is vivid for the "lower orders" in New York City, while Grant Thorburn's *Forty Years Residence in America . . .* (Boston, 1834) reveals a Scot who made good. For the frontier, Francis Adrian Vanderkemp's Journal of a Trip . . . 1792, MS, N.-Y. Hist. Soc., and Helen L. Fairchild, ed., *Francis Adrian Van der Kemp 1752-1829, An Autobiography* (N.Y., 1903) and John Lincklaen's A Journey . . . 1802, MS, N.-Y. Hist. Soc., are helpful. For the Hudson Valley life I am inclined to accept, although with a grain of salt, the observations of Hector St. Jean de Crèvecoeur, who farmed in Orange County before the Revolution and returned as French consul after it. His well-known *Letters from an American Farmer* (N.Y., 1912) is supplemented by *Sketches of Eighteenth Century America*, ed. Henri L. Bourdin *et al.* (New Haven, 1925) and *Eighteenth Century Travels in Pennsylvania and New York*, trans. and ed., Percy G. Adams (Lexington, Ky., 1961).

The first-person writings by York State residents are generally disappointing. An exception is the Diaries and Journals of James Kent, 4 MS vols., Lib. Cong., which have vivid capsule descriptions of the people and places Judge Kent encountered while riding circuit, 1791-1802. Small segments have been printed in *New York History*, 18 (1937), 22 (1941). Elkanah Watson's *Men and Times of the Revolution; or Memoirs . . . Including his Journals of Travels in Europe and America*, ed., Winslow C. Watson (N.Y., 1856), is more reliable for accounts of the frontier than for his own activities. Two diaries hint at the impact of Republicanism on New York professional men: Dr. Alexander Anderson, Diary, 1793-1799, 3 vols., Columbia Univ., Columbiana Collection, and that of the producer-playwright William Dunlap, Dorothy C. Barck, ed., *Diary of William Dunlap (1766-1839)*, 3 vols. (N.Y., 1929-31). For pioneer life, Levi Beardsley, *Reminiscences . . . of the Early Settlement of Otsego County* (N.Y., 1852), and the numerous first person accounts in Orsamus Turner's compendia, *Pioneer History of the Holland Purchase* (Buffalo, 1849), and *History of the Pioneer Settlement of Phelps and Gorham's Purchase and Morris' Reserve* (Rochester, 1852) are flavorsome. William Cooper's *A Guide in the Wilderness; or the History of the First Settlements in the Western Counties of New York . . .* (Dublin, 1810, Rochester, 1897) illuminates the unique position of the proprietors.

Newspapers. Historians have too often dismissed eighteenth-century newspapers as a source for political history. It is true that they were generally partisan, that seemingly unsolicited "letters to the editor" were often as not planted by politicians, that they usually did not report local events (which everyone knew about) and when they did, that they were often untrustworthy. Even so, the papers are indispensable for expressions of local opinions, for notices, for reports of meetings and election campaigns, for election returns (which for this period are available for New York in no other place), and for advertisements and commercial news revealing the life of the community.

I have attempted to read all the Republican papers extant and all "upstate" papers whatever their politics; for New York City, where there usually were a half dozen papers, besides the Republican papers, I read the *Daily Advertiser*, the best edited daily, and on key issues whatever else was published. I have of course given special attention to the leading Republican organs: at New York City to *N.-Y. Journal*, the short title I have used for the paper published weekly or semiweekly by Thomas Greenleaf as *New-York Journal, and Weekly Register* (1787-1790), as *New-York Journal and Patriotic Register* (1790-1794), and as *Greenleaf's New-York Journal* (1794-1800), and to its companion the *Argus, or Greenleaf's New Daily Advertiser*, a daily (1795-1800) which printed more or less the same articles; and at Albany to *Albany Register* published by John Barber and Solomon Southwick as a weekly (1788-1795) and then a semi-weekly (1795-1820).

The extant copies of the often shortlived small town weeklies are very few, especially for the western region. The fullest runs of the upstate papers are, for the Hudson Valley: *Albany Gazette* (1789-1797); *Catskill Packet* (1792-1797); *Goshen Repository* (1789-1797); *Hudson Gazette* (1792-1797); Kingston *Farmer's Register* (1793), Kingston *Rising Sun* (1793-1797); *Newburgh Packet* (1795-1797); *Poughkeepsie Journal* (1789-1797); and for the west: Cooperstown *Otsego Herald, or Western Advertiser* (1795-1798); and *Whitestown Gazette* (1796-1798); and for the north, Salem *Washington Patrol* (1795). I also examined most of the extant copies of some two dozen other small town papers for which only scattered runs exist and for New York City I also read the *Columbian Gazetteer* (1793-1794); *New-York Evening Post* (1794-1795); *Gazette Francaise* (1795-1797); *Mott & Hurtin's New-York Weekly Chronicle* (1795), and the *Time Piece* (1797-1798), all of varying hues of Republicanism, plus the *New York Magazine or Literary Repository* (1790-97), a monthly magazine. A complete list of the papers and the location of each extant copy is in the monumental work of Clarence Brigham, comp., *History and*

Bibliography of American Newspapers, 1690-1820, 2 vols. (Worcester, Mass., 1947), I, 527-757. The fullest collections of papers are at the N.-Y. Hist. Soc., N.Y. Pub. Lib., N.Y. State Lib., and Amer Antiq. Soc. Almost none, unfortunately, are yet on microfilm.

Imprints. The decade of the 1790's of course was a golden age of pamphleteering. Next to the newspapers the pamphlets and broadsides are most revealing of public opinion. I have attempted to look at all of the politically relevant imprints written by New Yorkers and brought out by New York printers for these years. These are of several sorts: (1) partisan tracts dealing with particular issues; (2) orations, sermons, and "discourses" before organizations and on public occasions; (3) the publications of associations; and (4) a miscellany of almanacs, collections of songs and poetry, etc. I have given less attention to works reprinted from other states and from Europe and to American religious imprints. The imprints I have used are identified in the footnotes. There is a partial listing in Young, The Democratic Republican Movement in New York State, 1788-1797 (unpubl. Ph.D. diss., Northwestern Univ., 1958), 928-35. Charles Evans, comp., *American Bibliography: A Chronological Dictionary of all Books, Pamphlets and Periodical Publications Printed in the United States of America . . . 1639 . . . 1820*, 14 vols., (Chicago and Worcester, 1903-59), locates the extant copies of imprints through 1800. Vol. 13 was compiled by Clifford K. Shipton, and Vol. 14, the index, by Roger P. Bristol. The imprints are now widely available in the microcard edition of the Amer. Antiq. Soc. The most helpful catalogs, however, listing many items not in Evans, are the imprint trays of the rare books room, N.Y. Pub. Lib. and Amer. Antiq. Soc., which are arranged by city of publication, by years. Douglas McMurtrie's check lists of early imprints, published in a variety of places, are available for Albany, Batavia, Brooklyn, Canandaigua, Geneva, Sag Harbor, Schenectady, and Whitestown.

Broadsides, single sheets issued at election time and for other political campaigns, have also been combed. The fullest collections are in the following libraries: N.-Y. Hist. Soc., N.Y. Pub. Lib., N.Y. State Lib., Lib. Cong., N.Y. State Hist. Assoc., and the DeWitt Clinton Collection at the Albany Institute of History and Art.

Government Documents. Federal. I have concentrated on the legislative record of New York's representatives, particularly in the House, which can be followed fairly well in *Annals of Congress* supplemented by newspaper reports. I have found *American State Papers* of value but have confined my foray into unpublished federal records to the Records of the Claims Commission Under Article VII of Jay's Treaty,

National Archives, for the record of depredations against New York ships, a factor of importance in understanding merchant politics. In light of the work on security holdings by New Yorkers by E. James Ferguson, Forrest McDonald, and Jackson T. Main, I have not felt it necessary to make a ritual trek through the treasury records that gave Charles Beard the evidence for his interpretation.

State. I have read the *Journals of the Assembly and Senate of the State of New York* for the eleventh to twentieth sessions (1788-97), each of which was published (occasionally together) after each session, usually in New York City. The sparse record of the motions, readings of bills, and votes must be supplemented by the debate reported in the newspapers. The laws are available in a volume published after each session and in several compendia: Samuel Jones and Richard Varick, comps., *Laws of the State of New York, First to Twelfth Sessions* (N.Y., 1789); *Laws of the State of New York, First to Twentieth Session* (N.Y. 1797); James Kent and Jacob Radcliff, comps., *Laws of the State of New York, 1783-1801* (Albany, 1802); *Laws of the State of New York, 1777-1801*, 5 vols., (Albany, 1886-87). I have listed all laws only by session number and chapter without regard to the compilation in which they appear. The major messages of Governors George Clinton and John Jay are in Charles Z. Lincoln, ed., *Messages from the Governors . . .* , 11 vols. (Albany, 1909), II. Hugh Hastings and J. A. Holden, eds., *Public Papers of George Clinton, First Governor of New York, 1777-1795, 1801-1804*, 10 vols. (N.Y., 1899-1914), is meager for the years of peace. A number of specialized volumes of state documents are listed in the footnotes to the two chapters in this study on the state and the economy. *Civil List and Constitutional History of the Colony and State of New York*, compiled by F. B. Hough (1855-63), S. C. Hutchins (1865-82), and E. A. Werner (1883-88), lists elected and appointed officers of both state and county government and is of value in any of its editions.

Several catastrophes befell the New York State Library; as a result such manuscript records of the legislative and executive branches as survive are literally often no more than charred fragments. The standard guide to the unpublished state records B.C. (Before Catastrophe) is Herbert Levi Osgood, comp., "Report on the Public Archives of New York," Amer. Hist. Assoc., *Annual Report for 1900* (Washington, 1901) , II, 67-147. Among state records I was unable to locate either the official election returns (and hence compiled them from the newspapers), or poll lists, or more than a handful of scattered county or township tax records.

Miscellaneous Collections. E. B. O'Callaghan, ed., *Documentary History of the State of New York*, 4 vols. (Albany, 1849-51), is a valuable potpourri. Nothing surpasses I. N. Phelps Stokes, comp., *The Iconography of Manhattan Island, 1498-1909 . . .*, 6 vols. (N.Y., 1915-28), which collects a day by day record of events in New York City from a variety of original sources. For New York City, the annual directories are indispensable to run down the occupations and addresses of individuals and for information about the private societies. They are worthy of analysis in themselves. I have referred to them uniformly as *New York Directory* by year. They were compiled by David Franks (1786-87), by Hodge, Allen and Campbell, publishers (1789-90), by William Duncan (1791-95), and David Longworth (1796-1801) and usually were published during the year of their title. Arthur E. Peterson, ed., *Minutes of the Common Council of the City of New York, 1794-1831*, 21 vols. (N.Y., 1917), is the only published city government record for the state I know of. Joel Munsell, comp., *Annals of Albany*, 10 vols. (Albany,1850-59), is the only collection of miscellany for a city outside of New York touching on this period. For New York City, Rosalie Fellow Bailey, *Guide to Genealogical and Biographical Sources for New York City (Manhattan), 1783-1898* (N.Y., 1954) is of exceptional value.

Secondary Authorities

The Federalist era in New York has received relatively little attention from scholars. Historians have generally treated it briefly as a prelude to later periods, and even the best of biographers have not had the patience or interest to depict the detailed political environment necessary for their subjects. One suspects others have avoided the period on the assumption that the deadly factionalism of the Democratic Republicans of the early nineteenth century was also characteristic of the 1790's.

The Revolutionary Era. For the period of the Revolution and Confederation there has been a good deal more research, but it may not be an exaggeration to say that scholars are living off a heritage of scholarship of the progressive school of the early twentieth century. The basic monographs for New York political history, with which every historian must still reckon, are: Carl L. Becker, *The History of Political Parties in the Province of New York, 1760-1776* (Madison, Wis., 1909), in which Becker first projected his interpretation of the revolution as a struggle of "who shall rule at home" as well as for "home rule"; A. C. Flick, *Loyalism in New York during the American Revolution* (N.Y., 1901); E. Wilder Spaulding, *New York in the*

Critical Period, 1783-1789 (N.Y., 1932), which followed the broad outlines of Charles Beard's economic interpretation of the Constitution and ratification; and Dixon Ryan Fox, *The Decline of the Aristocracy in the Politics of New York* (N.Y., 1919), which completed the Becker-Beard version of the conflict of radical vs. conservative and anti-Federalist vs. Federalist with the triumph of democracy in the Constitutional Convention of 1821 and the rebirth of Federalism as Whiggery.

The chapters in the cooperative work, *A History of the State of New York*, 10 vols. (N.Y., 1933-37) which A. C. Flick edited, only confirmed the status of the Becker-Beard-Fox interpretation. The chapters pertinent for this study were written by Evarts B. Greene on the empire, Edward P. Alexander on the provincial aristocracy (vol. 2), Flick on the making of the Revolution (vol. 3), Spaulding on the first state government and Frank Monaghan on the results of the Revolution (vol. 4), Spaulding on ratification (vol. 5) and Dennis Lynch and Dixon Ryan Fox on the growth of parties (vol. 6).

The monographs of the 1930's and 1940's in the Columbia University Studies in History, Economics, and Public Law, many supervised by Evarts B. Greene, were in the same mold. Irving Mark's *Agrarian Conflicts in Colonial New York, 1711-1775* (N.Y., 1940) portrayed bitter class conflict; Virginia Harrington, *The New York Merchant on the Eve of the Revolution* (N.Y., 1935), echoed Arthur Schlesinger, Sr.'s *The Colonial Merchants and the American Revolution, 1763-1776* (N.Y., 1917), a companion to Becker; Robert East, *Business Enterprise in the American Revolutionary Era* (N.Y., 1938), focused on the continuing thrust of New York merchants during the Revolution itself; Dorothy Dillon limned the divergent paths of provincial leaders in *The New York Triumvirate: A Study of the Legal and Political Careers of William Livingston, John Morin Scott, William Smith, Jr.* (N.Y., 1949). If Harry Yoshpe's findings in *The Disposition of Loyalist Estates in the Southern District of The State of New York* (N.Y., 1939) suggested that J. Franklin Jameson had overstated his thesis in *The American Revolution Considered as a Social Movement* (Princeton, N.J., 1926), they did not negate Becker's thesis of a continuing conflict over the fruits of the Revolution.

To be sure, there were some corrections of the progressive school. Spaulding as well as Thomas Cochran in *New York in the Confederation: An Economic Study* (Phila., 1932) pointed out a number of Beard's errors. But not until recent years have scholars directly challenged the traditional version of the Revolution and Confederation in New York.

Becker has been criticized primarily for the version of provincial politics prior to 1763 which he offered in his opening background chapter. The burden of the argument by Milton Klein in "Democracy and Politics in Colonial New York," *N.Y. History*, 40 (1959), 221-46, and by Nicholas Varga, "Election Procedures and Practices in Colonial New York," *ibid.*, 41 (1960), 249-77, is that the suffrage was broader and political practices more democratic than Becker allowed and that the aristocracy, if it dominated, did so by persuasion rather than coercion. These hypotheses await sustained proof. Varga in New York Government and Politics During the Mid-Eighteenth Century (unpubl. Ph.D. diss., Fordham Univ., 1960) gives more proof that politics was atomistic rather than democratic. Chilton Williamson, the most careful student of the suffrage, shows a much wider suffrage than was previously held, but also indicates a persistent demand in New York for more democratic election practices throughout the revolutionary era; see *American Suffrage: From Property to Democracy, 1760-1860* (Princeton, 1960). Scholars of late colonial politics have not yet come to grips with Beverly McAnear's Politics in Provincial New York, 1689-1761 (unpubl. Ph.D. diss., Stanford Univ., 1935), a study in the Becker tradition known only to specialists. Richard Morris's admonition in "Class Struggle and the American Revolution," *William and Mary Quarterly*, 3rd Ser., 19 (1962), 3-29, that historians might well give more attention to the "tone of politics" and less to the form seems especially applicable to New York.

Historians who deal with Becker's central concern, the politics of 1763-1776, seem to be correcting him without eliminating his basic thesis. Thus Roger Champagne, in The Sons of Liberty and the Aristocracy in New York Politics, 1765-1790 (unpubl. Ph.D. diss., Univ. of Wis., 1960) and the several articles cited above in ch. 1, shows the "liberty boys" to be less monolithic and more complex than portrayed by Becker; at the same time he lends weight to the thesis of Merrill Jensen of the emergence of an inadvertently democratic movement after 1774. Bernard Mason, *The Road to Independence* (Lexington, Ky., 1966), which I read as a doctoral dissertation (Columbia Univ., 1958), offers a different analysis of the sources of Toryism, yet documents the conflict in the making of the New York Constitution in 1777.

The most productive recent scholar of the Revolution in New York, Staughton Lynd, offers an analysis of class conflict more sophisticated than either Becker or Beard, in a number of articles which will appear in 1967-68 under the title, "Class Conflict, Slavery, and the United States Constitution: Ten Essays." Lynd portrays the tenants of 1776 in the role of radicals opposed by Whig landlords and popular Whigs and sees the anti-Federalists of 1788 as a coalition of popular Whigs of the middling sort and tenants against the Federalist "manor lords"; see his *Anti-Federalism in Dutchess County, New York: A Study of Democracy and Class Conflict in the Revolutionary Era* (Chicago, 1962), with additional evidence in "Who Should Rule at Home? Dutchess County, New York, in the American Revolution," *Wm. and Mary Qtly.*, 3rd Ser., 18 (1961), 330-59, and "The Tenant Rising at Livingston Manor, May 1777," N.-Y. Hist. Soc., *Quarterly Journal*, 48 (1964), 163-77. In New York City he sees the mechanics as consistently democratic and nationalistic; see "The Mechanics in New York Politics, 1774-1788," *Labor History*, 5 (1964), 225-46, developed at greater length in The Revolution and the Common Man: Farm Tenants and Artisans in New York Politics, 1777-1788 (unpubl. Ph.D. diss., Columbia Univ., 1962), Part II.

George Dangerfield, author of the major New York biography of recent years, *Chancellor Robert R. Livingston of New York, 1746-1813* (N.Y., 1960), also portrays New York's Revolution in strikingly Becker-like colors. The only new work on the land question, the articles by Beatrice Reubens and Catherine Snell Crary cited in ch. 1, revise Yoshpe to reveal the democratic or mixed results of the Revolution, and the only systematic analysis of the personnel of the legislatures, that of Jackson T. Main, reveals an unmistakable shift of political power away from the old landed-mercantile aristocracy; see "Social Origins of a Political Elite: The Upper House in the Revolutionary Era," *Huntington Library Quarterly*, 27 (1964), 147-58, and "Government by the People: The American Revolution and The Democratization of the Legislatures," *Wm. and Mary Qtly.*, 3rd Ser., 23 (1966), 391-408, part of a book length manuscript, The Upper House in Revolutionary America, in which ch. 6 deals with New York. Thus Becker's struggle for "who shall rule at home" in New York, whatever its oversimplifications, can hardly be dismissed.

Neither can Charles Beard. Beard clearly was wrong about a number of fundamentals in New York. His egregious error lumping the great landlords on the anti-Federalist side, corrected by Spaulding and Cochran as early as 1932, threw off his class analysis. He missed the importance of the mechanics, made the political structure less democratic than it was, and doubtless overemphasized the role of security holding, at least among the delegates to the ratifying convention. But if Beard is wanting, the analysis offered in his place both by his critics and by critics of the critics leaves something to be desired. In *We the People: The Economic Origins of the Constitution* (Chicago, 1958), Forrest McDonald's conclusion that both parties "included approximately equal numbers of large and small landholders and speculators in various forms of property" misses the distinction between established landed wealth and the new middle class entrepreneurial types. Jackson T. Main's suggestion in *The Antifederalists: Critics of the Constitution, 1781-1788* (Chapel Hill, 1961), that we return to Orin Libby's concept of commercial vs. non-commercial interests, like Lee Benson's suggestion in *Turner and Beard: American Historical Writing Reconsidered* (Glencoe, Ill., 1960) that the New York conflict was that of the "pure agrarian" as opposed to the commercial outlook, misses the commercial character of agriculture in anti-Federalist strongholds of the Hudson Valley. Linda Grant DePauw's argument in *The Eleventh Pillar: New York State and the Federal Constitution* (Ithaca, N.Y., 1966), which I read as a doctoral dissertation (Johns Hopkins University, 1964), that there were no parties, no fundamental differences and that the acrimony of 1788 soon dissolved into consensus can be sustained only by bypassing the perspective of the 1770's and the 1790's.

My reading of the evidence would leave intact some of Beard's interest group analysis of New York, the "hopes of the creditors" and "the commercial interest" Hamilton so clearly recognized. This has been amply demonstrated in E. James Ferguson's authoritative *The Power of the Purse: A History of American Public Finance, 1776-1790* (Chapel Hill, 1961), and is part of Forrest McDonald's analysis in his most recent book, *E Pluribus Unum: The Formation of the American Republic, 1776-1790* (Boston, 1965), which goes so far as to quote Beard on the existence of a coalition of business interests of the middle states as a dynamic source of nationalism. Unlike Beard I have placed more emphasis on the fears of the established class as a whole, on conservatism. This is certainly the thrust of Dangerfield's portrayal of Robert R. Livingston and is excellently documented in the new correspondence to and from Hamilton made available by the Syrett edition of *The Hamilton Papers*. The anti-Federalists it has seemed to me are best understood as middle class spokesmen a notch above "the middling sort" they represented. This is salient in Jackson T. Main's recent meticulous statistical studies and in Staughton Lynd's work. Even the evidence in Forrest McDonald's "The Anti-Federalists, 1781-1789," *Wisconsin Magazine of History*, 46 (1963), 206-14, about George Clinton's security funding plan of 1786 fits into this pattern. The New York evidence tempts one to say, as John Adams said on his deathbed of Thomas Jefferson, that somehow Charles Beard "still survives."

To solve the thorny questions of the character of the Revolution in New York, Edmund Morgan's suggestion in "The American Revolution: Revisions in Need of Revising," *Wm. and Mary Qtly.*, 3rd Ser., 14 (1957), 13-15, that we pursue research in local institutions:

county politics, important families, and particular social and economic groups, is still worth heeding. We could use studies of other great families as enlightening as Joan Gordon's exercise in historical sociology, Kinship and Class: the Livingstons of New York, 1675-1860, (unpubl. Ph.D. diss., Columbia Univ., 1959). Both the social structure and the economic operations of the landlord system are worth exploring. Staughton Lynd's study of Dutchess County would be worth emulating, for example, for Ulster-Orange, Albany, and Westchester. Local court and tax records have not been tapped for county history. Lee Benson's suggestion in *Turner and Beard* for "multivariate" analysis illustrated so strikingly in his own *The Concept of Jacksonian Democracy: New York as a Test Case* (Princeton, N.J., 1961) would be worth trying for the earlier period to measure the influence of religion and national origins in politics. The recent controversy over Beard has probably run its course, clearing the way for inquiry which will be most fruitful if it is neither pro-Beard nor anti-Beard but simply "beyond Beard."

The Federalist Era. For the Federalist period one must come to grips with Beard's companion volume to his book on the Constitution, *Economic Origins of Jeffersonian Democracy* (N.Y., 1915), the subject of scholarly criticism but not nearly as much controversy. Claude Bowers' *Jefferson and Hamilton: The Struggle for Democracy in America* (Boston, 1925), which has probably been as influential, has drawn some of the fire from Beard. The interpretations of the two men actually were quite different. To Beard the conflict between Republican and Federalist was between "agrarianism" and "capitalism" and continued that of anti-Federalist and Federalist down to the "Great Battle of 1800." Hamiltonian finance was decisive, and political and foreign policy issues only "reflexes" of the basic economic division; triumphant Jeffersonian democracy "simply meant the possession of the federal government by the agrarian masses led by an aristocracy of slave owning planters." To Bowers, by contrast an avowed partisan of Jefferson, the Republican party was shaped by his hero, Jefferson, the master politician, and the conflict revolved about eternal differences of principle between "aristocracy" and "democracy" personified by Hamilton and Jefferson. To set Beard, Bowers, and all other scholarship of Jefferson and the Jeffersonians into critical perspective, Merrill D. Peterson, *The Jefferson Image in the American Mind* (N.Y., 1960), is lucid.

Some important works of recent years modified these traditional pictures. Eugene P. Link, *Democratic Republican Societies, 1790-1800* (N.Y., 1942), called attention to the popular societies, the most important of which were urban and middle class, and not only agrarian; Manning Dauer, *The Adams Federalists* (Baltimore, 1953), analyzed with care a group Beard lost sight of in his harsh polarities, the agrarians in John Adams' wing of the party, distinct from the commercial Hamiltonians; Joseph Charles in the posthumously published essays taken from his thesis, *The Origins of the American Party System; Three Essays* (Williamsburg, Va., 1956), offered insights into the relative weight of the issues of the 1790's, emphasizing assumption as opposed to funding and the bank and excise as opposed to both, and foreign policy. Charles also suggested discontinuity between the party alignments of the 1790's and the earlier political factions, and he assigned a lesser role to Jefferson than had other writers.

Recent scholarship verifies some of these insights. E. James Ferguson's discerning study of public finance already cited, and Whitney K. Bates, The Assumption of State Debts, 1783-1793 (unpubl. Ph.D. diss., Univ. of Wisconsin, 1951), explain why funding did not become a political issue while assumption did, and why states behaved as they did. Bray Hammond's *Banks and Politics in America from the Revolution to the Civil War* (Princeton, N.J., 1957), while incomplete for New York, made clear that even for the 1790's the conflict over banking was not simply between agrarian and commercial elements but foreshadowed the better understood battles of the Jacksonian era. Alexander DeConde in *Entangling Alliance: Politics and Diplomacy under George Washington* (Durham, N.C., 1958) restored the importance of foreign policy as a partisan issue and of partisanship as a factor molding foreign policy.

Other scholarship has brought into sharper focus the Republican party and its leadership. Noble E. Cunningham, Jr., *The Jeffersonian Republicans: The Formation of Party Organization, 1789-1801* (Chapel Hill, 1957), shifted attention away from the components of the parties to "party leadership, party machinery and campaign practices," emphasizing the origins of the party in divisions in Congress. Cunningham, like the biographers of Jefferson and Madison, Dumas Malone and Irving Brant, and Adrienne Koch in *Jefferson and Madison: The Great Collaboration* (N.Y., 1950), agrees that of the two men Madison was more important as a party leader earlier in the decade and that neither was an organizer of the party as Claude Bowers would have it.

The extent to which this study of New York both corrects and leaves intact the conventional picture should be apparent from the conclusions drawn in the final chapter. Carl Becker was correct in projecting the conflict among New Yorkers of the 1770's for "who shall rule at home" into the 1780's and 1790's. My analysis of the classes aligned on the two sides, however, does not support Becker's contention that this was a clash between the "privileged" and "unprivileged" nor does it support his suggestion of an unbroken continuity of alignment. Similarly my findings for New York both uphold and challenge Beard's view of the 1790's. The Federalist-Republican conflict did and did not continue the alignments of 1787-88. Economic factors and interest groups were of obvious importance. Yet Beard's oversimplified dichotomy of "agrarian" vs. "capitalist" ignored the urban Republicans, especially the mechanics whom Beard considered politically passive, and obscured the role of the Hudson Valley landlords and the western land proprietors on the Federalist side. His insistence on the continuity of party alignment left no room for the desertion of the Livingstons and urban groups to the Republicans or the desertion of well-to-do anti-Federalists like Peter Van Gaasbeck and John Williams to the Federalists. Nor did it allow for the rapid underlying changes of the 1790's. And by stressing the primacy of internal economic issues he failed to account for the success of the Republican movement in response to the foreign policy crisis of the mid-1790's. As to Claude Bowers, it is quite apparent that he exaggerated the role of Thomas Jefferson and the issue of "democracy" vs. "aristocracy." My findings on New York support Cunningham in the distinctions he draws as to the degree of popular response to Federalist measures and the stages in the development of the Republicans, but not in his conclusion that the party was "a new growth that sprang from the divisions in Congress and the national government."

For guidance on the details of national developments I have relied most heavily on the recent multi-volume biographies of the major political figures: Dumas Malone, *Jefferson and his Time*, 3 vols. (Boston, 1948-62), II, III; Irving Brant, *James Madison, Father of the Constitution, 1787-1800*, 6 vols. (Indianapolis, 1941-61), III, and to a lesser extent Broadus Mitchell, *Alexander Hamilton*, 2 vols. (N.Y., 1957-62), II, and Douglas S. Freeman, *George Washington*, 7 vols. (N.Y., 1948-57), VI, VII, the latter completed by John A. Carroll and Mary W. Ashworth. These volumes are unsurpassed for grasp of detail, for tracing political issues on a day-to-day basis, and for nuances of contemporary points of view.

For particular issues of the period I have gotten special insights from a number of scholars: for the inter-relations of business and politics from Joseph S. Davis's lucid essays on William Duer and corporation chartering in *Essays in the Earlier History of American Corporations*, 2 vols. (Cambridge, Mass., 1917); for the phases of American reaction to the French Revolution from Kurt Beermann, The Reception of the French Revolution in the New York Press, 1788-1791 (unpubl. Ph.D. diss., New York Univ., 1960); and for the relation of the divisions over foreign policy to earlier rifts from Julian Boyd, "Two Diplomats Between Revolutions: John Jay and Thomas Jefferson," *Virginia Magazine of History and Biography*, 66 (1958), 131-46, and Ralph L. Ketcham, "France and American Politics, 1763-1793," *Political Science Quarterly*, 78 (1963), 198-223; for Jay's Treaty from the still incomparable Samuel Flagg Bemis, *Jay's Treaty, A Study in Commerce and Diplomacy* (New Haven, 1923, 2d rev. edn., 1962); and for the limitations of libertarianism manifest in the Keteltas affair from Leonard W. Levy's *Legacy of Suppression: Freedom of Speech in Early American History* (Cambridge, Mass., 1960).

New York. The best summary of New York politics in the Federalist era is the first five chapters of the first volume in Jabez D. Hammond, *The History of Political Parties in the State of New York . . . to 1840*, 2 vols. (Auburn, N.Y., 1842). I have used the fourth edition, the last (Cooperstown, 1846), which was "corrected and enlarged" by the author and contains an appendix of "Notes" by Erastus Root. A Yankee migrant to Otsego County in 1805, Hammond was a lawyer, Congressman, state senator, and county judge; he knew many of the politicians he wrote about; he certainly knew New York politics, and what's more, he read the legislative record and newspapers of the period. Although a Democrat, he was "too independent in mind to make a successful party man" and one can also agree with Dixon Ryan Fox in his sketch in the *DAB* s.v. "Hammond, Jabez," that Hammond's book was "distinguished for impartiality and candor." None of the multi-volume political histories of New York since then have improved on it. The relevant chapters in Flick, *History of the State of New York*, V, and in David M. Ellis, James A. Frost, *et al.*, *A Short History of New York State* (Ithaca, N.Y., 1957), testify to how little original research there has been on New York for the period from ratification to 1801.

A few works illuminate aspects of the New York Republican movement. Link's study of the Democratic-Republican Societies, noted above, provides excellent leads to the local varieties of the species; Edwin P. Kilroe, *Saint Tammany and the Origin of the Society of Tammany or Columbian Order in the City of New York* (N.Y., 1913), is unique, supplemented by Peter Paulson, "The Tammany Society and the Jeffersonian Movement in New York City, 1795-1800," *N.Y. History*, 34 (1953), 72-84; William Miller, "First Fruits of Republican Organization: Political Aspects of the Congressional Elections of 1794," *Pennsylvania Magazine of History and Biography*, 63 (1939),

118-43, is the only study of a New York election for this period. Happily there are two excellent studies of newspapers which complement each other: Milton W. Hamilton, *The Country Printer, New York State, 1785-1830* (N.Y., 1937), and Donald H. Stewart's enormous Jeffersonian Journalism: Newspaper Propaganda and the Development of the Democratic-Republican Party, 1789-1801 (unpubl. Ph.D. diss., Columbia Univ., 1950). George D. Luetscher, *Early Political Machinery in the United States* (Phila., 1903), provides some insight into party methods, a subject much in need of doing on the local level.

Local or regional studies and studies of particular economic groups have the best background to politics. For New York City, Sidney Pomerantz, *New York An American City, 1783-1803: A Study of Urban Life* (N.Y., 1938), proved an indispensable guide to all phases of city life. Richard Morris' *Government and Labor in Early America* (N.Y., 1946), remains the best introduction to the mechanics; I have attempted to pull this strand of urban politics together in "The Mechanics and the Jeffersonians: New York, 1789-1801," *Labor History*, 5 (1964), 247-76. For the Hudson Valley David M. Ellis, *Landlords and Farmers in the Hudson-Mohawk Region, 1790-1850* (N.Y., 1946), has three good opening chapters but necessarily focuses on the more dramatic conflicts of the nineteenth century. The gap in the history of landlord-tenant relations between Irving Mark's *Agrarian Conflict* which ends in 1775 and Ellis is only partially filled by Staughton Lynd's studies of Dutchess and of Columbia counties already cited. It is now possible for scholars to piece together the economics of the Hudson Valley estates and the politics of tenants and landlords on the basis of material in the Robert R. Livingston, Philip Schuyler, and Van Cortlandt papers.

For New York's frontier a number of books provide background: for Otsego County, James Frost, *Life in the Upper Susquehanna, 1783-1860* (N.Y., 1951); for the Genesee country, Neil A. McNall's *An Agricultural History of the Genesee Valley, 1790-1860* (Phila., 1952) and Royal Garff's Social-Economic Conditions in the Genesee Country, 1787-1812 (unpubl. Ph.D. diss., Northwestern Univ., 1939). Helen Cowan's *Charles Williamson: Genesee Promoter, Friend of Anglo-American Rapprochement* (Rochester, 1941) is a model that should be emulated for William Cooper, Phelps-Gorham, and others.

As to histories of counties, cities, and towns, I am indebted to generations of antiquarian historians too numerous to mention for tidbits of biographical and local history. Unfortunately almost none of these works provide such simple things as descriptions of landholding or consecutive accounts of elections, and the early national period is usually lost between the Revolution and the Civil War. The publications in the 1940's by the Lewis Historical Publishing Co., although by scholars, do not depart enough from the traditional mold.

There is very little scholarship on important nationality and religious groups, let alone what role they might have played in politics. The best introduction remains Thomas J. Wertenbaker, *The Founding of American Civilization: The Middle Colonies* (N.Y., 1938). Of the new immigrants of the 1790's the French alone are fairly well served by Frances S. Childs, *French Refugee Life in the United States, 1790-1800: An American Chapter of the French Revolution* (Baltimore, 1940), and T. Wood Clarke, *Émigrés in the Wilderness* (N.Y., 1941). Dixon Ryan Fox, *Yankees and Yorkers* (N.Y., 1940), distills a great deal of understanding about the New England migrants. I know of no scholarly study of a New York Protestant denomination for this period.

The farmer was the man in the eighteenth century and I have found several works valuable in recapturing his lost world: Ulysses P. Hedrick, *A History of Agriculture in the State of New York* (Albany, 1933), and Jared Van Wagenen, *The Golden Age of Homespun* (Ithaca, 1953). For this purpose nothing, however, compares to a visit to the restorations and Farmers' Museum at Cooperstown sponsored by the New York State Historical Association.

A number of studies deal with facets of economic life taken up by the state government, although invariably they leave out "politics." The best over-all study of the state and the economy is Beatrice Reubens's State Financing of Private Enterprise in Early New York (unpubl. Ph.D. diss., Columbia Univ., 1960), a worthy addition to the series guided by Carter Goodrich of the Social Science Research Council's Committee on Economic History. Mrs. Reubens's thesis, which I read after I completed my chapters on the state, in general confirms my findings. For canal policy, the opening chapter of Nathan Miller, *The Enterprise of a Free People: Aspects of Economic Development in New York State During the Canal Period, 1792-1838* (Ithaca, 1962), deals with the 1790's. Land policy is much in need of unraveling; there is little beyond Ruth Higgins, *Expansion in New York With Especial Reference to the Eighteenth Century* (Columbus, Ohio, 1931), and the specialized articles on the disposal of Loyalist estates.

The early reform movements are only beginning to find historians. For slavery and abolition there is Edwin Olson, Negro Slavery in New York, 1626-1827 (unpubl. Ph.D. diss., New York Univ., 1938), Edgar McManus, *Negro Slavery in New York* (Syracuse, N.Y., 1966), which I read in doctoral dissertation form, and a detailed article, Leo H. Hirsch, Jr., "The Negro and New York, 1783-1865," *Journal of Negro*

History, 16 (1931), 382-473. For humanitarian reform, David M. Schneider, *The History of Public Welfare in New York State, 1609-1866* (Chicago, 1938), is a guide. George P. Bauer, The Movement Against Imprisonment for Debt in the United States (unpubl. Ph.D. diss., Harvard Univ., 1935), is the only thing on this subject I know of. See also W. David Lewis, *From Newgate to Dannemora: The Rise of the Penitentiary in New York, 1796-1848* (Ithaca, N.Y., 1965). All these works miss the politics of the formative era. There is no modern scholarly history of the origins of public education in New York.

Biography. The best biographies are deficient for want of a knowledge of state and local politics of the 1790's. As might be expected Republicans are less well represented than their counterparts. An exception is Robert R. Livingston whose biography by George Dangerfield, in spite of the weaknesses I have suggested in a review in *Wm. and Mary Qtly.*, 3rd Ser., 19 (1962), 114-121, is outstanding. Joan Gordon's dissertation on the Livingstons already cited is rich with insight into the several branches of the family. William Hatcher, *Edward Livingston: Jeffersonian Republican and Jacksonian Democrat* (Baton Rouge, La., 1940), has a thin chapter on Livingston's career in Congress; E. Wilder Spaulding's *His Excellency George Clinton, Critic of the Constitution* (N.Y., 1938), is about as good as the sparse materials would permit. On the other hand Dorothie Bobbé's sketchy *DeWitt Clinton* (N.Y., 1933) points up the need for a new biography. Nathan Schachner does not do justice to the 1790's in *Aaron Burr: A Biography* (N.Y., 1937); hence one must still consult the *Memoirs of Aaron Burr* compiled by his amanuensis, Matthew Davis, and *The Life and Times of Aaron Burr*, 2 vols. (Boston, 1892, 2d. rev. ed.), by James Parton, a master biographer. In all these works Burr's later career casts too large a shadow on his early years. For lesser Republicans there are two dissertations worth mentioning: Robin Brooks, Melancton Smith: New York anti-Federalist, 1744-1798 (unpubl. Ph.D. diss., Univ. of Rochester, 1963), an incisive study, and Hugh Flick, Elkanah Watson: Gentleman-Promoter, 1758-1842 (unpubl. Ph.D. diss., Columbia Univ., 1958). For Jedediah Peck, there are only two articles, by Sherman Williams, N.Y. State Hist. Assoc., *Quarterly Journal*, 1 (1920), 219-40, and by Throop Wilder, *N.Y. History*, 22 (1941), 290-300. We could use articles or books about Brockholst Livingston (later a Justice on the United States Supreme Court); Abraham Yates, Robert Yates, and John Lansing of Albany; John Lamb, Marinus Willett, William Keteltas, and Tunis Wortman of New York City; and the editors Thomas Greenleaf and Solomon Southwick, as well as of others. A group biography might be a suitable form for men whose political lives were played out in the framework of a county or a city.

Of the several biographies of Hamilton, I found Broadus Mitchell's two-volume study, already cited, valuable for detail but so apologetic that it often needed the corrective of John C. Miller, *Alexander Hamilton: Portrait in Paradox* (N.Y., 1959), or Nathan Schachner, *Alexander Hamilton* (N.Y., 1946). For Hamilton's father-in-law, Don R. Gerlach's biography, the first volume of which is *Philip Schuyler and the American Revolution in New York, 1733-1777* (Lincoln, Nebr., 1964), fills a real need. For the third of the Federalist big three, Frank Monaghan's *John Jay, Defender of Liberty* (Indianapolis, 1935) must suffice. Hopefully a biography will emerge from Richard B. Morris's labors on Jay's papers. Professor Morris has already given us a volume on Jay as a diplomat, *The Peacemakers: The Great Powers and American Independence* (N.Y., 1965) and is currently at work on a volume on Jay and the courts. For Schuyler's other son-in-law, Stephen Van Rensselaer: The Last Patroon, William B. Fink's doctoral dissertation (Columbia Univ., 1950) focuses on the more important later career. As for the other Federalists there are first-rate biographies of two men: John T. Horton, *James Kent: A Study in Conservatism, 1763-1847* (N.Y., 1939), and Edward P. Alexander, *A Revolutionary Conservative: James Duane of New York* (N.Y., 1938). Unfortunately Duane's career was over even before he died in 1794 and Kent was not a central figure in the 1790's. A much needed biography of Rufus King, by Robert Ernst, will appear shortly. A biography of Gouverneur Morris by Max Mintz is in preparation. We have no more than sketches of William Cooper (by Lyman Butterfield, *N.Y. History*, 30 [1949], 385-408), Egbert Benson, Samuel Jones, Richard Varick, and Ambrose Spencer, all of whom left their mark on the state.

For sketches of lesser figures in New York, as my citations attest, *The Dictionary of American Biography*, Dumas Malone, Allen Johnson. et al., eds., 22 vols. (N.Y., 1928-1944), proved indispensable. Billy Bob Lightfoot, The State Delegations in the Congress of the United States, 1789-1800 (unpubl. Ph.D. diss., Univ. of Texas, 1958), fills in details on each New York senator and representative.

The best bibliographies of New York history are in Ellis, *et al.*, *A Short History of New York State*, and after each chapter in Flick, ed., *A History of the State of New York*. The cumulative ten-year indexes to the *Proceedings* of N.Y. State Hist. Assoc. and to *N.Y. History* (1925-1965) are a guide to recent scholarship. An incomparable guide to the extant historic buildings and sites of the period is *New York: A Guide to the Empire State* (N.Y., 1940), a volume in the American Guide Series compiled by the Writers Program of the Federal Works Projects Administration.

Index